# A–Z of GARDENING SECRETS

Reader's Digest

# A-Z of GARDENING SECRETS

techniques • flowers • tools
design • vegetables • containers

# CONTENTS

A .......... 8

B .......... 21

C .......... 45

D .......... 78

E .......... 93

F .......... 98

G .......... 112

H .......... 124

I .......... 135

J .......... 140

K .......... 144

L .......... 146

M .......... 160

N ............................................................................................................ 170

O ............................................................................................................ 178

P ............................................................................................................ 183

Q ............................................................................................................ 216

R ............................................................................................................ 217

S ............................................................................................................ 229

T ............................................................................................................ 261

U ............................................................................................................ 279

V ............................................................................................................ 280

W ........................................................................................................... 286

X ............................................................................................................ 306

Y ............................................................................................................ 307

Z ............................................................................................................ 308

INDEX ..................................................................................................... 310

## INTRODUCTION

In the ever-changing world of the garden, there is always something to discover. This is particularly the case if you're just starting on your journey in gardening. But even if you have a little knowledge or have been gardening for years, there'll be times when you feel the need for some trusted tips and advice. For example, one year your lemon tree doesn't flower. Or your trees have grown into mature specimens and turned sunny spots into shade. Or you want to grow a box hedge, or cover a pergola with flowering climbers. The changing environment of the garden is full of possibilities. The more time I spend gardening, and talking and writing about plants and gardens, the more I realise how much there is still to learn!

That's where *A–Z of Gardening Secrets* comes in. If you want to know how to keep your lawn in the best condition, prepare your soil for planting or grow perfect roses, then this is the book for you. It is an indispensable garden guide that gets straight to the heart of the problem with its handy A to Z format. Look up F for fertiliser to discover the best way to feed your plants, S for shade to find a shrub that can thrive in a tricky spot, or turn to C for caterpillars to learn how to stop these pesky critters eating your basil.

*A–Z of Gardening Secrets* is a book to keep close at hand. Dip into it when you've got a gardening problem to solve, want to learn a new technique or simply want to be inspired by the beautiful photographs and illustrations. Whatever your garden size, I'm sure it will become an essential part of your gardening tool kit.

### Debbie McDonald

Writer, horticultural consultant and horticultural editor at
ABC *Gardening Australia* magazine

# A

ABELIAS | ACID SOIL

## ABELIAS

The sweetly scented flowers of abelias are seen mainly in summer and autumn and are highly attractive to bees. The flowering stems can be picked and used indoors as they look attractive in flower arrangements.

### Abelias for hedges
Make a fast-growing, informal hedge by planting glossy abelia (*Abelia × grandiflora*) 1 m apart. After the second year, prune some of the older shoots near the base of each plant to allow for new growth, but otherwise let the plant develop its natural arching shape.

### A touch of gold
The gold colour of the variegated abelia cultivar 'Francis Mason' will be more intense in full sun and in poorer soils. It is an ideal choice for a hedge or border in a sunny spot. 'Francis Mason' grows to around 1.5 m. 'Sunrise' (1.8 m) has attractive red-bronze autumn colour, 'Prostrata' (60 cm) is a fragrant groundcover and 'Sherwoodii' (1.2 m) makes a good compact hedge.

Members of the Protea family, including the South African king protea and many Australian natives, have adapted to the acid soils common in those countries.

## ACID SOIL

### The acid test
You can find out the pH (acid or alkaline balance) of your soil by using a soil-testing kit, available from most nurseries. Acid soils show a pH less than 7 (neutral). Vegetation can also be a crude guide to soil acidity. The presence of carpet grass and dandelions, for example, usually indicates acid and infertile soils.

### Added sweetener
The best pH range for most plants is slightly acid at pH 5.5 to 6.5. Below this, you will need to add a liming agent or soil 'sweetener' unless you are growing acid-loving plants. The common liming agents are lime or dolomite. Dolomite is calcium magnesium carbonate which, like limestone, raises soil pH but also adds magnesium, an element often lacking in Australian soils.

### Plant selection
Instead of liming your soil, you could grow acid-tolerant plants. Plants in the Ericaceae family (azaleas, ericas, rhododendrons) are known for their preference for acid soils, as are camellias, citrus, gardenias, geraniums, magnolias and members of the Protea family. Lime these only if the pH is very

### Testing your soil pH
You can buy a simple kit to discover the pH value of your soil. Following the instructions, place a teaspoon of soil on the test card, then add drops of the indicator liquid. Stir it into the soil sample, adding more drops to form a thick paste. Dust the paste with the white powder provided, then wait for 1 minute until it changes colour. Match the colour of the soil sample with the nearest pH value on the colour card. Purple is alkaline, yellow is acid, and green is neutral.

severely acidic. Most Australian native plants are adapted to acid soil and in some cases are tolerant of extreme acidity. Only a few plants from coastal sand dunes and from the arid inland prefer alkaline soils.

*See also* Soil analysis

AFRICAN VIOLETS | AGAPANTHUS

## AFRICAN VIOLETS

African violets make ideal indoor plants. They flower over a long period, especially in spring and summer, with blooms of white, mauve, pink, purple or blue, and ruffled and double petals.

### The right conditions

Place pots in a warm room with a minimum temperature of 18°C, where they get bright but indirect sunlight. To create the humid conditions that these plants like, stand the pots on dampened pebbles. Fertilise from spring to later summer with a liquid feed at half strength.

### How to water African violets

Keep the soil moist but not soggy. When watering, carefully pour water into the dish under the pot. Alternatively, place the pot in a bowl of shallow water. Try not to wet the hairy leaves – they are easily marked.

### take leaf cuttings of African violets

1. African violets root easily from leaf cuttings. Carefully pull or cut off a leaf stalk and shorten it to about 2–4 cm long.

2. Bury each leaf stalk in propagating mix in a 13 cm pot. Cover the pot with a clear plastic bag or stand it in a closed and lightly shaded propagator. New plants will soon form. You can also root African violets by standing the leaves, with stalks, in a jar of water.

## AGAPANTHUS

### Divide clumps to line the driveway

Agapanthus are striking when planted to line a driveway or a fence. A quick way to increase your supply of agapanthus is to dig up a clump in late winter and divide it into separate plants using a sharp spade.

### Getting agapanthus to flower

Agapanthus that refuse to flower are usually growing in too much shade. Move the clump to a spot in full sun or enjoy the green leaves.

### Variety of flower colour

Good varieties to grow include 'Purple Cloud' (tall, with large heads of intensely purple-blue flowers), 'Strawberry Ice' (medium height with pure white heads of flowers blushed strawberry pink), 'Snowflake' (miniature to 50 cm with ice white flowers), 'Black Panther' (to 90 cm with dark violet-blue large flowers), and 'Silver Song' (white-striped blue flowers). Striking *Agapanthus inapertus* has pendulous deep blue flowers on tall stems.

### Variety of flower colour

Now there are also many dwarf agapanthus available for small gardens, pots or along a path. These dwarf agapanthus can be as small as 15 cm. Named varieties include 'Baby Blue' and 'Peter Pan', which have blue flowers in summer. 'Snowdrop' has white flowers. There are dwarf forms with variegated leaves, such as 'Tinkerbell', which grows to around 30 cm and has blue flowers that stand around 50 cm above the leaves.

# AGAVES | ALKALINE SOIL

## AGAVES

These striking succulents from tropical North America, Mexico and the West Indies produce rosettes of sword-shaped, often sharply toothed leaves with towering stems of flowers. Their frost tolerance varies, but all agaves require well-drained soil, doing well in the ground or pots. Although the flowering shoot dies when the flower is finished, the offsets continue to grow.

### Popular choices

One of the most popular agaves is the century plant, or foxtail agave (*Agave attenuata*), which forms compact pale green rosettes of spineless foliage that reach 1.5 m tall, with arching 3 m high stems of greenish yellow flowers. The royal agave (*A. victoriae-reginae*) is grown for its compact habit to about 60 cm high and attractive, lined foliage.

## ALKALINE SOIL

### The alkaline test

Alkaline, or limy, soil has a pH greater than 7. You can test the pH of your soil with a soil-testing kit, as shown on the previous page. Very alkaline soil can actually contain lime in the form of white nodules or a fine, white, sand-like substance. If you think the soil in your garden is alkaline, you can also test it by dropping a little vinegar or swimming pool acid onto a dry clod. If the liquid fizzes, the soil is alkaline.

### The effects of lime

The most obvious effect of an acid-loving plant such as camellia being grown in alkaline soil is a paleness in the young foliage, sometimes progressing to whiteness. This is chlorosis, caused by an iron deficiency and occurs because iron in particular is almost totally insoluble in alkaline conditions and thus unavailable to the plant.

Easier to grow are notable lovers of alkaline soils such as legumes (peas, beans and clovers).

### Growing acid lovers

You can still grow acid-loving plants if you have alkaline soil or even a truly limy soil. The secret is either avoidance – by building a raised bed of artificial acid soil, for example, or growing acid-loving plants in pots (but not concrete pots) – or management. This will mean keeping an eye out for iron chlorosis, especially on the plants' youngest leaves, and using a mixed chelated trace element spray to release nutrients locked in the soil.

*See also* Chlorosis, Soil analysis

### treat
## Alkaline soil

Mildly alkaline soils can be acidified quite easily. Acidic mulches such as eucalypt and pine bark can help. You can also apply iron sulfate, or in cases of severe alkalinity, agricultural sulfur. Use iron sulfate at about 100 g per m$^2$, water well and check the pH in a week's time. Repeat the treatment if necessary. Add agricultural sulfur at only 50 g per m$^2$ as it is more potent than iron sulfate. Dig it into moist soil and wait 6 weeks before testing again. Repeat if necessary to obtain the desired pH.

### When nothing works

In deep limy soils (those that fizz in acid) it is often not practical to acidify more than the surface and even then the lime will generally rise again, resulting in the same pH you started with. In this case, the solution is to grow alkaline-tolerant plants only.

ALOES | ANEMONES **A**

## ALOES

These handsome African natives are good accent plants. They add bold sculptural features to a garden as well as colourful blooms in autumn and winter. And like most plants with red, orange or yellow flowers, they attract native birds.

### In the hot spot

For a hot dry spot in full sun where little else grows, consider a collection of aloes. There are many forms, from the spreading, low-growing *Aloe brevifolia* and *A. nobilis* to the 3 m tall, single-trunked *A. marlothii* and *A. ferox*. While most aloes require full sun, those with speckled leaves need the protection of afternoon shade.

### Special needs

Rich soil, good drainage and regular summer watering are important, too. Only the hardiest species, such as *A. arborescens*, will survive frosty conditions. Most other species are damaged by low temperatures. Also check whether the aloe is suitable for summer or winter rainfall areas.

### heal with Aloe vera

The clear mucilaginous gel inside the aloe vera leaf has healing and anti-inflammatory properties. Probably best known for its ability to encourage the healing of burns, aloe vera gel can also be applied to wounds, abrasions, psoriasis, eczema and ulcers.

### Regeneration

Ultra-soothing for even the most dehydrated and parched skin, aloe vera is also a mild exfoliant, gently removing dead skin cells and stimulating cell regeneration, helping to prevent scarring and diminish wrinkles.

## ANEMONES

Anemones are all about colour. For very little effort, they provide red, blue, mauve or white flowers and add strong rich tones to the spring garden.

Anemones can be mass-planted in beds as a seasonal highlight, or grown in pots for a colourful cushion-like effect in spring. They are particularly decorative when planted in a sunny window box.

Some flowers are bicoloured, with a white eye and coloured outer petals. They do well amid other spring-flowering annuals, such as pansies, violas or forget-me-nots.

### Easy growing

Anemones are easy as well as good value. They are grown from tubers, called corms, which you can buy in bulk ready for mass planting. Plant the corms with the flat side upright in late summer or autumn (ideally from February to April) for spring flowers.

Select a spot in full sun protected from strong winds, so that the blooms, which sit atop stems up to 30 cm tall, are not damaged. Any well-drained soil with added organic matter is ideal.

### Water at the right time

The developing plants need to be kept well watered as the flower buds grow and develop. Water-stressed plants will only produce short-stemmed flowers.

# ANNUALS

Annuals complete their entire life cycle in a single season. Because their time is limited, they usually bloom with gusto.

### Where to plant
Annuals provide short-lived, easy-to-change colour schemes in beds, borders, window boxes, pots and containers. They are also excellent in mixed borders, where their blooms can bridge the gaps between perennials' flowering times. For newly planted shrub borders and new gardens, they can be used to great effect in the spaces that the developing shrubs will eventually spread to fill.

### Preparation is the key
Annuals are easy to grow and are not particular about soil type, but they all require good drainage. Also, if the soil is too hard or dry, annual seeds will have difficulty germinating. Work the soil well before sowing, raking it over until the surface forms a fine, crumbly tilth. Then water the drills well, before and after sowing. This will help the germination process.

Alternatively, raise seedlings in trays of propagating mix placed in a warm protected area. Water regularly. Harden seedlings off before planting out and water with a liquid seaweed solution.

### The importance of colour
Before planting annuals, give some thought to possible colour schemes. A single colour makes a strong statement. If you prefer a multicoloured display, choose harmonious shades or variations on a single theme rather than clashing contrasts.

White, yellow and pink flowers are at their best in the evening and early morning. A rich colour scheme is a mixture of reds, plum, maroon and purple. Blue and white is a cool combination during hot summer months.

### A good soak
Soak the roots before planting punnets of seedlings. Plunge the punnets into a basin of water, or water from above. Drain well, remove from the punnet and plant out late on an overcast day.

### Pinching out
To encourage the bushy growth of your annuals, pinch out the growing tips of young plants, just above the topmost pair of leaves. This encourages the plants to produce sideshoots and more flowers. Pinching out is particularly recommended for clarkias, cosmos, petunias, snapdragons and sweet peas.

See also Colour

## turn Annuals into biennials

A biennial is a plant that takes 2 years to complete its life cycle of growth, flowering and setting seed. This means that some plants grown in the garden may not flower in their first year of growth. For example, plants such as columbines, foxgloves and honesty tend to be biennials in cool-climate gardens.

In warm climates, however, many of the plants that are biennials in cool-climate gardens grow as annuals and die after flowering in their first season. Conversely, some plants that grow as annuals in cool climates may live longer in areas where winters aren't harsh.

Some of the commonly grown biennials that are considered annuals in a warm climate include campanulas, forget-me-nots, foxgloves, hollyhocks, honesty and mignonette.

## sow Annuals in semicircles

When growing annuals from seed, sowing them in straight lines will make it easier to distinguish them from weeds and to thin them out to the required spacing. However, straight lines of flowers can give a rather regimented appearance to your beds, so try marking out the area into overlapping semicircles, with one semicircle for each variety. Draw the drills in one semicircle at a different angle from those in the next semicircle. As the plants grow and spread, the lines of the drills will blur and you will have natural-looking drifts of flowers.

12

ANNUALS

## pick flowers all year with Annuals

With the right choice, you can have a succession of annuals in flower all year round, grown either from seed or as seedlings.

As a rule, annuals start to flower within 8 weeks from planting as seedlings. If growing from seed, sow the seeds in the season before flowering begins.

### Flowering season and colour

✲ **Alyssum** Year-round; purple, rose, white, yellow ✲ **Bedding begonia** Year-round; pink, red, white ✲ **Cineraria**\* Late winter to spring; blue, mauve, pink, red, white ✲ **Cosmos**\* Summer to autumn; pink, purple, white ✲ **Iceland poppy** Winter to spring; lemon, orange, pink, red, salmon, white, yellow ✲ **Ice plant** Summer; many luminous shades ✲ **Impatiens**\* Spring to autumn; mauve, pink, white, red, salmon ✲ **Larkspur** Spring to summer; blue, pink, white ✲ **Lobelia** Late winter to summer; blue, lavender, white ✲ **Marigold**\* Summer to autumn; brown, orange, yellow ✲ **Pansy and viola** Winter to spring; blue, brown, cream, orange, purple, white, yellow ✲ **Paper daisy** Spring; pink, white, yellow ✲ **Petunia**\* Summer to autumn; blue, mauve, pink, white, yellow ✲ **Polyanthus** Winter to spring; carmine, mauve, pink, purple, red, white ✲ **Salvia**\* Summer to autumn; blue, red, white ✲ **Snapdragon** Year-round; pink, white, yellow ✲ **Sweet pea** Winter to spring; pink, purple, red, white ✲ **Zinnia**\* Summer to autumn; green, orange, pink, red, white, yellow

\*Protect from frost when young or don't plant out until after the threat of frost has passed

13

# A

APHIDS | APPLES

## APPLES

Most apples need to grow in an area that has sufficiently cold winters. The low temperature is necessary to break the tree's bud dormancy, and if it is not adequate the buds may break at different times or not open at all. There are warm-climate apples available too, including 'Dorsett Golden', 'Anna' and 'Rome Beauty'.

### Something for everyone

Whether your garden is large or small, try to grow at least one apple tree. Some varieties are self-pollinating, such as 'Red Fuji', and in this case a single tree is all that you need to harvest a good crop. Some nurseries graft two or three different varieties onto the same tree to overcome the problem of pollinators.

A Ballerina apple has a slim, columnar shape. It can be grown in a narrow bed or container. Specialist tree nurseries or garden centres can advise you on suitable varieties for your site and pollination.

### Thin the fruit

Unless there is a late frost, apple trees will usually set too many fruit. Removal of some fruit (thinning) not only ensures that the apples that remain will grow to be a reasonable size and quality but also stops branches from breaking under the heavy load.

In addition, it encourages the tree to form fruit buds for the following year. In early summer, remove any abnormally shaped or damaged fruit. Then thin the fruit again in midsummer so that there is only one fruit remaining in each of the original clusters. The fruit should be left no closer than 10–15 cm apart.

### Picking apples

Apples on individual trees ripen at different times, so pick them over a few weeks. Fruit should be removed by hand and is ready if it parts with a gentle lift and twist. Early-ripening apples should be picked just before they are fully ripe or else they will become mealy. Later-maturing fruit must be fully ripe or they will shrivel when stored.

## APHIDS

### Plants affected
Most outdoor and indoor plants.

### Symptoms
Black, green, yellow, pink or grey 1–7 mm insects on new leaves and shoots. Young growth distorted.

### Treatment
✱ Wash insects off with a strong hose jet, squash with fingers, or prune off badly infested shoots.

✱ Encourage predatory ladybirds, hoverflies, wasps and lacewings.

✱ Use petroleum oil sprays, insecticidal soap, pyrethrum, synthetic pyrethroid, maldison, or a systemic spray – imidacloprid or acephate (NZ only).

✱ Apply a winter oil spray to deciduous shrubs and trees during the winter period.

✱ In Australian greenhouses, introduce the native green lacewing *Mallada signata*.

✱ Avoid the excessive use of nitrogen fertilisers.

## train an Apple tree

**1** When pruning a bush tree after planting, aim for a goblet shape, which should be open in the centre. Shorten branches by about a half to two-thirds back to outward-facing buds so that their tips are level.

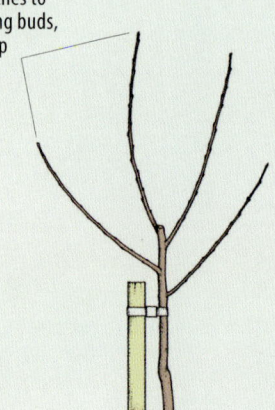

Shorten branches to outward-facing buds, level at the top

**2** The next winter, choose well-placed shoots as new branches and prune back to outward-facing buds. Shorten vigorous growth by a third, the rest by half. The tips of branch leaders should be about level.

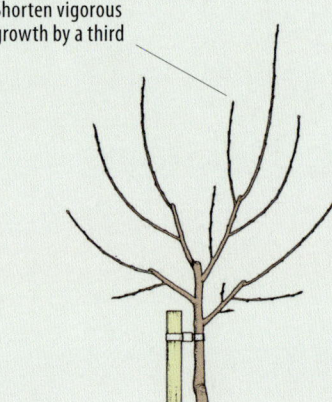

Shorten vigorous growth by a third

ANTHRACNOSE | ARBOURS AND ARCHES

# ANTHRACNOSE

### Plants affected
Beans, cucurbits, lettuce, tomato, avocado, mango, citrus, melons.

### Symptoms
Black or brown sunken spots on leaves, stems, pods or fruit; black veins, pinkish spores.

### Treatment
* Pull up diseased plants and destroy. Do not save the seed from affected plants.
* Handling plants in wet weather spreads the disease. Disinfect all tools. Also remove debris.
* Rotate crops.
* Plant resistant varieties.
* Sow disease-free new seed.
* Prune to keep canopy open and to increase air flow around plant.
* Spray with fungicides such as mancozeb, zineb or copper-based spray, depending on the crop, and observe the withholding period.

# ARBOURS AND ARCHES

### Creating an arbour
An arbour could simply be a favourite seat in the garden that is protected from the sun and wind. To enhance its restful qualities, you could surround it with screens made of trellis.

The best support for the open sides of arbours is wooden trellis with diamond- or rectangular-shaped latticework. This is ideal for supporting climbing plants.

### How to site an arch
Do not stand an arch all alone in the middle of a lawn – it should always appear to lead somewhere, or highlight a feature.

### A longer life
Because the plants that grow up the trelliswork of arbours will eventually become large and heavy, fix the poles that support the trellis firmly in the ground. Otherwise, strong winds could lead to the whole structure being blown down.

For your arbour or arch to last as long as possible, use treated pine or hardwood in the construction. To reduce the likelihood of rot, mount hardwood posts on post supports set in concrete. Treated pine posts can be set directly into concrete in the ground, but using supports is best.

# APRICOTS

Apricots can be grown as freestanding trees or they can be fan-trained on a wall that is at least 2.5 m high. A freestanding tree may grow to 5 m high with about the same spread. These trees should be pruned regularly to remove unproductive wood and to form the tree into a vase shape.

### Room to grow
Trees must be planted early in the winter before bud burst. The best soils for apricots are slightly alkaline with plenty of added organic matter. Dwarf varieties are available for gardens with limited space.

'Moorpark', 'Trevatt', 'Story', 'Hunter' and 'Riverbrite' are the most reliable – all are excellent for drying. 'Moorpark', 'Blenheim', 'Earlicot', 'Supergold' and 'Katy' are good for fresh eating.

### Routine care
Apply fertiliser in spring. For each year of the tree's age, apply a quantity of at least 0.5 kg up to a maximum of 5 kg.

Many varieties of apricot need some chilling in winter so they are best grown in cooler areas. They flower early and so are susceptible to frost damage. Water may be needed in spring to summer to avoid bud drop and produce good-quality fruit. Most varieties are self-fertile.

## A ASIAN VEGETABLES

Chinese flat cabbage

# ASIAN VEGETABLES

Chinese broccoli, Chinese cabbage, Chinese flat cabbage, bok choy, mizuna and mustard greens are all easy and quick crops to grow, provided the soil has been well dug and enriched with compost or well-rotted manure, and crops are watered regularly.

### Quick turn-around
These Asian greens are among the quickest vegetables to grow. They do best in full sun, and prefer a neutral or near-neutral soil. Mustard greens are especially resilient and will grow in soils that are not so well prepared. They will also tolerate more acidic conditions than the others.

### Crops from spring to winter
Chinese cabbage is best grown as a spring and autumn crop, but in the tropics it can also be grown as a winter crop. Seeds germinate rapidly in about 3 days. Mustard greens, bok choy, mizuna and mibuna all have similar growing needs. Mizuna and mibuna have enough cold tolerance to grow into the early winter months.

Chinese flat cabbage is grown as a winter vegetable and is planted in mid- to late autumn.

### Transplanting not necessary
Chinese broccoli can be raised as seedlings and then transplanted. The other Asian greens are sown directly in their allotted place. They should be thinned to a final distance of 35–40 cm between plants and 50 cm between rows.

If the hearts of Chinese cabbage plants seem loose as they grow, tie the leaves together with twine.

### The mustard deterrent
Because these Asian greens have a mustard component, they are less palatable to some insects. But they are still attacked by whitefly and cabbage white butterfly. Club root, nematodes and leaf spot can also be a problem.

### A regular harvest
Chinese broccoli is ready for a first harvest 8–10 weeks after sowing. Pick regularly to keep leafy heads tender. All other types can be harvested at any stage from thinnings and young leaves through to maturity, 50–60 days after sowing.

## Identify Asian vegetable greens

### Bok choy
Also known as pak choi and tsoi sum, the small-headed varieties are called baby bok choy. It is faintly hot in taste, and is stir-fried, braised, steamed or pickled.

### Chinese broccoli
Also known as gai larn, the young leafy tops and stalks are used particularly in stir-fries.

### Chinese cabbage
Also called wong bok, or celery, peking, shantung or napa cabbage, it has a sweeter, more delicate flavour than European cabbages. Stir-fry, or use raw as a wrap or in coleslaw.

### Mizuna and mibuna
Mizuna (right) is a traditional Japanese green, mostly used for salads. Its long, narrow, dissected leaves have a hot, mustardy tang. Mibuna is closely related, but its narrow leaves are not feathery like mizuna's.

### Mustard greens
Also known as gai choy, steam, braise or stir-fry this for its pronounced mustardy tang.

ARTICHOKES | ASTERS

## ARTICHOKES

The globe artichoke (*Cynara scolymus*) is worth growing not only for its culinary delights, but also for its ornamental leaves and dramatic visual appeal. In the vegetable garden it is grown for its fleshy, scaled, edible flower heads. These should be cut with a sharp knife when they are young and tender, but before the flowers come into bloom.

### Water well for tenderness
To ensure a tender crop, the buds of artichokes must grow quickly. Encourage this rapid growth by watering abundantly and often, and mulching with compost or well-rotted manure.

### Replenishing the stock
Artichoke plants are short-lived perennials, being productive for only 4 or 5 years. But you don't need to buy new plants or grow them from seed because the old plants can be replaced with suckers (sideshoots). These are taken from established plants in late autumn in frost-free areas or early spring in cooler regions and replanted at least 1 m apart.

### Start with the king
Mature plants produce ripe heads in November and December. Pick them, starting with the king head, when the bracts are still tightly wrapped. Use a sharp knife or secateurs to cut off a head with a 12 cm stem, then cut back each stem to about half its original length. The flower heads on the lateral shoots are best picked when about hen's-egg size.

## ASTERS

### Autumn flowers
The easiest asters to grow bloom in autumn. The masses of starry purple, pink or white blossoms with yellow centres often hide the leaves entirely. They make good cut flowers.

### Don't overdo the fertiliser
Asters are tough plants. Too much fertiliser can make them grow big but weak-stemmed, and short on flowers. Pinch back tall varieties at least once in early summer to encourage branching, then stake or tie up the stems when they reach more than 60 cm tall.

### In humid climates
Powdery mildew can be a worry in warm, humid climates. If you notice fuzzy or mouldy-looking spots on the foliage, prune back affected areas. Also space plants widely to increase air circulation. Or grow a disease-resistant aster, such as *Aster × frikartii*.

# Autumn colours

Autumn signals the beginning of the garden's slow saunter towards winter. Plants and gardeners alike welcome the return of cooler weather and lower humidity. The short days and cool temperatures signal an explosion of autumnal hues of gold, orange, rust and red.

## Making sure they are seen

In a cool climate plants with colourful autumn foliage are at their best between mid April and late May when you may be spending less time outdoors. Make the most of their beauty by planting them on both sides of a well-travelled path or in areas that can be seen from your house or where they are backlit by the sun.

## Not only trees

The processes that make trees such as maples and oaks turn red and gold also lead to changes in some perennials and shrubs. Shrubs such as forsythias glow a soft buttery yellow, while winged euonymus turn brilliant red.

Where space is tight, use deciduous trees as street trees and choose deciduous climbers with brilliant fiery colours for walls and trellises. After leaf-fall, the tracery of branches will provide winter interest.

## Autumn colour for warm areas

Foliage colour is not the sole preserve of cool districts. In warm or coastal climates crepe myrtle (*Lagerstroemia indica*) and Chinese tallow tree (*Triadica sebifera* syn. *Sapium sebiferum*) and European nettle tree (*Celtis australis*) all colour well. The latter two are weeds in certain areas, however, so check before planting them.

### pick plants with brilliant Autumn colour

- Japanese maples, especially *Acer rubrum*, *A. palmatum* 'Osakazuki' and 'Atropurpureum'
- Japanese barberry (*Berberis thunbergia*)
- Eastern redbud (*Cercis canadensis* 'Forest Pansy')
- Smoke bush (*Cotinus coggygria*)
- Maidenhair tree (*Ginkgo biloba*)
- Tulip tree (*Liriodendron tulipifera*)
- Oregon grape (*Mahonia aquifolium*)
- Nandina, sacred bamboo (*Nandina domestica* cvs)
- Tupelo (*Nyssa sylvatica*)
- Virginia creeper (*Parthenocissus quinquefolia*)
- Boston ivy (*Parthenocissus tricuspidata* 'Veitchii')
- Chinese pistachio (*Pistacia chinensis*)
- Flowering plum (*Prunus* spp. and cvs)
- Ornamental pear (*Pyrus* spp. and cvs)
- Scarlet oak (*Quercus coccinea* 'Splendens')
- Japanese glory vine (*Vitis coignetiae*)
- Grapevine (*Vitis vinifera* cvs)

# A

AVOCADOS | AZALEAS

## AVOCADOS

### Planting tips
Avocados thrive in a rich soil to which compost is added at least once a year. Young trees need regular deep watering until they are established, after which an occasional soaking is necessary only during long, dry periods. All avocados need good drainage, particularly in areas where the annual rainfall exceeds 700 mm.

### Buy from a nursery
Buy only grafted trees that are accredited free from root rot diseases, and buy from a reliable nursery. In gardens where there is only room for one tree, be sure to choose an A-type pollinator such as 'Hass', 'Wurtz' or 'Rincon'. This is because the avocado has a strange habit – the flowers change sex daily, either during daytime hours or at night. Unless there is a sufficient overlap of male and female flowers for pollination, there will be no fruit.

### harvest and ripen Avocados
Avocados do not ripen on the tree. When fruits look as if they have reached a mature size and shape, try picking a few as an experiment. Those that ripen within a week or so will serve as a guide for further harvesting.

### Slowing down the process
If you do not want to use all your fruit at once, leave a small section of the stem attached to some fruit: this seems to stop the avocado from ripening too fast.

## AZALEAS

These compact shrubs flower profusely in spring. Deciduous types do best in cool climates, while the evergreen azaleas generally prefer mild to subtropical climates.

### Best soil
Azaleas do best in acidic, moist, well-drained soils. Combine compost and well-rotted manure with the soil before planting, then dig a hole twice as wide and deep as the root ball. Plant your azalea no deeper than it was planted in the pot.

### Mulching to save roots
Azaleas are shallow-rooted plants that can easily dry out, whether growing in pots or in garden beds. Protect the shallow roots with a 5 cm thick layer of mulch; use compost or decomposed leaves and do not let it touch the plants' stems. Because of the shallow root system, always cultivate around azaleas with extreme care.

### Pot performance
Their shallow roots make most evergreen cultivars well suited to growing in pots or tubs. Select small-growing forms and use a good-quality potting mix.

### Sun or shade?
Most azaleas perform best in filtered light but they will not grow or flower well in deep shade. Their ideal spot is under deep-rooted deciduous trees or in a position that receives morning sun but not hot afternoon sun. Varieties marked 'sun hardy' will grow in full sun but perform best when they have protection from hot afternoon sun. Take care that azaleas growing in a sunny spot are not allowed to dry out.

### treat Azalea petal blight
Azalea flowers that seem to wilt even though the plant is well watered may be suffering from azalea petal blight. The wilted petals will turn brown and remain on the plant.

New cultivars seem to be more resistant. This disease can be controlled with a recommended fungicide. Begin spraying as the buds colour and continue throughout the flowering period following the manufacturer's directions. To avoid spreading the fungus, collect discarded or browning flowers and dispose of them in your garbage bin. When watering, avoid wetting flowers for the same reason. A month before flowering, rake up mulch and plant remains and discard.

# BALCONY GARDENS

### An elevated mini garden
You can create a mini garden on your balcony, complete with trees, shrubs and flowers. But remember that a balcony is a very different environment from a ground-level garden as it is usually covered and shady but also very windy.

### Make it safe
Before you start creating your balcony garden, it is important to check with your body corporate if there are any restrictions on balcony fixtures. Then make sure that everything – containers, furniture, structures – is securely fixed or is heavy enough that it will not blow away. Never place unsecured pots or window boxes on balustrades. Check whether water from your balcony can spill onto balconies below, as this will cause friction with neighbours. Always water carefully to be sure of minimising any run-off.

### Creating an attractive space
Furniture should be tough and reasonably heavy – plastic or resin furniture can blow around in high winds. Leave enough space so you can move easily around the furniture. De-clutter the space as much as possible and keep the colour schemes simple and co-ordinated with your apartment. After all, a balcony should not only be a comfortable place to spend time but also make an attractive picture from inside.

### Shelter from the wind
To shelter a balcony from the wind, you could line the open part that faces the direction of the wind with bamboo canes tied closely together or adapt a screen made from split bamboo. Also plant evergreen shrubs such as aucuba, box or pink Indian hawthorn (*Rhaphiolepis indica* 'Ballerina'). Eventually, these plants will grow into an attractive glossy-leaved hedge, creating a year-round natural windbreak.

### Interesting presentation
A balcony garden does not have to be dull. Even without colourful flowers, you can create interest with attractive foliage and clever presentation. Look for plants such as weeping figs, gardenias or azaleas grown as standards or presented in other interesting shapes. Ivy, honeysuckle and baby's tears (*Soleirolia soleirolii*) can all be trained into topiary shapes ranging from simple wreaths to ornate swans.

### Berries for colour
The long-lasting red-berried clusters of the shade-loving shrub the coralberry (*Ardisia crenata*) can make a strong statement on a shaded balcony. Train it to grow as a standard and use the space at the base to grow the dwarf mondo grass known as 'Mini Mondo'. Alternatively, try a small-leaved fig or a citrus tree. For a formal look, grow several plants in a long rectangular pot or place a pair of plants on either side of the balcony door.

## consider your Balcony's aspect

Your balcony's aspect – that is, the direction in which it faces – will determine how much sun it receives and what plants you can realistically grow there.

**North-facing** Sunny and warm, plenty of light and reflected heat. You can grow many plants; they will need lots of water.

**South-facing** Shady and cool. The choice of suitable plants is smaller; use foliage shapes, textures and colours for interest.

**East-facing** Gentle morning light, never subject to intense drying heat. You can grow a good range of plants, including flowers.

**West-facing** Full blast of the hot afternoon sun. Choose very tough coastal plants and succulents.

# BAMBOOS | BANANAS

## BAMBOOS

### Bamboos that take over
Running bamboos grow by sending out underground runners, or rhizomes, and can quickly take over whole areas of the garden, form dense thickets and become invasive. Many are weeds. Avoid planting them, or if you do, contain them in root barriers or plant in containers or troughs.

### Clumping bamboos
The clumping bamboos are non-invasive but they can form very large clumps over time. They spread by producing one culm (stem) from each new rhizome. If the clump is becoming too large, simply cut off the culm when you see it forming in summer.

These bamboos range from 1 m to a massive 35 m. They grow quickly and do well in narrow spaces.

### A useful hedge
Clumping bamboos can be grown as quick and stylish screening plants in a garden, pot or planter box. For a dense screen to about 6 m tall, you could try the slender weaver's bamboo (*Bambusa textilis* 'Gracilis'). Varieties with ferny, coloured or striped foliage are also available. Bamboo is an excellent soundproofer and carbon dioxide accumulator.

### Getting rid of a pest
Bamboo can be a problem as it is often fast-growing, invasive and very difficult to eradicate. While there is no shortcut to control, some things will make the task easier. Use a glyphosate herbicide on plants while they are actively growing. Either spray it on the foliage when plants are about 1–2 m tall or apply it to the cut stump. While the bamboo is actively growing, the herbicide will be carried to other parts of the clump. Keep reapplying to the leaves as new growth appears.

## BANANAS

### The sun-loving banana
Most banana varieties do well only in warm, humid climates, but some varieties, including 'Goldfinger' or 'Williams', thrive in cooler environments if they are protected from frost. Plant in spring, or any time of the year in tropical areas. They need good drainage, a well-composted soil with a pH around 6, protection from cold winds and either full sun or partial shade.

In some districts, you must seek permission to plant bananas from state agriculture departments. This aims to control serious diseases such as banana bunchy top and Panama disease.

### Anatomy of a banana plant
The banana plant is actually a giant herbaceous perennial, not a tree. It takes 12–18 months from when the suckers first appear above ground to when they bear fruit. The drooping mass of male flowers at the end of the stem is called the bell. Banana bunches form from the female flowers, which grow on the central stem. In cooler districts the developing bunch can be covered with a coloured plastic bag, open at the bottom, to protect against winter chill; this also protects against birds and flying foxes.

### Harvest before ripe
Ripening depends on the variety and the temperature – the cooler the climate, the longer it takes. A bunch is best harvested when the fruit at the top of the bunch begins to change colour. The easiest method is to cut off the bunch with a section of stalk for easy handling, and store under cover to ripen progressively. A single banana stem bears only one fruiting bunch, after which it is cut down to make way for new shoots from the underground rhizome. All parts of the plant can be chopped up and used as mulch.

BANKSIAS | BASIL

Scarlet banksia (*Banksia coccinea*)

# BANKSIAS

## Winter colour
As well as being evergreen, many banksias flower during winter. Most striking are the golden 'candles', or flowers, of heath banksia (*Banksia ericifolia*) and hairpin banksia (*B. spinulosa*) and its varieties and cultivars. Both carry their flowers for months.

Most banksias require well-drained sandy soils and prefer full sun. They respond well to annual pruning, which will keep them compact.

## Tall trees to groundcovers
Banksias range from tall trees to shrubs and groundcovers such as 'Birthday Candles'. Some good tree forms include the moderately frost-tolerant Menzies banksia (*B. menziesii*), which grows to 10 m high; and the iconic old man banksia (*B. serrata*), which is 3.5–12 m high.

## Seaside planting
The fast-growing coast banksia (*B. integrifolia*) grows naturally along the east coast of Australia. With its tolerance of dry soils and sea winds, it makes a good seaside screening hedge. Close to the sea, it grows as a small shrub. In a sheltered spot, with good soil, it can become a 10–15 m tall tree.

# BASIL

## Growing from seed
Basil is an annual easily grown from seed. In warm, frost-free climates it will grow year-round. In climates with cold winters and frosts, plant basil after all threat of frost has passed. If the weather turns cold after you've planted, protect the young plants with a plastic guard, which you can make from a cut-down plastic bottle (open at top and bottom).

## The secret of long production
Pinching back the shoots ensures bushy, long-producing basil. Pinch plants just above the point where two side branches leave the stem. Try not to allow flowers to develop because they sap energy from the plant's leaves.

## Basil and tomatoes
Some people think that basil and tomatoes make good companion plants. Planting them together will encourage better, stronger growth in each other. Basil grows well in large pots, and it is easy to raise a crop on a sunny balcony or patio.

## Choice of varieties
Sweet basil (*Ocimum basilicum*) is the most common form used in cooking. It includes large and smaller green-leaved varieties, purple or purple-splashed leaf forms, and the most intensely scented basils, such as 'Anise', 'Licorice' and 'Cinnamon'. Lemon basil (*O. × citriodorum*) includes a number of popular basils, not all of them lemon-scented. There is such an array of leaf form and colour, they can be used in garden beds and borders.

### make Basil pesto sauce

1. Blend 2 garlic cloves, ¼ cup pine nuts and ⅓ cup grated parmesan cheese in a food processor to combine.

2. Add the leaves and soft stalks of a medium bunch of basil and process until the basil is chopped and the mixture clumps together. Add 5 tablespoons extra virgin olive oil and process until combined. Serve with pasta.

# BAUHINIAS | BAY TREES

## BAUHINIAS

### From the tropics
These lovely trees grow 5–8 m high and have distinctive two-lobed leaves and flowers that resemble orchids or butterflies. Mostly evergreen or summer-deciduous, they like a tropical climate but will grow in drier areas if they have supplementary watering. They are easy to grow but need protection from frost and cold winds. They may also need training to develop a straight single trunk.

### Choice of colour
The Hong Kong orchid tree (*Bauhinia × blakeana*) has large cerise pink flowers during winter and spring, while *B. purpurea* has dark purplish pink flowers in autumn. The orchid tree or mountain ebony (*B. variegata*) has rose pink flowers in spring and summer; 'Candida' is a stunning white form. Pride of De Kaap (*B. galpinii*) is a fast-growing shrub with a sprawling habit. It is covered in small apricot orange to red flowers from late summer to autumn.

## BAY TREES

### Good conditions for growth
The bay tree (*Laurus nobilis*) originated in the Mediterranean region. It grows well in ordinary garden soil in a sunny, sheltered position in the garden and may reach its natural height of 6 m or more, with no need of pruning. The bay is remarkably hardy and will survive in all areas except those with very harsh winters. It will flourish even in coastal areas. It also does well in large tubs and containers, adding a touch of formality when trained as a standard or lollipop.

### Bay leaves for cooking
Aromatic bay leaves are an excellent herb for meats and Mediterranean recipes and for adding flavour to tomato dishes. If using the leaves whole, remove before serving.

## train a lollipop Bay tree

**1** Buy a young plant with a straight stem and plant it in a 10 cm container of good-quality potting mix. You must now look after the young plant so that it establishes and starts growing well – this may take a year or more.

**2** As the plant grows, pot it on into a larger container and trim off the lower sideshoots and leaves to start developing a clear trunk. Support the plant stem with a cane. Continue potting on and tying in the trunk to the cane as necessary.

**3** When the young tree is a little taller than the required height, prune off the central growing tip. Remove any shoots forming on the trunk, and cut the tips of sideshoots that will form the ball when they are about 15 cm long.

**4** Keep pinching out the tips of sideshoots to encourage a dense, well-shaped ball of leafy growth. Repot or top up with potting mix annually in spring, feed with slow-release fertiliser and trim with secateurs twice a year to keep the shape.

BEANS

# BEANS

### Preparing the ground
All beans do best in fertile, well-drained soil that has been enriched. Dig the ground deeply and work in well-rotted manure or compost the autumn before planting. In spring, when the soil has warmed and any danger of frost has passed, sow seed 5 cm deep in moist soil. To speed up germination, you can soak the bean seeds in warm water for one night before sowing.

### Watching the water
Although beans need plenty of water, take care when watering dwarf varieties. Their flowers are near the ground and can be damaged by water spray. It is best to wet the ground by letting water flow gently from a perforated hosepipe placed between the rows of beans.

### Good support
Where space is limited, you could grow runner beans on a bamboo-frame teepee. Many varieties have very pretty flowers, so a covered teepee will make a lovely edible display. This is a project that will appeal to child gardeners. Grow runner beans up a sturdy support of poles or canes, or use plastic, string or wire netting.

### Best yields
You will get the heaviest yields from picking beans regularly once they have reached their maximum length but before the seeds begin to bulge in the pods. The more you pick, the more the plants will produce. Once all the beans have been harvested, cut back the plant's stems and leave the roots in the soil – bean roots are a rich source of nitrogen and they will release this important plant nutrient into the soil.

## know your Beans
There are four basic types of bean, all with their own special features and needs.

**Runner beans** The easiest beans to grow well in cool conditions, runner beans are vigorous climbers with red or white flowers. Plant them in full sun.

**Broad beans** Broad beans are tough, hardy and very easy to grow in any good garden soil in a sunny place. Most grow to about 1 m tall and may need support, but a few varieties are much shorter.

**Dwarf (bush) French beans** Grown on a bush with a neat habit, these beans are generally stringless and have a fine flavour. They thrive in rich soil and full sun. Pick when small.

**Climbing French beans** Their flowers are self-pollinating and therefore more reliable than runner beans. Their flavour is often stronger than that of dwarf French beans and they crop for longer.

## make a cane support for Beans

Runner and climbing beans need support. Climbing beans are a heavy weight, so be sure to provide them with a well-constructed framework. For runner beans, canes, poles, string or wire netting work well.

**1** Hammer two pairs of 2.5 m stakes into the ground 2 m apart (or the length of the row you require). Angle each pair to form an X, 75 cm wide at the bottom. Lay a crosspiece over the top and tie it to each X with twine. Push angled pairs of bamboo canes into the ground at 30 cm intervals and tie them to the crosspiece.

**2** In spring, when the soil has warmed and any danger of frost is past, sow seed, 7–10 cm apart, at the foot of the canes. Once the plants are tall enough, begin guiding them up the canes from inside the structure.

# BEDDING PLANTS | BEDS AND BORDERS

## BEDDING PLANTS

### Making the best buys
Bedding plants are sold in pots, punnets or cellular trays. The best ones are those with green foliage, short branching stems, and a good root system set in a slightly moist potting mix. Avoid plants that are pale, have overly long foliage or roots protruding from drainage holes. Also avoid those growing in dry potting mix or in potting mix covered with algae or weeds.

### Potted colour
Annuals may be sold in bloom. These bedding plants, known as 'bloomers' or 'potted colour', are really grown-up seedlings. They are ideal for creating instant effects. Plant them straight into the garden.

### Getting the colour right
Before buying, check a plant's colour by examining the buds. The colour shown on plant labels may vary greatly from the actual colour of the plant's flowers. To grow beautiful bedding plants, deadhead frequently and feed them every 2–3 weeks with liquid feed, diluted as directed on the container. Plants in pots should be fed every 8–10 days.

## BEDS AND BORDERS
The easiest way to achieve an attractive, continuous display in a garden is to create a bed or border of mixed flowers – planting a whole range of perennials, bulbs and annuals around a framework of shrubs and small ornamental trees.

### Get the most from your beds
Following just two principles of design when planning a flowerbed or border will help you to create a pleasing effect. First, put most of your tall plants at the back of borders or in the centre of beds cut out of the lawn. Their height will offset smaller plants at the front of the border or around the edge of the bed. But don't be too rigid – two or three taller plants mixed with small ones can make a striking focus and add extra depth to the design.

Second, always group an odd number of flowering or foliage plants together. This will bring a more natural feeling to your planting scheme.

### Weird and wonderful
Add height and excitement to a low-lying flowerbed by growing annuals over structures made from bamboo or wire mesh. Spheres, cones or even animal-shaped structures will be covered quickly by dwarf nasturtiums, sweet peas, runner beans or other climbers for a flowerbed that looks a little out of the ordinary.

### Year-round interest
Make your flowerbed a centre of interest throughout the year by choosing plants that flower or produce decorative foliage at different times. Plan ahead to include bulbs that will bloom at the end of winter and in early spring, and also add some late-flowering perennials such as Japanese windflowers to brighten up your garden in autumn and early winter.

### Flowers of contrast
Give flowerbeds variety. Plant flowers with contrasting shapes together. Try spiked larkspurs, foxgloves, salvias or New Zealand flax with daisies, sedums and other plants that have flat-topped or rounded blooms.

BEDS AND BORDERS | BEES

### Creative colour
For a cohesive look when deciding on colour for a flowerbed, pick a single dominant colour and build a contrasting or complementary scheme around it. Add some white if you wish to highlight certain colours. Stronger tints work best at the front of a bed, with paler ones further back. This trick will make your beds look larger than they really are.

### Final check
Avoid creating a bed that is too large or awkwardly shaped by first covering the intended area with a light sprinkling of sand. This will let you see what the bed will look like before you start digging and sacrifice lawn space. To help you decide on the best position for your plants, insert stakes or canes into the ground to represent tall species and use pots for the smaller plants. You will gain an idea of the aesthetic effect of your planned bed.

### Decorative surround
Create an attractive surround with bricks. Dig a narrow trench about 15 cm deep round the bed or at the front of the border. Position each brick carefully, at an angle if desired.

### Avoid the stark look
If you plant a whole bed at the recommended spacing using young plants, the display will be rather stark until the plants fill out and cover the ground. For a good instant display, space the permanent framework plants at the correct distances and fill the gaps with disposable annuals, bulbs or groundcovers. Let the main plants grow and don't replace the annuals and bulbs. After two years the permanent plants will have filled all of the available space, smothering most of the temporary additions.

## BEES

### The great pollinators
Bees carry pollen from flower to flower, facilitating fertilisation in many edible and ornamental plants. Some bumblebees can take nectar from tubular flowers by making a hole in the back. To avoid harming these and other pollinating insects, confine any spraying of plants to the evening, when these insects are less active.

### Choosing the right plants
Bees are highly attracted to blue flowers, such as borage and campanulas, as well as gauras and wattles, and herbs including basil, comfrey and thyme. Native plants such as banksias, tea trees, bottlebrush and grevilleas tend to attract native bees, which are better at pollinating native plants than introduced honeybees.

#### Dealing with bee stings

**Act fast to remove a bee sting**
Either pull it out or scrape it off with a knife or your fingernail. The venom is pumped by the venom sac through the sting, so removing all of it or even just the part that is protruding will reduce the amount of poison entering the person's system.

**Taking the pain out of a sting**
The most effective remedy is a paste made from sodium bicarbonate and water. Done early enough, it neutralises acid from the sting and prevents swelling. Some people can have serious allergic reactions to stings, resulting in rapid and severe swelling, accompanied by difficulty in breathing. If this happens, take the victim to the emergency department of the nearest hospital immediately or call an ambulance.

## prepare a garden Bed

**1** Mark out the final planting area with sand, chalk, sawdust or the garden hose. Create smooth curves with a makeshift compass made from a piece of string tied to two wooden pegs.

**2** Using a sharp spade or half-moon cutter, slice into the ground, working along the marked line, then remove the grass from the planting area. The turf can be reused elsewhere to repair damaged patches of your lawn.

**3** Before planting, remove any weeds and grass runners, then thoroughly dig and loosen the soil, working in some well-rotted compost or manure. The bed can be bordered with edging stones, bricks or pavers.

# B

BEETROOT | BEGONIAS

## BEETROOT

### Globe and long
There are two main types of beetroot – globe and long-rooted. They will succeed in most fertile, well-drained soils in a sunny site. You can also grow striped, white and yellow varieties, which do not 'bleed' like the more common red-fleshed types. Baby beet is fast-growing and a good choice for a small garden or container.

### Soaking seeds
A beetroot seed is actually a fused cluster of up to four true seeds. Soak seeds in water for 2 hours before sowing. It is best to sow them – while wet – directly in the garden as transplanting is not always successful. Keep the bed damp until the seedlings emerge in 10–14 days. Use the tender leaves from beetroot thinnings in salads or cook the larger leaves as you would silverbeet.

### When to harvest
You can pick globe beetroot as soon as they reach the size of a golf ball. Pull by hand as needed in summer and autumn, but don't let them grow any bigger than a cricket ball as they become woody and lose flavour. In cold areas, lift long-rooted varieties with a fork in early winter and store; in mild winter areas, leave them in the ground and pull up as required.

## BEGONIAS

### For cool, humid summers
There are different types of begonia, requiring very different climatic and cultural conditions. Tuberous begonias (*Begonia × tuberhybrida*) need a cool but humid summer climate so they are not suited to hot, dry or tropical regions. In cool districts, you will find the best displays are in greenhouses or shadehouses.

### The choice with tubers
Never skimp on quality when buying tuberous begonias – the bigger the tuber, the more flowers it will produce. Make sure tubers are planted the right way up. The tops are concave and the bases convex. Look for the beginnings of the first shoots in the hollow tops and plant with these uppermost. Start tubers in late winter to early spring when they are dormant.

### Filling an awkward space
Tree begonias are also called angel's wing begonias, and they grow in most areas. Reaching 1–2 m tall, they are an ideal choice to fill a narrow garden bed in a shaded area. Their coloured and patterned leaves and pastel flowers provide year-round interest. For coloured foliage, you can grow the large-leafed rex begonias indoors or in a shaded part of the garden.

### Annual colour that lasts
Fast-growing and long-flowering bedding begonias (*Begonia × semperflorens-cultorum*) are hard to beat for annual colour or a border planting in a sunny spot. They are available as seedlings or potted colour and can be planted all year round.

## take flat leaf cuttings of rex Begonias

**1** A single colourful leaf of a rex begonia can produce several plants when laid on the surface of potting mix. Cut a leaf from the parent plant. Using a sharp knife, make cuts straight across the strongest main veins in several places on the leaf's underside.

**2** Spread the leaf, face up, on the surface of a tray filled with propagating mix. Weigh down the leaf with pebbles and keep warm and moist in a propagator. Young plants will soon appear where the cut parts of the leaf are in contact with the mix.

28

BELLADONNA LILIES | BENEFICIAL CREATURES

# BELLADONNA LILIES

### Ladies in the garden

Indigenous to South Africa, where they are known as March lilies because they appear in late February to March, these lilies are known to some gardeners as 'naked ladies'. This is because the beautiful trumpet-shaped flowers of *Amaryllis belladonna* – in light or dark pink or pure white – are carried on long, bare, bronze-coloured stalks, which appear before the leaves emerge.

### Dormant in summer

Belladonna lilies are easy to grow and relish those parts of the garden where other plants struggle. They need a period of late spring to summer dormancy with dry conditions, so grow happily in dry soils or even under the eaves of the house, sheltered from rain. But they need extra watering in their main growing season of late summer to autumn.

Plant the bulbs near the soil surface so that the bulb top – the slender neck – protrudes. Allow 15–20 cm between bulbs. Plant in early summer for flowers in late summer or early autumn.

# BENEFICIAL CREATURES

There are some creatures that should be welcomed into your garden because of their abilities to control pests and create good growing conditions naturally.

**Blue-tongue lizard**

**Earthworms** Burrowing by earthworms aerates the soil, improves drainage and reduces compaction; this discourages a number of insect pests and soil diseases. Earthworms can improve yields 20-fold.

**Frogs** Many entomologists think frogs and toads are the most important safeguard against insect pests. Provide a small, shaded pond for them to breed in.

**Hoverflies** Hoverflies are true flies, but they look like wasps and bees. The adults are valuable flower pollinators, while their brown, maggot-like larvae can eat 100 aphids a day.

**Insectivorous birds** Small birds such as flycatchers, honeyeaters and wrens tend to be both nectar and insect feeders. Create a safe habitat for them: a dense hedge of flowering shrubs is perfect.

**Lizards** Many lizard species feed either exclusively on insects or on insects and related arthropods. Geckos and skinks provide year-round pest control in the garden. Legless lizards inhabit the soil and feed on slugs.

**Parasitic wasps** These wasps lay their eggs inside the bodies of other insects, which then provide food for the developing larvae. A number of species are available as biological control agents.

**Ladybirds** A ladybird and larvae are voracious predators of aphids. The exception is the 28-spotted ladybird, which eats cucurbits. Ladybirds can be purchased for use as a biological control.

**Lacewings** Both the adult and larval stages of all lacewing species prey on aphids, sucking the juices from their prey.

**Predatory mites** Many predatory mites feed mainly on plant-eating mites. A number are available as biological controls – for example, *Phytoseiulus persimilis* is used to control two-spotted mites.

**Spiders** Ground-dwelling spiders are voracious insect hunters, and web spinners catch many flying insects, including mosquitoes and flies.

See also Biological controls

29

# BIOLOGICAL CONTROLS

## Balancing act
Instead of chemical treatments designed to eradicate garden pests, you can use biological control agents, which reduce the number of pests to an acceptable level without upsetting the balance of nature. The control agents' actions are very specific and they are harmless to other creatures. And because they can't survive without the pest on which they feed, there is no danger that today's predators may become tomorrow's pests.

## Parasitic pest controls
Parasitic pest controls use insects that lay their eggs in the larvae of other insects. Whiteflies are dealt with in this way by the parasitic wasp *Encarsia formosa*. When the wasp eggs hatch, they eat their whitefly hosts before the latter can emerge as adults.

## Moth and fruit fly traps
Pheromones are hormones that are naturally produced by insects to attract members of the opposite sex. Pheromones can be produced synthetically and used to bait traps, which attract male insects. Once in the trap, the insect cannot escape and is killed. These traps can be used to control and monitor pests such as codling moth and fruit fly. Hang moth and fruit fly traps in trees in early spring; one trap will protect five trees.

## Damage limitation
*Bacillus thuringiensis* is a deadly bacterium that infects and kills caterpillars of moth and butterfly pests. It is readily available in garden centres and is applied as a spray solution.

## All in the timing
For biological controls to work effectively, gardeners need to understand the behaviour of the pest they wish to control. In most situations, the control agent must be introduced as soon as the pest is noticed. If left for too long, pest numbers build so rapidly that they cannot easily be controlled by a predator.

# BIRDS

## Inviting them in
To encourage birds that will eat garden pests, create a protective cover of dense, prickly shrubs to protect the birds from predators. Dense groves of grevilleas, hakeas and prickly wattles create the perfect environment for small native birds. Also provide nesting boxes, birdbaths and feed tables.

## Installing a birdbath
A birdbath should be shallow – 5–15 mm deep – and will need to be refilled at least once a day. Place a few stones in the water for the birds to stand on. Position the birdbath where it will get full sun; in the open where predators cannot approach unseen, but not too far from hedges or bushes where the birds can perch to dry.

## Start with small portions
Avoid putting out too much food when trying to attract birds into your garden – uneaten seeds will quickly become damp and mouldy. Put out small quantities of seed to begin with, increasing the amount gradually as more birds begin to appear and the food is consumed more quickly.

## Keeping birds out
Old CDs strung from branches or sticks bearing rattling, glinting lengths of silver foil will deter birds for a short time, until they get used to them.

Protect newly sown seeds by inserting small wooden stakes into the ground at each side of the bed. Fit lengths of string, pulled taut, to stakes opposite each other, then lay pieces of pruned roses or prickly branches along the strings to deter predators.

To protect seedlings, cut flexible PVC-coated 15 mm mesh wire netting into lengths that will fit along the rows, then bend each length into a tunnel shape to fit over a row.

## temporarily protect fruit from Birds

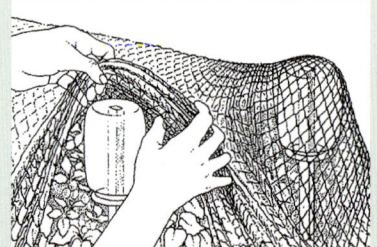

**1** Insert canes 1.2 m apart on either side of fruit bushes. Put glass jars over the top of canes. Peg the netting into the ground on one side and pull it over the canes.

**2** Pull the netting taut but make sure the canes hold it clear of the plants. Peg it down firmly all the way round, so birds can't find an entrance.

BLACKBERRY HYBRIDS | BLOOD AND BONE

## BLACKBERRY HYBRIDS

The blackberry has been bred from and crossed with other berries to create a range of hybrid berries.

### Prolific and delicious

Hybrids include the boysenberry, hildaberry, Japanese wineberry, loganberry, tayberry, youngberry, tummelberry and veitchberry. All are good for eating fresh when ripe or for making jams and pies. There are few fruits more prolific and easy to grow.

### A warning

The blackberry is a significant weed in parts of Australia and New Zealand. It should never be planted in areas where it is a declared weed, so always check with your local agriculture department or regional council. Fortunately, blackberry hybrids are not a weed problem.

Tayberry flower and fruit

### Protect the fruit

Some of these fruits are prone to sun scorch, so you may need to protect them with shadecloth. Birds love berries, too, so if you have plenty of bushes, it may be worthwhile investing in a protective 'cage' for your plants.

### Training fruit on wires

A simple way to grow plants is in a fan shape on horizontal wires. You can train the branches out on both sides of the rootstock, spacing them evenly on the wires. Fruit is on last season's growth.

Or you can separate them more clearly. Tie all the branches to the wires on one side of the rootstock, then as the new growth develops, tie these new branches to the wires on the other side. All the fruit for that year will be carried on the branches on one side, and after fruiting those branches should be cut out. The next year the berries will be on the branches on the other side.

Blackberry

## BLOOD AND BONE

### A boost for trees and shrubs

For a long-lasting boost, scatter a handful of blood and bone into planting holes and fork it in. This slow-release fertiliser is a rich source of phosphate, which helps development of roots, while the nitrogen that it contains provides food for leaf growth.

### Protect your hands

While the main ingredient of blood and bone – meat meal – is rendered at high temperatures and is safe to use, always wear gloves as an added precaution for good hygiene practice.

### Read the label

Products marked as blood and bone fertilisers should only contain organic products derived from blood and bone. In some areas laws are in force to protect consumers from products that contain other fertilisers or impurities. To find the fertilisers that really are pure blood and bone, check the label, ask at your local garden centre or contact the product manufacturer.

# Blue flowers

Truly blue flowers are hard to come by. Compared with most other colours, there are limited choices, and many gardeners substitute purple flowers and grey foliage to get similar visual effects. Blue has a calming effect and harmonises with most other colours in the garden.

## Contrast and complement

Blue encompasses a wide range of tones and hues. Within a genus of blue-flowering plants such as hydrangeas or campanulas, there are many shades. Blue contrasts with orange, and combinations of blue with orange, yellow and red create dramatic effects. Create a vibrant late summer combination with blue and red salvias, marigolds and rudbeckia.

Complementary to blue is purple and green, and planting schemes including these colours are calm and restful.

## At a distance

Blue recedes, so blue flowers give the impression of being further away. Take advantage of this by siting blue flowers at the end of the garden to make the space appear larger. Lining a path with blue flowers, such as lobelias, dampieras or dwarf agapanthus, makes it seem longer than it really is.

## Dark and light

Dark blue looks dramatic, while pale blue brings depth to combinations of pastel pink, lavender, silver and white in cottage-style gardens. In sunny spots, pale blue flowers often look washed out, so use deeper blues in those areas instead – hebes, cornflowers and delphiniums are good options. In the shade, lighter blue gives brightness, while darker colours can appear more intense. Combine blue and white, such as a border of blue and white irises, for a crisp, elegant look.

### choose Blue flowers

**For temperate and cool climates**
- Bugle (*Ajuga reptans*)
- Campanula
- Bluebeard (*Caryopteris* × *clandonensis*)
- Ceanothus (*Ceanothus* spp.)
- Cornflower (*Centaurea cyanus*)
- Chinese plumbago (*Ceratostigma willmottianum*)
- Moroccan glory vine (*Convolvulus sabatius*)
- Delphinium
- Iris
- Lobelia

**For warm and hot climates**
- Dianella (*Dianella caerulea*)
- Blue ginger (*Dichorisandra thyrsiflora*)
- *Duranta* 'Geisha Girl'
- Blue sage (*Eranthemum pulchellum*)
- Blue marguerite (*Felicia amelloides*)
- Hydrangea
- Blue lechenaultia (*Lechenaultia biloba*)
- Brazilian snapdragon (*Otacanthus caeruleus*)
- Plumbago (*Plumbago auriculata*)

Hydrangea

Iris

Ceanothus

Plumbago

# BLUEBERRIES | BOG GARDENS

## BLUEBERRIES

### Take your pick
There are four different groups. Low bush blueberries are suited to cold districts; high bush require some chill; southern high bush prefer warm districts; and Rabbit Eyes do well in very warm areas. Ask your nursery or garden centre for advice on varieties in the best group for your climate.

### Acidity is essential
All blueberries require an acid soil (pH 4.5–5), well drained and rich in humus. Add plenty of acidic compost, such as pine needles or composted woodchips, if your soil is alkaline. Or dig in sulfur or ammonium sulfate, following the quantities given in the manufacturer's instructions.

### Routine care
Fertilise 6 weeks after planting and then every spring. Blueberry roots form close to the soil surface so mulch to keep them cool. Water regularly so the berries are large and juicy. Because blueberries crop on older wood, no pruning is required until the third or fourth year except for cutting out any weak shoots. After this, regularly cut out older wood. Birds love the berries; cover the bushes with net.

### Plant in pots
Blueberries do well in tubs. Buy a potting mix for camellias or mix your own with 40 per cent pine bark, 40 per cent peat substitute and 20 per cent sharp river sand. Add a suitable fertiliser.

## BOG GARDENS

### Choose the place
If an area of your garden has naturally poor drainage, make the most of it by dedicating it to plants that thrive in damp soil. If no such area exists, you could create an artificial bog garden. These gardens need frequent watering so are not suitable for drought-affected areas.

### Natural plantings
Moisture-loving plants for a bog garden include water irises, especially the lovely Japanese iris (*Iris ensata*) and blue flag iris (*I. versicolor*), marsh marigolds (*Caltha palustris*), leopard plants (*Ligularia* spp.), forget-me-nots and hostas. For an exotic touch, you could use papyrus (*Cyperus papyrus*) or moisture-loving ferns such as *Blechnum camfieldii* or, in a cold climate, the alpine water fern (*B. penna-marina*) and royal fern (*Osmunda regalis*).

### Easy steps
Put stepping stones alongside and through a large bog garden so that you can tend the plants without getting your feet wet. Use a mixture of medium and large flat stones for easy walking.

See also Water plants

### Weed warning
Many introduced water and bog plants can become a menace or even a weed, quickly swamping native plants. Many vigorous-growing plants can be kept under control, however, if planted in a large pot which is then set into the bog garden. Even so, be very cautious with horsetails, reeds and rushes of all sorts.

### make a Bog garden
Dig a hole, at least 30 cm deep and as large as you require. Line it with heavy-duty plastic or butyl rubber liner. Trim so there is a 20 cm overlap on all sides. Make a few small holes in the liner to aid drainage. Mix the excavated garden soil with water-retentive organic matter, such as well-rotted compost or coir (use 3 parts soil to 1 part organic matter); use it to refill the lined hole. Incorporate 75 g slow-release fertiliser per square metre into the soil. Plant moisture-loving plants, then place stones all around the bog garden to cover the edge of the liner.

# BONSAI

## Choosing a specimen tree
Always check carefully that the roots of the tree are spread out evenly around the trunk and have not become entangled. Look for a tree structure that rises naturally and has an elegant habit. Plants with small leaves, flowers and fruit are best as they will be in proportion to the bonsai's height.

Although small, most bonsai trees are best kept outdoors in a sheltered but well-lit position.

## Wired for shape
Plastic-coated wire, spiralled around branches, helps to train young bonsai into a natural shape. Deciduous trees are most pliable in spring, evergreens in autumn. Check wires regularly and loosen them if necessary.

## Keeping a bonsai in shape
Once you've established a natural shape, only minimal pruning is necessary unless a new branch is required. Bonsai trees should be kept in shape by pinching back soft new growth during spring and summer. Keep an eye on plants with a vigorous growth habit as pinching back may be necessary three or four times during the growing season.

Major structural cuts to a bonsai tree should be made during late winter to prevent the sap loss that would occur if it were pruned during the growing season. No sealing compound is necessary – you'll find that the plant will heal naturally.

## repot Bonsai
Repot a bonsai every 2–5 years, depending on its age. Do this in early spring. Change the soil and cut off a third of the plant's roots. The older the bonsai tree is, the less often it needs repotting.

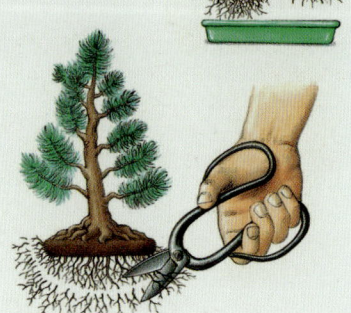

# BORAGE

## Edible leaves and flowers
This easy-to-grow annual is commonly associated with herb gardens. The young, tender leaves taste like cucumber and are often tossed in salads. The brilliant blue, star-shaped flowers can be used to garnish salads or frozen in ice cube trays and added to summer drinks.

## Increasing the bounty
Standing around 60–90 cm tall when in flower, borage will grow in almost any type of soil but does best in well-drained soil in a sunny position. It often wilts on very hot days but will spring back to life as soon as the sun sets. Borage is very easy to grow from seed. Sow directly into the garden in spring. Established borage self-sows enthusiastically but isn't invasive. If you don't want it to self-seed, clip off the flowers after they fade.

# BORERS

## Plants affected
Many trees and shrubs, including natives, cypress pine, fruit and nut trees.

## Symptoms
Sawdust; chewed wood; webbing on branches or trunks covering holes; ringbarking of twigs; wilting growth.

## Treatment
✽ Water, feed and provide good care for trees.

✽ Regularly check trees and shrubs if borers are active or if a tree is under some stress.

✽ Kill larvae in the tunnel with a flexible piece of wire, and plug the hole with butyl mastic putty, soft soap or wax.

✽ Prune off damaged areas; remove a badly infested plant.

# BOTTLEBRUSH

Bottlebrush (*Callistemon* spp.) are iconic Australian natives. They are trouble-free and quick-growing, and with so many types to choose from, there is one to suit any sunny position, whether you require a shrub or a small tree. Bottlebrush like moist soil but can be quite drought-tolerant once they are established. The stunning flower spikes in red, pink, purple, cream, white, yellow or green are loved by birds and bees, and form interesting woody seed capsules after flowering.

## Coloured new growth

Many bottlebrush have colourful new growth, an added advantage after pruning. 'Eureka' and 'Hannah Ray', both red-flowered forms, sprout new red leaves, while the pink-flowered 'Candy Pink' and the crimson-flowered 'Endeavour' (syn. 'Splendens') have young pink leaves. A recent cultivar, 'Great Balls of Fire', is grown for its spectacular bright red new growth.

## A fast hedge

A row of bottlebrush makes an excellent screen where a quick-growing hedge is required. Plant shrub forms around 1 m apart and taller growing bottlebrush about 2 m apart. Keep the plants well watered until they become established. For a uniform effect, plant all the same cultivar.

## Pruning tips

How you prune your bottlebrush will depend on the variety. Some bottlebrush develop hard woody seed capsules, and after several years of no pruning the stems can become gnarled with old seedpods. Pruning isn't essential, but many gardeners prune their bottlebrush after flowering to remove the woody seed capsules and to encourage bushiness, new colourful foliage and next season's flowers. There are some cultivars that don't set seed, such as the glorious red-flowered bottlebrush 'King's Park Special' and 'Harkness'.

---

### choose Bottlebrush by flower colour

Not all bottlebrush flowers are red. Here are some species and cultivars in other colours:

*Callistemon* **'Candy Pink'** Pink flowers; tall shrub, 3–4 m

*C. citrinus* **'Mauve Mist'** Mauve flowers; tall dense shrub, 2–3 m

*C. citrinus* **'Reeves Pink'** Pink flowers; round shrub, 2–3 m

*C. citrinus* **'White Anzac'** White flowers; low spreading bush, 1 m

*C. pallidus* Lemon flowers; loose shrub, 3 m

*C. pallidus* **'Austraflora Candle Glow'** Bright lemon flowers; groundcover, 60–90 cm

*C. salignus* White flowers; tree, 8–12 m

*C. salignus* **'Eureka'** Pink flowers; narrow compact shrub, 4–5 m

*C. viminalis* **'Rose Opal'** Rose flowers; dwarf shrub, 2 m

*C. viminalis* **'Wilderness White'** White flowers; weeping shrub, 2–3 m

*C.* **'Violaceus'** Rosy violet flowers; tall shrub or tree, 2–3 m

*C. viridiflorus* Yellow-green flowers; upright shrub, 1–2 m

---

# BOUGAINVILLEA

## A colourful covering

This showy climber for warm temperate to tropical climates brings a brilliant splash of colour to walls, pergolas, banks and fences. It needs strong support because of its heavy branches, so make sure your wall, fence or trellis is sturdy. It is generally fast-growing, although many new varieties are much less rampant than older types.

## Drain well

Ideally, choose a sunny position and plant in a light but rich soil. However, bougainvillea will do remarkably well in thin, sandy or rocky soils, provided it is watered regularly. It does not thrive in heavy clay soil and cannot stand prolonged waterlogging. Where drainage is poor, plants should be established in mounds or tubs.

## Specimen shrubs and standards

Although bougainvillea is best known as a climbing plant, it can also be grown as a specimen shrub or standard. Less vigorous-growing types are the best choice for shrubs, while pendulous forms make the best standards, giving a weeping effect. Regularly cut off all growth except a single bare stem, or leave two or more stems to be plaited together. Keep the canopy well trimmed if you want a formal look.

BOX | BROAD BEANS

# BOX

## Dividing the garden
Give your garden a formal air by surrounding the flowerbeds and even the vegetable garden with low box hedges. Box is ideal for this purpose because it does not mind constant hard clipping and it gives a neat edge.

## Different types
Japanese box (*Buxus microphylla*) is generally smaller in leaf and stature than common or European box (*B. sempervirens*). There are dwarf to taller cultivars suited to every form of hedge. Japanese box cultivars are best in coastal and humid-summer areas. In colder climates, choose common box.

## Make it uniform
Don't grow a box hedge or edging from seed because it is unlikely that all the plants will be the same colour and equally vigorous. Instead, take cuttings from a single plant so that all the new ones will be the same, or buy young plants from a specialist who will raise plants only from cuttings. To achieve a bicoloured effect, keep the two different sets of cuttings or plants separate.

## Speeding up growth
Box plants are renowned for coping with dry conditions. But be sure to water them copiously when they are young: they will grow twice as fast as they would otherwise, establish good roots and become very tolerant of any subsequent drought.

## When to prune
Clip hedges and topiary into the chosen shape from late winter to early spring. While box generally thrives on clipping, be careful not to clip it too severely at one time. Overpruning could retard growth.

See also Hedges

### Preparing to plant a hedge
Box hedges are long-lived and can be in place for a great many years, so prepare the ground well. In autumn or spring, dig a trench the depth and width of a spade. Then fork over the base, adding plenty of organic matter such as compost or well-rotted manure together with blood and bone. Also mix some organic matter with the soil from the trench, then replace it and firm in well. The ground is now ready for planting.

# BROAD BEANS

## Cool-season crop
Broad beans are a cool-season crop that are planted in late autumn to early winter, when other beans are finishing. In cool areas you can sow a second crop in early to midspring. These beans thrive in fertile, well-drained soil enriched with manure. Lime the soil if it is acid – broad beans love lime.

Hoe regularly to keep the weeds down and be sure to water well during dry weather. When the lowest pods are 8 cm long, pinch out the plant's growing tip. This encourages pod growth and also removes the part of the plant that is likely to harbour black bean aphid pests.

## Ready for picking
The earliest crops are ready in early spring. Start picking when pods are no more than 5 cm long. Then simply pick as required, feeling the pods to get an idea of the size of the beans inside.

## Provide support for broad beans
In an exposed garden, broad beans need support. Insert 1.5 m stakes or canes along both sides of the row, and tie two strands of string at suitable heights all around the row to act as a 'frame' for the plants.

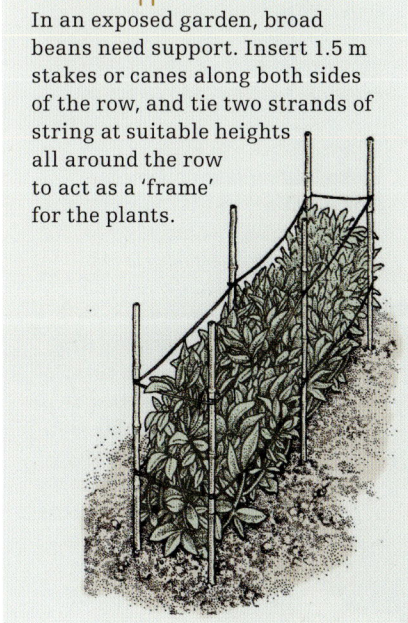

37

# BROAD MITES | BROMELIADS

## BROAD MITES

### Plants affected
Many, including beans, begonias, camellias, capsicums, cyclamens, chrysanthemums, dahlias, ivy, fuchsias, hibiscus and lemons.

### Symptoms
Twisted and puckered new leaves, sometimes also turning a bronze colour; damaged fruit.

### Treatment
* Encourage predatory mites and ladybirds as a first resort.
* Spray with wettable sulfur or dust with sulfur to kill mites and also help to combat fungal diseases, but do not do this in very hot weather.

## BROMELIADS

### Living on air
Despite originating in the tropical jungles of the Americas, bromeliads can survive with very little water so long as they have partial shade and very good drainage. Many are epiphytes, living on rocks or in the forks of trees, and surviving on moisture and nutrients obtained from the air. Certain *Alcantarea* species even have some frost tolerance.

### Spectacular shapes, colours and flowers
In some bromeliads, the rosette of stiff foliage can turn intense colours with sun or have striking spots, stripes and bands. Some produce tall flower spikes. The foliage rosettes of *Guzmania*, *Neoregelia* and *Aechmea* species form a vase; their central well must not be allowed to dry out.

Combine bromeliads with datura, frangipani, bougainvillea, cassia or jacaranda for a tropical garden with a colourful hot look. Or use them alongside other plants with distinctive shapes, such as New Zealand flax, dracaenas, yuccas and agaves, to create a dramatic architectural style.

### Instant drainage
Bromeliads need a fast-draining, highly porous and aerated soil. Plant them in a free-draining potting mix, with their rosettes sitting upright. Or plant them on top of your garden soil, in a light compost or a mulch of pine bark or coir. You can also simply bury them in mulch, still in their pot. Some types can be attached to old tree stumps or rocks.

## BROCCOLI

### A continuous supply
Because several varieties are available, it is possible to grow and harvest broccoli throughout most of the year. It grows best in fertile, loamy soil and prefers cool and cold climates. It is, however, more heat-tolerant than cauliflower and can be grown anywhere with a mild winter.

### Single versus sprouting
When buying broccoli seeds, look carefully at the type you are choosing. Single-headed broccoli generally produces one large head. Sprouting broccoli produces small heads, but once the first ones are cut off, a succession of heads will develop for many weeks afterwards to give a prolific cropping season.

### Fast and tender
Grow broccoli fast in order to keep it tender. It is a heavy feeder, so add plenty of fertiliser to the soil before planting. Side-dress or liquid-feed with a nitrogen-rich fertiliser during the growing season, but be careful because overfertilising can result in open, loose bud clusters.

Sprouting broccoli plants may be rocked by winter winds, which loosens their roots. Insert stakes on each side of the row, and tie strings between the stakes to support the plants.

### Harvest the heads
Harvest the heads of single-headed broccoli in autumn when the flower buds are green and tightly closed. Cut off the heads together with about 2.5 cm of stalk. You can harvest sprouting broccoli in winter, spring and beyond. Cut off about 10–15 cm of stem and cook this with the heads. Cut back the stem to a point just above a pair of sideshoots, which will then produce fresh spears.

Sprouting broccoli

BROMELIADS | BUDWORMS

*Neoregelia* sp.

*Guzmania* sp.

*Neoregelia* sp.

## BRUSSELS SPROUTS

### Tight buttons
Sprouts are sown throughout summer for winter picking. They need a cool to cold climate to perform at their best, and only grow well in fertile and reasonably limy soil. To encourage tight buttons, plant seedlings in soil that has been dug deeply and well manured the previous autumn. To ensure well-established roots, use a dibber rather than trowel to make the planting hole.

### Harvest from the bottom
Brussels sprouts are ready to pick when small, with their leaves tight and firm. They develop first at the bottom of the stem, so pick the lower ones first. You can encourage sprouts at the top of the stem to develop by cutting off the leaves at the top. Harvesting standard varieties after frost improves the taste.

## BUDWORMS

### Plants affected
Many, including carnations, roses and gardenias, fruit trees, crops such as beans, brassicas, hearting lettuce, peas, corn (corn earworm) and tomatoes (tomato caterpillars in New Zealand).

### Symptoms
Holes in flowers; buds and fruit bored by small caterpillars.

### Treatment
* If infestation is light, remove caterpillars by hand; destroy or release them outside the garden.

* Spray early with *Bacillus thuringiensis*, pyrethrum, carbaryl, permethrin or pyrethroids, depending on the plant attacked.

## BULBS

### Treat as annuals
Many cold-climate bulbs, such as tulips or daffodils, come from places where winters are very cold, and if they are grown in areas where winters are frost-free or barely frosty, they often decline after their first flowering. But you don't have to miss out on spring-flowering bulbs just because you live in a warm area. Instead, treat them as annuals and buy new bulbs each year. For best results, concentrate on early-flowering bulbs such as jonquils.

Or try South African and South American bulbs, such as sparaxis, babianas, bulbines, ixias, nerines and zephyranthes, which are well suited to warmer climates.

### Extend the display
You will lengthen the duration of your display if you plant bulbs that have successional flowering periods. Mix them with annuals, low perennials or creeping plants, which will later help to hide any yellowing leaves.

### When to plant
When spring bulbs are in flower it is time to plant autumn-flowering bulbs such as nerines. Similarly, when autumn bulbs are flowering it is time to plant spring bulbs, including crocuses, daffodils and tulips. Plant clusters together for the best show, but give more space to species that will multiply, such as grape hyacinths and crocuses. For a natural effect, plant the bulbs in informal groups rather than in symmetrical patterns or regimented rows.

### A lawn of flowers
Scatter clumps of bulbs in the lawn to extend the spring garden. Ideal bulbs for naturalising like this are ixias and freesias. In cool-climate gardens try daffodils and narcissus. Wait until the foliage dies down before mowing to ensure that the bulbs have absorbed the nutrients they need to flower again the following year.

### Stakes before planting
To avoid bruising or splitting bulbs, insert stakes for weighty flowers, such as liliums, before you plant the bulbs. If the bulbs are small, mark the planting area of each with a twig or small stake.

### Saving energy
Always deadhead flowers when they fade to conserve the bulb's energy for next year's display. Without deadheading, the flower will develop into a seedpod.

### plant **Bulbs** in a border

**1** Dig a planting hole large enough for a clump of bulbs, or use a slim trowel to make individual holes for each bulb. Position bulbs with their pointy end upwards and at the correct depth. Space bulbs in a clump at least their own width apart.

**2** Gently cover the bulbs with soil, taking care not to knock them over. Firm the surface with the back of a rake and mark the area, so you don't dig up the bulbs by accident.

BULBS  B

## plant Bulbs in a lawn

Drop handfuls of bulbs from waist height, then plant them where they fall using a slim trowel or a bulb planter (below). Or cut the outline of a large H with a spade and peel away the turf. Fork in blood and bone if you wish, then put the bulbs in place and replace the turf.

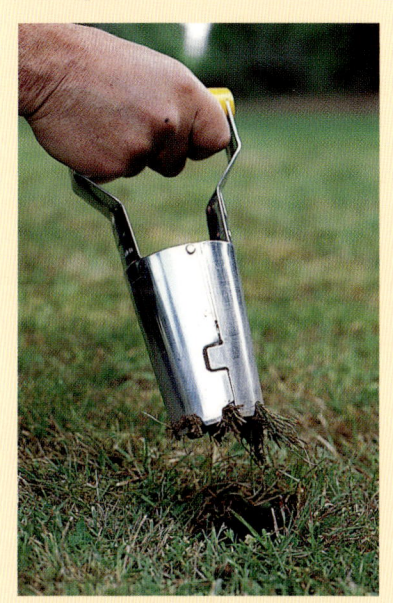

## The right depth for bulbs

As a rough guide, estimate the height of the bulb from tip to base, then cover it with two or three times that depth of soil. Plant a little deeper in light sandy soil and less deep in heavy clay. There are a few exceptions.

1. Grecian windflower (*Anemone blanda*)
2. Cyclamen (*Cyclamen coum*)
3. Spring starflower (*Ipheion uniflorum*)
4. Freesia
5. Grape hyacinth
6. Daffodil
7. Hippeastrum
8. Snowflake
9. Tulip
10. Lilium

## plant Bulbs in a pot

Pack a large pot with bulbs for a stunning display – a single variety is most striking. Fill the pot with a bulb potting mix or another potting mix with good drainage. For a dense, long show of blooms, stagger bulbs in two or three layers, 5 cm apart in a pot at least 30 cm deep.

## treat Bulb mites

### Plants affected
Amaryllis, dahlia tubers, gladioli corms, hyacinths, bulbs of hippeastrums, liliums, narcissus, onions and potatoes.

### Symptoms
Distorted leaves; rusty brown or red scars.

### Treatment
* Pull up and destroy infested plants.
* Store bulbs in dry, airy conditions.
* Expose dormant bulbs to frost for 2–3 nights before forcing, or immerse them in water heated to 45°C for 1–2 hours.

41

## BUSH REGENERATION

### Garden escapes
Many of the weeds in suburban bushland come from nearby gardens. If you live near a patch of bushland, consider removing and destroying problem species in your garden. These include plants that can break off and spread, and plants with seeds inside berries spread by feeding birds.

### Adopt a piece of bushland
Many councils offer incentives to those who want to look after and weed a piece of bushland. Contact your local council to find out about support groups, sources of indigenous native plants, rubbish removal and the like.

### Plan your attack
Weeding, whether in your own garden or in a patch of remnant bush, needs a systematic plan. There are three golden rules:

* Start where the native plants are holding and work towards the area of worst weed infestation.

* Make minimal disturbance.

* Stabilise each regenerated area before moving on to the next weed-infested area.

### Use of herbicides
Pulling out a weed is not always the best way to get rid of it. In many cases the disturbance this causes spreads weed seeds or bulbs further, which compounds your problem. Carefully used, glyphosate herbicides kill weeds without disturbing the soil. But always make sure that you keep glyphosate away from watercourses or use products that have been specially formulated for use on or near water.

If you can't remove a large weed, reduce its impact by removing its flowers. Then it won't be able to set any more seeds.

## BUSHFIRES

### Minimise the danger
Dry grass, leaves, bark, twigs and bush debris burn easily and are the first things to fuel a bushfire. Dead branches and leaves in tree crowns also provide easily lit fuel. It is important to take precautions to reduce the risk of spot fires if you live in a vulnerable area. Get information about the behaviour of local bushfires from your local bushfire brigade and council.

### Fire-resistant natives and exotics
All plants will burn eventually but some resist fire better than others. Plant fire-resistant trees on the side of your land from which bushfires will likely come; this will help block flying embers, which often start a house fire. Keep plants with a high volatile oil content, such as eucalypts, pines and some tea trees, clear of buildings, as well as plants with high fuel loads, such as hakeas and stringybark eucalypts.

### Clear a space
Trim lower branches to keep them out of reach of ground fires, and trim away dead material which could ignite in great heat, or be lit by burning flying debris. Consider creating pebbled courtyards and moss gardens. Groundcovers such as mown grass, bugle, pigface, gazanias, prostrate rosemary, ivy-leaved geraniums and cotton lavender help to keep fire at bay. And lush, wet vegetation is the slowest to heat up and burn.

### Before summer starts
Do as much preparation in the garden as you can before summer begins. Clear the ground, gutters and roofing of natural fuel and remove any flammable material near the house. Improve existing firebreaks by removing bushes, overhanging branches and any undergrowth close to the house.

### Water check
Check that hoses are long enough to reach all sides of the house and are attached to taps. Use heavy-duty hoses with metal fittings and wide-spray nozzles. Install a sprinkler system throughout the garden, and on the roof if you can afford it. Fill any ponds, tanks or dams – store as much rainwater as possible during winter. Fit a gate valve to the water tank and have a portable petrol pump, which fits the gate valve, to draw water if the power supply fails.

### Have a plan
Part of being ready for bushfire is discussing and deciding, well before any fire threatens, what you will do in the event of a fire. Get information and advice from your local bushfire brigade and your local authority to help you with making the decision.

# BUTTERFLIES

## Grow a butterfly nursery
Most butterflies lay their eggs only on plants that are in full sun, so if you hope to have a garden of beautiful butterflies, provide them with generous clumps of their favourite plants in the sun.

## Live and let live
Bear in mind that when you create a butterfly-friendly environment in your garden, you are also encouraging caterpillars, which will eat your plants. For example, cabbage white butterflies produce caterpillars that feed on brassicas and nasturtiums; the impatiens hawkmoth makes short work of impatiens. A solution is to plant so many cabbages, nasturtiums and impatiens that you don't mind losing a few. Other caterpillars munch a few leaves without doing much damage, which is a small price to pay for the pleasure of butterflies in your garden.

## Choosing blooms
Butterflies are attracted by red, purple, orange and yellow flowers. Remember that nectar is more accessible to a butterfly in single rather than double blooms – and some double blooms may produce no nectar at all. Also, butterflies find it hard to sip from flowers that hang downwards or have ruffled petal edges.

# BUTTERFLY BUSH

## Summer feature
Butterfly bush (*Buddleja davidii*) is a tall, easy-to-grow flowering shrub that, together with the many butterflies, bees and other insects that visit the nectar-rich blossoms, becomes a focal point in any summer garden. It combines with other shrubs, or even grows well in pots. While evergreen in frost-free areas, in areas with cold or frosty winters plants will be semi-evergreen to deciduous.

## Long flowering
The cones of white, yellow, pink, blue or purple flowers are up to 30 cm in length. They begin to open in early summer and will keep blooming until autumn if the spent flowers are clipped off every few weeks. They have an intensely sweet honey scent.

## Thriving on neglect
As long as they can bask in the sun and have well-drained soil, these plants thrive on neglect. They grow in most soil types and also tolerate dry conditions. Container-grown plants need regular watering and fertilising with a balanced fertiliser to remain at their healthiest. To ensure continuous flowers on a compact bush, prune the whole plant back hard in early spring. It will quickly recover height and be in bloom again by summer.

### A flower border for butterflies
* Create your butterfly border in a sheltered and sunny spot, as butterflies like still conditions and warmth.

* Butterfly bush (*Buddleja davidii*) is indispensable as a taller plant at the back of the border.

* Ceanothus, or California lilacs (*Ceanothus* spp. and cvs), with their exquisite deep blue flowers in spring, are a useful source of nectar.

* Perennials such as coneflowers (*Echinacea purpurea*), catmint (*Nepeta × faassenii*) and Michaelmas daisies (*Aster × frikartii*) have the blue-purple flowers that are so irresistible to butterflies.

* Showy sedum, or showy stonecrop (*Sedum spectabile*), with its flat, pink flower heads that mature to rusty red, are especially popular with small butterflies.

# BUYING PLANTS

## Where to shop
Buy from tidy, organised outlets that have weed-free plants and a high stock turnover. Try to use the botanical names to make sure that you're buying or asking about the right plant. Check the name on the label carefully, guard against expensive impulse buys and don't buy a substitute plant until you've researched it.

## When to shop
Shop early in the season when the selection is good, but avoid buying all your plants and planting out the entire garden all at the same time. Plants come into stock at nurseries when they are at their peak, so if you buy all your plants at one time, you'll select from a range of plants that always look their best at that time of year. It will be the same in your garden.

## Shopping from home
Mail order allows you to buy from specialist growers and nurseries. Many have websites where you can see photos of the plants, ask advice from expert staff and order by credit card through a secure page. But remember to check about any quarantine issues for your area before you order.

## Deliveries
Unpack deliveries straightaway, so the plants do not start to grow inside their packaging and become drawn and leggy due to lack of light. If you cannot plant out bare-root plants or cuttings immediately, pot or plant them temporarily for protection. Don't hesitate to reject goods if they are not good quality or if the package has been damaged during transit.

## check that you're Buying healthy plants

A good-quality plant looks the right size for its pot, with lush foliage and some new growth. To be sure you're buying a healthy plant, look for the following signs:

**Leaf colour** Look for green leaves that have no signs of yellowing (unless they are golden-leaved cultivars). Yellowing indicates plant stress from lack of fertiliser and water.

**Roots** A few small roots growing out of the pot's drainage holes are a sign of a strong root system. But avoid plants that have thick roots protruding from drainage holes or roots tangled around the base. Very carefully turn plants out of their pots to inspect the roots.

**Buds and flowers** Bypass any plants that have been in flower for several weeks as they may be 'bloomed out'. However, shrubs and perennials that are in bloom will transplant well because leaf growth is slowed during the flowering period.

**Plant size** The largest plant is not always the best choice. It may be leggy, lopsided or pot-bound, and its more mature roots will take longer to establish than the less advanced roots of a smaller specimen, which will catch up in size in one to two seasons.

**Weeds, pests and diseases** Avoid importing problems into your garden. Inspect the potting mix for any weeds, and examine the young leaves (including the undersides) and roots for signs of pests and diseases.

CABBAGES | CALLIANDRAS

# CABBAGES

### A year-round harvest
Cabbages are adaptable and can be grown in different climates. Choose varieties that mature at different times and sow seeds in succession for continuous crops. Most modern hybrids are very hardy and resistant to bolting when sown out of season.

### Early care
Transplant cabbage seedlings to the vegetable garden once they are around 5–7 cm high. Plant them deeply, covering the first two leaves, and firm the soil. New roots grow from the buried stems, resulting in more stable plants. Make sure the soil is moist and water thoroughly after planting.

### Harvest time
Different varieties mature at different rates, ranging from 8–16 weeks. Harvest them when their heads are firm and fleshy – squeeze the heads to test. Cut them off at the base with a sharp knife. Savoy cabbages are best eaten after a slight frost, which brings out their flavour.

Any stumps left in the ground will provide a further crop of greens, because new clusters of leaves will sprout from the stems.

*Savoy cabbage*
*Winter cabbage*
*Red cabbage*

---

### Prevent club root
Club root, the cabbage's worst enemy, causes swollen roots and yellow, wilting leaves. To help prevent it, ensure that lime levels in the soil are high and drainage is good. Rotate crops so brassicas are never grown on the same plot more than once every 4 years.

---

## treat Cabbage white butterfly

### Plants affected
Cabbages and all brassicas.

### Symptoms
Large holes in leaves, which can be skeletonised. The smooth blue-green caterpillars of the butterfly progressively eat through inner leaves, leaving behind soft green droppings.

### Treatment
* Manually squash caterpillars.

* Plant with strong-smelling herbs or French marigolds (*Tagetes patula*). Dill attracts wasps that control the butterfly, while sage repels the butterfly.

* Use a garlic and chilli spray or pyrethrum after bee activity ceases for the day.

* Spray plants with *Bacillus thuringiensis*. Note withholding period for vegetables.

# CALLIANDRAS

Long-lived and easy to grow, calliandras, or powder-puff bushes as they are also known, are essentially shrubs for tropical and subtropical climates, though some can be grown successfully in warm to temperate climates where severe frost does not occur. They are not fussy about soil, although drainage should be good. A sunny position suits them best and they appreciate regular watering in summer.

### Prune for neatness
Most species spread much wider than they grow tall, so position them with this in mind. If needed, they can be pruned quite severely to make them more compact – ideally, immediately after the main flowering period. In some cases a second flush of blooms will follow on the new shoots.

### Drooping leaves
Most species have the habit of folding their leaves up at night, although they are not 'sensitive' plants and do not react to touch. They also often close their leaves in rainy or very overcast weather. This is quite normal.

---

**CACTI**
*see pages 46*

## CACTI

### Where do they come from?
Some cacti, and some succulents, including *Cereus*, *Mammillaria*, *Opuntia* and *Rebutia* species, originated in the semi-desert and desert areas of North and Central America. Others, like *Epiphyllum*, *Rhipsalis* and *Schlumbergera*, grow among the trees of tropical forests in Central and South America. They have very different growing conditions, so you need to know the origins of your cacti.

### Desert versus forest
Desert plants need plenty of sun. Site them on northern or western window ledges in colder climates, or on a sunny patio or rock garden in warm areas. They need little or no water during their dormant period in winter, and only when dry during summer.

Forest plants like a bright but sunless situation. Try a south- or east-facing window ledge, a covered patio or under trees.

### Special soil requirements
All cacti need a quick-draining, very aerated soil. For pots, use a special orchid or succulent potting mix. In the garden, make a mounded or raised garden bed, or dig out a wide hole and replace heavier soil with an open, free-draining mix. Make sure that water can escape to a subsurface drainage channel. Mulch with gravel or pebbles so moisture does not build up around the cacti.

### New cacti from leaves
Cacti that have leaves can be propagated without difficulty. Any healthy leaves that fall should root easily if potted up immediately and watered well.

### Stop the mealybugs
White, woolly patches on your cactus mean that mealybugs have struck. These pests suck the sap and weaken the cactus. Dab with diluted methylated spirits.

See also Mealybugs

### repot Cactus
Ideally, repot in spring. Choose a pot that is big enough to allow for root growth. Its diameter should be equal to that of the plant, including its spines. If the plant is columnar, allow for a pot diameter equal to half the height of the plant.

### Repotting technique
Stop watering the cactus a few days beforehand. Then, holding the plant by its pot over a newspaper, gently push a pencil or knitting needle through the drainage hole in the base. The cactus should come out with its root ball intact. Repot so that the surface of the root ball is level with the new soil surface.

# CAMELLIAS

Camellias are treasures for the shady garden in climates with mild winters. Set off by glossy evergreen leaves, the flowers may be single, semi-double or double and come in white, pink, red or bicolour combinations. They bloom from late summer to early spring, depending on the climate and the species and cultivar.

## The key to success

Camellias flower best if they are mulched with well-rotted, lime-free organic matter every autumn. This provides a steady supply of nutrients, improves the soil and helps prevent plants from drying out in hot weather. Camellias are shallow-rooted plants and need regular deep watering, especially while in bud and flower.

Good drainage is important to ensure that the root area is kept moist, not wet. Dropped buds and browned flowers are usually an indication that the plant has been stressed and needs watering.

## Apples on camellias

As camellia seeds ripen, they develop into small, apple-like fruit. Left to mature, the seed can be collected and planted in autumn, or simply allowed to ripen, split and self-sow in the garden. Alternatively, clip off the 'apples' as soon as they appear.

## Other ways to make new plants

It is also possible to grow new camellias from cuttings. The two most common species, japonica camellia (*Camellia japonica*) and sasanqua camellia (*C. sasanqua*), and most of their cultivars grow readily in this way. Take cuttings of new growth in summer, and hardwood cuttings in autumn.

> ### Hedging plants
> Camellia hedges, particularly using sasanqua varieties, make attractive privacy screens or borders. Varieties range in height from dwarf cultivars (under 1 m), such as 'Little Liane', to several metres high, such as 'Jennifer Susan'. Clip regularly to create a dense, leafy hedge. For a uniform hedge, always use a row of a single cultivar.

# CANNAS

## Heat and damp lovers

Cannas thrive in hot weather but cannot tolerate the cold, and most die down over winter. Plants will reshoot in spring, once the cold weather has passed. Cannas can grow in average garden soil, but they prefer damp conditions and so are ideal for a pond edge or poorly drained spots.

## Growing from rhizomes

The best time to make new plantings is in winter in frost-free areas or in spring after the threat of frost has passed. Lay canna rhizomes on their side about 5 cm below the soil's surface, 30–40 cm apart. Keep the soil moist until they sprout.

Where cannas grow vigorously, cut off any old flowers to prevent them reseeding and monitor the edge of clumps to make sure they don't spread too far.

> ### Increasing the bounty
> Cannas are easy to increase by division. Separate the rhizomes in spring before planting, or dig up and divide established plants in late winter or early spring. Replant at the same depth at which the rhizomes previously grew.

## CAPSICUMS AND CHILLIES

### Picking your peppers
Capsicums, also called sweet peppers, are usually green and mild in flavour before they ripen. Depending on the variety, they may turn red, yellow or purple as they mature. They have a sweeter flavour when fully ripe.

Depending on their variety and your climate, chillies, or chilli peppers, can range from mild to fiery in taste. The colour changes as they ripen, but colour is no indication of 'heat'. That relates to the levels of capsaicin in the fruit, and that is determined by the genetics of the variety.

### When to grow
Capsicums and chillies originated in the tropics of Central and South America, so in a tropical or subtropical climate you can grow them all year round. In temperate climates, sow the seed from late winter to early summer. In cold climates, sow from early to late spring.

The plants are very frost-sensitive and should not be planted out until 2 weeks after the last frost date has passed and the soil temperature has reached 18°C.

### Protection from disease
Do not plant capsicums or chillies in soil where marrows, potatoes, eggplants, tomatoes or cucumbers were grown during the previous 3 years. This is because these plants share a susceptibility to the same diseases. If crops from earlier seasons had one of these diseases, there's a danger it could be transmitted to new plants grown in the same soil.

### Gentle harvest
Harvest the fruits in late summer to autumn at any stage from green to fully coloured. Do not pull them away from the stems as this may damage the plant and provide an entry point for disease. Use sharp scissors or secateurs and cut off fruits with a piece of stem. Wash your hands very well after harvesting chillies or wear gloves.

**Ornamental chillies**

Red and yellow capsicums
Banana capsicum
Cherry peppers
Bird's eye chillies
Long red and green chillies
Bird's eye chillies

## CARNATIONS AND PINKS

**Chinese pink**

### Understanding dianthus
The name 'dianthus' is used to cover the group of plants that are probably better known by their common names of carnation (*Dianthus caryophyllus*), Chinese pink (*D. chinensis*), cottage pink (*D. plumarius*) and sweet William (*D. barbatus*), which are grown for their long-lasting blooms.

### Simple to grow
For trouble-free plants, choose border carnations, garden pinks or sweet William rather than the perpetual-flowering varieties. All enjoy full sun and have long-lasting flowers. When planting carnations and pinks, bury only the bottom 6 mm of the stem, making sure that the lower leaves are above soil level. If planted deeply, they are susceptible to stem rot. Pinks are especially easy to grow as they rarely need staking or disbudding.

### Bushy growth
If young pinks do not put out sideshoots, pinch out the top of the main shoot in early spring, if possible early in the morning. This will delay blooming but is vital for strong, bushy growth.

# CARNIVOROUS PLANTS

Accustomed to the poor soil of their native bogs, carnivorous plants do not need a rich soil or extra feeding. Most varieties will grow in pure unfertilised peat or peat substitute, while some, such as Venus flytraps, prefer a mix of sand and peat substitute. For pitcher plants and other tropical species grown in hanging baskets, choose a fibrous potting mix like that used for orchids.

## Moisture lovers

Maintain high humidity for indoor plants, but shade them from bright sun. To create a warm humid environment, group pots on a bed of gravel sitting in 5 cm of water in a tray. In summer, be sure to maintain the water level and keep the soil damp, too. For constant heat and humidity, grow carnivorous plants in a greenhouse or terrarium.

Use distilled water or rainwater – both have a neutral pH – as often as possible when watering indoor carnivorous plants.

## Plant traps

Carnivorous plants use different methods to trap their prey.

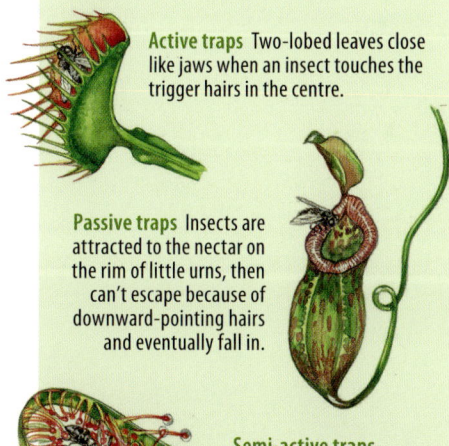

**Active traps** Two-lobed leaves close like jaws when an insect touches the trigger hairs in the centre.

**Passive traps** Insects are attracted to the nectar on the rim of little urns, then can't escape because of downward-pointing hairs and eventually fall in.

**Semi-active traps** Insects become more and more stuck in the sticky leaves and hairs while struggling to escape.

# CARROTS

## Range of colours and shapes

Carrots are traditionally orange or orange-yellow in colour, but there are also purple, yellow and white varieties. The flavour does not differ much.

There are three main types for different sites: round-, short- and long-rooted. Whichever variety you grow, look for one with some resistance to carrot fly if this is a pest in your area. In heavy, stony or shallow ground, avoid long-rooted varieties, which are likely to grow forked or malformed.

## Sowing season

In climates with a mild winter, carrots can be sown almost all year; in areas with cooler winters, spring and summer are best. Sow seeds in rows 30 cm apart, then thin seedlings to 3 cm apart.

When the plants are about 15 cm high, thin to 6 cm apart – use the thinnings as baby carrots. You can pull carrots as you need them after this, although full-sized carrots take about 12–16 weeks.

## Pulling them up

Always use a fork to loosen long- and short-rooted varieties before you pull them up. Harvest early, round-rooted varieties in early and midsummer. In cool regions, main-crop carrots are harvested in midautumn; use any damaged carrots straight away and store the rest for winter. In mild areas, simply pull them up as needed.

### What can go wrong

In the right conditions, carrots are an undemanding crop. But you may encounter the following problems, which have simple solutions:

**Forked roots** Your soil is too stony or contains too much unrotted manure or compost. Plant short-rooted varieties or use a site that has been manured for a previous crop.

**Short roots** You have not left enough space for carrots to grow. Next year, leave 2.5–5 cm between each plant. Compacted soil may also be a cause.

**Split roots** A dry spell has been followed by too much watering. Apply a mulch and water regularly during dry weather.

**A hard and woody heart** Not enough water or a variety unsuitable for late harvesting has been used. Water well; pull early carrots when they are young, and sow main-crop varieties for harvesting later.

**Lack of flavour** A variety for late planting has been sown too early.

## CATERPILLARS

### Plants affected
Wide range of plants, including vegetables, trees and shrubs.

### Symptoms
Large, irregular holes in leaves and flowers, fruit and curds.

### Treatment
* Leave alone unless doing real damage; remove by hand and release outside the garden to become moths or butterflies.

* Encourage natural enemies – birds, parasitic wasps, frogs, lizards, assassin bugs.

* Destroy if control is vital. Spray cabbage caterpillars with *Bacillus thuringiensis*, which is the best choice for all caterpillars susceptible to it.

* Otherwise, spray with garlic spray, rotenone, pyrethrum, permethrin or maldison.

* Apply grease bands to trees.

* Caterpillars of kowhai moths defoliate kowhais (*Sophora* spp.). Shake affected plants vigorously to dislodge. Collect and remove. Alternatively, spray carbaryl or acephate (both NZ only).

* Caterpillars of the New Zealand cabbage tree moth attack cordylines. Leave to predators such as hoverflies. Spray as a last resort only with either acephate or taufluvalinate (both NZ only).

## CATMINT

Catmint (*Nepeta × faassenii*) works well anywhere you want strong colour in the garden during the early summer months. After the prolific blooms pass, the dense, velvety, lightly fragrant foliage persists for the rest of the season. If you want catmint to rebloom, cut it back by a third just after the first round of flowers fades.

### Tough in tough conditions
Once established, catmint is a tough plant well adapted to poor but well-drained soil. But it grows best in soil of average fertility in full sun, or with afternoon shade in hot-summer areas. Mulch is unnecessary, and fertiliser and too much watering can cause it to grow long and lanky. Although catmint is in the mint family, it's not a water guzzler like its relatives. It is also virtually pest- and disease-free.

### Not for cats
Don't confuse catmint with its relative, catnip (*Nepeta cataria*), which is fascinating to felines but makes a comparatively unexciting garden plant for humans. Catmint is not so attractive to cats.

## CATS

In a garden, a cat will soil freshly dug, bare earth in preference to any other type of garden terrain. Keep borders and flowerbeds well covered with flowers and foliage to minimise this tendency.

### Seedling protection
To protect seedlings and young plants from cats, cover the beds with arches of protective wire mesh. Sheets of chicken wire will allow the seedlings to grow up through the holes.

Alternatively, use a covering of horticultural fleece, wire hoops draped with netting, small barricades of twigs or pea sticks, or prunings from prickly shrubs.

### Cat curfew
Cats can cause a lot of damage by stalking and killing native birds and animals. To minimise risks to themselves and other animals, apply a cat curfew. No matter how much your pet likes to go out and prowl at night, keep it inside from dusk to dawn.

If your cat catches a native bird or animal, place the injured creature in a small box and keep it warm to reduce the effects of shock. For advice, contact your nearest vet or wildlife rescue service.

### keep Cats off
Cats hate wet soil, so water your flowerbeds last thing at night. They also dislike the smell of citrus peel, eucalyptus and camphor, so put some orange or lemon rinds or a few mothballs, or even some old tea bags sprinkled with eucalyptus oil, around the garden. Pay particular attention to areas where cats congregate.

### A garden for your cat
Make a special place where your cat can play or bask by allocating a raised corner of a bed to a feline favourite, catnip (*Nepeta cataria*).

CAULIFLOWERS | CEANOTHUS

# CEANOTHUS

## Choose a ceanothus
To enjoy showers of minute, star-shaped blue flowers in spring and summer, plant a ceanothus, also known as a California lilac. These quick-growing shrubs from North America like cool to mild climates and can be short-lived in hot or humid climates.

For best results plant them in a sunny, sheltered site where they will be protected from the worst of the winter chill. They will tolerate a wide range of soil conditions as long as it is well drained. Many species will also tolerate exposed or coastal sites. Good air circulation is especially important in a humid climate.

## Scented and true blue
Ceanothus produce a showy display of scented, vibrant true blue flowers. There are paler blue or white forms, such as 'Snow Flurry', available, too. The very popular 'Blue Pacific' grows to a large shrub or small tree to 4 m high. 'Yankee Point' forms a spreading shrub to 1 m high. Several prostrate forms make excellent groundcovers.

# CAULIFLOWERS

## Rainbow effect
Purple, orange and green varieties of cauliflower are available, along with the more common white. Where space is limited, grow a few of these brightly coloured vegetables in the flower border for a stunning visual effect. Or grow the miniature-headed varieties, which are becoming increasingly popular and are just large enough to serve a small family for a meal.

## Soil preferences
Like all brassicas, cauliflowers prefer alkaline soil. Whether the soil is light or heavy is less important, but it needs to be well drained and generously enriched with compost or well-rotted manure. Crop rotation is vital for cauliflowers. Plant them where beans or peas grew previously.

## A cool-weather crop
Cauliflowers need cool weather to form their 'curds' – the edible flower heads – and so are best grown in temperate climates. Sow from midsummer to autumn, allowing 3–6 months to mature, depending on the variety. Transplant the seedlings, spaced 60–75 cm apart, and firm the soil well to help form compact curds.

## Keep them watered and fed
Cauliflowers are very susceptible to anything that causes a check in growth, such as drought, so make sure both seedlings and plants are well watered in dry weather. Also feed with a light dressing of fertiliser every 2–3 weeks.

## Harvesting firm curds
Cut the heads when they are firm. If left too long, the curds break up as the plant begins to flower.

### Sun shield
If curds are exposed to strong sunlight, they can discolour and scald, becoming yellow or brown. To prevent this, break a couple of leaves and place them over the developing curd or tie the upper leaves together over the curd. As the curd forms, the leaves will protect it from the sun. A number of newer cauliflower varieties produce inner leaves that naturally curl protectively over the curd to preserve its whiteness.

51

# CELERY | CHEMICALS

## CELERY

### Cool celery
Celery prefers a mild to cool climate. It can be grown as a winter vegetable in warm areas if planted in late summer or early autumn. Don't sow the small seeds too deeply or they will not be able to emerge easily after germination. Seedlings are small, take quite some time to appear and are slow-growing. When you are transplanting them, take care not to cover up the heart.

### To blanch or not to blanch?
The purpose of blanching is to encourage crisper, longer, less stringy stems, with a less bitter flavour. Self-blanching varieties are grown close together in a block, so that they shield each other from the sunlight. Only the outside plants need shading, either by banking straw against them or by planting the celery in an open frame.

### Feed and water well
Because it is shallow-rooted, celery dries out quickly. Even a short period of water stress or nutrient stress causes tough, stringy stalks. So grow in fertile soil, mulch heavily and give your plants a constant supply of water and food, watering daily in hot weather. Weekly liquid feeding is recommended.

## CHEMICALS

All garden chemicals should be treated with great care and respect, used strictly according to the manufacturer's instructions and only as a last resort.

Before you reach for one, ask yourself if there are equally effective, or better, ways to deal with the problem that do not require the use of chemicals and that cause less harm to insects, birds or even the soil.

### To each their own
Always read the information on the label very carefully before using. Labels on containers state clearly which pests or diseases the contents are intended to treat and the plants for which they are suited. Also, always match the treatment to both the problem and the plant. Failure to do this could result in an unsolved problem and a damaged or dead plant.

### Hazardous hoarding
Don't accumulate old containers of garden chemicals. Most have a fairly short shelf life (usually less than 2 years). Check all packages and bottles regularly and dispose of those you no longer require or that are out of date. Contact your local authority to find out about disposal facilities – never pour chemicals down the drain.

### Lethal mixtures
Never mix different chemicals, either in a sprayer or by spraying the same plant with a second chemical immediately after the first chemical. Allow a day for the first spray to dry. Where the label states that the chemical may be mixed with another, follow the instructions to the letter. Use the mixture immediately.

*See also* Insects, Pesticides, Safety, Spraying, Weed management

### Legal controls and availability
Many chemicals that were once widely available to the public have been withdrawn on health or environmental grounds. Some chemicals are available only for certified professionals to use on specified crops. Even techniques currently accepted as environmentally safe may in time prove to have detrimental effects on humans or native animals, bees or fish.

## know your Chemicals

When choosing a chemical remedy, consider its mode of action and the situation in which it is to be used.

### Insecticides and fungicides
**Contact action** The chemical comes into direct contact with the pest or germinating fungus spores. It is effective against pests that chew.

**Systemic action** The chemical is absorbed by the foliage and transported through the plant by the sap. It is effective against sap-sucking pests and fungi.

### Herbicides (weedkillers)
**Non-residual contact action** This type kills only the foliage that it touches and is effective on annual weeds.

**Non-residual systemic action** Absorbed through the leaves, this type is then passed to the roots. It is effective on annual and perennial weeds.

**Residual** Applied to the soil and absorbed by roots, it can be active for months. It is good for paths and clearing ground.

**Selective** It is used on lawns to kill broad-leaved weeds but not harm grasses.

CHERRIES

# CHERRIES

## Choosing the right cherry

Cherries are cool-climate trees, needing a cold winter in order to flower properly. There are three types: sweet cherries, for eating; sour cherries, which are used in preserves and cooking; and ornamental trees, grown for their lavish spring display of flowers.

They are usually grown as shaped trees. Dwarfing stocks are mostly used; this ensures that the trees grow to a manageable height and spread, and are easy to care for and to harvest. In cool-climate areas they are sometimes shaped into ornamental espaliers against north-facing brick walls to receive the reradiated warmth.

## Routine care

Little fertiliser is required if your tree is growing well. Prune sweet cherries in summer to restrict too much leafy growth. Sour cherries need to have old wood removed on a regular basis to encourage the growth of the year-old wood that produces fruit. Trees need regular watering or the fruit may split after heavy rain.

## Beware birds

Birds love cherries – especially sweet varieties – so you'll have to net the tree. If it is very large, you can keep at least some of the fruit safe by netting lower branches.

## Cherry ripe

Fruit will begin to appear on sweet cherry trees after 2 years, and on year-old sour cherry trees. Cherries are harvested along with their stalks and should be eaten right away.

Harvest sweet cherries in summer. Pull them off by hand. Sour cherries mature from summer to midautumn. Cut off the bunches with sharp scissors.

### choose ornamental Cherries

There are many varieties of ornamental cherry. Habit, or shape, and flower colour vary. Some truly magnificent cultivars include:

✳ ***Prunus* 'Amanogawa'** Upright; single and semi-double pink flowers
✳ ***P. campanulata*** Dwarf; single deep red flowers ✳ ***P.* 'Mount Fuji'** Weeping; double white flowers ✳ ***P.* 'Shirotae'** Spreading; single white flowers ✳ ***P.* 'Shogetsu'** Spreading; pink buds opening to semi-double white flowers ✳ ***P.* 'Ukon'** Spreading; semi-double pink-white flowers

## CHILDREN

### A garden of their own
There is an old saying that gardens grow children. Giving children their own plot of earth can develop a lifelong love of the living world as well as valuable life skills. Small children can have short attention spans, but digging holes rarely palls.

### Growing their own
Encourage children with seeds that are quick to grow, such as sunflowers, nasturtiums, zinnias, zucchinis and radishes. Making a butterfly garden, or a living teepee constructed with bamboo canes and covered with climbing beans, is the perfect summer project. With regular watering, the teepee will soon provide a leafy hideout.

Highly structured, neat gardens don't give a great deal of stimulus to children. Shady trees, a tree house, a wilderness of shrubs or a strawberry patch appeal far more.

### Don't forget the sandpit
No child's garden is complete without a sandpit. Locate it where it will receive summer shade, or erect a shadecloth sail overhead.

Cats love sandpits as much as children do. To keep them out and the sand clean, make a cover for your sandpit and keep it covered when not in use.

## CHINESE LANTERNS

The lantern-like flowers of *Abutilon* x *hybridum* give this shrub its common name of Chinese lanterns. The flowers range in colour from white to yellow and orange but there are also rose pink and crimson cultivars. They bloom almost all year round but are particularly dense from winter to summer.

The variegated trailing form (*A. megapotamicum* 'Variegatum') is ideal for a rock garden or as a groundcover and even works in a hanging basket. The variegated Chinese lanterns do not flower as well as those with ordinary green leaves, however.

### Pruning for a better shape
Even if it means sacrificing a few flowers, Chinese lanterns grow best if pruned in late winter, or in early spring in frost-prone areas. Cut wayward branches back to form a round bush. Excessive growth can also be trimmed back during summer.

### Holes in leaves
The round holes found in Chinese lantern leaves are usually the work of the metallic flea beetle, which also attacks hibiscus. The beetle is difficult to control – try using an insecticidal soap.

## CHIVES

Chives may be the smallest of the onion tribe but they have the sharpest flavour. The best known is the common chive (*Allium schoenoprasum*), with round leaves and mauve-pink flowers on stems about 20 cm tall.

Giant chives (*A. schoenoprasum* var. *sibiricum*) are milder and slightly taller, with larger heads of purple flowers, while garlic or Chinese chives (*A. tuberosum*) have flat leaves, a mild garlic flavour and white flowers.

### A steady supply
All prefer rich soil and sunshine and can be grown from seed, but it is easiest to buy plants from a nursery. Every 3 years, dig up the clumps in autumn, divide them into bunches of about six shoots and replant. For a fresh winter supply, plant a small clump into a 10 cm pot of potting mix and keep it on a sunny windowsill.

### Harvest one clump at a time
Cut the leaves close to the ground as required. Cut all the leaves from one clump before moving to the next; the plant will soon grow new leaves.

# CHLOROSIS

This iron deficiency turns leaves yellow or white, sometimes only between the veins, and is most noticeable on young leaves. It is usually caused by minerals being locked up in the soil. It often affects acid-loving plants grown on alkaline soil, but evergreen trees and shrubs growing in any type of soil may develop it.

## Plants affected
Ceanothus, gardenias, hydrangeas and acid-loving plants, such as camellias, rhododendrons and azaleas, growing in alkaline soils; evergreen trees and shrubs in any soil may also be affected.

## Symptoms
Foliage turns yellow or white, but veins remain dark.

## Treatment
* Avoid growing susceptible plants in alkaline soil – grow them in pots instead.

* Improve acidity by digging in pulverised bark, crushed bracken or an azalea food. In manageable small areas, use acidifying chemicals such as ammonium sulfate or sulfur, applied in several small amounts. To release nutrients locked up in the soil, water or spray the plants with iron chelates and trace elements or apply a granular formulation.

* Apply lime-free compost and leaf mould.

# CHRYSANTHEMUMS

Make a stunning display in the garden with late-flowering perennial chrysanthemums. Their vibrant colours, in shades of orange, rust, terracotta, red, purple, pink, yellow and white, are perfectly suited to the mood of autumn. The plants need full sun and well-drained soil.

## Making new plants
Chrysanthemums can be grown from cuttings. Take short cuttings (around 8 cm long with several internodes) in spring from new shoots. Do this every 2–3 years to renew ageing clumps or to increase your range of flower colours and shapes.

After flowering has finished, cut the plant down to just above ground level. In late winter or early spring when plants begin to regrow, sending out suckers, you can lift the clump, divide it into several new plants and replant.

## Compact but full of flowers
Chrysanthemums tend to be tall, rangy plants that usually require staking. To encourage plants to have a more compact, sturdy shape, regularly pinch out new growth. Start when the plants are about 20 cm tall to encourage side growth. Follow up with further pinching back when the new growth is around 30 cm long.

As soon as flowering is over, cut back the main stems of garden varieties to around 20 cm. This will encourage new growth and some small flowers for cutting.

## For big flowers
The technique of 'disbudding', which reduces the number of buds in each flower cluster, will mean fewer but larger flowers. To remove buds, just nip them out with your fingernails. The size of flowers will also be larger if the plants are kept well fertilised.

## grow mother's day Chrysanthemums

Chrysanthemums make long-lasting flowering pot plants that will bloom indoors or on a balcony or patio for 3–6 weeks. All they need is a well-lit spot, water when dry, and for spent flowers to be removed. When flowering ceases, plant them out in the garden, where they will flower again next autumn.

# CITRUS FRUITS

## Three-point plan for success
Citrus have three basic needs: full sun, excellent drainage and regular doses of fertiliser. If your soil is poorly drained, grow your citrus trees in a raised bed, on a mound or in a large tub. Fertilise twice a year in spring and late summer. Dwarf plants as small as 45 cm in height will grow in a pot, bear fruit and be decorative as well as productive.

## Young trees
To encourage good long-term growth and root establishment, do not allow a recently planted citrus tree to set fruit. If it does produce small fruits, simply clip them off. The following year the tree will be well established and should set a good crop of fruit.

## Too much too soon
If you see tiny fruits dropping from your tree before they begin to grow, don't panic. Citrus tend to produce an overabundance of both flowers and fruit. They offset this by discarding unwanted flowers and fruit at various stages of development. Flower buds may drop unopened, opened flowers may fall without setting fruit and the fruit itself can drop while still very immature. If plenty of fruit remains, just relax – it is simply nature at work.

## Store on the tree
With the exception of mandarins, which ripen quickly and fall, citrus fruit will store on the tree for months. So you do not need to harvest all your crop at once.

If your citrus fruit is meant to be sweetly flavoured but is rather tart, leave it for longer on the tree. The longer it ripens in the sun, the sweeter it will become. But if fruit fails to sweeten even after this, try an application of copper sulfate around the roots.

## No pruning
Citrus trees do not generally need regular pruning to improve growth or cropping. However, trees that have been damaged or become overgrown can be pruned hard to encourage new growth. This is best done during spring or autumn to avoid exposing freshly pruned branches to sunburn.

See also Grapefruit and pomelos, Lemons and limes, Mandarins and tangelos, Oranges

---

## deal with Citrus problems and pests

Yellowing leaves may be due to a lack of nutrients, especially nitrogen, or the soil is too cold or too alkaline. Citrus can also be troubled by leafminers, spined citrus bugs, scale and other pests.

### Bronze orange bugs
**Treatment**

✶ Encourage parasitic wasps, which kill the eggs.

✶ Kill small nymphs beneath leaves with a soap spray.

✶ Shake or prune off bugs with gloved hands and drop in a bucket of hot soapy water, but be wary of the acrid liquid they can discharge.

✶ Spray with insecticidal soap, a petroleum-based oil spray, pyrethrum or maldison and white oil, or the systemic imidacloprid.

### Citrus gall wasps
**Treatment**

✶ Interrupt its life cycle – prune off and destroy the affected parts.

✶ This must be done before the wasps emerge from the galls at the end of winter. Gardeners are required by law to remove galls by the end of August in some regions of Australia. Check your particular situation with the local agricultural authority.

---

### Some unusual citrus

**Citrons** The varieties of these low-growing shrubs to small trees include 'fingered' fruits that resemble a hand or starfish (right), and acidic and sweet varieties that look like a rough-skinned lemon.

**Cumquats** These small ornamental shrubs have dense glossy foliage, fragrant white flowers and prolific, brilliant orange fruit that make delicious tart marmalade and rich brandied preserves. Frost-tender, they are perfect in large pots on a patio or balcony.

**Satsumas** These are early-fruiting and cold-hardy, with intensely sweet and easy-to-peel fruit that are good for eating. Dwarf varieties will do well in small gardens or tubs.

# CLAY SOIL

## Improving a clay soil

Clay soils can be improved by working organic matter, perlite, vermiculite or very coarse sand into the topsoil, taking care not to compact the underlying soil. Clay soils that are dispersive benefit from calcium, which is added as gypsum (calcium sulfate). It is available from hardware stores and garden centres, and improves a clay's drainage and structure.

## When to add gypsum

To see whether your clay soil is a dispersive clay and will benefit from gypsum (source of calcium), do this simple test. Add about 2 cm of the dry soil to a tall jar, fill with rainwater, put on the lid, shake thoroughly, then set aside.

If the clay slowly disperses in the water, it is a dispersive clay. If the water in the jar then clears within 30 minutes, your soil needs no extra calcium. If the water clears in 1–2 hours, work 50 g gypsum per square metre into your soil. If the water remains muddy overnight, add 200–500 g gypsum per square metre, digging it in to at least a spade's depth. Irrigation or rain is then needed to wash the sodium out of the soil. Repeat the treatment every 4 weeks until fresh testing shows that the soil has improved.

However, if there is no change at all to the clay or water, your clay soil isn't dispersive and won't benefit from adding gypsum.

## Benefits of mushroom compost

Spent mushroom compost is ideal for adding to clay soil to improve its structure. It is quite cheap, available in large quantities, a perfect blend of organic matter and has a high calcium content.

Always test the pH of mushroom compost as some can be very alkaline. While this should not be a problem for acidic soils, it will make alkaline soils more alkaline. Never use it where phosphorus-sensitive plants such as banksias, proteas, grevilleas and waratahs will be planted.

## Raise the bed instead

If the clay soil in your garden is really not suited to digging and is not well drained, consider raising the level of your bed. A raised bed will be well drained and provide better growing conditions for most plants.

See also Raised beds

# CLEMATIS

A clematis likes a rich, well-drained soil and regular watering in dry summers. It should have its head in the sun and its roots in the shade. Mulch thickly with compost, and plant a low bush at the foot of the clematis to give cool shade while it establishes itself.

## Training and support

Clematis are not self-clinging like ivy, so a trellis or wire framework is needed when the plants are to be trained over a wall or fence. The branches of a climbing rose can also form a good support; this combination of clematis and rose is both traditional and beautiful.

## Perfect pairing

Two clematis growing together and flowering either at the same time or in succession are very attractive, but it is wise not to plant the two in the same planting hole. If clematis wilt attacks one of the plants, the disease could spread to the other. Plant the two clematis at least 1.8 m apart to minimise this risk.

## Clematis wilt

If flowers and leaves go brownish black and stems wilt, do not pull up the plant. It is suffering from wilt, but you may be able to save it. Cut back affected stems and leave it for several months to see if it recovers.

## C CLIMBERS

## CLIMBERS

Climbers have different climbing habits: self-clinging, twining leaf stalks, winding tendrils or scrambling.

### The right support
Be sure to match the climber you want to grow with the right type of support. Twining leaves and tendrils grow fastest around supports less than 1 cm thick. Clinging climbers need to attach to timber or masonry. Scrambling climbers, which use thorns or hooks, may need to be tied against a framework. Put up the support before planting, and make sure it is the correct size and strength for your chosen climber.

### Tying in to prevent damage
Tie in sideshoots before gusts of wind snap them. Do not tie too tightly, to allow for thickening of the stems as the plant matures. Use raffia or soft garden string, which will not damage the plant.

### Planting next to a support
Before planting a climber against a wall, check that the wall is not damaged in any way, because the climber will make this worse. The ground is usually dry under the eaves at the base of a house wall, so locate the planting hole about 30–50 cm from the wall, where the climber's roots can catch any rainfall. If using a trellis, pergola or fence, plant the climber as close as possible to it.

To help the shoots make contact with the bottom of the support quickly, settle the plant in the hole, angled towards the support. Don't remove the stake. The newly planted climber will use it to clamber onto the support.

### Covering up large areas
If you need fast-growing climbers to cover a large surface such as an ugly wall or fence, plant two or three climbers of the same variety 60–90 cm apart, and train the stems across the surface.

**Passionfruit**

**Bougainvillea**

**Sweet pea**

### find Climbers for every situation

**Fast-growing – cool climate**
✽ *Clematis montana*, *C.* × *jackmanii* ✽ Boston ivy (*Parthenocissus tricuspidata*) ✽ Chinese wisteria (*Wisteria sinensis*)

**Fast-growing – warm climate**
✽ Golden trumpet vine (*Allamanda cathartica*) ✽ Chinese trumpet vine (*Campsis grandiflora*) ✽ Flaming glory bower vine (*Clerodendrum splendens*) ✽ Carolina jasmine (*Gelsemium sempervirens*) ✽ Passionfruit cvs ✽ Runner beans ✽ Sweet peas ✽ Star jasmine (*Trachelospermum jasminoides*) ✽ Climbing nasturtiums (*Tropaeolum* cvs)

**Feature plants – cool climate**
✽ *Clematis* 'Perle d'Azur' ✽ *Rosa* 'New Dawn' ✽ *Wisteria floribunda* 'Multijuga'

**Feature plants – warm climate**
✽ Herald's trumpet (*Beaumontia grandiflora*) ✽ Bougainvillea ✽ *Mandevilla* 'Alice du Pont' ✽ Wonga wonga vine (*Pandorea pandorana*) ✽ Wreath plant (*Petrea volubilis*)

# CLIVIAS | CLOCHES AND COLDFRAMES

## CLIVIAS

### Plants for shady spots
Clivias thrive in shaded spots in a frost-free climate and are an ideal choice for massing under trees or on the shaded southern side of a house or wall. They form a dark green, leafy clump all year round. In late winter and spring they develop heads of spectacular flower clusters in salmon orange and other colours.

### New colours
Clivias have become popular in recent years, especially with the release of more cultivars of various colours, including white, yellow and red. However, because plants grown from seed take several years to reach a size that is mature enough to flower, the new coloured forms are expensive. Look for them in the catalogues of specialist bulb or perennial growers, particularly those bred from *Clivia miniata* var. *citrina*.

### Divide in spring
Traditionally, propagating clivias is done by division in spring after flowering. It is an easy task: simply dig up an existing clump, cut it up with the edge of a sharp spade and replant. Clivias can also be grown from seed but will take several years to flower.

## CLOCHES AND COLDFRAMES

Cloches and coldframes are invaluable for gardeners living in cold climates, especially if they don't have a greenhouse.

### Protection from cold and frost
Transparent cloches made from glass or plastic protect seedlings and young plants growing in the ground from the cold and rain. Also use them to heat up the ground before sowing and to maintain humidity. If overnight frosts are a problem, you can place cloches over frost-tender plants for the night, then remove them on warm or sunny days so the plants don't get burnt.

### Helping with propagation
Coldframes are the answer to the problem of propagating seeds and protecting cuttings and young plants if you live in a cold or frost-prone climate and don't have a greenhouse. Pots go inside the coldframe, which although it is unheated, gives extra humidity around plants.

The best place for a coldframe used for growing plants is facing north in full sun, where there is some protection from cold winds in winter. Slant the frame towards the sun. If possible, ventilate the frame on the side away from the prevailing wind.

### Warmth in the coldframe
Use pieces of old carpet or sacking over your coldframe to protect plants from frost. Covering the frame before sunset will help to trap the day's warmth inside. Another way to keep plants warm is to use insulation. Line the sides of the coldframe with offcuts of polystyrene sheeting. Remove the extra material when the day temperatures begin to warm up. In a small coldframe, a nightlight will protect plants from early, light frosts.

### Not too hot
In summer, use plastic netting or shading paint to protect plants from sun scorch and overheating. Ventilate the frame fully in very hot weather by opening the lid as widely as possible or by removing it altogether. But with the lid removed, your plants will still need shade from the sun.

# COASTAL GARDENS

Coastal gardens generally have a mild climate and enough rain. They can become home to a surprising number of plants if they are protected from salt and wind, and the soil improved.

## Beneficial windbreaks
To help reduce the effect of prevailing winds and salt spray, install a windbreak of fencing or a double row of suitable seaside shrubs and trees. A solid fence or very solid hedge forces the wind upwards, although it then swoops down further on with increased turbulence. A partly open barrier such as lattice or slatted fencing lets some wind filter through, reducing the general force. But any fencing or lattice must have sturdy supports that will survive occasional sea gales.

## Hedge protection
Two or three rows of tough plants that can cope with summer heat and winter gales and still stay upright will protect the garden planted behind them. As a general rule of thumb, a hedge protects for a distance equal to 20 times its height, so a row of shrubs 5 m high will protect a garden about 100 m wide.

## Hold it steady
Stabilise sand dunes and wind-blown sand by planting beach grasses and native beachside trailing plants at the edges of a garden close to dunes or beach. Local native dune-stabilising plants are always the best choice. Effective anchors include beach spinifex (*Spinifex sericeus*) and beach fescue (*Austrofestuca littoralis*). Pigface, fan flowers and native pelargoniums will dot the sand with colour and, once established, reduce erosion.

## Salt-tolerant windbreaks
Use salt-tolerant plants as the first line of defence. Look at the local coastal plants. They are acclimatised to the conditions, support local birds and animals and will help blend your garden with the natural landscape.

## Within sight of the sea
Many plants can stand a little wind and salt if grown behind windbreaks or further back from the sea. Plants grown in these conditions are generally slower, smaller and stockier than those in more hospitable environments but most will adapt and flourish. Also make the most of the natives and exotics that like sandy soils.

## Build up sandy soils
Soils in coastal gardens are usually sandy, porous and low in nutrients. It may take a few years to achieve a fertile soil. Each year spread masses of organic matter over all the garden, particularly several weeks before doing any planting. This will improve the nutrients, water-holding capacity and soil structure, and increase the organisms in your garden.

## Tree brace
Brace taller trees with three wire cables. To avoid damaging the bark, secure a piece of rubber hose around the trunk and attach the wires to it; then drive three stakes into the ground around the tree and secure the other end of the wires to them. Check regularly to ensure the collar isn't too tight.

## Plant care
Keep all natural vegetation and any other plants growing on the land, including weeds, until you are ready to replace them right away with better plants. Then clear a pocket for the first plants.

---

### choose plants for Coastal gardens

**Salt-tolerant plants**
✻ Fast-growing wattles (*Acacia longifolia, A. sophorae*) ✻ Coast banksia (*Banksia integrifolia*) ✻ She-oak (*Casuarina equisetifolia*) ✻ Mirror bush (*Coprosma repens* cvs) ✻ White correa (*Correa alba*) ✻ Tuckeroo, beach tamarind (*Cupaniopsis anacardioides*) ✻ White kunzea (*Kunzea ambigua*) ✻ Norfolk Island hibiscus (*Lagunaria patersonii*) ✻ Coastal tea tree (*Leptospermum laevigatum*) ✻ Silver cushion bush (*Leucophyta brownii* syn. *Calocephalus brownii*) ✻ Coastal beard heath (*Leucopogon parviflorus*) ✻ Coastal saltbush (*Atriplex cinerea, Rhagodia candolleana*) ✻ Broad-leaved paperbark (*Melaleuca quinquenervia*) ✻ Pohutukawa, New Zealand Christmas bush (*Metrosideros excelsa*) ✻ Japanese mock orange (*Pittosporum tobira*) ✻ 'Alba' and 'Scabrosa' rugosa roses ✻ Coastal rosemary (*Westringia fruticosa*)

**Plants with some wind and salt tolerance**
Rock rose (*Cistus* spp.) ✻ Pride of Madeira (*Echium candicans*) ✻ Escallonia ✻ Hebe ✻ Lavender ✻ Oleander ✻ Daisy bush (*Olearia* spp.) ✻ Rosemary

COASTAL GARDENS | COLOUR

Start with plants, not seeds or seedlings, to establish some cover quickly in the harsh conditions.

Make sure each planting pocket has at least 1 m of improved soil around it, and add some water-storing crystals. Water plants frequently until well established because sandy soil dries out quickly. Organic mulches about 10 cm thick and groundcovers will help to reduce the drying wind. Feed plants at least once a year in spring to compensate for nutrient loss from the sandy soil.

### Time for old favourites
To begin with, grow favourite plants that are not well adapted to seaside life in containers in a sheltered place. As the garden matures, the natural windbreaks develop and the soil improves, a greater variety of plants will do well in the ground and you can begin to plant out old favourites.

### No salt
Saltwater spray is a real problem for evergreens. Wash them down regularly with a forcible stream of fresh water from a hose.

### Exposed balconies
Balconies on high-rise buildings overlooking the sea or a harbour can be very difficult places to grow plants. Choose the toughest screening shrubs, such as Indian hawthorn (*Raphiolepis indica*) and mirror bush (*Coprosma repens* cvs) in large pots.

## COLOUR

### How to make colours work
Different hues and combinations produce quite different effects on the viewer. Intense colour tends to heighten the emotions; gentle, pastel shades relax. Reds and yellows are urgent and restless together. Blues and whites create a cool setting, while the warmer, primary contrast of blues and golden yellows is invigorating.

### Cool pale colours
Pale colours, in particular sharp lemons, blues and whites, work especially well in low light levels, gaining a luminosity that is not evident in the full glare of the sun. Also, don't underestimate the importance of foliage.

### Warm bright colours
Single colours are almost always more dramatic than a mix. Hot colours work exceptionally well against a drab, grey building. A bed of hot tones distracts from a more ordinary outline or an ugly feature elsewhere in the garden. Conversely, a foliage garden can merge into one dull mass unless something bolder, such as a group of red hot pokers, shouts for attention. Then the viewer will start noticing the subtleties. For this to work, abandon all thought of compromise and choose the boldest, most arresting hues.

### Deceiving the eye
You can make a small garden appear larger by placing soft colours farthest from the main viewing area and vivid colours in the foreground. Broaden a long, narrow garden by growing bright flowers in the background with paler plants at the front.

### Pastels and bright colours separated
Use the neutrality of white to separate uncomplementary colour schemes. Bright vivid colours in particular should be kept away from pastels as they make the latter appear lifeless. Soften large areas of blue with orange, which is blue's complementary colour, and offset the intense effect of an abundance of red with areas of restful green.

**Pastel shades in sun are refreshing, as seen in this grouping of soft pinks, blues and white. These colours also show up well in twilight.**

**Bright flowers make the most of a hot spot in full sun. Many need the strong light to bring out the intensity of the colour.**

### experiment with Colour
The options afforded by colourful modern materials are endless and can be used to create mood and drama in the garden. Blue pergolas smothered with pastel flowers and grey foliage conjure up the sun-faded look of yesterday's gardens. Wooden fences stained black will contrast dramatically on a sunny day with evergreen plants and bright flowers.

## COMPANION PLANTS | COMPOST

## COMPANION PLANTS

Some plants appear to have a direct effect on others growing near them. In some cases the effect is beneficial, while in others it is detrimental. Roses, for example, seem to be more sweetly scented and less prone to disease when surrounded by garlic, and less troubled by aphids when lavender is grown underneath them. Beans do not seem to do well when grown near onions. These phenomena are currently the subject of scientific study.

### Mixed planting benefits

Plants of different species, when grown together, compete less with each other than those of the same species, and make it more difficult for pests and diseases to spread. For example, planting potatoes and broad beans together can increase yields from both crops.

Flowers that attract pollinating insects can increase the yields from some other crops. Sweet peas and runner beans work as good companions in this way, and also look very attractive scrambling up bean poles together in flower and vegetable gardens.

### Weed beaters

Few weeds grow in pine woods because secretions from the trees prevent them from germinating. A mulch of pine needles on the strawberry bed will suppress weeds and may also improve the fruits' flavour. Rhododendron leaves produce secretions that prevent seeds in the soil nearby from germinating, and the leaves of dandelions appear to have the same effect.

### Space savers

Make good use of space in the vegetable garden by planting shallow-rooting vegetables alongside deep-rooting ones. Carrots and radishes do well together and occupy less space when planted side by side than when planted in separate rows.

### Disease resistance

Some plants can increase the ability of others to resist disease. Chamomile is beneficial to the health and fragrance of certain plants; foxgloves and golden feverfew (*Tanacetum parthenium* 'Aureum') are helpful to plants nearby; summer savory benefits beans; and onions can prevent mould on strawberries.

## COMPOST

Garden compost is one of the most effective ways of feeding the soil and improving its structure. It is nearly neutral in pH, so it helps to stabilise a soil's balance of acidity and alkalinity. It supplies varying amounts of plant nutrients for plants and soil micro-organisms to thrive in, and it has a disease-fighting ability.

### Solving compost problems

In cold weather the rate of decomposition will slow down. To keep the heap active, cover it with insulating material, such as an old blanket, a square of carpet or a layer of plastic bubble wrap.

If composting seems to stop, the heap may be too high in carbon or too dry. Add manure or blood and bone, and water in hotter weather. If the heap looks slimy and smells then it's too wet or low in carbon and has become anaerobic. Add high-carbon materials such as shredded paper or straw, cover during rain and turn to aerate.

COMPOST

## add to Compost

### Things you can use
✹ Weeds and plants (cut seedheads off first) ✹ Coffee grounds and tea leaves ✹ Eggshells ✹ Lawn mower clippings ✹ Manure ✹ Shredded paper and cardboard ✹ Straw and hay ✹ Stable litter ✹ Spent potting mix ✹ Uncooked kitchen waste such as fruit and vegetable peelings ✹ Dead flowers ✹ Shredded twigs and branches ✹ Plant trimmings

### Things you should avoid
✹ Colour magazines ✹ Detergents and chemical products ✹ Diseased plant material ✹ Perennial weeds ✹ Scraps of food that may attract vermin ✹ Thick paper or cardboard

Mulching with compost

## make the best Compost

1. Spread a thick layer of coarse, woody prunings in the base of the compost bin. Push it into the corners but don't press down. It raises the heap off the ground slightly, helping air to circulate so the material breaks down faster.

2. Spread a 5 cm thick layer of high-nitrogen material, such as shredded prunings, lawn mower clippings, weeds (minus seed heads and perennial roots), vegetable scraps and manures, on top of the heap.

3. Add a 25–30 cm layer of moistened high-carbon waste, such as shredded newspaper, straw, wood shavings, sawdust and dry leaves. Keep alternating thin nitrogen and thick carbon layers until the heap is 1.2 m high.

4. Sprinkle each layer with water. You can add compost activators such as comfrey liquid or diluted seaweed tonic. The material must be damp enough to encourage the bacteria that break it down, but not soaking wet.

5. Cover the heap to prevent moisture loss and also keep rainwater out. A lid helps the compost heat up more quickly, too. A piece of old carpet does the job well, combined with a sheet of plastic against the rain.

6. Leave for 1–2 months when the bin is full. Turn the heap often to aerate, forking the sides of the heap into the middle. (The centre is hotter and rots faster.) It is ready when moist, dark brown and of uniform consistency.

# CONIFERS

## Careful buying
Choose your conifer with care. A tree should be well balanced, so walk all around it to check that the branches are symmetrical and the stem is straight. A shower of fallen needles round the base could indicate an unhealthy plant or one suffering from severe root damage caused by dryness.

## Strong stem for healthy growth
To grow properly, an upright conifer needs one strong main stem. If yours develops two stems, cut off the weaker one. If the main stem breaks, train up the nearest young shoot so it takes over. If necessary, support this new main stem by tying it to a stake.

## Changing colours
Some conifers have foliage that changes colour. The leaves of *Cryptomeria japonica* 'Elegans', for example, change from green to purple or bronzy red in winter, while the green summer foliage of *Thuja orientalis* 'Rheingold' turns purple in winter and yellow in spring. *Juniperus* 'Plumosa' turns rich purple in autumn.

## find Conifers for every climate

### Cool climates
* *Chamaecyparis obtusa* 'Crippsii'
* Monterey cypress (*Cupressus macrocarpa*)
* Pencil pine (*Cupressus sempervirens*)

### Warm humid climates
* *Araucaria* spp.
* *Callitris* spp.
* *Podocarpus* spp.

### Hot dry climates
* Arizona cypress (*Cupressus arizonica*)
* *Juniperus horizontalis* 'Limeglow'
* Canary Islands pine (*Pinus canariensis*)
* Turkish pine (*P. brutia*)
* Stone or umbrella pine (*P. pinea*)

## trim a formal Conifer hedge

**1** Allow conifers to grow about 60 cm above the desired height before pruning. Run a string between two canes at the cutting height, which will be around 15 cm below the level you ultimately want. This will encourage new bushy growth at the top.

**2** Trim the sides of the hedge, starting at the bottom and working upwards, and making it narrower at the top than it is at the base. Wear gloves and even goggles when using a powered hedge trimmer and, if it is electric, always use a circuit breaker for your safety.

**3** Cut the top of the hedge along the guideline, tapering the edges rather than leaving a flat, wide top. Do not overreach; if you need to, set up a ladder or trestles on a firm stable base. Get a helper to steady the bottom of a ladder as you trim the hedge.

CONTAINERS

# CONTAINERS

Containers are the answer to a tough climate or unsuitable soil. They can help transform a courtyard, patio or balcony into a lush green space.

### Style and size
Choose large containers in a style that suits your garden space. Try to use fewer, bigger pots rather than lots of small ones. Bigger pots dry out more slowly, have more root space and are less likely to blow over. Some have a built-in reservoir that reduces watering. But good drainage via well-sized drainage holes is also important.

### The best shapes
Opt for a good stable design that makes repotting easy or use a plain plastic pot that fits inside a decorative pot. Avoid decorative containers that are impractical, very shallow or narrow. The old-fashioned shape of a truncated cone is the best proportion of depth to width for drainage and aeration of the potting mix.

## decide on the type of Container

**Terracotta** Porous and well-drained. It suits Mediterranean-type plants and styles, but needs more frequent watering and also cleaning. It is heavy to move and can be fragile.

**Plastic** Lightweight, easy to move, less evaporation, so less watering. It can become brittle after exposure to sunlight. There are good terracotta look-alikes.

**Fibreglass** Light, durable and well-insulated, in terracotta and stone finishes or bright colours and metallics. Fibreglass pots may need drainage holes drilled.

**Wood** Attractive and natural appearance. Choose either hardwood or pressure-treated softwood. It is usually heavy, so a good choice for top-heavy plants.

**Glazed** Earthenware and ceramic pots in attractive colours. They are heavy and fragile. Those without drainage holes are good for a simple water feature.

**Concrete** A wide range of designs and mouldings. It is robust, heavy and frost-resistant, so good for permanent plantings. Concrete is not suitable for acid-loving plants unless treated with sealant.

## CONTAINER GARDENING
see pages 66–67

# CONTAINER GARDENING

## CONTAINER GARDENING

Hundreds of plants will grow in the confined spaces of pots, hanging baskets and window boxes. By pairing these plants with the growing conditions they prefer, you can bring colour and texture to almost any space in the garden.

### Grouping for impact
Containers allow you to compose a picture and experiment in your garden. Instead of positioning them individually around the garden, you will make a greater impact by displaying them together in a collection. Adjust the height of the display by standing some containers on pot stands, bricks or upturned pots; mount flat-backed pots on walls. Make sure that they can be reached easily for watering and feeding.

### Unify for best effect
To achieve the best look from a container garden, choose pots that are the same colour rather than an odd assortment of pots and containers. This unifies the display, allowing the pots to recede into the background and putting the plants on show.

### Creating containers
Plant individual plants or group combinations of plants together in the one container, using plants that have similar light, fertiliser and water requirements. Spray a sealer inside new terracotta or concrete pots to minimise water evaporation before planting up.

### Drilling drainage holes
If you are planting directly into a container that has few or no drainage holes, make holes in the base before planting up. For a wooden container, make the holes with a hand or electric drill, working slowly to widen the holes gradually. If the container is made of clay or glazed terracotta, use a carbide-tipped masonry bit in the drill. To avoid cracking the container, do not apply too much pressure to the drill, and also withdraw the bit slowly and often to prevent overheating.

### plant up a Container

1. Spread a layer of fine mesh or shadecloth over the drainage holes of the container to keep the potting mix in while letting water drain out.

2. Add enough mix so that when the plant's root ball sits on it, the top of the root ball is about 2–3 cm below the pot rim. As you add the mix around the plant's roots, shake or rock the pot gently to help settle the mix.

3. Continue adding the mix and shaking until it is level with the top of the root ball. If you plan to top the mix with an ornamental mulch, leave 5 cm from the rim.

4. Water in well, using a fine shower from a water breaker or a watering can with a rose.

CONTAINER GARDENING     **C**

Containers can help enliven a shady spot. Choose perennials and annuals such as impatiens, lobelia, aspidistra, bugle and liriope for dappled shade.

## choose plants for Containers

These care-free plants will adapt easily to life in containers:

**Annuals** Begonia ✽ Calendula ✽ Coleus ✽ Cornflower ✽ Cosmos ✽ Impatiens ✽ Kale ✽ Marigold ✽ Nasturtium ✽ Pansy ✽ Paper daisy ✽ Petunia ✽ Polyanthus ✽ Portulaca ✽ Salvia ✽ Snapdragon ✽ Stock ✽ Sweet William ✽ Verbena ✽ Zinnia

**Perennials** African daisy ✽ Agapanthus ✽ Campanula ✽ Catmint ✽ Chrysanthemum ✽ Clivia ✽ Daylily ✽ Euphorbia ✽ Ferns ✽ Gazania ✽ Geranium ✽ Grasses ✽ Hellebore ✽ Hen and chicks ✽ Hosta ✽ Kangaroo paw ✽ Lamb's ear ✽ Rock rose ✽ Sedum ✽ Thyme ✽ Yucca

**Vines** Bleeding heart ✽ Clematis ✽ Jasmine ✽ Mandevilla ✽ Sweet pea ✽ Wisteria

**Bulbs** Bluebell ✽ Daffodil ✽ Grape hyacinth ✽ Hyacinth ✽ Lilium ✽ Snowflake ✽ Tulip

**Shrubs** Agave ✽ Azalea ✽ Camellia ✽ Coprosma ✽ Cordyline ✽ Fuchsia ✽ Hibiscus ✽ Hydrangea ✽ Japanese box ✽ Lavender ✽ Oleander ✽ Rose

**Trees** Citrus ✽ Conifers ✽ Crepe myrtle ✽ Japanese maples ✽ Palms ✽ Robinia

**Groundcovers** Bugle ✽ Deadnettle ✽ Ivy-leaved geranium ✽ Lobelia ✽ Mondo grass

### Drainage in plastic pots
To make or enlarge drainage holes in the bottom of a plastic pot, heat an old, slim screwdriver or a metal skewer that has a heat-resistant handle. Twisting it gently, push it carefully through the base of the pot. Because the plastic may give off noxious fumes, do this outdoors.

### Pluses of potting mix
Always use a specially formulated potting mix when planting in containers. Potting mixes replace garden soil in the artificial environment of a pot. They are specially designed to get the right balance between holding water and providing good drainage.

One benefit of using potting mix is you don't need to put drainage materials such as crocks in the base of pots. Also, it is sterilised, so weed seeds and diseases have been eradicated. Different mixes are tailored for particular plants.

### Best fertilisers
The best fertilisers for container plants are slow-release fertilisers, which provide regular small doses of plant food. Avoid forms that are not slow-release as they can burn roots if nutrients are dissolved all at once. You can also use liquid feeds every 2–4 weeks along with slow-release fertiliser to boost fast-growing annuals, perennials and vegetables.

### Watering strategies
All container plants need regular watering and their needs increase as they grow bigger. Add water-storing crystals to the potting mix if it does not contain them.

When plants are small, you can usually do a good job with a watering can with a sprinkler head, or rose, or a trigger hose with a water-breaker head. When the root system is more extensive, make sure that the roots are being thoroughly wet. A wetting agent will help; also cover the top of the mix with a thick mulch.

### Dealing with size and weight
A tall and bulky plant in a pot may topple over in the wind. Guard against this by placing a few heavy stones in the bottom of the pot before adding the potting mix. They will act as ballast to help the plant withstand the elements.

Place large containers in their final position before you plant them. And if you want to move it to a new position later, lift it onto a few round logs and roll it into place.

**Drought-tolerant perennials such as thyme, New Zealand flax, yarrow and sedum will thrive in a large pot in full sun.**

67

COPROSMAS | CORDYLINES

## COPROSMAS

### Varieties of form
The numerous coprosma cultivars provide a wonderful array of leaf shapes and colours. Many have highly polished leaves and make handsome foliage shrubs. Select the upright 'Beatson's Gold' for borders and hedge screens and low-spreading 'Prostrata' for banks and groundcovers. Some become small trees and can be clipped into oriental 'cloud' trees.

### Perfect for the coast
The many varieties of coprosma all tolerate salt and drought, so they make good coastal plants. They are ideal for a living screen along an exposed part of the garden, and can also be trimmed into a low formal hedge for an easy-care garden. When grown in pots, they are especially useful for an exposed patio, balcony or veranda – a row of them will protect more sensitive species from exposure.

### Group planting for bright berries
Several coprosma species produce beautiful berries in a range of hues. Examples include *Coprosma australis* (with orange berries), *C. brunnea* (blue berries) and *C. depressa* (reddish berries).

## CORDYLINES

### Frost resistance
Cordylines are mainly subtropical or tropical plants, but some, such as the cabbage tree (*Cordyline australis*), are fairly resistant to frost and can be grown outdoors in temperate climates. They prefer fertile, well-drained soil and a position sheltered from wind, although the cabbage tree is indifferent to conditions. Most cordylines will stand sunshine or partial shade, though coloured-leaf types prefer shaded positions.

The frost-tolerant cabbage tree and mountain cabbage tree (*C. indivisa*) create a tropical effect in temperate climates.

### Perfect in pots
Their slow growth, at least while they are young, makes cordylines excellent pot plants, though they should not be confined in too small a pot. For a more luxuriant effect, plant two or three of the same variety in a large pot.

### Keep it compact
Most species develop an attractive palm-like habit as they mature. If you want a more shrubby plant, cut it back to the height where you wish new growth to occur. For a multi-stemmed clump, cut it back almost to the ground. This pruning can be done at any time, though spring is best. Dead leaves can look unsightly, and it does not harm the plant to pull them off.

### New plants
Cordylines are easy to propagate from cuttings of 30–40 cm lengths of stem (with or without leaves). Cuttings can be taken at any time. Insert them in a pot of sandy soil and keep in a shaded place; transplant them when they have grown several new leaves.

### Scented flowers
While cordylines are grown mainly for their foliage and habit, the big sprays of tiny white or pale lilac flowers are attractive and usually sweetly scented. Don't be disappointed if flowers don't appear at first – they aren't produced until plants are several years old, and rarely indoors. Cut away spent flower heads.

CORIANDER | CORN

## CORIANDER

This hardy annual herb is grown for its fresh leaves and seeds. Before ripening, the seeds smell like the leaves, but as they ripen they develop a warm, spicy aroma – a sign they are ready for harvest.

### Growing techniques

The most important ingredient for this easy-to-grow herb is sun. All varieties produce leaves and seed, but if you want the leaves, choose varieties bred for leaf production that delay flowering. Coriander has a tendency to bolt (run to flower). This reduces the harvest of leaves, which can taste bitter.

To give a longer leaf harvest, make frequent plantings through warm months, use slow-bolting varieties, water well and protect from hot sun with shadecloth.

### Collecting seeds

Your nose is the best harvesting guide. When the seed heads emit a pleasant spicy odour, cut them off and leave to dry on trays in the sun or indoors. Or harvest when about half the seeds have changed from green to grey. Seeds will shatter less readily from the heads in the morning. When the seeds are dry, shake them out of the seed heads or rub them off and put them in an airtight jar.

## CORN

Corn is a warm-weather crop that needs a long growing season and does better in warm districts.

### Block planting

Corn is wind-pollinated and without good pollination it does not set full cobs. So, instead of planting corn in a single row, plant it in a block of four to eight rows to give the wind the best chance of pollinating all of them. Plants should be 30 cm apart.

To help with pollination, you can give the plants a good shake when the male flowers (the tassels at the top of the plant) are in full bloom. This helps the pollen fall on the female flowers below.

### Multipurpose

Corn takes up space and is a bit of a luxury in a small garden. But it can serve several purposes. By planting corn in a block (as above) it can act as a windbreak for the vegetable patch or garden beds. To maximise your space, plant some runner beans beside the cornstalks. Then, as the beans grow, the stalks will provide support for them.

### Sowing corn

Corn needs a sunny, sheltered position. It will grow in any soil that is well drained, but the soil does need to be enriched with compost or well-rotted manure. Sow the seeds about 2 cm deep and 10 cm apart in a block. The plants will usually emerge in 6–10 days, depending on the temperature and the variety.

### Extra sweetness

Supersweet varieties of corn are genetically different from traditional varieties and have at least double the sweetness. These are F1 hybrids, and they have largely replaced older varieties. They should be grown in isolation from older varieties, otherwise their extra sweetness may be lost.

The seeds of supersweet varieties cannot be saved because they will not breed true. Among the best are 'Sweet White F1', 'Honey & Cream F1', 'Breakthrough F1', 'Florida Supersweet F1' and 'Extra Early Sweet'.

### Perfect picking

It can be difficult to tell when corn cobs are ripe. Once the tassels have withered to dark brown, peel back the sheath around each cob and press an individual grain with a fingernail – if the cob exudes a watery liquid it is not yet ripe; a milky fluid signifies ripeness. If no liquid is exuded, the cob is past its best.

# Cottage gardens

The classic cottage garden is a mass of romantic informality, a glorious summer display of old-fashioned flowers. It suits any garden, large or small, and with plants left to self-seed and tumble over paths and edges, can be low on maintenance, too.

## Plant in layers

To create the cottage garden style successfully, you need to think of your planting as a system of layers. Use trees and shrubs for structure, and hedges to create frameworks. Plant climbers to scramble and clamber up arbours, arches and walls.

Use old-fashioned flowers and herbaceous perennials for the bulk of your planting. Include some vegetables and herbs, and fill gaps with annuals and bulbs for colour throughout the year.

## Formal or informal?

The prime feature of a cottage garden is 'controlled informality'. Aim for an almost overcrowded effect in your garden beds and borders. Set out plants in informal drifts and swathes, mixing species and colours to get a mass of flowers. Allow plants to grow and spread naturally. Repeat a number of key plants throughout the beds to link and give them rhythm.

## Flowers for cutting and scent

One of the joys of a cottage garden is having flowers to bring into the house. You could grow:

* Plants for drying – marigolds, roses, statice

* Flowers for vases – dahlias, gladioli, liliums

* Aromatic and honey-producing plants – pinks, carnations, lavenders, nicotianas, sweet peas.

### choose old-fashioned flowers for Cottage gardens

A selection of the following flowers will give you the classic cottage garden look:

* Bleeding heart
* Campanula
* Columbine
* Delphinium
* Foxglove
* Hollyhock
* Larkspur
* Lupin
* Mullein (*Verbascum* spp.)
* Wallflower
* Yarrow (*Achillea* spp.)

Lupins

Layers of flowers

Delphinium

Hollyhock

# COURTYARD GARDENS

## Walls, fences and sky
A courtyard is open to the sky but is sited within sheltering walls or fences. It may enjoy full sun or it may spend most of the year in shadow and receive only a gleam of sun in the middle of summer.

Sometimes it will have a wall that is tall and a little overwhelming, but the intimidating effect can be lessened by placing your seating area so that you face away from it. This also keeps the central part of the courtyard open, so it feels more spacious. High walls will also feel less overpowering if you create your own canopy with a small, spreading tree (perhaps in a large pot) or, in more limited spaces, a pergola or arbour.

## Breaking up the space
Break up a small, boxy ground area by using paving set on the diagonal or choosing different-sized paving. Making a raised seating area in front of a high wall will also achieve this. Place a bench in the centre with a pair of architectural plants on each side. Or frame the seat by training a plant on the wall into a fan shape or by fixing a decorative panel of metalwork or trellis.

## Protecting privacy
Enclosing a small courtyard with walls or fences about 1.5–2 m high gives maximum privacy but is not always the answer. Walls may block views outside the garden that add to a feeling of space, or cause stagnant air in small areas. Sometimes the right-shaped tree or shrub does a better job.

A bushy-crowned evergreen tree may screen out a neighbouring window, a line of shrubs increase terrace privacy. A climbing rose growing on a lattice fence lets in some light and wind, but gives privacy. Deciduous trees give winter light and summer privacy.

## Soil in the city
The soil in small gardens is often depleted and shallow, with pipes and building foundations below. Spread plenty of organic matter to help create the 15–30 cm of good topsoil needed for a fertile garden. Or build raised beds. Don't skimp on size as larger beds look better and hold more moisture.

## Pots and tubs
Small gardens look well furnished if well-placed containers are filled with flowering shrubs, topiary, trees and climbers. Do not scatter container plants about – arrange them as if in a still-life painting.

CRAB APPLES | CROWN ROT

# CREPE MYRTLES

The crepe myrtle is a deciduous tree for a warm climate, with distinctive gold and silver bark. It bears flowers in late summer and autumn in similar colours to those of the cold-climate lilac, ranging from white to mauve, pink, cerise and burgundy.

Crepe myrtle is easy to grow in well-drained soils. Varieties range from 2–8 m tall, ideal for a spot where a small to medium tree is needed. The naturally small size also reduces the need for pruning.

### Careful shaping
Traditionally pruned in winter to promote heavy flowering, the crepe myrtle is now more often seen unpruned and allowed to grow as a graceful tree. Restrict pruning to early shaping to create a multi-trunked tree.

### Avoid powdery mildew
One of the drawbacks of the crepe myrtle is its susceptibility to the disease powdery mildew, which disfigures the leaves and new growth of some forms. Look for plants in the 'Indian Summer' series, which have been bred for resistance to this disease.

See also Powdery mildew

# CRAB APPLES

### Blossoms for a cool climate
The crab apple is one of the most glorious of all flowering trees for a cold to temperate garden. In spring, trees are smothered in a cloud of pink or white blossoms. These are followed by small, serrated leaves which turn to yellow in autumn.

These deciduous trees grow 3–6 m high. They tolerate a wide range of soils but prefer well-drained, loamy soils. Once established, they are quite drought-tolerant.

### Best flowers and fruit
The Betchel crab apple (*Malus ioensis* 'Plena') has showy double pink and white flowers but few fruit, while 'Gorgeous' has small, single, white flowers and a mass of shiny red fruit. The Japanese crab apple (*M. floribunda*) and its cultivars 'Eleyi' and 'Golden Hornet' are also good choices for a lovely spring display.

### Fruit in autumn
Clusters of small yellow berry-like fruit appear in autumn. They are called 'crabs', and give the tree its common name. Crabs can be left on the tree to be enjoyed as an ornament in winter, or harvested when ripe in autumn and made into a tart jam.

# CROWN ROT

### Plants affected
Trees, shrubs, perennials and annuals, bulbs, vegetables, fruits and indoor plants.

### Symptoms
Base or crown of plant rots; pale foliage; plants wilt and eventually die.

### Treatment
✻ Dig up and destroy or safely dispose of entire plants that are affected.

✻ Avoid injuring plants near the base, through which soil organisms can enter.

✻ Plant at the right depth, and keep crowns and plant stems free of debris or mulch.

✻ Improve soil drainage.

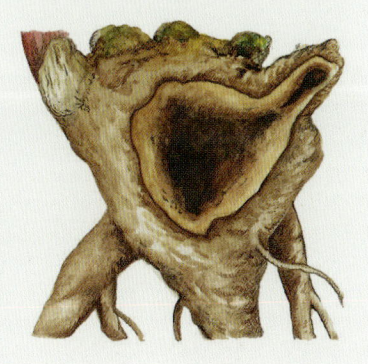

## CUCUMBERS

Cucumbers can bear long green fruit or round pale green or white fruit – the latter are called 'apple' cucumbers. 'Burpless' varieties have less acid than regular cucumbers and are preferred by people with digestive problems.

### Varieties for small gardens

Cucumber varieties are classed as 'vine' or 'bush' types. Vine types are usually spaced about 1 m apart and allowed to trail on the ground, but you can save space by training them up a trellis. Bush types do not trail and only need to be spaced about 40 cm apart. They do well in containers.

### Planting in spring

Cucumbers are a summer crop and should be sown in spring. In cooler areas wait until all danger of frost is over and the soil has warmed up. They do best in very rich soil and lots of sunshine. Mildew can be a problem if they are planted in sheltered positions, especially in humid climates. Most types mature in about 2 months from planting.

For an early crop, start the plants indoors on a sunny windowsill, sowing the seeds in peat pots to minimise shock when planted out. Alternatively, the young plants can be protected by covering them with plastic over wire hoops.

### Picking the best

Cucumbers are at their best if they are picked when crisp and sweet but before they reach their maximum size. Pick continuously to ensure a higher yield over a longer period. Don't pull the fruit off the vine as this can cause damage; harvest with a sharp knife.

### What is a gherkin?

Gherkins are immature green cucumbers picked young and pickled. Any green variety can be used, although the traditional type has rather short, spiny fruit and is highly productive.

## CUT FLOWERS

Always use scissors, sharp secateurs or a knife when cutting flowers. This gives a clean cut, through which the flowers can easily absorb water.

### Make cut flowers last longer

* Pick flowers early in the morning or in the evening.
* Remove all lower leaves that will be under water.
* Cut off the bottom 1–2.5 cm of each stem at a sharp angle, then soak stems in lukewarm water for 2 hours (use cold for bulb flowers).
* Make sure that your vases are scrupulously clean before use.
* Change the water every 2 days.

### Homemade flower food

All cut flowers benefit from a feed. You can make a good mix by blending 2 tablespoons of sugar, 1 litre of warm water and 1½ teaspoons of household bleach. Other aids thought to prolong cut flowers include crushed aspirin, a copper coin or sugar added to the water.

### Crushing blow

Using a sharp knife, slice the base of the hard stems of woody plants such as hydrangeas, lilacs, roses and viburnums. Some florists also recommend crushing the wound with a hammer, which is thought to help water penetrate.

To revive wilted flowers, cut off the stem ends under water, then plunge them into lukewarm water.

### The time to cut

The best time to cut flowers varies according to species. Cut daffodils when they are in bud and peonies when the buds are just showing colour. Never cut dahlias until the flowers have opened, and wait for the first gladiolus floret at the base of the stem to open.

This is true of all spike flowers and cluster flowers such as perennial phlox, agapanthus, yarrow and lilacs. If the top bud on gladioli remains closed, simply trim it off.

CUT FLOWERS | CUTTINGS

## send a message with Cut flowers

Flower meanings are steeped in folklore and mythology. A bouquet of flowers can be given special significance if the flowers convey a secret message to the recipient.

**Aster**  A first step

**Begonia**  Ethereal love

**Belladonna lily**  Pride

**Calendula**  Tenacity

**Candytuft**  Peace

**Chrysanthemum**  Truth

**Clematis**  Pure in mind

**Daffodil**  Chivalry

**Forget-me-not**  Fidelity

**Gladiolus**  Strength of character

**Honeysuckle**  Sweet disposition

**Hyacinth**  Play

**Iris**  Message

**Lavender**  Chastity

**Lilac**  First love

**Lily of the valley**  Purity

**Magnolia**  Dignity

**Marigold**  Happiness

**Primrose**  Sadness

**Rose**  Love

**Sunflower**  Haughtiness

**Sweet pea**  Gentleness

**Viola**  Love

Purple sage is raised from cuttings taken from early summer to midautumn. When cuttings root, they are put into individual containers, then planted out in spring.

## CUTTINGS

### New plants from old

When propagating new plants by cuttings, part of an existing plant is removed and grown so that it becomes a new plant that is a clone of its parent. Depending on the species, cuttings are usually taken in spring (softwood), late summer and autumn (semi-hardwood), or late autumn to winter (hardwood). Root cuttings are usually taken in winter. Some indication of the type of cutting that is most likely to succeed is usually given by the way the parent plant grows.

### Hormone rooting powder

You may not need it. However, if your previous attempts to root untreated cuttings have been unsuccessful, try using hormone rooting powder or gel. Only the smallest amount is necessary. Dip only the base of the cutting into the powder or gel, then tap it lightly to remove any excess.

### Testing for roots

Always allow enough time for cuttings to strike, or take root – this will vary according to the plant and the time of year. Examine the plants for signs of growth, such as new leaves or shoots, or roots showing through the bottoms of the pots.

### Poisonous plants

The sap of certain plants is poisonous or an irritant and great care should be taken to prevent any contact with your skin or eyes. Plants that require caution include euphorbias, dumb canes (*Dieffenbachia* spp.), croton (*Codiaeum variegatum*), tree ivy (× *Fatshedera*), hoyas, oleanders, philodendrons and gloxinia (*Sinningia speciosa*).

# CUTTINGS

## CUTTINGS continued

### Softwood cuttings
Naturally softwooded plants such as coleus (above), butterfly bushes, diosmas, fuchsias, hebes and impatiens, strike best from softwood cuttings.

In spring, cut off the tips of young, healthy, non-flowering shoots to about 10 cm long. Use a sharp knife to trim the base just below a leaf joint and remove the lower leaves. Lightly dip the base in hormone rooting powder if you wish. Fill a tray or 13 cm pot with propagating mix and make small holes in the mix. Insert a cutting in each hole, spaced so leaves do not touch. Water, drain well, cover with a plastic bag and keep warm.

### Semi-hardwood cuttings
Shrubs such as abelias, gardenias and lavenders (above) with harder stems will root most easily from semi-hardwood cuttings.

Take tip cuttings, 10–15 cm long, in late summer and autumn from shoots where the stem has become firm and brown. Remove all the leaves except the top five to ten. Dip the base into hormone rooting powder if desired. Make holes in a 13 cm pot of propagating mix or in soil in the ground and insert the cuttings 5 cm deep and 5 cm apart. Firm in, water well and cover with a plastic bag, cloche, or coldframe or propagator lid. Check the soil does not dry out.

### Hardwood cuttings
Hardwood cuttings are bare pieces of woody stem taken from deciduous shrubs while dormant in winter. They are ideal for roses.

Use a sharp knife to take cuttings in winter from shoots that have just completed their first season's growth. Trim each cutting just below a bud at the base and just above a bud at the top so it is 25–30 cm long. Remove a thin sliver of bark from the base. Dip in hormone rooting powder and insert in large pots of propagating mix or a shallow V-shaped trench lined with 2.5 cm horticultural sand. The cuttings should be half or two-thirds below the soil level.

## understand Cuttings

Follow these rules to ensure success when you propagate plants from cuttings:

✻ Always maintain a very high standard of hygiene in your working area, which should be disinfected before use.

✻ Ensure that propagating knives and secateurs are sharp and clean. Disinfect them before and after use.

✻ Take cuttings at the time of year appropriate to the plant.

✻ Select parent plants that are free from pests and diseases and growing vigorously.

✻ Always label your cuttings to avoid confusion later on.

✻ Prevent moisture loss by placing cuttings in a plastic bag as soon as they are removed from the parent plants. Maintain a high level of humidity around cuttings.

✻ Store hormone rooting powder in a cool, dark, dry place. Use it sparingly, lightly dipping the base in it and shaking off any excess.

✻ Only ever use good-quality propagating or seed-raising mix. Never use garden soil or recycled potting mix from other pots as the growing medium.

✻ Always make a hole in the propagating mix before inserting softwood cuttings.

CUTTINGS | CYCADS

## take root Cuttings

This type of cutting is a good method for perennials with thick fleshy roots, such as acanthus and Japanese windflowers.

**1** Dig up a strong, healthy plant and wash the soil off the roots. Select young, vigorous roots that are of pencil thickness and cut them from the parent plant near the crown.

**2** Cut each root into 7–10 cm lengths, cutting straight across the top and making a slanted cut at the bottom (so you know which way to plant them).

**3** Fill a deep 13 cm pot with moist propagating mix. Insert six to eight cuttings around the rim of the pot, 2–5 cm apart, with the tops of each cutting level with the surface.

**4** Cover the mix with a fine layer of sand or very fine gravel and place the pots in a coldframe, a sheltered place outdoors or on the windowsill of a cool room.

## CYCADS

### Living fossils

Cycads belong to an extremely ancient group of plants that preceded flowering plants by about 245 million years. Today, 23 per cent are either critically endangered or endangered – this includes Australian and African species – and another 15 per cent of cycads are threatened. Cycads should never be collected from the bush.

### Not palms

Cycads prefer protection from full sun in a woodland environment. They closely resemble palms but are gymnosperms – cone-bearing plants related to ginkgos and conifers. They do not have flowers. Instead, they develop huge, pine cone-like structures. The male and female cones are produced on separate plants. The male cones produce pollen. The female cones, which may take many months to ripen and split open, produce seeds that can be collected, then cleaned and propagated on top of seed-raising mix.

### Poison warning

Cycad seeds contain neurotoxins accumulated from a blue-green nitrogen-fixing algae in its roots. The seeds, ground and washed, have been used as a flour but the toxin is cumulative. Keep children well away, and wear rubber gloves when handling the seeds.

Once the seed has germinated the plant can be transplanted into a small pot. Place so that the young root is just in the potting mix.

# D — DAFFODILS, JONQUILS AND NARCISSUS | DAHLIAS

## DAFFODILS, JONQUILS AND NARCISSUS

Gardeners tend to use the name 'daffodil' to describe the spring flowers with the long trumpets, while the word 'narcissus' is reserved for those flowers with short, cup-like trumpets such as paper whites, jonquils and poet's narcissi.

### Narcissus for a warm climate
All these stunning spring bulbs belong to the genus *Narcissus* and are ideal for cool climates. But gardeners in a subtropical or warm climate can enjoy them, too. Try paper white narcissus, yellow jonquils and the daffodil varieties 'Erlicheer' and 'Golden Lion'. In a warm climate these bulbs may begin flowering from late autumn.

### divide Daffodils
When the number of flowers produced by a clump of daffodils begins to decline, the bulbs have probably become overcrowded. Lift the clump when the foliage has turned yellow, separate the clump into single bulbs and either replant them immediately or dry and store them.

### Plant early
Plant bulbs as soon as they are on sale in early autumn. They will root more quickly in soil that is still warm from summer, and by getting them off to a good start, they will last for many years.

### The importance of foliage
When the bulbs have finished their growing cycle, the foliage will begin to yellow. Do not cut the leaves down; they replenish the bulbs' energy reserves so they flower again the following year. Let the foliage die down naturally. But do deadhead faded blooms because they drain the bulbs' energy reserves.

Plant something around your daffodils and jonquils that will camouflage the dying leaves and, when they have finally withered, conceal the empty spot. Try geraniums and daylilies in sunny spots, or hostas under trees.

### Poor mixers
If you cut daffodils and jonquils for the house, do not put them straight into a vase with other flowers. The stems emit a toxic sap that shortens the life of other blooms. Cut 2.5 cm from the stems, then stand in water for 24 hours. The stem bases will seal and, once rinsed, can be combined safely with other flowers.

## DAHLIAS

### Early colour
If you want dahlias to flower in November or December, start them in late August or September. Pot new or stored tubers into 13 cm pots of good potting mix. Water well and keep them in a greenhouse or other well-lit, frost-free place. Once they start to shoot, stand them outside in a sheltered spot to harden off, then plant out.

Dormant tubers can be put directly in the ground in early spring, up to 6 weeks before the last expected frosts.

### Staking
These plants produce a great deal of foliage and are easily blown over by wind. When they flower, the sheer weight of the blooms can lead to broken stems unless the plants are well supported. The simplest method is to use three or four bamboo canes or stakes around each plant.

### Dahlias are thirsty plants
Prevent dahlias from wilting in hot, dry summers with copious watering. These plants are largely composed of water. To ensure maximum development, give them a bucket (9 litres) of water every other day during dry spells where water restrictions allow. Mulch heavily with compost to retain moisture in the soil.

# DAISIES

All daisies are members of the Asteraceae family. These are the cheery, happy-go-lucky flowers of the garden, with petals radiating distinctively around a central 'eye'. Given a sunny, well-drained position, most daisies are tough and even foolproof. They are good for starting a new garden as they grow quickly from cuttings and like full sun.

## African daisies *Arctotis × hybrida, Osteospermum fruticosum*

*Arctotis × hybrida* is a tough South African groundcover. Also known as veldt or arctotis daisies, these plants flower from autumn to spring in vibrant orange and red, burgundy, pink and creamy white. They tolerate hot, dry and coastal conditions.

*Osteospermum fruticosum* is a trailing perennial that loves a hot, sunny spot and grows in any soil. The dark-centred white, mauve or purple flowers, from spring to summer, open in full sun.

## Marguerite daisies
*Argyranthemum frutescens*

Colours and shapes range from single white flowers to anemone-centred flowers in white, pink and yellow. They flower for months; lightly prune after flowering to encourage a second flush.

## Cut leaf daisies *Brachyscome* spp.

These drought-tolerant Australian daisies make a tough groundcover. They are covered in a mass of small mauve, pink, white or lemon blooms in spring and summer. To avoid plants becoming straggly, replant from cuttings or layering every few years.

## Blue marguerites
*Felicia amelloides*

These South African evergreen groundcovers or low shrubs are frost-tender. The small blue flowers are produced from spring to autumn – deadheading will extend the flowering period.

## Daisy bushes *Olearia* spp.

The mass of tiny flowers – in pure white or shades of pink, blue and purple – on these hardy evergreen shrubs appear from spring to autumn. Some species even suit exposed and coastal sites.

## Paper daisies *Rhodanthe* spp., *Xerochrysum bracteatum* syn. *Bracteantha bracteata*

Also known as everlasting daisies or strawflowers, these annuals have dry papery petals in purple, pink, yellow, orange, white and brown. They flower profusely in early spring, then die down as the weather warms. Sow in swathes for colour in a waterwise garden.

**Marguerite daisies**

**Paper daisies**

**African daisy** (*Osteospermum fruticosum* cv.)

# D | DAPHNES | DEADHEADING

## DAPHNES

### Winter perfume
Winter-flowering daphnes (*Daphne odora*) are known for their beautiful fragrant flowers. They like a cool spot out of the hot sun, so plant them in the ground where they get morning sun only or grow them in a pot on a well-lit veranda. Picking the flowers for use indoors will stimulate bushy growth and is the only pruning needed.

### Going, going, gone
Daphne bushes have one major failing – they can turn up their toes and die without any explanation. Such sudden deaths are usually caused by root disease brought on by poor drainage. If a daphne dies, don't replant another in the same spot. Instead, consider growing a new plant in a pot filled with a good-quality potting mix.

## DAYLILIES

Few plants are as dependable as daylilies. Their trumpet-shaped flowers come in a rainbow of colours, from rich magenta to pale yellow, and are often enhanced by stripes, streaks or bands at the throat. The flowers, as their name indicates, usually last only a day, but you can count on the plants to keep on flowering for a month.

### Mass planting
Daylilies work well as a mass planting for a low-maintenance garden. They also bring long-lasting colour to a garden. Plant them with roses for a stunning summer garden.

When planted on a bank, daylilies provide good erosion control because their vigorous roots help hold the soil in place. They adapt readily to most soils, are drought- and heat-resistant, and virtually trouble-free.

### Look for two fans
Two young, fan-shaped sprouts are an indication that the plant is more mature, which will greatly increase the likelihood that it blooms in the first season.

In cold climates select deciduous daylily species to avoid damage from the cold in winter. In warm climates you can grow either evergreen or deciduous plants.

## DEADHEADING

As well as making the garden look tidier, deadheading will lengthen the flowering season of many plants. Plants put a lot of energy into seed formation. If you stop them from doing this, it can strengthen the plants and also encourage strong foliage. Resist deadheading any plants whose seed heads make good winter shapes or food for birds.

It is usually best to use sharp secateurs when deadheading. Clean them well afterwards to remove any sticky sap or disease-carrying organisms.

**Bulbs and corms** Deadhead flower stalks to ground level as soon as they fade. This diverts the plants' resources into the actual bulb (the underground storage organ). Keep well watered until the foliage dies down.

**Perennials** Remove dead flower spikes. In plants such as lupins and delphiniums this will encourage flowering sideshoots. Cut spring- and early summer-flowering perennials such as oriental poppies down to ground level after flowering. Some will flower a second time. Tidy up carnations and salvias.

**Annuals** Because they stop flowering once they have set seed, deadhead pansies, snapdragons and petunias to ensure continued blooms. Tidy up other annuals such as marigolds as flowers fade.

**Roses** Remove old flowers down to the first pair of leaves.

DECKS

# DECKS

Build your deck on the quiet side of the house and out of view of the neighbours. Site it for convenient access from the house: you won't want guests marching through the bedroom on their way out to the barbecue.

Plant an attractive climber for sun shelter and extra privacy, training it along a support to allow light breezes onto the deck. In warm to tropical climates use bougainvillea, potato vine (*Solanum jasminoides*) or 'Alice du Pont' mandevilla. In cooler areas try clematis or wisteria.

## Check your local building codes
In some cities or regions, you may need to apply for a permit from your local council to attach a deck to your house. Freestanding decks, however, are generally accepted and rarely require an application, but do always check with the relevant authorities first.

## Choose the right timber
A timber floor is more forgiving than other materials for building a deck. But never use flat-grain timber. Moisture will eventually raise the grain and cause the boards to cup and splinter. Use vertical-grain timber instead. Oregon is an excellent choice, as is western red cedar.

## Stain, don't paint!
For outdoor woodwork, staining is preferable to painting. Stains require less maintenance and they penetrate the wood to create a soft patina that enhances the natural grain. Many stains have an acrylic latex base that allows for easy clean-up with soap and water. Paints blister and peel over time and need scraping, priming and repainting.

## Tips for buying timber
It has a finite life, but timber can last longer if you take a few precautions:

**Buy from a reputable supplier** Check that all the components have been pressure-treated; most manufacturers offer a 10-year warranty. If there is no warranty, do not consider buying the product.

**Choose grooved** Decking boards are always grooved; this is partly to make them less slippery and partly to help with drainage. Ordinary wooden planks are not suitable for use as decking because they can be lethally slippery when wet.

**A question of length** Decking boards and other timber usually come in specific lengths, which may not exactly fit the area that you want to cover. Make sure that you buy longer rather than shorter lengths; you can use the leftover pieces to make other garden items.

# D

DECORATIVE FRUITS | DELPHINIUMS

*Persimmon fruit*

## DECORATIVE FRUITS

### Year-round colour
Some trees and shrubs have colourful flowers or leaves, and they also carry decorative berries or fruits in autumn and winter. They are usually brighter in colder climates and commonly red, orange or yellow. There are white berries on snowberries (*Symphoricarpos* spp.), and lilac or purple berries on beauty-berries (*Callicarpa* spp.).

### Fruits of the rainforest
The many different lillypillies decorate gardens with their fruits from summer onwards. One of the most striking for fruit is the riberry (*Syzygium luehmannii*), which has masses of edible bright pink pear-shaped fruit. It is native to the Australian rainforest but can be grown in all but the coldest areas. Also striking are the blue-black fruit of blueberry ash (*Elaeocarpus reticulatus*), which persist on the tree for a long period.

In warmer districts, try cherry guava, tree tomato, feijoa (or fruit salad bush) or Cape gooseberries for both beauty and food.

### Berry pyrotechnics
Display fruits and berries to their best advantage by making a hedge from berry-bearing shrubs. Or place a single specimen in front of evergreens or against a pale wall.

### Avoiding weeds and mess
Many autumn berry plants such as cotoneaster, hawthorn, holly and pyracantha are weeds. Do some research to ensure that you don't choose a plant that has weed potential in your area. For berries that don't pose a weed problem, consider planting beautyberries, clivias, crab apples, lillypillies, persimmons and rugosa roses.

Berries from elders (*Sambucus* spp.), crab apples and others can make a mess on the ground or when carried indoors on footwear. Plant them well back from paths.

---

#### Plants with bright berries
* **Coralberry (*Ardisia crenata*)** Scarlet berries * **Japanese beautyberry (*Callicarpa japonica*)** Purple berries * **Natal plum (*Carissa macrocarpa*)** Red fruit * **Persimmon (*Diospyros kaki*)** Orange fruit * **Cumquat (*Citrus japonica*)** Orange fruit * **Silk tassel bush (*Garrya elliptica*)** Purple-grey fruit * **'Golden Hornet' crab apple (*Malus* 'Golden Hornet')** Yellow crabs * **Rugosa roses** Red hips * **Riberry (*Syzygium luehmannii*)** Hot pink berries * **Snowball bush (*Viburnum opulus* cvs)** Various colours

---

## DELPHINIUMS

### Cuttings or seeds
The best delphiniums are the named hybrid varieties, which are propagated in spring by division or by cuttings. They can also be grown from seed, but the seeds collected from the garden produce variable results.

Three types are commonly grown:

* Belladonna group, frost-hardy perennials with rich blue or white, usually single, flowers in loose spikes

* Connecticut Yankees group, perennials that last 4 years, even in mild-winter districts

* Elatum group, frost-hardy perennials that bloom from summer to autumn, and include tall spike types.

### The richer the better
All delphiniums need a deep, rich, well-drained soil and a sunny position. Dig in plenty of bulky organic matter before planting the seedlings as delphiniums are big feeders. When watering, water the base of the plants. Do not sprinkle them from above, as water left on the leaves can encourage disease.

### Height needs help
Tall delphiniums will need staking. Tie each stem to a stout bamboo cane or surround the plant with canes spaced 15–20 cm apart and link them with wire or strong twine. Herbaceous supports are available from garden centres.

# DESIGN

Thoughtful design will help you create a garden that suits your needs, your taste and your site. Whether designing a garden from scratch or changing an existing garden, take your time.

## Plotting and planning

Using a pencil, draw the outline of your garden to scale on a large piece of graph paper. Then mark in the features that you wish to include in the design, such as flowerbeds, barbecue, swimming pool, vegetable garden and lawn. Include any existing features that you want to retain and indicate the proposed positions of other features, such as dividing hedges, steps and paths, that you wish to create. Rub out and revise the plan until you are fully satisfied.

You can experiment by drawing each feature on a separate piece of paper; as your ideas change, you can fit the pieces into place as you would a jigsaw.

## Careful curving

Curves are an effective way of creating some interesting borders and separating different areas of the garden. Lay out a hose or a piece of rope to give an idea of how the curve will look. View the shape from different parts of the garden and, if possible, from an upstairs window in the house. Use broad sweeps rather than tight curves, which are generally more difficult to maintain. But don't overdo it. Too many curves can look fussy.

## Plants to fit

Rather than make a list of plants by name, make a list of types of plants that you need, such as:

### A photographic guide

To help you design the layout of a new garden, a camera can be a useful planning tool. Take photographs of the garden from different angles and enlarge them. Draw your planned layouts on tracing paper and lay them over the photographs. Superimposing several designs over the existing space will help you to decide which design you prefer.

1 m high shrubs for sunny areas; narrow shrubs to 2 m high to screen an ugly wall along the side of the house; shade trees for the back garden. Take this list to your garden centre along with your plan and select the most appropriate plants for each area of your garden. If you are unsure

# D  DESIGN

Various design devices have been used to create a sense of width and depth in this garden, while keeping the beds narrow to give as much lawn as possible.

## Where to position it?

**Children's play area**  Within easy view of house; some shade

**Clothes drying area**  Breezy spot near house

**Compost area**  Hidden but accessible corner of garden

**Dog kennel**  Close to house, in shade

**Entertaining area**  Terrace or deck, possibly under cover

**Home office**  Close to house, out of breeze; ready access to electricity

**Lighting**  House or garage walls, paths, steps, patio, paved areas, shed, sculptural plants and outdoor art; access to electricity for plug-in transformer

**Rainwater tank**  Below rainwater downpipe at side of house or under deck

**Rubbish bins**  Hidden, but close to kitchen

**Shed**  Close to house, garden boundary or beside vegetable garden

**Sports**  Away from windows; on hard surface area such as driveway

**Swimming pool**  Level, private area; access to water and electricity; check your council's rules for distances from boundaries

**Vegetable or herb garden**  Sunniest part of garden, as close to house as possible

**Water taps**  Convenient for watering and cleaning

**Wildlife pond**  Semi-shade, away from falling leaves

## DESIGN *continued*

of which plants to choose, don't be afraid to ask for advice.

Do not be tempted to use lots of different plants if you have a small garden. Focus instead on a few plant types and a striking group of the same plant, such as a clump of daylilies or red hot pokers, to make a strong impact.

### Lawn or not?
When designing a new garden, think carefully before deciding to establish a lawn. A gravel or paved area may be more suitable, particularly if you want to be spared the bother of mowing. Or you could cover the area with a groundcover if you want an expanse of green without the constant maintenance.

### Consider different seasons
When establishing a new garden it is important not to buy all your plants at once. In order to have a garden that looks interesting all year round, throughout every season, visit your nursery at different times of the year. Make at least one visit in each of the four seasons to buy plants in flower then. Autumn foliage trees are best chosen in autumn.

*See also* Groundcovers, Paving

DIGGING | DILL

## DIGGING

### Why dig?
Digging is sometimes necessary to loosen compacted topsoil, destroy weeds, work in compost, manure and fertilisers, or create a seedbed. A soil newly used for gardening, or one that is too hard and compacted to push a hand trowel into, will need loosening, especially if you plan to grow vegetables, annuals or deep-rooted perennials there.

Do not dig wet or heavy soil; also do not dig when the soil is too dry and difficult to loosen. About 48 hours after rain or irrigation, you'll find the soil has the best moisture content for digging.

### Spade choice
A spade is the ideal tool for digging. When choosing a spade, make sure the shaft is a suitable length for you in order to avoid back strain when digging. Test whether a D-shaped, Y-shaped or T-shaped handle feels the most comfortable, although you may find that the T-shaped handle is not readily available.

### Comfort and health
First, be careful not to overdo it if you are not used to digging!

Wear gloves and strong boots or shoes. Do not push the spade or fork with your arms; instead, stand on the spade, keeping your back straight, and force it into the ground with your own weight. Then lever the spade backwards to break the sod off, lifting as much as you can easily handle. Throw the clod to the ground upside-down, which will cause it to shatter.

### Dig a large area
If you need to cultivate a large area, consider hiring a rotary hoe or power cultivator.

✸ A rotary hoe will do the work quickly, turning what would be a 4 hour job with a spade into a 50 minute task.

✸ The smaller hand-held models are ideal for the average garden.

✸ These machines are not difficult or strenuous to use and are powered by petrol motors.

✸ Equipment hire companies will have a range of models available at reasonable rates.

✸ When using, be careful not to overwork the soil – one pass is enough – and watch out that you don't damage major tree roots.

### Economise on spadework
Use a fork rather than a spade in heavy clays or where the surface is covered with a thick layer of weeds. Once loosened and heavily manured or composted, a soil should not need to be dug every year. If you mulch heavily with manures, composts and mulches, you will encourage earthworms and other soil organisms, which will do the work for you. Avoid compacting the soil: do not walk on it when it is wet. Stay on the paths instead.

### Think ahead
Try to plan ahead before any major planting projects so you dig the soil a few weeks before you intend sowing. This enables any manures or composts to rot down and gives the soil a chance to further crumble into a good seedbed. And you can destroy any weeds or stray roots that may surface in the meantime.

## DILL

### Hardy and trouble-free
This hardy annual herb with feathery blue-green foliage has a taste reminiscent of aniseed and parsley. It will grow in any well-drained soil in an open, sunny position, though it prefers a warm, dry summer. Incorporate plenty of organic matter into the soil to help it retain moisture during dry months.

### A good companion
If you sow seeds at monthly intervals in spring and summer, you will have a constant supply through summer and into autumn. Dill will often self-sow, and the vivid yellow flower heads are excellent for attracting pollinating insects.

It is usually trouble-free and can be a good companion plant to grow between rows of carrots as its strong aroma deters carrot fly.

### When to pick
The leaves will be ready for harvesting 8 weeks after sowing. Pick as needed to use fresh, and before plants flower for drying.

85

DIOSMA | DISEASES

## DIOSMA

Indigenous to Africa, diosma (*Coleonema pulchrum*) – also known as confetti bush – is hard to beat for effect when it is in full flower in early spring, smothered in tiny star-shaped pink flowers. The species will grow to 2 m but smaller compact forms that reach only 1 m, such as 'Compactum' and 'Nana', are available.

### Year-round colour

Choose dwarf golden diosma (*C. pulchrum* 'Sunset Gold') for an excellent small shrub where colour is needed all year round. It will grow in all areas, except where there are extreme frosts (–5°C and below). A true dwarf, this compact plant rarely grows more than 75 cm tall.

### Haircut to keep compact

All diosmas benefit from frequent light clipping. Left unpruned, the plants can become rangy. Start clipping when young. Regularly pruned, these plants make good informal hedges or borders. They can also be shaped into balls or other decorative forms with regular clipping.

Diosma won't thrive in poorly drained soils. If drainage is a problem in your garden, plant it in raised beds.

## DISEASES

### Radical action for bacterial and viral diseases

Plant diseases can be fungal, bacterial or viral. Bacterial diseases often show as brown, water-soaked spots on leaves and stems. They are untreatable, as are viral diseases. You can only prune off the affected plant parts or remove the entire plant.

### Fungal diseases on flowers and leaves

Common fungal diseases such as rusts, leaf spot and black spot, powdery and downy mildew, anthracnose, scabs and grey mould usually have symptoms of yellow, brown, red or black spots appearing on leaves, or furry mildew and mould growing on leaves and flowers.

These diseases thrive in humid, still conditions, so avoid any activity that increases humidity, such as watering in the evening. Also pick up infected fallen leaves and dispose of them safely to prevent spores spreading.

### The choice of fungicides

Unfortunately, there is no one-size-fits-all fungicide that will control all fungal plant diseases. Milk sprays and activated bicarbonate of soda spray (look for Eco-Rose or EcoCarb) are effective against powdery mildew.

Copper-based sprays, such as Bordeaux mixture, are effective against leaf curl and mildews, but they accumulate in the soil and are toxic to fish, bees and earthworms. Casuarina spray (boil 0.5 kg leaves in water and dilute with enough water to make 40 litres) helps to control fungal diseases, while lime sulfur spray forms a protective barrier.

Myclobutanil, triadimefon, chlorothalonil and triforine are systemic chemical fungicides approved for use against black spot, rusts and powdery mildew.

### Affecting roots, bark and plant stems

Fungal diseases that affect roots, bark and plant stems include types of armillaria, fusarium wilt and phytophthora, and cause plant dieback and splitting bark. Try to improve drainage, and pull all mulch and soil well away from the stems of plants. Anti-rot is a phosphorus acid spray that works against phytophthora root rot.

*See also* Downy mildew, Fungicides, Powdery mildew, Phytophthora root rot, Rose care and maintenance

**Powdery mildew**

**Rust**

86

# DIVISION

Division means separating a parent plant into pieces, each complete with roots, so that you can replant them as smaller, separate plants. It is used to propagate plants that naturally expand into thick clumps – mostly perennials and bulbs.

### Get the timing right
It is best to divide herbaceous perennials and deciduous plants from late autumn to early spring, although asters, delphiniums, chrysanthemums, sneezeweeds and red hot pokers are best left until spring. Clumping plants and grass-like plants, such as clivias, agapanthus and dianellas, can be divided at any time.

However, if your soil is heavy clay and particularly if you live in a cold area, it may be wise to divide all your plants in spring when the soil has warmed up.

### Use healthy stock
Use healthy plants only. If you propagate from diseased stock, infection will be passed on to the young plants. Before replanting any divisions, inspect the roots carefully to make sure that no pests are concealed among them.

When dividing an old plant, keep only the strongest, most vigorous young shoots from the outer edge and reject the old, woody centre. If possible, use only the divisions that have strong root systems, as the weaker ones may take a long time to establish and may never produce a good display.

### Saving time with smaller clumps
Do not pull up a whole plant if you want only one or two fragments. Instead, remove the soil on one side of the plant and use a garden fork to loosen the stems and roots as far down in the soil as possible. Use a knife to remove the pieces you want, then firmly replace the soil. Don't do this too often or the parent plant will become weak.

### Dividing bulbs
If a clump of bulbs becomes very congested, you can gently uproot it after flowering and divide it. This will give the mother bulb a new lease of life and generate a flush of new shoots. Shake the soil off gently and remove the young bulbs. These offsets should come away from the original bulb easily. If they don't, it is because they are not yet mature – in which case don't force them or you may end up damaging the roots.

## propagate perennials by Division

**1** Select a healthy plant that is free from pests and diseases. Use a garden fork to lift the clump (here cranesbills, or perennial geraniums, are being divided) and shake off the excess soil.

**2** The easiest way of splitting a large clump of perennials is to insert two garden forks back to back and lever them apart. Do this several times. Break these into smaller divisions if desired.

**3** Replant the small divisions in soil enriched with well-rotted compost or manure and a handful of slow-release fertiliser. Plant them at the same depth they were growing at previously.

# DOGS | DRACAENAS

## DOGS

### Keeping the lawn green
Canine urine can cause yellow patches on the lawn. Once a patch of grass has yellowed, it will soon turn brown and will almost certainly die. The only treatment is to dilute the urine with water as soon as possible. If you are too late and the grass dies, give the dead patch a good soaking and resow, or repair with a square of turf or runners.

### Barriers
To keep dogs out of your garden, surround it with thorny shrubs or climbers, such as bougainvillea, pyracantha and roses. Pepper dust will also discourage them. Make sure that garbage bin lids are kept firmly closed so that dogs are not attracted to your yard by the smell of food.

A picket fence can help to deter small dogs from scratching up seedlings in the vegetable patch. The fence can be covered with bright climbing annuals such as nasturtiums or runner beans.

### Bottle myth
Some gardeners believe that putting a bottle of water on the lawn will deter dogs from using the area as a toilet. Extensive observation has failed to find any truth in this.

## DOWNY MILDEW

### Plants affected
Brassicas, cucurbits, grapevines, lettuces, onions and roses.

### Symptoms
Yellow or brown blotches on upper surfaces of leaves, greyish white fur on undersides.

### Treatment
* Improve air circulation and drainage. Don't water overhead.
* Rotate crops and do not crowd.
* Destroy infected leaves and prunings (burn if permitted).
* Spray brassicas with mancozeb, or mancozeb and sulfur.
* Spray lettuces and onions with a copper spray, mancozeb, or mancozeb and sulfur.
* Spray copper oxychloride or zineb on cucurbits, and copper hydroxide or copper oxychloride on grapevines.
* Spray affected roses with zineb or furalaxyl.

## DRACAENAS

### Indoors and outdoors
These tropical foliage plants with thick stems and long, strap-like, striped leaves are popular plants for containers. They also thrive in hot-climate gardens. *Dracaena marginata* is particularly popular for indoors, with its variegated striped leaves in shades of red, pink, cream and green. It needs a medium light level and a free-draining potting mix; be careful not to overwater it.

Outdoors, most dracaenas grow best in rich soil and light shade so that their leaves are protected from bleaching and scorching by the sun. The leaf colour in the red-hued varieties will also be richer if they are positioned in shade. Be sure to feed and water dracaenas regularly.

### Add a tropical touch
Their tidy habit makes dracaenas perfect for poolside plantings, particularly when protected from afternoon sun by taller plants or nearby buildings. They add a truly exotic touch to gardens when combined with palms, yet their sparse, uncluttered look makes them equally suitable as feature plants in both oriental-style and Mediterranean gardens.

The dragon tree (*Dracaena draco*) is a tree-sized dracaena that hates humidity and tolerates drought. This makes it a good choice for inland areas.

# DRAINAGE | DRIED FLOWERS

## DRAINAGE

### Combating clay
If the soil in your garden is heavy clay and water is slow to drain away after a downpour, there are several remedies. The best, but most labour intensive and costly, is to install a drainage system using agricultural pipe. In very cold climates, you could dig the soil in autumn to penetrate any compacted layers, then allow frost to break the soil down in winter.

Working in plenty of well-rotted organic material will improve the soil structure.

### Land drain
You may have a mature tree or shrub that is suffering the effects of badly drained soil. Improve the drainage by digging a circular trench, as wide as the spade and 15 cm deep, in the soil around the tree or shrub, in line with the outer edge of the foliage. Shovel a thick layer of gravel into the bottom of the trench and top up with a mixture of garden soil and well-rotted compost or manure.

### Lift up your herb bed
Most herbs need a well-drained soil. A badly drained small herb bed can be improved if it is raised within a retaining wall two bricks high with at least a couple of drainage holes on each side. Fill with well-rotted compost and manure or a good-quality garden soil mix from your local garden centre or a landscape supplier. When the mixture has settled, the bed should drain well and your herbs should flourish.

### Sloping sites
A commonly held misconception among gardeners is that a sloping site is well drained. This may not be the case. Drainage is actually related to the type of soil rather than the lie of the land.

See also Clay soil

**Drying lavender**

## DRIED FLOWERS
You can preserve the beauty of many garden flowers by drying them by air or by silica gel, or by pressing them flat between heavy books.

### Air drying
✱ Pick flowers before they are in full bloom.

✱ Strip off untidy lower leaves.

✱ Secure in bunches of up to 10 stems with an elastic band (the stems will shrink as they dry and fall out if tied with string). Tie to hangers with string of different lengths and hang in a dark, warm, well-ventilated place for 2 weeks.

### Using silica gel
✱ Line an airtight container with 2.5 cm of silica gel. Push trimmed flower heads in, face upwards and spaced well apart.

✱ Cover with another 2.5 cm layer of gel, seal and leave for 3–5 days.

✱ Alternatively, microwave on High for 2 minutes for delicate blooms and 4 minutes for fleshier ones. Cool for 20 minutes.

✱ Check that flowers are totally dry before removing from the gel.

### Pressing with books
✱ Put four sheets of newspaper on a tray and cover with a sheet of blotting paper. Place the flowers, stems or leaves on top of the blotting paper, well spaced out.

✱ Cover with another sheet of blotting paper and four sheets of newspaper. Place heavy books on top and leave for 2 weeks in a cool, dry place.

✱ Remove blotting paper with care to avoid damaging your specimens. Leave for another week if not completely dry.

### Prevent colours from fading
Preserve the colours of large leaves from maples, liquidambars and such trees by ironing them with a moderately hot iron. Slip smaller leaves, still attached to their stems, between a double thickness of newspaper and press gently with a slightly hotter iron.

### Drying roses
To dry roses, pick them either when they are in bud or just as they begin to open. Hang them in bunches and air dry them as described above. Alternatively, leave them in the oven, at an extremely low heat and with the door open, for about 5 hours. Pink roses keep their colours best. Reds, yellows and oranges tend to darken with drying, and creams and whites turn beige.

89

# Drought-tolerant plants

Certain plants are well adapted to survive in dry or hot conditions. Some store water, some reduce the amount of water lost through evaporation. Plants in extreme desert conditions use combinations of these mechanisms. These are nature's water misers.

## Leaves

**Tough leathery or waxy** Plants with waxy or leathery leaves, such as eucalypts, daphnes, banksias and oleanders, resist evaporation.

**Light-coloured** Silver and grey leaves reflect intense light and heat for plants such as lamb's ears, olive trees and the silver wattles.

**Hairy** The downy hairs on the leaves and stems of plants such as lavenders shade the leaf surface and slow down wind, thus trapping more humid air.

**Small** Tiny leaves reduce the surface area that can lose water vapour, as in the leaves of tea trees, ceanothus and jacarandas.

**Shiny** Very glossy leaves reflect hot summer sun off plants such as murrayas, photinias, lillypillies and abelias.

**Deciduous when dry** Trees from subtropical areas with distinct dry seasons drop their leaves to protect themselves from water stress. Examples are flame trees, jacarandas and silky oaks.

**Water-storing** Some leaves hold water for dry periods. Pigface and jelly bean plants do this.

## Flowers

**No petals** Instead of water-losing petals, some plants have brightly coloured tepals, styles and perianths, as found on grevilleas and banksias. Others have fluffy flowers of stamens, a common feature of eucalypts and paperbarks.

**Flowers that aren't flowers** Rather than having flower petals to attract pollinators, some plants have coloured modified leaves, known as bracts. Poinsettias and leucadendrons are examples.

## Trunk or stems

**Water-holding** Many plants have water-holding stems that store water for drought protection, such as begonias and geraniums, or massively swollen trunks, such as bottle trees and baobabs.

## Root system

**Deep-rooted** Perennials and clumping grasses have deep root systems, which help them make the most of any soil moisture. They include mondo grass and strelitzias.

**Swollen and water-storing** Some perennials, such as agapanthus, clivias and orchids, have swollen, fleshy roots that hold water.

## Life cycle

Many drought-tolerant plants become 'summer dormant'. Others escape drought by growing quickly and seeding after cool-season rain, such as California poppies, or by lying dormant until winter rain, as many native orchids do.

Geraniums

Banksia

Jelly bean plant

Lavender

# D
## DRY CONDITIONS | DWARF PLANTS

## DWARF PLANTS

### Deceptive dwarfs
The term 'dwarf' can sometimes be a misnomer. Many so-called dwarf conifers, for example, are really slow-growing trees, and in time they will grow as big as the standard forms. Given that many conifers are forest giants, smaller versions can grow into alarmingly big trees.

To make sure that the dwarf plant you buy will stay that way, go to a reputable garden centre.

### An orchard on the patio
If space is tight for fruit trees, grow them in pots on the patio. A few varieties are naturally dwarfing and are ideally suited to large pots. But any apple or plum that has been grafted onto a dwarfing or semi-dwarfing rootstock can be grown in a pot.

Also useful are columnar apples, sold as 'Ballerina' apples. Or use the naturally dwarfing cherry, 'Compact Stella'. Dwarf peaches and nectarines such as 'Pixzee' and 'Nectarzee' are about 1.2 m tall. Select the 'Meyer' lemon for a potted citrus. All need large pots at least 45 cm in diameter.

## DRY CONDITIONS

### Coping with arid conditions
If you live in a dry area, work with your climate to create a garden that will survive on rainfall alone or with minimal additional watering. This can be achieved by using plants that grow naturally in arid regions and designing your garden to reduce water use. This form of gardening is called 'xeriscaping'.

### Grey water
Recycled bath and clothes washing water can be used on lawns and gardens. Bath water may have to be taken out by bucket; diversion valves are available from plumbing suppliers to direct water from the washing machine out to the garden. Grey-water diverters will capture excess water from bathroom and laundry taps, washing machines and showers and divert it to the garden.

Select a laundry powder or detergent that is low in phosphorus and boron. Alternatively, only use the final rinse water – and use it in different areas to avoid any build-up of salts in the soil.

### Beating water restrictions
Prepare for times when drought occurs and water restrictions come into force by installing a tank or tanks to collect as much water as you can from the roof of your house, garage or shed. To provide good pressure in the hose, you will need to install a small domestic water pump. Check with your local authority about any restrictions that may apply.

### How much water?
To prepare for dry conditions, it is better to water plants and soil thoroughly or not at all. If only the top couple of centimetres of soil is dampened, plants will develop roots in this shallow layer, where they are vulnerable to the drying effects of the sun.

Instead, moisten the soil to a depth of at least 30 cm. Roots will then grow downwards, deep into the layer of soil that is insulated from the sun and that will remain damp for longer.

### Mulch to retain moisture
A thick layer of mulch spread over all bare soil and around plants (including trees) will help retain soil moisture and also minimise changes in soil temperature. Cover your beds and borders with a rich organic mulch – at least 10 cm thick – after heavy rain or watering, when the soil is moist.

### Let the lawn look after itself
Cutting lawn too short makes it less drought-tolerant. In times of drought, either mow it with the mower blades set high or do not mow it at all. The more grass left on the lawn, the longer it will take to turn yellow. It will quickly turn green again after the first rains.

See also Drought-tolerant plants, Water tanks, Waterwise gardening, Xeriscaping

EARTHWORMS | EDIBLE FLOWERS

# EARTHWORMS

## Friends of the soil
Earthworms and a myriad other organisms live in the soil. They are mostly beneficial because they help to create good soil structure by eating and excreting organic matter. In doing so they dig holes and open the soil to rainfall and air. Worms are a sign of healthy soil and an active compost heap.

## Encourage worms
Earthworms cannot survive without moisture and food. If the soil is too dry or there is not enough for them to eat, they will head downwards and form a little ball surrounded by a mucus sack to keep them from drying out. When rain comes they will emerge and set about aerating the soil and eating dead plant material again. Mulching the soil surface is a way of providing earthworms with their food in the garden.

One of the quickest ways to build up earthworm numbers is to use a high-quality hay, such as lucerne or green oaten hay, as mulch when the weather warms up in spring. Keep the soil continually moist to encourage the growth and reproduction of earthworms.

See also Worm farms

# EDIBLE FLOWERS

## The edible garden
You can mingle edible flowers and culinary herbs with vegetables in the kitchen garden to create an eye-catching and edible display. They can also be grown in a tub, window box or hanging basket for a bright display. Heartsease, nasturtiums and calendula (*Calendula officinalis*) will all flower more vigorously if they are deadheaded frequently.

## Eat with caution
Eat only flowers that you can definitely identify as edible – and those you can be certain have not been contaminated with chemical sprays of any kind. Pesticide-free flowers, grown specifically for eating, are now available in some markets. Never eat flowers from the florist.

## Small doses
Some people may have an allergic reaction to certain edible flowers. Only eat a small quantity of a flower if you have never eaten it before. It is also said to be unwise to eat the flowers of calendula or thyme during pregnancy.

## Petal-strewn salads
Flowers give a special appeal to salads. Think about what colours and flavours will harmonise with the rest of the salad ingredients. You can use the peppery-tasting nasturtium and the petals of calendula to bring prominent splashes of scarlet, orange or yellow to green salads. You can also add a subtle flavour and visual impact to fruit salads by using petals from heartsease, roses or violets.

### grow Edible flowers
These plants from the herb garden and ornamental border have edible flowers:

#### Herbs
* Anise hyssop (*Agastache foeniculum*)
* Basil * Bergamot (*Monarda* spp.)
* Borage * Chervil * Chives * Dill
* Elder * Fennel * Garlic chives * Hyssop
* Lavender * Marjoram * Mint * Rosemary
* Sage * Salad burnet * Savory * Thyme

#### Ornamental plants
* Calendula (*Calendula officinalis*)
* Carnation * Chrysanthemum
* Clove pinks (*Dianthus* cvs) * Heartsease (*Viola tricolor*) * Hollyhock * Jasmine
* Nasturtium * Scented geraniums
* Violets (*V. odorata*)

**Heritage roses** such as Bourbon, Centifolia, Damask and Gallica are all edible. Modern roses are bitter and should not be used.

# E | EGGPLANTS | ENTRANCES

## EGGPLANTS

### A hot-weather plant
Eggplants are also known as aubergine or brinjal, and come from tropical Asia. They need warm temperatures, sunshine and very rich soil to grow.

When you are pricking out the delicate eggplant seedlings, make sure that you handle them by their seed leaves only, or you may bruise the stems, which will kill them. Seedlings should be planted deep, with the first set of leaves just at soil level.

### Avoiding problems
The developing fruit of eggplants is very attractive to fruit fly in those areas where this pest occurs. Commercially available lures and homemade traps will give some protection and avoid the risk of contaminating the fruit.

The soilborne fungus known as verticillium wilt may attack the base of the plants, causing them to wilt and die. Crop rotation is the best preventative. Do not grow eggplants in the same bed 2 years running. Better yet, allow 3 years between crops.

### No more than eight
Unless you are growing small-fruited varieties, restrict each plant to a maximum of eight fruit. Allow only one fruit on each branch, removing all further flowers, buds and sideshoots once the first eight fruit have set. This will encourage the eggplants to reach their maximum size.

### Taking out the bitterness
Pick eggplants as soon as the skins are firm and glossy, because they may taste bitter if they are left on the plants for too long.

## ENTRANCES

The front garden is your link with the street; the bridge between the outside world and your house. As such, it should be welcoming and an appropriate reflection of your home. It may also be a place to park bicycles and cars and store garbage bins.

Choose a layout that is easy to keep tidy, as this will save you time and effort. Paths should be kept clear and should be solidly constructed. In planting schemes for front gardens, you would generally have low-growing plants in the foreground and taller plants towards the rear, allowing easy access.

### Colour harmony
Choose plants to complement the exterior materials and colours of your house. Dark red and blue blooms can appear dull against new, raw brickwork, whereas pale flowers would stand out against it with heightened clarity. Keep darker flowers as a dramatic foil against a pale wall.

### The front door
Bring the doorway into focus. Keep a generous open space in front of the door if possible; this is where visitors wait. You could grow flowering climbers around the doorway, or arresting stands of hollyhocks or lilies on either side, or window boxes of blazing pink petunias or geraniums on nearby windowsills. For a formal approach, place a clipped shrub or tree, such as box or bay, on either side of the door.

### Planting plan: an enclosed front garden
The front gate opens straight onto a shady garden. A neatly trimmed standard or an elegant sculpture in the centre adds interest. The wide, ample path is flanked by temperate-climate perennials in shades of soft blues, purples and white, which will make the garden appear larger than it is.

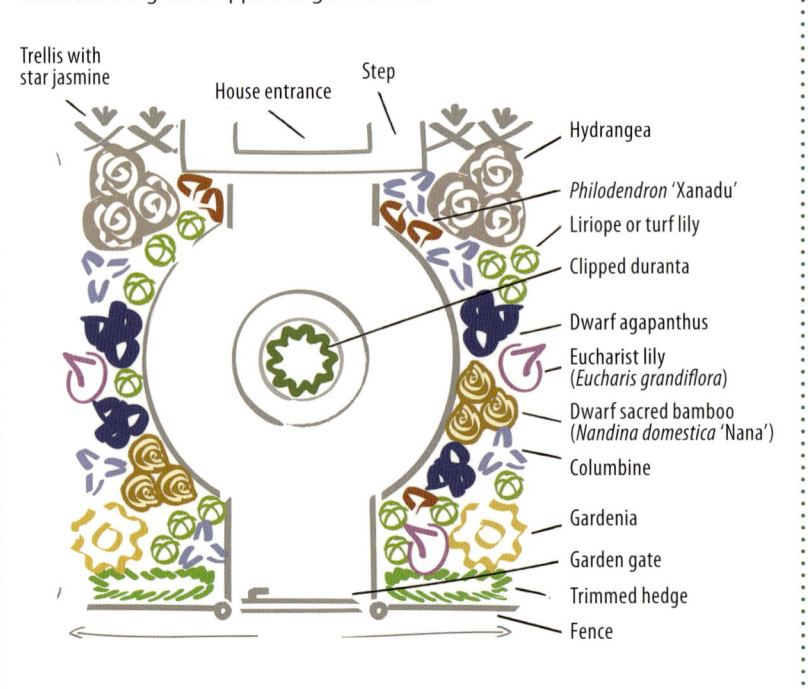

Trellis with star jasmine
House entrance
Step
Hydrangea
*Philodendron* 'Xanadu'
Liriope or turf lily
Clipped duranta
Dwarf agapanthus
Eucharist lily (*Eucharis grandiflora*)
Dwarf sacred bamboo (*Nandina domestica* 'Nana')
Columbine
Gardenia
Garden gate
Trimmed hedge
Fence

94

# ESPALIERS

## Space-saving fruit
Make the most of your wall space by using it for an espalier – a fruit tree with 'tiers' of three or more horizontal branches trained to grow flat against a support. This is very useful for growing apples, citrus fruit and pears in small gardens, where every centimetre of space needs to be used fully.

## Simple shapes
A horizontal design is the easiest espalier shape to begin training. Horizontal shapes can be grown against a wall or a paling fence. They can also be freestanding if the wires are stretched between two stout poles.

Fan shapes may look complex to achieve, but with support wires arranged in a diagonal pattern, they are quite straightforward. Peaches and nectarines work well trained as fans.

## Other suitable plants
Although traditionally used for fruit trees, many ornamental shrubs and trees can also be trained in these ways – to make the most of limited space or hide an ugly wall. Sasanqua camellias, redbuds (*Cercis* spp.), lemons, crab apples and laburnums all work well as espaliers.

## Setting up wires
Before beginning to train an espalier, stretch the wires into position, selecting a design that suits the plant and the space you have available. For a horizontal espalier, stretch three or more wires horizontally along a wall or make a freestanding fence.

The wires should start about 30–45 cm above ground and be spaced about 30 cm apart in rows. If using a plant already partially trained by a nursery, match the lower wires with the existing height of the espalier. If the wall gets hot, keep wires at least 30 cm from the masonry surface.

## Strong support
Check that the supporting posts are sturdy, pressure-treated with preservative and driven well into the ground. Use galvanised wires; fix them to the posts with vine eyes, and ensure they are pulled taut by using tensioning bolts.

## Planting angle
When planting a plant against a wall or fence for espalier training, place it about 25 cm out from the wall to allow for future growth. Lean the stem slightly inwards to make it easier to attach the branches to the espalier wires.

See also Fan-training

## train an Espalier

1. After planting, choose two strong, young, outward-facing side branches at the same height as the first wire. Tie in with soft ties. Cut back the main stem to a bud 5 cm above the top wire, which will hold the top tier of branches.

2. As growth starts next summer, choose two buds – one pointing left and one pointing right – below the cut made to the main stem at planting. As these shoots grow, tie them to the guide wire.

3. When the tree is well established and the tiers have reached the desired length, cut back the previous year's growth to 1 cm each May. In late summer, prune shoots from tiers to three leaves from the basal cluster, and shoots from laterals to one leaf. Remove all unwanted side branches as they appear.

**ESCALLONIAS**
see page 96

# E
ESCALLONIAS | EUCALYPTS AND GUMS

## ESCALLONIAS

### Withstanding wind and salt
These tough evergreen garden shrubs are tolerant of wind and salty air, making them invaluable as hedges or screens for seaside gardens. They also thrive in cool-climate gardens that are buffeted by chill winds.

If growing a row of escallonias as a hedge, use only one named variety to ensure uniformity. They grow readily from cuttings taken in spring or autumn.

### Attractive all year
Despite the toughness of these plants, they are very pretty when in flower. Masses of dainty pink, red or white flowers cover the plants over many months from spring to autumn. All escallonias can be pruned and shaped to maintain a rounded compact habit. Even when not in flower, they are attractive, with small, shiny and serrated leaves that closely hug the stem.

### Easygoing escallonias
Escallonias grow well in any soil, even poor soils, but perform best in full sun. In areas with hot and dry summers, provide extra water when plants are dry. They are rarely attacked by major pest or disease problems, but they do need protection from extremely cold, frosty weather.

## EUCALYPTS AND GUMS

### Forest giants or garden plants?
For many gardeners, gum trees fell from favour when the species they used in their garden grew far too big for the available space. The tallest eucalypts are forest giants that can reach 100 m in height. But with around 800 species, you can find eucalypts that are suited to small gardens.

These sun-loving Australian natives are quick-growing and easy to establish as shade trees. They adapt to a wide range of soils, and all are drought-tolerant once established. Some come from tropical and subtropical areas, while others are best in arid zones, so choose a variety that suits your conditions.

### Don't move
Eucalypts do not transplant successfully. If a tree has grown too large for its position, it will need to be removed completely.

However, there are certain species that can be coppiced. *Eucalyptus gunnii* produces attractive silver-blue foliage in its first 1–2 years. You can encourage the plant to continue producing this juvenile growth by stooling – pruning stems back to ground level – or by cutting side stems back to the main stem, 1.2–1.5 m from the ground, in early spring each year.

### Red-flowered clones
Among the most attractive of all the eucalypt flowers are red-flowering gums. Several species produce red flowers, but as they are mostly seed-grown, there can be a huge difference in flower colour, from pale pink to strong watermelon pink or red.

New propagation techniques are now making it possible to grow selected forms of red-flowering gum trees. Look out for these to be assured of the best red flowers. Note that *E. ficifolia* has been reclassified as *Corymbia ficifolia*.

### Eucalyptus leaf mulch
Fallen eucalyptus leaves or prunings make a good mulch for a native garden. Use it on garden beds and around shrubs and also as a surface for informal paths.

### Tips for growing 'Silver Princess'
One of the most popular eucalypts is *E. caesia* 'Silver Princess'. It is also a plant that has broken many hearts because it can be hard to grow. The beautiful small-growing weeping tree produces clusters of huge red flowers followed by huge seedpods. It thrives in a Mediterranean climate in extremely well-drained soil. In more humid areas, or where drainage is poor, grow plants in large planters or tubs filled with a very well drained sandy potting mix.

EUPHORBIAS | EVERGREENS

## EUPHORBIAS

The extremely diverse *Euphorbia* genus includes trees, shrubs, perennials, groundcovers, annuals and even succulents that resemble cacti. They vary greatly in their soil and growing conditions and their tolerance of frost. All have a milky sap, which deters pests but also irritates the skin and eyes and can cause allergic skin reactions. Be sure to wear gloves when handling these plants.

### Bracts, not flowers
What appear to be colourful flowers are actually flower bracts. These can be borne singly or in large showy heads. Crown of thorns (*E. milii*) and poinsettia (*E. pulcherrima*) have vivid red flower bracts – cultivars of the latter also come in shades of cream, salmon and pale pink. Some euphorbias make good cut flowers, such as the annual snow on the mountain (*E. marginata*).

### Colourful effects with spurges
Spurges are shrub euphorbias that bring long-lasting and often unusual colour to gardens. They grow into mounds of green, bronze or golden leaves ranging in height from 30–180 cm. These plants adapt to poor soil, tolerate drought and appear impervious to pests and diseases. Among the most dramatic are Mediterranean spurge (*E. characias* subsp. *wulfenii*), with blue-green foliage and large flower heads; cushion spurge (*E. polychroma*), with bright chartreuse flower bracts and red autumn foliage; and *E. dulcis* 'Chameleon', with purple foliage topped by chartreuse flower bracts.

## EVERGREENS

### Evergreen versus deciduous?
Trees and shrubs are broadly divided into two groups, based on whether the plant loses its leaves completely before new leaves are formed (deciduous) or the plant's leaves are gradually replaced so it is never bare (evergreen). In some evergreen species leaves may even colour before being discarded, just like deciduous plants. This is natural and not a sign that something is amiss.

Selecting evergreen trees or shrubs for your garden will mean year-round shade and protection. This is important if hedges or screens are needed for privacy or for shelter from prevailing winds. On the other hand, a deciduous tree or shrub will allow sunlight to shine through during the coldest, darkest months.

### A time for planting
Gardeners with a light soil can plant container-grown evergreens through the year – except during the heat of summer – provided the ground is not waterlogged and the climate is frost-free.

If soils are heavy or seasonally wet, or your area experiences extreme cold or frost, avoid planting new evergreens until spring. But if early planting is essential for some reason, cover the ground with thick plastic sheeting in advance to maintain an adequate moisture level and soil temperature. Remove the sheeting before beginning to plant your new shrubs.

### Rejuvenating cuts
Some ageing and straggly evergreen shrubs and trees will develop new and youthful growth if they are cut back severely in spring. Those plants that respond well to this are azaleas, camellias, mahonias and viburnums. When the pruning is complete, apply liquid fertiliser to the soil around the plant.

### choose Evergreens for their scent

**Perfumed flowers**
✱ Yesterday, today and tomorrow (*Brunfelsia* spp.) ✱ Mexican orange blossom (*Choisya ternata*) ✱ Winter daphne (*Daphne odora*) ✱ Gardenia ✱ *Mahonia japonica* ✱ Murraya (*Murraya paniculata*) ✱ Japanese mock orange (*Pittosporum tobira*) ✱ Sweet box (*Sarcococca* spp.)

**Aromatic leaves**
✱ Wormwood (*Artemisia* spp.) ✱ Lavender ✱ True myrtle (*Myrtus communis*) ✱ Waxflower (*Philotheca myoporoides* syn. *Eriostemon myoporoides*) ✱ Mint bush (*Prostanthera* spp.) ✱ Rosemary

Gardenia

97

**F** | FAN FLOWERS | FAN-TRAINING

## FAN FLOWERS

### Fans of mauve-blue
Fan flowers are also called by their botanic name, *Scaveola*. They are spreading perennials that flower in spring and summer, producing hundreds of small mauve-blue blossoms shaped like old-fashioned, opened fans. They are ideal for pots, window boxes and hanging baskets, or growing in rockeries or over banks and walls in the garden. Some are even suited to coastal conditions.

### Tough groundcovers
Fan flowers are self-branching, drought-tolerant and wind-resistant. They can endure hot blasts of scorching weather. With amazing speed and no fuss, each plant spreads into beautiful 50–100 cm wide mats or mounds. All require well-drained soil, and pruning keeps the plants compact and stimulates fresh growth.

Provide water during heatwaves and a bit of extra fertiliser during the second half of summer to keep them blooming at their peak.

## FAN-TRAINING

### A good start
Fan-training is an attractive way of growing apricots, nectarines or peaches. Take advantage of the expertise of nursery staff and buy a fan-trained tree that has its two main ribs (trained branches) in place so that you do not have to tackle the specialist job of creating the initial shape. Plant the tree against a sunny wall.

### Maintain the shape
An established fan-trained tree needs pruning each winter to help it produce regular crops and high-quality fruit. Cut out some overcrowded spurs completely and cut back others to reduce their size. For summer pruning, wait until new growth is woody, at least 23 cm long and has dark green leaves. Then cut back to one leaf beyond the cluster of leaves at the base of each new shoot.

### train a Fan

**1** In late winter, before new growth begins, cut the two main ribs (trained branches) back to 30–45 cm, making each cut just above a growth bud. Secure two canes to the nearest wires at an angle of about 40 degrees and tie the branches to the canes.

**2** In the summer after planting, tie in the shoots that grow from each end bud. Let two well-spaced shoots grow upwards from each branch and one shoot grow downwards. Tie these to canes secured to, and fanning out from, wires. Rub out all other buds.

FAST-GROWING PLANTS | FENNEL

## FAST-GROWING PLANTS

### Establish 'the look' quickly
If you want to create a new garden without having to wait too long for it to look good, plant some fast-growing perennials. Choose from Marguerite and African daisies, asters, daylilies, geraniums, larkspurs, yarrows (*Achillea* spp.) and any of the salvias. Also put in some of the prolific groundcover plants, such as bugle, deadnettles, fan flowers, gazanias, lamb's ears, Moroccan glory vine (*Convolvulus sabatius*) and snow-in-summer (*Cerastium tomentosum*), which will speedily stop the ground looking bare.

From the first year, sow fast-growing annuals such as cosmos, alyssum, nasturtiums and poppies to fill in gaps between young shrubs and perennials.

### Nurse plants
Fast-growing plants adapted to harsh conditions can protect, or 'nurse', more slow-growing or vulnerable plants while they get established. Wattles, grevilleas, native rosemaries (*Westringia* spp.) and paperbarks make good nurse plants. They will rocket away, giving shelter. But think of them as temporary – at some point it will be time to remove them.

*Asters*

#### For a fast hedge
No hedge or topiary is instant. However, if you want faster-growing plants, try:

* **Abelia** About 1.5–2 m * **Diosma** (*Coleonema pulchrum*) About 80 cm * **Pittosporum, kohuhu** (*Pittosporum tenuifolium* cvs) Up to 5 m * **Cotton lavender** (*Santolina chamaecyparissus*) About 25 cm * **Bush germander** (*Teucrium fruticans*) About 1 m
* **Native rosemary** (*Westringia fruticosa*) About 1 m

## FENNEL

### The vegetable
The plant *Foeniculum vulgare* var. *azoricum*, also known as florence fennel or finocchio, is fennel the vegetable, with the swollen bulb that can be eaten raw in salads or braised or baked. It does not transplant well, so sow the seed directly in the ground in early spring. Sow the seed very thinly, 5 mm deep, in rows 45 cm apart. When 5 cm tall, thin the seedlings to 20–25 cm apart.

Fragile though they appear, these plants are greedy feeders and will swell quite rapidly at the base. Water regularly and well, and apply liquid seaweed fertiliser or diluted manure tea every 4 weeks. If any flowering stems appear on the spring crop, cut them out. This will concentrate all the plant's growth into the swelling stem bases, the edible bulbs.

### Harvesting the bulbs
Begin harvesting once the bulbs are the size of your fist. Use a sharp knife to cut below the bulbs. They will keep for several days in the crisper section of the refrigerator. Do not harvest the aniseed-scented foliage during the growing period, as this can cause it to bolt (run to flower).

### The herb
The herb is the tall, perennial variety of fennel, *F. vulgare* subsp. *vulgare*. It is grown for the fine flavour of its feathery leaves, seeds and stems. Its flowers are also very attractive to a range of beneficial insects that will prey on garden pests.

The foliage and stems can be harvested for use as a flavouring at any time. Gather seed heads when pale brown, on a dry day in early autumn. Hang them for 1–2 weeks until really dry, then store in an airtight container.

**FENCES**
*see page 100*

# F FENCES

## FENCES

### Check local restrictions
Before erecting a fence around your property, check your local regulations. In some areas, front fences are not permitted. There are also restrictions in most areas on the maximum height for fences.

Both neighbours are responsible for boundary fences and jointly bear building costs. The style and quality should be determined by other fences in the area. Extra costs for more expensive fences are borne by the neighbour who wants the upgrade. If a dispute arises, seek legal advice or contact your local authority.

### Cope with a slope
To put up a fence on a slope, erect it section by section, stepping down the height of posts evenly. Place a spirit level on a length of timber laid between two posts, then use a wooden block at the lower post end to raise the timber to the height of the higher post. Dig out or build up soil at the base for even gaps under each section.

### Maintaining timber fences
A timber fence will last much longer with regular upkeep. Every 2–3 years, cut out and replace rotted sections. Close-boarded fences need a gravel or concrete base strip to protect the panels from dampness in the soil. Leave a space between the fence and the base strip so air can circulate.

## select a Fence material

**Timber** Hardwood and treated pine are popular for paling fences. Be sure to choose the correct durability level in hardwood or the correct hazard level in treated pine.

**Metal** Designed to be erected in panels, metal fences usually comprise three sheets locked into a top and bottom rail. They are prepainted and available in a range of colours. In coastal areas, this type of fence will be battered by high winds and the effects of salt corrosion, so sufficient post strength and protection are essential.

**Brick** The toughest fence, offering the most privacy and security, is brickwork – either a double or single skin. It can be rendered and painted to match or complement the home. But a brick wall more than 1 m high requires council approval and the cost of the materials and construction can be high.

**Brushwood** Brushwood fencing is best erected by a professional for a good-quality, long-lasting finish. Panels of brushwood, or even bamboo, are supported on metal posts, with strands of tough wire holding the panels together. Prefabricated panels are also available if you want to do the installation yourself.

**Powder-coated aluminium** Often called tubular fencing, this comes in many styles and colours. Its open design does not provide soundproofing or privacy but makes an excellent choice around swimming pools, offering good visibility as well as security. It is susceptible to coastal corrosion, however.

FERNS  **F**

*Silver tree fern (Cyathea dealbata)*

*Maidenhair fern (Adiantum aethiopicum)*

## FERNS

Ferns are among the oldest plants on Earth and, when grown in suitable sites, are tough, durable and vigorous. They are the perfect solution for filling low-light pockets in foundation plantings, bedding beneath dense shrubs, or ground shaded by buildings or a thick canopy of trees.

### Running or clumping

As a general rule, ferns prefer a shady spot out of direct sunlight and a moist, well-mulched soil. They can be classified in two groups based on their growth habit. The running ferns grow from creeping stolons that push outwards through the soil, producing new fronds as they creep. The clumping ferns produce new fronds in clusters that spring up close to the mother plant.

### Tree ferns

With their tall trunks and tufts of spreading fronds, tree ferns bring height and architectural interest to gardens. Underplant with other ferns or shade-loving flowering plants, such as tree begonias and impatiens. *Cyathea* species have tall slender trunks and rosettes of long fronds. They and the soft tree fern (*Dicksonia antarctica*) are widely grown.

### Divide and grow

If a fern grows too large for its place in the garden, it can be divided. In a cool climate this is best done in spring, whereas in warmer climates divide ferns when they are actively growing. To do this, lift the clump, cut it in half with a saw, then replant. If the clump is very large, push two forks, back-to-back, into the centre of the clump, then lever them apart to split it in two.

### Spring cleaning

Prune old growth in autumn or winter, except in cold climates, where it is best to let old fronds protect the plant base from winter frost and cold, then prune them once new shoots appear in spring. At the end of winter, spread 5 cm of well-rotted compost or leaf mould over the base of ferns. This will help the soil retain moisture so the ferns will only need to be watered during dry spells.

### A humid home

Indoor ferns need a humid atmosphere. Place pots on trays filled with damp gravel and spray the leaves with tepid water each time you water.

## get to know Ferns

**Maidenhair fern (*Adiantum aethiopicum*)** It will grow in all areas and naturalise in moist environments such as beside a pond.

**Bird's nest fern (*Asplenium australasicum*)** This epiphyte develops a large nest shape and can be grown on rocks, logs or in pots in shade. In tropical areas grow *A. nidus*.

**Hen and chicken fern (*Asplenium bulbiferum*)** A feature of this easy-to-grow fern is the way it produces new ferns (plantlets) on its fronds.

**Blechnum articulatum** It is grown for its striking red new growth. Grow in a fernery in cold areas.

**Fishbone water fern (*B. nudum*)** This tall-growing fern forms clumps in wet areas. *B. tabulare* is good for deep shade.

**Cyrtomium spp.** This widely grown group of ferns is well suited to a range of climates. The holly fern (*C. falcatum*) has distinctive holly-shaped pinnae.

**Hare's foot ferns (*Davallia* spp.)** These ferns spread by rhizomes. The new growth is furry like a hare's foot, hence its name.

**Brake ferns (*Pteris* spp.)** Most species are easy to grow outdoors with shelter, and form attractive clumps. Some cultivars have variegated fronds.

# F FERTILISERS

## FERTILISERS

### The right time
Only apply fertilisers to plants before and during their growing period. Never apply when plants are about to become dormant and their growth is slowing down – in late autumn and winter. Apply granular fertilisers when the ground is wet because moisture aids the release of the nutrients and the absorption process. Water thoroughly if there is no rainfall within 2 days of application.

### More or less
Reapply fertilisers, particularly those that are nitrogen-based, more frequently if your soil is light and free-draining. These soils, which are usually sandy, lose nutrients quicker than other types, particularly during rain.

The more clay your soil contains, or the more organic matter that you dig into it, the less fertiliser you will need to apply. This is because both trap the nutrients and release them over time.

### Storage
Keep fertilisers in a dry but airy garage or shed, stored in plastic bags, tubs or covered containers that are raised off the ground. Do not store paper bags of fertiliser on concrete or against walls. Make sure you always close the bags firmly after use.

### Green lawns
Spread lawn fertilisers evenly, according to the manufacturer's instructions, and water in unless rain is forecast. Aerating the lawn before applying fertiliser helps the nutrients to penetrate the soil, as well as improving drainage and preventing compaction.

### Tree time
To feed a tree, spread a general slow-release fertiliser in the area beneath the edge of the leaf canopy. Alternatively, make holes in the ground directly below the canopy edge and fill these with the fertiliser. Unless the weather is rainy, you will need to water the fertiliser in.

## choose a Fertiliser

**Complete or compound fertilisers** These are also known as general fertilisers and contain the three main plant foods – nitrogen, phosphorus, potassium – plus the trace elements that are essential for plant growth. Some are specially mixed to suit the needs of particular plants.

**Organic fertilisers** Derived from wholly natural sources, some organic fertilisers are quick-acting, while others release their nutrients over a period of time. They are generally used as dressings before sowing plants, or as top-dressings for crops.

**Inorganic fertilisers** Inorganic fertilisers are derived from chemical sources. They can consist of a single chemical that stimulates growth in part of a plant, or a compound of two or more chemicals. Some give an instant boost, while others are effective for longer periods.

**Manures** Consisting mainly of animal dung, these are rich in organic matter and improve the condition of the soil. All manures should be well rotted before use.

**Liquid feeds** Once diluted, these can be applied as foliar feeds, or watered in to the roots to provide a regular supply of plant foods and also help to correct nutrient deficiencies. They are particularly beneficial to container plants and newly planted specimens.

**Controlled-release fertilisers** These release nutrients over a specific period. Those formulated for fast-growing annuals provide nutrients for only 3–4 months; others, for more general garden use, can last longer, depending on the formulation.

See also Nutrients

FIGS | FLOWERING PLANTS

## FIGS

### The versatile edible fig
A rocky hillside in dry country is the natural home of the edible fig, although this ancient tree is surprisingly adaptable. It prefers dry summers and winter rainfall but some varieties do well in the subtropics, particularly away from humid coastal areas.

Water well from spring onwards until fruit begins to ripen, but too much water at this stage can cause fruit to split and increases the risk of fungal disease.

### Varieties
There are four types of fig, all coming from the same species, *Ficus carica*. Caprifig must be pollinated by a particular species of wasp; Smyrna is cross-pollinated by Caprifig; San Pedro is an intermediate type; and the most commonly grown type has female flowers only and does not need cross-pollination.

### Protect yourself
The sap from the fruit, stems and leaves contains a substance that may irritate the skin and eyes. Wear gloves when working on the tree, and do not allow the sap to come into contact with your eyes.

### Pick when ripe
When fully ripe and ready to pick, figs will be soft, fully coloured and the apical pore at their base may begin to split open. Once they have been harvested, figs do not ripen any further. Clip from the tree to avoid bruising.

### consider ornamental Fig trees
Popular species such as Hill's weeping fig (*Ficus microcarpa* var. *hillii*) and weeping or Benjamin's fig (*F. benjamina*) add a formal touch to the garden, patio or entranceway when planted in ornamental tubs and pots.

Australian rainforests produce several species of fig, including the Port Jackson fig (*F. rubiginosa*) and Moreton Bay fig (*F. macrophylla*). These massive trees make attractive features in parks but easily outgrow home gardens, causing damage to drains and walls.

## FLOWERING PLANTS

To achieve a pleasing, continuous display of flowers, plant a whole range of annuals, perennials and bulbs around a framework of shrubs, roses and small trees.

### To dig or not to dig
Once flowering annuals and perennials are established, do not dig the soil around them. If you cut through the surface roots, the plants will have to use up their energy renewing them. Instead, use a hoe to get rid of weeds, or apply an organic mulch.

### Promote and prolong flowering
If you burn logs in a fireplace, save the ashes and scatter them around flowering plants. Wood ash contains 5–10 per cent potash, which promotes flowering.

To extend the flowering period, remove a plant's flowers as soon as they fade. Unable to produce seed and thus ensure its survival, the plant will bloom again. Also apply a complete fertiliser and water frequently.

### Check plants daily
Make a daily inspection of plants in summer; cut off fading flowers, water where necessary and support weak stems with canes.

### Staying power
Some flowering annuals and perennials produce a succession of blooms for many months. Gaura (*Gaura lindheimeri*) will flower from late spring to autumn. In warmer areas marigolds (*Tagetes* spp.) and petunias will do the same, while pansies can bloom year-round in a cool climate.

# F FLOWERING TREES

*Yulan magnolia*

*Judas tree*

## FLOWERING TREES

It is difficult to imagine a garden without trees. They provide shade and structure. Trees with flowers create a spectacular show that makes them the centre of attention for a time.

### Small specimens

There are many flowering trees grown for their stunning blooms that are ideal for small gardens. Choose a single specimen that will have a low to moderate eventual height, such as magnolia or an ornamental cherry in a cool to mild district, or a bauhinia or crepe myrtle in a warmer area.

### Extra attraction

Blooms on tree are often followed by berries in late summer and autumn. In cool areas, mountain ash (*Sorbus aucuparia*) produces large bunches of globular orange-red berries in late summer. Other flowering trees with attractive berries include blueberry ash (*Elaeocarpus reticulatus*), crab apples (*Malus* spp.), riberries (*Syzygium luehmannii*) and other lillypillies (*Syzygium* spp. and *Acmena smithii*).

### Effective filling

Take advantage of the space in a large garden to plant several trees that flower at different times. In a cool climate choose from (in order of flowering) winter-flowering peaches, magnolias, ornamental cherries, flowering pears, crab apples, mountain ash, laburnums, robinias and catalpas for flowers from late winter to early summer.

In a warm to tropical climate go all out for colour. Bauhinias, crepe myrtles, frangipanis, jacarandas, poincianas (subtropics and tropics only, but check for weediness) and trumpet trees (*Tabebuia* spp.) will provide flowers from winter to late summer and beyond.

*Crab apple*

## choose a spring Flowering tree

If you have room for only one tree, choose one that offers especially beautiful blooms as a focus for your spring garden.

**Cape chestnut (*Calodendrum capense*)** Height 10 m, spread 4 m; slightly scented pink-mauve open flowers with purple-wine red markings.

**Judas tree (*Cercis siliquastrum*)** Height to 12 m, spread 10 m; a mass of small, pea-shaped pinkish purple flowers along bare stems.

**Pompom tree (*Dais cotinifolia*)** Height and spread 6–7 m; densely crowded sugar pink inflorescences; tough, frost-hardy and drought-resistant.

**Jacaranda (*Jacaranda mimosifolia*)** Height and spread 12–15 m; clusters of mauve, bell-shaped flowers.

**Yulan magnolia (*Magnolia denudata*)** Height 7–10 m, spread 5–6 m; hundreds of cream lily-shaped flowers touched with rosy carmine.

**Crab apple (*Malus* spp.)** Height and spread 3–8 m; pink, white or purplish flowers, depending on the variety; colourful fruits in autumn.

# FOLIAGE | FOUNTAINS

## FOLIAGE

### Don't forget leaves
Leaves last for much longer than blooms, so select plants that have attractive foliage as well as flowers. You can even compose plantings where flowers are not used at all, and where all the interest comes from leaf shape, size, texture and colour.

The leaves of some plants are variegated, striped, speckled or marbled, and will light up a shady corner. Others range from purple, silver and blue to lime green, and in tropical plants such as crotons (*Codiaeum variegatum*), yellow, orange and red.

### Shape and texture
Plants with enormous leaves, such as the ornamental rhubarb (*Rheum palmatum*), spread to make compelling architectural shapes. Tall foliage plants, such as cordylines, dracaenas, New Zealand flaxes and tree ferns, can be used like a living fountain.

To create a soft, billowing effect, use plants with feathery foliage, such as wormwoods (*Artemisia* spp.) and bronze fennel. Choose columbines, love-in-a-mist and many of the ferns for their masses of delicate leaflets.

### Soften and give movement
Carefully selected ornamental grasses and bamboos can be used to soften displays and give a sense of movement and height. The blue grasses *Festuca glauca* and *F. valesiaca* 'Silbersee' are particularly useful, with their dense spiky tufts and drought tolerance. The colours and flower heads of sterile fountain grasses (*Pennisetum* cvs), Chinese silver grass (*Miscanthus sinensis*), switch grass (*Panicum virgatum*) and lomandras will add interest for many months.

*Crotons*

## FOUNTAINS

### Match the style
Look for a fountain that will complement the style of your garden. If it is a formal garden, a traditional fountain could work best. In a natural or wildflower garden, a rock waterfall might be better than a fountain.

### Choose gentle droplets and low jets
Moving water helps to oxygenate a pond but falling droplets can harm delicate ornamental plants, and floating plants can be sucked underwater by the force of the fountain's pump. So install the pump well away from vulnerable plants and protect floating plants by opting for a fountain with a bell jet, which produces a gentle cascade of water.

A jet that is too powerful can cause water to flow over the edges of the pond, which will turn the surrounding garden into a bog. To prevent this, regulate the fountain so that the jet is no higher than half the width of the pond.

### make a child-friendly pebble Fountain

This small water feature is both safe and fun for children to play with because the reservoir is securely covered. You can use any large, watertight container for the reservoir – a plastic bin, metal drum or extra-large bucket to hold the pump and enough water for the fountain to work.

1. Dig a hole to fit the reservoir so the top is about 2.5 cm below soil level. Position the reservoir and fill in any gaps around the edges to support its sides.

2. Slope the surrounding area down towards the reservoir. Line this area with a flexible pond liner that will lead the bubbling water back into the reservoir.

3. Position a small pump in the bottom of the reservoir so the head of the jet will be above the water but hidden by the pebbles.

4. Make sure that you use a transformer at source to supply low-voltage electricity to the pump. Bury the cable safely, right across the garden.

5. Fill the reservoir with water. Use an upturned plastic laundry basket to cover the pump and be a platform for the pebbles.

6. Wedge large pebbles in between the laundry basket and the reservoir rim. Add a complete surface of pebbles to thoroughly disguise the fountain jet and basket, as well as cover the catchment area.

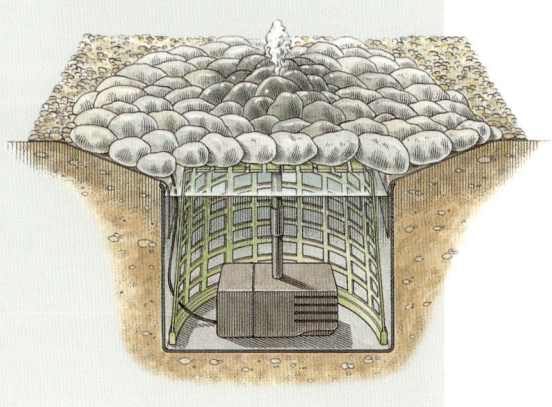

105

# F

FOXGLOVES | FREESIAS

## FOXGLOVES

Foxgloves, with masses of bell-shaped flowers aligned on 1–1.5 m spires, are perfect for the edge of a woodland or a shaded entrance. Note that all parts of the foxglove, which is the source of digitalis, a prescription heart medication, are poisonous if eaten. Avoid siting them where children or pets may be tempted.

### Foxgloves for ever

The common garden foxglove (*Digitalis purpurea*) is technically considered a biennial: it grows from seed one year, then the flower spike appears, blooms, sets seed and dies the next. Varieties abound in a range of colours and sizes, and many are now grown as bedding annuals. The longer lived perennial yellow foxglove (*D. grandiflora*) has glossy foliage and buttery flowers with reddish speckles on the throat.

### Start from seedlings

Set out purchased seedlings, apply mulch to protect them from extreme dryness, and wait for them to bloom the following year. Common foxgloves will self-seed year after year. Learn to recognise the seedlings and transplant them while they're small because these self-sown seedlings will be most likely to settle well in the garden.

## FRANGIPANIS

### Taste of the tropics

The frangipani (*Plumeria rubra*) is the no-fuss tree to grow for the scent and colour of the tropics – even in a cool or temperate garden. The ideal situation where winters are cold is against a west- or north-facing masonry wall or in a sunny courtyard. Frangipanis will grow to 8 m in height and 5 m in spread, but are around 3 m high and wide in cool areas.

### Colour choice

The most commonly seen form has fragrant, white, propeller-shaped flowers with a clear yellow throat. There are many other flower colours, which mostly fall into the sunset range of deep red, orange, apricot, pink and yellow. Some flowers are striped.

Most of the frangipanis grown in Australia and New Zealand are sold as unnamed varieties, selected by colour. In Hawaii, where they are widely grown, there are many named varieties.

### Frangipanis from cuttings

Frangipanis can be bought as potted plants. Alternatively, take cuttings around 30–60 cm long; they are easiest to strike in winter when the tree is bare. Leave them to dry for a day or two until the cut end stops exuding milky sap. Place each cutting in a 20 cm pot filled with moist propagating sand. When roots have formed and new shoots appear, plant out in the garden.

### Native frangipani

Native frangipani (*Hymensporum flavum*) is a quick-growing tree from the subtropical east coast of Australia and New Guinea. It prefers moist, rich soil but adapts remarkably well to a wide range of conditions. It needs some frost protection, and may shed leaves during extremes of heat or cold if grown outside the subtropics. In spring, it is smothered in fragrant cream flowers that age to yellow.

## FREESIAS

Freesias are the classic 'plant and forget' flower. They grow and naturalise readily, and flower with an exquisite perfume that says spring has sprung.

### Best fragrance and colour

The freesia with the best scent is the old-fashioned *Freesia refracta* var. *alba*, which has intensely perfumed white flowers. Hybrid freesias are available in pink, apricot, blue, lavender, purple, rosy red, carmine, brown, orange, yellow and white, often with a contrasting throat colour.

### Growing from corms

The plants are easy to grow from corms, which are widely available at nurseries and from mail-order specialist growers. Plant the corms in late summer or early autumn. Freesias will tolerate any soil but do better in soil that has been improved with compost. They can be grown in sun or shade. In hot, dry climates, a little shade is recommended.

Freesias can be left undisturbed for years and will self-seed or spread by corms. Split clumps every 3 years, in summer.

FROST | FRUIT DROP

## FROST

### Plant protection

Frost protection is most likely to be needed when species are grown in areas that are much cooler than their natural environment – for example, tropical and subtropical plants grown in inland areas. Young plants with soft, unripened wood are particularly susceptible.

To protect vulnerable shrubs and young trees, insert four stakes in the ground around the plant, then wrap a piece of hessian, heavy-duty plastic or sacking around the stakes. Natural materials are best as they let the plant breathe. Fill the space inside, around the plant, with straw or leaves.

For tender perennials, apply a protective blanket of straw and weight it down with stones, pipes or wire netting.

### Other anti-freeze ideas

You could water heavily before nightfall, or cover susceptible plants with newspaper, plastic sheeting or even bed sheets, then remove the cover in the morning when the frost has thawed. Bury pots of susceptible plants in soil and cover overnight.

### understand how Frost and cold help your garden

**Spring bulbs**  The cold stimulates bulbs into growth. They do not need frost protection until their first shoots begin to show.

**Fruit tree flowers**  Frost can protect flowers from rapid changes in temperature. Professional growers sometimes spray water onto blossoms as soon as the temperature approaches zero. Ice forms around the flowers and protects them. Make sure you do this continually until the frost is over.

**Easy digging**  Cycles of freezing and thawing in winter help to break down lumps in freshly dug heavy soils. This improves the soil texture and makes the soil easier to work in the spring.

**Pest control**  Cold kills off many harmful insects and disease spores, which means fewer problems when the weather warms up again.

## FRUIT DROP

### Seasonal drop

Many trees may lose flowers and fruit during the season. This is natural and may be due to a variety of causes. The tree may be getting rid of poorly pollinated or badly positioned fruit or a surplus of fruit. Well-fed trees support more fruit, so feed your trees in spring and water regularly.

### Citrus drop

Citrus trees often shed surplus fruit at the end of flowering, when the fruit is pea-sized, and again when the fruit is about 20 mm in diameter. Careful attention to watering, fertilising and pest and disease control helps avoid this.

### Pesticide damage

Dimethoate is commonly used in Australia to control fruit fly, codling moth and other pests. However, this pesticide can damage early varieties of stone fruit and may cause leaf and fruit drop. Look for environmentally friendly oil sprays instead.

### Trapping codling moths

Falling apples and pears may be an early warning sign of codling moth. The caterpillars burrow into fruit, ruining the crop. They move down the tree in summer searching for a suitable site to pupate and can be trapped by wrapping a band of sacking or corrugated cardboard around the trunk. Remove and destroy the bands in winter. Collect and destroy fallen and infested fruit and use chemical sprays as necessary.

107

# FRUIT FLY | FRUIT TREES AND BUSHES

## FRUIT FLY

### Legal requirement
In Australia, both commercial growers and home gardeners are required by law to control fruit fly in order to protect the commercial fruit industry.

### Three types of fly
The Queensland fruit fly is the most problematic pest. The wasp-like fly grows to approximately 7 mm and is reddish brown with yellow markings. The smaller Mediterranean fruit fly is yellow with brown bands on its wings. It is the prevalent species in Western Australia. Papaya fruit fly is a serious threat to fruit and vegetables in North Queensland. Gardeners in that area should seek out information on how to identify and control this pest.

### Fruit and vegetables affected
Almost all summer-fruiting trees as well as many vegetables, especially tomatoes, capsicums and eggplants, can be affected. The fly lays eggs in the developing fruit, which is particularly susceptible a few weeks before harvesting. The eggs hatch and the maggots burrow through the fruit, making it inedible.

### Preventative measures
Good garden hygiene will help prevent fruit fly problems. Pick up any fruit on the ground daily and any left on the tree after harvest. Destroy the collected or infested fruit, or seal it in an airtight plastic bag and leave in the sun for 5 days. Or place it in a bucket, cover with boiling water and leave submerged for a few days until all the larvae have emerged. Don't bury the fruit or put it on the compost heap, as this will allow flies to complete their life cycle and multiply.

### Organic control
Some gardeners use a repellent mix of kerosene, creosote and mothballs placed in cans hung in trees or on vegetable stakes. A deep mulch around fruit trees and in the vegetable garden makes it more difficult for flies to emerge from the ground underneath.

### Chemical control
Dimethoate or fenthion can be used. Spraying must commence 4–7 weeks before harvest and be reapplied at weekly or fortnightly intervals, depending on the type of fruit tree and the product. It is important to begin spraying when the fruit is just starting to develop. If you start the process too late, flies may have already infested the fruit.

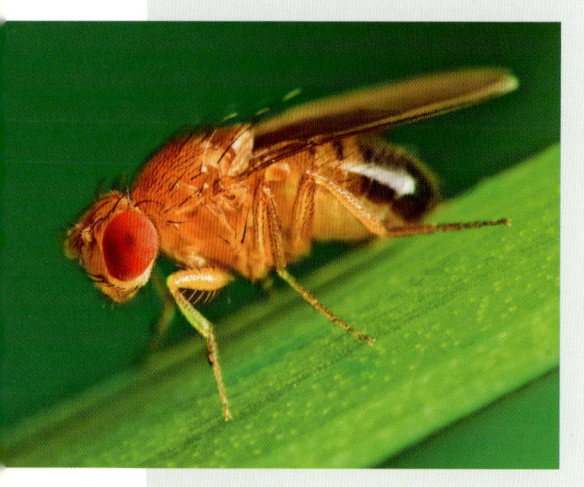

### How to catch fruit flies
Traps will not only kill off some fruit flies but also indicate their presence. Fruit flies like anything that is wet, sweet and yeasty. Place some beer or a mixture of sugar, Vegemite and water in some lidded plastic soft drink bottles. Punch a few holes in the bottom and hang them upside down. Inspect the traps daily and spray when fruit fly numbers become critical.

**Peaches**

## FRUIT TREES AND BUSHES

### Coping with damp soils
Fruit trees and bushes need a well-drained soil if they are to thrive. A heavy soil can become waterlogged, causing roots to die and shoots to wilt. Improve the drainage. Or try raising the roots above the waterlogged area by creating a small mound of soil, then plant the tree so that the upper part of the roots are about 10–20 cm above ground level.

### Potted fruit
There are fruit trees for even the smallest garden. Apples, apricots, peaches, avocados, yellow cherry guavas, nectarines and quinces can all be bought grafted onto a semi-dwarfing rootstock, making them suitable for growing in containers. Most citrus trees also make useful and decorative container plants. Strawberries

## FRUIT TREES AND BUSHES

**Apples**

**Pears**

and blueberries do very well in pots. Use a terracotta pot rather than a plastic one as terracotta is sturdier, more pleasing to the eye and also gives a better degree of protection from frost. Mulch the soil surface and be careful not to let the soil dry out in hot areas.

### Fruit trees need feeding
Give fruit trees a general fertiliser at the end of winter, at the rate of 70–140 g per m² of ground beneath the spread of the tree. If the soil is cultivated, spread the fertiliser evenly, leaving it for the rain to wash down into the soil. If not, use a bulb planter to make a circle of holes in the ground 30 cm apart to match the outer extent of the branches above. Fill the holes with fertiliser mixed with old potting mix or good soil.

Fruit trees will also benefit from a mulch of compost or well-rotted manure or mushroom compost in October or November.

### Protect berries from hungry birds
Birds have voracious appetites for soft fruit of all kinds, which makes protecting crops essential. This is easiest for bush fruit, such as raspberries or blueberries, and for low-growing strawberries. Make a cane framework around the bed or bush, drape netting over the top and pull taut. For strawberries, push sturdy hoops into the ground and stretch the netting over. Peg it down firmly.

### The challenge with fruit trees
Trees such as cherries and plums are much more difficult to protect, but you can throw netting over a small tree for short periods. Old CDs, strands of cassette tape or pieces of scrunched-up foil hung from branches will work for a while. For a large area, think about constructing a fruit cage high enough to walk inside.

See also Birds

### Take the strain
Fruit trees may produce more fruit than they can support. This can lead to small fruit, or it can stunt the tree's growth or cause branches to break. Wait until the summer drop period – the time when the tree rids itself of badly pollinated, diseased or surplus fruit. If the crop is still overly heavy, cut off any damaged or stunted fruit. Leave one or two of the best fruit to ripen on each fruiting spur.

The fruit on a tree mature at different rates. So picking should be carried out on several occasions. By the end of the harvest, all fruit should be cleared from branches and underneath the tree to minimise pests and diseases.

# FRUIT TREES AND BUSHES | FUCHSIAS

## FRUIT TREES AND BUSHES continued

### prune Fruit trees and bushes

#### Fruit bushes
Well-pruned fruit bushes will stay healthy and produce maximum yields. Prune soft fruit according to their time of fruiting and the type of wood on which the fruit grow.

**Raspberries** For summer-fruiting types, remove dead canes after fruiting. For autumn-fruiting varieties, cut back to ground level in autumn or early spring.

**Currants** Blackcurrants fruit on new wood, so prune the bushes as you harvest them, leaving eight to ten branches less than 3 years old to grow and fruit next year. Red and white currants fruit on old wood. Prune them in winter, shortening tall new growth by half. Cut side branches (laterals) back to one bud.

#### Fruit trees
**Winter pruning** Prune to create a strong framework. Remove crossing branches, those blocking light or air, and any dead wood. To promote new growth, prune back the main growing shoots (leaders) to just above a healthy growth bud, slanting the cut upwards. Prune back sideshoots (laterals) to form a fruiting spur or leave them to grow into new branches. Growth buds are easily distinguished from fruit buds because they lie flat to the stem; fruit buds are plumper and stand more upright by comparison.

**Summer pruning** You can prune apple trees in summer to promote fruiting. Prune new sideshoots to about six or seven buds, cutting just above a plump fruit bud.

**Training** Training fruit trees against walls and fences saves space and is ideal for warmth-loving types, such as peaches and apricots. Hybrid blackberries, raspberries and other bushes that grow untidily are best trained onto wires spaced 30 cm apart, cutting out any dead wood each autumn after fruiting.

*See also* Espaliers, Fan-training

## FUCHSIAS

### Weather warning
Fuchsias need to be protected from frost and cold. In very cold areas grow them in a glasshouse or shadehouse. In milder areas plant them in a frost-free part of the garden (for example, near a masonry wall) or move pots to a sheltered patio.

Fuchsias are also extremely sensitive to hot conditions and will suffer badly during summer heatwaves. Plants in garden beds need to be kept cool and well watered. Mist lightly with the hose and keep the root area cool with mulch. Hanging baskets should be taken down on hot or windy days and 'rested' in a cool, moist place.

### Light pruning for less stress
To avoid stressing fuchsias during the worst of the summer heat and humidity, don't overdo the pruning. Lightly cut back, removing any diseased foliage. Plants will reshoot in autumn for a flush of flowers.

### Care after winter
The right time for their main hard pruning is in late winter in frost-free areas or early spring in colder zones. This encourages strong new growth from the base of the plant and many flowers through spring. Be sure to feed well after pruning. The *Fuchsia magellanica* hybrid cultivars are frost-tolerant and need no pruning.

FUCHSIAS | FUNGICIDES

### Pick up flowers and leaves
In very humid climates fallen leaves or flowers encourage fungal problems such as rust to develop. Regularly pick up spent flowers and leaves from the plant or the ground nearby. To avoid diseases, remove and dispose of any rust-infected leaves immediately.

### choose Fuchsias for a warm, humid climate
Several fuchsias have proven themselves as long-lived garden plants for a shady spot, even in a warm, humid climate:

*Fuchsia* '**Annabel**' Large white flowers; grow as a shrub or in a hanging basket.
*F.* '**Derby Imp**' Long single flowers in crimson and violet-blue.
*F.* '**Display**' Single pink flowers; grow as a standard or shrub.
*F.* '**La Campanella**' Small semi-double white and purple flowers; grow as a shrub or small standard, or in a basket.
*F.* '**Lord Byron**' Small red and purple flowers.
*F. magellanica* **and hybrid cvs** Tall, well-established shrubs; can be grown as dense hedges in cooler areas.
*F. triphylla* **cvs** 'Coralle' (coral red flowers), 'Gartenmeister Bonstedt' (scarlet flowers) and 'Thalia' (orange-red flowers); reliable, long-flowering shrubs.

## FUNGICIDES

Fungicides are used to treat diseases, such as rust or mildew, on flowers, leaves, fruit and even roots. Unless combined with an insecticide, these chemicals will not control insect pests.

### Take quick action
Fungi reproduce themselves by airborne spores, minute dust-like bodies composed of a single cell. Most fungicides do not actually kill fungi. Instead, they prevent the spores from spreading. At the first signs of a fungal disease, prompt spraying of the whole plant and any other plants of the same type that are planted nearby should give adequate protection from infection.

Apply preventative spray early in the season to plants such as roses that are susceptible to attack. A protective coating of fungicide on the leaves will ensure that any fungus spores that land do not infect the plants.

### Use fungicides sparingly
An overdose of fungicide can be fatal to plants, so always follow the manufacturer's instructions to the letter. When using an aerosol or a sprayer, hold it at arm's length and spray from the bottom of the stem upwards, making sure that you coat the undersides of the leaves, where most diseases occur.

### Sensitive plants
Some plants can be sensitive to certain chemicals that are used in fungicides. The leaves may drop or develop various spots and scorch marks. This can be the result of incorrect dosage, so be sure to follow the manufacturer's instructions exactly. Also, always check the product label for any warnings about plants known to be susceptible to fungicides.

Do not spray in bright sunlight, in very hot weather or when plants are dry at the roots. If in doubt, test a small area of the plant first. When treating a group of plants, first try the chemical on just one.

### Practical control tips
Your plants will be far less susceptible to fungal diseases if you follow these tips:

✱ Choose plant varieties that have some in-built resistance.

✱ Give plants the amount of light, space and food that they require.

✱ Always rotate your crops in the vegetable garden.

✱ Be scrupulous about garden hygiene, picking up and disposing of diseased leaves, weeds or fruit.

## GALL MIDGES

### Plants affected
Acacias, cypress pines, daisy bushes (*Olearia* spp.), hebes, eucalypts and other native plants.

### Symptoms
Galls, thorn-like lumps or pimples deform leaves, stems or flowers.

### Treatment
* It is difficult to spray the larvae of the tiny flies which create and are protected within the galls, so prune off and destroy affected plant parts.

---

### make a Garden drawer seat

Rescue a battered old chest of drawers that have deep bottom drawers to transform these into seats with storage.

**1** Cut a piece of 19 mm thick radiata pine to fit on top of the drawer space and form a lid. Attach brass hinges to the lid and drawer so you can use the space inside for storage.

**2** Paint the piece of wood and drawer, inside and out, with gloss paint. Allow to dry, then place a thick cushion on top.

---

## GARDEN FURNITURE

### A site for a seat
Think carefully when siting a garden seat. Consider the top of a flight of steps, the end of a path or in front of a warm wall. The seat could be in sun or shade and may be a focal point, or tucked away in a secluded corner. For greater effect, place the seat on a raised half-circle of granite cobbles mixed with gravel, which will dry out quickly after rain. Plant with aromatic thyme and alyssum. In shade, plant lady's mantle and creeping campanulas.

If you want a garden seat on the lawn, stand it on flat stones or blocks of wood to keep it level and to prevent the legs from sinking into the ground. Lay stones in front of the seat to avoid an ugly worn patch in the lawn.

### Room with a view
If you have space, you could erect a gazebo and surround it with climbing scented plants. It will give shelter from the rain and shade from the sun, while offering views of the entire garden. Install chairs and a table inside, if you like. Gazebos can be bought ready-made or in kit form.

### Choosing wood
A wooden bench seat makes a good focal point and, if properly sited, can draw attention to your garden's best view. Teak or other imported hardwoods, from managed plantations, are most expensive, but the seat will last a lifetime and become increasingly attractive as it weathers. It can be left outdoors throughout the year, requiring only a quick scrub at the end of each winter.

### Rustic comfort
A garden seat need not be overly expensive. A simple heavy flitch of timber fixed to a couple of well-embedded logs is effective, especially when it has a well-clipped hedge as a backdrop.

In a less formal garden, a seat made from timber, weathered bricks or old railway sleepers is more fitting than one made from metal. You could construct a brick seat as you would a low raised bed: infill it with good garden soil, firm in well, then cover with a layer of fine lawn turf, creeping thyme or lawn chamomile.

GARDEN HYGIENE | GARDENIAS

# GARDEN HYGIENE

## A tidy garden

While there are some areas of your garden that can safely be left untended to encourage wildlife, never leave piles of rubble and accumulations of dead leaves and prunings lying around. They will soon harbour unwanted spiders or slugs and snails.

The regular removal of dead, diseased or pest-infested leaves will help to prevent diseases from taking hold. It also makes plants look more attractive.

## Cleaning stakes, pots and garden tools

After clearing crops such as peas and runner beans, always clean the stakes. Brush off the soil, remove plant debris and dislodge any insects. Overnight, soak the ends that were in the soil in a bucket of household detergent or horticultural disinfectant. Rinse and allow to dry, then store them in a dry place.

In the warmth of a greenhouse, young plants are particularly vulnerable to attack by diseases. Clean, disinfected pots are vital for raising seeds, young plants and cuttings. Also use a solution of 1 part household bleach to 9 parts water to sterilise garden tools. This prevents diseases being spread from plant to plant by contaminated tools.

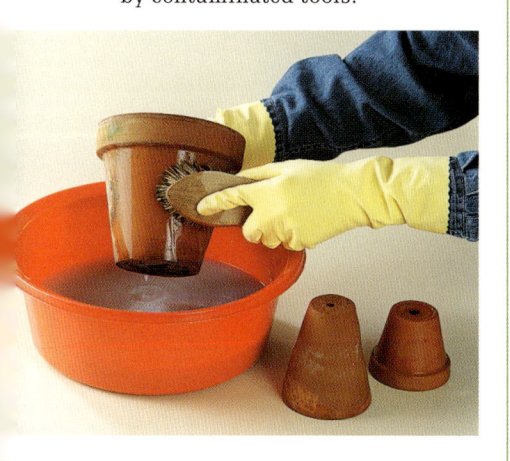

# GARDEN ORNAMENTS

## In harmony with your plants

Complement the style of your garden by choosing appropriate ornaments. Terracotta pots on patios and terraces will enhance a Mediterranean garden, classical statues and fountains are perfect in a formal setting, while a statue of an oriental divinity and a bamboo waterspout will evoke a Japanese garden.

## Features to surprise

Some elements of surprise are welcome in any garden. A bird table or birdbath at a turning in a path can be eye-catching. For a touch of humour, tuck a tall bird sculpture away behind bamboo, or let bronze frogs and snakes lurk among low groundcovers.

A stone nymph looks especially charming when glimpsed through sprays of roses, wisteria or ivy.

An evergreen backdrop for a statue or a fountain will make it stand out beautifully. Clipped lillypillies, ivies, yew or box are especially effective.

## Dignified stone

A stone statue, a sundial, or an urn with ivy-leaved geraniums can lend an air of quiet dignity to your garden, and make an interesting focal point at the end of a path. If you place stone or concrete statues or ornaments in a cool and shady place, algae will soon spread over them and soften their starkness. You can apply a coat of liquid yoghurt to speed up the process.

# GARDENIAS

## Gardenias for summer perfume

Gardenias, particularly cultivars of *Gardenia augusta*, have strongly perfumed flowers that appear mainly through summer. The plants flower best in a tropical to subtropical climate in a position that is sheltered from the full heat of the sun. Place a gardenia under a window or near the front door to fully enjoy its wonderful perfume.

A low-growing form of gardenia called *G. augusta* 'Radicans' is suited to edging paths or spilling over the ground or a wall. The evergreen, summer-flowering star gardenia (*G. thunbergia*) will tolerate cool conditions.

## Care when picking

Gardenia flowers bruise easily and the petals will turn brown. Every care should be taken when picking flowers not to touch the petals, nor to handle the flowers. Instead, gently handle them by their stems.

## Yellow leaves

Gardenias can develop yellow leaves, particularly in spring. This may be due to a magnesium deficiency, which can be treated with a dose of Epsom salts (which is magnesium sulfate) dissolved in water. However, the yellow leaves are more often a sign that the plant needs a general feed. Fertilise in spring or when you notice the yellow leaves with an all-purpose fertiliser for flowering plants.

# GARLIC | GAZANIAS

## GARLIC

### Growing from bulbs
Named varieties of garlic are not always easy to buy. The best place to acquire planting stock is the greengrocer, where an array of garlic from various sources can be found throughout the year. There are Italian, French, Chinese and Mexican varieties available. Be sure to select plump, fresh bulbs.

Garlic requires a cold spell to grow well, so in late autumn divide bulbs into cloves. In a sunny spot, plant each clove about 15 cm apart in drills 7.5 cm deep. Cover the nose with a thin layer of soil. Garlic is hardy and needs little attention other than watering during dry spells. If the soil is very heavy, wait until early spring to plant the cloves.

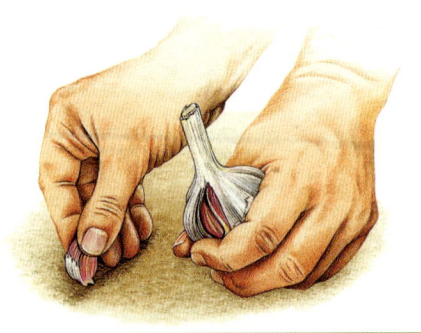

### Lift in late summer
Lift garlic after the foliage dies down in late summer. Ease the plants out of the ground with a fork to avoid damaging the bulbs. Dry the bulbs thoroughly in the sun, then store in a cool, dry place – never in the kitchen.

### Good for you and the garden
As well as being an invaluable culinary plant that won't be out of place in an ornamental garden, garlic has other fine properties. Some gardeners claim that garlic grown between other plants will help ward off pests and diseases. Roses, particularly, seem to benefit from the proximity of garlic, which is said to give them a sweeter scent and a greater resistance to disease and may also help to deter aphids and other pests. It is also thought to benefit raspberry bushes and brassicas, but to stunt beans.

### Continuing the crop
When harvesting, leave two or three bulbs in the ground where they will overwinter. Then, when the green shoots start to show above the soil, dig up the bulbs, split them into cloves and replant them in a different section of the garden. Because these cloves already have roots, they will grow quickly and produce a crop that should be particularly fine.

## GAZANIAS

These bright, bold perennials form a dense, almost mat-like groundcover. They thrive in harsh conditions and in most areas with mild winters, including inland gardens. They seem to prefer dry sandy soil and do particularly well in a seaside garden.

### Flowers in the sun
The flowers have a habit of closing up when the sun sets and may fail to open on cloudy days. Flowering will be poor in shade, so save gazanias for sun-drenched spots. Make the most of the bold shades in yellow, orange, deep red and rusty brown to add seasonal colour to foliage and succulent gardens. Plant them with hen and chicks (*Sempervivum* cvs) in the narrow beds under house eaves, and mulch the ground with gravel or pebbles. Gazanias also do well in containers and window boxes.

### Low-care gazanias
Gazanias are not fussy about soil, provided it is well drained. Other than occasional watering and applying mulch once a year in spring, established plants need little care. Some species self-seed and have become weeds. To prevent this, remove spent flowers or grow non-seeding cultivars, such as 'Montezuma', 'Sunset Jane', 'Sahara' and 'Sun About'.

GERANIUMS AND PELARGONIUMS | GLADIOLI

# GERANIUMS AND PELARGONIUMS

### Get the name right
The plants that are classified botanically as *Pelargonium* are commonly called geraniums or sometimes pelargoniums. They are divided into three groups: Ivy-leaved Hybrids (commonly called ivy-leaved geraniums), Regal Hybrids (commonly referred to as regal geraniums or simply pelargoniums) and Zonal Hybrids (usually called zonal geraniums).

The plants that are classified as *Geranium* are called cranesbill or species geraniums. They are more delicate-looking plants with less spectacular flowers.

When buying geraniums, look for sturdy specimens with one or two flower buds already open, so you can see what colour they are and select the shade of your choice.

### Cascading geraniums
The best geraniums for hanging baskets and window boxes are the F1 hybrid cascading varieties. Both will produce flowers through the summer. Ivy-leaved geraniums make a quick, colourful cover-up for a wire fence in full sun in all but the very coldest areas.

### Food and drink
Geraniums need little attention other than a general tidy up to remove woody stems and spent flowers. Most of these hardy, easy-to-grow plants originate from South Africa, so do not overwater. To encourage flower production, add a little tomato fertiliser to the water, following the manufacturer's instructions.

In frost-prone areas plant them where they will be protected or grow them as annuals.

### Taking cuttings
Geranium cuttings can be taken at almost any time but autumn is ideal. Cleanly cut off healthy, non-flowering shoots below a leaf joint. Use pieces around 10 cm long with at least two nodes. Remove the lower leaves.

Insert five or six cuttings around the edge of a pot filled with coarse propagating mix. Water carefully and cover with a clear plastic bag for moisture and warmth. The cuttings should be established in 2–3 weeks, at which stage transfer to 10 cm pots of potting mix.

*Regal geranium*

## select scented Geraniums

The leaves of scented geraniums can be used to create potpourris and perfumed pillows or to make an infusion for flavouring jellies and jams. Pick them just before the flowers open. The different scents include:

- Rose-scented *Pelargonium capitatum, P. graveolens*
- Lemon-scented *P. citronellum, P. crispum*
- Nutmeg-scented, with a hint of pine *P. 'Fragrans'*
- Coconut-scented *P. grossularioides*
- Apple-scented *P. odoratissimum*
- Orange-scented *P. 'Prince of Orange'*
- Incense-scented *P. quercifolium*
- Rose lemon-scented *P. radens*
- Peppermint-scented *P. tomentosum*

## GLADIOLI

### Summer-long supply
Plant the first batch of gladioli corms from May in hot climates or late June in warm climates in well-manured soil. Make sure to position them in a sunny place. Three or four further batches of corms can be planted at fortnightly intervals up until about August. In a cool climate delay planting until August or September to avoid any frosts, but then continue planting through until late spring.

This staggered system of planting will give you a steady supply of cut flowers throughout summer. The gladioli will flower around 90–100 days after planting.

### Stem support
Plant the corms more deeply than other bulbs, at least 10–12 cm into the ground. This will give the flower stems more support. The small nubble of new growth at the top of the corm should point upwards. As plants grow, stake them within a ring of canes and rings of soft garden twine. Or push a cane in near the plant and use string to gather the stems together. Never tie an upper stem to a cane as it could snap off.

# GRAFTING

Grafting is a propagation method that differs from other methods in that it joins two living portions from two separate plants to form a permanent join. One portion is part of a plant with roots and is called the 'stock'; the other is a piece of the previous year's wood of another plant and is called the 'scion'. When properly joined to the stock, the scion forms the aerial parts of a new plant – that is, the branches, leaves and buds.

It is essential that the stock and the scion be compatible. This usually means that they should be of the same botanical genus, but sometimes different genera within the same botanical family can be grafted.

## Splice grafting
One of the simplest methods of grafting is called splice grafting. It involves joining a stock and a scion of the same diameter so that the cambium layers (the green growth layer underneath the bark) match on at least one side.

## Grafting and budding knives
A good-quality grafting knife or budding knife can be an excellent investment if you are interested in grafting new plants regularly. Horticulture suppliers stock many styles. A budding knife with a finger guard is ideal.

## A quick, clean match
There are many types of grafting. Success relies on matching the cuts being made quickly and cleanly. Practise your technique on branches that can be cut easily using a budding or grafting knife. Once the essentials are grasped and after some practice, anyone can use these grafting methods.

## make a wedge Graft
Wedge grafting is done in autumn or late winter. Try to avoid large wounds as they will take a long time to heal. It is better to insert new scions into two smaller limbs of the stock than one large one.

1. Take shoots from the plant variety you wish to propagate and make slanting cuts at the lower end of each shoot. Prune the upper ends just above a bud.

2. Using a hammer or mallet, insert a sharp wedge obliquely (ensuring that it does not extend across the branch) into the top of the stock. Insert the slanted end of the scions; ensure that they make good contact (picture A).

3. Tie the grafts in with budding tape and cover with grafting wax or petroleum jelly to exclude wind and rain (picture B).

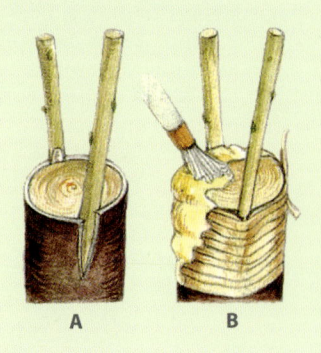

## try a budding Graft
This is another form of grafting, using a single bud for the scion. It is a good way to propagate roses, fruit trees and some ornamental shrubs. Employ this method from mid- to late summer.

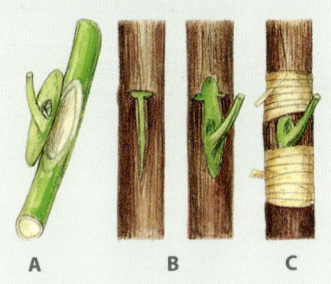

1. Remove shoots from the stock and prune to 30 cm. Select a bud on a well-ripened shoot of the plant to be propagated. Push a knife beneath the bud and cut behind it, making a 5 cm slice to remove it. Leave about 1.5 cm of the bud stalk for you to hold when inserting the bud (picture A).

2. Make a T-shaped cut in the stock, just penetrating the bark, and peel back the flaps. Insert the scion. Trim the top to be flush with the T (picture B).

3. Tie in with budding tape until the graft takes (picture C).

*The new leaf growth on multiple wedge grafts to a cherry tree shows that the grafts have been a success.*

# GRAPEFRUIT AND POMELOS

## Try these varieties
The grapefruit (*Citrus × paradisi*) has many varieties available. The yellow 'Marsh's Seedless' is very reliable – vigorous and heavy bearing, with large, juicy, sweet fruit. It is best suited to warm areas. The sweet-tasting pink grapefruit varieties have become popular in recent times and are excellent for juicing. Varieties to grow include 'Star Ruby', with seedless, thin-skinned fruits and deep red flesh; 'Rio Red', which has variable colour intensity; and the highly productive 'Flame'.

## Dwarf trees and crosses
There are also dwarf grapefruit trees, usually grafted onto 'Flying Dragon' rootstock. A grapefruit–orange hybrid called 'Honneff's Surprise' gives large crops. The fruit has deep orange skin and is exceptionally juicy and sweet.

See also Citrus fruits

### What is a pomelo?
A tropical citrus, the pomelo, or shaddock (*C. maxima*), resembles a large grapefruit and is often mistaken for one. The segments are much larger and sweeter. Excellent varieties to grow include the seedless 'Nam Roi' from Vietnam; the white-fleshed 'Flick's Yellow'; the juicy, lime-scented 'Tahiti'; and pink-fleshed 'Carter's Red'.

# GRAPEVINES

Grapevines do best in climates with cool winters, where summers are dry and humidity is low. In humid coastal areas they are very prone to fruit splitting, fungal fruit rots and mildew. At least choose a mildew-resistant variety.

Grow grapevines in full sun in well-drained soil. They prefer alkaline soil (with a high pH) and should be planted in winter. Place fruiting vines 3 m apart.

## Water requirements
Established vines are drought-resistant but young plants will need summer watering. Fruit crops will be reduced if they are deprived of water during their flowering period. Avoid overhead watering when fruit is ripening as this encourages fungal disease.

## Ornamental grapevines
An ornamental vine trained over a pergola gives shade in summer, colour in autumn and, being deciduous, sun in winter. The grapes are not edible. Vines only need pruning to train them and restrict rampant growth. Prune them back quite hard in winter when they are dormant, then lightly in summer if necessary.

## Training fruit vines
Table grapes are traditionally shaped into a T-shaped cordon – a trunk with two arms supported by a fence or trellis. Let the strongest shoot grow up the wire, removing all competing growth. Cut back this cane to two buds. Train growth from these buds along the wire in each direction for about 1 m.

Correct pruning is necessary for successful fruiting. Most varieties bear fruit on the current year's wood arising from permanent spurs, which become established on a framework cane. Each winter, prune new spur canes back to two buds and remove all other growth from the framework canes.

### choose Grapevines
Whether you want a fruiting or ornamental vine, choose one that suits your climate.

#### Ornamental species
* *Vitis amurensis* Vigorous; tall walls and fences with some support; cold climates.
* *V. coignetiae* Crimson glory vine; best for cool climates.
* *V. vinifera* Several ornamental hybrids and cultivars; best in dry, cool climates.

#### Table grape varieties
Unless stated otherwise, these varieties are best in dry, cool climates: * 'Blush Seedless' * 'Crimson Seedless' * 'Flame Seedless' * 'Italia' * 'Isabella' (subtropics) * 'Muscat Hamburg' * 'Purple Cornichon' * 'Red Globe' * 'Ruby Seedless' * 'Thompson Seedless' (sultana grape) * 'Waltham Cross'

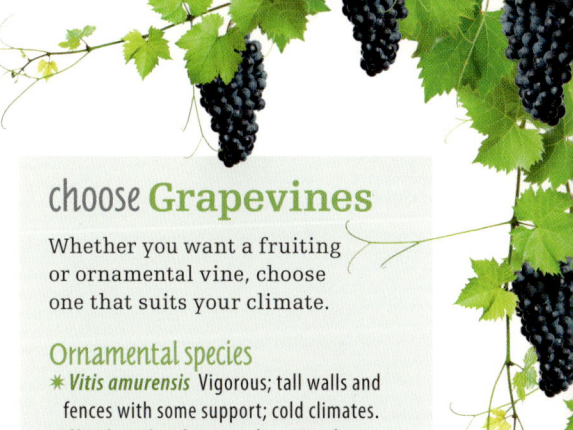

# GRASS TREES | GRASSES

## GRASS TREES

### Add a sculptural element
If you are looking for a talking point in your garden, the grass tree (*Xanthorrhoea australis*) could be it. A tall, spear-like flower grows from the centre of the grassy foliage atop the trunk. Flowering usually occurs after a fire in its natural habitat.

To grow grass trees successfully, excellent drainage is essential. They do best in a sunny spot but will tolerate dappled light. Plant them in a group in the ground or use one in a tall terracotta pot.

### A word of warning
Be wary of plants offered for sale at markets or by the roadside. Many are harvested illegally from the bush. If harvesting is not done carefully the plants may die after planting. Large specimens with established trunks that are sold with a licence have been salvaged from areas where development would otherwise destroy them. These plants have been removed carefully and held in wholesale nurseries before being sold to ensure that the plants transplant successfully. Only buy grass trees from a reputable garden centre.

## GRASSES
Soaring and spiky, or willowy and arching, ornamental grasses bring undulating and eye-catching height and mass to gardens.

### A grass for every border
Leaf colours include blue-grey, bronze, bright green, green-grey, reddish green, silver or yellow. The more unusual grasses will need to be grown from seed or bought from specialist nurseries. Tall perennial grasses such as *Helictotrichon sempervirens*, *Miscanthus sinensis* 'Zebrinus' and *Stipa gigantea* will bring a touch of grandeur to a border.

However, many grasses have weed potential, so be careful not to choose varieties that are a weed risk in your area.

### Massed tussocks
Many native Australian and New Zealand grasses are highly ornamental. The lomandras and tussock grasses (*Chionochloa* and *Poa* spp.), for example, adapt to a wide range of soils and climates and will tolerate dryness.

*Restio* is a genus of ornamental reed-like grasses indigenous to South Africa and Australia. They form attractive tussocks 30 cm – 4 m in height. Grow as half-hardy perennials in well-drained soil and an open, sunny aspect.

### Dark green wave
The dark green of mondo grass (*Ophiopogon japonicus*) makes a lush grass-like edging for a shaded garden. The dwarf form, sold as mini mondo, makes a distinctive dark green line when planted among paving.

### Colourful flower heads
There are some striking annual and perennial grasses with bold or vividly coloured flower heads. The Australian swamp foxtail (*Pennisetum alopecuroides*) has purple flower spikes all year. Many other forms of *Pennisetum* are also grown for their colourful foliage, such as purple fountain grass cultivars (*P. advena* cvs).

### Spring trim
Cut back ornamental grasses to the ground in spring rather than in autumn. As well as protecting the roots from frost, this later trimming lets the leaves bring a decorative note to winter gardens.

### choose Grasses by colour
**Blue** *Festuca glauca* ✻ *Helictotrichon sempervirens* ✻ *Poa poiformis* 'Kingsdale'
**Red, especially in autumn** Japanese blood grass (*Imperata cylindrica* 'Rubra') ✻ *Panicum virgatum* 'Rubrum'
**Silver to white** *Carex* 'Frosted Curls' ✻ *Miscanthus sinensis* and cvs
**Yellow** *Calamagrostis* × *acutiflora* 'Karl Foerster' ✻ *Carex morrowii* 'Evergold' ✻ *Hakonechloa macra* 'Aureola' ✻ *Miscanthus sinensis* 'Zebrinus'

Japanese blood grass

GRASSES | GREENER GARDENING

## divide Grasses

**New edges** For those grasses that produce new rooted plants around the edges of the parent plant, carefully pull away the new growth complete with its roots. Plant in pots or replant elsewhere.

**Dead centre** If the centre of a clump of grass has died and the plant is growing only around the outer edges, lift it and divide it in two using two garden forks.

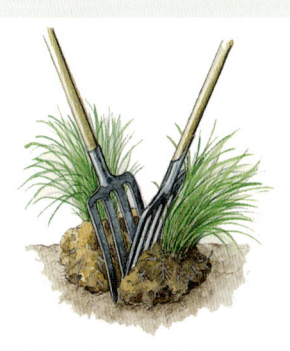

**Large clumps** Slice up large clumps of grass while still in the ground with a sharp spade. Then lift and replant elsewhere.

## GREEN MANURES

### Grow them, then dig them in

Don't leave soil bare for long, particularly over winter or if you're breaking up new ground. Instead, sow one of the many green manure crops to improve the soil. When the plants have grown and before the stems become woody – usually just before flowering – dig them in to add organic matter and some nutrients to the soil. Then wait 3 weeks to make new plantings.

Trouble-free choices are rye, mustard, clover, lupins, crown vetch, comfrey, field or garden peas and broad beans, from which you can first take a crop. Simply buy seeds and sow.

## GREENER GARDENING

### Almost chemical-free

It's not difficult to use 'greener' gardening methods. Even without out-and-out organic techniques, you can take steps towards an environmentally friendly garden.

Chemical-free or almost chemical-free gardening leads to stronger, more self-sufficient plants in the long run. Most pesticides kill both pests and the beneficial creatures that feed on them, so pesticide use may even increase the number of garden pests. Some weedkillers may leave poisonous residues and even weaken the plants they are intended to protect.

### Steps to greener gardening

✱ Use green manures and compost made from your garden and household waste to improve soil structure, help retain soil moisture and replenish nutrients.

✱ Help reduce the number of pests by growing plants that attract natural predators – such as frogs and birds – or change to more varied planting schemes. Use pest controls as a last resort – preferably biological controls.

✱ Check your plants regularly and act in sympathy with the natural balance between plants, soil, bacteria, insects and their predators in your garden.

*Frogs eat many insect pests and slugs. Welcome them to your garden with a gently sloping pond and native plants.*

### Nature's air conditioner

Save on household energy bills by planting deciduous trees to the north side of the house. They ameliorate the heat of midsummer and their green colouring soothes the eyes. After their vivid autumn display and winter leaf drop, they let in sun, which warms the house.

### Solar power

Make life easier and help the environment by buying solar-powered fountain pumps and garden lights. These are no more expensive than conventional items, but use free energy and can save you money in installation costs. A solar panel on the shed roof could be used to top up the batteries of garden equipment.

**GREEN VEGETABLE BUG** *see page 120*

119

## GREEN VEGETABLE BUG

### Plants affected
Many, including vegetables such as beans, peas capsicums and pumpkins; fruit such as tomatoes and passionfruit.

### Symptoms
Wilting shoots, deformed leaves, stems and fruit; tomatoes are mottled.

### Treatment
* Encourage any of the natural predators, including assassin bugs and small wasps, that parasitise the bug's eggs.

* Keep weeds down and remove vegetable crops when finished.

* Spray with either carbaryl or maldison, if severe infestations make it necessary.

## GREENHOUSES AND SHADEHOUSES

A greenhouse is very useful in cooler climates because it lets you raise plants all year round. It does require attention, but modern materials and equipment can be used to automate some tasks. Larger greenhouses take less work than smaller ones, which are prone to extremes of temperature and hard to ventilate. Glass is the best cover; polythene panels don't age as well. Aluminium frames need little care.

### Think big
When choosing a greenhouse or shadehouse, buy the biggest you can afford and fit in your garden – its larger volume of air will help to better control the growing environment. You will find that your enthusiasm for cultivation will grow, and a small structure will only cramp your efforts.

If you'd like to grow plants under glass but don't have garden space for a full-sized greenhouse, buy a mini version that can be attached to the sunny side of the house.

### Space-saving shelves
If it is possible, fit shelves as well as staging into your greenhouse to hold seed trays and potted plants. Then you will be able to tend all your seedlings and plants without bending over, and more floor space will be left free.

### Shading a greenhouse
A greenhouse needs to be shaded from hot sun during the summer months. A simple method is to coat the glass with limewash. Apply it with a brush in spring, but sponge it off in autumn. Never use acrylic white paint or any other type of domestic paint. Alternatively, cover the roof with fine-mesh plastic netting.

### Keep the greenhouse damp
During hot, dry weather, dampen the benches and paths in the greenhouse twice a day to increase the humidity available to the plants. Alternatively, wet an old towel and hang it in the greenhouse with the lower end dangling in a container of water. The towel will constantly draw up water, stay wet and provide humidity.

### Types of shadecloth
Use knitted rather than woven shadecloth for a shadehouse because it will last longer. Make sure all elements, even the clips used to join shadecloth lengths, are UV-stabilised. For shade-loving plants such as fuchsias and ferns, choose a shadecloth that will provide about 70–80 per cent shade.

# GREVILLEAS

### All-purpose plants
If you could only choose one type of plant for your garden, grevilleas would be a good choice. They are tough, long-flowering, and there is one for just about every climate and every niche, from tall trees to groundcovers. Do match the species or cultivar to your garden's climate as some are cold- or frost-sensitive.

### Spidery or brush-like
The spectacular, nectar-rich flowers are spidery or brush-like, and come in all shapes, sizes and colours. Birds adore them. Foliage varies greatly between different species, too. The shrubs are fast-growing, making them excellent for establishing a new garden, and for hedges and screens.

Popular cultivars include 'Honey Gem', 'Coconut Ice', 'Molly', 'Misty Pink', 'Sandra Gordon', 'Robyn Gordon', 'Superb' and 'Winpara Gem'. The prostrate forms, such as *Grevillea* 'Poorinda Royal Mantle', make good groundcovers. There are towering tree forms such as the silky oak (*G. robusta*). Several varieties are grafted as weeping standards and make for an eye-catching centrepiece.

### Care when planting
Most grevilleas need full sun and good drainage. Remove competitive plants such as grass and weeds before planting, then mulch around each grevillea with an organic garden mulch. Water grevilleas well when first planted but reduce watering as the plants become established.

### When to feed
Don't fertilise grevilleas until they have begun growing well. In general, you can feed these plants annually, usually after flowering, with a low-phosphorus slow-release fertiliser. (Like many Australian natives, grevilleas are sensitive to phosphorus.) But if your plant is growing well in a good soil, it may not need extra fertiliser at all.

*Grevillea banksii*

*Grevillea juniperina*

### Pruning tips
Most grevilleas should be pruned regularly. If you have neglected a grevillea, cut it back hard, preferably in spring. It will reward you with new growth and a more compact shape. This is particularly important with tall-growing shrub forms.

The best approach is to clip lightly over the plants after flowering (either in spring or autumn). Adjust the amount you cut to suit the size of your plant. Certain cultivars, however, demand much harsher treatment. 'Sandra Gordon' and 'Honey Gem', for example, can be cut back to about 2 m each year after flowering. If a grevillea fails to thrive, simply replace it.

# GREY MOULD, OR BOTRYTIS

### Plants affected
Most flowering plants, shrubs and trees; raspberries, strawberries and other selected soft fruits.

### Symptoms
Furry or velvety grey mould on leaves, flowers or fruit. Rotting shoots, covered in a grey, velvety mould. Rapid deterioration and rotting.

### Treatment
✽ Cut out and destroy affected shoots, or entire stem on roses.

✽ Remove and destroy affected perennial plants; clear away any dead and dying material around plants; maintain good hygiene.

✽ Remove and destroy affected fruits.

✽ Ensure good drainage and air circulation around plants.

✽ Keep weeds under control.

✽ Ventilate the greenhouse.

✽ Spray with mancozeb or chlorothalonil (if it is registered in your area), but it is better to remove plants such as perennials entirely. As flowers on roses open, spray with mancozeb or a suitable rose spray, if necessary.

# Groundcovers

Any plant that carpets the ground with foliage, stays under 30 cm in height, and grows so thickly that it chokes out weeds qualifies as a groundcover. Creeping shrubs and vines, ornamental grasses, perennials and herbs will become hard-working groundcovers when planted where they can spread.

## Hardy and handy

Many groundcovers will grow where other plants and lawn grass fail to thrive, for example in heavy shade, on slopes and under thirsty trees. Use flowering perennials, such as pinks, gazanias or star jasmine, if you'd like to add flowers to the show.

## Instead of a lawn

If you want the aesthetic appeal of a green space without the high maintenance of a lawn, try a spreading groundcover. Groundcovers won't take a lot of foot traffic, but once they are established and forming a thick cover, you will only need to water when necessary and pull out the occasional weed. Bugle and native violets are good in shade, and for sunny areas try Moroccan glory vine (*Convolvulus sabatius*) or snow-in-summer. Mini mondo grass can be used for a no-mow lawn. Or try lawn chamomile or creeping thymes for a herb lawn.

## Covering a slope

To prevent erosion on a slope, choose groundcover plants whose root systems will help to bind the soil together. Among those suitable for this type of site are the tough ivy-leaved geraniums, ivies, groundcover roses such as the 'Flower Carpet' or 'Sunsation' series, bougainvilleas, lesser periwinkle (*Vinca minor*) and prostrate junipers and rosemaries.

### make good Groundcover choices

**Sun lovers**
- Snow-in-summer (*Cerastium tomentosum*)
- Hen and chicks (*Echiveria elegans*, *Sempervivum* cvs)
- Seaside daisy (*Erigeron karvinskianus*)
- Non-seeding gazania cvs (*Gazania* 'Montezuma', 'Sunset Jane')
- Prostrate junipers (*Juniperus horizontalis*, *J. procumbens*)
- Ivy-leaved geranium (*Pelargonium* Ivy-leaved Hybrids)
- Lamb's ear (*Stachys byzantina*)
- Star jasmine (*Trachelospermum jasminoides*)

**Shade lovers**
- Bugle (*Ajuga reptans*)
- Hellebore (*Helleborus* spp.)
- Deadnettle (*Lamium maculatum*)
- Liriope, turf lily (*Liriope* spp.)
- Mondo grass (*Ophiopogon* spp.)
- Pratia (*Pratia pedunculata*)
- Plectranthus (*Plectranthus* spp.)
- Native violet (*Viola hederacea*)

Bed planted with hen and chicks and chamomile

# H HANGING BASKETS

## HANGING BASKETS

### Strong means of support
A large, well-watered basket can weigh 10 kg or more so ensure hooks and brackets can withstand the weight and that they are fixed securely to the wall. Never attach brackets to crumbling brickwork or rotting wood.

### The right site
Wind and strong sun, especially sunlight reflected off a white wall, will cause baskets to dry out even more rapidly than usual. If possible, choose a site that is sheltered from wind, and where the baskets will receive some shade for part of the day.

### Solving the watering problem
Use a water-retentive potting mix or a mix specially formulated for hanging baskets. Water-storing crystals can be added to the mix to improve water retention. Basket liners made of plastic or coconut fibre also help to retain moisture. After fitting the liner in the basket, place a plastic saucer about the size of a dinner plate in the bottom. This will form a valuable water reservoir.

Once the potting mix in baskets has dried out completely, it can be difficult, if not impossible, to water adequately with a watering can or hose. The only remedy is to take them down and stand them in a container of water until the potting mix is thoroughly wet.

### Swinging salads
Hanging baskets filled with trailing flowers are a delight, but for something a little different, you can plant a few baskets with herbs such as oregano, chives, basil, thyme and curly parsley. For a splash of colour you could try adding cherry tomatoes; 'Sweet 100' is ideal for a hanging basket. Strawberries, including alpine strawberries, do especially well in hanging baskets.

### Coping with heat
On very hot or windy days, you will need to water your hanging baskets frequently. One way to protect them in a heatwave is to take them down completely and stand them on the ground in a sheltered spot until the heatwave has passed.

### plant a Hanging basket

**1** If possible, remove the detachable hanging chains and stand the basket on top of a bucket. Thoroughly wet a pre-formed coconut fibre liner so it expands and line the basket with it. (You can also buy rigid cardboard or cellulose liners, flexible ones made of felt, jute or other fibres, or use a piece of hessian.)

**2** Starting from the bottom, create a series of holes in the liner with a knife or piercing tool. If the plants are delicate, wrap them in plastic and carefully push them into the holes. Add premium potting mix as you go, gently pressing it into place to ensure that all the air pockets around the roots are filled. Space the plants evenly, staggering them in rows.

**3** Put the tallest plants in the centre at the top, making a depression in the potting mix around them to help retain more moisture. Plant more trailing plants around the rim, using hairpins or loops of stiff wire if necessary to attach stems to the frame, encouraging them to hang down.

**4** Drench the basket with water and allow excess to drain through. Attach the chains, then hang the basket, taking care not to squash any plants with the chains.

# HEAT

## When to water?

Early morning is usually the optimum time to water, but you should water your garden when the plants need it and when your time permits. If you see a plant wilting, don't wait for the evening or morning, water it right away.

While a deep soak is the best way to water garden beds and lawns, extremely hot conditions may mean plants need more frequent watering. Pots and new plantings in particular should be checked and watered when they need it. In very hot or windy weather, water may be needed two or three times a day. Ponds and birdbaths will lose a lot of water due to evaporation. Check them regularly and top them up as needed.

## Delay new plantings

It is best not to make new plantings in hot weather. If it is unavoidable, protect them with shadecloth, and keep watering them as if they are still in a pot while the hot spell lasts.

## Protect yourself

If you are gardening during hot weather, make sure you protect yourself by having frequent cool drinks of water and wearing protective clothing including a broad-brimmed hat. If possible, do your gardening in the cooler parts of the day.

# HEATHS

## Take your choice

The heather family includes genera such as *Erica*, *Calluna* and *Daboecia*. In Australia and New Zealand, the heaths are represented by four genera: *Styphelia*, *Sprengelia*, *Woollsia* and *Epacris*.

## Where to plant

Most heaths do not like alkaline conditions, preferring a slightly acid soil. The majority of ericas are from South Africa and they generally tolerate only moderate frosts. The European species are more cold-hardy.

Plant heaths in a sunny to partly shaded position in a light soil with good drainage. During prolonged dry periods they will need to be watered thoroughly but infrequently. Mulch plants to conserve moisture and to reduce the need for cultivation, which can cause root disturbance.

## Group planting

For almost year-round colour, you could plant heaths in bold groups of individual species or cultivars, making the most of the variety of colours, shapes and sizes, from low-growing groundcovers to tall shrubs.

The old flower heads should be trimmed or sheared regularly each year to keep plants compact and tidy. Be careful, though, not to prune back into old wood.

### Banned from sale

In New Zealand there is a ban on the sale and propagation of Scotch or red heather (*Calluna vulgaris*) to reduce the risk of plants spreading in subalpine areas where they readily naturalise. It is also on the weed alert list in Australia for the same reason. Double-flowered cultivars cannot seed and do not pose a problem. Gardeners are encouraged to replace existing plants with something else.

# HEDGE TRIMMERS | HEDGES

## HEDGE TRIMMERS

### The tool for the job
Hedge trimmers will cut a small-leaved hedge well. However, they can damage large leaves and make the hedge untidy, so use secateurs on large-leaved plants.

### Which hedge trimmer?
An electric or petrol-powered trimmer can save time and effort if you have a large hedge. They are available to buy or hire. Fitted with either single- or double-sided reciprocating blades, these powerful machines require great care during use. Always keep power cables safely out of the way, use a circuit-breaker, and wear thick gloves, goggles or a faceguard, and ear protection.

### Essential maintenance
Ensure that the hedge trimmer cuts cleanly by having the blades sharpened in winter. After use, remove dried resin and sap from the blades with a cloth soaked in white spirit, then apply a thin film of oil. Always turn off the power and disconnect first.

### Garden shears
There are lightweight and heavy-duty models for trimming hedges, shrubs and small areas of grass. Straight-edged types are easy to sharpen and maintain. Those with wavy cutting edges (below) are effective on thicker stems, but need care when being sharpened.

## HEDGES

Hedges create borders and boundaries in a garden. They can be clipped and formal or left to grow in a more relaxed style.

### How much pruning
If you want a formal hedge, you can limit the amount of trimming by choosing resilient plants that have a slow growth rate, such as aucuba or box, or plants with a naturally neat habit, such as 'Pink Pixie' escallonia. An informal hedge only needs an occasional trim to stop it looking straggly.

### Colourful privacy
An informal flowering hedge could use grevilleas, hibiscus or oleanders. If you'd like a formal hedge of spring flowers, consider escallonias or sweet viburnum (*Viburnum odoratissimum*); for flowers in autumn and winter, choose sasanqua camellias. Plants that have colourful new growth, such as *Photinia glabra* 'Rubens' or 'Red Robin' or many of the lillypillies, will bring colour to your hedge after each clip.

### Conifer hedges
Conifers make handsome, dense hedges that will act as a screen or windbreak throughout the year. However, don't plant boundary hedges of fast-growing conifers in urban gardens – they are too big, can block out light and breezes, and also create difficult growing conditions for nearby plants. They are a good choice for a windbreak on a country property.

126

## plant a Hedge

**1** Before planting a hedge, mark out its proposed length with a piece of string. Dig a trench along this line, making it twice the width of the shrubs' root balls and the same depth.

**2** Place the shrubs at evenly spaced intervals along the trench, using a tape measure for accuracy. Refill the trench with the excavated soil and press down firmly around each plant.

**3** Remove any stakes and ties. Prune long, non-sprouting branches to encourage vigorous new growth. For future low bushy growth, prune each plant down by half. Water well and mulch.

### Spacing and good growth

Place shrubs that are to be grown as a clipped hedge between a fifth and a quarter of their fully grown width apart. Also leave a space of at least 50 cm to 1 m from any walls or fences.

Shrubs planted this close together will need additional water and fertiliser for strong growth. You could lay a drip-watering system for ongoing care. Regularly tip-prune plants all over during their first few growing seasons for a thick, healthy hedge.

## trim a Hedge

Hedges need trimming to maintain their set width and height. Doing this in mid- to late summer allows new growth to ripen before winter sets in.

**1** Tie strong string along the hedge on one side to mark the desired height. Make sure it's taut and horizontal, and fix the string to long bamboo canes or to strong stems within the hedge.

**2** Cut the sides of the hedge with shears or a hedge trimmer using an upward motion. Taper the hedge slightly towards the top. Cut the top to the string level.

HEDGES H

# H
## HEIRLOOM VARIETIES | HELLEBORES

## HEIRLOOM VARIETIES

For thousands of years gardeners have saved seeds from the best, strongest, most nutritious and delicious of their crops.

### Gourmet delights
After millennia of crop selection, those vegetables and fruit still survive, and are now known as heirloom varieties. They have an extraordinary range of flavours, sizes, shapes and colours: think golden celery, capsicums 30 cm long, rainbow corn, intensely flavoured black, green or striped tomatoes, and purple carrots.

There are hundreds of apple varieties, some dating back to Roman and medieval times. If you want to grow stone fruit and strawberries with intense flavour and fragrance, look for renowned old varieties.

### Seed savers
It is estimated that in the last 75 years the world has lost about 75 per cent of all varieties of vegetables and grains, and even more fruit varieties. But over the last 30 years in particular, serious attempts have been made to save them because they represent a huge amount of genetic diversity, which is irreplaceable once lost.

There are seed-saving groups and networks around the world. Through them, you can share and swap a wide range of rare old varieties. There are also seed and nursery businesses that specialise in heirloom plants.

### Saving your own seed
You can save the seed of heirloom varieties from year to year. If you keep seed of your best plants only, that variety will become better adapted to your conditions.

### Adopt a variety
You could adopt a variety and share it with other gardeners every year – this will help to save that variety. Never dry seed in a domestic oven. Air-dry it instead, but keep it out of direct sunlight.

*See also* Seeds and seedlings

## HELLEBORES

### Flowers in winter
Hellebores are tough perennials that bloom in winter and early spring, when most perennials are dormant and flowers are rare. Their lovely five-petalled blossoms can last for 3 months. The flowers of Christmas rose (*Helleborus niger*) open creamy white and age to pink. Lenten rose (*H. orientalis*) blooms in shades of rose, pink, lavender, burgundy and lettuce green, with petals that are often speckled with a darker colour.

All parts of the plants are toxic if eaten, so keep them away from young children and pets.

### Winter sun, summer shade
These perennials are a favourite for growing under deciduous trees. Choose a spot that receives some winter sun then becomes shady when trees leaf out and temperatures rise. Dig in compost, leaf mould or other organic matter before setting out plants in spring or autumn. Hellebores often need at least 2 years to settle in before they start blooming prolifically, so be patient. Once established, they are quite tough and will even tolerate drought.

HERBS

# HERBS

## Where to grow herbs

Herbs are so adaptable that they can be grown in any number of ways, although almost all of them enjoy plenty of sunshine. You can grow them in the traditional way, in their own self-contained herb garden, or plant them among the flowers in your garden beds and borders, where their foliage will provide contrasting, cooler tones among the bright colours.

Lavender or rosemary, with their culinary, fragrance and insect-repelling uses, makes an excellent border to paths and a traditional edging for herb beds. Or put herbs in pots or tubs on a patio, or in window boxes or hanging baskets. You do not need a very rich soil or compost, just a reasonably fertile and free-draining one. Ideally, site your herb garden near the kitchen door, where you can pick leaves as you need them.

## Planning a herb garden

Before planting an ornamental bed of herbs, sketch a plan so that you make the best use of the contrasting leaf shapes and colours. Remember to place taller herbs such as dill and fennel at the back and smaller ones, such as chives, marjoram, parsley and thyme, at the front.

## Ease of harvesting

Make sure your herbs are within easy reach for picking. Place stepping stones in an ornamental bed, or use a chessboard design in which different herbs are placed in the 'black' (soil) squares, with paving or gravel filling the 'white' squares. Or make a cartwheel design in which bricks form the dividing 'spokes' of the wheel.

## A potted herb garden

Herbs love growing in pots. Indeed, for herbs such as mint and parsley, which spread easily and can take over beds, pots are best. Put the containers in a sunlit position, use good-quality potting mix, and water and feed as necessary. Your herbs will flourish.

Although the most convenient place indoors is the kitchen window ledge, the constant changes in temperature and moisture levels can be bad for the plants. Basil, chives, marjoram, mint, parsley and thyme will do best in these conditions.

129

# HERBS *continued*

## Collecting seeds for cooking
Collect the seeds from coriander, dill, fennel and lovage to use in cooking. Select a dry day when the flower heads are turning brown. Carefully cut them from the plant, turn them gently upside down and shake the seeds into an open paper bag. Store fully dried seeds in airtight containers, in a cool, dry place out of direct sunlight.

## Drying methods
Dry herbs by hanging them in bunches or placing them on drying trays. Herbs that dry well include bay, lovage, marjoram, rosemary, sage and thyme. Lay a piece of muslin over a cake rack, or stretch muslin or fine netting over a wooden frame and secure with nails. Place the rack or frame in a well-ventilated, warm place and lay individual sprigs or leaves of herbs on the muslin. When brittle, they are ready to store.

## Freeze for winter
Freezing preserves the flavours and colours of herbs, making it very useful for basil, coriander, chervil, dill and parsley, which do not dry well. Either freeze whole leaves, in plastic bags, in the quantities needed for recipes, or chop them finely and freeze them, in a little water, in ice cube trays.

## Propagating methods for more herbs
Seedlings and small plants are available at garden centres. But if you want to raise your own, many can be propagated easily from cuttings, division, layering or seed.

**Cuttings** Take cuttings of bushy herbs, such as lavender, rosemary, sage and thyme, from late spring to early autumn. Cut off shoots 5–7.5 cm long and strip leaves from the lower half of cuttings. Fill pots with propagating mix and insert three cuttings around the edge of each pot. Water in. Cover each pot with a clear plastic bag and put in bright, warm shade.

**Sowing** Herbs such as basil, coriander, dill and parsley are raised from seed. Sow three seeds in each small pot of seed-raising mix in spring and place in a warm spot. Keep moist.

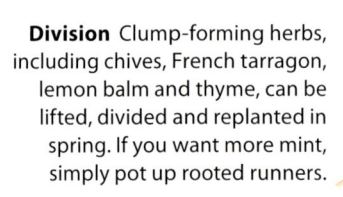

**Division** Clump-forming herbs, including chives, French tarragon, lemon balm and thyme, can be lifted, divided and replanted in spring. If you want more mint, simply pot up rooted runners.

**Layering** A few shrubby herbs, such as thyme, rosemary and sage, can be propagated without any equipment. In summer, lay a shoot down onto soil that has been enriched with compost and hold it in place with a stone. It will root naturally by autumn and can be separated from the parent plant.

HERBS

## get to know some culinary Herbs

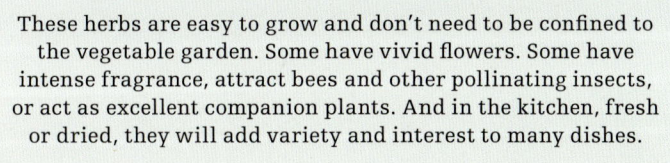

These herbs are easy to grow and don't need to be confined to the vegetable garden. Some have vivid flowers. Some have intense fragrance, attract bees and other pollinating insects, or act as excellent companion plants. And in the kitchen, fresh or dried, they will add variety and interest to many dishes.

### Angelica *Angelica archangelica*
This tall biennial flourishes in well-drained, compost-enriched, moist soil. Seed must be sown fresh or stratified. The flower stems are candied.

### Hyssop *Hyssopus officinalis*
The small, hardy evergreen shrub has pretty blue, pink or white flowers. Grow in full sun. Harvest the leaves from early summer and use sparingly to season salads, vegetables, white meat and fish.

### Chervil *Anthriscus cerefolium*
Chervil is an easy-to-sow hardy annual; it often self-seeds if you let a few plants go to seed. Plant in a shady spot and pick the leaves 6–8 weeks after sowing. The finely chopped fresh leaves are good with salads, soups, and grilled fish or meat.

### Horseradish *Armoracia rusticana*
This is a hardy perennial that spreads rapidly. Plant it in any rich soil and it will continue to grow there for many years. Harvest the roots in autumn and winter. Grated, it serves as a hot and piquant condiment, or make a sauce with it to replace mustard. The young leaves have a bitter taste.

### Lovage *Levisticum officinale*
This hardy, herbaceous perennial is rather like a huge celery plant. It grows best in rich soil and in sun or partial shade. Chop up the leaves for salads and soups.

### Lemon balm *Melissa officinalis*
Lemon balm thrives in well-drained soil in partial shade. It is a perennial that loses its leaves in winter, but it self-seeds and can be quite invasive, so cut plants back regularly. Harvest the leaves and young shoots in summer and use in soups and marinades, or make a drink with it.

### Savory *Satureja hortensis, S. montana*
Summer savory (*S. hortensis*) is an annual and reseeds every year; winter savory (*S. montana*) is a hardy perennial. Both grow well in light soil in a sunny position. The spicy-flavoured leaves are excellent for stuffing, or add them to dried beans, pulses or meat dishes at the end of cooking.

See also Basil, Bay, Chives, Coriander, Dill, Lemon grass, Marjoram and oregano, Mint, Parsley, Rosemary, Sage, Tarragon, Thyme

## HIBISCUS

### Subtropical beauty
Thought to be typically tropical, the many flamboyant varieties of the best known hibiscus species, *Hibiscus rosa-sinensis*, are in fact most at home in the coastal subtropics. They flourish where winters are cool and dry but not cold and frosty, and summers are warm and wet with sea breezes to disperse the humidity.

The flowers do not last long after picking but the bushes are so prolific, you can pick fresh blooms as you need them.

### Tree and shrub forms
There are many different species of hibiscus throughout the world. Some are small trees. Cottonwood (*H. tiliaceus*) grows into a large tree that makes an excellent coastal windbreak. The cup-shaped flowers are yellow with a maroon centre. *H. arnottianus* is a small tree with white or pale pinkish mauve flowers. It can tolerate light frosts.

Other cooler climate hibiscus include frost-tolerant herbaceous *H. moscheutos* varieties such as 'Dixie Belle'; *H. coccineus*, with huge red flowers; and the popular rose of Sharon (*H. syriacus*), a tall deciduous shrub that has many varieties. For tropical gardens, try *H. schizopetalus* or *H. mutabilis*.

### Feed for flowers
Start feeding plants in spring with a high-potash fertiliser to ensure good flowering. Feed every 3 weeks at the rate recommended on the packet, but don't exceed this or the plants will suffer. In subtropical and warm temperate areas do not feed during the cool season. In tropical areas continue fertilising while flowering lasts.

### Water with care
Hibiscus are thirsty drinkers so water well during dry weather but try not to wet the leaves as this encourages fungal diseases.

### Good for hedges
Hibiscus make good informal hedges. The top of the hedge can be kept trimmed, leaving the sides to flower freely. After flowering, give the whole hedge a good clip. For a hedge with a tropical touch, use just about any strong-growing variety of *H. rosa-sinensis*. The tree types can be used to make a taller hedge.

### treat **Hibiscus** flower beetles

**Plants affected**
Hibiscus, magnolias and sometimes pale roses.

**Symptoms**
Holes in petals, deformed flowers, as beetles eat pollen.

**Treatment**
* Collect and dispose of any fallen flowers.

* Manually remove insects, or spray with garlic to discourage them and metallic flea beetles. Use pyrethrum or carbaryl.

* Cultivate the garden well, and keep it free of debris.

* These small black beetles differ from metallic flea beetles, another hibiscus pest, which make holes in the leaves.

## HOLIDAYS

Try to take your annual holiday at a time when the garden is at its least productive. That way, your plot will be at its best when you are at home to appreciate it.

### Postpone delicate tasks
Plants need extra care straight after repotting or planting out, so never do these jobs just before going away. Instead, leave them for a time when you can provide that essential extra care.

### Help the waterer
Spend some time weeding and mulching your beds before you leave – this will reduce the need for watering. To make sure pots of precious plants are not overlooked by the person watering while you're away, group them together. This will reduce drying out and also make the task of watering that much easier.

If you are going to be away for any length of time, it is a good idea to invest in a watering system with an automatic timer. This will enable your plants to be watered regularly while you're gone. If necessary, you can arrange for a neighbour to override the system if there is heavy or constant rain during your absence.

### Humidity for indoor plants
Indoor plants can be kept alive in the bath. Line the bath with plastic, then a thick layer of newspaper. Wet the papers and place the thoroughly watered pot plants on top. The wet papers and clustered plants raise local humidity and help prevent the potting mix from drying. If the plants are lower than the bath rim, a sheet of clear plastic over the top will act as a mini greenhouse.

HOSTAS | HYACINTHS

## HOSTAS

### Foliage colour and texture
Hostas make handsome foliage plants for a shady garden. Many have plain green leaves, in shades ranging from pale lime to deep forest. But there are alternative foliage colours, including 'Krossa Regal' with solid blue leaves and 'August Moon' with golden ones. Others are variegated: marked with edging, marbling or centre splotches in white or yellow that are luminous in shade. Some hostas have ribbed leaves, while others are puckered or quilted.

### Bulb cover
Hostas unfurl their leaves in late spring, making them ideal for interplanting with spring bulbs. They quickly and effectively hide the spent leaves of daffodils and jonquils. Then in summer, they send up long, slender flower stalks lined with fragrant lavender or white flowers that linger for several weeks.

### Easy growing
The secret to growing hostas is good soil and good but indirect light. They can tolerate moist or dry shade. Plant in early spring, or in autumn in mild areas. Don't overwater, but do water during a drought, and control snails and slugs, which are their main pest.

## HYACINTHS

### Spring perfume
Hyacinths are among the most elegant spring-flowering bulbs, with a sweet spring perfume. They bloom year after year in cool climates, but the flower spikes often become slightly longer and less densely packed with blossoms after the first year.

In warm climates, new hyacinth bulbs may need to be planted each autumn. If potted up in autumn and kept in a place that's cool but remains above freezing – or in a refrigerator – for 12–14 weeks, hyacinths will eagerly bloom indoors during winter.

### Small is good enough
When buying hyacinth bulbs for the garden, do not be tempted to spend more money on bigger bulbs. Small bulbs grow just as well, and they are considerably cheaper. Another advantage is that their blooms will be more in proportion with the plant's size, and less likely to be damaged by wind or heavy rain.

### Growing on air
To grow a hyacinth in a glass of water, leave a 1.5 cm gap between the surface of the water and the bottom of the bulb. This will prevent the base of the bulb from rotting.

Take precautions when handling hyacinth bulbs, because they can irritate your skin and eyes. Wear gloves when planting the bulbs and be sure to keep the bulbs out of the hands of children.

# HYDRANGEAS

### Hydrangea choice
The mop-headed hortensias and flat-headed lacecaps of the common hydrangea (*Hydrangea macrophylla*) are worth growing for their showy clusters of star-shaped flowers. They do best in a sheltered position in a sunny or partly shaded area of the garden but need protection from the hot westerly sun. Both types flower on shoots from the previous growing season and bring colour to the garden in summer.

The deciduous oak-leaf hydrangea (*H. quercifolia*) has white flowers that age to purple, and leaves that turn yellow and red in autumn. A tall shrub perfect for cool areas is *H. paniculata* 'Grandiflora'. It spends most of summer covered in dense clusters of creamy pink flowers that resemble fairy floss.

### Bluer blues
There are two ways to make pink hydrangeas turn blue. Either spread aluminium sulfate around the roots or water with a blueing agent, which you can purchase from garden centres. The colour of your hydrangeas is an indication of the pH value of your soil. Blue flowers mean the soil is acid, pink that it is alkaline. Using an acid mulch of pine needles or oak leaves will help maintain the blue colour, as will dusting soil around the roots with sulfur.

### Water well
Hydrangeas are very forgiving but they do like regular watering. As soon as they run short of water, they will wilt and look unsightly. Give hydrangeas in flower a deep watering twice a week. On hot summer days water well in the morning to prevent the plants from wilting during the day. Keep the soil around the fibrous roots well mulched to reduce loss of moisture from the soil.

### Pruning versatility
Traditionally, hydrangeas are pruned in winter while they are leafless and dormant. They can, however, be pruned any time after the flowers have finished. Leave shoots that haven't flowered and cut others back to two plump buds on each stem. Hydrangeas don't need to be cut back hard but this technique can be used to renovate plants which have become spindly and unsightly. Just remember that a hard prune may reduce flowering next season.

# HYDROPONICS

### Something completely different
This method of growing indoor ornamentals and greenhouse crops employs expanded clay granules or scoria, rockwool, vermiculite or perlite instead of soil to support the plants. Instead of being grown in conventional pots, the plants are fed on a nutrient-rich water solution and cultivated in special stands or watertight containers, each of which has a float that indicates when the growing solution should be replenished.

### Soil transfer
A soil-grown plant can be moved to a hydroponic system. All you have to do is gently wash away all soil and pot the bare-rooted plant into a hydroponic pot. Special kits are available from some garden centres or specialist hydroponic shops. Although expensive at first, once installed, the system is relatively maintenance-free.

### In the greenhouse or balcony
Hydroculture can be worthwhile in the greenhouse. Plants that respond well to it include cucumbers, eggplants, lettuces, capsicums, strawberries and tomatoes. Hydroponic systems are also a good way of growing plants on a sunny balcony. Invest in a vertical stand to grow as many plants as possible.

### The right fertiliser
It is essential to follow the instructions and to use only the nutrient solution especially manufactured for hydroponic growing. Ordinary fertilisers aren't suitable and should never be used.

IMPATIENS | INDIGENOUS PLANTS

## IMPATIENS

### Colour for shade
Impatiens, also known as busy lizzies, brighten up shady garden spaces, with more than 20 flower colours, including white, pink, cherry, lavender, orange and salmon. There are also varieties with contrasting edges, blotches, streaks or swirls of more than one colour, and double-flowered types, too. The New Guinea hybrids are larger and showier than regular impatiens, and they also tolerate a little more sun.

### Shade and moisture
All impatiens need fertile soil that retains moisture. Container-grown plants in particular benefit from regular fertilising. In most coastal, subtropical and tropical gardens, impatiens will grow and flower all year round. In frost-prone areas, plant seedlings in spring for flowers until autumn.

### Raising from seed
Seed is the cheapest way to obtain a mass of impatiens for your summer bedding. Fill a seed tray or other container with seed-raising mix and sow the seeds on top, making sure that they are not covered by the mix. Place the container in a clear plastic bag and put it in a warm room, out of direct sunlight. The extra humidity created in the bag will encourage the seeds to germinate quickly.

Impatiens cope badly with root disturbance, so transplant the seedlings into pots when they have grown leaves, and then to the garden when 5–7 cm tall.

### Doubling up
Seeds of double-flowered varieties are sold, but only about a quarter of the plants that develop will have double flowers. To build up a collection of double-flowered impatiens, buy pots in the nursery and then take cuttings from them at home. In frost-prone areas you may need to keep some impatiens in pots in a protected area to nurse them through winter.

### Quick cuttings
Nothing could be easier than propagating impatiens. From spring to early autumn, take a cutting below a leaf joint, remove the tips of the bottom leaves, put the cutting in water and stand it in the light. When it has developed a root system, plant it out.

## INDIGENOUS PLANTS

### Finding your indigenous plants
Indigenous plants are plants native to a specific locality. Some will be found over a wide area but others may be local variations, best adapted to the soil and climatic conditions of only one place. To grow plants that are indigenous to where you live, you need seeds and cuttings from plants growing naturally in undisturbed bushland. Remember, though, that you need permission from landowners to enter their land and collect material, and that it is illegal to take plants from national parks and reserves.

### Creating a natural environment
If you are building on a new block of land, collect seeds or cuttings from any plants that will not survive the building. To avoid damaging trees, carefully mark all those that are to be protected and discuss them with your builder. Rope them off with brightly coloured tape and do not allow heavy equipment to be used nearby. Avoid changing soil levels around existing trees when you lay out your new garden as this will cause the trees to die.

### Preserving topsoil
In a previously undeveloped area the topsoil will contain a seed bank of plants indigenous to your locality. To preserve this important resource, retain any topsoil that has to be cleared for building on your block. Store it in a mound in an out-of-the-way spot to be respread in the garden later.

# I INDOOR PLANTS

## INDOOR PLANTS

### Understand differing needs

Just like plants grown in the garden, different indoor plants have differing needs for light, food, humidity and water. Some thrive in full sun while others may scorch unless shaded from bright light or sited away from the window. Equally, while many plants respond to frequent watering, a few will flourish only if they are allowed to dry out in between watering.

Understanding these differences is the key to success with indoor plants. So always keep the plant label in a safe place to remind you of the plant's botanical name and also of its light, watering and feeding requirements.

### Settling-in period

Help a new plant to settle in to a new situation by placing it in a position free of draughts and out of direct sunlight for at least 2 weeks. It can then be moved to its permanent home.

Plants do not like change, so refrain from constantly moving them about the house. Not only could a plant be damaged – for example, a move into bright sunlight could lead to leaf scorch – but changes in temperature, light and humidity can also affect growth. For example, a reduction in temperature could chill and shock a plant, and the plant's growth be retarded.

### Group benefits

Clustering pots in a group looks attractive and also helps to create the right environment for plants to survive indoors. Healthy plants that like the same conditions will benefit from being grouped together. Moisture will evaporate from the potting mix and provide a humid atmosphere for them all.

Plants that require a very humid atmosphere should be placed on a waterproof tray half-filled with small pebbles, pea shingle or clay balls. Pour a shallow layer of

*Mother-in-law's tongue*

---

### provide good care for Indoor plants

Follow these basic tips to help your indoor plants have a long and healthy life:

✽ Regularly remove faded flowers and damaged or dried leaves.

✽ Do not overwater your plants; let the potting mix dry out a little before rewatering.

✽ Feed plants frequently during the active growth period (between spring and autumn).

✽ Do not use leaf-polishing products too often as they may clog leaf pores. Wipe the leaves with a damp sponge instead.

---

*Cyclamen*

*Moth orchid (Phalaenopsis sp.)*

*Croton*

136

INDOOR PLANTS

water into the tray to create some humidity around them. Replenish the water in warmer weather.

### Light seekers
Some plants and germinating seeds require a lot of light during winter when the light quality can be low. To ensure they receive the maximum available, site them on a north- or west-facing window ledge; also keep fertilising to a minimum. It is also a good idea to rotate indoor pot plants by a half-turn every few days to help ensure even leaf growth.

To increase the light that reaches a plant during the dull winter months, position a mirror, or a sheet of aluminium foil mounted on a piece of cardboard, behind the plant or to one side of it. The extra light that the mirror or foil reflects will encourage the plant to grow more upright.

### Fortnightly feed
Plants in containers soon absorb the nutrients in potting mix. Add a slow-release fertiliser to the potting mix when repotting, or feed frequently with a liquid fertiliser during the growing season. If you find that flowering is disappointing, try feeding the plants with a tomato fertiliser.

### Water signals
Use one of the many products, widely available from garden centres, that is inserted into the pot and changes colour as the soil dries out. Treat it as an indication only, and always water according to the plant's individual needs.

To make sure the water goes around the base of the plant, use a small watering can with a long, slender spout. This prevents splashes on the plant's leaves and your furniture. If the potting mix has dried out, immerse the pot in a bucket of water until bubbles stop rising to the surface. Drain well and place on a saucer.

### Keeping leaves clean
Give glossy-leaved plants an occasional light spray of tepid water to remove dust. Wipe the leaves individually to remove surplus water. Don't do this to grey foliage plants.

### Useful guests
Plants can help to clear the air. After painting and decorating, banish paint smells by placing pots containing azaleas, ivies and mother-in-law's tongue in the room. Their leaves absorb and break down toxins.

### Indoor show
Potted plants such as evergreen azaleas, miniature camellias, orchids and gardenias can be brought in from outside when they are in flower so you can fully enjoy their attractive temporary display. Return the plants to their outdoor location when the flowers have finished.

## choose Indoor plants
Foliage plants offer an array of leaf shapes, sizes, colours, markings and textures. This is complemented by the seasonal diversity of flowering plants.

### Flowering indoor plants
* Lipstick plant (*Aeschynanthus speciosus*)
* Flamingo flower (*Anthurium* spp.) * Zebra plant (*Aphelandra squarrosa*) * Bromeliads
* Cyclamen (*Cyclamen persicum*) * Painted lady (*Echeveria derenbergii*) * Orchid cactus (*Epiphyllum* spp.) * Poinsettia (*Euphorbia pulcherrima*) * Persian violet (*Exacum affine*)
* Hoya, wax flower (*Hoya* spp.) * Kurume azaleas, dwarf indica azaleas * Orchids
* Primula * African violet (*Saintpaulia ionantha*) * Zygocactus (*Schlumbergera* spp.)
* Peace lily (*Spathiphyllum wallisii*)
* Cape primrose (*Streptocarpus* spp.)

### Indoor foliage plants
* Maidenhair fern (*Adiantum raddianum*)
* Cast-iron plant (*Aspidistra elatior*)
* Rosary vine, string of hearts (*Ceropegia linearis* subsp. *woodii*) * Grape ivy (*Cissus rhombifolia*) * Croton (*Codiaeum variegatum*)
* Cabbage tree (*Cordyline australis*)
* Umbrella plant (*Cyperus alternifolius*)
* Dumb cane (*Dieffenbachia* spp.) * Corn plant, happy plant (*Dracaena fragrans*)
* Devil's ivy (*Epipremnum aureum*)
* Ivy tree (× *Fatshedera lizei*) * Polka dot plant (*Hypoestes phyllostachya*) * Desert cacti (*Echinopsis*, *Mammillaria* and *Rebutia* spp.) * Boston fern (*Nephrolepis exaltata* 'Bostoniensis') * Heart-leaf philodendron (*Philodendron scandens*) * Mother-in-law's tongue (*Sansevieria trifasciata*)
* Piggyback plant (*Tolmiea menziesii*)

Flamingo flower

Desert cacti

137

# INSECTS

## Good insects
Don't think of all insects as pests. Some, such as bees, may pollinate flowers; others are predators and feed on garden pests. They include assassin bugs, lacewings, ladybirds and hoverflies. Centipedes, which are closely related, break down plant debris. They have one pair of legs on each body segment. Don't confuse them with millipedes – pests that feed on plant roots and have two pairs of legs on each segment.

## Protect the predators
Some insecticides will kill useful insects as well as insect pests, so do not use them unless absolutely necessary. If possible, choose to use non-persistent soap-based insecticides or insecticides that are toxic only to the specific pest.

You can also reduce your reliance on insecticides if you set out to encourage insect predators into your garden. Poached egg plant (*Limnanthes douglasii*), fennel, dill, calendulas, marigolds and other nectar- or pollen-rich plants all provide food for predators.

See also Beneficial creatures, Biological controls, Pesticides, Spraying

### repel Insects naturally
Many herbs have aromatic oils with chemical compounds that repel pests, but you need to brush against them to release the scents. Position these plants in high-traffic areas, such as alongside pathways:

* Wormwood repels mosquitoes.
* Tansy banishes flies or ants.
* Basil wards off both flies and mosquitoes.
* Both fennel and pennyroyal repel fleas.

# IRISES
The golden rule with irises is to plant a single variety in a mass or swathe rather than dot single plants around the garden.

## Tall bearded irises
The best known irises are the tall bearded types, named after the fuzzy, caterpillar-like 'beard' at the centre of each outer petal, or 'fall'. These are easygoing plants. All they need is a sunny, free-draining position and a spring dressing of slow-release fertiliser. Most varieties require a cool winter to flower well.

## Sunlight for rhizomes
Make sure that the top of each rhizome is exposed after planting. Check them regularly to ensure they remain clear of the soil while the plants are establishing themselves, otherwise flowering will be affected. To minimise wind rock after planting, use secateurs to reduce the foliage by about half.

## When to divide
Divide bearded iris rhizomes every 3–5 years, after flowering. Cut out and discard the old centres of the rhizomes, keeping just the healthy, outer parts, which produce the new growth. Replant 30–40 cm apart.

## Water irises
Water irises include flag irises such as the blue *Iris versicolor* and yellow *I. pseudacorus*, the prolific Siberian flag (*I. sibirica*) the Japanese flag (*I. kaempferi*) and the Louisiana Hybrids. They grow best in damp conditions, such as a bog garden or the shallow edges of a pond. They are truly stunning in water gardens.

## Growing water irises
These attractive, dainty plants prefer a neutral or slightly acid soil, especially one that is rich in plant foods – as many waterside soils are. Transplant them from their pots in spring, just as the green shoots start to develop from the rhizome.

### identify bulb Irises
There are three groups:

**Dutch, Spanish or English irises** These are tall, late spring types. The Dutch hybrids are the best known, being easy to grow in any temperate to cool climate. The other two types need cold winters to flower well.

**Dwarf species** The small, winter to spring types, which include *I. reticulata* and *I. danfordiae*, are very beautiful but need a cold winter to grow and flower well.

**Juno irises** Uniquely formed, these irises are difficult to grow and propagate and are only available from specialist bulb growers. They need cold winters.

Bearded iris

IRISES | IXORAS

## IVY

### Coat for a wall
A garden wall can be made into a feature or a backdrop for other plants if contrasting variegated and green ivies are trained to scramble up it. Before planting ivy, inspect the wall thoroughly and renew any defective pointing. Ivy will find its way through cracks and faults but will not harm a well-maintained wall.

### Unwanted ivy
Ivy can be invasive on house walls and under roof tiles. Keep growth under control; cut back yearly on walls to 50 cm below the level of the gutter. If growing near a tree, don't let it climb up the trunk.

Where ivy has got out of control, it can be removed by applying a herbicide containing glyphosate. Nick the stem and paint the chemical onto the exposed area. While you will not need to treat every stem, you may have to cut back sections that have not been in contact with the chemical after a couple of weeks.

### Itch warning
Ivy leaves can play host to a microscopic insect called an ivy mite, which will cause itchiness. Cover your head, arms and legs before tackling ivy.

### Quick carpet
Create a handsome green carpet that stifles weeds and brightens a sunless corner by planting large-leaved *Hedera canariensis* or the variegated *H. helix* 'Goldheart' or 'Glacier' as a groundcover. Use one plant to every square metre for quick cover.

Dwarf iris (*Iris reticulata*)

### Cover the bases
Each spring, limit weed growth, retain moisture and provide nutrients for water irises growing in a bog garden by covering the bases of the plants with plenty of mulch or compost.

### In deep water
To grow water irises in deep water, plant the rhizomes in a mesh basket filled with rich garden soil and cover with a layer of pea gravel. This will stop the soil from being washed out and also prevent any fish from uprooting the plants. Place some bricks on the base of the pond and lower the basket to sit on top. Make sure the rim of the container is no more than 7.5 cm below the surface of the water.

## IXORAS

### Easy to grow
One of the most colourful and undemanding shrubs for warm climates, ixoras are deservedly popular in the home garden and in public spaces. Well-known varieties such as 'Coral Fire', 'Prince of Orange' and 'Sunkist' grow well in subtropical climates; 'Malay Pink' needs a sheltered, warm spot with plenty of water and humidity. Many of the dwarf varieties only grow and flower well in the tropics.

### Sun or shade?
In the garden, ixoras can be used as single specimens, borders, low hedges and mass plantings. They can be grown in sun or shade; full sun promotes flowering but some protection from direct sunshine in the afternoon helps flowers last longer and prevents them fading.

### Regular care
A rich, well-drained soil gives the best results, but ixoras tolerate most soils if they are regularly fertilised and watered. Use any balanced slow-release fertiliser. If you live in the tropics, use this slightly more frequently than the recommended rate or choose a fertiliser specially formulated for the tropical conditions.

139

# J

JACARANDAS | JASMINES

## JACARANDAS

### A tree of variable size
Perhaps the most widely admired of all tropical trees, *Jacaranda mimosifolia* also grows well in warm to temperate areas, being able to withstand an occasional light frost once it is established. However, it does not grow nearly as large in those areas as it does in the subtropics, and before planting you should look at mature trees in your area to get an idea of what size to expect.

Although deciduous, jacarandas hold their leaves through winter, only dropping them in spring.

### A white jacaranda
While blue jacarandas are more admired and commonly seen, a beautiful white variety, 'Alba', is now available. It does not grow quite as tall as blue jacarandas.

### Bonus flowers
Although the main flowers are borne in late spring and early summer, jacarandas will often also bear flowers in autumn. It depends on the particular season and the individual tree. When the flowers fall, they cover the ground beneath the tree in a spectacular coloured carpet. If you can, site your tree in the middle of lawn and enjoy the carpet without the hazard of wet, slippery flowers on a path or pavers.

### Give the tree its head
A young jacaranda grows very fast and upright for the first 3–4 years. Cutting it back during this time to force branching can cripple it. Leave it alone and it will develop a shapely crown in its own good time. Never lop an established tree to try to control its size. It will grow back strongly but it will be years before it flowers again.

### Easy to grow
Jacarandas are easily propagated from seed, and in climates where the trees flourish you will need to be vigilant about self-sown seeds unless you want a jacaranda forest. If you do wish to keep the seedlings, transplant them to the desired position when they are quite young as large seedlings are more difficult to establish.

## JASMINES

Jasmines are renowned for their superb scent and their beautiful flowers. They vary greatly in their habit, size and perfume. Most originate from tropical and subtropical areas and only some of them are frost-hardy.

### Coping with the cold
Carolina jasmine (*Gelsemium sempervirens*) This frost-hardy evergreen twining climber from the southern United States is neat and not too vigorous. It has glossy green foliage and small trumpet-shaped, scented yellow flowers in spring and autumn.

Common jasmine (*Jasminum officinale*) This easily cultivated semi-evergreen climber from China is frost-hardy. Its evening-scented white flowers bloom from summer to early autumn, set off by glossy foliage.

Pink jasmine (*J. polyanthum*) The tall, twining, frost-hardy pink jasmine from China is very vigorous and can become invasive. The pink buds open to almost overpoweringly perfumed white flowers in spring and summer.

Star jasmine (*Trachelospermum jasminoides*) A tough, versatile, twining evergreen climber from China, it is moderately frost-hardy and makes an effective groundcover. Dark green foliage sets off the sweetly scented white flowers over a long period in late spring and early summer.

Winter jasmine (*J. nudiflorum*) The most cold-tolerant of all jasmines, best suited to cool to cold climates, winter jasmine is a deciduous, rambling climber. Masses of vivid yellow flowers appear in winter and early spring.

### Prefers warmth
Angel wing jasmine (*J. nitidum*) The delicately star-shaped white flowers are scented and about 2 cm across. This jasmine grows

JASMINES

Carolina jasmine

Star jasmine

Pink jasmine

best in the subtropics, flowering from late spring through summer.

### Lemon-scented jasmine
(*J. azoricum*) This evergreen climber has highly scented white flowers, which appear in summer, opening from deep pink buds. Here is a jasmine that is easy to control and will grow as a shrub when pruned.

### Shrubby jasmines
Yellow or primrose jasmine (*J. mesnyi*) is a tall shrub with arching branches. It makes a good informal hedge, and tolerates hot and dry conditions. The Arabian jasmine (*J. sambac*) is a small shrub or vine with superbly fragrant white flowers in spring and summer. It thrives in a warm to tropical climate. There are lovely double-flowered forms.

**JAPANESE WINDFLOWERS**
see page 142

141

# J

JAPANESE WINDFLOWERS | JERUSALEM ARTICHOKES

## JAPANESE WINDFLOWERS

### Protect from heat
Japanese windflowers (*Anemone × hybrida*) grow best in a cool to mild climate in a semi-shaded position. These beautiful plants will grow and flower well in milder subtropical areas if they are given protection from hot sun and drying winds in summer. Although they grow well in cool frosty areas, mulch the root area in winter in very cold districts.

### Autumn flowers
The delicate windflowers come in a wide range of colours, from white through pinks to a rosy red, with golden centres. Many named varieties are available, and they will enliven your garden with flowers in autumn. They make good cut flowers as they have long stems and last well indoors. Unfortunately, the flowers have no perfume.

### Woodland situation
Perhaps the best way to grow Japanese windflowers is in a woodland garden where they are allowed to grow and spread in clumps under trees. When the plants finish flowering and die back in winter they can be lifted, divided and replanted. Indeed, they will spread even without this attention.

## JERUSALEM ARTICHOKES

### Confused identity
Jerusalem artichokes are not artichokes and they have nothing to do with Jerusalem. They are a species of sunflower, and native to tropical America. They have edible potato-like tubers with a sweet, delicate flavour, which is thought to be slightly reminiscent of the globe artichoke.

### Two good reasons
The plants are easy to grow, and a row of their golden, sunflower-like flowers, to a height of at least 3 m, makes an attractive screen or windbreak for the vegetable bed in summer. In exposed areas, support these tall plants with wire stretched between two posts.

### Harvest time
Jerusalem artichokes need a long growing season of 5–6 months. The tubers can be harvested from midautumn, after the plants have died down. Cut the stems back to within 30 cm of the ground, and dig up the tubers with care as their skins are thin.

You can leave the tubers in the ground until needed – their cut stems will tell you where they are. Or store them in a box of dry sand or sawdust in a cool, dry place for up to 3 months. But be sure to dig up even the smallest tubers if you don't want Jerusalem artichokes popping up year after year.

# JUNIPERS

## Hardy evergreens

These reliable evergreens have a very wide natural distribution, from the Arctic to the tropics. They come in so many forms and colours that there's bound to be exactly the right one for any site you have in mind. Adaptable and hardy, they ask only for sun and good soil drainage. They'll thrive for many years without pruning, watering or other maintenance.

## Getting to know junipers

With most garden plants, it makes sense to begin with plant names when deciding which plants to grow in your garden. However, this can lead to unnecessary confusion with junipers, because several major species are very similar in terms of hardiness, diversity of form, and practical use in the landscape. So rather than sorting through hundreds of cultivar names, it's better to decide on the size, shape and colour of juniper, and then shop around to see what's available.

Junipers may be blackish green, medium grass green, blue-green, grey-green, yellow-green or have bold chartreuse leaf tips.

## Getting off the ground

Many junipers grow into medium-sized shrubs and small trees. For an unusual juniper with an upright habit, grow the greyish green dwarf tree *Juniperus communis* 'Compressa'. It would look effective in a rock garden, but you'll need to be patient as it takes a decade to grow to 60–90 cm. For a vertical shape or an accent plant in front of a wall or on either side of a set of stairs, choose the pencil-like blue-grey *J. scopulorum* 'Skyrocket'.

Dwarf junipers do very well in containers and always look good on a patio. The many spreading conifers, which generally grow 30 cm tall and to 3 m wide, make hardy groundcovers. Use shore juniper (*J. conferta*) in coastal gardens as it tolerates salt spray.

## Keeping junipers healthy

Junipers prefer acid soils that are moisture-retentive, free-draining and in the pH range 5.5–6.0. They will not grow in the tropics.

Prune only to remove damaged stems. Junipers look best when allowed to follow their natural growth patterns, and severe pruning can result in brown patches that never fill out with fresh green growth.

## Action against pest problems

Most junipers grow for many years without any pest problems. However, they can be prone to attack by a range of insects and diseases, including borer, canker, aphids, scale, two-spotted mite, rust and dieback. The prompt treatment of any problems, with a targeted pesticide if necessary, will help to ensure the plant's survival. Plants are much less susceptible to pest and disease attack when grown in a suitable situation and looked after well.

*Prostrate juniper*

*Juniperus × medea* 'Plumosa Aurea'

*Juniperus procumbens* 'Nana'

# K

KALANCHOES | KANGAROO PAWS

## KALE

### A winter green
Kale, also known as borecole, provides greens from midwinter to the middle of spring, a time when other greens may be scarce. Kale varieties are extremely hardy, surviving conditions that would harm the related broccoli and brussels sprouts. Indeed, it is generally thought that frosts improve their flavour. The leaves may be either curled or plain.

### Getting a good crop
Kale grows best in a well-drained, medium or heavy loam that has been well manured for a previous crop. It thrives in alkaline soil. Sow seeds in 1 cm drills in mid-spring; transplant the seedlings to the permanent bed in summer, spacing them 60 cm apart.

Harvest from winter to midspring. Cut the centre of each plant first to encourage the production of fresh sideshoots. When they start to flower, pull up the plants and discard.

### Ornamental types
Ornamental kales are unusual members of the cabbage clan. They are cold-hardy, tough-leaved foliage plants that bring colour to autumn and winter flowerbeds and containers. The frilly leaves often start out green and then turn red, purple, pink, white or a mixture of these shades. The colours, concentrated on the inner leaves, intensify with the cool weather and contrast with the green outer leaves.

## KALANCHOES

### Showy succulents
These succulents have showy foliage and flowers, and are mostly natives of subtropical and tropical Africa. They vary in their frost tolerance and growing conditions, but all kalanchoes need well-drained soils. They do well in the garden or in pots.

### Shrubs to groundcovers
Plants range from architectural tree-like shrubs up to 3.5 m high, such as velvet elephant's ears (*Kalanchoe beharensis*), which is grown for its large, triangular, velvety olive green leaves, to dwarf shrubs 30 cm high, such as *K. blossfeldiana*. This makes an excellent bedding plant with its brightly coloured flowers, and is also common in containers and as an indoor plant.

Other varieties include flapjacks (*K. thyrsiflora*) and panda plants (*K. tomentosa*). There are also numerous kalanchoes that make popular and useful groundcovers.

## KANGAROO PAWS

### Colour choice
Kangaroo paws (*Anigozanthos* spp.) bring colour to a perennial garden. The plants form leafy green clumps, and the furry, paw-shaped flowers come in striking colours – from lime green and gold to red and orange. Borne on flower stems 20 cm to 1.5 m high for a long period in spring and summer, they make long-lasting cut flowers and also attract birds.

Small-growing kangaroo paws such as 'Dwarf Delight' and 'Bush Joey' make good potted plants.

### Best position
These plants prefer sandy, well-drained soil with an acidic pH. They grow best in full sun, but in very hot, arid areas plants will appreciate shade during the hottest time of the day. Hot soil temperatures can cause rhizomes to rot, so keep them well mulched.

Water well, particularly in late winter and spring when flowers are forming; don't wet the foliage to minimise ink spot disease.

### Pruning tip
If your clump of kangaroo paws begins to look untidy, a quick way to prune it back is with a lawn mower. Simply mow the clump down to ground level. Although this may sound like a drastic remedy, the plant will regrow with strong, healthy new growth.

144

KIWI FRUIT | KOWHAIS

# KIWI FRUIT

## A decorative vine
The kiwi fruit, or the Chinese gooseberry, grows on a vigorous woody vine with handsome leaves that turn yellow before falling in autumn. The cream and gold flowers make a lovely display in spring and the fruit ripens from early autumn to winter.

The golden kiwi fruit is a recent hybrid. It has smooth skin, a tropical fruit salad flavour, and the flesh is golden yellow rather than the emerald green of the common kiwi fruit.

## Give them space and support
Kiwi fruit are best suited to temperate climates. They need warmth, shelter and plenty of space – the vines grow to at least 7.5 m. Support them on a post-and-wire framework, trellis or pergola, on which the long stems will make a shady summer canopy. Prune the dormant wood in winter.

In the past, varieties were either male or female and you had to have at least one of each to ensure cross-fertilisation. Today's self-fertile varieties mean that you need only one plant.

## Harvest when ripe
Pick the ripe fruit from mid- to late autumn. Store them in single layers in trays and boxes or in the refrigerator for about 6 weeks, by which time the flavour will have developed fully. Kiwi fruit are ready to eat when the surface yields slightly to the touch.

## treat ink spot disease in Kangaroo paws

### Symptoms
Black streaking; black marks on leaves.

### Treatment
* Use trickle watering, or water in the early morning. Don't water the foliage.

* Do not overwater.

* Remove badly affected leaves or plants.

* Choose disease-resistant cultivars, such as 'Bush Gem'.

* *A. manglesii* is the species most susceptible to attack. It needs very well drained soil and open, airy conditions in sun or dappled shade.

# KOWHAIS

## A New Zealand beauty
Regarded by many people in New Zealand as their national flower, kowhais (*Sophora* spp.) make a striking display in full bloom. The nectar-rich flowers are a delight to honey-eating birds.

## Flowers can take time
Kowhais can be slow to flower. *S. microphylla* takes between 10 and 17 years to mature. Many cultivars have been developed to flower earlier, including the compact *S. microphylla* 'Early Gold' and 'Goldilocks'. Kowhais like either full sun or partial shade and need to be sheltered from cold, drying winds.

## Attractive but destructive
If you notice your kowhai being defoliated, take a closer look. The pretty pale green kowhai moth caterpillar can soon strip a plant of its leaves. The foliage generally grows back quickly, but a suitable insecticide is recommended for use on young plants. Alternatively, shake the tree and the caterpillars will drop off easily; they can then be collected and disposed of.

## Raise from seed
Most kowhais can be propagated from seed. Like wattles and other leguminous plants, they have a hard coat, which needs to be broken down to allow germination to occur. Pour boiling water over seed and leave to soak overnight, or carefully nick the seed coat with a sharp knife before sowing. Cultivars can be propagated by semi-hardwood cuttings.

# LABELLING

## Label your plants
To avoid later confusion, always label the plants you propagate. The most secure types of labels are plastic or metal tags that loop around the stems of plants. These can't be removed easily or become lost. Use a permanent marker to write on the labels.

## Quick reference
When your seeds have been sown, impale the packets on small sticks or thin garden canes and cover each with a transparent plastic bag. Secure the top of the bags with an elastic band or twine, then push the stakes into the soil at the end of each row. They will provide a means of locating and identifying the seeds in each row, along with growing instructions. Alternatively, use purpose-made packet holders.

You can cut up rigid, straight-sided plastic food containers into narrow strips to make weather-resistant plant labels. Use flat paddle pop or craft sticks as plant labels when propagating cuttings.

## Colour coding
Try different-coloured permanent marker pens for different types of plants when you're inscribing plant names on labels. You might, for instance, use yellow for bulbs, red for perennials and blue for biennials. Seal with a coat of clear nail varnish.

# LADYBIRDS

## Voracious visitors
Ladybirds are especially welcome in the garden because they and their larvae devour two garden pests – aphids and two-spotted mites. Their large numbers are partly due to the fact that they have few natural enemies: their striking colouration serves as a warning to birds that they taste bad and are poisonous.

While most ladybird species are considered the gardener's friend, feeding on aphids and other pests, the leaf-eating ladybird, which has 26 or 28 spots, is not. Both the adults and larvae of this species feed on the leaves of cucurbits such as pumpkins and zucchini. The most commonly seen ladybird beetles have 2, 11 or 18 spots.

## Organic control
A female ladybird lays about 200 eggs on aphid-infested plants. Her larvae eat hundreds of aphids in their 3 week lives. Providing your garden is not overrun with aphids, ladybirds can provide an efficient and organic way of controlling them.

Pesticides should be strictly withheld as they kill the adults and larvae as well as their food.

# LANTANA

## Declared weed
*Lantana camara* is a serious problem in many warm-climate areas, and has been declared a Weed of National Significance in Australia. The sale of it and all its cultivars is banned throughout the country. Trailing or creeping lantana (*Lantana montevidensis*) is considered weedy in northern Australia; its sale is restricted in some states.

## Removing lantana
It is hard work getting rid of lantana that has become a weed. It has barbed stems and forms impenetrable barriers up to 5 m tall. Birds spread lantana when they eat its purple-black berry. Its long canes root where they touch the ground, so it can regenerate quickly if not removed completely.

The best way to attack lantana is to cut out the root ball and any sections that have layered. Cut stumps can be treated with a glyphosate herbicide. If thickets are dense, spray with glyphosate (in a 1:100 concentration) in summer when the plant is actively growing, but not during drought.

# LAVENDER

## A good home
Warm, dry conditions suit lavender best. Plant in any well-drained soil in a sunny position where the roots will seek moisture deep in the soil. Lavender will often do well in heavy soil for a while, but winter waterlogging may well shorten its life.

## Extra lime
Many lavenders come from poor soils around the Mediterranean, an area with soils that are well drained but rich in lime. A small piece of concrete rubble placed beside plants will provide lime. In acidic soils lavenders will appreciate the addition of lime to the soil, although if your soil is very acidic, you will need to grow them in containers.

## Varieties
Most lavenders need dry heat in summer to grow well. In areas with wet or humid summers, look for tolerant species and varieties, including Allard's lavender (*Lavandula × allardii*), cultivars of *L. canariensis* such as 'Sidonie', and fringed lavender (*L. dentata*) and its cultivars.

French lavender (*L. stoechas*) has showy, leaf-like purple tufts at the top of each flower spike, which remain after the dark flowers have faded. This species is a weed in some parts of rural southern Australia. In those areas, plant other species, or French lavender cultivars instead. 'Fairy Wings' makes a decorative fringe planted at the foot of standard roses.

A cool-climate alternative is the pure white-flowered 'Nana Alba', a variety of English lavender (*L. angustifolia*). The deep purple 'Hidcote' variety is more compact than the species and reaches a height of 60 cm.

## grow new Lavender plants

Grow new lavender plants by taking semi-hardwood cuttings in early autumn.

**1** Gently pull off 10 cm long sideshoots. This will leave a short 'heel' of tissue at the base, where it has been torn from the main stem. Trim the heel with a sharp knife to give a clean edge, and remove all except the top five to ten leaves. Dip the base of each cutting in hormone rooting powder and shake off any surplus.

**2** Fill a 13 cm pot with propagating mix, then use a dibber to make holes in the mix, 4–5 cm deep and 5 cm apart, around the rim of the pot. Insert the cuttings and firm them in.

**3** Water in well and cover with a clear plastic bag, cloche or lid of a coldframe or propagator. Keep the cuttings enclosed, but check weekly to make sure that the soil is not drying out.

## A neat trim
Cut off the dead flower stems and lightly trim the plants in late summer. Straggly plants can be cut back hard in early spring to promote bushy growth and encourage new shoots. However, lavender plants are inclined to grow leggy with age and will need replacing after 5–6 years.

# LAWN

### Laying turf
Laying rolls of turf is the quickest way to create a lawn, but it is relatively expensive and a large area is best left to professionals. Lay it in spring or autumn when the soil is warm and moist. Run turf across slopes – not up and down – starting at the bottom.

### Sowing grass seed
This is a cheaper way to start a patch of grass or even an entire lawn, but it takes several months from sowing before you can use it. Sow cool-season grasses in early autumn, warm-season grasses in spring. Hire a seed spreader and distribute the recommended amount of seed evenly, first going crosswise, then lengthwise. Rake over the surface lightly to partly bury the seed, then water well. Don't let the soil dry out, and protect the seed from birds, if necessary, with netting. Once the grass is more than 6 cm long, you can trim it lightly.

### The right way to water
As a rough guide, water the lawn thoroughly at weekly intervals during its main growth period from late spring to early autumn. Regular thorough watering will help the grass to develop deep roots. Avoid frequent shallow watering, as it will encourage shallow rooting.

The weather and your garden's soil type will determine whether the lawn needs watering.

### Seasonal feeding
If you want to encourage slow, steady growth, use a granular slow-release fertiliser specially formulated for lawns – twice a year is usually sufficient. Apply after rain in spring or autumn, when the grass is growing, then water in well.

Spring and summer lawn fertilisers have a high nitrogen content to promote lush green growth. Only apply it to grass when the ground is moist; if it is applied to dry soil, it will burn the grass. Autumn lawn fertiliser is low in nitrogen but high in phosphates, which stimulate root growth and help the grass survive a severe winter.

### Top-dressing
Top-dressing is an old lawn care tradition. But it is done to level an uneven lawn, not to promote growth. Top-dress uneven lawns with sand – never use soil – to prevent the mower scalping raised areas and creating bald patches.

### De-thatching
Thatch is a spongy layer of old, partially decayed grass roots and stems that stops water and fertiliser from penetrating the soil. If thatch builds up thicker

### Aerating is vital
Lawns can become compacted from foot traffic, and this limits aeration and water penetration. Break up compacted soil by coring it – piercing the surface with numerous tiny holes.

For small areas, push in a garden fork, then wiggle it back and forth to enlarge the holes. For large lawns, hire a spiked lawn roller or a lawn corer, which pulls up plugs of soil and grass, leaving them on the lawn. Fill holes with top-dressing sand to keep them open. Early spring is the ideal time to aerate and decompact your lawn.

than 1–2 cm, the grass roots will grow in the thatch rather than the soil and the grass will wilt easily. Remove thatch by raking the lawn vigorously with a special thatch rake. For large lawns, it is worth renting a power de-thatcher, scarifier or vertimower.

## lay a Lawn

1. Level the soil at about 5 cm below the level of any hard surfaces that the turf will adjoin. This will let water run off the hard surfaces onto the lawn. Make sure heavier soils are not compacted. Don't spread fertiliser now as it will burn the grass's fine root hairs. Screed the area with a screed board to make it level.

2. Position the turf around the edges of the area, then fill in the centre using a straight brick-like pattern. Use a sharp spade to cut and trim the rolls of turf, and butt the edges together without overlapping or leaving gaps. Go over the turf with a lawn roller to improve root contact with the soil.

3. Water immediately and deeply. Then during the first weeks, water twice a day if possible and don't let the lawn dry out. Wait 4 weeks before fertilising with a good handful of complete lawn food per square metre.

4. Do not cut the grass for up to 4 weeks. Couch should be left to grow up to 3 cm high, buffalo and kikuyu to 5 cm. Cut 25 per cent off the grass's blade length on the first mow, then gradually cut it shorter.

### Dead centre
If a bald patch develops in the middle of your lawn – perhaps as a result of a mower petrol spillage – do not make the mistake of reseeding it. You are unlikely to find seed that will match the surrounding grass, and in such a conspicuous spot, the new grass will be obvious. Instead, cut out a piece of turf around the bare patch and replace it with a piece of the same size and shape taken from a less obvious part of the lawn. If you make the repair in autumn, the turf will blend in imperceptibly, whereas it is unlikely to root well in summer. Don't forget to fill in, level and reseed the place from where you took the turf.

### Damaged lawn edges
If an edge of your lawn is worn or damaged, cut out a rectangular section of turf that includes the spoiled area. Slide a spade underneath and lift the turf, then reverse it so that the bare patch is turned in towards the lawn. Line the healthy side up with the edge and firm in gently. Sift some soil on the patch to level it with the lawn and sprinkle on a little grass seed. Make sure that you water the area thoroughly.

### Spring flourish
For a splash of spring colour in the lawn, plant drifts of freesias, ixias and daffodils. You may want to restrict them to a single area, because you won't be able to cut the grass until the bulb foliage dies down in summer.

### In the shade
It is difficult to successfully grow grass in shade under trees. There is one lawn grass, Durban grass (also known as LM or Berea), that does. It is coarse-textured and should be cut longer than the rest of the lawn. Because it is only available as turf or plugs, it is an expensive lawn to establish over a large area. Once you have some growing, however, you can take runners to use in other areas.

# LAWN | LAWN MOWING

## LAWN continued

### choose the right Lawn grass

As with any plant, lawn grasses differ in their hardiness and growth habits. Find the type that best suits your climate, conditions and usage.

#### Cool-climate grasses

**Bent, Creeping bent** Fine texture; high moisture and fertility requirements; good shade tolerance.

**Chewings fescue** Fine-leaved, low-growing; often used in fine grass mixes.

**Kentucky bluegrass** Not good for close mowing but dark green and hard-wearing; needs water during dry periods; look for improved cultivars.

**Perennial rye (fine-leaved)** Tolerates wear and tear; not able to cope with high summer temperatures or moisture stress.

**Tall fescue** Drought tolerant in cool to mild climates; green in winter; not suited to hard wear and tear; some shade tolerance.

#### Warm-climate grasses

**Buffalo** Easy care but coarse; can cause skin irritations; has some shade tolerance; look for improved cultivars such as 'Shademaster' and 'Sir Walter'.

**Carpet grass** Rough, easy-care lawn for frost-free gardens in a warm to tropical climate.

**Couch cultivars** Fine-leaved grass; some cultivars stay green throughout winter, including 'Casablanca', 'Windsor Green' and 'Wintergreen'; needs water in dry times.

**Dawson's creeping lawngrass** Best in subtropical areas; good drought tolerance.

**Kikuyu** Good drought and wear tolerance but needs frequent mowing; very invasive.

**Queensland blue couch** Fine turf; best choice in a warm to hot climate; not cold tolerant.

## LAWN MOWING

### Variable height
The optimum height for your lawn depends on the grass species and the lawn use – from display to high traffic. The basic rule is to cut off no more than one-third of the blade each time you mow. So if the ideal height for your grass species is 5 cm, mow when it reaches 7–8 cm. Cutting grass too short makes it more susceptible to attack from pests and diseases.

### Lawn clippings
There is no need to catch grass clippings as you mow. If left uncollected, they return nutrients to the soil and improve the lawn. The clippings only take a day or two to break down in fine sunny weather. To speed up the process, use a mulching mower, which transforms the clippings into mulch as you mow.

Compost lawn clippings before you use them on the garden as mulch. To compost them quickly, add them to a compost heap along with dry material such as leaves and mix together well.

### Reaching awkward places
An electric or petrol-driven line trimmer, or whipper-snipper, which cuts with a rotating nylon line, is useful in places where a mower is too big to reach, as well as for trimming edges and around trees. Wear goggles as protection from the stones and dust often thrown up by the trimmer.

LAWN MOWING

### Protecting young trees
Trees can be damaged by knocks from the lawn mower and line trimmer. The smaller the tree, the easier it is to damage. If it is in a vulnerable position, protect the stems with lengths of hot-water pipe insulation. For its first 4–5 years, a young tree will grow best in a small well-mulched bed with no grass around its base, competing with it for nutrients and moisture.

When using a line trimmer near established trees, lean a plastic pipe, cut in half lengthwise, against the tree to protect the bark from being scarred.

### Safety first
Whatever type of mower you use, never do any maintenance work without first immobilising the motor. If it is a petrol mower, this means removing the lead from the spark plug. If it is an electric mower, always check the mower is switched off and unplugged before you examine or clean it. Don't forget to wear stout shoes or boots; they will guard against the most common cause of accidents.

When using an electric mower, plug a circuit breaker into the socket, then plug the mower lead into the circuit breaker. Never use the mower when the grass is wet.

### Routine maintenance
It is important to thoroughly clean the blades and catcher after use. First disconnect the power if using an electric mower. Clean with a strong jet of water from the hose. Wear gloves if using your hands to remove built-up crusts of grass. The machine can then be dried and wiped over with an oily rag before being put away.

### Worn blades
Regularly inspect the mower's blades and change them as needed. Damaged blades cut badly and also use more fuel. When you change worn blades, change the nuts and bolts at the same time, as they will be worn, too.

### A mower to suit your lawn
Choose a mower that suits the type and size of your lawn.

**Hover** This is good for small or fiddly lawns and banks. The mower can be moved to the side, back and forth, and the blades glide over lawn edges, speeding up mowing around beds and borders.

**Rotary** A large area of unobstructed grass suits the rotary mower best. Rotary mowers are ideal for longer grass, but their wheels make it difficult to get right up to lawn edges. Petrol models are the most powerful.

**Cylinder** If you want a top-quality lawn, the cylinder mower is the only mower to make well-defined stripes in grass. It needs a level surface and dry grass. Small electric and large petrol versions are available.

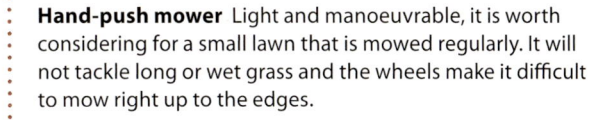

**Hand-push mower** Light and manoeuvrable, it is worth considering for a small lawn that is mowed regularly. It will not tackle long or wet grass and the wheels make it difficult to mow right up to the edges.

# LAYERING

Layering is a simple method of propagation that encourages roots to form where a stem that is still attached to the parent plant has been wounded or nicked.

## Simple layering
In simple layering, the stem is brought down to the soil or the propagation mix so the wound or nick can be buried. It is suitable for propagating climbing or trailing plants, such as clematis and philodendron, or low-growing shrubs with branches that are easily bent to touch the soil, such as gardenias, box, blackberry hybrids and the woody herbs rosemary and lavender.

## Timely separation
Shoots layered in spring should form plantlets at the cut joints by autumn or the following spring. Separate them from the parent plant, and from one another, and plant out. Do not let the plantlets become too well established because it will be hard to uproot them without damaging them.

## Transplanting made easy
A stem layered in a plastic pot is very easy to transplant once the new plant has formed. Bend the stem down to a pot of propagating mix buried in the ground. When the plantlet has formed, sever it from the parent plant, dig up the pot and replant as required.

## Aerial, or air, layering
If a stem cannot be layered at soil level, take the soil to a stem. In aerial layering, propagating mix is brought up to the wound on the stem, then wrapped in plastic. This method works well for thick-stemmed plants, and for plants, such as azaleas, rhododendrons and camellias, with stems that are difficult to bend down to make contact with the ground. Autumn and spring are the best times to carry out this sort of layering.

### do simple Layering

1. Take a young supple stem that is not too thick, long or tangled, and tear or nick the bark slightly to wound it.

2. Peg the nicked section of stem down in the soil using a loop of stiff wire, then cover with fine soil or fresh propagating mix.

3. Bend the end of the shoot upwards and tie it to a vertical cane to start training the new shrub. Water well, and keep moist in dry weather.

### do aerial Layering

1. Choose a 10 cm section of stem no more than 60 cm from the tip of the plant. Remove any leaves on the section, then make a shallowly angled nick, about 1 cm long, into the bare stem, directly below a leaf junction.

2. At the bottom of the bare stem section, tie or tape a plastic bag or other type of transparent wrapping around the stem, then fold it back, out of the way. Dust the wound with hormone rooting powder using a paintbrush.

3. Work damp coir or other peat substitute into the wound, using the back of a knife. Then roll the plastic wrapping up into position around the wounded part of the stem, and fill it with more damp coir or peat substitute.

4. Tie the top of the plastic wrapping around the stem. After about 2 months, roots should be visible through it. Sever the rooted layer from the parent plant below the bottom tie, then unwrap it and pot it up.

# LEAFHOPPERS

### Plants affected
Many, including indoor plants, trees and shrubs, flowers, fruit trees, tomatoes and vegetables.

### Symptoms
Coarse white flecks on leaves, insects' skins may be found underneath; honeydew or sooty mould may be present.

### Treatment
* Encourage parasitic wasps.
* In most cases, no action is needed.
* Use sticky yellow traps in the greenhouse.
* Spray with insecticidal soap.

# LEEKS

### Adaptable leeks
Leeks are the most undemanding member of all the onion family. They will grow in both very cold areas and tropical climates. In temperate and cold climates seed can be sown from spring to autumn, but in warmer regions it is best to sow in late summer and autumn so the plants can grow in the cooler months.

### Raising seedlings
Raise leeks outdoors as seedlings in a seedbed. Grow them to 20 cm in height and pencil thickness before transplanting them to the vegetable plot.

Several factors govern the size of a leek crop. The young plants should be as large as possible when they are planted. The soil must be rich and fertile, so add organic matter and a balanced fertiliser before planting and dress regularly with nitrogenous fertiliser or apply liquid feeds every 2–3 weeks. Water regularly and keep the bed free of weeds to encourage quick and even growth.

### Baby leeks
Leek seedlings that are spaced close together (as shown) will be small and can be harvested and used as baby vegetables or instead of spring onions.

### Blanching the stems
In autumn, use a hoe to draw soil up around the base of each plant and its developing stem to exclude light from the stem and increase the length of the blanched part. This is known as earthing up.

### Careful lifting
Start lifting leeks when they are about 2 cm thick. Ease them out of the soil with a fork, otherwise they may break. Continue lifting the leeks throughout the winter months as you need them. They will keep growing in winter, although only slowly during the coldest months.

# LEMON GRASS

### Lemon scent from the tropics
Lemon grass (*Cymbopogon citratus*) is a tropical perennial clumping grass that smells powerfully of fresh lemons and can grow to 1–1.8 m high under ideal conditions. These include a sunny position, well-drained soil, warm growing conditions – ideally between 18°C and 38°C – and high humidity.

In cooler areas this herb will do best if grown in a large pot and overwintered indoors. It will go dormant in winter outside of the tropics. Prolonged temperatures below –2°C will kill the plant tops and then the whole plant.

### Harvesting and preparing
The plump, white, fleshy base of the stalk is used in cooking. Harvest at any time by cutting stalks away from the clump. Remove the roots and tough outer leaves. Slice the white part thinly, then bruise with a knife blade to release the flavour.

153

# LEMONS AND LIMES | LEUCADENDRONS

## LEMONS AND LIMES

Lemons and limes originated in subtropical and tropical South-East Asia and many varieties prefer a warm climate. Excellent drainage and a protected, sunny position are also essential. Prepare the soil well with plenty of compost.

### In a cold climate

Lemon trees are reasonably tough plants and some can withstand quite low temperatures, though they do not do well in frost. For cold-hardiness, the best hybrid cultivar is 'Meyer'. 'Lisbon' is also fairly cold-tolerant. 'Rangpur' is the most cold-resistant lime.

Smaller varieties of lemon, such as 'Meyer', grow well in large pots or tubs and are highly ornamental. In a cold climate, potted plants can be placed in a warm, frost-free position or overwintered in a greenhouse.

### On or off the tree

Lemons can be stored on the tree and picked as needed, almost year-round. If you do pick lemons that won't be used immediatcly, always cut them off with a small section of stalk attached. This reduces the likelihood of rot.

Limes are best used fresh, when the skin has a pale green-yellow colour. Clip fruit from the tree.

### Fertilise regularly

Lemons and limes growing in the ground produce the best fruit when they are fertilised in early spring and again in early autumn. Use a specially formulated citrus fertiliser or a slow-release fertiliser. When grown in pots, they respond to more frequent feeds. Be sure to water before and after applying fertilisers.

### make Lemon butter

1. Wash 2 large lemons well. Finely grate the zest. Juice the lemons and strain. Put the zest and juice in a heatproof bowl over a saucepan of gently simmering water; do not let the base of the bowl touch the water. Add 90 g unsalted butter, cut into small pieces, and 1¼ cups caster sugar. Beat 3 eggs, then strain through a nylon sieve – to remove any white threads – into the mixture.

2. Cook over medium heat, stirring continuously, for 20–25 minutes, or until the mixture is thick enough to coat the spoon and hold a light ribbon trail. Do not let it boil or it will curdle.

3. Remove the pan from the heat. Pour the mixture through a fine nylon sieve into thoroughly cleaned jars. There is no need to sterilise the jars by boiling in water. Store in the refrigerator; the lemon butter will keep for up to 6 weeks.

For lime butter, replace the lemons with 4 large limes and use ¾ cup caster sugar. Follow the steps above.

## LETTUCES

### Avoid bolting

Lettuces are particularly prone to bolting – that is, running to seed before they are ready to harvest. It is caused by a check to growth during their development, which could be due to a transplanting delay, hot weather, fluctuating temperatures, overcrowding or insufficient watering. Always plant lettuces in light shade if possible and ensure they are well watered and mulched, especially in hot weather. Pick looseleaf lettuces regularly to stop them from bolting.

### Fertilise and water well

It is important to keep lettuces growing fast, otherwise they become tough and bitter. Water them copiously in the early morning, making sure that you apply the water directly to the root zone, where it is needed most. Heavy preplanting additions of fertiliser and regular applications

## LEUCADENDRONS

### Create a long-lasting show

These hardy South African shrubs are grown for their striking blooms, which make long-lasting cut flowers. The true flowers on the end of the branches are quite small, but they are surrounded by large colourful bracts, which create the show.

### Dry and well-drained soil

Leucadendrons vary in their frost hardiness, but all prefer dry summers, winter rain, full sun and very well drained sandy soil. There are many cultivars, such as 'Red Devil', 'Devils Blush', 'Corringle Gold' and 'Safari Sunset'. Flowers vary in size and come in shades of red, burgundy, lime green and gold. The silver tree (*Leucadendron argenteum*) makes a stunning feature plant with its silver foliage and flowers.

LETTUCES | LICHEN

of high-nitrogen liquid feeds will also keep them growing rapidly.

### Constant supply
For a constant supply, make small sowings of lettuces every 3 weeks. Grow looseleaf or semi-hearting butterhead lettuces, which can be harvested by regularly picking the outer leaves. As the leaves are picked from the outside, more leaves develop in the centre.

### When to harvest
Start harvesting a crop of lettuces as soon as the first hearts form. They should be picked and used as needed. Morning is the best time to gather them. Either cut the lettuces with a sharp knife just above ground level, or pull the whole plant up and cut its roots off afterwards. Harvest looseleaf and semi-hearting butterhead types a few outer leaves at a time, as needed.

### Different types of lettuces
There are several types and hundreds of varieties of lettuce. Choose those that suit your tastes and growing conditions.

**Looseleaf (cut-and-come-again) lettuces** Many leaves but no heart; produce new leaves if a few leaves are picked regularly. Varieties include 'Salad Bowl', 'Red Salad Bowl', 'Lollo Biondo' and 'Lollo Rosso'.

**Iceberg (crisphead) lettuces** Traditional lettuces with crisp leaves and a cabbage-like head. Varieties include 'Great Lakes', 'Webb's Wonderful' and 'Lakeland'.

**Butterhead lettuces** Soft tender leaves, loosely packed into heads. Varieties include 'Green Mignonette', 'Red Mignonette', 'Tom Thumb', 'Buttercrunch' and 'All the Year Round'.

**Cos lettuces** Upright, narrow, tight-packed heads with a distinctive flavour; can be picked a leaf at a time or harvested whole.

## LICHEN

### Easy removal
Lichen does no harm to trees – it takes its nourishment from the air, not its host, and is a sign that the air is pure and clean. If lichen grows on trees with ornamental bark, however, you may wish to remove it with a stiff scrubbing brush and water.

On paving and tiles, it can be more of a problem since it makes them slippery. Remove it with bleach and a stiff broom, taking care that the bleach does not go near your plants. Alternatively, buy a proprietary moss control from the garden centre.

### LIGHTING, LILAC
*see page 158*

155

# Lilies

Lilies have the nickname of 'queen of the bulbs', thanks to their spectacular – and sometimes fragrant – trumpet-shaped blossoms in white, pink, yellow and orange. With an upright habit, they mingle easily with shrubs, roses, perennials and annuals. Site them prominently in a bed, pot or by a path, where you can enjoy their blooms all summer.

## All in the family

Most modern lilies are hybrids and are organised into groups. Oriental lilies have huge, fragrant blossoms and grow to 1.5 m high. Asiatic lilies grow to 1 m and produce smaller flowers over a long period. Trumpet lilies reach 1.5–1.8 m high, have smaller but more numerous flowers, and grow into vigorous clumps in a few years.

## Among the lily species

The November lily (*Lilium longiflorum*), known as the Easter lily in the Northern Hemisphere, blooms in spring with long white trumpets. A good choice for the back of the border is the 2.4 m tall Turk's cap lily (*L. superbum*), with its freckled orange petals folded back into little turbans. The golden-rayed lily (*L. auratum*) is a standout, its late-season white flowers streaked in gold and spotted with crimson.

## Planting the bulbs

Most lilies grow well in a range of soils, although good drainage is essential. Plant bulbs in autumn in sun or partial shade, depending on the type of lily. The exception is the lime-loving madonna lily (*L. candidum*), which is planted in late summer to give its foliage time to grow before winter. Dig a hole three times as deep as the bulb is high, gently set the bulbs 15–20 cm apart, and cover with soil.

## Ensuring beautiful blooms

Stake tall lilies as the stems develop to keep them from toppling in the wind. When cutting the flowers, take short stems and leave the remaining foliage to nourish the bulb. Clip off spent flowers to keep energy from going into producing seeds.

**Tiger lily**

**November lily**

**Asiatic hybrid lily**

**Oriental hybrid lily**

# LIGHTING

## Illuminating garden features

With the right type of lighting, features such as ornaments, statues and fountains, as well as individual plants, can become the stars of your night-time garden. The simplest option is to use lighting that doesn't need cabling, such as garden candles or solar-powered lamps.

Uplighting is particularly good for picking out individual garden features; place a light right at the base of the item. Spike-mounted lights work well for illuminating pathways or lighting a garden bench. Water features take on a new lease of life if lit at night, especially with submersible lights, to which coloured lenses can be fitted.

## Lights around the garden

A number of small lights will be more effective than a single spotlight and, as a general rule, a warm light is best. The exceptions might be lighting a barbecue area, a patio or a party, when you could try weatherproof party lights.

## Garden lighting safety

✸ Make sure mains-powered lighting is installed by a qualified electrician, and have all mains cabling checked by a qualified electrician every few years.

✸ Bury cables under walls, lawns and paths to protect them from damage. It is easiest to do this when creating a new garden.

✸ Know where mains cables run to avoid accidental damage when digging in the garden.

✸ The safest form of lighting for a garden is a low-voltage system in which a transformer reduces power to 12 volts. Low-voltage lights are easier to install, as the cable need not be buried. DIY kits are available with a transformer that just plugs in to an existing electrical socket indoors.

## Money-saving bulbs

For all garden lighting, it is worth investing in energy-saving 11 or 13 watt bulbs, which have the equivalent light output of 60 watt bulbs. Although more expensive to purchase, their life expectancy is up to 10 times longer.

### try Lighting with candles and flares

**Garden flares** Flares are best used in a sheltered spot and are easily positioned for scenic lighting. Anchor them firmly.

**Pots and pails** Garden candles in pails and flowerpots can be used time and time again.

**Lanterns** A glass hurricane lamp or metal storm lantern gives candles decorative shelter from garden breezes.

**String of lights** String up lights for a festive occasion.

# LILACS

## A wealth of choice

Thousands of cultivars of the common lilac (*Syringa vulgaris*) exist. Single, double and semi-double fragrant flowers in purple, blue, pink, yellow and white – all have cottage-garden charm. Place them near doorways or along paths, where the sweet fragrance will greet passers-by. Lilacs bloom in late spring and will only grow well in areas that are cold in winter. Select a site with a moist, loamy soil and an alkaline pH, that receives 6 hours of sun daily and has good air circulation.

## Energy conservation

Deadhead lilac bushes after flowering. This directs the shrub's energy into making new shoots rather than producing seeds.

## Pruning policy

Lilacs can become rather leggy without effective pruning. Plants should be multi-stemmed from the base and have a total of five to seven stems. Cut out one of these main stems each autumn so that a succession of new growth from the base is achieved. After you have finished pruning, apply a balanced slow-release fertiliser to encourage new growth.

**LILLYPILLIES | LOOPERS AND LEAFROLLERS**

# L

Broad-leaved lillypilly

## LILLYPILLIES

Lillypillies are evergreen trees from tropical and subtropical rainforests of Australia, Asia and Africa, grown for their lush foliage, colourful new growth and berries, and delicate blossoms. They prefer fertile, well-drained soil in frost-free areas, and can tolerate dry conditions once established or if they are grown in a more sheltered position.

### Attractive flowers and fruit
Lillypillies produce fluffy, creamy white flowers through spring and summer, followed by edible white, pink or purple berries. All fruits are edible, although some are tart and best eaten as jams or jellies.

### Species and cultivars
Some species, including the riberry or small-leaved lillypilly (*Syzygium luehmannii*), can develop into large trees, while the broad-leaved lillypilly (*Acmena smithii*) is medium-sized.

Cultivars that do well in garden conditions include 'Hinterland Gold', 'Elegance', 'Minipilly', 'Dusky', 'Allyn Magic' and 'Hot Flush'. 'Resilience', 'Cascade' and 'Tiny Trev' have good resistance to lillypilly psyllid. Lillypilly cultivars have a compact habit and range from tall hedging plants 2–4 m high to miniatures that grow to only 50 cm high.

### Tall hedges
Some lillypillies make good fast-growing hedges. The brush cherry (*S. australe*), for example, can reach 15 m in just 3 years. Plant tall-growing varieties around 3 m apart if a hedge or windbreak is required.

### Pimpled leaves
Pimples on lillypilly leaves should not cause you too much concern, although they are unsightly. They are the work of a psyllid, a small sap-sucking insect that attacks new growth. Spraying is usually unnecessary. The offending leaves can be pruned off or ignored as they will not affect growth and will become less noticeable as the tree grows. Alternatively, select species and cultivars that have resistance to the pest.

## LOAM SOIL

### The right balance
The ideal soil is called a loam. Loams have a good balance of clay and sand, which is what makes them fertile as well as being easy to work. They are usually dark and contain plenty of humus. This mixture combines large and small particles of clay, lime and sand that, along with the humus, bind together, holding on to moisture and nutrients while also draining freely. When moist, loam soils feel neither gritty nor sticky. They break down to a good tilth when dry, but they will become lumpy if worked too soon after rain.

### Porous and open
A loam soil is a well-aerated soil, which allows for the strong, deep growth of plant roots. It is also the perfect environment for micro-organisms; the resulting healthy micro-organism activity breaks down organic matter into humus, releasing nutrients into the soil.

## LOOPERS AND LEAFROLLERS

### Plants affected
Many vegetables, annuals and perennials, and indoor plants.

### Symptoms
Extensively chewed leaves and transparent patches from caterpillars feeding beneath the leaf; defoliation. Also watch for dry brown droppings on lower leaves or on surfaces beneath indoor plants. These caterpillars move with a looping motion.

### Treatment
✳ Search beneath leaves and remove by hand.

✳ Spray with carbaryl or *Bacillus thuringiensis* but remember the withholding period for vegetables.

✳ Encourage parasitic wasps.

## MAGNESIUM DEFICIENCY

### Plants affected
Fruit such as tomatoes, citrus and apples; vegetables, including beans, onions, potatoes and turnips; gardenias.

### Symptoms
Yellow, orange, red or brown patches between leaf veins; sometimes bright colouring at leaf edges; leaf fall. Signs show first in oldest leaves.

### Treatment
✻ Acid sandy soils in high rainfall areas or soil heavily fed with potash may be deficient.

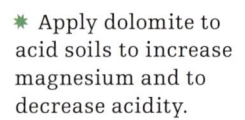

✻ Apply dolomite to acid soils to increase magnesium and to decrease acidity.

✻ For quick results, or on neutral or alkaline soil, apply magnesium sulfate (Epsom salts) to the soil, or spray plants with it.

## MAGNOLIAS

### Room for expansion
Large magnolia species, both deciduous and evergreen, are among the most beautiful of the flowering trees. Most tall-growing species also spread quite wide, so they need plenty of space to develop their elegant forms.

The deciduous Yulan magnolia (*Magnolia denudata*) grows 7–10 m tall and 5–6 m wide. The popular *M.* x *soulangeana* grows almost as big. Perhaps the largest of all is the evergreen or Bull Bay magnolia (*M. grandiflora*). In warm climates it can reach 20 m high and 10 m across, though it will be smaller in cooler areas (7 x 5 m). Its large creamy flowers appear in summer and autumn.

### Small magnolias
The star magnolia (*M. stellata*) grows as a shrub about 3 m tall. In early spring its bare branches are laden with fragrant white flowers. It can be grown in a large pot. The richly fragrant port wine magnolia (*M. figo*) also grows as a shrub and is at its best in a warm climate.

To appreciate their beauty, plant magnolias at least 5 m from the house and about 7 m from any other tree. Allow even more room for the larger magnolias in a warm-climate garden.

### Growing magnolias
Magnolias thrive in sun to partial shade and slightly acid soil with average to good drainage. If exposed to hot conditions, the leaves of the deciduous magnolias may become burnt and damaged. Sun can also damage the bark and may lead to scald. Shelter magnolias from hot winds and afternoon sun.

Magnolias need no pruning and, indeed, hard pruning can destroy the natural shape of the plant. Dwarf evergreen magnolias, such as 'Little Gem', grown as a hedge or screen can be lightly trimmed to maintain the shape and size.

### Provide protection
Magnolias have no serious pest or disease problems if sheltered from hot winds and kept well watered through dry times. Also mulch deeply through the summer with compost and well-rotted leaf mould. Birds may peck holes in buds and possums can graze on new growth. Deter birds with netting and use motion-sensitive lights to deter possums.

### Propagating methods
Magnolias can be difficult to propagate from cuttings. You could try taking ripe heel cuttings in midsummer and rooting them in a heated propagator. Layering is more reliable, however. Peg low branches into a fertile soil in autumn, or use aerial layering. The new plants should be ready to transplant a year later.

See also Layering

**Evergreen magnolia**

# MAHONIAS

### Cool-climate drama
These striking plants range from tall shrubs 3–4 m high to creeping dwarf shrubs to 40 cm high. In cool climates they are hardy in sun, but in warmer areas they do better in semi-shade. They like fertile, well-drained soil.

### Dramatic leaves and berries
The beautiful large, blue-green, holly-like leaves make for a useful shrub in the landscape. Yellow flower clusters open in early spring and develop over summer into bunches of dark blue berries that persist until eaten by birds. The most popular is Oregon grape (*Mahonia aquifolium*). Its new spring leaves have a reddish hue, then in autumn they turn bronze and some stems glow bright red.

# MANDARINS AND TANGELOS

### Best for kids
Because mandarins have a sweet flavour and are easy to peel, they make an ideal fruit for children. So if you have a family, consider including a mandarin tree in your garden. Seedless varieties are available, although many remain seedless only if they are grown by themselves.

### Alternate bearing
The characteristic of alternate bearing (also called biennial bearing) is a heavy crop one year followed by a lighter crop the next. It can cause disappointment. The main mandarin variety to be affected is the early-maturing 'Early Imperial'. Thin heavy crops before they develop to reduce alternate bearing and also to produce larger fruits.

### Harvesting tips
Unlike most citrus, mandarins don't store well on the tree. They ripen quickly and must be picked at once. Always leave a little stem when clipping the fruit from the tree. If you notice that a mandarin is puffy, it has been left on the tree for too long and will quickly become dry and lose flavour.

### Tangelos, too
The tangelo is a mandarin–grapefruit cross that produces large, orange-skinned, intensely juicy fruits with a rich, slightly tart flavour. 'Minneola' is a popular variety. Tangelos dry out if left on the tree for too long, so pick them once they've ripened.

# MANDEVILLAS

### Tropical display
These mostly evergreen, tropical climbers are native to Central and South America. They produce a spectacular show of large, open trumpet-shaped flowers, from red to pink, over a long period. The Fantasy and Aloha series are very popular cultivars. Chilean jasmine (*Mandevilla laxa*) is a deciduous, frost-hardy species with scented white flowers.

### Twining climber
Mandevillas, sometimes known as Brazilian jasmines, will twine up a pillar or over an arch to create a focal point in the garden. They can be trained onto a trellis to separate the garden into parts or screen a fence. Smaller cultivars, such as 'Scarlet Pimpernel' with bright red flowers, make excellent plants for balconies or patios as they can be grown in large tubs or planter boxes.

### Warm sheltered spot
Mandevillas are easy to grow with frost protection and free-draining soil. Poor drainage can lead to root rot problems and poor growth. A warm, sheltered spot with morning sun and afternoon shade is ideal in summer. You will find flowering is more profuse in sun and sparser in shade.

## MANGANESE DEFICIENCY

### Plants affected
Many.

### Symptoms
Yellowing between veins; veins pale green; water-soaked spots.

### Treatment
* Spray affected plants 2–3 times at fortnightly intervals with a manganese sulfate solution, or apply manganese sulfate directly to the soil.

* Sometimes soil will have been given too much lime, so acidify it with sulfur.

* Check soil pH before planting; do not add lime if it is 7.5 or over.

## MANURES

### Leave it to rot
Animal manures make excellent soil conditioners. However, fresh animal manure (less than 60 days old) must be allowed to rot down before it is applied, otherwise it will scorch the plants' roots. If you can collect only a small amount at one time, add it to the compost heap. Stack large quantities on a solid base, water well if dry, and cover with plastic to keep moisture in and rain out. When the material stops smelling, it is ready to use.

### Dried and bagged
You can buy dried manure in bags from garden centres. Scatter it on flower and vegetable beds or add it to the compost heap to act as an activator. When using bagged products, always follow the application rate on the packaging. Many contain a mix of manure and other organic matter, such as blood and bone or fishmeal.

### Manure-go-round
If your vegetable garden works on a rotation system, make sure that you always have enough well-rotted manure to cover the section of the plot where you plan to grow beans, celeriac, celery, garlic, leeks, lettuces, onions, shallots, peas, spinach and tomatoes. As these crops move around from year to year, a different part of the soil is fed and enriched regularly.

See also Green manures

## MANGOES

### Wanted!
One of the world's most sought-after fruits, the mango is also a handsome tree for home gardens in warm climates. It provides dense shade and bears flushes of attractive new reddish foliage as well as panicles of creamy or reddish spring flowers.

Make sure trees are not planted where dropped fruit can pose a messy problem. Mature trees can withstand brief temperature drops down to 0°C, but young fruit and flowers can be killed by frost and low temperatures.

### Good varieties
The most popular variety is 'Kensington Pride', also known in Australia as the Bowen mango. It has a very large fruit flushed with yellow and red. The Australian-bred 'Kensington × Kent' hybrid 'R2E2' is more cold-tolerant than most mango varieties, as is the 'Valencia Pride'. Other popular varieties include early-season 'Calypso', 'Tommy Atkins' and mid- to late-season 'Kent', 'Palmer', 'Brooks', 'Keitt', 'HoneyGold' and 'Pearl'.

### Growing from grafts
Grafted varieties are best and bear faster than seed-grown trees, producing fruit when around 3 years old.

### Thirsty in summer
Plenty of water is needed during the summer, and irrigation is required in dry areas. However, dry warmth is needed for fruit set so water sparingly in late winter and spring. Many older gardeners say that a dry spring means a good flower set and therefore heavy fruiting later.

### Ripe for picking
When mangoes are ready to be picked, they have a distinctive fragrance and are fully coloured. This is usually from 4–5 months after flowering. They should be cut off the tree with a 5 cm stem. Watch out for the sap, which can stain nearby fruit and clothes, and also cause skin problems.

### Disease control
A fungal disease called anthracnose, or bacterial spot, is the main problem for mangoes in tropical areas. The symptoms are dead flowers, leaf blackening and dropping of rotting, immature fruit. It is more prevalent during prolonged wet weather and is controlled by the application of an appropriate fungicide spray. A fungicide may also be needed to control powdery mildew.

MANURES | MAPLES

### Good sources of manure

**Horse manure** The best horse manure comes from horses bedded on straw. Manure from horses bedded on wood shavings takes longer to rot down; stack it for at least a year before using.

**Goat manure** Goat and horse manure are similar.

**Poultry manure** Poultry litter is alkaline and should always be rotted down first. Even then, don't use it near Proteaceae plants, including banksias, waratahs, grevilleas and proteas. Its smell makes it unsuitable for city gardeners.

**Sheep manure** This manure is excellent for making liquid manure.

**Cow manure** Cow manure contains small amounts of plant nutrients and acts as a good compost activator.

**Pigeon manure** This manure has higher nutrient levels than most and is an excellent compost activator. Always let it rot down before using.

## MAPLES

### Something for everyone

Among the 200 species of maple are trees and shrubs ranging from the dwarf 1.5 m high *Acer palmatum* var. *dissectum* to the stately 18 m tall Norway maple (*A. platanoides*). You can choose from columnar, conical, erect, mop-headed, pyramidal, rounded or spreading shapes.

### Check special growing conditions

Before buying a maple, check the conditions that it needs to grow. Species such as the Japanese maple (*A. palmatum*) need humus-rich soil and a sheltered spot, while others will tolerate windy or waterlogged sites – the sycamore maple (*A. pseudoplatanus*), for example, tolerates exposed sites.

Similarly, some maples prefer acid soils; others thrive in alkaline soils. Box elder (*A. negundo*), trident maple (*A. buergerianum*) and Japanese maples are among the more accommodating and easy to grow.

### Range of colours

Leaves range from variegated green and cream to purple, and in autumn have spectacular hues of red, gold, orange and purple. The beautiful shape of maple trees means that they can also look majestic in winter when they have lost their leaves. In some species the bark may also be coloured.

### Japanese maples

Japanese maples have fine leaves, which are extensively divided in some varieties. If exposed to wind or prolonged hot or sunny days, the leaves are easily burnt and fall off. These maples do best in sheltered spots and cool climates. Autumn colour also develops best in cold climates.

163

# MARIGOLDS | MARJORAM AND OREGANO

## MARIGOLDS

### One for the pot, two for the plot
The name marigold is commonly used to refer to two completely unrelated plant species. African and French marigolds belong to the *Tagetes* genus; calendulas or pot marigolds are *Calendula officinalis*. Flower colours are the same in both, and the flowers of some *Tagetes* varieties look very similar to calendulas. But only calendula flowers are edible.

### Green guardians
Some organic gardeners believe the French marigold (*T. patula*) protects nearby plants from whiteflies. Although there is no scientific proof of this, there is some evidence to suggest that French marigolds can help to control soil nematodes. If you discover nematodes infesting plant roots, mass-plant the area with French marigolds.

### New colours for modern gardens
As well as bold oranges and yellows, marigold (*Tagetes* spp.) flowers come in bright lemon yellows and soft whites. They begin blooming a few weeks after sowing and continue to produce their blossoms from spring to autumn in cool areas, and all year round in warm climates. Few flowers are as easy to cultivate, which explains why they are often a child's first experiment in the garden.

## MARJORAM AND OREGANO

### Marjorams identified
Several related herbs are called marjoram, but all are species belonging to the *Origanum* genus. Sweet marjoram (*O. majorana*) is a tender perennial mostly grown as an annual from seed. It has a sweet, warm, spicy fragrance and goes particularly well with cheese and tomato dishes. The true pot marjoram (*O. onites*) has a strong, less sweet flavour. It is also grown from seed.

### Culinary oregano
There are a number of culinary oreganos, which are perennials mostly propagated by cuttings. They include oregano, also known as wild marjoram (*O. vulgare*); the strongly flavoured Greek oregano (*O. vulgare* subsp. *hirtum*); the attractive golden oregano, also called 'Aureum'; and the highly fragrant Lebanese or white oregano (*O. syriacum*).

### Full sun
These herbs grow best in full sun and a well-drained, fertile soil. They will grow readily in a sunny spot in the garden and also thrive in large pots. The leaves can be picked from spring to autumn.

MEALYBUGS | MELONS

# M

## MEALYBUGS

### Plants affected
A wide variety, including indoor and conservatory plants, ferns, cacti, succulents and fruit trees.

### Symptoms
Small pink insects, covered with woolly white wax; often on leaves.

### Treatment
* Encourage natural predators.
* Replace affected indoor plants.
* Spray with insecticidal soap, petroleum oil sprays or maldison.
* Spray with imidacloprid or pirimiphos-methyl (NZ only) for citrus mealybug or long-tailed mealybug.
* Discourage ants, which transport them.
* Apply winter oil to dormant vines in winter.

## MELONS

### Warmth essential
Melons need temperatures of 18°C to germinate and 21°C to grow well. But even in cold districts, some varieties can be grown in a greenhouse. In warmer districts all three groups – the rockmelons, cantaloupes and winter melons – will flourish.

Winter melons include casaba melons; the honeydew melons with their green flesh; and an assorted group of Crenshaw, Canary and other types, which keep exceptionally well.

### Drainage is essential
To ensure good drainage, mound the soil into individual 'hills' 1 m apart and plant two to three seeds, about 2 cm deep, in each hill. Or sow them in raised beds. Fruiting takes place on the sideshoots. Pinch out each plant's growing tip two or three times during the season to encourage as many sideshoots and, therefore, as much fruit as possible.

### Signs of ripeness
Short-season varieties take about 65 days for fruit to ripen, but most varieties need 75–85 days. Winter melons ripen later and can be stored for longer than the others.

Rockmelons separate from the stem when ripe, at slip stage. Cantaloupes are ripe when fully coloured and the non-stem end is slightly soft; cut from the stem. Carefully cut winter melons from the vine to prevent rot bacteria being introduced during storage.

## MEDICINAL PLANTS

### Wise precautions
Many common garden plants have medicinal properties. When gathering plants for this use, avoid any that have been treated with chemical insecticides or exposed to traffic pollution. Never use a plant unless you are 100 per cent sure of its identity and botanical name. Remember that some culinary herbs can be harmful if taken in large doses.

If you have any doubts about a plant's properties, always be sure to consult a qualified herbal practitioner or a reputable book on herbal medicine before taking it or administering it to others. Be particularly careful when treating young children and pregnant or nursing mothers. If the illness or symptoms persist, do not delay in consulting your usual medical adviser.

### Calming chamomile
Chamomile's relaxant properties can help relieve the after-effects of overeating and symptoms of migraine and arthritis. Use fresh flowers as soon as they open.

### Antiseptic mouthwash
A cold tea of fresh or dried thyme makes a good mouthwash and can relieve the discomfort of mouth ulcers and inflamed gums. Gather just before flower buds open.

### Garlic for good health
Extract the juice from garlic cloves and take a teaspoonful with honey to soothe a sore throat or ease a cough. Garlic's antiseptic action on the liver and digestive system is effective against stomach disorders, and it is known to lower blood sugar levels and reduce blood pressure.

## METROSIDEROS

### Good coastal plants
Given that these shrubs and trees are native to coastal parts of New Zealand and some other Pacific Islands, they make a good choice for coastal gardens. Most species tolerate a range of soil conditions and withstand strong winds and salt spray. They are excellent screening plants or street trees. However, they can be frost-tender away from the coast, and in dry climates they will need extra watering for strong growth.

### Spectacular displays
The pohutukawa, or New Zealand Christmas bush (*Metrosideros excelsa*), the ratas (*M. robusta* and *M. umbellata*), the shrubs and the clinging climbers (*M. carminea*) reward with magnificent mass displays of crimson to scarlet red flowers. Some cultivars, such as *M. excelsa* 'Aurea' (5–8 m), have orange or yellow blooms, while others, such as *M. kermadecensis* 'Sunninghill' and 'Variegata' (both about 3 m), have attractive green and creamy yellow variegated foliage, as does *M. angustifolia*.

## MINT

### Aromatic selection
If you have the space, it is fun to try several varieties of this useful plant. Lemon mint flavours tea, eau de cologne mint scents the bath water, ginger mint adds zest to salads when used sparingly, peppermint makes mint tea, pineapple mint looks good in hanging baskets, while apple mint and spearmint – the commonest variety – are used for mint sauce and jelly, and in iced drinks.

### Almost anywhere
Mint thrives in a deep, moist soil in a semi-shaded position, but it will grow almost anywhere, including damp, dark corners where few other plants survive. You can also grow mint in a large pot or a window box, and those with variegated leaves look attractive in hanging baskets.

### Control an invasive plant
The challenge with this plant lies not in obtaining a crop but in preventing it from spreading. Plant it inside a large pot, a bottomless bucket or a plastic bag that has been filled with soil, then sink the container in the herb or garden bed, leaving 5 cm above the soil surface. This will stop the invasive roots from spreading.

### Unusual and useful
Pennyroyal (*Mentha pulegium*) is a low, spreading member of the mint family with an unusual aroma, which some people find unpleasant. A handful of fresh or dried leaves, rubbed gently into the fur of cats or dogs, is said to repel fleas.

### Creeping groundcover
Plant tiny creeping Corsican mint (*M. requienii*) in the rock garden. Alternatively, you could grow it through gravel around a garden seat, where light treading will release its peppermint aroma.

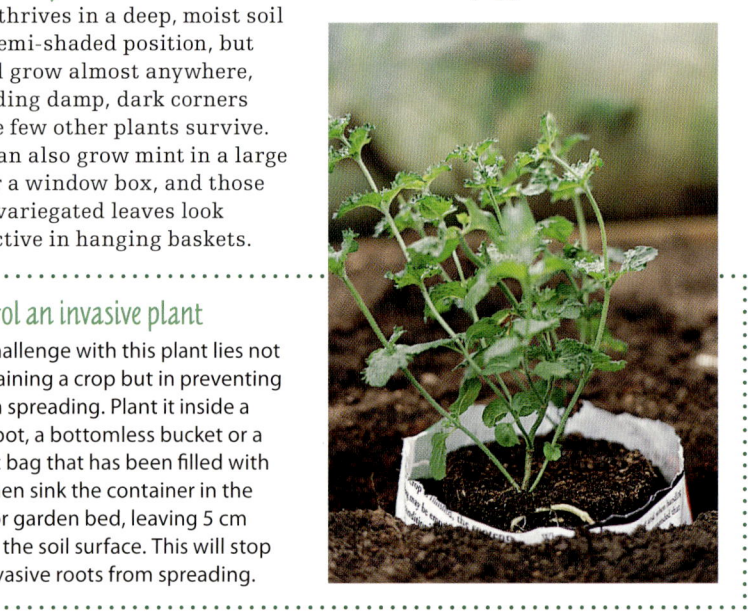

## MOSQUITOES

### Tadpole fallacy
Many people believe that tadpoles will eat mosquito larvae. But tadpoles are vegetarians, which means they don't eat insects. To keep mosquito numbers down in ponds, rely on small native fish such as the Australian mountain minnow, available at aquariums or pet stores. Avoid the so-called 'mosquito fish', which can become a pest in waterways and will compete with native fish.

### Look close to home
Most mosquitoes spend their entire lives within a radius of about 1.5 km from where they hatched. They need water in which to complete their life cycle and it is therefore likely that any mosquitoes annoying you are breeding nearby. Check all places where water may be lying, such as gutters and pot plant saucers, and clean birdbaths regularly.

### Slow-burning scent
Burn candles and tea lights that contain citronella oil, or light citronella coils and position them around your seating area. They will give off a scent that acts as a mosquito repellent. The coils also repel other flying insects.

## MULBERRIES

### Black and white
Mulberry trees have a graceful habit, attractive foliage and abundant delicious fruit. They mature into very large specimens so are not suitable for a small garden. The black mulberry (*Morus nigra*) can be exceptionally long-lived, bearing fruit for centuries. The white mulberry (*M. alba*) was the species used in the silk trade to feed the silkworms.

### Care for the crop
Mulberries are tough and unfussy. Only in really cold districts will they fail to thrive. Plant a young tree in an open, sunny position in well-manured soil, taking care not to damage the roots. Don't plant it near paths as the fruit is messy.

These trees tend to bleed when cut, so it is best to avoid heavy pruning. Between late autumn to early spring, remove dead wood or inward-growing branches that rub against other branches.

### Tree house
Mulberry trees are strong and have low branches, which makes them ideal for supporting a tree house for children. Don't use nails or wire; instead, lash the house frame to the tree with nylon rope threaded through holes drilled in the frame of the platform. Check regularly that the rope is not biting into the tree.

### Gathering mulberries
Wait until the mulberries ripen in early autumn, then spread a cloth or large sheet of plastic beneath the branches and shake the tree gently. Unripe fruit will remain on the tree to be gathered later.

## MOSS

### Eliminate a lawn problem
Moss on a lawn is a sign that the ground is poorly drained and that the grass has been badly treated. Moss killers based on iron sulfate and dichlorophen are available, but no matter how often you use them, the moss will return unless you cure the underlying problem. First apply the moss killer, then wait until the moss is dead before vigorously raking it up. If you do this when the moss is alive, you simply spread the spores.

Prevent moss from growing on a lawn by improving drainage. Spike the lawn with lawn corer or, for a small area, a garden fork. Drive it 7–8 cm into the soil, allowing about 15 cm between each spiking, then scatter a top-dressing of sand at 1 kg per m². On a larger lawn a roller-type or power aerator will save time.

### High-pressure help
Hire a high-pressure hose to remove moss from drives, patios and low roofs. Then spray the area with a moss killer that does not contain iron sulfate, which leaves a stain. Brush patios frequently to discourage moss and algal growth.

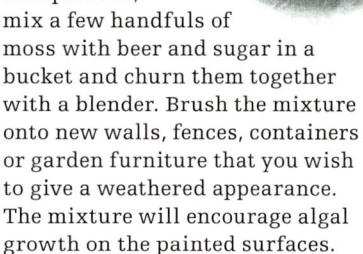

### That antique look
To give new ornaments an antique look, mix a few handfuls of moss with beer and sugar in a bucket and churn them together with a blender. Brush the mixture onto new walls, fences, containers or garden furniture that you wish to give a weathered appearance. The mixture will encourage algal growth on the painted surfaces.

# M | MULCH | MURRAYAS

## MURRAYAS

### Sweetly scented
Some common names of *Murraya paniculata*, such as mock orange or orange jessamine, reflect the perfume of this evergreen shrub with its overwhelmingly fragrant cream flowers. It is ideal if you need a fast-growing front hedge, or to screen a fence or divide up garden areas.

### Warm and frost-free
Murrayas flourish in warm, frost-free climates. They do best in fertile, well-drained soil, so when planting, dig in plenty of compost or well-rotted manure. They usually reach around 2–3 m tall, and have small, dark, glossy

## MULCH
A layer of mulch spread over your garden beds will conserve soil moisture and reduce your garden's water needs. And because it excludes light, mulch will also suppress the growth of weeds.

### Natural or artificial
Loose organic materials, such as compost, straw or woodchips, are easy to apply and often improve the soil; inorganic materials such as pebbles and gravel last well and create a dry environment. There are also living mulches and sheet mulches. Choose a mulch to suit your garden based on the mulch's function and appearance.

### Living mulch
Groundcovers form a living mulch of plants that spread out, shade their own root zones and prevent weeds from germinating. Plant them at the closest recommended spacing to give quick coverage.

### Sheet mulches
Sheet mulches smother perennial weeds and stop windborne weed seeds. You can use old carpet or newspapers (only pages without coloured ink), or buy mulch mat or weed mat in rolls or pre-cut squares. Cover a new bed with the sheet mulch before planting, then cover it with a thin layer of gravel or bark chips.

### First things first
The time to apply mulch is when the soil is moist but not cold. Fertilise your garden beforehand, and if you are installing dripline irrigation, lay the dripline first, too. When working with organic mulches, damp down the material and always wear gloves and a dust mask to protect against airborne *Legionella* bacteria.

### Applying mulch
The mulch should be deep enough to exclude light completely from the soil surface. Loose mulch should be 5 cm thick. It can be laid straight onto the soil or on top of overlapping thicknesses of wet newspaper or mulch mat. Never pile mulch up around plant stems or tree trunks, as the high humidity this creates can cause fungal diseases.

### use Mulch mat

1. Thoroughly prepare the soil in a new garden bed and rake it level. Add any slow-release fertiliser and also install dripline irrigation if using.

2. Spread out the mulch mat over the soil. Secure it well by burying the edges or anchoring them with pins or stones.

3. Cut a cross in the mat and peel back the flaps. Plant the plant through the hole, then tuck the flaps back so weeds can't grow in the gaps.

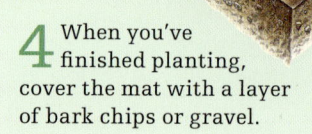

4. When you've finished planting, cover the mat with a layer of bark chips or gravel.

168

green leaves right to the ground. But they can be kept clipped to any size with occasional pruning during the growing season, or even clipped into topiary shapes.

## MUSHROOM COMPOST

### Where does it come from?
Commercially grown mushrooms are cultivated on a compost made up mainly of horse manure. When the mushrooms have been harvested, the compost is sold in bulk by the cubic metre or, more expensively, in prepacked bags at garden centres and nurseries.

### Mulch or manure
Mushroom compost is a good garden mulch or manure, as it contains both humus and plant foods. However, it can be overly alkaline and cause burning or chlorosis. Always check the pH before using it in your garden – it should not exceed 8 when applied to most soils. Sometimes, it can be as high as 11.0.

# MUSHROOMS

### Fungi kits
Mushroom enthusiasts can raise their favourite fungi at home. Kits are available that will provide regular crops for 8–12 weeks. A kit consists of mushroom spawn, some coarse compost, a growing container and a bag of soil-like material called 'casing', which is a mixture of peat and chalk or peat and lime. Mix the spawn with the compost; add the casing 2 weeks later and lightly water during the final stages of growth. The first crop should be ready 8–9 weeks after the spawn and compost are mixed, provided the temperature does not drop below 16°C.

### Gourmet varieties
Oyster, shiitake, chicken-of-the-woods and other more unusual mushrooms can be raised on logs, which can be bought already inoculated with the fungus as kits from specialist suppliers. All you have to do is place them in a shady spot in the garden and wait for mushrooms to start sprouting. Also check on the internet to see the latest varieties on offer.

### Proper picking
Snap off mushrooms at the base or twist them free of the soil; do not take the heads alone. Also, to minimise rot, do not cut the stems. Remove any stumps, little pieces of stem and other debris to minimise the growth of moulds, which may stop new mushrooms forming. To encourage further cropping, it is a good idea to fill any holes in the compost.

### For best flavour
Mushrooms taste best if cooked and eaten immediately after they are picked. They will store for a few days in a paper bag in the refrigerator, but they should be used as soon as possible.

> ### Take no chances
> Be wary of folklore tests for edible fungi such as 'If the cap peels, you can eat it'. Many such tales have proved to be wrong – sometimes fatally so. To be safe, you should never eat any fungus unless it has been positively identified as edible.

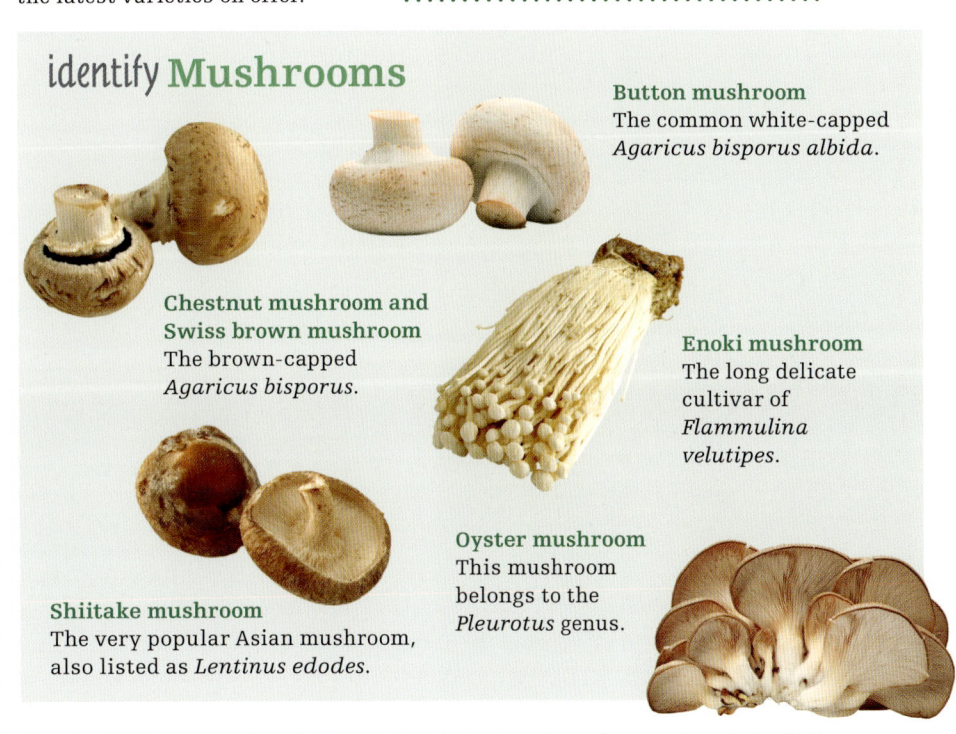

## identify Mushrooms

**Button mushroom**
The common white-capped *Agaricus bisporus albida*.

**Chestnut mushroom and Swiss brown mushroom**
The brown-capped *Agaricus bisporus*.

**Enoki mushroom**
The long delicate cultivar of *Flammulina velutipes*.

**Shiitake mushroom**
The very popular Asian mushroom, also listed as *Lentinus edodes*.

**Oyster mushroom**
This mushroom belongs to the *Pleurotus* genus.

# NANDINAS

## Foliage and berries
Nandina (*Nandina domestica*) is an evergreen plant from China and Japan with cane-like stems and ferny foliage that takes on autumnal tints in the cooler weather. It grows to 2 m high and tolerates dry conditions. Sprays of white flowers are produced in summer, followed by vivid red berries. It and its cultivars are hardy and easy to grow, and they make lovely accent plants.

## Good choices
The most common cultivar is 'Nana', known as dwarf sacred bamboo. It forms a neat, rounded mound 45 cm to 1 m high, and the foliage takes on vibrant autumnal tones. Cultivars 'Gulfstream' and 'Moonbay' have the ferny foliage of *N. domestica* but a compact dwarf habit.

# NASTURTIUMS

## Time and money savers
Nasturtiums grow fast, self-sow, actually prefer poor soil and need no feeding. In rich soils they produce plenty of leaves but few flowers. Use them to brighten up a dull corner, make a colourful screen or fill a new garden, and add the peppery leaves and petals to salads. They are a great choice for children's gardens.

## Weed problem
The old-fashioned trailing forms self-seed and can become a weed. The compact, non-trailing forms such as 'Alaska' and 'Jewel' don't have this problem. 'Alaska' has mottled green and cream foliage and flowers in shades of orange, red, yellow and apricot.

## Bright and useful
Cabbage white butterflies like to breed on nasturtiums. Plant them in the vegetable patch near your cabbages and other brassicas, where they should entice the butterflies to lay their eggs away from the vegetables. Nasturtiums are also thought to keep whiteflies away from tomatoes.

### Floral 'big top'
Fill a wooden half-barrel or a large tub with a good-quality potting mix. Position a stout stick in the centre and drive it into the potting mix. Cut a groove around the stick, near the top, and then attach 12 pieces of string to it. Use drawing pins to secure the other ends of the strings at regular intervals around the edge of the barrel, then sow nasturtium seeds of a semi-trailing variety beside each string. In 8–10 weeks you will have a display of flowers in the shape of a circus 'big top' tent to brighten up a sunny area.

NATIVE ANIMALS | NEMATODES

## NATIVE ANIMALS

Having native animals and birds visit your garden can be a delight, so long as they don't dine on your most precious plants.

### Safe haven
To make your garden attractive to native animals, provide food, water and shelter. Make sure it is a safe haven, free from predators such as domestic cats and dogs. Keep your pets indoors, especially at night and at the main feeding time for native birds and animals.

### Green corridors
If you live near bushland you will see a diversity of native animals. If you are separated from the bush and would like to encourage native creatures into your garden, talk to your neighbours or your local authority about ways of creating safe links between your garden and the bush. These links are often called green corridors.

### Best line of defence
There are several tricks you can use to keep native animals away from precious plants or from damaging your house. Stout fences between your garden and the bush should keep larger animals out. If this is too costly, focus on fencing the vegetable patch. Bird scarers such as humming lines or white plastic bags tied to stakes can give some protection. Plastic snakes arranged on eaves or balcony railings will deter cockatoos – move them around from time to time.

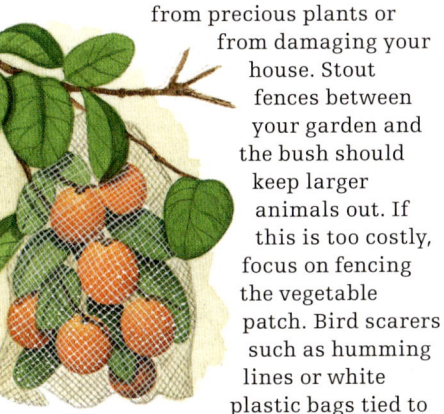

Birds and flying foxes can also wreak havoc on fruit trees and bushes. The plants will need the protection of nets or permanent cages. Motion sensor lights can work well in protecting plants from nocturnal predators such as possums.

### Share and share alike
Native fruiting plants will give the animals and birds in your garden a food source that they can eat to their heart's content. Consider lillypillies, blueberry ash and other native fruit trees.

### Care for injured animals
If you find an injured animal, immediately place it in a small box in a quiet, dark place and keep it warm (for example, by placing a hot water bottle beside the box). Call your local wildlife rescue service or the nearest vet, who can then assess the animal for injuries and arrange for the necessary care. Most veterinary surgeons do not charge for care given to injured wildlife.

### Lizard-friendly
To make your garden lizard-friendly you need to provide a variety of holes in hollow logs or terracotta pipes. Lizards also need flat, sunny spaces where they can bask. Both basking sites and holes will need to be scattered through the garden. To make the area safe, you'll need to stop using chemicals, including snail baits, as these can be very harmful to lizards.

*Rainbow lorikeet*

## NEMATODES
Nematodes, also known as eelworms, are microscopic worm-like organisms that dwell in the soil. Most species are harmless and some are even beneficial, but some are plant pests.

### Root knot nematodes

**Plants affected**
Many, including annual flowers, bulbs, fruit trees, ornamental trees and shrubs, and vegetables.

**Symptoms**
Stunted and wilting plants; galls or swellings on roots or tubers.

**Treatment**
* Dispose of affected plants.

* For 2 years, plant tolerant or non-susceptible vegetables, such as chives, broccoli, onions or corn, where infected vegetables were previously growing.

* Destroy soft bulbs.

* Keep weeds under control.

* Leave the soil fallow for a year, but cultivate it. Rotate crops over a 3-year rotation cycle.

* Plant a cover crop of French marigolds (*Tagetes patula*) on the site to discourage nematodes.

**NATIVE PLANTS** *see pages 172–173*

# NATIVE PLANTS | NEW ZEALAND FLAX

## NATIVE PLANTS

Native plants have spent hundreds, if not thousands, of years developing the unique forms that make them ideally suited to the local environment. Enjoy the benefits of their low-maintenance qualities, and take advantage of their unique shapes, textures and colours in your garden.

Kangaroo paw

### Using native plants
Native plants, especially local indigenous plants, are well suited to the climate, soils and local conditions, needing less time and money spent on maintenance, fertilisers and supplementary water once they are established. They will also support the local ecosystem, which means native birds and insects and perhaps even native animals will want to call your garden their home.

### Beyond bush
The sheer variety of native plants can give a garden splendid visual impact. They can be used to create native gardens that look very reminiscent of the local bush. But they don't have to. Native plants are just like any other plant – they can be pruned, hedged, layered, even used for topiary, to create a wide range of garden styles. So don't be afraid to experiment. You can combine them with suitable exotics as part of a more highly defined, less bush-like garden.

### Design basics
Successful gardens usually begin with a balance of strong uprights and broad horizontals. Verticals might be supplied by eucalypts in Australia, and the horizontals by grevilleas and tea trees. New Zealand gardens can use kanukas (*Kunzea ericoides*) or graceful, fast-growing lacebarks (*Hoheria lyallii* and *H. populnea*). Hebe cultivars will fill in the gaps.

This well-proportioned setting is the background for accent plants. For architectural drama, try gymea lilies and grass trees in Australia, New Zealand flax in New Zealand. For outstanding colour focus, include kangaroo paws, bottlebrushes and wattles; or the extravagant kaka beaks (*Clianthus* spp.), metrosideros and kowhais (*Sophora* spp.).

See also Indigenous plants

Cordyline

## NEW ZEALAND FLAX

### Just as tough
New Zealand flax (*Phormium* spp.) is not the same as the flax (*Linum usitatissimum*) used by early European settlers to make linen, fibre and cloth. The Maori people, however, used it in a similar way to weave fabric that is both tough and durable.

### Hardy plants
New Zealand flaxes are extremely hardy plants, growing in almost any soil and situation, including swampy and coastal conditions. Groom them occasionally by cutting back any unsightly leaves. Their flowers, which tower above the foliage on long stalks, are a good source of nectar for birds.

### Great form
The clumps of distinctive long, leathery, sword-like leaves, 3–6 m high, can be put to dramatic use in any garden, and also do well in containers. Some cultivars hold their leaves upright, while others have graceful arching foliage. Cultivars such as the 'Maori' series, 'Variegatum' and 'Sweet Mist' come in an array of foliage colours, from green, cream and gold to pink, copper, bronze and burgundy, as well as striking variegated combinations.

# find Native plants for every situation

|  | Australia | New Zealand |
|---|---|---|
| **For coastal areas** | Coastal wattle *Acacia longifolia* subsp. *sophorae*<br>Coast banksia *Banksia integrifolia*<br>Coastal she-oak *Casuarina equisetifolia*<br>Screw pine *Pandanus tectorius*<br>Coastal rosemary *Westringia fruticosa* | Brachyglottis, daisy bush *Brachyglottis greyi*<br>Coprosmas *Coprosma* spp.<br>Purple hebe, napuka *Hebe speciosa*<br>Pohutukawa *Metrosideros excelsa*<br>Karo *Pittosporum crassifolium* |
| **For shady areas** | Common maidenhair fern *Adiantum aethiopicum*<br>Necklace fern *Asplenium flabellifolium*<br>Dog rose *Bauera rubioides*<br>Soft tree fern *Dicksonia antarctica*<br>Elkhorn fern *Platycerium bifurcatum* | Rosy maidenhair *Adiantum hispidulum*<br>Rough tree fern, wheki *Dicksonia squarrosa*<br>Machaerina, pepepe *Machaerina sinclairii*<br>Chatham Island forget-me-not *Myosotidium hortensia*<br>Five finger, whauwhaupaku *Pseudopanax arboreus* |
| **For colour** | Wattles *Acacia* spp.<br>Banksias *Banksia* spp.<br>Cut leaf daisy *Brachyscome multifida*<br>Red-flowering gum *Corymbia* 'Summer Red'<br>Grevilleas *Grevillea* spp. | Kaka beak *Clianthus puniceus*<br>Coprosma *Coprosma* 'Karo Red'<br>Hebe *Hebe* 'Blue Gem'<br>Tea trees *Leptospermum* spp.<br>Pohutukawa *Metrosideros excelsa* |
| **For screening and privacy** | Lillypillies *Acmena smithii*, *Syzygium* spp.<br>Bottlebrushes *Callistemon* spp.<br>Grevillea *Grevillea* 'Orange Marmalade'<br>Paperbarks *Melaleuca* spp. | Manuka, tea tree *Leptospermum scoparium*<br>Pohutukawa *Metrosideros excelsa*<br>Ngaio *Myoporum laetum*<br>Kohuhu *Pittosporum tenuifolium* |
| **Climbers** | Climbing flame pea *Chorizema diversifolium*<br>Goat's beard *Clematis aristata*<br>Hardenbergia *Hardenbergia violacea*<br>Bower of beauty *Pandorea jasminoides*<br>Wonga wonga vine *Pandorea pandorana* | Native clematis *Clematis forsteri*, *C. paniculata*<br>Kaka beak *Clianthus puniceus*<br>Crimson rata *Metrosideros carminea*<br>New Zealand jasmine *Parsonsia heterophylla*<br>Three kings climber *Tecomanthe speciosa* |
| **For boggy areas** | Christmas bells *Blandfordia cunninghamii*<br>Crimson bottlebrush *Callistemon citrinus*<br>Native frangipani *Hymenosporum flavum*<br>Knotted club rush *Isolepis nodosa*<br>Broad-leaved paperbark *Melaleuca quinquenervia* | Carexes *Carex* spp.<br>Giant umbrella sedge *Cyperus ustulatus*<br>Giant rush *Juncus pallidus*<br>Swamp musk *Mazus radicans*<br>Bartlett's rata *Metrosideros bartlettii* |
| **To attract birds** | Wattles *Acacia* spp.<br>Banksias *Banksia* spp.<br>Illawarra flame tree *Brachychiton acerifolius*<br>Grevilleas *Grevillea* spp.<br>Hakeas *Hakea* spp.<br>Paperbarks *Melaleuca* spp. | Kaka beak *Clianthus puniceus*<br>Cordyline, cabbage tree, ti kouka *Cordyline australis*<br>Tree fuchsia, kotukutuku *Fuchsia excorticata*<br>Kunzeas *Kunzea* spp.<br>New Zealand flax, harakeke *Phormium tenax*<br>Kowhais *Sophora* spp. |
| **For architectural form** | Kangaroo paws *Anigozanthos* spp.<br>Tree ferns *Cyathea* spp., *Dicksonia* spp.<br>Gymea lily *Doryanthes excelsa*<br>Burrawang *Macrozamia communis*<br>Grass trees *Xanthorrhoea* spp. | Spaniards *Aciphylla* spp.<br>Renga lily, rengarenga *Arthropodium cirratum*<br>Tree ferns *Dicksonia* spp.<br>Pukanui, puka *Meryta sinclairii*<br>New Zealand flax, harakeke *Phormium tenax* |

Grevillea

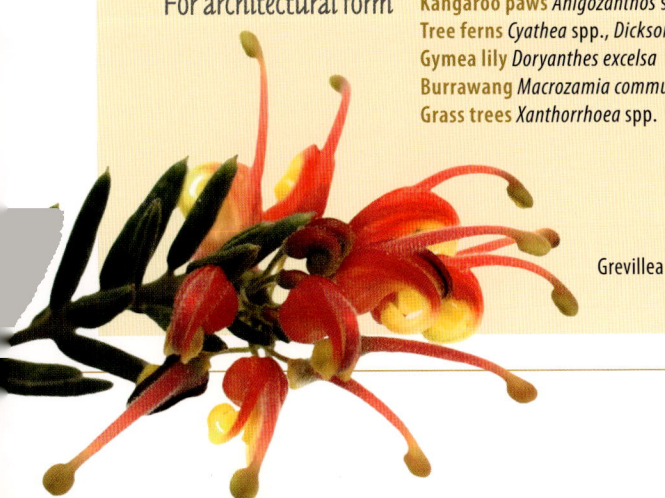

# NEWSPAPERS

## Make them wet
Newspaper makes an excellent mulch for anywhere in the garden. In the ornamental garden, it can be covered with bark chips for aesthetic reasons. Where the appearance is less important, cover it with grass clippings or use it uncovered and held down securely with stones. Make sure that the paper is thoroughly wet before being laid out because it is extremely difficult to dampen layers of newspaper once they are on the ground.

## Wrap up for winter
Garden tools will last longer if you buy quality products and maintain them properly. Before putting your tools away at the end of the growing season, remove all traces of soil and dirt, then clean them thoroughly with an oily rag. Oil any moving parts and tape newspaper around the metal parts to protect them from rust.

## Creating darkness for seeds
After sowing seeds that require darkness to germinate, such as pansies, cover the trays or pots with sheets of glass and lay newspaper on top. Remember to turn the glass each day to prevent moisture from condensation causing damping off.

# NICOTIANAS

## Annual aroma
Grow a clump of nicotianas, also known as tobacco plants, where you sit on warm summer evenings so you can enjoy the lovely scent from this annual. The flowers of species such as *Nicotiana alata* open only in the evenings, when their sweet scent attracts night-flying moths. The white flowers of woodland tobacco (*N. sylvestris*), however, remain open throughout the day and night.

## Green flowers
For something a little out of the ordinary, grow 'Lime Green', which has vivid greenish yellow flowers through late summer and into autumn. Many of the old-fashioned nicotianas are tall, rangy plants. If you'd like a more compact look, select cultivars in the Sirocco series. Plant from spring to summer and they will provide colour into autumn.

## Tough in the sun
All nicotianas are tough and extremely heat-tolerant, although they'll need a generous watering during hot, dry spells. They flower best in full sun but can adapt to sites with half a day of shade.

# NITROGEN

## An essential element
Nitrogen is the most abundant and important plant nutrient, building proteins, vitamins and plant cells. Because nitrogen is washed out of the soil quickly by rain, it needs to be replaced constantly. Dig in plenty of well-rotted compost or manure, then add a sprinkling of blood and bone or the slower-acting hoof and horn. But don't overdo it – too much nitrogen from excessive fertiliser use results in deep blue-green leaves, floppy leaf growth, and poor fruiting and flowering.

## Sources of nitrogen
Slower acting, organic forms of nitrogen include blood and bone, hoof and horn, fishmeal and dried pelleted poultry manure. Ammonium sulfate, urea and nitrate of soda are inorganic fertilisers that act quickly.

### Warning for sensitive plants
Ammonium-based fertilisers such as urea and ammonium sulfate can be harmful to some plants. Ammonia-sensitive plants include acacias, azaleas, camellias, carnations, lettuces, pansies, phlox, snapdragons and verbena. Use only organic or nitrate forms of nitrogen on these plants.

# NO-DIG GARDENING

## Proponent of no digging

The Australian gardener Esther Deans developed a form of no-dig gardening, which depends on building up layers of mulch, manure and compost instead of digging down. This method makes vegetable gardening possible for people who either don't want to, or simply can't, do the hard work of digging a vegetable plot.

Raised beds can be constructed on grass or any unprepared, solid surface. With non-porous surfaces such as concrete, a layer of gravel will improve drainage.

## make a No-dig vegetable plot

**1** Mark out the position of the bed or beds with a spade or string. Nail together timber boards to make the sides of each bed, which should be 20–30 cm high. Cover with a layer of newspaper about 5 mm thick.

**2** Spread a 10–20 cm layer of lucerne over the paper and water thoroughly. Apply organic fertiliser, such as blood and bone, at the recommended rate.

**3** Spread a 20 cm thick layer of loose straw. Water well and sprinkle with a different organic fertiliser, such as dried pelleted poultry manure.

**4** Add a 10–12 cm layer of compost. It may come up to higher than the frame but will soon shrink down.

**5** Leave for at least 2 weeks, watering regularly, so the materials have time to rot down and the layers settle.

**6** Plant seedlings through the layers; add a trowel-full of potting mix and plant them in it.

**7** After harvesting the crop, add a fresh 10 cm layer of compost or potting mix and plant again. You never need to dig the bed.

### Added extras

To make a path between beds, lay a sheet of mulch mat and cover with gravel or bark chips. You can tend the plants without walking on the beds. If you want to mulch the beds, use organic materials such as mushroom compost, well-rotted compost, or shredded paper.

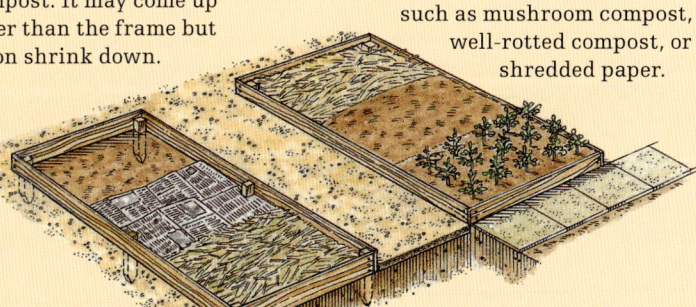

### Bed covers

The secret of successful no-dig gardening lies in continuous growing. Never allow the soil to lie fallow and exposed to the elements. As soon as one crop has been harvested, sow a follow-on crop or a crop of an annual green manure, such as crimson clover (*Trifolium incarnatum*) in spring or winter field beans (*Vicia faba*) in autumn. The green manure can be chopped down once it's grown and left on top of the soil as a nutrient-rich mulch.

### Make more compost

Finding sufficient raw materials to make enough compost can be difficult. Collecting household and garden waste from friends and neighbours or discarded vegetable matter from local greengrocers and market stalls can help, but if you have space, use part of the garden to grow a perennial green manure that you can turn into compost.

### Rotation of crops

If you have more than one no-dig bed, it is an advantage to follow a rotation plan. If you grow the same crop in the same place year after year, there is a risk of crops passing on pests and diseases from one season to the next.

# NURSERY AREAS

### For the serious gardener
A plant nursery is something no serious gardener should be without, and it is quite easy to create one. In a nursery you can raise new plants from seeds and cuttings, and propagate trees, shrubs and ornamental plants to keep your garden stocked and have plants to give to friends.

### Choosing a site
If you have space, turn part of your vegetable garden into a small nursery. Choose an area that has some shade and easy access to water. Since the young plants may need to be moved about, raise them in containers. To reduce the need for weeding, stand the containers on a heavy-duty black plastic sheet or a piece of old carpet. In colder areas it may be necessary to move young plants into a coldframe to protect them from frost.

### Label your plants
To avoid confusion when trying to identify plants later, always label the plants you grow in your nursery. The most secure type of label is a plastic or metal tag that loops round the stem of a plant.

#### Easy to set up outdoors
This garden propagator is ideal for softwood or semi-hardwood cuttings. In a sheltered site out of direct sun, dig a 5 cm deep trench and fill it with river sand. Insert the cuttings and water well. Push in wire hoops and cover with white plastic weighted down with bricks.

---

# NUTRIENTS

### Survive and thrive
Plants need 16 nutrients, or plant foods, to survive and thrive. They are divided into macro-nutrients, micro-nutrients and trace elements. Each is essential, and either too little or too much of any one of them can cause poor plant growth or toxicity.

### Macro-nutrients
Nitrogen, phosphorus and potassium are used by plants in relatively large amounts. Nitrogen (N) encourages leafy growth and the formation of branches and stems. It gets used up quickly by leafy plants and also leaches easily from soil. Phosphorus (P) is needed for seed germination and vigorous root development. It is especially important for young plants. Potassium (K) promotes flower and fruit production, and gives plants resistance to disease and adverse conditions.

Carbon, hydrogen and oxygen are absorbed from the air and water. Most plants take up all the other nutrients through their roots.

### Micro-nutrients
Plants need lesser amounts of these: calcium for cell structure and cell division; magnesium for photosynthesis; and sulfur, a part of all plant proteins.

### Trace elements
Plants also need manganese, iron, boron, zinc, copper, chlorine and molybdenum in tiny, or 'trace', amounts for robust health.

### Explaining 'NPK'
Packets of proprietary fertiliser display the amount and ratio of N:P:K that they contain. For example, an 18:8:8 fertiliser contains 18 parts of nitrogen and 8 parts each of phosphate and potassium. Choose a fertiliser with the best balance for your particular plants – and that also contains essential nutrients such as magnesium and copper.

---

## recognise common Nutrient deficiencies

**Nitrogen** Growth is poor. Shoots are short and leaves are small. Older leaves are yellow.

**Phosphorus** Plants are stunted. Leaves and stems can turn purple. Brown spots may also appear on leaves, or edges may turn brown.

**Potassium** Older leaves pucker and turn dull, often combined with yellowing between veins (a sign of chlorosis) and browning at the tips.

**Magnesium** All leaves yellow between their veins, although the leaf base often remains green.

**Manganese** Young leaves start to yellow and develop a greyish sheen. Manganese deficiency occurs in sandy and alkaline soils, frequently in combination with iron deficiency.

**Iron** Yellowing occurs on young shoot tips and on leaves between veins, but veins remain green. Eventually, shoots die back. It is common in alkaline soils.

**Zinc** Leaves are small and crowded on stems.

NUTS  **N**

# NUTS

A small nuttery can make an attractive and useful addition to the garden, and most nut trees are easy to grow. Pecans and macadamias thrive in warm climates. Almonds are excellent for Mediterranean-climate areas. And in cool-climate gardens, hazelnuts, walnuts and chestnuts all perform well.

Almonds

## Hazelnuts

Hazelnuts do well in open sun or partial shade, sheltered from cold winds. Any well-drained soil is suitable, although they prefer slightly acid soils. Choose two varieties that will cross-pollinate, and opt for bush forms if you have an average-sized garden.

Pecans

## Almonds

Almonds like a Mediterranean climate of cool winters and hot, dry summers. The blossoms are vulnerable to late frosts. Choose a sunny position with good air circulation and deep, well-drained soil; enrich with compost the winter before planting. The fragrant spring blossoms make these trees a good choice for an ornamental garden, although most almonds are not self-pollinating, so you will need to plant at least two varieties.

Hazelnuts

## Macadamias

These long-lived, attractive trees can grow to 10–15 m tall. They require a deep, rich soil in a subtropical to tropical climate, although they can be grown further south if protected from frost in their first years. Before planting, incorporate generous quantities of compost and some ground rock phosphate into the soil. They are self-pollinating, so you only need to plant one.

## Pecans

Pecan trees make a handsome medium-sized deciduous tree in an ornamental garden. The trees need a long, hot summer. They are quite frost-hardy and flowering occurs late enough to avoid all but the most exceptional frosts. They prefer deep alluvial soils and need a deep planting hole for the long tap root. Most varieties need cross-pollination, so you'll need to plant two varieties.

Walnuts

Chestnuts

Macadamias

## Walnuts

Walnuts make handsome trees that grow slowly to 15 m tall. They must spend 600–800 hours at temperatures between 7° and 0°C during dormancy in order to flower. They need a deep, rich soil, as they are very deep rooted, and a sunny position. Most varieties are self-fertilising but will cross-fertilise with other varieties if you grow more than one. Modern grafted varieties can produce nuts by the second or third year; older varieties can take up to 12 years.

## Chestnuts

Both European and Chinese chestnuts prefer a well-drained loamy soil with high humus levels. Dig the soil deeply, adding plenty of compost. All species are cold-hardy and wind-pollinated, so plant more than one variety.

177

OFFSETS | OLIVES

## OFFSETS

### Potting up plantlets

Offsets, also known as sideshoots, are a type of plantlet produced from a main plant. These can be detached and potted up separately, whether they have roots or not. This is the best way to propagate many cacti, succulents such as aloes, and bromeliads. Before splitting offsets from the parent, water the plant, then remove it from its pot or carefully lift it out of the ground. Prise the offsets away from the root ball and plant out or pot up individually.

## OLIVES

Olive trees make very attractive garden specimens and, once established, are drought-resistant and tolerate poor, infertile soils. In fact soils need to be well drained, not overly rich – so restrict compost use – and preferably on the limy side. A semi-mature tree will have quite a large spread, so take this into account when deciding where to plant it.

*Ripe olives*

### Temperatures for flowers and fruit

Olives need a warm, sheltered situation in full sun. However, they usually only produce flowers when average temperatures are below 10°C for at least 2 months of the year. They also require 12–15 weeks during which there are fluctuations between daytime and night-time temperatures. And they need a warm to hot summer to set fruit. This means that olives can be grown with reasonable success in open gardens and on farms in many parts of Australia.

### Fruit, not oil

You can purchase young olive trees and bushes from many nurseries and garden centres, by mail order or via the internet. Ask for plants for fruit harvest, not for oil production. The trees don't begin fruiting until they are about 5 years old, so the larger the specimen, the sooner it will produce fruit.

*Unripe olives*

### Good for containers

Olives do well and also look very attractive in large containers or tubs. Plant in a free-draining mix of loam and compost. Regular liquid feeding, from spring to late summer, is essential for pot-grown olive trees if they are to produce fruit regularly.

## OLEANDERS

### Mediterranean benefits

The oleander (*Nerium oleander*) is native to the Mediterranean. This is an extremely versatile, tough and useful plant that can be grown as a hedge or screen planting almost anywhere. It will thrive even in highly polluted areas such as beside roadways, on sites exposed to sea winds or in very dry areas.

All through summer it is clothed in flowers ranging from white to pink, apricot or red. New dwarf varieties such as 'Petite Pink' and 'Petite Salmon' make excellent pot plants or low hedges. There are double-flowered varieties, too.

### Keep in shape

Oleanders can be pruned hard in winter to encourage a bushy look and good flowering. This hard pruning should be done only about once every 3 years. At other times restrict the annual pruning to cutting away flower stems that have finished their show.

OLIVES | ONIONS

### Pick when purple
Only commercially grown olives are harvested when green, and they then undergo a chemical treatment process to remove the worst of the bitterness. For the home gardener, harvest olives when they turn purple and are fully ripe. They don't need to be treated with chemicals, and you can pickle your olives in brine to make homemade preserved black olives – although this is a long, complicated process.

### Oleander warning
Oleanders produce an irritant, milky sap and have a poison in their leaves and flowers. These qualities deter predators and are what make oleanders pest-free garden plants. Even so, it's worth taking a few precautions. Be especially careful if children are in the garden. Always wear gloves when pruning and clearing away oleander stems, and never burn clippings as the fumes are harmful.

## ONIONS

### Many types
Onions grown from seed include spring onions, or scallions, onions used for pickling, as well as Welsh onions and globe onions. They take a long time to mature, so if space is limited, consider growing other, faster crops. Alternatively, grow spring onions.

### Plant at the correct time
Sowing onions at the wrong time can result in plants that bolt into flower, which ruins the bulbs. To ensure success, choose varieties that are suited to your climate. In warm areas, early-maturing varieties are best; sow them from late summer through autumn. In temperate areas, sow early varieties in autumn and mid-season types in winter. In cool climates, sow early varieties in late autumn, midseason varieties in winter and late-maturing ones in spring. As a general rule, the late varieties keep longest after being harvested.

### Cut back on nitrogen
Onions planted in nitrogen-rich soil will put out lush foliage at the expense of bulb growth. If your vegetable bed has high nitrogen levels, interplant onions with leafy vegetables such as lettuces, which will help to absorb the excess nitrogen. High nitrogen also encourages disease in onions and reduces storage life.

### Spring onions and shallots
Spring onions, or scallions, are simply regular onions grown for their leaves rather than their bulbs. To produce them, sow seed of any onion variety thickly, pulling up the young plants when the leaves are about pencil-thick and long enough for use. Sow at any time of year; make successive sowings for a continuous supply.

Spring onions are also called shallots, but true shallots are a different, perennial species grown for their clusters of mild-tasting yellow bulbs.

### Ripening onions
Onions that form a bulb must be ripened. When the outer leaves begin to yellow, bend over the leaf tops to encourage early ripening. Two weeks later, push a fork under the bulbs to loosen the roots. After another fortnight – or sooner if the weather is wet and your onions show any sign of splitting – lift the bulbs and spread them out in a greenhouse or shed to ripen fully. This will take days, even weeks with large bulbs. Handle bulbs carefully to avoid bruising, as this encourages disease. Complete the ripening by hanging in a cool, dry place.

*See also* Shallots

179

# ORANGE FLOWERS | ORANGES

## ORANGE FLOWERS

### Dare to be bold
Add excitement to your garden with orange flowers. This hot colour appears to leap out from its surroundings; it always creates a cheery atmosphere. Unfortunately, many gardeners discount orange from their garden, believing it to be too bold and brash. But without a touch of orange, a colour scheme can appear monotonous.

### Colour combinations that work
For a border that really sizzles, combine orange with red, yellow or hot pink. If you prefer a more harmonious effect, contrast it with blue and purple, for example try sneezeweeds and daylilies with lavenders and salvias. If you're worried about orange looking garish, avoid using it en masse and instead strategically dot your orange flowers around the garden as an accent. It can also be softened by white or creamy yellow flowers.

### Working with shades of orange
In sunny spots in hot climates, use bright orange because the intense light can make paler tones appear washed out. In cooler, often cloudy areas, the paler apricots, salmons and peaches will look best.

### Choosing orange flowers
**For temperate and cool climates**
- Calendula (*Calendula officinalis*)
- Flowering quince, japonica (*Chaenomeles speciosa*)
- Flame pea (*Chorizema cordatum*)
- Gazania
- Avens (*Geum* spp. and cvs)
- Sneezeweed (*Helenium* cvs)
- Red hot poker (*Kniphofia uvaria*)
- Mollis azaleas
- Iceland poppy (*Papaver nudicaule*)
- Nasturtium

**For warm and hot climates**
- Kangaroo paw (*Anigozanthos* spp.)
- Bougainvillea
- Clivia
- California poppy (*Eschscholzia californica*)
- Grevillea
- Hibiscus
- Ixora (*Ixora* spp.)
- Flame vine (*Pyrostegia venusta*)
- Bird of paradise (*Strelitzia reginae*)
- Zinnia

**Bird of paradise**

**Hibiscus**

## ORANGES

### Worth trying
Orange trees are worth growing, as much for their decorative value and scent as for their fruit. They can withstand a degree or two of frost. Pink- to red-fleshed blood oranges are usually juicier and sweeter than orange oranges.

### Water regularly for good fruit
One of the fatal errors to make when growing oranges is to water them erratically, so the plants sometimes get too much water and at other times don't get enough. While lack of water will cause stress, which can leave the tree vulnerable to pest or disease attack, or reduce its crop, too much water can cause fruit to split. Many navel oranges are especially susceptible to this.

### Extra copper
Copper deficiencies may also contribute to splitting that is not the result of too much water. Copper deficiencies lead to fruit that develops a hard skin, which will not then grow with the expanding flesh. Fertilising your tree regularly with a complete citrus food and additional trace elements should provide adequate copper and solve the problem.

### Green, not orange
Colour is not always a good guide of an orange's ripeness. Fruit that has ripened in warm temperatures can have a green skin. The colour change, from green to orange, is influenced by low temperatures. Early-ripening navel oranges may also fail to colour up regardless of the temperature even though they are ready. Also, oranges that have coloured to orange and are left on trees may re-green if there is a spell of hot weather. Valencia oranges and the variety 'Lanes Late Navel' are most susceptible to this phenomenon.

### Feast or famine
Valencia oranges can produce a heavy crop one year and a lighter crop the next. Sometimes, only part of the tree is affected. There is nothing wrong with plants that do this but clever pruning can reduce the effects of what is called alternate bearing. Prune off some flowering shoots, thin the developing fruit and harvest early when the crop is heavy. This should help to improve the size of the crop the following year.

See also Citrus fruits

ORCHIDS | O

## ORCHIDS

The exoticism and beauty of orchids can make them expensive to buy, but with proper care they should flower again and again.

### Pay for quality
Orchids are difficult to grow from seed so are best bought as container plants. Because they can be expensive, check the plant carefully before buying. Look for healthy leaves and a flower spike that has some unopened flowers. You can propagate more orchids from your plant, so it is worth investing in good stock to begin with. For orchids that offer the best repeat flowering, choose the moth orchid (*Phalaenopsis* spp.) or hardy cymbidiums.

### Light and water
Position orchids in good light but not full sun, and in a humid environment, ideally provided by standing pots in trays filled with moist gravel. Mist them regularly with rainwater. Keep plants moist between spring and autumn by plunging the pots into a bucket of rainwater once a week, but water only sparingly (about once every 14 days) in the winter months.

### Health check
Many orchids have aerial roots, which are an excellent indicator of the plant's health. If the ends of the roots are white or green the orchid is healthy, but if they are yellow or brown the plant needs attention. Check the position of the orchid – good ventilation is essential to its wellbeing but a cold draught may cause it to die. Other things that could affect an orchid include too much sun, an excess or lack of food or water, or temperatures that are too low.

### Exotics for the garden
Orchids such as cattleyas, cymbidiums and miltonias can be grown in the garden or in a shadehouse. Most grow best in pots but many can also be grown in orchid bark on a rock or log or in a tree. In warm and tropical climates cymbidium orchids grow well outdoors in the shelter of trees. If grown in pots, they can be brought indoors as decoration while they are in flower.

### Australian natives
Australian native orchids, such as the striking rock lily or rock orchid (*Dendrobium speciosum*), grow well in the garden if they are positioned on a rock in dappled sun. In cooler climates, try *Bletilla striata* or *Pleione formosana*, which can tolerate low temperatures during their winter rest period.

---

### Potting mix is important
Never pot up orchids using soil or regular potting mix and never plant orchids into the ground. As most orchids grown by home gardeners are epiphytic in their natural habitat – and get nutrients from air and water, not soil – they need a special well-drained mix. Specially formulated orchid mixes tailored for different types of orchids are available from garden centres.

---

## treat Orchids for dendrobium beetles

### Plants affected
Orchids, including cymbidiums, and particularly dendrobiums, such as rock lilies.

### Symptoms
Damage to leaves, flowers, shoots and pseudobulbs.

### Treatment
* The orange and black beetles are easy to see. Pick them off, but be ready with a catcher or a hand beneath them because they will drop to the ground or circle in flight to elude capture, before returning to the plant.

* Search for tunnelling by larvae in pseudobulbs and shoots, and destroy old flower spikes.

# ORGANIC GARDENING

## No chemicals
Begin by safely disposing of any chemicals that you have. To be successful, you must adopt the organic system throughout the garden. Banning chemicals from the kitchen garden only may provide you with vegetables that are free of pesticide residues but it won't restore the balance of nature that is essential to the control of pests and diseases.

## Help plants stand up for themselves
Healthy, well-fed plants that are grown in the situations suited to their needs can better withstand pests and diseases than plants that struggle in poor soils or the wrong growing conditions or climate. Check the pH of your soil and provide plants with the conditions they need, or grow only those that require what you can provide. To improve soil fertility and structure, apply well-rotted compost and manure each year.

## Pest and disease control
In a well-balanced, established organic garden, pest and disease control is mostly carried out by natural parasites and predators, such as birds, beetles, ladybirds and parasitic wasps. Encourage these creatures into the garden. Learn to distinguish between insect friends and foes and grow plants such as lavender, rosemary or thyme, which will provide these beneficial creatures with food, shelter and breeding places. Practise companion and mixed planting and, whenever possible, choose plant varieties that are resistant to pests and diseases.

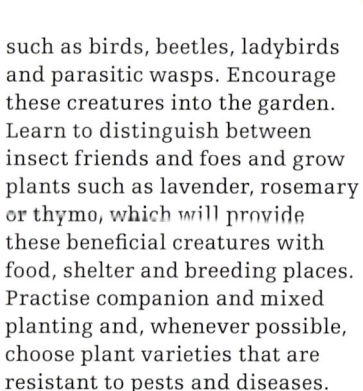

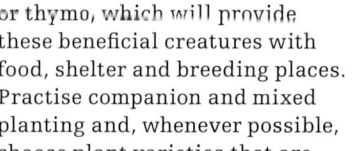

## Rotating your crops
Moving annual crops around the garden on a rotation system is important for organic growing. The more years you are able to leave before returning a crop to its original site, the better it will be for the crop. It helps maintain a balance between soil fertility and the needs of the plants.

## Dealing with diseases
Prevention is easier than cure, so always check any plants you buy or any cuttings or seedlings given to you, to ensure that they are not infected with a disease. Some species, such as tomatoes and strawberries, are susceptible to viruses so choose certified virus-free varieties even if they're more expensive. Be alert for signs of fungal disease and remove affected plant parts immediately. If this doesn't stop the outbreak, you'll need to spray. This should always be a last resort, as there are really no truly non-toxic organic fungicides.

*See also* Beneficial insects, Biological controls, Companion plants, Insects, Manures, No-dig gardening, Permaculture

## use sprays approved for the Organic garden

Organic gardeners do not use chemicals to deal with pests and diseases, but there are some non-chemical sprays that are approved for use.

**Copper** A naturally occurring element; controls diseases including potato blight and damping off.

**Pyrethrum** Made from the *Tanacetum cinerariifolium* flowers; controls a wide range of pests, including aphids and caterpillars.

**Quassia** Derived from the bark of a tree, *Picrasma quassioides*; controls numerous leaf pests, especially aphids.

**Bacillus thuringiensis** This bacteria attacks a range of caterpillars, leaving predatory insects unharmed; controls leaf-eating caterpillars.

**Soaps** Made from organic fatty acids and organic salts; controls a wide range of pests, including aphids, mealybugs, two-spotted mites, scales and whiteflies.

**Sulfur** A naturally occurring element; controls fungal diseases; may damage some plants, so check warnings on product labels.

PALMS | PANSIES AND VIOLAS

## PALMS

### An exotic touch
There is nothing quite like a palm tree for adding an exotic touch to a garden. There is a species to suit almost any site, indoor or out. While often clumped informally near a swimming pool or outdoor entertaining area, they can also be grown in formal rows along a driveway or street frontage.

### choose Palms for your climate
To get the most from palms in your garden, always select varieties that are best suited to your climate and your site.

#### Tropical and subtropical areas
* Carpentaria palm (*Carpentaria acuminata*)
* Bamboo palm (*Chamaedorea microspadix*)
* Sealing wax palm (*Cyrtostachys renda*)
* Foxtail palm (*Wodyetia bifurcata*)

#### Temperate areas
* Alexandra palm (*Archontophoenix alexandrae*)
* Bangalow palm (*A. cunninghamiana*)
* Golden cane palm (*Dypsis lutescens*)
* Kentia palm (*Howea forsteriana*)

#### Cool areas
* Chinese fan palm (*Livistona chinensis*)
* Dwarf date palm (*Phoenix roebelenii*)
* Nikau palm (*Rhopalostylis sapida*)
* Chinese windmill palm (*Trachycarpus fortunei*)

### Clump for effect
Palms do not provide good shade unless they are densely planted. Before selecting a palm for your garden, check on its eventual height. Place several different species together to give a range of heights and create a natural-looking clump. By using lower growers with taller species, you can hide the long, bare stems of the taller growing species. Some good low-growing, clumping palms include the lady palms (*Rhapis excelsa* and *R. humilis*), which are both reasonably cold-tolerant and thrive in temperate gardens, and the window pane palm (*Reinhardtia gracilis*), with its distinctive holed leaves.

### Don't prune
Palms shouldn't be pruned. If their tops are removed they will die. Restrict any pruning to the removal of spent leaves.

### Trees from seeds
Palms can be grown from seed. Remove the fleshy seed coat, then soak the seeds in lukewarm water for 24 hours. Viable seeds will sink to the bottom of the bowl. Discard the floating seeds and push the others into a mixture of equal parts of sand and potting mix in a seed tray. Put the tray in a warm greenhouse and keep the mix moist. Germination will take at least a month and possibly as long as a year.

**Chinese fan palm**

## PANSIES AND VIOLAS

Perfect for a quick spark of colour from autumn to spring, pansies (*Viola* × *wittrockiana*) are the modern hybrids of violets. Smaller flowered forms with clear colours are usually called violas. The tiny-flowered forms, such as the 'Tinkerbell' and 'Harbour Lights' series, are hybrid forms of the old-fashioned Johnny-jump-ups, or heartsease (*V. tricolor*).

### Year-round colour
Modern breeding techniques have increased heat tolerance. In areas that have a mild to warm summer, it is now possible to enjoy pansies all year round. If you want plants to continue growing throughout summer, keep them well watered and regularly remove any spent flowers. Also provide some shade from the late afternoon sun, particularly in warmer areas.

#### Constant picking
The old saying – the more you pick pansies, the more they will flower – may sound strange but is true. Frequent picking stops the plant producing seed and instead encourages it to stay in flowering mode. So you can have your pansies and pick them, too.

# PAPERBARKS

### Good drainage
Ranging from tall trees to small shrubs, there is a paperbark, or melaleuca – they are also known by their genus name – to suit any sunny position. These Australian evergreens do prefer well-drained soil, but there are varieties that can tolerate poor drainage and even cope with 'wet feet'. Those that don't can be short-lived and may succumb to soilborne root fungus, especially phytophthora. To reduce the likelihood of this, ensure that they grow in well-drained soil.

### Popular hedge
Paperbarks are well known as hedging plants. They are fast-growing, can be struck readily from cuttings and will develop a dense screen in less than 2 years. They can be kept in shape with regular pruning.

### Many colours
The bottlebrush-like flowers are very attractive to nectar-feeding birds. They come in a range of colours, including red, white, purple and yellow. Particularly attractive are the fluffy mauve flowers of *Melaleuca laxiflora*. Also interesting are the lemon yellow flowers of *M. citrina* and the red flowers of *M. coccinea*. These species are 1–2 m high rounded shrubs that are native to Western Australia.

Also good for flower colour are *M. nesophila* (mauve), *M. lateritia* and *M. hypericifolia* (red), *and M. incana* and *M. linariifolia* (cream). *M. bracteata* 'Revolution Gold' has golden yellow foliage.

See also Phytophthora root rot

### Tea tree oil
The widely used tea tree oil is distilled from the leaves and branches of melaleucas, particularly *M. alternifolia*. This plant grows naturally in Australia, on the New South Wales north coast and in south-east Queensland, and tolerates poorly drained or boggy soils.

**Tea tree plantation**

---

# PARSLEY

### Choose from two
There are two types of parsley. The most decorative and slowest to bolt is curly parsley, with dark green, tightly crinkled foliage. It can be used in the garden as a low decorative border or edging. The flavour of the flat-leaved, or Italian, parsley is stronger and more intense, but the leaves are not as attractive.

### Getting moving
Parsley seeds take a long time to germinate – about 4 weeks in warm soils and much longer in colder ones. Speed up the process by soaking the seeds in lukewarm water for several hours before sowing to help soften their tough outer shells. Dry the seeds before sowing. Alternatively, buy parsley seedlings in pots or punnets. It doesn't like root disturbance, so transfer the seedlings to a larger pot or the garden with care.

### Parsley in winter
Parsley is invaluable in the kitchen throughout the year. To ensure a winter supply, make a late sowing outdoors in February; the parsley will be ready to pick from autumn onwards. Or you could grow a few seedlings in pots on a sunny balcony or a sunny window ledge.

Curly parsley

Flat-leaf parsley

PARSNIPS | PASSIONFRUIT

# PARSNIPS

### Long growing season
Parsnips occupy the ground for almost a year. However, they are hardy and demand little attention once the seedlings have been thinned. And they are harvested when fresh vegetables are scarce.

### Success in sowing
Parsnip seeds rapidly lose their viability, so buy fresh seeds every year. They are winged and light, so keep your hand close to the ground when sowing and avoid sowing on windy days. Never sow into freshly manured soil as this is likely to cause the roots to fork. Sow the seeds along the drill in groups of three and lightly rake over the soil to cover them. When the seeds germinate, gently pull out the two weakest seedlings from each group, leaving the strongest to develop into a good-sized plant.

### Frost for flavour
Parsnips can be used as soon as the leaves die back in autumn, but it is best to wait until frosts improve their flavour. When lifting the roots, take care not to damage them with the fork.

# PASSIONFRUIT

### Passion in the garden
Passionfruit, or grenadilla, is a climbing plant that produces delicious fruit as well as lovely white and mauve flowers. The passionfruit vine is a useful and decorative addition to any frost-free garden. Its dense foliage can be used to cover unsightly objects such as garbage bins and old sheds, or you could make an appealing entrance to the herb or vegetable garden by growing it over an archway or trellis.

### Popular varieties
The most common type is black or purple passionfruit (*Passiflora edulis*). Popular grafted varieties in the subtropics and tropics are 'Panama Red' and 'Panama Gold'. Some old favourites include 'Black Beauty' for warm areas, and 'Black Magic' and 'Nellie Kelly' for cooler areas. Also good in colder areas is the banana passionfruit (*P. mollisima*), which tolerates light frosts and is fast-growing.

In some areas vines can spread easily and have weedy tendencies.

### Where to plant
Plant passionfruit in a warm, sunny position protected from the wind. The soil should be light but enriched with compost and very well drained – vines planted in heavy, poorly drained soils are likely to die from root diseases. In hot or dry weather, give plants a thorough soaking once a week, particularly during the summer growing season.

### Train as they grow
The vines require strong support. They can be grown over fences, pergolas, walls, archways or any other strong structure of wire, mesh, lattice or timber supports. A simple trellis can be built with two horizontal wires, about 1–1.2 m high and 2 m apart and supported by posts.

### Pick when ripe
Harvest black passionfruit when fully sized and coloured – they are at their best when slightly wrinkled. The 'Panama' varieties, however, are ripe when they are still smooth. The pulp can be extracted and frozen.

# PATHS

## Path style
Paths provide lines of movement around the garden. Straight paths are business-like, being direct and formal in appearance. Curved or winding paths will give a more relaxed, informal feel, gently leading you through the garden.

## Planning a path
A main path should be at least 1.2 m wide, while minor paths should be at least 60 cm wide. The slope of a path and drainage should be taken into account when deciding on materials. Any type of material can be used on level ground, but where there is an incline of more than 6 per cent, a solid surface is best.

Decide whether you want a porous path (such as gravel) or a solid paved one, and whether it should have a brick or other decorative edging. If you need to deal with a slope, a curved path could wind up the slope, but a straight path will need steps or a ramp.

See also Paving

## make a simple gravel Path

For a simple permanent path that is easy to keep tidy, install edging boards and lay gravel over mulch mat. Stepping stones could be bedded into the gravel for variety and to give a firmer feel underfoot. Many plants will self-seed in the gravel for a softer, more natural effect.

1. Use pegs and string to mark the path's line. Excavate the area to a depth of 80 mm.

2. Construct the sides with pressure-treated 75 mm wide timber planks. Brace this framework with 200 mm pegs hammered in and nailed to planks at both ends.

3. If you do not want a sharp turn, create gentler curves by cutting the edging planks into shorter lengths.

4. Staple or tack mulch mat to the inside of the edging planks.

5. Cover the mulch mat with no more than 50 mm of gravel – or use bark chips. Level and tidy with a plastic rake.

# PATIOS

### Choosing the site
Before beginning work on a new patio, consider what aspect it will have. If the garden is north-facing, you can build as close to the house as you like because it won't cast shadow on the patio. If the aspect is southerly, it may be better to site the patio far enough from the house to prevent its shadow falling across the patio.

### Levelling up
If the patio will adjoin the house, the level of the paving must be at least 15 cm below the damp course. If the site slopes sharply away from the house you may need to build a low retaining wall to contain the soil and hardcore needed to raise the patio's outer edge. If it slopes towards the house, you will need to level the ground and build a retaining wall to hold back the soil.

### Rain and the patio
Good drainage is vital. When laying the patio, allow for a fall away from the house of about 2.5 cm in every 1.5 m. If the fall is towards the house and levelling the site is impossible, you must construct a drainage channel between the edge of the patio and the house wall. This will take rain run-off into an existing drain or a specially constructed soakaway.

### Weed prevention
For a timber deck, check that the timber has been pressure-treated. Before laying the deck, cover the area with mulch mat or heavy-duty plastic sheeting, perforated to allow water to drain away. This will prevent weeds from growing up through the slats.

On paved patios, joints between the pavers are usually filled with mortar, which obstructs weeds. But if the gaps are filled only with sand, you may need to treat them occasionally with a herbicide.

### Sunny patio plants
Grow drought-tolerant plants in large containers to minimise watering. Try African daisies, agapanthus, lavender, rosemary and succulents. On a small patio, use only a few large pots and make the most of hanging baskets and window boxes.

### Providing shade
From midspring to midautumn, overhead shade is essential for comfort and safety. Solid shade is cast by walls, fences or densely foliaged trees. Lattice screens provide lighter, dappled shade. A pergola with deciduous climbers provides all-day dappled shade in summer, while a plant-clad arch creates a pleasant arbour.

Often it is best to experiment with temporary shade before investing in a more permanent screen. For example, an umbrella can be moved about the patio and put away when not needed. You may decide to have an awning erected. Awnings can be wound out by hand or electric motor, and provide protection from light rain, too. A canvas gazebo protects from sun and light rain but is time-consuming to erect.

### make space on a Patio

Just a few square metres of patio are enough to create a seating area adjacent to a house. Remember to leave enough space for people to push back their chairs from the table.

A patio that acts as an entertaining area adjacent to the house should have space for tables and chairs and a sun umbrella without blocking access from the house to the garden.

187

# PAVING

**Sandstone**   **Stamped concrete**   **Recycled bricks**   **Concrete pavers**

## PAVING

### Slabs or blocks?
Paving slabs – flagstones – are the most common material for paths and patios, although smaller stone or concrete blocks and brick pavers have become popular more recently. Slabs, blocks and pavers are laid on a bed of sand; slabs are secured with mortar while blocks and pavers are laid dry, directly onto the sand. They are kept firmly in place by their neighbours – a little sand brushed into the cracks also helps.

### Stability for the drive
Blocks or pavers are best for driveways and parking areas. If paving slabs are used for a drive, they need a firm foundation and must be well anchored to prevent them from rocking or cracking. On areas that will bear weight, they should be laid on concrete. Or lay stencilled or stamped concrete, which uses pattern, texture or colour for a decorative finish. The stencilled concrete looks like tile, brick or crazy paving; the stamped resembles slate, rock or bricks.

### Working with paving
As a general rule, the larger the paver, the better it will bed down, although it will be heavier and more difficult to handle. The thickness of the paver should be taken into account when working out the height of the path or patio, especially if it is to abut the wall of the house. To prevent rising damp, any paved area should be at least 15 cm below the level of the damp course.

### Tiling the indoor–outdoor room
The idea of the indoor–outdoor room has resulted in interior tiling being extended outside. Patios, courtyards and pool areas can be surfaced to match the interior decor with tiles made from ceramic, terracotta, concrete or natural stone, such as slate and sandstone.

### Flowering 'islands'
In large paved areas, you could remove the occasional slab and fill the gaps with different plants. These plant 'islands' add interest and soften the harsh expanse of stone. Dig over the soil in the gap and add a mixture of potting mix and compost. Plant with carpeting groundcovers, cushion-style rock garden plants or low-growing grasses or shrubs.

## choose the right Paving

**Clay pavers** Great strength and hardness; warm, earthy colours that don't fade; corrosion-resistant around swimming pools.

**Concrete pavers** Made from a combination of sand, cement and aggregates, with oxide added for a range of fade-resistant colours; surfaces resemble natural products; interlocking shapes give driveway strength; can take weight.

**House bricks** Versatile alternative to commercial pavers; decorative effects; great for paths and courtyards; recycled sandstocks provide rustic charm.

**Granite** Hard-wearing igneous rock; available as small cobbles; great border feature or inset.

**Sandstone** Soft, easy-to-work sedimentary rock; natural non-slip surface; split stone for crazy paving or cut stone for a formal look.

**Slate** Metamorphic rock; difficult to stain; range of colours; relatively easy to cut.

**Terracotta or unglazed ceramic tiles** Fade-resistant surface; rich earthy colours.

**Glazed ceramic tiles** Wide range of colours; hard-wearing; slip-resistant surfaces.

**Concrete pavers**

PAWPAWS | PEACHES AND NECTARINES

# PAWPAWS

## What to plant
Trees of the pawpaw (*Carica papaya*), also known as the papaya, may be male, female or hermaphrodite. True females bear large ivory flowers, one per short stalk, and the ovary resembles a mini pawpaw. Males bear profuse flowers on long, drooping stems. Some may produce hermaphrodite flowers, which self-pollinate and produce long delicious fruit.

Plant two or three female plants with one male plant, or plant a couple of bisexual trees. They can be spaced as close as 1.5 m.

## Subtropics and tropics
Pawpaws need a subtropical to tropical climate and thrive in a sunny position with a rich, well-composted, freely draining and slightly acid soil of about pH 6.5. Adjust very acid soils with an application of dolomite.

## For quality fruit
Trees need reliable watering and thick mulching to ensure good fruit quality. Under ideal conditions, they start producing fruit within 9–12 months of being planted. They reach peak production at 2 years, declining gradually from then onwards.

You can harvest pawpaw almost year-round, once the tree is 9–12 months old. To test for ripeness, press your thumbnail into the top of the fruit at the stem end. If a milky exudate appears, it isn't ready yet.

# PEACHES AND NECTARINES

Peach

Nectarine

## When a peach is not a peach
The difference between a peach and a nectarine is that the peach has a downy skin, whereas its close cousin, the nectarine, is smooth. They are often described as freestone or clingstone – the flesh of the latter adheres to the stone, the former separates.

## High or low chill?
Traditionally, peach and nectarine trees needed periods of winter cold to fruit satisfactorily. These are known as high chill varieties, which need about 850 hours of chilling (below 7°C). Now medium chill varieties and low chill varieties have been bred, which are ideal for temperate and subtropical areas respectively.

Peaches and nectarines fruit well for 12–15 years. Most varieties are self-pollinating, so you can plant just one tree. Recent breeding for harder fleshed, easy-to-transport commercial crops means that you must seek out older varieties if you want melting, juicy fruit.

## When to plant
Peach and nectarine trees should be planted in early winter. They will thrive only in a sheltered, sunny position and well-drained, enriched soil. Because the trees flower in late winter or early spring, there is a danger in cool climates that the flowers may be damaged by frost. Take care not to plant them in frost pockets.

## Flowering peaches
Ornamental peaches produce spectacular displays of flowers in colours ranging from white to pink and red before the leaves appear. Some varieties flower in winter and suit warm climates, while the later spring-flowering varieties are best for colder areas.

### Watch out for these
Stone fruit trees suffer from several pests and diseases. Fruit flies are a serious pest, and peach leaf curl disease, silver leaf and crown gall can all infect trees.

# PEARS | PEAS

## PEARS

### Two types
Two species of pear are commonly grown – the European pear (*Pyrus communis*) and the nashi or Asian pear (*P. pyrifolia*). European pears are grown in a similar climate to apples while nashi pears can be grown in slightly warmer areas.

Most varieties are somewhat self-fertile, but plant a second variety to ensure good pollination. In fact, two varieties can be grafted onto the same tree.

### Similar to apples
Both species can be trained like apples – as a vase-shaped tree, a central leader, cordon or espalier. Plant them in a sunny, sheltered position, preferably in deep loamy soil that will retain moisture in summer. They tolerate humidity and warmth better than apples.

### Testing for ripeness
Harvest European pears in late summer to early autumn, before they are fully ripe. To test, lift each fruit in your hand and give it a slight twist. If it parts readily from the spur, it is ready. Store in a cool, dark place until fully ripe.

Nashi pears can be picked when fully ripe, which is when the skin begins to turn yellow and the flesh gives slightly when touched. They are easily damaged at this stage so handle them with care.

## PEAS

### Tough or tender pods
The common shelling peas are peas that rapidly develop their seeds (the peas) within a tough, fibrous pod. Those that delay seed development and keep a crisp, tender pod for some time include the snow peas (mangetout, or 'eat all'). An intermediate group has been developed – the sugar snap pea is an example. They retain a tender pod while the seeds develop normally.

### Ensuring a good crop
Peas grow best in rich, well-drained soil, with a pH of 6.0–6.5, in a sunny position. They are cold-resistant but will rot in cold, wet conditions. You will get better crops from soil where peas have not been grown for at least two seasons, because planting in a different area each year helps to prevent the build-up of soilborne pests and diseases.

### Deterring birds
Birds can be a problem for emerging seedlings. Protect recently sown seeds by covering the rows with netting or clusters of twigs. Water lightly once, then not again until the seedlings have emerged (overwatering can cause seeds to rot). You should remove the netting or twigs once the seedlings are 10 cm high.

### Sturdy support
Support for climbing and dwarf varieties is essential. Without it, the plants will collapse onto the ground where they will attract slugs and dirt, and you may lose a large part of the crop.

### Picking peas
When the pods of shelling peas seem to have reached their full length, check daily to feel if the peas are swelling inside. Aim to pick the pods when the seeds are well developed but before they are fully mature. Harvest snow peas and sugar snap peas when the pods are about 5–10 cm long. Snow pea pods should be full but flat, the seeds not yet swelling. For sugar snap peas, wait until the seeds are well developed. Go over your plants every day because regular picking will prolong flowering and help maintain the supply.

'Kelvedon Wonder' shelling pea

'Early Onward' shelling pea

## support Peas

**1** Use short, twiggy sticks as the first support. The sticks will help the peas start climbing when they are about 7–8 cm high

**2** Once plant growth is strong, provide taller sticks, wires or plastic mesh to suit the ultimate height – from 45 cm to 1.8 cm – of the pea variety you are growing.

190

# PEAT AND PEAT SUBSTITUTES

### The future of peat
Until recently, peat was widely used in potting mixes. But with increasing environmental concern about the importance of wetlands, its use is being discouraged in many parts of the world. In New Zealand peat is abundant, and while it is still being harvested and used, significant areas are protected. Australia is subject to a code of practice. Some good peat substitutes are now on the market. They include coconut coir, composted pine bark and, in New Zealand, punga fibre, made from ground tree-fern stems.

### Using peat substitutes
Coconut coir comes in bales or compressed blocks and is used to increase water retention in potting mixes, particularly in seedling and propagation mixes. Simply soak the block in water to swell it back to its original size. Many coir products are deficient in calcium and will benefit from the addition of gypsum (a source of calcium).

### Sphagnum moss
Sphagnum moss peat, a very high-quality coarse peat, is available in bulk for use in potting mixes in New Zealand. But in Australia it is confined to use in specialist orchid and epiphyte mixes or for disguising the top of pots.

# PEONIES

### Peony types
There are two types: herbaceous peonies, which grow to 50–75 cm and flower in late spring; and tree peonies, deciduous, soft-wooded 1.2–2.5 m shrubs that bear very large flowers. Both prefer cool to cold climates, a deep, rich, moist soil and a sunny or lightly shaded position sheltered from winds. They need heavy feeding and dislike root disturbance.

### Establishing new plants
Propagate herbaceous peonies by dividing the roots in winter. Set divisions no deeper than 2.5 cm in enriched soil, mulch in spring and water well in dry spells. They may not flower for 2–3 years. Tree peonies are grafted onto pieces of herbaceous peony root, a slow process that explains their price.

### Why peonies fail to flower
If peonies fail for flower, check:

✽ Your winters may be too warm. The plants grow, but flower buds shrivel. Plant tree peonies, which tolerate slightly warmer winters.

✽ Your garden soil is too dry. Mulch and water regularly.

✽ The plants are young. New plants flower in their third year.

✽ The plants get too much shade. Transplant to a sunnier position.

# PERENNIALS

Cannas

## PERENNIALS

### What are they?
Perennials are long-lived plants with flexible rather than woody stems that grow each year from hardy rootstocks. The parts above ground usually die back in winter or are cut back in late autumn or winter as they become untidy. They flower year after year in the same spot, the backbone of a herbaceous border.

### Extended colour
Most commonly grown perennials flower in spring to early summer, when many begin to fade. Extend flowering by pruning back spent flowers to encourage reflowering in plants such as penstemons and many salvias, and by including heat-tolerant and late-flowering agapanthus, rudbeckia, red hot pokers and purple coneflowers. Japanese windflowers (*Anemone* × *hybrida*), sedums, dahlias and perennial asters will flower in late summer and autumn.

### Looking ahead
Most perennials are quite small when sold in pots in winter, but within 2–3 months they may have grown to 1 m or more. When you are buying, check catalogues or plant labels for eventual sizes to ensure that you have the space to plant them and they won't obscure other plants in the bed.

### Planting potted perennials
Water thoroughly to give both roots and stems a boost. When planting out, soak the bottom of each planting hole, especially during dry weather. Make sure that the crown of the plant is level with the surface of the soil.

### Self-sown for savings
Increase your plant stock at no cost by growing self-seeding perennials. Among these are dwarf campanulas, columbines, fennel, cranesbills and lupins. When tidying up the garden, collect seedpods from plants and sow them elsewhere in the garden.

### Increasing flower power
Disbud perennials with large flowers, such as chrysanthemums, to produce a showy single bloom. Wait until most of the side buds have emerged, then remove all buds except the central one. The flower will be magnificent.

## know the hardiest Perennials

Perennials can thrive in difficult conditions and are remarkably long lived. Here are some of the toughest:

### In poor and dry soils
❋ *Anthemis* spp. ❋ Dietes ❋ Gazania ❋ Gaura ❋ *Potentilla* spp. ❋ Red valerian (*Centranthus ruber*) ❋ Seaside daisy (*Erigeron karvinskianus*) ❋ Yarrow (*Achillea* spp.)

### In shade
❋ Acanthus ❋ Bergenia ❋ Blue ginger (*Dichorisandra thyrsiflora*) ❋ Clivia ❋ Foxglove ❋ Gingers (*Alpinia*, *Etlingera* and *Zingiber* spp.) ❋ Hellebore ❋ Lady's mantle (*Alchemilla* spp.) ❋ Lungwort (*Pulmonaria* spp.) ❋ Monkshood (*Aconitum* spp.) ❋ Plectranthus

### In hot summer areas
❋ African daisies (*Arctotis* × *hybrida* cvs, *Osteospermum fruticosum*) ❋ Agapanthus ❋ Aster ❋ Canna ❋ Catmint ❋ Clivia ❋ Cut leaf daisy (*Brachyscome* spp.) ❋ Daylily ❋ Dietes ❋ Euphorbia ❋ Gaura ❋ Gazania ❋ Kangaroo paw (*Anigozanthos* spp.) ❋ Penstemon ❋ Purple coneflower (*Echinacea purpureum*) ❋ Red hot poker ❋ Rudbeckia ❋ Russian sage (*Perovskia atriplicifolia*) ❋ Salvia ❋ Sea holly (*Eryngium maritimum*) ❋ Sedum ❋ Strelitzia ❋ Thrift (*Armeria* spp.) ❋ Yarrow (*Achillea* spp.)

# PERFUMED PLANTS

All too often, when planning a garden, scent is an afterthought or even an accidental inclusion. With a careful choice of plants, you could enjoy a perfumed garden through most of the year.

### Fragrance to the fore
Ensure that your fragrant plants are placed well to the fore, and don't waste their sweetness at the back of a border. Also choose plants whose scents complement one another and do not clash.

### Scented strategy
Site fragrant plants where they will do the most good – outside a window that is often left open in summer, on an arch over a path that is used most, or in sunny, sheltered spots where their scent won't be dispersed by the wind. Drape a rambling rose over the front door, or grow gardenias and lavenders in pots on the patio.

### Not only flowers
When you are planning a fragrant garden, don't just think about the scent from flowers. Many plants have fragrant leaves, which will add perfume to your garden for most of the year. Sometimes the leaves have to be crushed to release their scent, but plants such as lavender, rosemary, some sages, scented geraniums and thyme only need to be brushed against. To make the most of fragrant foliage, place the plants in beds near a path so the leaves are easily brushed or touched and the fragrance released.

### Hidden delights
Not all fragrant plants have spectacular flowers. Some flowers use their fragrance to attract pollinators and so plants such as osmanthus have no use for large or showy flowers. These plants can be hidden among other, more visually interesting specimens but their scent will still perfume the surroundings.

### Not always wanted
Some floral perfumes are very strong and may not be pleasant. Privets, cestrums, particularly the night-scented form, and hawthorn can be cloyingly sweet; they are weeds in many areas and should be removed from gardens or bushland.

### Added pleasure
Someone with fading eyesight will enjoy a gravel path – so they know where they are – bordered with plants of contrasting scents. Try rosemary and thyme, pinks and stocks, phloxes and nicotianas, as well as roses, mock orange (*Philadelphus* spp. and cvs) and murrayas. In cool-climate areas substitute Mexican orange blossom (*Choisya ternata*).

Roses

Mock orange

## select Perfumed plants through the seasons

### Spring
* Carnations and pinks * Freesia
* Hyacinth * Paperwhite narcissus (*Narcissus papyraceus*) * Wallflower

### Summer
* Alyssum * Chocolate cosmos (*Cosmos atrosanguineus*) * Gardenia * Lavender
* Madonna lily * Nicotianas (*Nicotiana alata*, *N. sylvestris*) * Night-scented stock (*Matthiola longipetala*)

### Autumn
* Butterfly bush (*Buddleja davidii*)
* Chaste tree (*Vitex agnus-castus*) * Sage

### Winter
* Mignonette (*Reseda* spp.) * Sweet box (*Sarcococca hookeriana*) * Sweet daphne (*Daphne odora*)

Phlox

193

# PERMACULTURE

## What is permaculture?
The Australian pioneer of organic gardening, Bill Mollison, coined the term 'permaculture' for a system of sustainable gardening without inorganic fertilisers or heavy use of pesticides. In a permaculture garden, you grow the widest possible variety of species and use every space. This discourages pests and gives you a constant source of organic matter in trimmings. Combine these with kitchen waste in compost and you return to the soil all the goodness taken from it by your crops.

## Ten permaculture principles
* Improve the soil before you plant the garden, using plenty of well-rotted organic matter. In poor clay soil, planting potatoes or sweet potatoes is a good way to start improving it.

* Grow different plants and crowd as many as you can onto your piece of land.

* Use every surface, horizontal and vertical, for your plants.

* Have a compost heap and use it to recycle all the organic waste from your home and garden. Spread the compost on the soil to encourage worms and to improve its fertility.

* Attract birds and bees by providing clean water and plenty of flowers.

* Intermingle different types of vegetables, rather than planting them in blocks of one variety.

* Destroy pests by hand, keeping a constant eye out for them.

* Keep chickens, although first check with the local authority on regulations. Feed them kitchen scraps and let them scratch in the garden beds after harvest. Add their manure to the compost.

* Plant near the house those herbs or vegetables that you use most often, or the ones that need the most regular attention.

* Include a pond for insect-eating frogs and for aquatic crops such as water chestnuts. However, do not introduce goldfish.

# PERGOLAS

## A seat in the shade
A pergola is a framework of columns and beams designed to carry climbing plants and provide a sheltered walkway or a shaded place in which to sit. It can be either freestanding or anchored to a wall. In some areas building permission is required to erect a pergola, so check your local authority's requirements before beginning construction.

## Building a pergola
You can buy ready-made kits from many hardware stores. In general, pergolas consist of uprights supporting horizontal beams and crossbeams (struts). Most are built of timber, although uprights may be made of stone or metal. Timber is the easiest option if you plan to do it yourself – make sure it has been pressure-treated.

## Wind warning
If a pergola will be attached to the house, make the framework strong but light and the foundations firm. When fully grown, the foliage of clematis, climbing roses and wisterias can exert a weighty pull, which increases in intensity in high winds.

## Sound barrier
A pergola erected on a terrace or balcony will reduce noise. Having built the frame, place a tub at the foot of each upright and plant climbers. When fully grown, their foliage will muffle traffic noise and neighbourhood sounds.

## Covering the pergola
Choose low-maintenance climbers, such as jasmines or wisterias, for a pergola. Bougainvillea and mandevillas are ideal in warm, frost-free climates. Plant climbers leaning towards the supports so that they grow upwards quickly.

See also Climbers

### Height and footings
The height of the pergola should be at least 2.2 m to enable an adult to move around freely underneath. The crossbeams should be of the same strength as the uprights.

Larger pergolas need concrete footings to hold the uprights securely in place. There are several types of bracket for fixing the upright to the concrete, but all prevent the wood from rotting below ground.

# PESTICIDES

## What is a pesticide?
A pesticide is any substance or mixture of substances intended to prevent, destroy, repel or control a pest. In the garden, a 'pest' might be insects, mites and slugs, or a disease or a weed.

## The thing about pesticides
Pesticides are not only potentially dangerous to users but may also be harmful to beneficial creatures and wildlife. Pests may become resistant to pesticides over time if they are overused or misused.

For these and other reasons, pesticides may be deregistered and withdrawn from sale. It is important to check that any pesticides you have stored in your shed are still registered for use. Also note that it is the active ingredient of a pesticide that is registered, not the product name.

## When to use
Before using a pesticide, you must correctly identify the pest that is causing the problem. First, you should attempt to control it by methods such as pruning, picking grubs off plants and removing weeds by hand. Then you should select the correct type of pesticide for the specific problem, choosing the least toxic. If you are not sure, seek appropriate advice first.

Pesticides include:
* Fungicides for fungal diseases
* Herbicides to control weeds
* Insecticides to control insects
* Miticides to control mites
* Molluscicides for slugs and snails
* Nematicides for nematodes.

## Biological pesticides
The active constituents are living organisms, usually a bacteria or a virus, and are mostly insecticides. They target a specific pest or pest group and are not harmful to people and 'good bugs'. The most common products are those containing *Bacillus thuringiensis*.

## Botanical pesticides
The active constituents are plant extracts. The best known are the pyrethrins. They are contact insecticides, which knock down insects immediately. They break down quickly, which means they don't persist in the environment.

## Horticultural oils
Petroleum oil products work by suffocation and are particularly effective on scales and mites.

## Insecticidal soaps
The active constituents are the salts of fatty acids, which disrupt an insect's cell membranes so the cells leak, which kills the insect. They are sprays, and must make direct contact with the pest. Best on soft-bodied pests, they have no residual effects, so once dry, you can reintroduce beneficial insects.

## apply Pesticides
Here are some of the most common application methods:

**Pressurised aerosol cans** Premixed pesticides can be pointed and sprayed to spot-treat minor problems.

**Hose-end sprayers** They fit on the end of a garden hose and mix pesticides with water from the hose. They are convenient for treating large areas.

**Pressure sprayers** Both canister (below) and backpack models are hand-pumped to deliver a solution of liquid concentrates or wettable powders and water. The nozzle can be adjusted for either spot application or broad coverage.

**Dusters** Containers fitted with a shaker top sprinkle the pesticide over a small area.

## Mineral pesticides
These products are usually fungicides and/or miticides and contain such minerals as copper and sulfur. Avoid using them in hot weather or for about 2 weeks after applying a horticultural oil spray. Some vegetable crops are particularly sensitive to sulfur, so read the label carefully.

## Synthetic pesticides
These manufactured chemicals need to be handled carefully, as some are extremely toxic and will have lasting effects on beneficial species. They include carbamates, organophosphates and synthetic pyrethroids. Read the label and have a good reason for using them.

# P — PESTS | PETUNIAS

## PESTS

### Large herbivores
Wallabies, possums, fruit bats and rabbits can all be problems. You must never harm native animals, but you can deter them with unpleasant-tasting sprays, better fencing or tree collars that stop them climbing.

### Leaf and flower eaters
Caterpillars, beetles, weevils, grasshoppers, earwigs, slugs, snails and crickets eat leaves. Leafminers and sawfly larvae tunnel inside the leaves, creating wiggly lines, dead patches or leaf skeletons. Budworms (which are moth larvae) eat out the inside of flower buds. Each is controlled by a different method, which is why correct identification is crucial.

### Sap suckers
Scales, aphids, leafhoppers, whiteflies, mealybugs, lace bugs, psyllids and bronze orange bugs feed on plant sugars in leaves, stems, flowers or fruit. Plant growth is stunted, leaves become twisted or pimply, fruit develops brown patches, and leaves and flower buds wilt. Some pests are specific to one plant, while others attack a range of plants. They all secrete sticky honeydew, which falls onto surrounding leaves and grows black sooty mould. Ants 'farm' sap suckers for honeydew, so look for ants on plants, too.

### Mites and thrips
These tiny insects cause fine bronze or silver mottling of leaves.

### Stem and trunk eaters
Stems and tree trunks are chewed by beetle or moth larvae, bark weevils and slaters. They often girdle the stems of small plants. Larvae enter larger trees through damaged bark to feed on sap.

### Root attackers
Plant roots are attacked by curl grubs, black beetles, weevils, slaters, millipedes and nematodes. Seedlings can collapse overnight, and larger plants die back.

### diagnose Pest problems
- Irregular holes, chewed leaves; black droppings: Caterpillars or loopers
- Meandering silver lines across distorted leaves: Leafminers
- Discoloured or distorted leaves: Thrips; lack of nutrients
- Speckled dots on leaves and 'cobwebbing': Two-spotted mites
- Flowers dropping off before blooming; brownish marks on petals: Petal blight (a fungus)
- Stunted, wilted plant: Soilborne fungus
- Stunted plants; yellow, mottled leaves: Mosaic virus
- Orangey brown powdery pustules underneath leaves: Rust (a fungus)
- Sticky leaves, black 'soot' and ants: Sooty mould (a fungus) growing on a secretion produced by aphids, scale insects or mealybugs. The insects are the problem, the fungus a by-product.
- Buds not opening; leaves twisted and distorted: Aphids

## PETUNIAS

### Summer colour
Petunias are annuals that bring colour to gardens from late spring to autumn. In warm, frost-free climates they grow almost year-round, but in mild areas they are planted in early spring for flowers from summer to autumn. In cold climates wait until late spring or early summer before planting.

### Single or double
Single-flowered petunias come in either pure colours or they are bicoloured. There are double-flowered forms in tones of purple, amethyst, pink or white. They look particularly decorative in a pot or hanging basket, as do the trailing Pendula and Cascade types or the perennial 'Colorwave' petunias.

PETUNIAS | PHOTINIAS

**P**

### Snail protection
Snails and slugs enjoy feasting on petunias. Newly planted seedlings must be protected immediately (with a barrier or snail trap) or they may be wiped out. Snails will not destroy a mature plant, but they will make it look unsightly and can destroy the flowers.

### Prune and rejuvenate
Once seedlings are established (at around 10 cm tall), nip out the main shoot. This will encourage sideshoots to branch. Many new cultivars will self-branch, so only nip out any long straggly stems on them. Remove flowers on newly planted petunias so they put all their energy into bushing out.

If petunias become rangy in late summer, lightly prune all over and apply a liquid fertiliser every 2 weeks. The new growth will mean flowers for many weeks.

### Wet weather blues
After heavy rain petunia flowers become a wet, soggy mass. To avoid this, plant Multiflora types. Although the flowers are smaller, they bounce back after rain.

## PHOTINIAS

### For a hedge
These tall, hardy, easy-to-grow evergreen shrubs from eastern Asia make popular hedge plants, forming a dense hedge 2–3 m high when trimmed. They do best in fertile, well-drained soil.

### New growth
Photinias are grown for their showy red or bronze new spring growth, which trimming will encourage. They also produce heads of creamy white flowers that have a rather overpowering scent, followed by blue-black berries. *Photinia glabra* 'Rubens' has vivid red new foliage, while *P. × fraseri* 'Robusta' has larger, bronze red foliage. 'Red Robin', which grows to 2 m high with improved reddish-coloured new growth, is not as frost-hardy as the other cultivars.

## PHOSPHATES

### Source of phosphorus
Phosphorus is an essential nutrient and, with nitrogen and potassium, one of the principal elements for plant growth. Phosphate, which contains phosphorus, aids fruiting and stimulates early root formation and growth. Where soils lack phosphate, initial growth may be weak and plants poorly developed with stunted growth. Phosphate-deficient plants may have reddish leaf colours.

### When to add phosphate
Australian soils are very low in phosphorus. The high phosphate content of most fertilisers is intended to compensate for this. New Zealand soils are generally richer in phosphorus, and in many areas, only maintenance applications may be required.

### Phosphate fertilisers
There are organic and inorganic, quick-acting and slow-release forms. They include:

✱ Blood and bone (organic, breaks down slowly)

✱ Heavy applications of manure and garden compost

✱ Liquid phosphate fertilisers (quick-acting)

✱ Rock phosphate (exceptionally long-lasting)

✱ Superphosphate of lime (inorganic, fairly quick-acting and yet long-lasting).

### Be careful
The Proteaceae family of plants, which includes many Australian natives (acacias, banksias and grevilleas) as well as proteas, are sensitive – to varying degrees – to excessive phosphorus. The addition of soluble phosphates to soil near these plants should be strictly avoided. On very poor soils, the use of some slow-release phosphates, such as blood and bone and rock phosphate, is sometimes justified. Plants showing phosphorus toxicity can be helped with additions of iron to the soil or perhaps a chelated spray.

197

# P

## PHYTOPHTHORA ROOT ROT | PINCHING OUT

## PHYTOPHTHORA ROOT ROT

### Plants affected
Trees, shrubs such as maples, native plants, rhododendrons, strawberries.

### Symptoms
Roots die back, turn black; dead tissue shows up on stems and trunk; yellow leaves; dieback of shoots; leaf fall and wilting.

### Treatment
* Avoid heavy watering, and improve drainage where soil is wet or waterlogged.

* Dig up and destroy affected plants.

* Choose resistant plants, such as cabbage tree (*Cordyline australis*), some eucalypts, some paperbarks, willow myrtle (*Agonis flexuosa*).

## PINCHING OUT

### The kindest cut
Certain annual bedding plants and herbaceous perennials benefit from pinching out. This should be done early in the season before the plants grow too tall. Early pinching out encourages strong basal growth and plants that are compact and bushy. This will result in the production of many more flowers and the improved quality of the blooms.

### Size and strength
Trailing varieties of marrows, pumpkins, squashes and zucchini can grow very large, making them unsuitable for smaller gardens. If you wish to grow these in a limited space, pinch out the tips of the main shoots when they are 60 cm long. When the sideshoots grow to 60 cm, pinch them out in the same way.

### Pinch these plants
Some plants will produce better, sturdier growth if the main shoot is pinched out and the sideshoots are left to develop.

#### Flowering plants
* Begonia * Campanula
* Carnations and pinks
* Chinese lantern (*Abutilon* × *hybridum*)
* Chrysanthemum * Coleus * Dahlia
* Fuchsia * Geranium * Impatiens
* Penstemon * Petunia * Poinsettia
* Salvia * Snapdragon * Sweet pea

#### Vegetables and herbs
* Basil * Capsicum * Chillies
* Eggplant * Lemon balm * Marjoram
* Marrow * Mint * Oregano * Pumpkin
* Sage * Summer squash * Tarragon
* Tomato * Zucchini

Eggplants benefit from pinching out. It encourages bushy growth while limiting the number of fruit.

### Pinch out tomato sideshoots

**In cool climates** You need to maximise the exposure of tomato fruit to light and air. Regularly pinch out the sideshoots that develop in the leaf axils when they reach about 3–5 cm long.

**In hot climates** Retain at least some sideshoots to protect fruit from sun scald.

Eggplants and capsicums produce many flowers, not all of which yield fruit. To strengthen the crop, pinch out some of the flower buds as they form, leaving no more than six to eight on each plant.

### Fruit trees and roses
Train fruit trees by removing young, unwanted shoots that, if left, will develop into an untidy tangle of branches. Pinch back any strong shoots that grow from spurs to encourage more fruit buds to develop. To prevent any sideshoots developing on the stems of standard roses, snap them off with a downward tug at an early stage. Suckers from the base should be treated similarly.

### When not to pinch
During damp weather, plants can develop grey mould. Pinching out may squash the stem, leaving it susceptible to reinfection, so trim sideshoots with scissors instead. Note that bush tomatoes, also known as determinate tomatoes, have no leading shoot and so need no pinching out.

PINK FLOWERS

Dahlia

Flowering dogwood

Azalea

# PINK FLOWERS

## From pastel to hot
There seem to be more flowers in pink than in any other colour. From pale pastel and romantic to bright, bold and brilliantly hot, there's a pink to suit every spot in the garden. Pink is usually a soft colour that can be used in great swathes. But be more sparing with bright, bold pinks because they draw the eye and can become overpowering en masse.

## A shade of red
Pink is not a primary colour. Rather, it is a shade of red. It is a warm colour when mixed with yellow – think coral or salmon – but cool when mixed with blue. Combining flowers that share the same undertone works best. So, for example, you would mix blue-based pinks with blue and purple flowers.

## Bring it to life
If you want to enhance a pink flower, plant it with white – even delicate pale pinks will come to life. Opposite pink and red on the colour wheel is green, and a combination of pink, white and green is elegant and fresh. If you want pink to really stand out, mix it with grey and grey-green foliage. A beautiful combination is a carpet of silver-leaved lamb's ears, anthemis or cotton lavender (*Santolina chamaecyparissus*) planted beneath pink roses.

## Made for each other
Blues of all shades are effective with pink. Be bold when using bright pinks and combine them with other saturated colours, such as deep purples and blues. Add drama with touches of bright orange. For a striking summer border, combine hot pink zinnias, blue salvias and bright orange calendulas or California poppies.

Among the lighter shades, pale pinks are beautiful with soft blue and purple. Add yellow and white to bring the scheme to life.

### Choosing pink flowers

**For temperate and cool climates**
✱ Thrift (*Armeria maritima*)
✱ Pink boronia (*Boronia floribunda*)
✱ Flowering dogwood (*Cornus florida* cvs)
✱ Dahlia ✱ Carnations and pinks (*Dianthus* spp.) ✱ Sweet pea
✱ Ornamental fruit trees (*Malus* and *Prunus* spp. and cvs) ✱ Peony (*Paeonia* spp.) ✱ Azaleas ✱ Roses

**For warm and hot climates**
✱ Shell ginger (*Alpinia zerumbet*)
✱ Begonia ✱ Bougainvillea
✱ Camellia ✱ Crowea (*Crowea* spp.)
✱ Pompom tree (*Dais cotinifolia*)
✱ Brazilian plume flower (*Justicia carnea*)
✱ Fringe flower (*Loropetalum chinense*)
✱ Bower of beauty (*Pandorea jasminoides*) ✱ Paper daisy (*Rhodanthe chlorocephala* subsp. *rosea*)

Sweet pea

# PITTOSPORUMS

## A good selection
The numerous cultivars of these evergreen trees and shrubs provide shades of foliage colour in green, silver, yellow, white and red, many of which are more pronounced in winter. Plants vary from medium-sized trees, such as *Pittosporum rhombifolium*, to small shrubs, such as kohuhu (*P. tenuifolium* 'Tom Thumb').

## Sticky seeds
Although pittosporums are grown mainly for their handsome foliage, their sweetly scented flowers and attractive fruits are a bonus. Seeds can be used to raise new plants. To aid handling, remove the sticky substance by pouring hot water over the seeds, or simply mix the seed with fine sand. Cultivars are usually propagated by semi-hardwood cuttings.

## Planting position
While most pittosporums are cold-hardy, *P. rhombifolium* and a few other species require milder climates. Most grow best in full sun or partial shade and should be watered thoroughly during dry periods.

## Many uses
Plant larger forms as specimen trees or for background effect in shrub borders. They are also useful for screening and hedging. The kohuhu and tough evergreen Japanese mock orange (*P. tobira*), from Japan and China, make excellent formal hedges.

# PLANT NAMES

## Avoiding confusion
The botanical names of plants, written in a form of Latin, may irritate gardeners who cannot understand why they cannot be labelled simply, with a common name. The reason is that the same plant is available in many other countries, each of which has its own common name for the plant.

Even in the same country, the same plant may have a different common name. For example, the weedy Paterson's curse (*Echium plantagineum*) of some parts of Australia is known in other areas as salvation Jane. If gardeners are to communicate, they need to know what each other is talking about, regardless of nationality, custom or folklore – hence the botanical names, which are added to as new species are discovered and new cultivars are introduced.

## Where the names come from
In its simplest form, a botanical name consists of two parts, a noun and an adjective, which are written in italics. The noun, such as *Salix*, is the name of the genus to which a plant belongs. The adjective, such as *alba*, is a label that narrows the name down to a single species – for example, *Salix alba*, the white willow.

# PLANTING

## The best time to plant
Autumn and spring are optimal times for planting container-grown plants. Autumn is best because it gives plant roots more time to establish over winter, before the rapid growth period of spring, then the heat and drought stress of summer. Deciduous trees, shrubs and vines can be planted in winter while they are dormant.

If you're planting in spring in cool regions, don't plant out tender plants until the last frosts have passed (in very cold areas, this may not be until early summer). In warm areas, planting in winter is fine, especially as any spring plantings may need more water by early summer. In tropical zones, the latter part of the wet season is best.

## Limit drying out
Whenever possible, plant in the evening to limit the drying effects of the sun. If you are planting a large garden bed, try to wait for periods when some cloud cover or light rain is forecast. While you can plant in summer, it is hard to keep new plants, especially small ones, growing in the heat. Check the forecast to avoid extra-hot, windy days.

## Dealing with bare-root plants
Bare-root plants, such as roses and fruit trees, are available from winter to early spring and must be planted as soon as possible after they are delivered, while they are still dormant. First prepare, or 'dress', the roots: cut off any broken or damaged roots and trim any larger roots. Do not touch little roots, as these will take up water from the soil.

To plant, dig a wide, shallow hole and make a mound of soil in the bottom. Spread the roots over the mound, then backfill with soil, giving the trunk a gentle shake now and then so the soil fills up all the spaces. To make sure that

PLANTING   P

## Plant out a container-grown specimen

Once you've prepared your garden beds, it's time for planting out. Soak the plant in a bucket of water beforehand so the roots absorb as much water as possible.

**1** Ensure the soil has plenty of organic matter, such as compost or well-rotted manure, then dig a hole that is wider but not deeper than the root ball.

**2** Tease out the roots and loosen the potting mix so the roots will seek out nutrients and moisture from the soil around them.

**3** Position the plant in the hole carefully, making sure it sits at the same level in the ground as it did in the pot. Don't cover the crown.

**4** Backfill around the root ball, starting at the base to hold the plant in position. Gently firm in the soil around the plant by hand. Water immediately, soaking the area until the ground can take no more. Finish with a liquid seaweed fertiliser, then apply mulch. Water regularly in the following days until well established.

you don't plant too deeply, lay the handle of your spade across the hole. The neck of the plant – that place between the roots and the trunk with a soil mark – should be at that level. Any grafting point needs to be 10 cm above the soil.

### Heeling in
Never attempt to plant bare-root plants when the soil is frozen or waterlogged. Instead, dig a trench, lay the roots in it at an angle and cover them with soil until conditions improve.

### Turning out well
If a plant resists all attempts to remove it from its pot, do not try to lever it out, as this is likely to break the pot or damage the plant's roots. Instead, plunge the pot up to its rim in water and leave it to soak for a couple of hours. Cut any protruding roots from the base, then try again. Holding the pot upside down with one hand supporting the soil surface, sharply tap the rim of the pot on a bench edge, turning the pot several times. If it still won't come out, break the pot carefully. Use secateurs on plastic pots.

### Whatever the weather – water!
Newly planted plants should be watered thoroughly immediately after planting, even if rain is imminent. Watering eliminates pockets of air in the soil and ensures that all a plant's roots come into contact with the soil. Water the plant well in the following weeks – as often as a potted plant. Apply at the base of the stem to make sure it soaks right into the root system.

### Replacing plants
When you have to replace a dead or diseased plant, never plant the new plant in the same hole. Instead, dig a new hole at least 1 m away. This should eliminate any risk of contamination. If there isn't enough space in the bed to do this, remove as much soil as possible from the area around the hole (dispose of it safely) and replace it with fresh soil from another part of the garden.

### Leave enough space
The labels on plants will include advice on how far apart plants should be spaced in the garden, based on the width that each particular plant will grow to. However, this advice is only a rough guide because the same plant may grow larger and faster in some climate zones and conditions than in others. Before you start digging the planting holes for your new plants, set them out, still in their pots, on the soil surface to see how they will look.

PLANTING PLANS | PLUMBAGO

## PLANTING PLANS

### A planting scheme
Plants for beds and borders need to be planned carefully, especially if you want to include groups of trees and shrubs. Before choosing the exact location for plants, check on their height and spread at maturity so that they will look good together in a few years' time and will be easy to maintain. When planning hedges, take into account how far apart the plants must be positioned from one another and how much they will spread, remembering to leave enough space so you can get easy access for maintenance.

### Colour coordination
Make a note of the colour of any existing flowers and their flowering period to help you plan a coherent and harmonious scheme around them.

### Drawn to scale
By using a plan drawn to scale and different symbols to depict different types of plants, you can produce a clear planting plan. The symbols for trees, shrubs and flowering plants can be added to with information on colour and flowering periods.

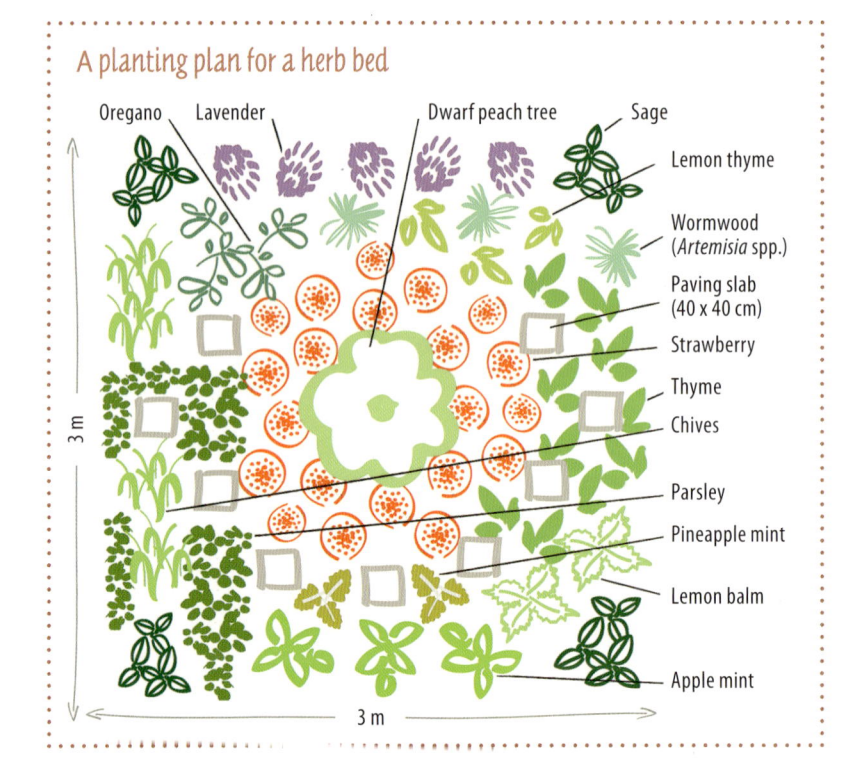

### A planting plan for a herb bed

Oregano, Lavender, Dwarf peach tree, Sage, Lemon thyme, Wormwood (*Artemisia* spp.), Paving slab (40 x 40 cm), Strawberry, Thyme, Chives, Parsley, Pineapple mint, Lemon balm, Apple mint

3 m × 3 m

## PLUMBAGO

### Show of blue flowers
This showy plant (*Plumbago auriculata*) from South Africa is grown for its massed display of blue flowers over a long period from spring to autumn. Needing a frost-free area and well-drained soil, it forms a shrub 2 m high. The most popular form is 'Royal Cape', with deep blue flowers and a more compact habit. It appears to have greater frost and drought tolerance than other types. There is also a white-flowering form.

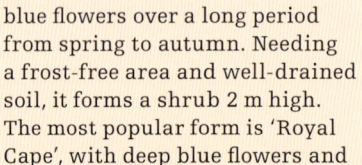

### Easy hedge
This easygoing, sprawling shrub can be trained into a soft, informal hedge. Place plants 1 m apart in a sunny position and trim lightly to keep dense. Within 12 months you will have a hedge about 1 m high. For a patterned look, plant white and blue plumbagos alternately.

### Pruning tips
Plumbago can be pruned lightly after the main flowering in summer to keep it dense. It will flower again through autumn. Do the main pruning in late winter or early spring to encourage new growth and good flowers.

PLUMS | POINSETTIAS

# P

'Santa Rosa'

'Green Gage'

## PLUMS

### Pick of the plums
Plums are easy fruit trees to grow so long as the right varieties for the climate are chosen. Check with your local nursery to find out which varieties suit the climate where you live. European plums are smaller and hardier than Japanese plums, with slightly drier but richly flavoured flesh, making them an excellent choice for conserves, cooking or drying for prunes. Japanese plums are generally large and juicy and are usually eaten fresh; the trees are highly productive.

The related gages are usually sugary sweet and much juicier than plums, while damsons are small, richly flavoured and mostly used in pies and conserves.

### Chilling needs
All varieties of plums, gages and damsons require high chilling hours to set fruit, apart from the Japanese plums, which are ideal for warmer climates because of their low chilling requirements. Note that only damsons will succeed in exposed positions in wet districts.

### Plant one or more?
These fruit trees tolerate a wide range of soils, including heavy soils. Plums and gages are highly productive. Most European varieties must be planted with a second variety for pollination to occur, as must the Gulf series of Japanese plums. However, all other Japanese plums and all the damsons are self-pollinating, so only one tree needs to be planted for a crop.

*'Czar' is self-pollinating but produces an even better crop when crossed with another plum variety.*

> **Ornamental plums**
> Ornamental plums make a spectacular spring display with their masses of single, double or semi-double blooms ranging in colour from white to deep pink. Flowers usually appear before leaves, which are often purple, in early spring. Good varieties include *Prunus* 'Nigra' (single pink flowers), *P.* 'Pissardii' and *P.* 'Elvins' (single white flowers), and *P.* × *blireana* (double bright pink flowers). Some grow into tall trees with an equally wide spread, while others are ideal for a shrub border.

## POINSETTIAS

### Indoor decoration
Poinsettias, from the *Euphorbia* genus, are flamboyant winter-flowering plants that can be enjoyed as indoor pot plants all year round. Use them to cheer up the house in the colder months or to add colour to a traditional red and green Christmas theme.

Poinsettias will last indoors with little care for weeks or even months. Water them only when the potting mix is dry to the touch. If planted in the garden they will grow into a normal-sized plant several metres high.

### High elevation origins
While they may look tropical, poinsettias are found at high elevations in Mexico, which means they can withstand some cold. Use them in a cool climate to bring a lush, tropical feel to your garden in winter but remember that in cool districts, they will lose their leaves in winter.

### Leaves, not flowers
The showy red 'petals' are in fact coloured bracts that grow around the true flowers, massed together in the centre of each cluster. The bracts can range in colour from white to yellow and through all sorts of reds, pinks and salmon. Some cultivars, such as 'Henriette Ecke', have double red leaves.

203

# POISONOUS PLANTS

### Keeping things in perspective
Poisonous plants are much less of a threat to children's safety than traffic. But it makes sense to instill in youngsters' minds the idea that some things in the garden can be a danger, and that berries and fruits should not be eaten without first checking with adults. Plant shrubs with bright berries at the backs of borders, out of reach of children, and it's best to ban the house plant dumb cane (*Dieffenbachia* spp.) where there are children and pets.

### Quick action
If a child shows any symptoms of poisoning, telephone a doctor or the Poisons Information Centre immediately. Or take the child to the closest emergency department of a hospital, together with leaves and fruit from the plant.

### Cover up
Wear long-sleeved clothing and gloves before handling plants that irritate the skin. Never wear shorts when working in strong sunlight among such plants.

## know the possible effects of Poisonous plants

Many familiar plants have irritant or toxic properties. Poisoning by some can be fatal, but many will cause only minor skin irritations.

*Aconitum*  All parts; even small amounts, if eaten, cause severe or fatal poisoning.
*Aesculus*  All parts; respiratory paralysis, mild gastrointestinal effects if eaten.
*Alstroemeria*  Foliage; irritation to skin if handled continuously.
*Brugmansia*  Leaves, berries; hallucinogenic effects.
*Clivia*  All parts; nausea, vomiting, very severe diarrhoea.
*Colchicum*  All parts; burning in the mouth and throat, vomiting and diarrhoea if eaten, weak pulse, low temperature, death.
*Convallaria*  All parts; headache, nausea, vomiting, slow pulse, excessive urination.
*Delphinium*  All parts; nausea, vomiting, blurred vision if eaten.
*Dieffenbachia*  All parts; sap dangerous if it enters the mouth or eyes.
*Digitalis*  All parts; headache, convulsions, vomiting if eaten; heart failure.
*Euonymus*  Berries; diarrhoea, vomiting, sleepiness if eaten.
*Euphorbia*  All parts; burning in mouth and throat, vomiting, diarrhoea if eaten.
*Grevillea*  Foliage, stems; contact dermatitis when handled or cut.
*Helleborus*  All parts; irritation to skin if handled; digestive upsets if eaten.
*Hyacinthus*  All parts; diarrhoea if eaten; sap causes dermatitis.
*Ipomoea*  Seeds; stomach ache, nausea, blurred vision if eaten.
*Laburnum*  All parts; vomiting, drowsiness, headache, increased heartbeat if eaten.
*Ligustrum*  Berries; vomiting, diarrhoea if eaten.
*Lupinus*  Seeds; nausea, vomiting, dizziness if eaten.
*Narcissus*  All parts; vomiting, convulsions if eaten; irritation to skin if handled.
*Nerium oleander*  All parts; nausea, vomiting, headache, weak pulse, heart failure.
*Primula*  Foliage; dermatitis if handled; digestive disturbances if eaten.
*Prunus laurocerasus*  Berries; vomiting, convulsions, can be fatal if chewed.
*Taxus*  All parts; vomiting, diarrhoea, dilated pupils, low blood pressure, heart failure.
*Thevetia*  Berries; poisoning.
*Toxicodendron*  All parts; severe skin irritation and swelling.
*Wisteria*  All parts; nausea, vomiting, headache, diarrhoea, collapse.

# POLLINATION

### Planting the pollinator
When planting fruit trees, check that the varieties are suitable pollinators for each other or, if not, that they can be pollinated by a single tree added to the group. In a small garden, the pollinator should be planted in the centre of the group or grafted to an existing plant. In a larger garden or orchard, place the pollinating tree at the end of a row – the end that faces the prevailing wind. This will assist the distribution of pollen and also encourage pollinating insects to move along the rows in the right direction.

### Single parents
If you only have room for one tree, plant a 'family tree' on which two, or sometimes three, mutual pollinators have been grafted. An alternative is a self-fertile variety, but the choice is limited and harvests are often mediocre.

### Aiding pollination
If vegetables are slow to form, you can help nature. Pollinate plants manually using a small dry brush to transfer pollen to the female part of the flower. In pumpkins and zucchini, pollen is carried in separate male flowers so must be transferred to the female flower.

POLYANTHUS AND PRIMULAS | POSSUMS

# P

Polyanthus

## POLYANTHUS AND PRIMULAS

### A plethora of choice
There are nearly 500 *Primula* species. The cheery polyanthus (*P.* × *polyantha*) are bedding plants that grow in full sun or light shade and brighten gardens in late winter and spring. In cool moist summers, they may last for 2–3 years but are mostly treated as annuals, planted each autumn.

Primulas (*P. malacoides*) are annuals with white, pink or crimson flowers in winter and spring. They prefer more shade and in moist conditions will grow in quite dense shade. They are easygoing and will even self-seed out of cracks in paving.

### Cool and moist
The easiest way to establish polyanthus or primulas is to buy seedlings or small plants. Prepare the planting area by digging in rich compost, well-rotted manure or leaf mould. Keep the soil moist.

### Mixed blessings
Planting different strains of primulas or primroses together will result in new specimens of different colours the following year. Primulas hybridise easily. In later years, the plants will bear little resemblance to the original varieties, but the results could be very attractive.

## POMEGRANATES

### Flowers and fruit
The pomegranate is an attractive small tree or large shrub with glossy leaves and showy scarlet blooms from spring to summer. Some ornamental varieties bear only small or sparse fruit, but 'Wonderful' is a good cultivar for fruit quality. While the plant can be grown in warm to tropical climates, including semi-arid areas, the fruit will only ripen in hot, dry summers. It makes a good container specimen, especially the dwarf variety 'Nana'.

### Using the fruit
Pomegranate kernels are used in Middle Eastern and sometimes Indian cookery, as a garnish, in salads or desserts, and the jelly-like pulp of the fruit can be eaten or juiced. Pick the fruit when they are an orange-brown colour. They will split if left on the tree for too long.

**PONDS AND POOLS** *see pages 206–207*

**POPPIES** *see pages 208–209*

## POSSUMS

### Plants affected
Rosebuds, flowers and shoots, fuchsias, geraniums, magnolias and many other plants.

### Symptoms
Partly eaten flower buds, fruit and shoots.

### Treatment
✽ Use decoy feeding plants as far away from your favourite plants as possible, and add vegetable and fruit scraps to a designated feeding area.

✽ Plant banksias and small eucalypts as natural food in this area.

✽ Repellents, such as quassia spray, can be tried but they need to be reapplied regularly.

✽ Wide metal collars around trunks will help to protect fruit.

✽ Electrified fencing can be used as a barrier around a vegetable garden. Cover small plants with sheeting or netting at night.

✽ Motion sensor lights can deter visiting possums.

# PONDS AND POOLS

A water feature adds a completely new dimension to a garden. Choose a shape and design that complements your garden.

## Keep in style
If your garden is formal in style, a traditional fountain or a formal pond based on symmetrical shapes will probably suit it best. In a natural garden, a rock waterfall or informal pool or pond will blend into the natural landscape.

## Choosing a site
Site the pond at the lowest point of the garden if you want it to look natural, in an open situation that gets full sun for most of the day. Don't put it near buildings or trees that throw deep shade. The area must be clear of underground installations, pipes or cables, but do arrange the electricity supply before you build a feature with a pump or lights. Don't choose a site that has a high water table.

## The right depth
A pond that is to be stocked with fish should be not less than 45 cm deep at the centre. When you're excavating the site, remember to leave a shelf about 20–25 cm from the top and 30 cm wide on which to grow shallow-water (marginal) aquatic plants. It can go around all sides or one or two sides only. In larger, deeper ponds, a second shelf about 30 cm deep and wide could also be constructed.

## Nitrate warning
Take care when siting a water feature at the bottom of a slope. Nitrates in the soil can be washed into the pond and will turn the water green. A plastic barrier at the foot of the slope is the easiest way to avoid this problem.

## A choice of liners
The life expectancy of rigid and flexible liners varies according to the materials they're made of. Preformed plastic liners are cheap but may last for only a few years. Fibreglass is more expensive and should last for at least 10 years.

There are several types of flexible liners – butyl rubber (or EPDM), polythene and PVC. Butyl is made from synthetic rubber and is the best material to use. It has an

## Ornamental fish
Before choosing ornamental fish for your pond, calculate how many the pond can accommodate. As a rough guide, allow 5 cm of fish to every 1 m² of surface area of water. Initially, however, it is better to understock than overstock to allow for growth of both fish and aquatic plants. If you wish to attract wildlife to the pond, don't choose predatory fish such as golden orfe or koi carp. Instead, use small native fish, available from pet stores and aquarium shops.

PONDS AND POOLS

anticipated life span of 50 years and is usually guaranteed for up to 20 years. Polythene is weak and not suitable for a permanent pond but can be used for a bog garden. PVC is fairly strong and about half the price of butyl. Heavy-duty PVC liners should last up to 15 years.

### Concealing the edge
When edging a pond with paving slabs or stones, lay them so there is an overhang of about 5 cm to hide the liner. The paving will protect the liner from damage and shield it from sunlight, which can cause deterioration. When choosing the materials for the edging, check with the supplier that the surfaces of the paving slabs or stones will not become slippery when wet.

### Topping up
The water in a pond must be topped up frequently, especially in summer when the evaporation rate is high. Avoid tap-water if possible. Rainwater from a tank is best. If filling from a garden tap where the water pressure is high, soften its impact as it fills the pond by putting the hose nozzle in a bucket in the pond.

### Dispatch debris
Use a mesh scoop or small fishing net to scoop debris out. If it isn't removed, it sinks to the bottom, rots and contaminates the water. In autumn, stretch mesh over the pond and peg it to the surrounding soil. This will prevent lots of dead leaves falling into the water.

### Algae control
Algae thrive on sunlight and mineral salts. About a week after filling your new pond, introduce oxygenating plants to absorb these salts. However, until plants become established, the water in a recently filled pond will acquire a green film of algae very quickly. Remove it with a mesh scoop and use as a fertiliser on the garden. In spring, plant a waterlily to provide shade on the surface.

### Keep plants in proportion
When selecting plants to grow in and around the pond, bear its dimensions in mind and choose plants whose final size will be in proportion to their surroundings.

### Accommodating wildlife
Make a gently sloping beach of cobblestones or gravel or pile up some stones in one corner of the pond. This lets native animals drink easily, and helps birds to bathe and frogs to hop in and out.

### Clean up with snails
When your aquatic plants are established, introduce a few water snails to the pond to patrol the sides and bottom, cleaning up algae and fish waste. Don't add them to the pond while plants are young as they may damage them.

See also Fountains, Water plants

## make a simple Pond
Use a freestanding half-barrel on a firm, level site for a simple pond.

1 Paint the barrel with preservative and allow to dry thoroughly. Raise it on bricks to let air circulate underneath and prevent the base from rotting.

2 Insert a thick black polythene, PVC or butyl rubber pond liner and carefully trim it with a sharp knife.

3 Half-fill with water, then fold over the top edge of the liner and staple or tack it to the inside of the barrel, just below the rim.

4 Cover the bottom of the liner with gravel to protect it. Then top up the barrel with water.

5 Let stand for a week to allow chemicals in the water to dissipate, then add your choice of plants and fish.

## edge a Pond
Providing a neat and practical edge can greatly improve the appearance of a pond. Create an edge to suit the style of pond you want to construct.

**Natural edge** A shallow beach of pebbles allows easy access for wildlife and is better than soil, which tends to muddy the pond. Behind the pebbles, long grass provides hiding places for wildlife and a natural transition to a lawn.

**Formal edge** A neat, formal edge can be made with paving laid on a bed of mortar. The liner is securely trapped between the soil and the paving, above the water level of the pond.

**Informal edge** Plants behind a brick or stone edging, laid on a bed of mortar, soften the rim's harshness and is ideal for an informal pond. The plants eventually spill over the bricks and disguise the edge of the liner.

207

# Poppies

Poppies are among the easiest flowering plants to grow and they often reseed each year if you let the attractive lantern-shaped seedpods mature and dry on the plants. Harvest them and shake the seeds into an envelope for replanting.

### Iceland poppies
The best known of all garden poppies are the Iceland poppies (*Papaver nudicaule*), which flower in a rainbow of colours from winter to spring. As well as looking bright and cheery in the garden, they make long-lasting cut flowers. For a good range of colours and stout stems that will stand up well, look for the 'Matilda' varieties.

### Flanders poppies
The red field poppies are known as Flanders, corn or field poppies (*P. rhoeas*). They bloom in late spring. To have them in flower for Armistice Day (11 November), sow seeds on Anzac Day (25 April). These poppies are a good choice for a meadow garden. As well as the simple red flowers of the species, there are flowers with large black blotches at the base of each red petal.

### Shirley poppies
Also popular are the silky, nodding Shirley poppies, cultivars of the Flanders poppy that come in pastel shades of white, mauve, pink and salmon, often with contrasting edges to the petals. For double flowers in a range of colours, look for 'Double Mixed'.

### California poppies
Not true poppies, but bringing colour to even the hottest and driest of gardens, are California poppies (*Eschscholzia californica*). Traditionally, they have orange flowers, but now they also come in pinks, yellows, apricots, white, cream ('Milkmaid') and even with double flowers ('Apricot Chiffon'). These poppies are a good choice for wildflower meadows or to extend flowering in perennial beds.

Shirley poppies

## POTASH

### The importance of potash
Potassium, found in potash, is a crucial element in photosynthesis, the chemical process by which plants use sunlight to fuel growth. It also helps to protect plants against disease, improves the colour of flowers and fruit, and ensures a balanced use of the essential plant food, nitrogen.

### Healthier fruit
Potash is important for fruit formation. Too much foliage and not enough blossom on a fruit tree could mean an excess of nitrogen. Sprinkle potash on the ground around the edge of the roots. For annual plants such as tomatoes and capsicums, feed with liquid tomato food, which is rich in potash, once the first flowers have set and continue to feed at weekly intervals. Stop feeding when night temperatures begin to fall.

---

#### Sources of potash
Potash is available in a number of forms:

**Comfrey** Use the leaves fresh, as a mulch or in planting holes, or soak in water for a liquid feed.

**Muriate of potash (potassium chloride)** A cheap form, but not suitable for soft fruits and vegetables such as beetroot and potatoes.

**Nitrate of potash (potassium nitrate)** Provides nitrogen and potash at the same time, and is very quick-acting.

**Sulfate of potash (potassium sulfate)** The safest and most widely used form, fast-acting and also remains in the soil for some time.

**Wood ash** Potash content varies greatly, depending on the source. Nutrients last longer if ash is added to compost heap.

---

## POTATOES

### Double the benefits
Potatoes thrive in temperate or cool climates, but are adaptable and can actually be grown in most locations, although they are very susceptible to frost. They take up a lot of space. But if you do have room to cultivate them, potatoes will not only provide you with a good harvest, they also break up the ground and clean it of weeds for future cultivation.

### Buy certified seed
Potatoes can be affected by a number of plant diseases, so try to buy certified disease-free seed potatoes at a nursery. Purchase them in winter, take them out of their bags at once and place in a cool, well-ventilated room. After a week or two, set them in seed trays with their 'eyes' (from which the sprouts will grow) facing upwards. Place the trays in a cool room. In 4–5 weeks the sprouts should be sturdy and, ideally, 1–2.5 cm long. When sprouted, or 'chitted', in this way, the potatoes will have a longer growing season and produce a heavier crop.

### Earthing up
When the plants are about 25 cm high they should be earthed up. This drawing up of the soil with a hoe supports the plants, protects the tubers from being exposed to light and turning green, and helps to prevent the caterpillars of the potato moth from eating them. The green flesh areas of light-exposed tubers are toxic. Cultivate between the rows with the hoe to destroy weeds and gradually pile the loose soil up against the haulms (leafy stems).

### Harvesting
Most potato varieties can be harvested 16–20 weeks after planting. The hotter the climate, the sooner they'll be ready. Insert the fork carefully, close to the haulm, and lift gently. Shake the fork gently to remove the soil.

In temperate areas potatoes are best stored in the ground. In other areas lift the tubers on a dry day and dry them in the sun for 2–3 hours before storing them. Remove excess soil and discard any potatoes that are blemished or damaged because broken skin will let disease enter the tubers. Store in a cool, dry, dark place.

---

### plant Potatoes
You can plant your sprouted, or 'chitted', potatoes in a 10 cm deep trench at 30 cm intervals. You can also plant them in individual holes at the same depth and distance apart.

POTTING MIX | POWDERY MILDEW

## POTTING MIX

### Why potting mix?
You will need a potting mix when potting up plants in containers. It takes the place of natural soil and transmits water, nutrients and oxygen to the roots of the plant. It should be light in weight, absorb water readily and also retain nutrients. It should contain no disease organisms.

### Explaining the standard
To buy the best possible potting mix, look for a bagged mix that is accredited under the national Australian Standard in Australia. Two grades are available. The premium mix contains water-storing crystals and fertiliser for 1–2 months of growth without the addition of further fertiliser. The regular mix will need water-storing crystals and fertiliser added at the recommended rate.

### Tailor-made mixes
Different potting mixes are available for growing different plants. When you buy a potting mix, remember to check that it is the right one for the plants you are planning to grow. The name will indicate whether a mix is suitable for your plants (for example, orchid potting mix), or read the description on the bag.

Potting mixes are developed especially for propagation and are usually sold as seed-raising mix or propagation mix. Ingredients include sand, vermiculite, perlite, coconut fibre, coco peat or coir.

### Health and safety
Potting mix contains micro-organisms. Some, such as tetanus, can be extremely harmful. This is no different to soil and the normal precautions of washing hands before eating should be observed. Those people prone to respiratory infections should avoid inhaling dust and water droplets – wear a dust mask and don't hose down potting areas vigorously.

### The need to repot and rest
A potting mix doesn't last forever. If you get a year's life from a good-quality mix you should be satisfied. Some plants become root-bound or outgrow their container. They will need 'potting on', or moving to a larger pot.

### Some common potting mix myths

**Peat** Many books will tell you peat is essential for potting mixes. This is not so – composted bark and sawdust are often the main products used.

**Crocking** There is a belief that putting broken pottery shards (crocks) at the bottom of the pot will improve drainage. Today, potting mixes are specially formulated for good drainage. No professional nurseryman ever crocks a pot, which should debunk this myth.

**Soil** Almost no professional growers use soil in mixes as dormant seeds can contribute weeds, and the denser soil particles block pore space and make the mix heavy.

## POWDERY MILDEW

### Plants affected
Many, especially annuals, apples, azaleas, crepe myrtles, grapevines, perennials, roses and vegetables.

### Symptoms
Shoots, leaves and, sometimes, flowers covered with white powdery coating.

### Treatment
✽ Water and mulch soil often to help it retain moisture.

✽ Remove affected plants and do not grow susceptible plants on damp, humid sites.

✽ Avoid using nitrogen-rich fertilisers.

✽ Spray apples with lime sulfur at green-tip stage.

✽ As soon as symptoms appear, spray with a suitable fungicide, such as wettable sulfur or myclobutanil (NZ only) for flowers, grapevines and shrubs.

211

## PROPAGATION EQUIPMENT

A certain amount of electrical equipment is almost essential for creating the climate-controlled environment that is necessary for germinating seedlings and propagating cuttings.

**Electric mat** Place the mat on a shelf. Put pots and trays of seedlings on top of it to keep the root areas warm. It can be rolled up after use.

**Propagator** Choose one with a thermostat. Useful accessories include a water mat (to raise humidity) and tray covers (to reduce moisture loss).

If you are propagating plants in a greenhouse, you may also need lighting to extend the growing season. A specially designed electrical fan heater with a thermostat will provide reliable, safe heating of the greenhouse – it also circulates air, which reduces the risk of disease.

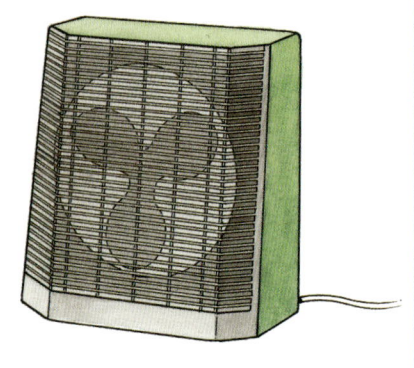

## PRUNING

Pruning is a way of controlling a plant's growth. It may encourage its vigour and health, alter its size and shape, or increase the amount and quality of its flowers and foliage.

### When to prune

All plants respond differently to being cut back, but there are some simple guidelines. Pruning at the right time of year is crucial. It ensures that new growth is not damaged by frost or heat, and that you don't cut off next year's flower buds. If you're not sure of the correct time to prune a particular plant, always do it after flowering – unless it produces fruit.

Don't cut plants back by more than a third if you aren't sure what you're doing. If the plant is a focal point of your garden, get specific advice on what to do from a trained horticulturist.

### Some pruning tips

* Make as clean a cut as possible.
* Prune out all dead or diseased wood before starting to shape.
* Remove all-green shoots on variegated shrubs so they don't take over the plant.
* You don't need to prune to a bud if the plant has thin, wiry stems.
* Don't prune on wet, cold days, because wet foliage makes the job unpleasant. Choose a fine, dry day.
* Prune a little at a time. You can't stick it back afterwards.

### For trees

The best time to prune trees is at the start of the growing season – August or September, depending on your climate. That is when the tree's sap is rising and pruning wounds grow over more quickly.

Avoid hard pruning into thick, older limbs, as inexpert lopping will encourage a rush of weak growth, which spoils the overall shape. If a tree is blocking a view or has grown too dense, selectively remove entire branches to lighten the canopy rather than lop back all over. Always seek advice from a qualified tree surgeon and hire them to remove branches from large trees. In Australia, most local government authorities must approve the pruning of any tree's canopy if it is to be cut back by more than one-third.

### No pruning of conifers

Firs, cedars, pines and most other conifer varieties do not respond well to pruning and often fail to

# PRUNING

produce healthy new shoots if pruned too severely. The yew tree is an exception – it can withstand vigorous pruning.

### For shrubs, perennials and annuals
Some overgrown large shrubs can be rejuvenated by cutting back hard into older wood, although it's best not to prune a branch back to where there is no foliage or buds. Thin out branches of old shrubs gradually over 2–3 years.

**Tip pruning or pinching out** Regularly prune off the tips of new growth to force buds further down the branch to develop into new stems and flowers. The result is increased branches and leaves, making a plant bushier.

**Deadheading** This removes spent flowers, which then promotes new flowers. Cutting fresh flowers for the house does a similar job.

**Shearing** Shear plants that you want to grow into dense hedges or neat shapes. When hedge plants have joined together, use hedge shears or a hedge trimmer to create geometric shapes and a smooth, even surface.

**De-caning** For shrubs with long cane-like stems, such as abelias and nandinas, remove old canes at the plant's base using secateurs; this gives a more open framework.

## make the correct Pruning cut

Pruning will cut through the bark, which is what protects a plant from disease. The cleaner the cut, the faster the wound will dry and heal, so it is important to keep your tools sharp and to avoid ragged cuts and torn bark. Plants have natural defences against injury that are concentrated in certain places, such as in the joint where a bud or a leaf grows. Cutting close to this point helps the wound to heal quickly and results in healthier plants.

**Just above a bud** Always prune a plant just above a bud, angling the cut so that water will be directed away from the bud.

**Two buds** Where buds are in pairs on either side of the stem, make the cut straight across, no more than 5 mm above the buds.

**An incorrect cut** A pruning cut made with blunt secateurs will produce a ragged cut and torn bark. It will heal slowly and be more susceptible to disease entering.

**Annual cut-down** Many grasses must be cut back to their base in late winter or before the growing season starts. Cut perennials down when they start to die back.

**Framework pruning** Plants that have a definite dormant season, such as roses, need to be pruned back to a strong, basic framework. This will create enough space for vigorous new growth in spring.

### Encouraging a hedge
One year after a new hedge has been planted, cut back the new growth severely. The hedge will thicken up much more quickly because each shrub will then push out vigorous new shoots.

### Recycling garden waste
Chop up your tree and shrub prunings and branches with an electric shredder. Add this to the compost heap or use it for mulch to recycle your garden's nutrients. If anything is diseased or insect-infested, put it in the rubbish bin to stop the problem spreading.

*See also* Shrubs, Trees

## know the Pruning toolbox

These are the tools you'll need for successful pruning.

**Secateurs** Use for cutting stems less than 1.5 cm thick. Bypass secateurs have a scissors action; anvil secateurs have a single sharp blade that cuts against a flat surface. Flower snips have thinner blades, ideal for deadheading.

**Pruning saw** It cuts through woody branches 3 cm thick. A tri-saw cuts quickly but will get jammed in thick wood. A pull saw is better for thicker cuts.

**Loppers** Long-handled loppers are for cutting woody stems up to 3 cm thick. Ratchet loppers have gearing to cut through thicker branches.

**Garden or hedge shears** Both lightweight and heavy-duty models, with straight or wavy cutting edges, are available for trimming hedges, shrubs and small areas of grass.

**Hedge trimmer** Electric, battery or petrol models are available, as are pole handles that extend to 2 m. They make fast work of shearing but are very heavy.

### PROTEAS
*see page 214*

PROTEAS | PUMPKINS

## PROTEAS

### A big family
The term 'protea' usually refers to the more than 100 species of the South African genus, *Protea*. The shrubs and trees are grown for their magnificent flower heads of colourful bracts. Flowering can last for many months.

The term is also sometimes used to refer to members of the entire Proteaceae family, which includes *Protea* as well as the South African leucadendrons and the leucospermums; the Australian banksias, grevilleas, hakeas and waratahs; and the New Zealand rewarewa (*Knightia excelsa*).

### The key to success
*Protea* species are thought of as difficult to grow. But if you follow a few basic rules, you will find them very hardy. Be sure to plant them in a well-drained (sandy or gravelly) acidic soil that is low in nutrients. They come from areas with poor soils, so fertilisers, and phosphates in particular, can be harmful. They need a sunny, open position and benefit from periodic deep watering during dry spells, especially during the first 2 years after they are planted. Sugarbush (*P. repens*), *P.* 'Pink Ice' and *P.* 'Special Pink Ice' are among the hardiest, and easiest, to grow.

### Proteas for colder climates
In frost-prone areas select species originating from colder habitats such as the mountainous areas of South Africa – for example, the king protea (*Protea cynaroides*). Protect from frost at night for the first 2 years after planting.

### Prune as necessary
Most proteas only need a yearly light trim after flowering to keep them in shape and to promote new growth. The degree to which they are pruned depends on the plant's age and the species. Younger plants often respond better than older ones.

## PUMPKINS

There are hundreds of types – not all are good for eating.

'Queensland Blue'

'Blue Hubbard Squash'

### Winter squash
Pumpkins are a type of winter squash; the fruit is hard-skinned and can be stored for months for eating in winter. The related summer squash – zucchini and marrows – are picked and eaten when tender and young.

### Space hungry
Pumpkins need a very enriched and well-drained soil in an open, sunny spot. Many varieties have scrambling vines, which can spread and occupy a great deal of space. In smaller gardens, help vines to climb along a fence or over a trellis or shed. Or use bush pumpkins, such as 'Cinderella', 'Golden Nugget' and 'Butterbush', rather than vine types. They can even be grown in large containers.

### Heavy feeders
These vegetables are heavy feeders – the top of a compost heap is an ideal growing site for them. Being shallow-rooted, they can easily become water-stressed and fruit quality will suffer, so water regularly and well, and help retain soil moisture with mulch. Pinch out the tips of overly enthusiastic vines to contain their growth.

### Halloween lantern
There are Halloween varieties of pumpkin, such as 'Jack o'Lantern', which have bright orange ribbed skin and flesh that is easy to carve, although the flesh of some isn't edible. Choose a large pumpkin. Cut off the top, scoop out the flesh and carve a face in the skin. Put a lighted nightlight inside and replace the top.

# PURPLE FLOWERS

## The illusion of distance
Purple ranges from the palest mauve, to brilliant violet and deep, moody, velvety purple. Like blue, it recedes in a garden and makes plants look further away, so position purple flowers at the end of a garden to make it seem larger.

## A royal touch
Purple is made by mixing red and blue, and every purple shades towards one or the other. Purples with a red undertone add a royal touch, and tone down colours such as red and orange that can clash. A scheme of orange and purple is a brilliant combination.

## Complementary colours
Blue-dominated purples lend a cooling effect to planting schemes and work best with blues, greens and cool yellows. On the colour wheel, yellow is complementary to purple; it lightens and brightens a mainly purple colour scheme. Purple is the perfect partner of lime green flowers and foliage, which can be tricky to use.

## Don't let it disappear
Be careful in shady spots. Use paler bright mauves and violets in shade rather than deep purples so they bring in light instead of disappearing into the shadows.

**Heliotrope**

**Pride of Madeira**

**Tibouchina**

### Choosing purple flowers
**For temperate and cool climates**
* Bugle (*Ajuga reptans*) * Aster
* Campanula * Clematis * Pride of Madeira (*Echium candicans*)
* Perennial wallflower (*Erysimum* 'Winter Joy') * Heliotrope (*Heliotrope* 'Lord Roberts') * Statice (*Limonium perezii*) * Pincushion flower (*Scabiosa* spp.) * Common lilac (*Syringa vulgaris*)

**For warm and hot climates**
* Blue hibiscus (*Alyogyne huegelii*)
* Hardenbergia (*Hardenbergia* spp.)
* Jacaranda (*Jacaranda mimosifolia*)
* Liriope (*Liriope* 'Evergreen Giant')
* Plectranthus (*Plectranthus* spp.)
* Mint bush (*Prostanthera ovalifolia*)
* Salvias (*Salvia leucantha, S. sclarea*)
* Fairy fan flower (*Scaevola aemula*)
* Tibouchina (*Tibouchina* spp.)

## Gourds
Gourds are annual vines native to tropical America with fruit in weird and wonderful shapes and brilliant colours. They make good table decorations and great conversation pieces, and are grown in a similar way to the other squash. Sow the seed after frost, and train plants up a fence, tripod or trellis.

## Grow to full size
Harvest pumpkins and winter squash in mid- to late autumn when they are full sized and fully coloured. Cut off the fruit with a sharp knife, leaving as long a stalk as possible. Store in a dry, cool, airy environment.

## Harvest festival
To create a vibrant harvest festival display, grow a selection of the many different pumpkins, gourds and other winter squash that are available. Mail order seed companies will supply a packeted collection or assortment. Add the final touch – a Halloween lantern.

# Q QUINCE TREES

Flowering quince

## QUINCE TREES

### Which quince is the true quince?
Among gardeners, there is much confusion about quince trees. The true quince, *Cydonia oblonga*, has crooked branches and dark green leaves, and is grown mainly for its edible fruit, which can be cooked with meat or made into delicious quince paste or jam.

Flowering quinces, or japonicas, of the genus *Chaenomeles* are quite different plants. They are much smaller, and are grown for their ornamental flowers, which look like apple blossoms, and their decorative yellow fruit.

### Feed and mulch
The edible quince (*C. oblonga*) grows to 4.5 m. While it does best in good moist loam, it will survive in any garden soil. In colder areas plant it in a sunny, sheltered position, such as a corner bounded by two walls. Keep it healthy and productive by working bonemeal into the soil in late winter, and apply a mulch of well-rotted compost in spring.

### Picking and storing
Quinces should be harvested from midautumn onwards, or before the first frosts. By then they will be either yellow or green, depending on the variety. Store them in a cool, dry, frost-proof place. They continue to ripen after harvesting and usually last for 6–8 weeks.

Store quinces away from other fruit, such as apples and pears, which may be tainted by their strong aroma.

### Colour for a shady wall
*Chaenomeles japonica* makes an excellent wall shrub and will tolerate shade. *C.* × *superba* 'Knap Hill Scarlet' has large, orange-red flowers in spring. If the weather is fairly mild, it may produce a second flush of blooms on its leafless branches during winter. The small, yellow fruits ripen in late summer and can be harvested to make preserves or left to brighten the garden through winter.

## make Quince jam

1. Peel and core enough quinces to make 2 kg quince flesh. Cut into small cubes or grate coarsely. Put in a large saucepan with 2 litres water, cover with a lid and bring to the boil. Reduce the heat to low and simmer gently for about 30 minutes, or until tender.

2. Remove the lid and simmer until reduced to a pulp. Do not stir during cooking. Slowly add 3 kg sugar, stirring constantly, and the juice of 2 lemons. Stir until the sugar has dissolved.

3. Increase the heat and rapidly bring the jam to boiling point. Boil rapidly until setting point is reached, from 5–15 minutes, stirring occasionally and testing for setting point from time to time. To do this test, put a little jam on a chilled saucer. A skin will form on the jam's surface. Push it with your finger: if it wrinkles, the jam has reached setting point.

4. Remove the pan from the heat and leave the jam to settle for 10–15 minutes. Then remove the scum that has risen to the surface with a perforated spoon.

5. Give the hot jam a final stir, then pour it into sterilised, warm, dry jars, filling them right to the top. Wipe the rims of the jars clean, then cover them while the jam is still hot with baking paper or plastic wrap and then the lid.

Quinces

RADISHES | RAISED BEDS

'Scarlet Globe'

White summer radishes

'French Breakfast'

Winter radish

## RADISHES

There are three main types of radish. The small, summer varieties are grown for salads. Larger winter radishes can be eaten raw or cooked like turnips. The long white daikons, or oriental radishes, are up to 50 cm long and may be spherical or cylindrical.

### Healthy growth
In spring and autumn, sow summer radishes in a sunny spot. In summer, choose a position in light shade. Winter radishes grow best in soil that has been manured for a previous crop; sow seed from mid- to late summer. Daikons require a deep, well-dug, fertile, moist soil. They are sown in early spring for summer harvest and again in late summer for harvest in autumn to early winter.

### Radishes to mark the rows
Sow summer radish seeds where you are also growing carrots, onions, parsley and parsnips during spring. The radishes will grow quickly and clearly show the vegetable rows within a few days. Pull the young radishes 4–6 weeks after sowing, to make space for the other vegetables.

### Harvest and store
Harvest summer radishes when young and tender. In summer they tend to ripen all at once, so aim to harvest them daily. Washed and placed in a refrigerator, they will keep for up to a week. Winter radishes can be left in the ground until needed. Daikons require a growing period of about 10 weeks and will keep well in a sealed container in the refrigerator.

## RAISED BEDS

### The biggest container
A raised bed is the biggest type of 'container' for growing plants in a courtyard. It holds a much larger volume of soil than a pot, so plants need less watering and feeding. It has space for perennials and shrubs, so there is less replanting.

### Drainage guaranteed
A raised bed minimises the need for stooping, raises low-growing plants closer to nose and eye level, and ensures good drainage. It doesn't need to be built on a soil surface – although drainage and plant rooting will be better if it is – so it's a good choice if your courtyard is covered in concrete or paving.

### Choosing materials
Choose a style and materials that complement the house and the space. Materials include concrete blocks, brick, railway sleepers and natural stone. There are also prefabricated kits in powder-coated or galvanised steel, timber, plastic panels or recycled plastic.

Build the bed at least 60 cm high to minimise bending. You should be able to reach the back of the raised bed, but do not build it less than 45 cm wide, as this will not hold a sufficient volume of soil. Fill with good-quality topsoil or a mix of potting mix and soil, and let it settle for a few weeks before topping up and planting. Because potting mixes 'shrink', you'll need to top up the bed every year.

### Create a raised vegetable bed
If you have only a small space for growing vegetables, then pack them into a raised bed full of nutrient-rich soil. At the base, layers of coarsely broken branches and twigs, moistened paper and coarsely chopped garden waste provide ventilation. An optional layer of manure provides warmth and a long-lasting supply of nutrients. Shredded fresh garden waste mixed with dead leaves form the next layer, which stimulates growth in the first spring. Vegetables thrive in the topmost layer – soil enriched with compost.

See also
No-dig gardening

## RAINFOREST GARDENS *see pages 218–219*

217

# RAINFOREST GARDENS

A rainforest garden is a haven from the hustle and bustle of suburban life – a green retreat providing coolness and privacy.

## A world apart
A rainforest garden can be a taste of the exotic, an adventure land for children and a protective habitat for birds and wildlife. The dense screen of vegetation also keeps external noise at bay and helps reduce air pollution.

## Moderate drinkers
Despite their reputation as heavy water users, well-established rainforest trees in an area with good seasonal rainfall should rarely, if ever, need watering. Indeed, one of the characteristics of rainforest plants is their efficiency in taking up, using and storing water and this means that most of them can withstand dry periods. Australian native rainforest plants are particularly well adapted to quite long periods (up to 3 months) with no rainfall. Alternatively, consider installing dripline irrigation, which will allow you to water the rainforest garden deeply once a week during its establishment period and in prolonged drought.

*Staghorn*

## Trouble-free
Once established, rainforest gardens should be virtually pest- and disease-free. Because this type of garden becomes a micro-environment, plants can maintain a better balance with nature. The variety of plant life encourages a range of beneficial birds and

## create a Rainforest garden

**1** Build up and protect the soil. Add lots of organic matter and water-holding soil improvers, including compost, manures, mushroom compost, prunings, vermiculite and rock dusts.

**2** Mulch well before planting. Rainforest plants typically grow partly in soil and partly in the rotting organic matter of fallen leaves. Use as deep a layer of mulch as you can afford – at least 30–40 cm thick. Try bark chips, sugarcane, tea-tree or coir mulch, even old wool carpet.

**3** Establish the canopy and windbreaks with fast-growing or mature palms and trees, which will provide dappled shade and protection for the understorey plantings that will follow. Plant right through the mulch.

**4** When the canopy provides enough protection, usually after 1–2 years, plant slower growing and smaller trees. Select those that have colourful foliage, flowers or fruit.

**5** Add an understorey planting. Use shade-loving low-growing shrubs and groundcovers.

**6** Once the tree trunks start to mature, after about 3–4 years, add vines and attach epiphytes such as staghorns and rock orchids to well-established trees.

*Bromeliad*

# RAINFOREST GARDENS

predatory insects, which help control pests. Also, the density means that occasional insect attacks are not all that noticeable and the plants usually recover.

### Pick and choose
There is a large range of plants with which to create a rainforest in the garden. They include small trees, palms, ferns, tree ferns, plants with fleshy and colourful leaves, groundcovers that flower in shade, climbers and epiphytes.

### Palms
Palms play a vital role in tropical and subtropical rainforest gardens. Their slender stems look graceful and don't take up much room. Both native and exotic palms are suitable. Most do best in light soils with good drainage. To create a tropical rainforest effect, single-stemmed species can be teamed with palms that form clumps. Rainforest palms that like temperate conditions include the Bangalow palm (*Archontophoenix cunninghamiana*), the walking stick palm (*Linospadix monostachya*) and the cabbage tree palm (*Livistona australis*). Try the royal palms (*Roystonea* spp.) and golden cane palm (*Dypsis lutescens*) in tropical and subtropical areas.

### A rainforest for cool climates
While rainforests are usually associated with the tropics and subtropics, they are also found in Tasmania and New Zealand, and the plant species from these forests can be used as the basis for rainforest gardens in cooler regions. Here, tree ferns usually take the place of palms as the main structural plantings, while ferns are the main groundcover.

### Life at the top
The canopy is the top layer of tall trees and palms and it has to be established first to provide shelter and dappled (not heavy) shade for the understorey plants. This requires patience, but fortunately many rainforest plants are fast-growing and thrive in either sun or shade. Many palms also have speedy growth habits. Smaller types, such as the *Rhapis* palms, which only grow in shade, should not be planted until sufficient cover is established. Include some bird-attracting varieties.

### Ferns for many climates
Ground ferns common in the warm humid shade of rainforests include *Adiantum*, *Athyrium*, *Cyathea* and *Lastreopsis*. Species such as *Doodia* and *Pellaea* are more drought-hardy. The cool temperate rainforest is sometimes called fern forest and it provides a wide choice of ferns for cool damp microclimates, including *Todea*, *Asplenium*, *Blechnum*, *Dicksonia* and *Polystichum*.

See also Ferns, Palms, Tropical gardens

**Bird's nest fern**

**Hoya**

### Plants for a rainforest garden

**Canopy trees**  Lillypillies (*Acmena* spp., *Syzygium* spp.) ✹ *Backhousia* spp. ✹ Ivory curl tree (*Buckinghamia celsissima*) ✹ Davidson's plum (*Davidsonia pruriens*) ✹ Blueberry ash (*Elaeocarpus reticulatus*) ✹ *Eugenia* spp. ✹ Silky oak (*Grevillea robusta*) ✹ White cedar (*Melia azedarach*) ✹ Pink-flowered corkwood (*Melicope elleryana*) ✹ Puka (*Meryta sinclairii*) ✹ Native palms and tall, single-stemmed, fast-growing palms ✹ Celerywood (*Polyscias* spp.) ✹ *Pseudopanax laetus* ✹ Native gardenia (*Atractocarpus fitzalanii*) ✹ Umbrella tree (*Schefflera actinophylla*) ✹ Rose apple (*Syzygium jambos*) ✹ Golden penda (*Xanthostemon chrysanthus*)

**Mid-level fillers**  Clumping bamboos ✹ Shrub-sized lillypillies (*Acmena* spp., *Syzygium* spp.) ✹ Gingers (*Alpinia*, *Etlingera* and *Zingiber* spp.) ✹ *Clerodendrum* spp. ✹ Croton (*Codiaeum variegatum*) ✹ Dracaena ✹ Cassava (*Manihot esculenta*) ✹ Philodendron ✹ New Zealand flax (*Phormium* spp.) ✹ Dwarf umbrella tree (*Schefflera arboricola*) ✹ Small clump-forming palms

**Understorey groundcovers and low growers**  *Aglaonema* spp. ✹ Elephant's ear (*Alocasia* spp.) ✹ Cunjevoi, spoon lily (*Alocasia brisbanensis*) ✹ Native ginger (*Alpinia caerulea*) ✹ Bromeliads ✹ *Calathea* spp. ✹ Coleus ✹ Swamp lily (*Crinum pedunculatum*) ✹ Dianella, flax lily (*Dianella* spp.) ✹ Hosta ✹ Forest lobelia (*Lobelia trigonocaulis*) ✹ Mat rush (*Lomandra hystrix*) ✹ Prayer plant (*Maranta* cvs) ✹ *Syngonium* spp. ✹ Plectranthus ✹ Native violet (*Viola hederacea*)

**Climbers**  Gum vine (*Aphanopetalum resinosum*) ✹ Herald's trumpet (*Beaumontia grandiflora*) ✹ Kangaroo vine (*Cissus antarctica*) ✹ Flaming glory bower vine (*Clerodendrum splendens*) ✹ Native monstera (*Epipremnum pinnatum*) ✹ *Faradaya splendida* ✹ Golden guinea vine (*Hibbertia scandens*) ✹ Hoya, wax plant (*Hoya carnosa*) ✹ *Pandorea* spp.

**Epiphytes**  Bird's nest fern (*Asplenium australasicum*) ✹ Cymbidium orchids ✹ Rock lily, rock orchid (*Dendrobium speciosus*) ✹ Staghorns and elkhorns (*Platycerium* spp.) ✹ Pink rock orchid (*Thelychiton kingianum*)

219

# RASPBERRIES

## The right spot
Raspberries are suited to cooler areas. A site in full sun will produce the best crops, but the canes will also thrive in partial shade and yield well even in a cool, damp summer. For the space they occupy, raspberries give a higher yield than any fruit other than strawberries.

## Summer and autumn fruit
There are two raspberry types: summer-fruiting varieties that produce fruit on the previous season's shoots in summer; and the lighter-cropping autumn varieties that fruit on the current season's growth from early autumn onwards. A few varieties fruit twice, in summer and again autumn. Some have golden berries.

## Pest control
Several pests attack raspberries. If you notice aphids, leafrollers, light brown apple moths or thrips and you must spray, use a pest-specific insecticide and keep it to a minimum so beneficial insects are not harmed. Raspberries are also highly susceptible to viruses, and it is important to purchase 1-year-old canes that have been certified disease-free. Only buy stock from a reputable nursery.

## Ripe berries
Ripe but still firm berries are needed for preserves and freezing, while fully ripe berries are best for eating. Harvest every other day so that they are in peak condition and not overripe. Pick by gently squeezing a berry between your thumb and first finger so that the fruit detaches from its central plug.

# RECYCLING

## Using foil again
Attach strips of aluminium foil to strings to make bird scarers. Lay squares around the base of plants to deter flying insect pests. Wind 15 cm long strips around brassica stems to minimise damage from cutworms, and around the stems of runner beans and marrows to deter snails. Use sheets as light reflectors to prevent seedlings raised on a window ledge from becoming leggy.

## Bottling plants
With a little ingenuity, empty plastic bottles can be used in a multitude of ways. Cut large ones in half and use as mini cloches. Or remove the bottoms, pierce holes in the tops and upend them in the soil close to plants to make an irrigation system. Use the bottom halves as plant pots by piercing holes for drainage. Any opaque bottles can be cut into strips to make plant labels.

To make slug and snail guards for seedlings, cut out the bottoms and tops from transparent plastic bottles, then push the remaining cylinder into the soil to encircle a seedling. Remove before the plants become too large.

## Net protection
Drape old net curtains over your fruit bushes to protect them from birds. Alternatively, place the curtains over slightly tender plants as protection from frost.

## Eliminate weeds
Lay old carpets, underfelt or rugs over weed-infested land to smother weeds. Use them between rows of beans, peas and soft fruit bushes to keep the soil weed-free and retain moisture.

## Pots for plants
Use washed yoghurt containers, disposable plastic cups or milk cartons instead of plastic plant pots. Pierce drainage holes in the base. Cardboard egg cartons are the perfect shape for holding seed potatoes while they are chitting. Or fill the carton with seed-raising mix and sow seeds in each cell. When the seedlings are ready, divide the carton into cells and plant – the cells will decompose.

## Window cloches
Old windows make an ideal top for temporary coldframes, or you could remove the panes of glass and use them to make cloches. You can buy special clips to hold the panes together.

RED FLOWERS **R**

*Red-flowering gum*

*Flaming glory bower vine*

*Snapdragon*

*Waratah*

## RED FLOWERS

### Go for impact
If you want to make an impact in the garden, choose red. This is the colour of excitement and danger, and all eyes are drawn to it. Red flowers add brilliance and drama. But be warned – it's easy to overdo it, which is why these blooms should be used carefully in the garden.

### Bring it up close
Red gives the impression of being closer than it really is. You can see this effect if you look at a photograph of a garden with red flowers – they almost leap off the page. Take advantage of this by planting a red-flowering tree at the end of a narrow garden to make the garden appear shorter than it is. Or dot red-flowering plants around a large garden to create a feeling of intimacy. But conversely, if you don't want to shorten the perspective, restrict red to the foreground where its warmth can be enjoyed without destroying any illusion.

Because it attracts attention, splashes of red can also be used to draw you through a garden or to highlight an entrance, doorway or garden feature.

### Good combinations
The best colour to combine with red is green: it is complementary on the colour wheel. A backdrop of green foliage frames and enhances red blooms. For visual drama and moodiness, combine deep purple or dark orange with red. *Dahlia* 'Bishop of Llandaff', in a single plant, has the dramatic combination of dark purple foliage and red flowers. Yellow, lime green, silver and white will calm red down and provide a crisp contrast.

Be careful when mixing different red flowers. Reds based on orange tones can clash terribly with reds that have a blue undertone. Keep orange reds with orange reds, and blue reds with blue reds – don't mix them together.

*Hibiscus*

### Choosing red flowers
**For temperate and cool climates**
- Snapdragon (*Antirrhinum majus*) ✳ Red valerian (*Centranthus ruber*) ✳ Dahlia
- Poinsettia (*Euphorbia pulcherrima*) ✳ Daylily ✳ Cardinal flower (*Lobelia cardinalis*) ✳ Pohutukawa, New Zealand Christmas bush (*Metrosideros excelsa*)
- Oriental poppy, Flanders or corn poppy (*Papaver orientale, P. rhoeas*)
- Geranium (*Pelargonium* 'Big Red') ✳ Waratah (*Telopea speciosissima*)

**For warm and hot climates**
- Kangaroo paws (*Anigozanthos* spp. and cvs) ✳ Illawarra flame tree (*Brachychiton acerifolius*)
- Red tassel flower (*Calliandra tweedii*) ✳ Bottlebrush (*Callistemon* spp. and cvs) ✳ Canna
- Flaming glory bower vine (*Clerodendrum splendens*) ✳ Red-flowering gum (*Corymbia ficifolia* syn. *Eucalyptus ficifolia*, *C.* 'Summer Red') ✳ Hibiscus (*Hibiscus rosa-sinensis* cvs, *H. schizopetalus*)
- Red justicia (*Odontonema callistachyum*) ✳ Jacobean lily (*Sprekelia formosissima*)

221

# REPOTTING | RHUBARB

## REPOTTING

### Monitoring roots
Unpot a plant and check its roots when it can't take up water or has simply stopped growing. Crowded roots are the most common problem, but occasionally insects or diseases are to blame.

### To repot or not to repot
Allow the soil in the pot to dry out, then tap the pot gently and jiggle the plant to remove it without pulling too hard on the main stem. If the roots are badly matted, spiralled in a tight mass inside the pot, or so thick that you can hardly see the potting mix, it's time to repot the plant.

### Into a new pot
If you are 'potting on' – repotting in a new, larger container – select a slightly larger pot that is still in proportion to the plant's size. Fill with fresh potting mix, tease out the plant roots and plant as you would a new specimen.

If you want to put the plant back in the same pot, trim the roots first to stimulate growth. Lie the plant on newspaper. Gently pull away some mix, hold the plant upright, and slice from top to bottom around the root ball with a knife to cut off old roots. Fill the pot with new mix and replant.

## RHODODENDRONS

### A share of the sun
The natural habitat of most rhododendrons is light woodland in a cool or mountain climate. Most grow best in a semi-shaded position in cooler areas, but large-leaved species need more shade than others and do best in gardens with plenty of trees. In general, exposure to sun for about half the day promotes abundant flowering.

### The right situation
Most rhododendrons prefer a lime-free soil. Where soil is too limy, the best solution is to grow them in large tubs or half-barrels filled with lime-free potting mix. The best varieties for tubs are the smaller, slower growing types such as the *Rhododendron yakushimanum* hybrids.

### Light pruning
Rhododendrons don't need regular pruning. However, to promote good bushy growth, lightly prune young plants after flowering. Remove fading blooms, otherwise they will produce seed and reduce the quantity and quality of next year's blooms. Avoid damaging the buds that grow just below the old flower heads, and gently snap off this year's faded blooms between your finger and thumb once the new buds appear.

### Surface roots
Rhododendrons have surface roots and enjoy regular mulching with leaf mould or compost. If they outgrow their space in the garden, relocate them rather than prune them back – their shallow roots make them one of the easiest plants to move. If possible, move the plant in early autumn so the roots can establish themselves before winter sets in.

## RHUBARB

There are several strains of rhubarb, with leaf stalks ranging in colour from bright red to green. All stalks can be eaten but the leaves cannot as they contain oxalic acid, which is poisonous, although they are safe to compost.

### Seed or 'sets'
Rhubarb is best grown in cool climates and can survive several degrees of frost, especially if it is covered with straw. If grown from seed, the plants are likely to be variable. It can also be grown from segments, or 'sets', which you can buy from some nurseries or take by dividing the thick fleshy roots of an existing plant. Plant the sets in a well-manured site, leaving the bud just above the soil surface.

### Wait a year to harvest
Do not pull any of the stems in the first year. In subsequent years pull the fully grown outer stems as needed, by placing your thumb inside the stem as far down as possible and twisting it away from the clump.

ROCK GARDENS

## ROCK GARDENS

### Solution for a slope
A rock garden is a good solution for a sloping site, showcasing the natural beauty of stone and plants and creating pockets of retained moisture. You can even use rocks to make planting brackets on slopes that are almost vertical.

### Choosing stone
Choose quarried local stone so that it blends in seamlessly with the surroundings, especially if you are adding rock to an existing outcrop. But make sure you don't use illegally collected bush rock. Weathered, uncut stone gives a natural look, while cut stone creates a formal mood.

### Placing rocks
To make the most of an existing rocky outcrop, you should clear away all the unwanted vegetation first. Then add additional stones in a similar material if this is necessary to create a balanced look, starting at the bottom of the slope and working your way upwards. Choose the largest, heaviest rocks for the base of the slope, and decrease the size of the rocks as you go up. This trick of perspective will increase the perceived distance and height of your rock garden.

### Try to imitate nature
Make the stones as stable and natural-looking as possible. Dig out small holes and position the rocks so they are half-buried in the soil. If they are flat in shape, angle them backwards towards the slope. This encourages water to flow back into the soil behind the stone, where plants can use it.

### Plants between rocks
The most successful way to mix and match a variety of plants with stone is to balance nearly equal areas of stone and plants. The soft textures of the foliage and the flowers are framed and flattered by the heavy, smoother surfaces of stone.

### Carpets of colour
Many rock garden plants creep or cascade to form low carpets of colour between stones. Choose those that are easy to establish but not invasive, such as alyssum, candytuft, pinks, gazanias, lamb's ears, ivy-leaved geraniums, ice plants, spillover rosemaries and prostrate grevilleas.

To avoid a patchwork look, group similar-looking plants together so they'll interweave as they mature. Small pockets are ideal for clumps of little bulbs, such as miniature daffodils and freesias. Where the soil is shallow on top of large stones, plant with shallow-rooted hardy succulents, such as jelly bean plants and hen and chicks.

### build a Rock garden

1. Position the first rocks at the base of the slope. Let the natural lines in the stone all flow in the same direction.

2. Place the next row of rocks in position. Always use a strong stick or crowbar to move them so you don't hurt your back.

3. Fill around each new row of rocks with soil mixed with compost or rotted manure. Tamp this down well between the rocks.

4. Tuck the plants into the pockets of soil between the rocks. Cover any bare earth around them with gravel.

# R

ROCKET | ROSEMARY

## ROCKET

### Wild about rocket
Rocket (*Eruca sativa*), also known as arugula, has a smoky, peppery flavour. It is easy to grow and resembles a looseleaf lettuce, with lobed leaves that can be harvested a few at a time. Another species, wild rocket (*Diplotaxis muralis*), is common in northern Italy. It has much smaller leaves with an intense rocket flavour. Both are delicious used fresh in salads – the flowers can be, too.

### Position
Both types of rocket require a sunny position, although it is best to provide them with some light shade in midsummer. They are quite unfussy otherwise, thriving in average garden soil that has good drainage.

### Spread the harvest
Sow rocket in successive plantings each month, from spring to autumn, as it tends to run to seed fairly easily. If it doesn't self-seed in your garden, carry out monthly plantings to maintain your supplies. Pick the leaves before the plants start to flower. You can harvest the flowers as required for use fresh, and collect seeds when ripe.

## ROOFTOP GARDENS

### Can it take the weight
First make sure that your roof area is constructed sturdily enough to take the extra weight that a roof garden will involve. Also check access difficulties for bringing materials up narrow stairwells or in lifts. Consult your local authority or a surveyor or structural engineer for any restrictions on structures, weight, drainage and appearance.

### Don't forget drainage
Water must be able to drain away safely. You will need to install a waterproof membrane before putting planters or pots on the roof, with unimpeded drainage channels for rainwater to run off. Also bear drainage in mind when you choose the 'ground' surface. Lightweight tiles in a restful colour are good, while decking in clip-together sections can be both attractive and practical.

### Plants around the edge
A flat roof is strongest at its perimeter, so put the largest containers around the edges. No matter how light the containers – and plastic and fibreglass are particularly useful – potting mix weighs a considerable amount, although special lightweight mixes are available.

When planning your roof garden, include protection from the wind and sun – panels of trellis or slatted timber, a canvas awning or screen on the most exposed side, a sail or awning for a 'ceiling'. Always make sure that it is attached securely.

See also Balcony gardens

## ROSEMARY

### A touch of the Mediterranean
Rosemary, a hardy evergreen shrub with sweetly fragrant leaves, originally came from the shores of the Mediterranean. The pretty blue flowers appear from early spring to autumn. Pink, white and lilac varieties are also available. It can be planted as a hedge, while spillover varieties are excellent over retaining walls or in rock gardens.

### Good drainage essential
Rosemary will grow in any well-drained soil in full sun. It is salt-tolerant but will not recover if the soil dries out. Also avoid excessive watering and poor drainage, and keep mulch away from the stem to avoid fungal diseases. Many growers use a pea gravel mulch, which creates the dry, non-humid conditions that this plant likes. It does well in large pots but can become pot-bound easily and need repotting.

### An asset in the vegetable garden
This robust plant is largely untroubled by pests and diseases. If you want to protect cabbages, carrots and turnips from attack by root flies, grow some rosemary nearby. The scent of the herb is thought to confuse the female flies as they hunt for places to lay their eggs. The carrot fly detests the scent of rosemary.

# ROSE CARE AND MAINTENANCE

Although their blooms may appear delicate, roses can be extremely hardy in the right conditions. They love climates with hot, dry summers and cold, wet winters. They also prefer heavier but well-drained soil that has been improved with plenty of organic matter.

## How to avoid problems
With careful attention to plant selection, planting site, pruning and fertilisation, you can grow at least a few roses without constant problems. Set out dormant bare-root roses in early to midwinter, before the first leaves appear. Container-grown roses can be planted all year round.

## Planting at the correct depth
In prepared soil, dig a generous hole for a new rose and mound the soil in the centre slightly before positioning a bare-rooted rose on top and spreading the roots out carefully. Place a cane across the top of the hole before filling it, to ensure the rose will be planted with the grafting point about 10 cm above the soil surface when the hole is filled. The graft looks like a swollen area between the stem and root of the plant.

## Effective watering
Once established, roses can survive dry periods with little or no supplementary watering, although their repeat flowering will be reduced. If you have water available, try to give the base of each plant a good deep soak every week or two during the flowering season, depending on the climate. Mulching will also help conserve soil moisture.

## Get a good start
To promote early growth, dig plenty of organic matter into the soil when planting a rose. Mulch with an organic mulch such as lucerne hay, then once growth begins, add a liquid tomato feed or special rose food high in potash every 3 weeks in the first season to encourage flowering.

*continued page 228*

## Different roses, different pruning
To prevent your roses from turning into shapeless, tangled shrubs with very few flowers, prune them annually. The type of rose will determine the pruning methods required.

**Hybrid teas** Limit the main stems to about five per bush, and shorten these to four or five buds from the base of each stem, or just two buds for extra vigour and fewer, superior flowers.

**Floribundas** Keep five or six stems on each plant, and prune older stems to five or seven buds long. Trim young new shoots or leave them unpruned.

**Standard roses** These should be pruned according to type. Weeping standards are mostly grafted forms of rambling roses, and are pruned in the same way as them.

**Climbing roses** Prune the stiff stems in winter to retain a framework of mature branches. The flowers come in flushes or are borne continuously throughout the summer months.

**Rambling roses** In late summer, prune to replace flowered stems with young healthy shoots.

**Shrub roses** Lightly prune to shape, thin any overcrowded shoots, and cut one or two of the oldest branches to ground level or to a low sideshoot to stimulate new growth.

**Groundcover roses** Treat like shrub roses, but cut out any vigorous upright stems that disturb the low profile.

**Miniature roses** Prune lightly to maintain the size, or fairly hard for improved flower quality, cutting all the stems back to four or five buds.

# Roses

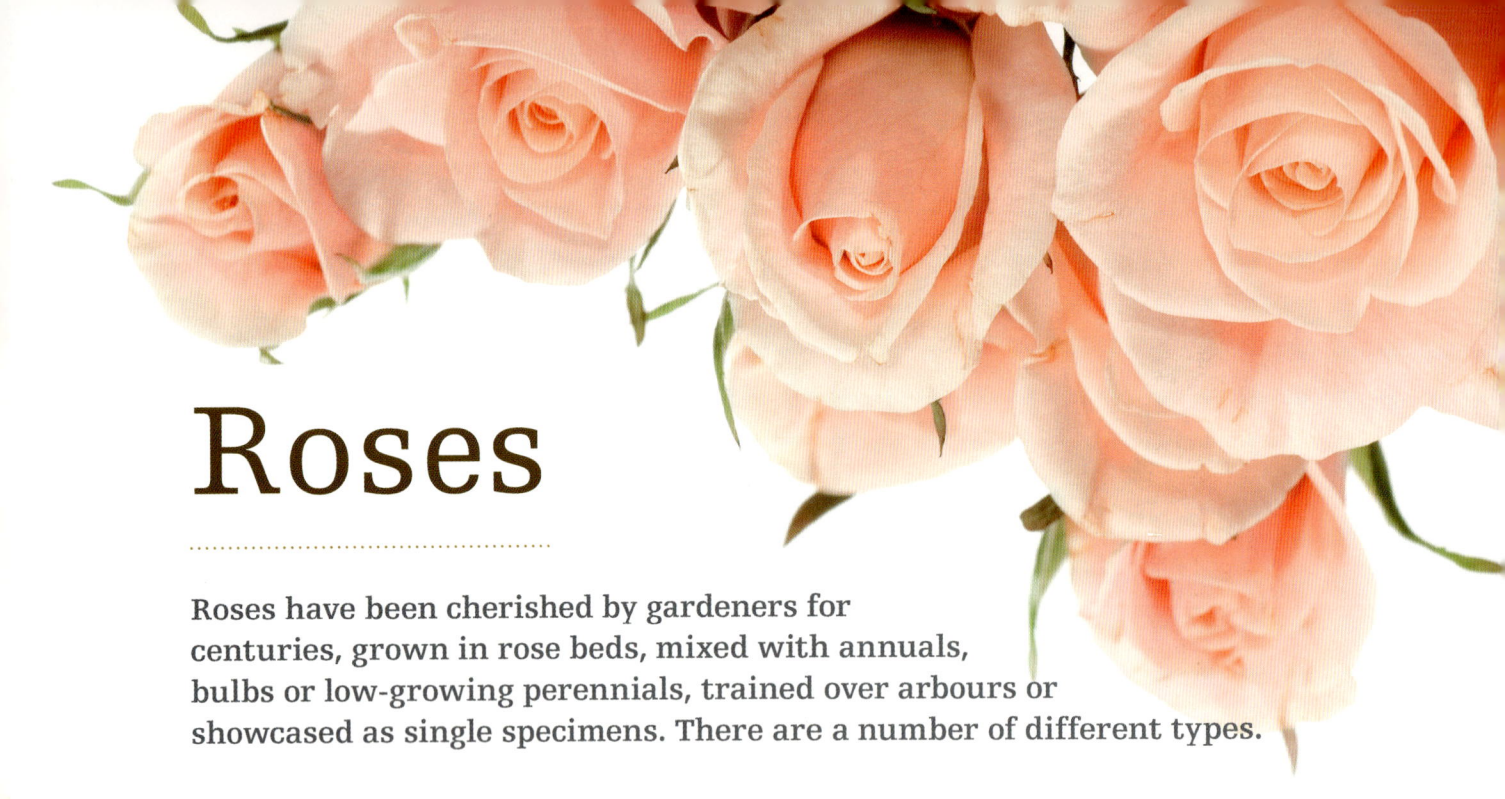

Roses have been cherished by gardeners for centuries, grown in rose beds, mixed with annuals, bulbs or low-growing perennials, trained over arbours or showcased as single specimens. There are a number of different types.

## Floribunda roses

Floribunda, or cluster-flowered, rose bushes will give continuous colour throughout summer and autumn. They produce multiple blooms on each stem, which are carried all over the bush.

✻ 'Bonica' ✻ 'China Doll' ✻ 'Friesia' ✻ 'Iceberg' ✻ 'La Sevillana' ✻ 'Pink Parfait' ✻ 'Sexy Rexy' ✻ 'Regensberg'

## Miniature and groundcover roses

Miniature roses have small blooms and foliage, usually borne on small bushes less than 60 cm high. Groundcover roses have a low, dense growth habit, with spreading rather than upright branches. They often grow to 1 m high by 1.5 m wide.

**Miniature** 'Cricket' ✻ 'Dresden Doll' ✻ 'Magic Carousel' ✻ 'Miss Daisy' ✻ 'Pride 'n' Joy' ✻ 'Starina'

**Groundcovers** 'Gold Magic Carpet' ✻ 'Hot Chilli' ✻ 'Meidiland' ✻ 'Nozomi' ✻ 'Ralph's Creeper' ✻ 'Sea Foam' ✻ 'White Flower Carpet'

## Hybrid tea roses

The blooms of hybrid tea, or large-flowered, roses have the classic rose shape, with one large flower borne at the top of a long, straight stem that is ideal for picking. They flower in distinct flushes from early summer to autumn.

✻ 'Aotearoa' ✻ 'Blue Moon' ✻ 'Diamond Jubilee' ✻ 'Double Delight' ✻ 'Fragrant Cloud' ✻ 'Ingrid Bergman' ✻ 'Just Joey' ✻ 'Maria Callas' ✻ 'Midas Touch' ✻ 'Mister Lincoln' ✻ 'Papa Meilland' ✻ 'Pascali' ✻ 'Princesse de Monaco'

## Climbing and rambling roses

These roses add an extra dimension to the garden. Climbers can be grown on a wall, fence or screen, while supple-stemmed ramblers can be trained over arbours and pergolas.

**Climbers** 'Albertine' ✻ 'Altissimo' ✻ 'Gold Bunny' ✻ 'Golden Showers' ✻ 'Handel' ✻ 'Lamarque' ✻ 'Lorraine Lee' ✻ 'Pierre de Ronsard' ✻ 'Titian'

**Ramblers** 'Paul's Scarlet' ✻ *Rosa banksiae* 'Lutea' ✻ 'Seagull' ✻ 'Veilchenblau'

## Old-fashioned roses

Heritage Roses were bred before 1867, while Old World Roses look similar but were bred after that date. These old-fashioned roses have blooms of exquisite shape with a delightful scent. They include the Gallica, Damask, Moss, Alba, China, Tea, Bourbon and Hybrid Musk roses.

✻ 'Charles de Mills' ✻ 'Felicia' ✻ 'Heritage' ✻ 'La Reine Victoria' ✻ 'Lady Hillingdon' ✻ 'Mutabilis' ✻ 'Quatre Saisons' ✻ 'Tuscany'

## Wild or species roses

These are roses as found in the wild. Their flowers may not be big or showy but they are beautiful because of their simplicity. Most wild roses are single-flowering. They often have added features, such as interesting foliage or colourful rose hips.

✻ *R. canina* ✻ *R. chinensis* ✻ *R. moyesii* ✻ *R. rugosa* and cvs

**Floribunda rose 'Honey Perfume'**

**Gallica rose 'Charles de Mills'**

**Hybrid tea rose 'Double Delight'**

**Wild rose**

## ROSE CARE AND MAINTENANCE
*continued*

### When to feed
Mature roses should be fed in early spring, midsummer and again in early autumn (that is, September, January and March). Use a slow-release fertiliser that is specially formulated for roses. Keen rose growers will also liquid-feed roses every 6 weeks from spring to autumn while the plants are flowering. During the growing season also remember to top up mulches.

### Training time
To grow ramblers or climbers up poles, train the stems in a spiral around the support, bending them almost horizontally to encourage flowering all the way up. Tie into the support regularly to keep them in place and prevent wind damage.

### The trouble with roses
The list of every rose pest or problem would be long, but the three most common ones are black spot, powdery mildew and aphids. After the winter prune and before any new growth appears is the time to deal with black spot and other fungal diseases and to reduce scale pests, even if they are not in evidence. Spray the dormant trunk and the ground around the rose bush with lime sulfur or a copper-based fungicide such as Bordeaux mixture.

### Deadhead for a second flowering
Encourage a second flush of flowers on floribunda and hybrid tea roses by prompt and frequent deadheading. Cut faded flower stems with secateurs just above the fourth leaf below the flower. The dormant bud in the joint of the leaf will develop and flower.

## plant a climbing Rose

**1** Soak a bare-root or container-grown climbing or rambling rose in a bucket of water for 1–2 hours. This allows the roots to absorb a maximum amount of water. Dig compost or well-rotted manure into the soil in the planting area.

**2** Dig a generous planting hole at the base of the arch, trellis or other support. Loosen the soil at the bottom of the hole. For a bare-rooted plant, make a mound in the centre of the hole.

**3** Place the rose in the hole; angle it slightly towards the support and spread the roots of a bare-rooted plant over the mound. Check planting depth – the grafting point should be 10 cm above the soil. Backfill with soil and water in well.

### Time your pruning
Winter is the main season for rose pruning. It should be timed so there is no likelihood of the new growth that comes after pruning being burnt by frost. In warm or coastal areas roses can be pruned from early July. In cold or inland areas pruning should be delayed until late July or early August.

Use a pair of garden shears to cut back mature shrub roses such as rugosa rose cultivars, Musk hybrids, groundcover and bedding roses, much as you would cut a hedge.

*See also Aphids, Powdery mildew, Pruning*

## treat Rose black spot

### Symptoms
Dark brown or black spots on leaves, which turn yellow and fall prematurely.

### Treatment
✳ Rake up and discard diseased leaves and always maintain good garden hygiene.

✳ Encourage plant vigour by spraying regularly with a foliar feed. Mulch to reduce reinfection from spores being splashed up onto rose stems by rain.

✳ Increase air circulation; water early in the day around the base.

✳ Spray with a copper-based fungicide, mancozeb, triforine, zineb, myclobutanil or a combined rose spray. Spray with lime sulfur in winter.

## SAFETY

### Wear the right clothing
Wear a wide-brimmed hat, long sleeves, gloves and a sunscreen. Also wear stout shoes, especially when using machinery or sharp, heavy tools. Don't wear a loose-fitting jacket, scarf or jewellery that might catch in machinery. Always wear gloves when potting up or planting out plants, and when pruning and trimming.

Also make sure that your tetanus injections are up to date. Tetanus bacteria may lurk in soil at the roots of the finest rose as readily as on a rusty garden fork.

### Save ears and eyes
Earplugs or mufflers are a good idea if using machinery for long periods. Goggles should be worn for tasks that send splinters and pebbles whirling, when using a chainsaw, hedge trimmer, mower, whipper-snipper or line trimmer.

### Extra care with power tools
Power tools are safe in the garden provided you observe a few basic rules. Always attach electrical equipment to a residual current device (RCD) or circuit-breaker, but never use power tools when it's raining. Loop cables over your shoulder and keep them behind you while working. Use extension leads that have a three-core flex and are connected to purpose-made rubber plugs and sockets. Always turn off the power supply and remove the plug from the socket before you adjust or clean a power tool.

Have your electrical equipment serviced regularly by an approved agent. Finally, never let children touch the equipment or distract you while you're working.

## use chemicals with Safety

Many chemicals that were once widely available to the public have been withdrawn on health or environmental grounds. Some chemicals are available only for certified professionals to use on specified crops. Even techniques accepted now as environmentally safe may in time prove to have detrimental effects on humans or native animals, bees or fish.

All pesticides, fungicides and herbicides are poisons. If you use them, follow these precautions:

✱ Choose the least toxic option, but remember that even these may kill beneficial insects.

✱ Homemade remedies can also be dangerous, so mix carefully.

✱ Follow the manufacturer's instructions carefully. A stronger solution of a chemical or more frequent spraying is not better.

✱ Wear recommended protective clothing and a mask. Do not eat, drink or smoke during application.

✱ Never spray when the weather is wet, windy or very hot, or there has been a hard frost.

✱ Spray only the infected plants or the infected parts of plants. Do not spray plants in flower.

✱ Keep children and pets away from the area during treatment and for a few days afterwards.

✱ Clean equipment thoroughly after use. Use separate equipment for herbicides and pesticides.

✱ Store chemicals in a safe place in the original labelled, sealed container. Do not store homemade remedies at all.

✱ Use chemicals by the use-by date as recommended on the label.

✱ Dispose of all containers and residues carefully.

✱ Thoroughly wash your hands and face after using chemicals.

## SAGE

### Sun for sage
The leaves of the hardy common or garden sage (*Salvia officinalis*) can be picked all year round. This attractive evergreen perennial grows to at least 60 cm high and produces tall spikes of violet-blue flowers – or occasionally white, lilac or pink – in summer. Grow it in full sun so it stays compact and develops the best aroma.

### Sage advice
Sage is an appealing plant for a flower border or container, as well as the herb garden, especially if you plant varieties with colourful leaves. These have the same flavour as the green-leaved types. 'Icterina' has yellow variegated leaves and 'Purpurascens' is dusky purple. 'Tricolor', with variegated leaves in pink, purple and cream, is not as vigorous as other sages.

### Regular renewal
Cut back plants in winter or trim in spring to keep them dense and bushy. Common sage is naturally short-lived, so replace it every 3–4 years. Sometimes low shoots will layer and root themselves. Otherwise, take 7.5–10 cm long cuttings in summer.

# S SALAD LEAVES

## SALAD LEAVES

### Grow a colourful medley
Choose different types of leafy greens to provide a variety of colour, texture, shape and taste in your salads. For a sweet taste, include lettuce or corn salad; add rocket, mizuna, mibuna or cress for spice; and endive, radicchio or chicory for a bitter flavour.

### Cut and come again
Pick all salad leaves when they are young and tender. Many lettuces and leafy greens can be picked by the repeat harvest method – leaf by leaf, all year round. The open-hearted lettuces can be cut back to the ground and the leaves will 'come again' up to five times.

### Great for small gardens
Salad crops are ideal if you don't have a full-sized vegetable patch and don't want to bother sowing seed. Buy four or five different types in mixed punnets and add them to your herb garden or tuck them away in a flowerbed.

They can also be grown in a container on a sunny balcony. Use a good-quality potting mix; add slow-release fertiliser and water-storing crystals if the mix doesn't already contain them.

### Nurture salad crops
The secret of successful crops is to plant your salad vegetables in rich soil containing plenty of organic matter and nutrients. Apply liquid fertiliser every 2 weeks and water copiously, as this will keep them growing fast and constantly. If growth is checked and they wilt, they will become tough and bitter. It is best to water them in the coolest part of the day – early morning or the evening. And if they start to run to seed, cut off the flowering stem and fertilise the plant.

See also Lettuces, Rocket

## identify Salad leaves

**Endive and chicory** They are grown in the same way and share a hint of bitterness. Endive varieties with plain leaves are called broad-leaved endive. A second group is known as curly endive, or frisée endive. Looseleaf chicory includes asparagus chicory, radichetta and the ruby-coloured radicchio. A group called heading chicory grows like a conical cabbage and is often known as witlof.

**Lamb's lettuce** Also called corn salad and mâche (*Valerianella locusta*), this salad vegetable makes a good substitute for lettuce. It grows during autumn and winter, when most other fresh salad leaves are scarce.

**Watercress** Although watercress (*Nasturtium officinale*) has a natural environment of a running stream, this peppery salad leaf can easily be grown in well-composted soil when given plenty of water.

**Miner's lettuce** It is also known as spring beauty or winter purslane (*Claytonia perfoliata* syn. *Montia perfoliata*). Although mainly used in salads in spring, it can also be cooked and used like spinach.

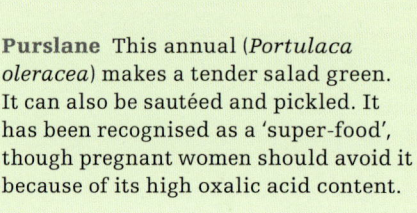

**Purslane** This annual (*Portulaca oleracea*) makes a tender salad green. It can also be sautéed and pickled. It has been recognised as a 'super-food', though pregnant women should avoid it because of its high oxalic acid content.

# SALVIAS

## 700 species
There are around 700 species of salvia, which include annuals, biennials, perennials, evergreen shrubs and culinary herbs. Each type makes a useful contribution to the garden. They range from 50 cm to 3 m high and vary in flower colour, flowering period and foliage. Many bloom over a long period and attract birds.

## A variety of situations
This group also varies greatly in its growing conditions and requirements. Some prefer poor, dry, well-drained soils, while others like moist, fertile soils. Frost tolerance also varies.

## Encourage flowering
When young plants reach about 5 cm tall, pinch out the growing tips to encourage bushy growth. Alternatively, for earlier colour, allow them to produce the main flower spike but remove it as soon as it starts to fade. You can also prolong flowering by lightly shearing off spent flowers.

## Dot plants
To add interest and height to summer bedding, use varieties of scarlet sage (*Salvia splendens*) in intense reds, or mealy sage (*S. farinacea*) with white, light or dark blue flowers, as dot plants.

You can grow them from seed sown in seed trays in spring or early summer, but they are easier bought as punnets from spring to summer. Look for young plants that have not yet begun to bloom. In frost-free areas the plants will survive winter and flower in the following season.

## A touch of blue
The strong blues of many of the herbaceous salvias, such as the gentian blue of *S. patens*, go well with yellow-flowered perennials such as daylilies for an easy-care, long-lasting display.

## Beware the bog sage
The dainty light blue flowers of bog sage (*S. uliginosa*) disguise this plant's true nature. Far from being delicate and dainty, it can spread rapidly to become invasive in a garden. It grows well in shade and in heavy soils.

## Good choice
Mexican sage (*Salvia leucantha*), with its woolly silver-green leaves and spires of purple flowers, is one of the easiest salvias to grow. It grows in sun or partial shade, flowers from summer to autumn and is drought-tolerant once established. It grows to around 1 m tall and, with its creeping rhizomes, forms a large but not too invasive clump in the garden.

*See also Sage*

# SAWDUST

## Sawdust in the garden
Local sawmills or cabinetmakers can often be a source of sacks of untreated sawdust, which is very good in the garden. It decomposes very slowly and absorbs large quantities of water, so small amounts of composted sawdust will improve the soil. Mix it through as you dig it into the vegetable plot or flowerbed.

## Compost and mulch
Composted sawdust is ideal as a mulch around fruit trees and flowering bushes, including roses. As it rots, sawdust takes nitrogen from the soil in the short term before releasing it again in the long term. As an interim measure, add some high-nitrogen fertiliser to keep plants well supplied with nutrients until the sawdust breaks down.

### Speed up decomposition
Spread alternate layers of sawdust and chicken manure in a compost heap, where the acidity of the sawdust will compensate for the manure's alkalinity. The resulting soil improver has the high nutrient content of chicken manure with the organic bulk of sawdust. Do not use it until the sawdust has decomposed and the mixture looks like rich, dark peat.

**SANDY SOIL**
*see page 232*

## SANDY SOIL

### The pros and cons
Sandy soils drain freely because of their high sand content. They are well aerated and don't have drainage problems, are easy to cultivate and have good rooting depth. They also warm up more rapidly in spring, allowing for earlier planting of warm-season annuals. The disadvantages are that they do not retain water or nutrients well and they also dry out quickly. They are so very porous that plant nutrients are constantly leached, or washed, out of them.

### Attractive to nematodes
Sandy soils can harbour parasitic root knot nematodes, also called eelworms. Affected plants will develop stunted roots with small swellings, thickenings and other deformities. Nematicides are available but control is difficult and can be expensive.

The most effective method to control nematodes is to only grow the affected host species every year in three. Leave the soil fallow but cultivated for a year or so, and rotate crops over 3 years. For 2 years, plant non-susceptible or tolerant vegetables, such as chives, broccoli, onions or corn, on the site where the infected vegetables have been growing. Or try companion planting – a cover crop of French marigolds (*Tagetes patula*) or pyrethrum daisies on the site can discourage them.

---

### Nutrient deficiencies
Sandy soils, particularly those containing some lime, are prone to deficiencies in iron and other trace elements. If plant foliage is pale, and particularly if young foliage displays any yellowing between the veins, think about using an application of trace elements. Also feed plants at least once a year with a slow-release fertiliser.

---

### Feeding sandy soils
Digging in compost and manure is the main way sandy soil can be improved. A small amount of clay (no more than 5 per cent) can also be worked in. Regularly grow green manures such as mustard, clover, lupins, comfrey, field or garden peas and broad beans, and add compost to keep sandy soil in good condition.

### Mulching sandy soils
Keep sandy soils mulched to conserve water and also prevent evaporation. Any coarse mulch can be used – straw, woodchips, chipped garden waste or pebbles.

### Natives will thrive
Many native plants are well suited to sandy soils. In Australia these include coast wattle (*Acacia sophorae*), coast banksia (*Banksia integrifolia*) and swamp she-oak (*Casuarina glauca*). In New Zealand try pohutukawa, also known as New Zealand Christmas bush (*Metrosideros excelsa*), the large-leaved kowhai (*Sophora tetraptera*) and Chatham Island akeake (*Olearia traversii*).

### Perennials, bulbs and annuals for sandy soils
Among the perennials, bulbs and annuals that do well in sandy soils are agapanthus, wormwoods (*Artemisia* spp.), catmints, dianellas, freesias, blanket flowers (*Gaillardia* spp.), gazanias, pinks, sea hollies (*Eryngium* spp.), cut leaf daisies (*Brachyscome* spp.), strawflowers and most types of succulent.

See also Coastal gardens, Nematodes, Soil analysis

---

## SCALE INSECTS

### Plants affected
Many, including bay trees, citrus and other fruit trees, camellias, daphnes, eucalypts, ferns, roses.

### Symptoms
Pink, brown, red or white scale on stems, twigs or leaf undersides.

### Treatment
✽ Encourage predators, such as parasitic wasps, flies or ladybirds.

✽ Spray affected plants with petroleum-based sprays, such as white oil, or with organic plant-based oil sprays.

✽ Use wettable sulfur to control white louse scale.

✽ Sprays of lime sulfur, or permethrin and oil, or maldison and oil can be used.

✽ Time non-dormant sprays to destroy young scale while mobile.

✽ Discourage ants, which defend some scale to get their honeydew.

✽ Sponge indoor plants with soap and water or move them outside and use petroleum oil sprays.

*Pohutukawa, or New Zealand Christmas bush*

SCREENS AND COVER-UPS | SECATEURS

# SCREENS AND COVER-UPS

### A camouflage curtain
A climbing vine quickly produces a dense curtain around unsightly areas, drainpipes and garbage bins. A trellis with an evergreen climber, such as star jasmine (*Trachelospermum jasminoides*), provides a robust screen all year. Fix a collar of plastic-coated open mesh around a drainpipe, then train a vigorous climber up the mesh to quickly hide the pipe.

### Bin solutions
A small pergola or sections of trellis trained with ivy, especially the variegated varieties, can be turned into a screen that will hide garbage bins from view. On a hard surface, you could grow a hedge of dwarf conifers in a 45–50 cm wooden trough for an elegant screening touch.

See also Climbers

## create a Screen

**1** Drive metal post holders into the ground where the posts supporting the trellis are to be sited. Secure the posts in place.

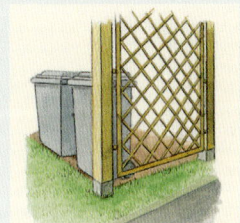

**2** Screw the trellis to the posts. For a 1.8 m post allow three screw fixings per post. Most trellis kits come with the screws and fittings.

**3** Dig a hole beside each post. Plant, angling the plants slightly towards the trellis. As they grow, tie their shoots in with twine or string.

# SEAWEED

### Collecting seaweed
Seaweed has a similar value in the soil as composted manure, but with a higher potassium and trace element content. Kelp seaweed contains growth hormones and growth regulators, acids and trace elements. Check with the local authority first for rules about collecting seaweed. Stack for 1–2 months to allow rain to wash out the alkaline, salty sand, then dig it into the soil at the rate of about one bucketful per square metre. Or add it to your compost.

### Seaweed-lovers
Artichokes, asparagus, beetroot, cabbages and brussels sprouts thrive on seaweed, as it provides them with a lot of potassium, calcium, magnesium and the trace elements boron, chlorine, iodine, sodium and sulfur. For these plants, rake the seaweed directly into the bed, without first leaving it to decompose.

### Liquid feeds
Seaweed liquid fertilisers are rich in growth stimulants, help protect plants from drought, frost and fungal attack, and also activate micro-organisms in the soil. Use them to stimulate growth in trees or shrubs that are not growing well or are being attacked by pests and diseases. They also help seedlings and mature plants to overcome transplant shock when applied after new plantings have been watered in.

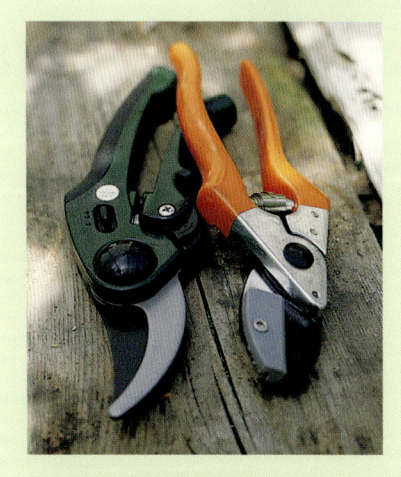

# SECATEURS

### A gardener's essential tool
Use secateurs on stems up to 1 cm thick. Ratchet types can make cutting easier, as does a rubber stop fitted between the handles. Check that the hand grips are comfortable and fit the span of your hand when open. Avoid cheap models, which are suitable only for light work. You'll find left-handed models available, too.

**Bypass secateurs** Operating with a scissors action (top left), these secateurs are used for most kinds of pruning and deadheading, and trimming plants to size and shape.

**Anvil secateurs** A single sharp blade cuts against a flat surface (top right), making these ideal for cutting hard, woody stems.

### Good hygiene
Viruses can easily be spread on secateurs, so always clean them in a weak bleach solution after use. To minimise the spread of disease in your rose garden – roses are very prone to viruses – be extra-vigilant. Give your secateurs a quick dip in bleach solution before you use them on each rose bush.

# SEDUMS
*see pages 236–237*

## SEEDS AND SEEDLINGS

Growing plants from seed is rewarding and economical. Some are easier to grow from seed than others – many vegetables and annual and biennial flowers offer a good chance of success, while perennials, shrubs and trees can take longer to establish.

### Sowing seed
Seeds can be sown into pots or trays, or directly into the ground in the warmer months. Sow in spring or summer for a summer or autumn harvest, and autumn for crops that will mature the following year. If the weather is still cool and there's a risk of frost, cover with frost cloth, cloches or a mini poly-tunnel – but be sure to water regularly.

### Directly into the ground
Seeds of some annuals, such as cornflowers and California poppies, don't transplant well. They are best scattered directly onto garden beds and raked in lightly. Use sand to mark out areas for each plant, overlapping for a natural look, and sow in drifts, not in regimented rows.

Many vegetable seeds can be sown directly into the well-prepared soil of a vegetable bed once the soil and the weather has warmed up. They are sown in drills.

### Help the germination process
Help seeds germinate and produce stronger plants with these tips:

❋ Before planting, rub sweet pea seeds with sandpaper or nick each seed with a clean sharp knife.

❋ Plant the flat seeds of melons, cucumbers and other cucurbits on their sides.

---

## prevent damping off in Seedlings

### Plants affected
Most seedlings, especially small bedding plants, such as begonias, lobelias, petunias, snapdragons, and young lettuces.

### Symptoms
After sprouting, seedlings collapse as stems or roots darken and rot; rapid spreading on seed tray; fungal growth may appear; seedlings do not emerge.

### Treatment
❋ It is difficult to control once started, so take preventive action. Use clean sterilised trays and tools washed in a weak bleach solution.

❋ Dispose of all seedlings and growing medium from trays where infection has occurred, even if seedlings appear healthy.

❋ Use sterilised seed-raising mix.

❋ Ventilate seed trays; water early in the day and be careful not to overwater.

❋ Water seedlings with copper oxychloride after pricking out.

❋ Water a seedbed with copper oxychloride or furalaxyl before sowing seeds.

SEEDS AND SEEDLINGS

* Soak hard-skinned seeds such as lupins, wattles, beans and peas in warm water for 24 hours before planting to soften them.

* Plant seeds that develop deep roots, such as runner beans, in root trainers. These are individual reusable cells that can be folded open to remove seedlings without damage to roots or stems.

### After sowing
If birds are a problem, cover the seedbed with horticultural fleece, or fasten wire or plastic netting to canes set just above soil level.

### Sowing vegetable seeds in a drill
Rake prepared soil of a fine tilth in the vegetable bed. Use pegs and twine to mark straight lines; space them the correct distance apart according to the packet instructions. Following the twine, create a shallow V-shaped groove, or drill, with the corner of a hoe. If the soil is dry, trickle water into the drills, then sow seeds thinly, at the recommended distance, and lightly cover with soil. Water with a fine mist and label the rows.

## sow Seeds in a seed tray

**1** Fill a seed tray with quality seed-raising or propagating mix. Gently smooth the surface with a piece of dowel but do not compact the mix. With the dowel, make a shallow channel. Gently shake seeds evenly over the mix or, if large enough, drop them in one at a time.

**2** Smooth the mix so the seeds are just covered, or use a sieve to add a light covering of seed-raising mix. Very fine seeds may not need any covering. Select the fine spray setting on a spray bottle and water the tray thoroughly. Label the seeds.

**3** Place in a warm, dry location with natural indirect light. To retain moisture and humidity, cover trays with plastic wrap or a sheet of glass. Add a tag with the plant name and the date of sowing. Remove the cover when the seeds begin to germinate.

### Buying and saving seeds
Seeds are usually sold loose in packets, but some vegetables are now also supplied on tapes that you bury in the ground, with no thinning or transplanting needed.

To save seed from garden plants, allow seed heads to ripen for as long as possible. Collect directly from the plants or cut off the seed heads, dry them in a warm place, then shake or pick off the seeds.

### Storing seed
Don't throw away seeds that you haven't used. Store them properly for later use. Put leftover seeds in paper packets and wrap in aluminium foil, then place them in an airtight container in a cool room or in a screw-top jar in the vegetable part of the refrigerator. Add a packet of desiccant.

### Pricking out
Seedlings in trays must be given room to develop by spacing them out in other trays or in pots. Do this 'pricking out' as soon as the seedlings are large enough to handle, when the first true leaves – rather than the seed leaves, which are the very first two leaves – appear. Fill trays or pots with a good-quality propagating or potting mix. Carefully lift each seedling with the point of a pencil or dibber, holding it by a leaf, not the stem. Use a pencil or stick to make a hole in the new mix. Plant the seedling at the same depth as it was. Water gently and keep out of direct sunlight for 2 days.

### Hardening off
Frost-tender plants or plants raised in a greenhouse, coldframe or cloche must be hardened off before planting out. Gradually expose them to full sunlight for a week, but protect them at night. Also water them more frequently.

*See also* Sowing, Transplanting, Vegetable gardens

# SEDUMS | SHADE

## SEDUMS

### Tough succulents
Sedums are a large family of flowering succulents that come in many forms. As long as there is good drainage, they will tolerate a variety of soils. They will adjust to growing in sand and gravel and can persevere during drought, thanks to their thick, fleshy, water-storing leaves. Sedums are also salt-tolerant and grow well in coastal gardens.

### Good for groundcovers
The evergreen groundcover sedums look effective in a rock garden, containers or hanging down a retaining wall. They are even being used in roof gardens on 'green buildings'. The jelly bean plant (*Sedum rubrotinctum*) and its colourful cultivars provide very dense coverage. Baby donkey tail (*S. burrito*) and donkey tail (*S. morganianum*) look especially good growing in a hanging basket. *S. dendroideum* makes a small spreading shrub; *S. palmeri* forms bright green rosettes.

### Growing sedum
Don't fertilise sedums, and water them only when a serious drought is in progress. They need to be divided only when the centres of ageing clumps begin to grow and flower less vigorously. It is easy to root stem cuttings taken in early summer.

### Late show
The very popular perennial showy sedum (*S. spectabile*), also known as showy stonecrop, is topped with large, showy long-lasting heads of tiny flowers from midsummer to autumn. This is a lovely, versatile plant with a tough constitution to suit difficult sites. 'Autumn Joy' has 60 cm stems of pink blossoms that darken to russet red in autumn. 'Matrona' has pinkish flowers and burgundy-flushed foliage.

## SHADE

### Shade calculations
Before planting a large hedge, calculate the amount of shade it will cast 10 or more years from now. To do this, hold up branches or poles of the height you estimate the hedge will reach and note the length of shadow that these cast throughout the course of a day. Remember that the sun is lower in the sky in winter than in summer and the shadows will be longer. Hedges on the north side of your property are most critical as they will shade the garden in winter.

### Growing instant shade
Enjoy shade beneath a pergola from the first year of planting by interspersing fast-growing climbers, such as cup and saucer vine (*Cobaea scandens*), black-eyed Susan vine (*Thunbergia alata*) or climbing nasturtiums (*Tropaeolum* cvs), with clematis, rambling roses or perennial climbing plants, which will take longer to establish themselves and clothe the pergola.

### Improvised protection
To make a temporary sunshade for leafy green vegetables such as lettuces and spinach, drive stakes into the soil around them and put a wooden crate, a cardboard box or tightly woven netting on top. Alternatively, plant the vegetables in a spot where they will receive

SEDUMS | SHADE TREES

## SHADE TREES

### Natural air-conditioning
Trees planted on the northern and western sides of your house will provide a natural air-conditioning system throughout summer. Deciduous trees will let in the warm sunlight during winter when they are leafless. When the heat of the sun returns, the leafy canopy will offer shade.

### Lawn under trees
Trees that provide shade can be frustrating for gardeners who want to grow lawn under trees. One solution is to use Durban grass, a long-bladed coarse grass that grows well in shade. An alternative is to replace grass with shade-loving groundcovers or a mulch of gravel or leaf litter.

### Let the light in
Thin out the lower branches of trees to let light and rain filter through so the plants underneath can flourish. If the area beneath the tree is grassed, raising the canopy will make mowing easier.

### Shade umbrella
In the hot tropics, where shade is at a premium, make the most of beautiful bauhinias, poincianas (*Delonix regia*), trumpet trees (*Tabebuia* spp.) or tulipwoods (*Harpullia pendula*). In a cooler climate the naturally spreading shape of box elder (*Acer negundo* cvs), redbuds (*Cercis canadensis*) or Chinese pistachios (*Pistacia chinensis*) creates a good canopy.

### Don't forget to water
In periods of prolonged or unseasonable dryness you may need to water established trees and shrubs that do not normally require water. Street trees are particularly vulnerable during drought. Before making a decision not to water lawns during a drought, consider the effect this may have on surrounding trees, which are generally watered by run-off from the lawn.

### Light shade
Trees that create dappled shade, such as jacarandas, Japanese maples and many eucalypts, can be planted to provide light shade for shrubs that like semi-shade. These include many camellias, azaleas and rhododendrons. Avoid trees with dense foliage, as they will cast a thick blanket of shade where few plants will thrive.

---

### Effective heat shields
To lower the temperature inside a greenhouse in summer, put up roller blinds on the outside of the sunny, north-facing roof, fastening them to the ridge of the greenhouse roof. On dull days, the blinds can be raised as needed to let in light.

To help prevent plants becoming too hot during the summer when growing under the protection of coldframes and cloches, apply a shading paint or limewash to the outside of the glass when the weather becomes hot. In autumn, wipe the paint off.

---

shade during the hottest part of the day, from noon to 3 pm.

You could also plant tall-growing vegetables on the western side of the vegetable plot. Corn can be used in this way. Leafy vegetables will thrive between rows of taller vegetables – runner beans or Jerusalem artichokes are ideal for this – or grow flowers such as dahlias or sunflowers.

**Japanese maple**

# SHADY GARDENS

There are areas of partial or permanent shade in every garden, caused by trees, buildings, walls and fences. Because there are so many plants for the open, sunny parts of the garden, shade is often considered difficult. It doesn't have to be so.

### Shade-loving flowers
In a cool to temperate climate make a show in the shade in spring and early summer with lungworts (*Pulmonaria* spp.), Solomon's seal (*Polygonatum × hybridum*) and foxgloves. From late summer to late winter you can enjoy clivias, hellebores and Japanese windflowers (*Anemone × hybrida*). In warm climates use billbergias and other bromeliads along with native ginger (*Alpinia caerulea*) for an exotic look in the shade. For a carpet of vivid colour all summer, choose impatiens.

### Evergreen shrubs
A number of evergreen shrubs are suited to a heavily shaded garden: aucubas, with their glossy oval leaves; *Buxus sempervirens* 'Marginata', whose leaves are yellow-edged; bushman's friend (*Brachyglottis repanda*), with dull green leaves and fragrant cream flowers in spring; osmanthus (*Osmanthus fragrans*), with tiny but intensely fragrant flowers; lily-of-the-valley shrub (*Pieris japonica*), with tassels of delicate white to pink flowers and coppery red new growth; and Japanese skimmia (*Skimmia japonica*), which has oval leaves topped by large bunches of red berries.

### Shrubs with flowers
There are many flowering shrubs that need dappled shade to look their best – try azaleas, boronias, camellias, hydrangeas, forest bell bushes (*Mackaya bella*), kalmias and rhododendrons. Use Vireya rhododendrons in subtropical and tropical shade. Hardy laurustinus (*Viburnum tinus*) makes a good hedge even in deep shade.

### Don't forget foliage
Flowers are important, but don't underestimate foliage plants. Their shapes and textures can be put to good effect in positions of low light. You can use some variegated plants to create colour contrasts. Variegated forms of euonymus, hosta and ivy are particularly useful. Gardeners in frost-free climates can add begonias, caladiums, crotons, variegated gingers and bloodleafs (*Iresine herbstii*). In fact, many yellow-leaved plants prefer semi-shaded positions, as their foliage can be scorched by the sun.

### Vegetables for shade
Most vegetables will produce a good crop only if they are grown in full sun, but spring cabbages, Hamburg parsley, leeks, winter lettuces and shallots will grow fairly well in slightly shady conditions. Mint and lemon balm thrive provided the soil is moist.

### Lighten up
Plants, furniture and even pathways can help brighten up a dull corner. Grow plants with silver or pale leaves and white, yellow or pink flowers. Paint trellises, fences and garden furniture white and construct walkways using pale-coloured bricks or paving stones. White gravel will reflect the light and make an attractive pathway.

### Mulch to improve conditions
Where small plants are being grown underneath larger ones, apply a good mulch every year to improve the water- and nutrient-holding capacity of the soil. The

## pick flowers for Shady gardens

Some flowers are well adapted to growing in shade but fussy about the soil conditions.

### Perennials for light shade, dry soil
❋ Bromeliads ❋ Bugle (*Ajuga reptans*) ❋ Clivia ❋ *Euphorbia amygdaloides* var. *robbiae* ❋ *Geranium macrorrhizum* ❋ Hellebore ❋ Heuchera ❋ Hosta ❋ Lungwort (*Pulmonaria* spp.)

### Perennials for light shade, moist soil
❋ Gingers (*Alpinia* and *Zingiber* spp.) ❋ Japanese windflower (*Anemone* x *hybrida*) ❋ Goat's beard (*Aruncus dioicus*) ❋ Rex begonia ❋ Tree begonia ❋ Leopard plant (*Ligularia* spp.) ❋ *Rodgersia pinnata* ❋ Meadow rue (*Thalictrum* spp.) ❋ Violet (*Viola odorata*)

### Perennials for light shade, wet soil
❋ Astilbe (*Astilbe* x *arendsii*) ❋ *Houttuynia cordata* ❋ *Persicaria affinis* 'Superba' ❋ White arum lily (*Zantedeschia aethiopica*)

### Bulbs for shade
❋ Golden garlic (*Allium moly*) ❋ Italian arum (*Arum italicum*) ❋ *Corydalis flexuosa* ❋ *Cyclamen coum* ❋ *C. hederifolium* ❋ Dog's tooth violet (*Erythronium* spp.) ❋ Amazon lily (*Eucharis grandiflora*) ❋ Paintbrush lily (*Scadoxus puniceus*)

### Bedding plants for shade
❋ Bedding begonia ❋ Foxglove ❋ Impatiens ❋ Lobelia ❋ Honesty (*Lunaria annua*) ❋ Monkey flowers (*Mimulus* spp.) ❋ Forget-me-not ❋ Nicotiana ❋ Primula ❋ Viola

# SHADY GARDENS

best time to mulch is in early spring, using compost, well-rotted manure, spent mushroom compost or composted bark. If mulching alone is not enough to retain soil moisture through summer, you could install a timer-controlled soaker hose or dripline irrigation system under the tree.

## Trees and their shade

Deciduous trees cast heavy shade in summer, but let light in from autumn until their leaves return in spring. The shade of evergreens is permanent, but varies with the species. Many eucalypts cast only dappled shade; conifers and rainforest trees cut off almost all sunlight. Often the gloom can be lightened by judicious thinning of the branches, a task best done in winter or late summer when the tree is not in active growth.

## The underrated fern

Ferns are attractive plants for shady places. There are ferns for both moist and dry sites, though some need frost protection. While none offers flowers, they display a wonderful range of leaf shapes, textures and shades of green.

Tree ferns are plants of such character that they can set the theme for the entire garden. To discourage the taking of tree ferns from the bush, always buy them from a reputable grower.

## Coping with dry shade

The combination of drought and shade can be challenging. Areas under a well-established tree or at the foot of a sunless wall are often difficult because of the dry soil that accompanies the gloom. You'll need to improve the water-retaining capacity of the soil by adding copious amounts of well-rotted compost and leaf mould. You could also install a watering system to provide regular water for the shade-loving plants.

> ### Think of woodlands
> Many favourite garden flowers grow wild in deciduous woodlands, and their life cycle is adapted to that of the trees overhead. They grow and flower during winter or early spring, becoming dormant for the summer when shade is heaviest and the tree roots most competitive. They include bluebells, columbines, daffodils and primroses. Add some shade-loving groundcovers and perennials, such as hellebores, hypericums, plectranthus and lesser periwinkle (*Vinca minor*), to clothe the ground for summer.

# SHALLOTS | SHRUBS

## SHALLOTS

### The real shallot
Known as an eschalot in classic French cuisine, a true shallot is a small perennial brown-skinned bulb of the onion family that grows in clusters. Shallots can be roasted or fried and are often used for sauce making. They are milder flavoured than onions.

### Growing shallots
Most garden centres only stock one or two varieties of shallots for sale by weight. There is a bigger choice of prepacked shallots sold through mail order. For a good crop, they need enriched, well-cultivated soil. Plant individual bulblets 20 cm apart in drills, ensuring the tips are just below the surface of the soil and leaving 30 cm between each row.

### When foliage dies down
When foliage dies back in late summer or early autumn, lift the clumps and lay them out to dry for a few days. When the foliage has withered completely, split the clumps into single bulbs and leave to ripen for a few days. Store in a net or basket in a cool, dry place.

## SHRUBS

Long-lived and resilient, shrubs add structure to the landscape and create a backdrop for garden beds. Depending on the shrub, you can get showy flowers, fragrance, autumn colour, brilliant berries or fruit, and food and shelter for wildlife.

### Making the case for shrubs
Shrubs are permanent and do not have to be replanted each year. They are much less susceptible to disease and weather extremes than annuals and perennials, and those with evergreen foliage offer interest throughout the year.

They are the perfect choice for small gardens where there may not be room for trees. They can also be planted in a tub on a patio, courtyard or balcony. In a large garden, they are the ideal way to divide the space with a hedge, a framework or a specimen plant.

### Planting shrubs

* Always choose shrubs to match your garden conditions. Keep in mind your soil type, the climate and how much space you have, and read labels carefully.

* Don't skimp on hole size.

* Water often and generously until plants are well established.

* Put in supports or stakes if necessary before planting, not after, to avoid damaging the roots.

### Mistakes to avoid
To give shrubs the best chance, avoid these common pitfalls:

* Don't plant new shrubs too close together. They will become overcrowded after 2–3 years and you will have to dig some of them up just when they are settling in.

* Avoid autumn feeding in cold climates. This encourages soft, sappy new shoots to form, which may be damaged by cold or frost.

* The best time to plant most shrubs is autumn, while the soil is still warm but temperatures are falling. The root system will have time to become well established before the increased temperatures and growth of spring. The only exception is frost-sensitive shrubs in cold climates – with them, you should wait until spring.

240

SHRUBS

### Trial shrub positions
To avoid the mistake of siting a shrub badly and then having to transplant it later, pot it up in a large container of quality potting mix and stand it in a few selected spots first. Plant it out later when you have had time to decide where it will look best.

### Scent and colour
Select a shrub that offers scent as well as showy flowers. Sometimes it's the flowers that are scented, such as murrayas or mock orange (*Philadelphus* spp.); sometimes it's the foliage, as with lavender, mint bushes (*Prostanthera* spp.) and rosemary.

### Rejuvenating a shrub
When a shrub is growing slowly and not flowering well, it may need radical treatment. First, cut out any dead or diseased wood as well as any spindly shoots, then remove the oldest branches, which are usually the thickest and darkest in colour, cutting them out at the base with a saw. To reshape the plant, cut back the current season's growth to within a few centimetres of a strong branch and also remove any crossing or rubbing branches. Do all this in spring when growth is just beginning. Finally, apply a general slow-release fertiliser, mulch well and keep well watered during the spring that follows.

### Combinations for year-round interest
Create a planting scheme that has something to offer throughout the year. This shrub grouping for cool or temperate climates will need only minimal pruning.

**Winter into spring** The red flowers of flowering quince and the yellow blooms of mahonia take over in spring from the witch hazel's spider-like, fragrant flowers.

**Summer into autumn** The flowering quince's fruit start to swell in summer. By the time they are ripe, the witch hazel, mahonia, nandina and small Japanese maple have taken on their autumnal tints.

### Keeping leaves variegated
If you have a shrub – or, for that matter, a tree – in a variegated form, cut out any branches on which plain green leaves appear. These branches are very vigorous and, if left, will take over from the branches with variegated leaves.

### Multi-season attraction
In small gardens, choose shrub varieties that give two or three seasons of colour. Some, such as 'Robyn Gordon' and 'Honey Gem' grevilleas and 'Wiri Mist' and 'Autumn Glory' hebes, flower over a long period. In a cool climate the deciduous dogwood *Cornus alba* 'Spaethii' has red stems in winter, variegated foliage and creamy flowers in summer, and white fruits in autumn. Some lillypilly varieties, such as 'Cascade', have large pink or yellow powder-puff flowers, a mass of pale or bright pink berries and pink new growth at different times of the year.

## prune Shrubs

Before pruning a shrub to shape it, cut out all dead and diseased wood – this can be done at any time of year. Overgrown shrubs can be rejuvenated by pruning over several seasons.

**Shrubs that flower before midsummer** Early bloomers such as weigela and mock orange (*Philadelphus* spp.) produce flowers on the previous season's growth. They should be pruned as soon as flowers fade, cutting back the stems only to the highest new shoot or bud. This gives the shrub time to grow mature wood, ready to flower again next season.

**Shrubs that flower after midsummer** Late bloomers such as butterfly bush (*Buddleja davidii*) should be pruned in early spring, before new growth starts. Cut back last year's flowering stems and any weak shoots. The harder you prune, the more new growth – on which flowers will develop – will be produced.

**Evergreen shrubs** Prune plants such as azaleas, box, camellias, gardenias, grevilleas, lillypillies and photinias to keep them in shape, shorten overly long shoots and thin out congested plants. The pruning is usually done in spring and summer, after flowering.

**Shrubs with coloured stems** Some shrubs, such as red-barked dogwood (*Cornus alba*), are grown for their colourful stems. Prune in early spring, cutting back all last year's growth to near ground level or to an established framework.

### SHEARING PLANTS
*see page 242*

241

# SHEARING PLANTS

### Why shear?
Shear plants that you want to grow into dense hedges or neat shapes. When hedge plants have joined together, use hedge shears or a hedge trimmer to create geometric shapes and a smooth, even surface. Box, lavenders, murrayas, plumbagos and other shrubs with a tight, compact form will benefit from shearing.

### Super-speedy deadheading
When you have a mass of plants that need deadheading, shearing with hand-held hedge trimmers makes quick work of the job. In midsummer, shear back petunias, cut leaf daisy (*Brachyscome* spp.), alyssum and verbena by half their height. Many groundcovers can be cut back with a lawnmower or line trimmer. A new flush of healthy leaves and maybe even flowers will appear a few weeks later.

## Shear lavender

**1** When lavender bushes are coming towards the end of their flowering, clip them all over if you want to maintain a dense, compact shape.

**2** Use shears to clip the entire plant. Cut off the dead flowers complete with stems and top few centimetres of new shoots.

# SLOPES

A garden on a hill can have drainage and erosion problems. You can treat a slope as one straight fall or as a series of terraces, especially if the slope descends towards the house.

### Ensure proper drainage
Plan a drainage system for water at the bottom of a slope, especially if you live in an area subject to heavy storms. A pond or a pool may be the ideal collection point for water streaming down a slope.

### Wet slopes
A commonly held misconception is that sloping land drains well, but this is not necessarily the case. If the soil is heavy it will not drain even if it is steeply sloping. Indeed, springs and hanging swamps can be found on hillsides. To improve drainage in poorly drained soil, build raised beds or install subsoil irrigation.

### Dig from the top of a slope
When digging a sloping site, start at the top and work downwards so that any soil that washes down can be thrown back towards the top again. Trample the soil down well and it will remain in position for longer.

### Dig small hollows
To ensure that plants do not dry out, plant them in small hollows dug into the slope. These will collect rainwater and also make it easier to individually water each plant with a watering can if necessary. A deep mulch will also help to keep the soil moist and prevent erosion.

### Right plant, right place
North-facing slopes are ideal for planting Mediterranean shrubs and other sun-loving plants, including many spring bulbs. West-facing slopes are best for

SLOPES | SNAILS AND SLUGS

# SNAILS AND SLUGS

### Effective barriers
Slugs and snails will not cross a rough-surfaced barrier, such as one made from gravel, crushed eggshells, nut shells or oyster shells, sharp sand, ash or lime. Spread any of these around the most vulnerable plants in your garden. Or cut out the bottoms and tops from transparent plastic drink bottles, then push each bottle into the soil to encircle a seedling. Remove them before the plants get too large.

### Use slug pellets sensibly
Modern slug pellets are effective. They are usually coloured blue – not a natural food colour – and also contain a chemical deterrent to deter animals from eating them. The pellets are best used sparingly in the garden; do not pile up pellets in small heaps, but scatter them so that each is distributed about 10–15 cm apart.

Never put snail pellets where pets, especially cats and dogs, can find them and don't leave the packet lying around. The dead and dying snails also pose a hazard to pets and wildlife in your garden, so each day, collect up any poisoned snails and dispose of in the bin.

If you suspect that your pet has eaten pellets or poisoned snails, take it to the vet immediately.

### A citrus trap
Create a snail and slug trap by placing inverted empty grapefruit or orange halves near threatened plants. (You could cut little doors in the halves, to ease the snails' or slugs' entrance.) Attracted by the smell, they will congregate inside, ready for collection and disposal.

### Death by drowning
Slugs and snails find beer irresistible, even if it is flat! Bury a plastic cup half filled with beer in the soil close to vulnerable plants. Don't sink the cup to soil level, otherwise creatures that are beneficial to the garden, such as slug-eating ground beetles, will fall in. Cover the cup with an upturned plastic flowerpot with a large hole in the bottom as further insurance against any beneficial insects falling in. Renew the beer every 3 days.

---

rock gardens or, in a cold climate, alpine plants. Ferns and tough evergreens are a good choice for south-facing slopes. East-facing slopes are the best site for shade-loving plants. For a coastal site, try white correa (*Correa alba*), fan flowers (*Scaevola* spp.) and pigface (*Carpobrotus glaucescens*) to bind the soil.

### A retaining structure
To retain earth on a slope, erect a series of low barriers or hurdles from treated pine logs or sleepers. If you'd like an informal look, use brushwood. Hammer 60 cm stakes into the ground, leaving around 30 cm above ground to support the logs or brushwood. The steeper the slope, the closer together the structures should be placed– between 1 m and 3 m. Planting groundcover plants or dwarf shrubs in between will give additional stability.

### Groundcovers for slopes
It can be simpler and cause less land disturbance to plant the natural slopes of your garden with plants that ramble and scramble. They'll form a thick carpet of foliage that excludes weeds, retains moisture and also protects the soil against erosion.

Simplicity is the key. Slopes planted with broad bands of only a few varieties will also be much easier to maintain than many different plants.

### Waterfall feature
For rock faces or cliffs that are so steep there is really little hope of being able to create and maintain a garden, turn this into a feature by creating a waterfall.

*See* Groundcovers, Rock gardens, Terraces

### Other snail control methods
* Encourage natural predators, such as frogs, ground beetles, lizards, native Australian snails and birds. Or keep ducks.

* Clear the ground of debris and of plants that provide moist, shady hiding places, such as ivy.

* Hand-pick at night or trap by day under moist flowerpots.

## SMALL CITY GARDENS
*see pages 244–245*

# SMALL CITY GARDENS

A garden in the city can be a private haven of beautiful flowers, a shady retreat, even a kitchen garden full of edible plants. Moreover, a small space is easier to landscape and look after, and to create the particular mood or style that you want.

### Borrowed landscape

To help your small garden seem bigger, make a focal point of a feature beyond your garden fence, such as a view or a distant tree. This is known as a borrowed landscape, and it's a much used technique in landscaping.

Use climbers, shrubs and small flowering trees to shield out neighbours, and stretch space by linking indoor and outdoor living areas with a terrace or deck, so that friends and family can spill into the garden or dine outdoors.

### Let in light

Let in the sun and light that plants need, especially flowering and edible plants. Put tall shrubs and evergreen trees that have year-round shadows to the south of the garden, and deciduous ones to the north and east, so you will get winter sunshine.

### Choose your trees

Urban gardens, especially those behind terraced houses, tend to be shady. Plant small trees or tree-like shrubs that won't add to the gloom. Choose a columnar tree like the Japanese cherry *Prunus* 'Amanogawa', or a delicate and feathery tree that won't resent being cut back hard if it grows too large. In a warm climate consider frangipani, jacaranda or *Tabebuia chrysantha*. In cooler climates try a deciduous Japanese maple.

### Buffer against noise and pollution

Solid walls are most effective against noise but can block views or cause stagnant air in small spaces. Dense hedges of abelias, murrayas, photinias or camellias, particularly sasanqua camellias, will make a lovely noise-muffling screen. Planting thick banks of groundcovers, such as ornamental grasses, mondo grass, bugle or sedum, will help to clean the air and deaden street noise.

Use street beds and container plants as extra noise mufflers. Plants that cope well with smog include hydrangeas, lavenders, mock orange (*Philadelphus* spp.), marigolds, petunias and roses. The tinkle of a water feature or fountain can also mask the noise of traffic or neighbours.

### Banish the lawn

With shade and concentrated foot traffic to contend with, a lawn in a small city garden will struggle. Consider replacing the grass with paving or gravel, which can better withstand the wear and tear. You can soften the effect with crevice or container plantings.

### All-year evergreens

In a small city garden every shrub must pull its weight for as much of the year as possible. Evergreens are indispensable but choose them carefully with this purpose in mind. Shrubs that are smaller in scale will make the garden seem airier and larger.

### Make less work

In some city gardens, the whole area may have been concreted over. It can be an enormous task to remove the concrete and then dig over and improve the soil to make it ready for planting. If you

### Skilful use of mirrors

A carefully placed mirror will extend a garden without you having to buy an extra plot of land. It draws the eye to a fresh view that is nothing but illusion. However, the view above the mirror and the supporting structure must be masked or the magic is broken.

SMALL CITY GARDENS

decide on the positions of beds and borders first, you can break up the concrete in these areas only and construct raised beds. The remaining concrete will serve as paths. Or simply build raised beds on top of the concrete.

## Lift into the light

If your city garden has limited sunlight, raised beds will help your plants capture more light. This is essential if you want to grow vegetables and herbs. A few well-placed beds raised up to 45–50 cm and edged attractively will grow much better crops than those growing at ground level in shade. Plant miniature vegetable varieties to optimise space, along with heirloom varieties that are noted for their resilience.

## Pots and tubs

Pots of perennials and annuals let you put flowers where you want them when you have limited space – lifting a dull corner or a patch of shade beneath a tree where roots prevent concentrated planting. Choose a range of compatible and beautifully shaped pots. There are many well-made lightweight copies of expensive pots available.

## Plants for pots

Camellias and azaleas take well to pots, as do hydrangeas if given shade and water. Other plants to consider include bougainvilleas, citrus, coleus, cordylines, ferns, fuchsias, impatiens, succulents, bulbs, palms and many herbs.

## Ornamental and edible

When space is tight, choose plants that are both ornamental *and* edible. Plant fruit trees, choosing varieties suited to your climate. Cumquats and standard bay trees look handsome in tubs. Along the edges of paths, try prostrate rosemary, alpine strawberries, chives, curly parsley, thymes and coloured basils.

Interplant flowers with attractive vegetables – open-hearted lettuce varieties, rainbow chard, 'Tuscan Black' kale and leeks. Soft fruit bushes can be sited at the back of borders. Add drama with silver-leaved artichokes, while a patch of tall corn or sunflowers gives height and colour.

Use fences to support climbing beans and peas. Grow pumpkins, squash and passionfruit on wires or lattice. Mints, lemon balm, alpine strawberries or gingers make good groundcovers in shade.

*See also* Courtyard gardens, Patios, Paving, Raised beds

## plan a Small city garden for the front yard

Lack of space does not mean lack of options. In this square front yard, an imaginative use of materials and plants makes for three very different designs.

**Colour without flowers** The straight herringbone path is set with terracotta bricks, which are also used to edge the decorative diamond. Four matching plants balance the diamond; these could be either standard bays or roses.

**Green and gold** Honey-coloured paving gives a warm-toned surface in a neatly squared plan. The large container next to the side plantings provides a focal point from the window and door and breaks up all the rigid geometric lines.

**Soften straight surrounds** The decorative surfacing – brick paving laid in a basketweave pattern among large grey pavers – is the strongest design element. The two parallel areas of plantings soften the straight lines of the path.

245

# SNOWDROPS AND SNOWFLAKES

A clump of snowdrops or snowflakes is a welcome sight at the end of winter, right on the threshold of a new gardening year.

### Where it's warmer
Snowdrops (*Galanthus nivalis*) do well in a very cold mountain garden but are hard to grow in warmer or coastal areas. If it's too warm, they may flower in the first year but gradually fade away as the weather warms up. The giant snowdrop (*G. elwesii*) tolerates warmer climates better.

### Snowdrop alternative
A plant with a similarly white nodding flower is the snowflake (*Leucojum aestivum*). Each petal is marked with a green dot. These plants tolerate slightly warmer conditions. They grow as a leafy clump that becomes dormant over summer. The flowers last from autumn to spring, held on straight stalks among or above the leaves.

### Let them naturalise
Snowflakes are such easygoing plants that they thrive even in moist, shaded soils. They also grow well with more sun. Allow the bulbs to naturalise in clumps with daffodils, which also flower in late winter and spring.

*Snowdrops*

# SOIL ANALYSIS

### Identify the soil in your garden
Knowing what type of soil you have in your garden is essential for gardening success. There are suitable plants for every soil type. Your local nursery should be able to advise you on your particular area. You can also do a number of simple tests to check soil texture, pH (the acid/alkaline balance) and the presence of lime.

### Different types of soil
First you need to know what soil type you are dealing with. Soils fall into three general groups: clay, loam and sand. Most larger gardens have a mixture of soils, but often there is one type that predominates. You can identify the composition of your garden soil by observing and feeling it.

### The soil's profile
Dig a hole about 60–70 cm deep, or down to the bedrock, and clean one side of the hole so you can examine your soil profile. This is

## test your Soil texture
The easiest way to determine what sort of soil you are dealing with is to pick up a handful and rub it.

**Clay soils** Have a smooth, soapy texture if moistened and rubbed between your finger and thumb.

**Loam soils** Are crumbly and fibrous when handled, due to the high level of organic matter.

**Sandy soils** Feel rough and gritty when rubbed. They crumble and fall apart easily in your hand.

# SOOTY MOULD | SOWING

## SOOTY MOULD

### Plants affected
Most garden and greenhouse plants, fruiting and ornamental trees and shrubs, and especially tea trees such as manuka (*Leptospermum scoparium*).

### Symptoms
Black mould on upper surfaces of leaves and stems.

### Treatment
* The mould develops on honeydew, a sugary excretion of sap-sucking insects such as aphids and scale – so start by controlling these insects.

* Hose off the sooty mould, as it dries out once the honeydew is removed. Wipe greenhouse plants with a soft damp cloth.

See also Aphids, Scale insects

## SOWING

### Getting organised
After buying packets of seeds, arrange the packets in the order of sowing to make sure that you remember seed-sowing times. Check the guide on the back of the packet. It can be frustrating to find you've missed a favourite plant's sowing date.

### Test for viability
If you want to sow an old packet of seeds, do a test to make sure you are not wasting your time. Put a few of the seeds on a piece of damp paper towel laid in the bottom of a clean margarine tub, replace the lid and leave in a warm place. Check every day for signs of germination. If none of the seeds germinate on the paper, throw the rest away. However, if some germinate, the proportion showing signs of life indicates how many of the remaining seeds you need to sow to get the number of plants you require.

---

the soil layers, which will usually be in two and sometimes three distinct horizontal layers.

**Topsoil** Under the top cover of leaves and mulch, you'll find the uppermost and darkest layer. This is the topsoil, and it can range in depth from 3 cm to 60 cm. This is where the root systems of most plants are located.

**Subsoil** Below the topsoil layer, a well-marked change of colour indicates the compacted subsoil. Large trees and deep-rooting shrubs can force their roots deep down into this layer. Some deeper soil profiles may have an extra, transitional layer between the topsoil and subsoil.

**Parent bedrock** In gardens that have shallow soils, a third layer may be visible, the underlying parent bedrock. This is the rock that, through weathering from wind, rain, ice and rivers, has contributed the mineral content of the soil.

### Altered layers
In a garden of a newly built house, where excavation and heavy machinery have packed down and churned up the soil, the original soil profile may have been altered completely. The topsoil may have been pushed aside, stripped and removed, or buried under the subsoil. This can cause plants to wither for no apparent reason and can be time-consuming and expensive to fix. Before you have major building work done, clear the topsoil on your block and store it in a mound in an out-of-the-way spot. Respread it in the garden when work is complete.

See also Acid soil, Alkaline soil, Clay soil, Sandy soil

### Testing the pH level of your soil
You can purchase a simple colour indicator kit from garden centres. By following the kit's instructions, you will be able to test and get a reasonable idea of the pH of your soil. This will help you decide which plants to grow and if there are any you should avoid. For example, if your soil is alkaline or limy, acid-loving camellias and azaleas won't thrive without extensive soil modification and are probably best avoided.

# SOWING | SPICES

## SOWING continued

### Sterile sowing medium
Never use garden soil for sowing seeds in pots. It contains bacteria, fungi, pests and weeds, which will damage your seedlings as they germinate. Always be sure to buy bagged propagating or seed-raising mix from a garden centre or nursery to give your seedlings the best possible start.

### Warm up the soil for early sowings
Vegetable seeds will germinate much more readily after winter if the soil in the vegetable garden is warmed with a sheet of black plastic for 2 weeks in advance of sowing. If the weather is still cold when the seeds have germinated, protect the young seedlings with cloches or horticultural fleece. Resist planting too early.

### Controlling the flow
Small seeds tend to stick to the fingertips, with the result that they are sown unevenly and germinate in clusters. Fold a piece of stiff white paper to make a channel for the seeds. Use the tip of a knife to push them singly into the drill or hole, moving the paper along to ensure even spacing. Try mixing sand with fine seed, such as carrot seed, for even sowing.

### Ensure germination
When sowing seeds in individual pots, sow two seeds in each pot in case only one seed germinates. If both seeds germinate, gently remove the weaker seedling so that the stronger one is left to develop fully.

### Nature's way
Seeds that fall to the ground naturally are buried only to the extent that the wind blows a light covering of soil over them. Imitate nature's way when sowing seeds by covering them afterwards with no more than their own depth of seed-raising mix.

### Firming in
Use the back of a rake to cover the seeds and the drill where they're sown with soil, and to firm it in gently. The mix in pots can be firmed in with the bottom of another pot. Alternatively, you could use a purpose-made presser consisting of a disc of plywood nailed to a piece of dowel.

### Speed germination in dry weather
Seeds sown in dry soil will not germinate until rain provides moisture. Water seed drills before sowing, then sow the seeds and return the soil to the drill with the back of a rake. If your soil is poor, cover the drill with fresh seed-raising mix. Water carefully with the rose on the watering can.

### The right temperature
The optimum temperature for the germination of most seeds is 21°C. After sowing, place seed trays in a greenhouse or a warm place indoors and check them every day. Better still, use a thermostatically controlled seed propagator in the greenhouse or on the window ledge to keep the seeds at exactly the right temperature to help germination. Move them into cooler conditions with good light once seedlings start to develop.

### Light and dark for germination
Most seeds will germinate in light or dark as long as moisture and warmth are provided. It is usual to cover seeds in a pot or tray with a little seed-raising mix or vermiculite, more to ensure they don't dry out than to cut out light. A few seeds, including begonias, impatiens and lobelias, need light to germinate; sow on the surface of the mix and do not cover.

## SPICES

### Tender cumin
Cumin, a popular cooking spice, is produced from an annual plant (*Cuminum cyminum*) that grows to 15–30 cm high. It needs a long growing season and should be sown in spring in the place where it will grow. Not only will it produce seeds for cooking, but it is also a highly ornamental plant.

### A tropical quartet
Four plants widely used as spices in cooking – ginger (*Zingiber officinale*), turmeric (*Curcuma longa*), galangal (*Alpinia galanga*) and cardamom (*Elettaria cardamomum*) – are all members of the Zingiberaceae family and are all similar in habit. Though they will grow in any frost-free

# SPINACH AND SILVERBEET

### True spinach
English spinach (*Spinacia oleracea*) is a cool-season crop mostly grown in cool or cold areas. In warmer areas it is grown as a winter crop. So-called New Zealand spinach (*Tetragonia tetragonioides*), also known as Warrigal greens, can grow in hot summers and cooler conditions.

### Not spinach but silverbeet
Silverbeet, or Swiss chard (*Beta vulgaris cicla*), belongs to the beetroot family. It is often called spinach (incorrectly) in Australia but has larger, darker, coarser and more crinkly leaves and thicker stalks than English spinach. It has a longer cropping period and does better in warm climates.

### Garden ornament
Rainbow chard, also known as rainbow silverbeet, looks very striking growing among purple basil, nasturtiums or ornamental cabbages. Try varieties such as 'Rhubarb' and 'Bright Lights', with red, pink, orange, yellow or multicoloured stalks. They both look and taste good.

### Water supplies
Spinach and silverbeet require enriched soil and copious water, particularly in dry weather, but soil must be well drained. Mulch to help retain soil moisture. A mulch of hay or lucerne will also prevent the leaves getting gritty from soil splash.

Fast, vigorous growth in English spinach indicates good nitrogen levels in the soil, while pale green, limp leaves signal that the soil is low in nitrogen.

### Keep it cool
Cool soil temperatures are crucial for successful seed germination of English spinach. It also tends to bolt, or run to seed, in warm weather. Gardeners in warmer climates should grow it during the winter months, or find a cool, partly shaded position to plant it during the warmer months.

**Rainbow chard**

climate, these tropical perennials need year-round warmth for good yields. In spring plant rhizomes 5 cm deep in rich soil and a sunny or semi-shaded site, and water and fertilise through summer.

Gather cardamom seedpods as soon as they ripen in late summer and dry them carefully. Harvest ginger, turmeric and galangal by digging up the rhizomes in late summer to autumn. Trim off the foliage when it withers. Save the plumpest rhizomes and replant segments for next season's crop.

### Grow your own saffron
Corms of the saffron crocus (*Crocus sativus*) are occasionally available from specialist bulb growers. This is the world's most expensive spice, and it is not difficult to grow in a temperate climate. Just don't expect huge harvests – it takes the stigmas of hundreds of flowers to yield just a few grams of saffron threads.

Plant the corms as soon as they become available in late summer, setting them about 5 cm deep and 5 cm apart in fertile, well-drained soil in a sunny position. When the flowers appear in autumn, carefully snip out the three orange stigmas from the centre of each flower and spread them to dry in a warm but shaded spot. Fertilise the corms after flowering, and divide them every 2 years. Don't water during summer when the plants are dormant.

### Pods from a climbing orchid
Vanilla pods come from an orchid, *Vanilla fragrans* syn. *V. planifolia*, which is quite easy to grow in humid tropical conditions and a lightly shaded position. It needs distinct wet and dry seasons, as flowers are initiated after the dry period. It is a climbing orchid, up to 7–8 m high before it begins flowering – so some support, such as a pole or lattice, is essential.

**Galangal**

# S

SPRAYING | SPROUTING SEEDS

## SPRAYING

### Keep them separate
Keep one sprayer for misting plants and a separate one – that is clearly labelled – to use solely for applying pesticides. Always wear protective clothing and a mask when spraying any kind of chemical.

### Extend the range
For controlling pests or diseases, feeding plants or killing weeds over a large area, buy a sprayer that can be worn on the back and pressurised while in operation. A knapsack sprayer holds a far greater quantity than a hand-held one yet is comfortabe on the back.

Add an extension or telescopic lance to your sprayer to help treat pests and diseases on out-of-reach trees. These are available from garden centres.

### Make a quick killing
Invading grasses, such as kikuyu, and other persistent shrubby weeds in the flowerbed can be killed quickly and safely with the help of a large, bottomless plastic bottle. Cut back the weed to a few centimetres above the ground. Wait until it has resprouted, then slip the bottle over it. Spray a systemic herbicide through the neck of the bottle, then replace the lid. The bottle directs the herbicide onto the weed and also provides protection for nearby plants.

### Fine-weather spraying
If rain is forecast, don't carry out any spraying job in the garden. Chemicals require several hours of dry weather in order to be absorbed by plant leaves or through the body of an insect. Never spray in windy or hot conditions either. Spraying early in the morning or in the evening will minimise damage to beneficial insects such as bees, who are less active at that time.

### A rainforest in the home
The sprayer has a vital role for epiphytic rainforest plants such as tropical orchids, bromeliads and certain ferns, which take no sustenance from the ground but instead draw their moisture and nutrients from the air around them. To help reproduce these conditions, mist the plant's leaves with rainwater every day or two, especially in summer. Add a few drops of liquid fertiliser to the water every 3–4 weeks.

### Foliar feeding
If your plants are growing in compacted soils or have diseased or damaged roots, they may be unable to take up nutrients and will benefit from foliar feeding. This uses fertilisers designed so a plant absorbs nutrients through the leaves; they are applied to the plant's leaves.

## SPROUTING SEEDS

### Sprouts on the windowsill
Even in the depths of winter you can have fresh greenery to add to your salads by growing cress or salad sprouts on a windowsill. Many types of bean sprouts, alfalfa and mustard seeds can also be grown in this way.

### grow Sprouting seeds in a jar

1. Wash the seeds well and soak overnight in warm water. Drain, rinse well, place the seeds in a jar and secure damp muslin over the top with an elastic band. Place the jar on its side in a warm, dark place.

2. Rinse the seeds from once to five times a day, depending on the type of seed. To do this, half-fill the jar with water.

3. Replace the muslin, swill the seeds gently in the water then drain through the muslin. Repeat daily until the sprouts reach the desired size; always return the jar to a warm, dark place.

4. If the sprouts need 'greening' in sunlight, place the jar on a shady windowsill for 1–2 days. When the sprouts are ready, empty them out and rinse well in a colander. Store in the refrigerator for 1 week.

# STAKES AND STAKING

## Lasting stakes
The best stakes are made from hardwood. They are straight and will last well. Canes or thin, twiggy branches, usually called pea sticks, make ideal supports for perennials and bulbs that reach a height of up to 1.2 m and tend to flop over. Push two or three pea sticks firmly into the soil around the edge of the plant. If a plant tends to sprawl after heavy rain, loop twine around the outside of the sticks to encircle it and provide additional support.

## Staking a bare-root tree
Before positioning a bare-root tree in a prepared planting hole, drive a 5 cm thick stake 40 cm into the ground, ensuring first that it is tall enough to support the tree's trunk up to the point where it branches. Putting the stake in first avoids damaging the roots. Plant the tree and tie it securely to the stake.

## Staking for a strong trunk
Trees with a tall, narrow root ball or trees in very windy areas will be damaged if they're left to rock in the wind. However, they do need some lateral movement in order to develop strong trunks.

To provide this limited lateral movement, drive two hardwood stakes 40 cm into ground that has not been dug, on opposite sides of the tree, outside the area of the root ball. Use three stakes in very windy areas. At a height equal to a third to halfway up the trunk, staple a hessian tie to each stake. Loop each tie around the trunk and staple the end back to the stake. You can use three stakes in very windy areas. Remove ties and stakes within a year of planting.

> ### A tie for all seasons
> Tree ties should be strong enough to resist the force of wind but should not cut into the bark. Suitable ties include a plastic or webbing strap with a plastic or rubberised buffer, a pair of old stockings or tights, or a wide rubber or plastic strip held firmly in place with string or wire.

# STANDARDS | STEPS

## STANDARDS

### Training a shrub
Drive a stake into a planting hole or into a pot filled with potting mix, then plant a young shrub that has a straight, sturdy stem. Train the shrub into a standard by cutting off the lowest branches so they are flush with the main stem. When the shrub is a little taller than the desired height, prune off the central growing tip to make the head branch out and form a ball. Cut the tips of the sideshoots that will form the ball.

### The key to success
Standards require ongoing care. Remove any sideshoots on the main stem and adjust the ties as the stem gets thicker. Check that the stem is not rubbing against the stake as this can weaken the plant and allow an entry point for fungal diseases. A pruned standard should be roughly ball-shaped and well balanced. This will encourage vigorous growth.

If growing a standard plant in a pot near a wall, hedge or fence, turn the pot once a week to prevent uneven growth and flowering.

### Suitable shrubs
Evergreen shrubs, including bay trees, box, euonymus, lillypillies and yews, make particularly striking standards and look good all year round. The main stem will need support while it is growing and even when it is mature. Standards let you grow large shrubs in a small garden. You can restrict the size of the head and also have space to grow other plants underneath.

### Desirable and decorative
Roses and fuchsias are good plants for flowering standards. Standard 'lollipop' trees, such as lillypillies or bay trees, which are trained into a ball of foliage on a bare stem, make elegant potted specimens on either side of the front door. Climbers, including honeysuckle and wisteria, and rambling roses, pruned regularly, also make colourful standards.

*See also* Bay trees

## STEPS

### Versatile bricks
Using bricks as your material enables you to make steps of all sizes. Build brick steps on firm ground or concrete bedding.

### Seasonal considerations
Log, slate and smooth stone steps can become slippery in very cold or wet conditions. For a non-slip surface select textured materials, such as raised-pattern concrete slabs. The best treads are made from natural or constructed stone slabs, positioned on stable risers of stone or brick. If slabs wear, lift and turn them over to expose a new surface.

### Teaming up heights and depths
Make risers a minimum of 10 cm and a maximum of 18 cm high. The lower the height you choose, the deeper each tread will need to be from front to back. For example, team up a 10 cm riser with a tread depth of 45 cm, and an 18 cm riser with a tread depth

## prune a **Standard** rose

**1** Always prune above the graft for standard roses. Start in the middle, cutting back any branches growing in towards the centre.

**2** Trim outward-growing shoots by about two-thirds, cutting any dead or diseased branches back to the main stem.

**3** Cut shoots back to just above a healthy, outward-facing bud so the shoots are less likely to become congested in the centre.

# STEPS | STOCKS

of 30 cm. For safety, each tread should overhang its riser by at least 2.5 cm and slope slightly downwards so that rain runs off. Build steps starting from the bottom and work up.

### Winding steps
If you are building steps on a steep slope, set them across the slope diagonally rather than straight up. By doing this, the steps can be made to wind and will look more attractive.

### Recycled steps
Hard-wearing, second-hand wooden railway sleepers will make excellent, attractive risers for shallow steps and they also provide a generous width. They are available from many landscape suppliers. Railway sleepers or timber boards can become slippery, especially when sited under trees or in other shady areas. To give a good grip even after rain, cover the tops of the steps with chicken wire, wrapping it down the sides and stapling it securely in place.

### Soften the edges
Border concrete steps with fragrant flowering shrubs, such as lavender and rosemary, and colourful annuals, such as nasturtiums or petunias. In dry and coastal areas, seaside daisy (*Erigeron karvinskianus*) is charming. Let hardy creeping plants, such as native violets (*Viola hederacea*), chamomile, gazanias, lamb's ears, rockery pinks, snow-in-summer (*Cerastium tomentosum*) and thymes, spread over the edges of steps and in between stones or blocks; trim as necessary once flowering ends. Give wide steps the appearance of being narrower by planting hardy, undemanding climbers, such as star jasmine (*Trachelospermum jasminoides*), at the edges.

## STOCKS

### Doubles are best
Stocks (*Matthiola incana*) with double flowers produce the most attractive spikes. They are dense and colourful, and the double flowers also last much longer and usually have a more intense scent than single-flowered stocks.

You can select seedlings that will produce double flowers at an early stage. Remove seedlings that have dark green leaves, as these are usually single-flowered, whereas seedlings with pale leaves will usually produce double flowers. Stock seedlings are susceptible to diseases caused by overwatering, so don't let the potting mix or soil get too wet. Also, pick plants up by their leaves, not their stems.

### Secret stocks
Try planting night-scented stocks (*M. longipetala*) – which have small, insignificant flowers but a wonderful scent – behind more colourful flowering plants. The latter will provide a good show, while the stocks' scent wafts all over the garden.

### Fast colour
The Virginia stock (*Malcolmia maritima*) has dainty flowers in a mix of white, pink, lavender and purple. It grows easily from seed planted from autumn to spring. Simply sprinkle the seeds over a garden bed where you need some colour.

## STONE | STORAGE

## STONE

### Stone mulch
A light covering of small stones, pebbles or gravel slows down the evaporation of moisture from the soil and, at night, releases the heat that it has absorbed during the day. In places where even grass will not grow, stop weeds taking over by covering the area with a weed mat and a bed of attractive pebbles.

### Rock mobility
Move a heavy rock by rolling it along on five or six logs or metal pipes. As you progress, bring the log or metal pipe that is at the back around to the front.

### Reusable stone
When knocking down walls or other features, never throw the stone away. It could be used to create an attractive raised bed or stepping stones in the garden.

### Platform for maintenance
Install a paving stone in a flowerbed so you can stand on it when watering, weeding or doing any maintenance task and avoid trampling over the soil and treading on plants. Lay the stone on a bed of sand so that the top is flush with the soil; eventually it will blend in with the foliage.

### Keep features to scale
When using a hard landscaping material such as stone in a small garden, bear in mind the scale of the garden and the existing features to ensure that an overall impression of equal proportions is maintained.

## lay stepping Stones

**1** Position the stepping stones on the lawn along the intended route of the path, at intervals equivalent to an average adult stride. Cut around each slab neatly with a spade.

**2** Lift the turf for each stone, scoop out the soil below and level the surface. The hole should be twice the depth of the slab, to accommodate a base of gravel and to allow the surface of the slab to sit just below the lawn.

**3** Half-fill the hole with fine gravel and position the slab on top. Check that it is level and build up or scoop out more earth as necessary. Hammer it firmly into place using a rubber mallet so it is level with the soil surface.

## STORAGE

### Clean up storage boxes
Before using wooden boxes for storing fruit and vegetables, brush them clean, wash them with disinfectant, then rinse thoroughly with fresh, clean water and leave to dry. Paint each box with a wood preservative.

### Fumigate the storage shed
Kill off any germs or fungal spores in your shed before storing fruit and vegetables there. Empty the shed in early summer, before fruit is ripe and after hibernating insects have gone. Seal up any cracks, then use an insecticidal and fungicidal greenhouse fumigant to destroy any pests and diseases. Fumigants are sold in cones and are set off in a similar way to fireworks. Place a warning sign on the door and leave it closed overnight, then ventilate the shed in the morning.

STORAGE | STRAWBERRIES

**S**

**Complete the ripening of onions by securing them to a piece of rope and hanging them in a cool, dry place.**

When storing vegetables, make use of the natural preservative qualities of garlic by peeling cloves and placing them around the cellar or shed. Alternatively, you can use bay leaves, which will also help to keep your crops fresh.

### Tidy tools
Hanging shoe holders are a cheap and efficient way to help keep the shed tidy. Nail to the wall and use the plastic pockets to store seed packets, small tools and labels.

### Cloche storage
If you are not using them in the garden, store polycarbonate or polythene cloches in a dark place. This helps to prevent the rapid breakdown of the ultraviolet inhibitor that preserves them and will prolong their useful life.

## STRAWBERRIES

### Choose wisely
Strawberries are easy to grow and give a quicker return than any other fruit. There are two varieties of garden strawberry: those with a single large crop in summer, and those that are 'everbearing', and start cropping in early summer, peak later in summer and continue through autumn. Choose varieties suited to home growing, with plenty of fragrance and flavour.

### Planting young plants
Strawberries need a rich, well-drained soil in a sunny position. Plant in freshly dug soil that has been enriched with well-rotted compost or manure.

### Keeping berries clean
Tuck fresh straw under the leaves as the fruit begins to form, or use black polythene or mulch mat. This will keep the strawberries from rotting when in contact with the ground.

When all the fruit has been picked, clear away the straw from underneath the leaves and cut back plants to remove old foliage and runners.

### Propagating strawberries
As long as you are sure that the parent plant is healthy, encourage plantlets that form on strawberry runners to root by pegging them into the soil with pieces of wire that have been bent into U shapes. After the runners have rooted, remove the new runners from the parent plant and plant directly in the bed or pot up before planting.

### Handle gently
Strawberries are particularly delicate fruit. Pick them by the stalk to avoid bruising and eat them as soon as possible.

**STRELITZIAS**
*see page 258*

### plant a Strawberry pot
Cultivating strawberries in a strawberry pot keeps the fruit off wet ground and away from slugs.

**1** Fill the strawberry pot with a good-quality potting mix up to the first holes.

**2** Gently push the roots of a strawberry plant through each of the lowest holes, then cover the roots with potting mix and firm in around them. Add more mix and plants for the holes higher up the pot.

**3** Once all the holes are planted, fill the pot with mix to about 5 cm below the rim. Set several strawberry plants in the top of the pot, placing them about 15 cm apart, and firm in. Water well with a watering can with a fine rose, then water regularly.

255

# Succulents

Succulents come in all shapes and sizes, from groundcovers to spiky shrub-like agaves, aloes and yuccas. The huge range of foliage colours includes green, grey, silver, blue, yellow, gold, orange, pink, red and even black. Some have spectacular daisy-like or spire-forming flowers.

## The great survivors

Succulents, which also include all the cacti, are superbly equipped to deal with dry conditions. Many have features or structures to prevent water loss, such as a waxy surface, downy hairs or a felty covering over the leaf. As well as providing weather-proofing, these features are what help make them such colourful and interesting plants.

## Drama and architecture

The dramatic and often bizarre shapes and textures make for exciting garden plants. Yuccas and agaves provide strong foliage contrasts and height. Eye-catching colour highlights can be created by mixing together plants with different foliage colours. For example, the fabulous burgundy-black rosettes of *Aeonium arboreum* 'Zwartkop' planted in swathes alongside the silver-blue of blue chalk sticks (*Senecio serpens*) makes for a bold statement.

## The waterwise choice

Most succulents are an ideal basis for a water-saving garden in a sunny, dry situation. They need a quick-draining, very aerated soil. Make a mounded or raised garden bed, or replace heavier soil with an open, free-draining mix. If growing in containers, use a special orchid or succulent potting mix.

### choose sensational Succulents

- *Aeonium*
- *Agave*
- *Aloe*
- *Cotyledon*
- *Crassula*
- *Echeveria*
- *Euphorbia*
- *Graptoveria*
- *Haworthia*
- *Kalanchoe*
- *Sedum*
- *Sempervivum*
- *Senecio*
- *Yucca*

*Echeveria* cv.

*Agave macroacantha*

*Echeveria* 'Blue Curls'

*Graptoveria* cv.

*Haworthia attenuata* cv.

*Aeonium* cv.

*Echeveria* cv.

*Aloe polyphylla*

# S | STRELITZIAS | SUPPORTS

## STRELITZIAS

### Different sizes
Probably the best known strelitzia is the orange-flowered plant commonly known as bird of paradise (*Strelitzia reginae*). But there are several others. The giant white bird of paradise (*S. nicolai*) can grow to 3–4 m tall. With its banana-like foliage and dramatic blue and white flowers, it makes a good choice in a tropical garden. *S. juncea* has slender, rush-like leaves and orange flowers.

### No flowers?
Keep plants looking stunning by removing spent flowers, so new ones can open. Also remove old leaves regularly. If plants become a large clump of leaves without flowers, the main reason is that they are getting too much shade. Move them to a sunnier spot for more flowers.

### Favourite conditions
While strelitzias tolerate dry and adverse conditions, they do best in a sunny spot, sheltered from cold winds, and watered well when it is hot or dry. They need well-drained soil with compost.

### Dividing for more
Grow new plants by dividing an old clump, simply separating the rhizomes. The disturbed plants can 'sulk' after replanting, so grow in a pot in a sheltered spot until they show signs of regrowth.

## SUNFLOWERS

### The best way to plant
Sunflower seeds should be sown in rich, well-drained soil in a sunny position, in groups of two or three. Thin out to keep the strongest seedling in each group. Make sure young plants are protected from slugs and rabbits, which are particularly fond of them.

### Moisture-absorber
Although the sunflower is a plant that thrives with its head in the sun, its roots will tolerate damp conditions. Make the most of this ability to absorb moisture by planting groups at the base of walls or fences, where there are often damp spots.

### Small sunflowers
If you don't have room for the traditional 2–3 m tall sunflowers, there are a number of dwarf and medium-sized varieties available. They include 'Sungold' (about 1 m, with shaggy double yellow flowers), 'Bronze Shades' (about 1.5 m, with gold to brown single flowers) and 'Teddy Bear' (65 cm, with double yellow flowers).

The perennial sunflower species, including *Helianthus salicifolius* and *H.* × *multiflorus*, form clumps to about 1.8 m high and have multiple flowers.

## SUPPORTS

### Ready-made supports
Wall-mounted or freestanding plant supports can make a feature out of a climbing plant in any part of the garden. There are numerous ready-made types of support for sale, made from timber, wrought iron, plastic-coated tubular steel and ornately decorative wirework. Whatever you choose, make sure it is strong and well anchored.

### Prop appeal
If timber props support the heavy branches of fruit trees in your garden, plant a climbing annual that does not need to be in an especially sunny position at the foot of each prop for a striking visual effect. Climbing French beans would be suitable.

### Woven willow supports
Willow twigs are very flexible and can be woven in bands around a tripod of thin rustic stakes to create an attractive climbing plant support for an informal cottage-style garden. To make them more flexible, soak the twigs in water for a few hours before using them. Remove any twigs that start to shoot, as they may be developing roots.

### Going geometric
To grow a decorative column of flowers or foliage, position a cylinder of rigid netting in the container holding the plant and secure it with slender stakes. Alternatively, roll the netting into a cone and position it firmly in the mix, securing the cone shape at the top with small twists of wire.

258

SUPPORTS | SWEET PEAS

S

## SWEET PEAS

### If seeds fail
Sweet pea seeds are large and can be handled easily, so it is best to sow them directly in the garden bed where they are to be grown. Occasionally, however, the seeds fail to germinate. This usually occurs if there is moisture after planting. To ensure successful germination, water the soil well before sowing the seeds, then wait until the first small leaves appear (around 10 days later) before watering the soil again.

Cut sweet peas as they flower or fade to promote further flowering, but leave some flowers to set seeds if you want them for the following year.

### Create a miniature wigwam
Four or five bamboo canes angled in a large container of potting mix and tied together at the top make a climbing frame for sweet peas. Loop garden twine around the canes halfway up to ensure stability as the plants grow.

### Creeping peas
For hanging baskets or for edging borders, choose 'Cupid', a pink and white bicoloured variety that grows only about 15 cm high but spreads to about 45 cm across.

Dwarf or semi-dwarf varieties of sweet peas require little or no support. Depending on the size, they can be candidates for flower borders or containers.

### Sweet peas for scent
The best varieties for fragrance are the old-fashioned ones. They come under a variety of names, so check mail-order seed catalogues for mixtures such as 'Antique Fantasy', 'Old Fashioned Mixed', 'Old Spice Mixed' and 'Old Fashioned Scented Mixed'.

## consider creative plant Supports

**Lattice trellising** Panels in various widths, in diamond-shaped or square patterns, add interest to a wall or are useful for dividing a garden into sections.

**Post and rope** Fence posts with finial tops linked by rope are ideal for dividing a garden without creating a lot of shadow and for adding height in a flowerbed.

**Obelisk** Ready-made designs are available in wood and metal, or you could make your own out of lattice. An obelisk will create a focal point or add height to a border.

**Single post** Secure a timber post in the ground for a quick and easy way to add colour, variety and height to a border.

259

# SWEET POTATOES | SWIMMING POOLS

## SWEET POTATOES

### Orange or white
Sweet potatoes (*Ipomoea batatas*) are known by many local names, including kumara in the Maori language. The plants cover the ground densely because of their vining habit. In subtropical to tropical areas there is no stopping them – they make a thick, weed-excluding groundcover. Sweet potatoes produce orange or white tubers underground – often well away from the base of the original plant – that have a high sugar, or starch, content.

### Planning the crop
Sweet potatoes are easily grown in a sunny position in districts with warm nights. Plants require a raised bed with a well-drained, preferably slightly acidic soil that has been dug through with well-rotted compost. They develop more and larger tubers in soil that is not overly rich, and they are not demanding in terms of water.

### When leaves turn yellow
Harvest your sweet potatoes progressively after the leaves begin to yellow. The vines die with the first frost, and the crop must be pulled before then. Sweet potatoes can be stored for up to 4 weeks in a cool, dry place.

White sweet potato

Orange sweet potato

## SWIMMING POOLS

### Pick your style
A swimming pool can have any style or character you desire, from formal to natural. Choose a pool that matches the style of your house and garden. There are many design options on the market, so take time to investigate them.

When the budget is tight, an above-ground pool can be an economical option. These pools can be difficult to blend into a backyard, however. One way to soften the look of such a pool is to surround it with decking.

### Safety measures
The safety of your family and your visitors is of paramount importance – especially where children are concerned. Ideally, site the pool where it can be seen clearly from the house. In most areas pool fencing and childproof gates are mandatory.

When it is not in use, it is a good idea to cover a swimming pool if you have children. An insulated cover will keep the pool clean and will limit the reduction in water temperature. Whichever type you choose, make sure the cover is easy both to put over the pool and to remove.

### Water restrictions and pools
Periods of severe drought and climate change have resulted in strict water restrictions being adopted throughout Australia. Water usage conditions vary, but filling a swimming pool usually requires a permit, or may be banned completely. Check what restrictions apply in your area.

### A garden around the pool
Plant several varieties of plants in mass groupings, positioning them so that none overhang or shade the pool. Palms such as slender bamboo and Bangalow palms, underplanted with pygmy date palms, will give a tropical backdrop; they have non-invasive roots and do not drop litter. Tropical perennials such as *Calathea*, *Ctenanthe* and *Maranta* thrive under palms. Disguise any walls with scrambling groundcovers, and the fence with tall members of the ginger family and cannas.

# TARRAGON | TEA TREES

## TARRAGON

### Question of identity
The only tarragon seeds available are those of Russian tarragon (*Artemisia dracunculus*). This has less aroma and a coarser flavour than French tarragon, or estragon (*A. dracunculoides*), the true gourmet herb whose dark fragrant leaves are preferred by cooks. French tarragon does not set seed, so you will need to buy a plant by name from a reputable source and propagate it either by cuttings or by root division.

### A shovelful of sand
French tarragon grows best in temperate to cool climates. It needs light, well-drained soil in a sunny position if it is to thrive. Waterlogging is the main cause of fatalities, so if you have poorly drained or waterlogged soil, grow it in pots of good-quality potting mix. Pick fresh leaves from late spring until midautumn. Sprigs can be dried or frozen but will have less flavour.

### Keep plants going
To ensure a continuous supply of French tarragon, pot up some 5–7.5 cm long cuttings in spring. Or cut the plant down in late autumn and cover with straw until any risk of frost has passed. Lift, divide and replant every 2–3 years in spring.

## TEA TREES

These hardy, easy-to-grow plants are native to Australia, New Zealand and Malaysia. They vary from dwarf weeping plants perfect for a rock garden to tall, upright, screening shrubs and small trees. Different plants have varying frost tolerance, but all prefer rich, well-drained soil.

### Useful screens
Many tea trees (*Leptospermum* spp.) make excellent screening plants because of their compact growth. If you are dealing with harsh or seaside conditions in Australia, the coastal tea tree (*L. laevigatum*) is a good choice.

### Oil-filled leaves
Tea trees gained their common name from the use of their leaves as a tea substitute in colonial times. However, tea tree oil does not come from a *Leptospermum* species. Despite its name, this essential oil is derived mainly from *Melaleuca alternifolia*. The foliage of a tea tree, *L. liversidgei* 'Mozzie Blocker', has citronella oil, which deters mosquitoes.

### New Zealand tea tree
The oil of the manuka, or New Zealand tea tree (*L. scoparium*), is strongly antimicrobial and can be diluted and used to disinfect wounds. A particularly important complementary remedy is manuka honey, which is produced by bees that graze on manuka.

### treat Tea tree web moth

**Plants affected**
Tea trees and sometimes bottlebrushes, grevilleas and paperbarks (*Melaleuca* spp.).

**Symptoms**
A mass of webbing on shoots and leaves where the night-feeding caterpillars shelter during the day. If disturbed, they may drop to the ground.

**Treatment**
* Encourage bird predators.
* Prune or knock off webbing (it repels sprays) and discard or destroy it.
* Leaves rolled together by a mass of webbing on plants other than those listed above may be from leafroller caterpillars. Shoot tips, leaves and fruit are chewed. Prune off, or spray with *Bacillus thuringiensis* or maldison.

## TERRACES

### The slope solution
A terraced garden may be time-consuming and expensive to have built, but it can be an excellent and stylish solution to a steep sloping garden that will also slow run-off and erosion.

Terraces create the illusion of space. By separating a single sloping area into a series of level areas, they give maximum usable flat ground and add considerable visual interest to your garden. They can be linked by shallow steps and will allow easy access to all planting areas.

### Split the slope up
Terracing will split the slope into a series of manageable, flat growing areas that are packed with attractive plants thriving in ground that is easy to maintain. Each terrace can be reached from the one below via steps, and you can tend the beds without having to bend or stretch. You could put a patio at the base or the top of the slope, or have a level area of lawn.

### A job for the professionals
Terracing needs to be carefully planned and managed. Don't do it yourself unless the retaining walls are low because if it is not done properly, it can create serious problems. The weight of damp earth pushing against a retaining wall is enormous, so walls must have substantial footings and drainage behind them. Indeed, any structure that is more than 600 mm high may require a building permit and an engineer's drawings – check with your local authority. This type of work is best done by a professional contractor who has the skills and equipment to do the job properly.

### Holding back the slope
The deeper the terraces, the gentler the slope will be, and the shallower the steps, but the gentler the gradient, the more space you will need. Play around with your dimensions until you find a design that works.

### Choosing your materials
Brick walls may be more in keeping with an area that has mostly brick houses; where stone is the predominant building material, natural or artificial stone would fit perfectly. If cost is an issue, a neutral or rustic brick or even concrete blocks painted with stone paint could work.

### Don't forget
Ask your contractor about important construction details, such as the size of foundations, making the step, the provision of drainage materials and 'weep holes' for the lower terraces, and how they will prepare the soil for planting. Ask them to retain and replace as much topsoil as they can salvage, rather than filling the terraced beds with subsoil. If necessary, buy some good topsoil or garden mix for finishing off the beds.

## THINNING

### Gentle handling
Thinning is the removal of excess seedlings from beds, pots or trays in order to help the growth of the seedlings that remain. Carefully loosen the soil around the roots of an excess seedling, then hold down the soil with the fingers of one hand and gently remove the seedling with the other.

### Waste not
Always thin seedlings in stages to allow for loss from diseases or pests. Clear away the thinnings, as their odour may attract pests. Both carrot flies and onion flies can detect the scent of crushed leaves from a long distance.

When you are making the final thinnings of carrots, onions and lettuces, eat the baby carrots raw, use the thinned onions as spring onions, and add the miniature lettuces to leafy green salads.

### Watering time
Water seedlings thoroughly the evening before you intend to thin them out. Thin them in the early morning, then water all the remaining seedlings well to help settle the soil round their roots.

### Thinning for perfect fruit
Fruit trees including apricots, nectarines, peaches and plums set too many fruit. A certain amount of fruit drop will occur naturally when the fruit is still small. But if the branches remain overloaded, the crop will not develop normally unless it is thinned by hand. Also, the weight can cause branches to break. First, thin any fruit that is awkwardly placed or particularly small. Only keep six to ten fruit for each metre of main branch.

## TIBOUCHINAS

### What's in a name?
Tibouchinas come from South America. Some gardeners still use lasiandra (a previous genus name) as a common name, giving it also to closely related plants such as the pink lasiandra (*Melastoma malabathricum*). Tibouchinas are also known as glory bush.

### For mild climates only
With their lavish autumn displays of purple flowers, tibouchinas are gorgeous evergreen shrubs or trees, but they are suitable for frost-free climates only. In cool areas, the more compact types can be grown in large containers and brought inside for winter. They like fertile soil, regular watering in summer and a sunny or lightly shaded, sheltered position.

### Attractive combinations
Plant *Tibouchina granulosa* or *T.* 'Alstonville' alongside crepe myrtles with pink or lilac flowers. The spreading 'Skylab' cultivar looks wonderful trained through the branches of a large-flowered pink or yellow climbing rose.

### Versatile plants
Most tibouchinas can be grown either as large shrubs or as small single- or multi-trunked trees, depending on how you prune them. For shrubs, trim after each burst of flowers and prune more severely in spring. To train as trees, gradually remove the lowest branches, a few each year, until the crown is lifted as high as you wish. The rather open-growing *T. urvilleana* and cultivars make excellent informal espaliers.

## THYME

### Fragrance and flavour
There are an astonishing number of aromatic thyme species and cultivars with a wide variety of fragrances, flavours and uses. Most do best in poor but well-drained soil in full sun. Garden or common thyme (*Thymus vulgaris*) is the most well known culinary type; it forms a wiry-stemmed, low-growing evergreen bush that lives for 3–4 years. Lemon thyme (*T. × citriodorus*) also grows into a small bush.

### Cut back or clip
Cut flower stems back after the plant has bloomed to encourage new shoots. If left unclipped, thyme bushes become leggy. Leave carpeting varieties unclipped.

### Blooming thyme
Use close-growing thyme varieties to outline the front of a flowerbed, where the aromatic flowers will attract butterflies and bees to the garden. Plant lemon-scented or variegated varieties or the pink-flowering *T. serpyllum* in the cracks between paving stones, or even use them as a low-traffic lawn alternative. When crushed underfoot, they will release their delightful aroma.

### Winter aid
As befits their Mediterranean origins, thyme plants hate cold and wet weather, and tend to die back in hard winters. If they do, leave the dead stalks as some protection against any further damage and add a layer of straw for extra protection.

# TOMATOES

'Black Krim'

'Banana Legs'

'Brandywine'

## Great to grow
If you have only ever tasted supermarket-style tomatoes, you won't know what a taste sensation a home-grown, vine-ripened, eaten-straight-from-the-bush tomato can be. Even if you grow no other vegetables in your garden, it is worth trying a few tomatoes. The plants are widely available from garden centres. Look for short, sturdy plants with healthy green foliage. To grow luscious heirloom tomatoes in an array of colours, sizes and shapes, seek out specialist nurseries and seed companies.

## What tomatoes want
Tomatoes need a sunny and fairly protected site. They thrive in a well-drained, compost-enriched soil and prefer acid conditions. Incorporate a bucket of well-rotted compost into each square metre of growing area and water plants well every day unless it rains. Also mulch around them to prevent evaporation.

## A planting tip
When planting tomato seedlings, borrow an old tip from Italian gardeners: bury the stem up to the first set of leaves. Adventitious roots will develop on the buried section of stem and provide an additional root system. Spindly, overgrown seedlings are easily rescued in this way, too.

## Patio tomatoes
You can grow tomatoes in tubs or containers on the patio or balcony. 'Tiny Tim' produces ornamental fruit on a compact bush and does well in pots. Cherry tomatoes are ideal for hanging baskets.

## Pinch and prune
It is important to prune out the lateral growths that appear between a plant's leaf axils. Pinch these out when they are small or cut them if they have grown too large. Prune plants to one or two main stems or leaders, using the lateral immediately below the first flower truss for the second leader. Pinch out the growing tips when plants have set five or six trusses. Bush varieties do not need their tips pinched out.

Cherry tomatoes

### Staking for support
All except dwarf tomatoes should be supported with 1.8–2 m stakes. Regularly tie in the growing plants to their stake with soft ties that are loose enough to allow for the stems to increase in size.

## Watch for pests
There are several pests that can damage tomato plants and fruit, including mites and whiteflies. Tomato caterpillars or budworms can be difficult to control because they enter the fruit, where they can't be reached by insecticide. For organic control use *Bacillus thuringiensis*. Cherry tomatoes are less likely to be attacked by fruit fly, so plant them if you live in affected districts.

Basil is a good companion plant for tomatoes, as it deters aphids and tomato hookworms. Some other useful companion plants for tomatoes include borage, chives and nasturtiums.

## Disease-prone
Tomatoes are prone to numerous problems, especially wilts and root knot nematodes. Choose resistant varieties. A number of diseases are common to plants in the Solanaceae family, which includes tomatoes, tomatillos, eggplant, chillies, capsicums and potatoes. To minimise the risk of disease occurring, do not plant tomatoes on a site where any of these crops have been planted in the previous 3 years.

## Harvesting tomatoes
Unless fruit fly or imminent frosts are a problem, it is best to leave tomatoes on the plant until they are fully ripe. If you must pick them when green, you can ripen them on a sunny window ledge.

# TOOL CARE AND MAINTENANCE

## Work in comfort
There are many garden tools available, but only you can choose the ones that will be comfortable for you to work with. When you're buying, go through the motions of planting, raking and so on to make sure the tool fits your build.

## A quick shine
Put a shine on rusty or dirty tools. Add oil to a bucket of sharp sand. Brush the worst of the dirt from your tools then, one at a time, move them up and down several times in the mixture until the sand has removed the tarnish.

## Handling handles
Metal handles on tools are stronger but not as warm to the touch as wooden or plastic ones. Check wooden handles for splits, rough patches and abrasions; to prevent blisters, smooth them down with sandpaper, then coat with polyurethane varnish for a comfortable grip. Treat quality handles annually with linseed oil.

## Saw size
When using a bow saw, don't tackle branches that are too thick. A 60 cm bow saw should not be used to cut branches that are more than 10 cm in diameter.

If your saw is very dirty from tree sap, spray it with oven cleaner and leave it on for a few minutes before removing with an old toothbrush. To keep the saw in the best possible condition, wrap it in oil-coated newspaper when you're not using it. Also avoid dropping a saw on the ground.

## Lawn rakes
Rakes with thin metal tines tend to clog up quickly with leaves, whereas plastic rakes have wider tines, which do not clog up so readily. Plastic rakes are usually lighter than metal ones and so are less tiring to use.

## Bright beacon
Losing small tools among plants and in undergrowth is a frequent annoyance for gardeners. Make tools easier to see by painting their handles in bright colours that stand out from the greenery.

## Safe use of a wheelbarrow
Wheelbarrows are usually fitted with a single wheel; if you are using it frequently over long distances, a pneumatic tyre will be more comfortable than a solid one. Two-wheeled barrows are more stable on uneven ground.

Load the barrow so the weight is mainly over the wheel, and bend your knees, not your back, to lift and lower. When not in use, stand a metal wheelbarrow on its wheel and lean the handles against a wall. Or turn it upside-down.

## Easy on the knees
Avoid gardener's backache by kneeling down to plant or weed, rather than bending over. Buy a kneeling pad with handles to help you get up. Or make your own: fold an old hessian bag into a pad and cover it with plastic to keep it dry; stuff a strong plastic bag with rags; or partially fill an old hot-water bottle with sawdust.

---

### Clean up after use
Get into the habit of cleaning your garden tools after working with them. They will be easier to use next time and will also last longer. Before you put tools away for any length of time, remove traces of soil with newspaper or a brush. If you wash tools, dry them thoroughly and apply oil to all metal parts with a paintbrush or soft rag. Treat wooden handles with linseed oil, which should be left on to feed the wood until the tools are needed again.

# T TOOLS

## TOOLS

Begin with a collection of basic gardening tools, then add to it as your interest and experience grow. Here are the essentials: a spade and fork for digging the soil, a Dutch hoe and hand fork for weeding, a lawn rake and lawn shears, a trowel for planting, and shears and secateurs for trimming and pruning hedges or shrubs.

Each tool should be comfortable to use and suit your height and strength. It is worth buying quality products made from sturdy materials because most will last a lifetime if they are properly maintained.

**Fork** Multipurpose tool.

**Garden rake** Preparing seedbeds and levelling soil.

**Long-handled pruner** Cutting through branches too thick for secateurs.

**Spade** Breaking up or removing soil; digging planting holes.

**Pruning saw** Wide-set teeth easily cut through green wood.

**Hand shears** Trimming hedges and small patches of grass.

**Secateurs** Pruning thin branches or deadheading.

**Bow saw** Cutting through large branches.

TOOLS **T**

**Draw hoe** Loosening heavy weed growth, making drills and earthing up plants.

**Dutch hoe** Using a push-pull action to sever weeds at soil level.

**Daisy grubber** Digging out weeds.

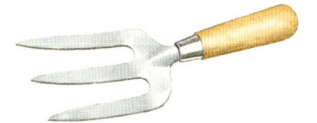

**Hand fork** Cultivating and weeding around small plants; also lifting them.

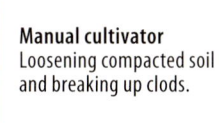

**Onion hoe** For delicate work between seedlings and rock plants.

**Manual cultivator** Loosening compacted soil and breaking up clods.

**Garden line** Marker for sowing or planting in a straight line. Cord is held taut between two spikes.

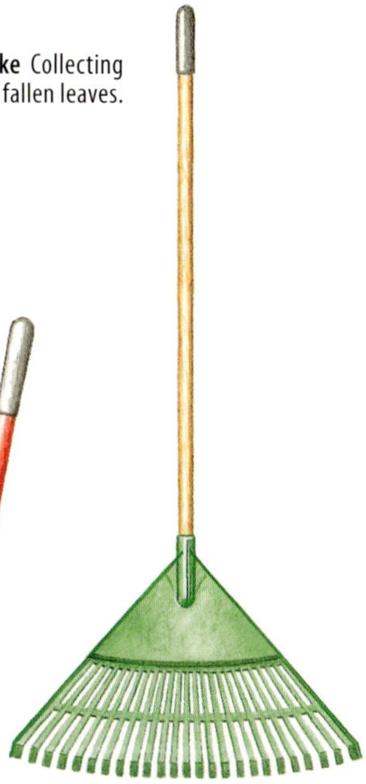

**Edging knife** Used with a garden line for cutting a straight edge in turf.

**Lawn rake** Collecting fallen leaves.

**Measuring rod** Spacing plants, seeds and vegetable rows correctly.

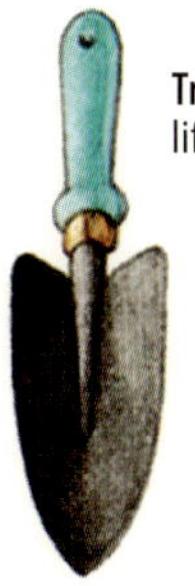

**Trowel** Planting and lifting small plants.

**Bulb planter** Making a bulb planting hole then replacing soil on top.

**Dibber** Hole-making tool for transplanting.

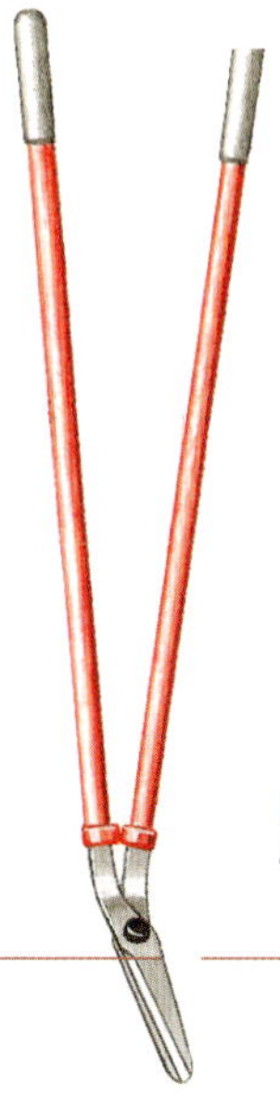

**Lawn shears** For edging and trimming.

267

# TOPIARY

## Living sculptures
Topiary is no longer the stiff, formal art it once was. If you like the idea of living sculptures in your garden, choose a sunny, sheltered position where strong winds will not be able to distort the specimen's shape. Make sure you can access it from all sides.

## Choosing plants
Evergreen shrubs such as bay, rosemary and lillypillies are suitable for simple shapes. Good small-leaved evergreens include boxleaf honeysuckle (*Lonicera nitida*) and myrtle (*Myrtus communis*). If you want to create more complex sculptures, use box or yew, which are slow-growing and easy to clip and train.

The variegated box cultivars, including 'Argenteovariegata', 'Aureovariegata', 'Elegantissima' and 'Marginata', can look very attractive when clipped into small balls or pyramids.

### Begin with the basics
If you are a newcomer to topiary, begin with a simple shape, such as a cone, pyramid or ball. Buy a ready-made frame or make one using wooden stakes and chicken wire. Place the frame over the shrub and, as the shrub grows, use secateurs or sheep shears to trim all the shoots that protrude through the frame. In a short time, the shrub will begin to take on the shape; then you can remove the frame.

## Topiary techniques
It takes about 5–10 years to train and clip evergreen shrubs into simple geometric shapes such as balls and cubes, and a little longer for more complex figures such as birds and small animals. Start with an existing bushy specimen that is larger than the finished shape, and carve it freehand with secateurs or one-handed sheep shears. Alternatively, plant a smaller container-grown bush inside a ready-made frame or wire former; they are available from specialist suppliers and some garden centres. Then use this as a guide for your cutting.

## Precise but limited pruning
While the topiary is taking shape, cut back half the annual shoots to ensure that the shrub's new growth remains bushy. Once the shape has been created, most topiary specimens need clipping at least twice a year, in midspring and then again in late summer. More frequent trimming will be rewarded with a precise outline and bushy growth; fast-growing species such as lillypillies may need four or five trims a year. Feed your topiary in early spring with a slow-release fertiliser.

## Creating a spiral
Topiary spirals are not so very difficult to create. Choose a plant such as fastigiate yew (*Taxus baccata* 'Fastigiata'), which grows naturally to form a slim column. Plant a young specimen and drive a stout stake into the ground on each side of the plant and 15 cm apart. Bend the main shoot around one stake and tie it firmly in place. As it grows, continue to twist the shoot around the other stake in turn and tie in, to form a spiral. Use sharp scissors to keep the plant in shape when young, and pruning shears as it matures.

## Sheep shears
On small plants, use sharp sheep shears in preference to large hand shears. They are held in one hand, so clipping and shaping are much easier. They are available from garden centres.

TOPSOIL | TRANSFORMING A GARDEN

## TOPSOIL

### The top layer
Topsoil is the uppermost and darkest layer of soil. It can be from 3 cm to 60 cm deep and contains the most organic matter and soil organisms. The roots of most garden plants, particularly annual and perennial flowering plants and vegetables, occupy this layer only.

### When topsoil is shallow
It takes on average a century to build 2.5 cm of topsoil in nature. Many naturally occurring soils in Australia have shallow topsoils (less than 15 cm deep), which means there is less good growing medium for plants. But if you plan to do intensive gardening, you can use certain techniques to build up the thickness and fertility of a shallow topsoil.

### Building up topsoil
Incorporate as many bulky organic materials as possible into your soil, including compost, well-rotted manures, mushroom compost (often very alkaline so use it sparingly) and washed, composted seaweed. Keep soil covered with organic mulches such as straw and lucerne hay. Also use green living mulches such as densely planted crops of fenugreek, mustard or lupins to cover beds left fallow, then dig the plants into the soil. To avoid creating a poor environment for soil organisms, don't dig soil too frequently (more than once every 1–2 years) and don't walk on the soil as this will compact it.

*See also* Soil analysis

## TRANSFORMING A GARDEN

Here are steps you should follow if you want to transform your garden. Wait until Step 4 before you start buying any plants.

**1** Clear up the garden. Remove all unwanted plants, debris and rotting fences from an established garden. If it is new, clear away any rubble that may have been left behind by the builder. Put bricks and old stones to one side for possible reuse as paths or other landscaping.

**2** Dig over the ground and remove any building debris and rotting tree roots. Install or renovate boundary walls, fences and hedges. Carry out any earth-moving that is necessary for making raised beds, changes of level, steps, banks or pools.

**3** Make or repair any permanent features that you want to incorporate, such as walls, fences, pools, paths, steps, seating areas, garden buildings and play areas. Install any necessary outside plumbing and electrical fittings, or make future provision for them by laying conduits before building paths and paved areas.

**4** Mark out and dig or rotary hoe new planting areas; remove all weeds and incorporate plenty of compost or well-rotted manure as you go. Allow time for the soil to settle before planting the framework – hedges, trees, larger shrubs and key plants. Revitalise existing plants with pruning, fertilising and mulching.

**5** Plant a new lawn in spring or autumn. Mark out and prepare the lawn areas before seeding or turfing. Keep off the new lawn or use boards if you must walk on it.

**6** Add the finishing touches to your garden. Position any statues, wall fountains, garden furniture and containers. At the appropriate time of the year, plant smaller shrubs, perennials, annuals and bulbs. Clean and fill the garden pool or pond, adding plants after a week and any fish a few weeks later.

**TRACE ELEMENTS** *see page 270*

269

## TRACE ELEMENTS

### How to recognise a deficiency

Plants need manganese, iron, boron, zinc, copper, chlorine and molybdenum in tiny, or 'trace', amounts. They usually get enough of these elements from the soil. But occasionally, they may suffer from a lack of a particular trace element. The main symptoms are yellowing between the veins of the leaves, particularly in young leaves (lime-induced chlorosis); yellowing between the veins of older leaves (manganese deficiency); and yellow bands between the leaf veins that turn brown (magnesium deficiency). Keep an eye on your azaleas, citrus, gardenias, murrayas and rhododendrons for any of these signs. Generally, deficiencies are worse in cool weather conditions.

### Avoiding deficiencies

Some trace elements become unavailable to plants in soil with a pH above about 7. Many plants are adapted to this pH level, so rather than trying to change your soil's natural pH, it's often better to choose plants that are suited to your conditions.

Trace element deficiencies are most common in pot plants and in plants growing on sandy or limy soils. Some regions are naturally deficient in certain trace elements. Your local nursery should be aware of local problems.

*See also* Chlorosis, Manganese deficiency, Magnesium deficiency, Nutrients

---

#### Seaweed cure-all

It can be difficult to decide which problem is causing a deficiency. In such cases, water the plant with a seaweed liquid feed. This contains a wide range of trace elements and will often cure the problem.

---

## TRANSPLANTING

### Successful seedlings

When transplanting seedlings to their permanent position, choose plants that are stocky, sturdy and well hardened off. Discard weak or damaged plants. Check that the soil is moist and firm. If possible, wait for mild, still, fairly overcast weather or the cool of the evening, and give protection from winds or hot sunshine. Use a small dibber or trowel to make holes for the new plants. Lift the plants with a trowel and set each in a hole at the same soil depth as it was previously. Firm in gently with your fingers and water in well.

### A gentle touch

It can often be tempting to firm seedlings in well but this might damage the young roots. After gently replacing the soil, thorough watering will settle it sufficiently. The exception is members of the Brassica family, such as broccoli, brussels sprouts and cauliflower; always plant them firmly.

### Minimising transplant shock

Here are some tips for easing your plants into the garden.

✻ Gradually 'harden off' plants by moving them into stronger light while they are still seedlings and before transplanting them out in the garden.

✻ Certain plants don't like their roots being disturbed. Grow them in small pots or individual cells so you won't need to thin them out from other seedlings.

✻ Don't transplant – simply sow seeds directly in the garden bed.

✻ When watering, add a seaweed-based solution to increase your plants' resistance to drought, heat and frost, and improve their root and stem development.

✻ Apply an anti-transpirant foliar spray to foliage to protect it from drying winds, water loss and heat and to also reduce the effects of transplant shock. These products are biodegradable and the effects last for several months.

### New homes for shrubs and trees

Sometimes a plant is obviously growing in the wrong place. Move deciduous shrubs while they are dormant, and evergreens in autumn or winter. An overcast or rainy day will limit moisture loss and the trauma of disturbance.

### A year of preparation

If you intend to transplant an established tree, prepare it for the move a year in advance. Dig a narrow, circular trench halfway between the trunk and the outer limit of the branches, and use the spade edge to sever any roots that you encounter. Refill the trench with well-rotted compost and keep well watered. This will encourage the tree to form fibrous roots close to the trunk, which will help it to establish quickly after it is dug up and moved.

# TRANSPLANTING | TREE REPAIRS

## Transplant an established shrub or small tree

**1** The day before moving day, water the plant well. Tie up the branches or prune the canopy down to a manageable size, but leave at least two-thirds of the canopy. In the new site, excavate a saucer-shaped hole 30 cm wider all round than the root ball. Work in some well-rotted compost.

**2** Dig a trench around the shrub or tree in a circle 60–75 cm in diameter, cutting through the roots cleanly. Dig down at an angle and underneath the root ball, working all the way around until the root ball is free. Ease the plant onto strong hessian or heavy-duty plastic. Wrap the root ball if desired and lift or drag the plant to its new planting site.

**3** Plant the shrub or tree as you would a container-grown plant, making sure it is at the same depth as before. Stake if necessary, water thoroughly and apply mulch. Spray with an anti-transpirant to minimise moisture loss, and protect evergreens from drying winds with a windbreak of netting attached to stakes.

## TREE REPAIRS

### Canker wounds
Check fruit trees early in the year before leaf fall for signs of canker wounds. Use a sharp knife or pruning saw to cut away all affected bark and wood, at least 15 cm behind the canker into clean wood. Dispose of the infected material safely and sterilise your equipment. Spray the tree with Bordeaux mixture at budburst in spring and again in autumn.

### Split trunks
Split tree trunks are usually caused by sudden, severe late frosts, or a long period of hot, dry summer weather followed by prolonged heavy rain. In many cases the split runs deeper than the bark, and such damage can lead to rotting of the heartwood. It is best just to let the tree heal naturally, cutting back any dead wood the following autumn. If a broken branch leaves a ragged snag, remove the snag as it can be an entry point for disease.

### Prevent honey fungus
When you have to cut down a tree entirely, always remove or kill the stump that is left. Honey fungus can infect stumps, then spread through the soil to healthy trees, and may eventually kill them.

### Lopping branches
Never remove large branches with a single cut. It is much safer to use a sharp pruning saw to saw off a branch in manageable sections until you are left with a stub about 30–45 cm long. Remove the stub close to but not quite flush with the trunk. (This is called the branch collar and is the swelling where the branch meets the trunk.) To do this without tearing the bark, saw in an upward direction one-third of the way through the stub, then saw down to meet it. Trim any ragged edges from the wound with a sharp knife.

**Play it safe: call an expert.** For the removal of damaged trees or branches from large trees, get advice from a qualified tree surgeon and hire them to do the work.

# TREES

### Take expert advice
Most trees will live and grow for many years. So that you make the right choice before planting one, consult staff at a specialist tree nursery. They should be able to provide information about the most suitable varieties to grow in your area and in your type of soil. They can also advise on the growth rate and eventual height of particular trees.

### Strike a balance
If you have enough space, plant some evergreen and deciduous trees. They will provide you with a year-round structure as well as colours, shapes, shade and light that change with the seasons. A ratio of two-thirds evergreen to one-third deciduous will give a good balance.

### A long-term investment
Select and site trees with extra care. After all, they will form the backbone of your garden. Also, their roots can cause structural damage to nearby buildings, walls, drains and foundations, especially if they are less than 3 m away, while their crown can grow into overhead wires. Over time, roots can cause a nearby paved surface to lift.

Remember, too, that a tree planted on your boundary could have some impact on your neighbour, causing unwanted overshadowing or invasive tree roots, or it may block valuable views.

### At the nursery
When buying a young tree, choose one that has only one main stem. If the plant has two main stems, they will compete with each other as the tree grows, and this will reduce its overall quality. Always buy small, relatively immature trees. As well as being much less expensive than larger ones, they are easier to move about, more likely to re-establish themselves successfully and will always grow quickly once they're planted.

### Drip-watering trees
Agricultural (ag) slotted pipe can be looped around the roots of a tree at the time of planting, with the end left sticking out of the ground. Or lengths of rigid slotted pipe can be pushed into the soil around an established tree's root zone. Then you water the tree through the pipe and the water reaches right down to its roots, encouraging them to establish more quickly.

### Safety in the small garden
It may be impossible to allow the recommended safe distances between trees and buildings in a small garden. Planting closer, especially if insufficient building foundations have been laid, can result in damage to the buildings. Instead of standard trees, you should choose dwarf varieties or specimens that have been grafted onto dwarfing rootstocks.

### Shade considerations
Think carefully about the sun's orientation before you plant evergreen trees or tall conifers. If planted on the north boundary, they may cast unwelcome shade over the garden in winter.

See where the shade of the mature tree will fall by placing a stick of the same height in the proposed planting spot. On a sunny day, look at its shadow at different times, paying close attention to flowerbeds or sitting areas that you wish to keep in the sunshine.

### Autumn planting
Container-grown trees can be planted at most times of the year – provided the ground is not too dry or frozen – but autumn is best.

TREES

The soil is moist and will still retain some of summer's warmth. Maintain soil moisture, and avoid planting during cold dry winds.

### Protect other plants
Tree roots are greedy, soaking up moisture and nutrients. If you are worried that nearby plants could suffer, select plant types that will tolerate dry soil conditions.

### Loosen the tie
Check tree ties regularly to make sure that they have not become too tight. Such constriction can damage the wood fibres and weaken the tree trunk, which could then break in a high wind. Remove ties and stakes after about 2 years, by which time the tree will have rooted firmly.

## plant a Tree

**1** Loosen the soil around the planting area and dig in compost or well-rotted manure. Dig a planting hole about twice as wide as the root ball. Set the tree in the hole at the correct depth and spread out the roots. Insert a stake on one side (or both sides if using two stakes) of the root ball.

**2** Backfill the planting hole, starting at the base to hold the plant in position, and gently firm in the soil with your hand as you work. Water immediately, slowly and thoroughly, using at least 20 litres of water. Finish off with a solution of seaweed and water.

**3** Tie the tree trunk to the stake (or stakes), ensuring that the ties are firm but not cutting into the trunk. Finally, cover the area around the base with a layer of mulch.

### Protection for a young tree
Put a sleeve protector, made of either perforated plastic or fine mesh wire, around the base of a young tree. Alternatively, if the trunk is not too thick, cut open a plastic bottle lengthwise and secure it around the trunk with twine. These guards will protect the tree's bark from being eaten by rabbits and from accidental damage by whipper-snippers, line trimmers or lawnmowers.

### Action against poor growth
If a young tree appears to make no growth after planting, it may be because it is establishing badly. Make sure that it has the best conditions for growth. Mulch the soil round the roots and water regularly. Also reduce the crown by about a third – pruning can help to stimulate growth.

### Keep trees watered and fed
Water a mature tree beneath the canopy, which is where the roots are, rather than close to the trunk. Do not let a newly planted or young tree suffer from drought as this will weaken its root system. Mature trees growing in their natural habitat are unlikely to require feeding, but young trees, whether ornamental or fruit varieties, will benefit from a slow-release fertiliser in early spring.

### Remove suckers
If your tree produces suckers, cut them off cleanly with secateurs. Pinch out any shoots or suckers that subsequently appear with your finger and thumb.

### Tree preservation
Heavy machinery left leaning against a tree can damage the trunk or affect growth because of pressure on the root plate. The careless use of mowers, whipper-snippers or line trimmers can damage the surface roots.

*See also* Flowering trees, Planting, Pruning, Stakes and supports, Transplanting

## choose Trees for a small or medium garden

When space is limited, choose a tree that won't grow into a giant and will give you as much year-round interest as possible. The trees listed here are generally trouble-free and will suit a small or medium-sized garden.

**Ornamental plum (*Prunus* spp. and cvs)**
Deciduous; to 9 m; lovely autumn foliage; single or double, perfumed white, pink or red flowers from early winter to spring.

**Chinese tallow tree (*Triadica sebifera* syn. *Sapium sebiferum*)** Deciduous; to 8 m; orange-red or yellow leaves in autumn; weed potential in some areas.

**Flowering gum (*Corymbia ficifolia* cvs)**
Evergreen; 4–5 m; spectacular creamy white, pink, orange, red or scarlet flowers in summer; attractive bark and large seedpods.

**Irish strawberry tree (*Arbutus unedo*)**
Evergreen; to 10 m; attractive bark; white flowers and red fruits in autumn.

Golden penda

**Golden penda (*Xanthostemon chrysanthus*)**
Evergreen; to 10 m; showy yellow, bird-attracting flowers in summer and autumn; red new growth.

**Crepe myrtle (*Lagerstroemia indica*)**
Deciduous; to 8 m; white, mauve, pink, cerise or burgundy flowers in summer; orange-tinted leaves in autumn.

**Golden shower tree (*Cassia fistula*)**
Semi-deciduous; to 8 m; pendulous yellow flowers in summer; some autumn colour; weed potential in some areas.

TRELLISES | TROPICAL FRUITS

## TRELLISES

Trellis, also known as lattice, is a quick way of extending walls and fences. It also makes an ideal screen for less attractive parts of the garden, such as sheds, clotheslines and compost heaps.

### Add a little distance
Do not place a trellis directly onto a wall. Attach it to vertical 5 x 5 cm wooden battens fitted to the wall. This lets air circulate, which helps to prevent plants becoming infected with mildew.

### Easy access
Hinged trellis is a wise precaution if you will need access behind the trellis to paint the wall. The trellis is attached to the wall by hinges at its base and hooks at the top. Just unhook it at the top and fold it down carefully when you need to reach the wall behind.

### Selecting trellis
Select the type of trellis that is most suitable for a plant. Unless you want the trellis itself to be a feature, select a colour that will blend into the background.

### Choosing climbers
Rambling and climbing roses can display their blooms to the best advantage when trained on a trellis. You will need to tie in new shoots before they become so long that they obstruct paths or patios, where their thorns may cause injury. Clematis is ideal trained on a trellis because its leaf stems curl around and cling to the wooden struts.

For a quick flowery cover, select the orange-flowered trumpet vine (*Campsis grandiflora*) or white-flowered potato vine (*Solanum jasminoides*). Mandevillas or star jasmine (*Trachelospermum jasminoides*) are also stunning. Passionfruit will provide dense leafy growth, exotic large flowers and tasty fruit.

### Training for even coverage
It takes only a few seconds every few days to train climbers so they cover the trellis evenly. Weave the stems horizontally along the bottom. At the edges, allow a little upward growth before resuming the horizontal training. Once the trellis is covered, you will have a permanent even screen and a framework to prune back to.

See also Climbers, Supports

## TROPICAL FRUITS

For those living in subtropical and tropical climes, it is possible to plant a home orchard full of tropical fruits. There is a rich variety of exotic forms and flavours to choose from.

### Pineapple *Ananas comosus*
Pineapples grow well in the subtropics and tropics. They are bromeliads and need an open, sunny position in enriched, very freely draining soil, with good air circulation. Harvest the fruit when it changes from green to pale green, with a hint of orange through to fully orange.

### Custard apple
*Annona reticulata*
Custard apples do well in the coastal tropics and subtropics. The tree is short and spreading, with clusters of scented, pale yellow trumpet flowers. The knobbled fruit has flesh that is soft, custard-like, sweet and aromatic when ripe.

### Soursop *A. muricata*
The soursop, also known as graviola or guanabána, is a close relative of the custard apple. The compact tree reaches about 4.5 m high and must be grown in warm, tropical conditions.

### Lychee *Litchi chinensis*
So long as the correct varieties are chosen, lychees can be grown from the southern subtropics to the tropics. They need a cool, dry autumn and a winter that does not fall below 10°C for flowering to be initiated. The fruit has very thin, red skin and delicious, translucent white flesh.

274

TROPICAL FRUITS | TULIPS

### Black sapote  *Diospyros digyna*
The black sapote is an evergreen tree to 25 m. The tomato-sized fruit turn yellowish green when ripe, with a delicious pulp that has a colour and texture just like chocolate custard pudding. The tree will grow in the southern subtropics to the tropics if protected from cold winds.

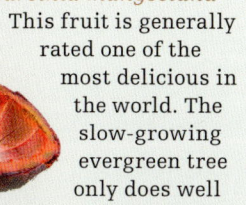

### Mangosteen
*Garcinia mangostana* 
This fruit is generally rated one of the most delicious in the world. The slow-growing evergreen tree only does well in the wet tropics. It is sensitive to cold and killed by temperatures below 7°C. The fruit has a hard, deep purple skin with luscious white edible flesh inside.

### Rambutan
*Nephelium lappaceum*
This is a close relative of the lychee. Its flesh is translucent white, jelly-like, sweet, luscious and fragrant. Rambutan trees need frost-free conditions and will flourish in hot, high-rainfall coastal areas north of 18 degrees South latitude.

### Tamarillo  *Solanum betaceum*
This cousin of the tomato forms a small tree and grows well in a warm to hot climate. It has large, heart-shaped leaves and produces continuous flushes of egg-shaped crimson or orange fruit from spring through to autumn.

See also Bananas, Mangoes

# TULIPS

Tulips are the quintessential spring bulb for cool to cold regions. Choose tall-stemmed types sold as Monet tulips in warmer areas. The bulbs of countless varieties are available by mail order.

### Small tulips
If your garden is very windy, choose smaller growing varieties such as 'Apricot Beauty' or *Tulipa liniafolia*, *T. turkestanica* or *T. tarda*, which attain a height of 20–30 cm. Both the Single Early and Double Early groups are short-stemmed, too.

### Lifting and replanting
Don't leave bedding tulip bulbs in the ground. They will degenerate from year to year and yield fewer flowers as time passes. Wait until the foliage has yellowed before lifting them and storing them in a dry place until autumn, when you can plant them out again. The exceptions are wild species or varieties derived from them; they can remain in the garden all year round unless the soil is very wet.

### Easy lifting
Before planting a clump of tulip bulbs, line the planting hole with a piece of wire mesh or plastic netting, or purchase a purpose-made bulb-planting basket. Leave the edge of the liner protruding slightly above the soil. After the foliage has died back, it is easy to lift the bulbs by pulling gently on the edges of the liner.

### Leave the leaves
Once the tulip blooms have faded and been deadheaded, you may not like the untidy look of the old foliage. Even so, do not cut it down because the old leaves will replenish the bulb's strength and ensure it blooms again next year. Deadheading stops energy being lost to seed development.

**TROPICAL GARDENS**
*see pages 276–277*

275

# Tropical gardens

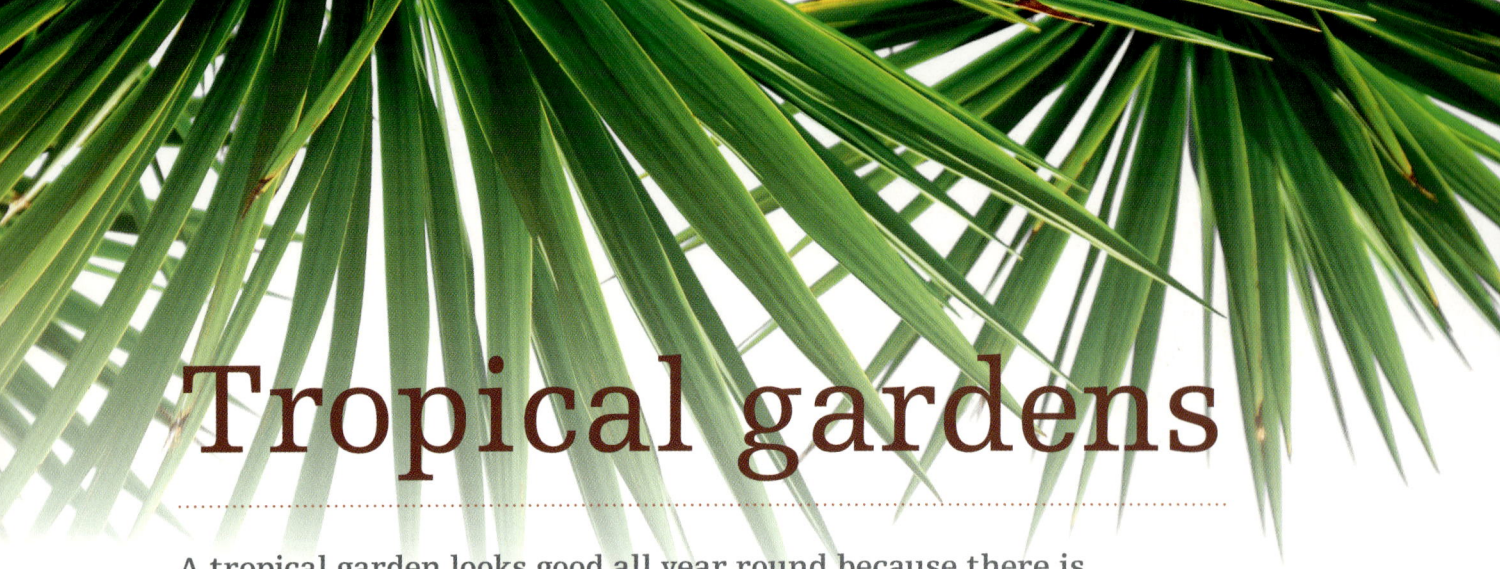

A tropical garden looks good all year round because there is no season when growth is not happening and no period when something is not in flower or putting out fresh lush greenery.

## Style of the tropics

The tropical garden can have a lush, cool rainforest look, with palms, groundcovers and vines; or a rich, colourful, hot look, with bromeliads, orchids, crotons, cordylines, hibiscus and frangipanis.

## True tropicals and look-alikes

Many plants suited to the tropical garden style originate from the zone either side of the Equator, which is the true tropics. In those regions rainfall is heavy and constant, day length varies little throughout the year, and the climate is hot and steamy. Fortunately, many tropical plants do surprisingly well outside their narrow zone.

There are also plants that originate in tropical mountain areas or in arid zones that look 'tropical' and do well in cooler, drier climates. And there are plants from subtropical and warm temperate areas with the same appearance. They can all be used to create tropical-style gardens outside the true tropics.

## Creating the look

Lush greenery, sometimes with vibrant colour, is the main characteristic of tropical gardens. They often have water features to make the landscape feel and appear cool. Traditionally, gardens in the tropics are bounded by a screen of palms, tall trees and leafy shrubberies. If there is a view, such as the sea at the bottom of the garden, it should be framed – but not obstructed – by plantings on either side.

### choose plants for a Tropical garden

**Palms**  Bamboo palm (*Chamaedorea microspadix*) ✻ Golden cane palm (*Dypsis lutescens*) ✻ Triangle palm (*Dypsis decaryi*) ✻ Date palms (*Phoenix* spp.) ✻ Royal palms (*Roystonea* spp.) ✻ Foxtail palm (*Wodyetia bifurcata*)

**Trees**  Cassias (*Cassia brewsteri, C. marksiana, C. fistula*) ✻ Jacaranda (*Jacaranda mimosifolia*) ✻ Frangipani (*Plumeria* spp.) ✻ Traveler's palm (*Ravenala madagascariensis*) ✻ Trumpet tree (*Tabebuia* spp.)

**Shrubs and perennials**  Gingers (*Alpinia*, *Etlingera* and *Zingiber* spp.) ✻ Angel's trumpet (*Brugmansia* spp. syn. *Datura* spp.) ✻ Cordyline ✻ Croton (*Codiaeum variegatum*) ✻ Heliconia spp. and cvs ✻ Hibiscus (*Hibiscus rosa-sinensis* cvs) ✻ Vireya rhododendrons

**Groundcovers**  Elephant's ear (*Alocasia* spp.) ✻ Bromeliads ✻ *Calathea* spp. ✻ Bloodleaf (*Iresine herbstii*) ✻ Prayer plant (*Maranta* cvs)

**Climbers**  Bougainvillea ✻ Glory bower vines (*Clerodendrum splendens, C. thomsoniae*) ✻ Jasmine ✻ *Mandevilla* spp. ✻ Purple wreath (*Petrea volubilis*) ✻ Rangoon creeper (*Quisqualis indica*)

*Heliconia* cv.

Traveller palm

Elephant's ear

*Zingiber* sp.

# T | TURNIPS AND SWEDES | TWO-SPOTTED MITES

## TURNIPS AND SWEDES

Turnips and swedes are so similar and closely related that many gardeners think they are identical.

### Close relatives
The turnip has white roots, while the slightly larger swede is usually flushed with purple. It keeps better after harvest than the turnip, and some cooks think it superior in flavour. They are grown in the same way, the main difference being that turnips mature in 6–12 weeks, while swedes take about 16 weeks.

### Sowing and growing
Both turnips and swedes are sown in autumn so that the plants mature in cool weather. Prepare the soil with fertiliser before sowing and, if the soil is acid, add lime. Give plants plenty of water to keep roots tender and prevent the plants from running to seed.

### Tops for crops
Young turnip leaves make a delicious spring vegetable. Sow the seeds thickly in winter, and crop the leaves when they are about 10–15 cm tall. Give the plants a dose of liquid fertiliser and they will regrow and provide two or three harvests. Swede leaves are coarse and bitter.

### Keep turnips apart
Grow turnips and swedes away from other root vegetables. They belong to the Brassica family and are susceptible to club root, a serious soil-borne fungal disease. Grow them in the same part of the vegetable plot as other brassicas (cauliflowers and cabbages) so they can all be rotated together from year to year to prevent a build-up of club root in the soil. Water in a diluted lime solution to deter the fungus, too.

### Time to harvest
Depending on the variety, turnips are ready from 40–90 days after sowing. Pick regularly, never letting them become larger than a tennis ball. Swedes need at least 150 days to reach maturity. Lift as needed from autumn to spring.

### In the kitchen
Some turnips are crisp and sweet, ideal for salads, while others are suited to soups or stews. Swedes can be roasted or puréed. Add both to cornish pasties.

*Swede*
*Globe-shaped turnip*
*Flat-rooted turnip*

## TWO-SPOTTED MITES

### Plants affected
Many plants, including annuals, some perennials, roses, some shrubs, trees, fruit trees and vegetables. Plants that are grown indoors or in a greenhouse, coldframe or polythene tunnel are most vulnerable to mites. Dryness can increase infestations.

### Symptoms
Light mottling of upper leaf surfaces; leaves turn yellow and may fall; fine silk webbing on plant. The mites are microscopic.

### Treatment
* Encourage natural predators into your garden – lacewings, ladybirds, predatory mites and predatory thrips.

* Spray deciduous fruit trees with winter oil when dormant.

* Sprays of insecticidal soap or maldison may control two-spotted mite, but these also kill predators.

* Maintain a humid atmosphere, as they flourish in dry heat.

* In the greenhouse, release the predatory mite *Phytoseiulus persimilis*. However, do not spray insecticides or use any yellow sticky traps.

**UNDERPLANTING**

Bluebell woodland

## UNDERPLANTING

### Carpet with periwinkle
In shady spots under bushes, you can make a fine spring showing with lesser periwinkle (*Vinca minor*). It comes in green-leaved and variegated forms and has blue, purple or white flowers.

### Violet undercoat
The Australian native violet (*Viola hederacea*) is a useful plant for underplanting. It thrives in cool, moist conditions and flowers throughout the year. Another violet that is excellent for this situation is the rock garden violet (*V. labradorica*). Its white-throated lilac blooms rise above purple-tinged leaves. It seeds freely to give good coverage.

### Woodland natives
To find plants that can cope with the dry soils and shady conditions common under trees, look at those that are native to woodland areas around the world. Depending on your climate, this could include azaleas, bulbs such as bluebells, daffodils and grape hyacinths, perennials such as Japanese windflowers (*Anemone* × *hybrida*) and columbines, and bromeliads in warmer areas. In cool climates hellebores will flower in winter and early spring in shades of pink, plum, green and white.

Hostas and ferns will create a carpet of green in the shade under trees; the sheer variety of foliage texture, shape and shades of green will provide plenty of interest.

### Spreading scent
For scented underplanting in a cool climate, grow the spring-flowering lilies of the valley (*Convallaria majalis*). They prefer to grow under deciduous trees, where they spread by creeping horizontal rhizomes. You could also consider planting sweet violets (*V. odorata*), which thrive in partial shade. The fragrant purple flowers bloom in winter and spring.

See also Groundcovers, Rainforest gardens, Shady gardens

### Rainforest understorey
After the canopy of a rainforest garden has become established and these fast-growing or mature tree specimens have begun to provide shade and protection, and once the slower growing trees have been planted, it is time to start putting in the rainforest understorey. Shade-loving low-growing shrubs, perennials and groundcovers are perfect for this purpose. Plants such as elephant's ears (*Alocasia* spp.), native ginger (*Alpinia caerulea*), bromeliads, *Calathea* and *Caladium* species, dianella or flax lilies (*Dianella* spp.) and plectranthus are all good choices for a rainforest understorey.

*Caladium bicolor* cv.

# VEGETABLE GARDENS

Freshly picked home-grown vegetables are full of flavour and immensely satisfying to cultivate. You can grow vegetables almost anywhere in the garden beds, borders or containers. If you have enough space, however, a traditional plot will give better results and be easier to maintain. Raised beds are also excellent for growing vegetables.

## Site in the sun

A sunny position is vital, ideally sheltered from the wind, as it can impede plant growth and pollination. Vegetables prefer a well-drained soil, so you'll need to add generous amounts of organic matter if you have a heavy clay, very light sand or chalk. Easy access to water is also essential.

## Permanent features

You'll need one or two compost bins, a space to stack manure or other bulky materials such as leaf mould, paths between beds for easy access, and gardening tools – and, ideally, somewhere to store them. In a small garden, choose tall compost bins that take up less ground space.

## Test case

Most vegetables do best at a pH of 6.0 to 7.0, although potatoes prefer a more acid soil and the brassicas (broccoli, cabbages and cauliflower) and celery like a slightly alkaline soil. In regions where the soil is acid and there is high rainfall, such as coastal areas, add lime or dolomite to the vegetable patch every year or two, ideally after the summer crops have finished and you're preparing the bed for a cool-season crop. Use an inexpensive soil-testing kit to test the soil's pH.

## Coarse feeding

Applying bulky organic matter annually will benefit vegetable gardens greatly. Use well-rotted manure or compost or provide nourishment by sowing a green manure, such as lucerne, lupins, oats, field peas or annual clover. These can be sown in winter when the vegetable garden is empty. Sow seed quite densely. When the plants die down in spring, you can either sow your crops through the mat of dead vegetation or dig it in.

## Feeding habits

In addition to adding organic matter, non-organic gardeners may also want to add a balanced general fertiliser to the vegetable plot in August before the main sowing and planting season gets underway in spring and summer. Many growing crops will need additional feeding with a side dressing or regular applications of liquid fertiliser.

## Break out of the mould

Traditionally, vegetables were grown in square plots. One reason for this was that it is easier to water and care for vegetables if they are grouped together. You can make a vegetable plot more decorative by creating a round bed and planting in circular patterns. Or, if you don't want a separate vegetable patch at all,

# VEGETABLE GARDENS

you can tuck the vegetables in among the flowering plants in your garden beds.

### No-dig plot
You can make a vegetable garden without doing any digging. The key is to ensure that the existing grass or perennial weeds in your plot cannot grow. This is done by excluding light. Start by spreading about 10 layers of newspaper over the area you have chosen, ensuring good overlap between them. Then add layers of lucerne hay, hay or pea straw. Scatter chicken manure pellets and blood and bone between the layers until it reaches a height of 30 cm. Add 10–15 cm of compost. The plot is now ready for planting.

### What to plant
Begin with the vegetables you most like to eat, and match them to your space. Quick-growing salad leaves, spinach and snow peas are good to start with. On a small plot, choose vegetables that can be grown close together, such as lettuces, beans, garlic and onions. Or grow crops that will provide fresher, more nutritious and cheaper produce than that available from the greengrocer or supermarket. These crops include Asian vegetables, dwarf beans, runner beans, snow peas, sugar snap peas, spinach, silverbeet, corn and tomatoes.

### Buy healthy specimens
Make sure that the vegetable seedlings you buy are well grown and sturdy. Choose those that are grown singly in pots or in cell punnets as this will minimise disturbance to the roots when the seedlings are planted out. Reject any pots or punnets that contain seedlings with yellowing leaves, leggy stems or are past their best.

### Planting know-how
Plant low-growing vegetables on the sunny side of taller ones in your vegetable patch to ensure that both receive the light they need and that space is maximised. In addition, intercrop vegetables that reach maturity at different times. For example, plant quick-maturing radishes or spring onions between slow-growing parsnips or brussels sprouts.

### Mark the rows
It pays to mark out rows with string or sticks before sowing. This enables you to plant straight rows, which not only look neater but help you to locate emerging seedlings and distinguish your plants from weeds.

### Thinning
To give your plants the best chance of success, sow more seed than is required then thin excess seedlings as soon as they are big enough to handle, first removing malformed and weak plants. Only do this when the soil is moist, then water after thinning to settle the remaining plants back in. If possible, thin seedlings in two stages. With crops such as onions, carrots and beetroot, the second thinning can yield small crops – spring onions, baby carrots and beets – for eating.

> ### Seed or seedlings
> Buying your vegetables as seeds is cheap and gives you the choice of a huge array of varieties. Don't confine yourself to the packets available in supermarkets or garden centres. Read mail-order seed catalogues from specialist companies for the latest selections. The seed packets will give you the information you need on the sowing date, depth and spacing.
>
> Buying seedlings is easier and quicker for busy gardeners, but gives you a more limited choice. Many vegetables do best when seed is sown directly where the plants are to grow as this avoids transplant shock and checks to growth. Seedlings may be more convenient for those vegetables that are usually sown in seed trays and transplanted out into beds later.

## sow Vegetable seeds in a drill

**1** Use pegs and twine to mark straight lines at the correct distance apart. Create a shallow V-shaped groove, or drill, with the corner of a hoe.

**2** If the soil is dry, trickle water into the drill grooves before sowing. Sow the seeds and cover lightly with soil. Water gently through a fine rose.

281

## VEGETABLE GARDENS *continued*

### Tall, vivid screens
Attractive flowering vegetables help to blend the vegetable plot with the rest of the garden. For an ornamental divider, it is hard to beat tall, twining runner beans with their scarlet or white flowers or their colourful pods, such as 'Purple King' and 'Blue Peter', or crimson-streaked borlotti beans.

### Companion crops
Almost all vegetable crops benefit from a border of strong-smelling herbs, such as lavender, rosemary, sage or thyme, or from clumps of French marigolds (*Tagetes patula*) planted in their midst. These plants support many beneficial insects and their smells confuse some pests. Many vegetables are prone to invasions of pests and diseases; companion planting may help minimise problems. There is little scientific evidence to support it, but it is worth trying to see if it works for you.

### Climatic considerations
To achieve a successful crop, all vegetables need to be sown and grown at the right time of year. In tropical and subtropical locations many vegetables can be grown all year round. Use the advice on seed packets as a guide and adapt this to your local conditions.

### Warm- and cool-season vegetables
In temperate locations warm-season vegetables such as beans, capsicum, corn, cucurbits and tomatoes do best in temperatures of 20°C and above, so they are planted in spring to grow through summer. Cool-season vegetables such as broad beans, brussels sprouts, cauliflower, onions and peas must be sown so they grow through the cooler months. There is an intermediate group, which includes beetroot, carrots, celery, leeks and lettuces, and they are adaptable, although they tend to bolt and run to seed if sown too early or too late.

### Plant in groups
If you grow a wide range of vegetables, you can put them in the following groups to practise a 3- or 4-year cycle of crop rotation:

**Hungry crops and salad leaves** Beans, celeriac, celery, leeks, lettuces, onions, peas, shallots, spinach, corn, tomatoes, zucchini.

**Brassicas** Broccoli, kale, brussels sprouts, cabbages, cauliflowers.

**Root crops** Beetroot, parsnips, potatoes, carrots, swedes, turnips.

### Growing vegetables in containers
You can grow some crops successfully in containers. Pots need to be at least 20 cm deep and filled with a good-quality potting mix that is formulated for vegetables and herbs. Start with easy crops such as runner beans, early potatoes, carrots, tomatoes, spring onions and salad leaves. Vegetables in pots will need regular watering and liquid feeding every 2–4 weeks: use a balanced liquid feed for leafy crops and a tomato food for fruiting crops.

**Beans** Dwarf varieties, such as 'Brown Beauty' or 'Gourmet's Delight', grow best in pots. Use large pots and keep plants well watered.

**Spring onions** The best variety is actually called 'Spring Onion'. Harvest 12–14 weeks after sowing.

**Carrots** Plant a short-rooted variety, such as 'Baby Carrot', in grow bags. Pull up when 5–7.5 cm long.

**Tomatoes** Dwarf tomatoes, such as 'Tiny Tim', will do well in large containers. Choose cherry tomatoes or a trailing variety, such as 'Sweet Tumbler', for a hanging basket. Plant after the last frosts and never allow the potting mix to dry out.

**Potatoes** Buy seed potatoes that are certified virus-free. In late winter or early spring, leave them in the sun until they begin to sprout, then plant in a container at least 50 cm deep. Stake the tops.

# VEGETABLE GARDENS

### Practice crop rotation
A crop rotation system ensures that these large plant groups move to a different position in the vegetable garden every year and are grown in the same spot only once every 3–4 years. This limits the build-up of pests and diseases and ensures that the different plant groups receive the differing soil treatment and quantities of various soil foods that they need. Old gardening books tend to recommend strict rotation, but this is less critical now that there are so many excellent fertilisers and organic materials available to provide crops with the nutrients they need.

### Slight rotation
Gardeners who grow only small quantities of a few crops have less need to practise a crop rotation system. However, try to avoid growing the same crop in the same place 2 years in succession.

### Feast or famine
No matter how hard you try, you will likely end up with not enough of one type of vegetable and a glut of another type. If you have an overabundance of a particular crop, try to find time for freezing, pickling, bottling or preserving. One way of avoiding gluts is to successively sow or plant small amounts at regular intervals (2–3 weeks), or to grow different varieties of the same vegetable with different maturing times.

### Keep a record
It pays to record everything you do in the vegetable patch – the varieties you plant, sowing and planting dates, planting distances, harvest dates and anything else you want to remember. This will help you with crop rotation as well as plan future crops and adapt to your particular conditions. Also include comments on flavour.

### Small and tender
Vegetables are best harvested when they are small and tender. Root vegetables, in particular, soon become woody in texture if left to grow too large. Regular picking increases the yield of repeat-cropping vegetables such as beans.

### Be organic
A great advantage of the home garden vegetable plot is that you can minimise or avoid the use of chemicals, especially pesticides. Organic gardening or farming avoids the use of synthetically manufactured fertilisers and pesticides and uses crop rotation, crop residues, animal manures, green manures and biological pest control to maintain soil health and productivity, supply nutrients and control pests and diseases.

You can do this by making your own compost or buying organic materials, using companion planting techniques, picking off insects such as caterpillars by hand, controlling snails and slugs without using pellets, and trying different non-chemical sprays, such as those based on garlic or soap flakes. Keep the patch weed-free and learn to accept that there will be some losses or reduction in harvest quality.

### Chemical control of pests
If you do use pesticides, correctly identify the problem first and use the correct chemical. Try to use the least toxic options, such as horticultural oils and soaps, before more lethal chemicals. If you use chemicals on vegetables, observe the label instructions about the withholding period – the time between spraying and harvesting (and eating) the crop. This is the length of time it takes for substances that are harmful to humans to break down.

*See also* Biological controls, Companion plants, Fertilisers, Organic gardening, Raised beds, Seeds and seedlings, Soil analysis, Sowing

# VERTICAL GARDENS | VIRUSES

## VERTICAL GARDENS

### Make the most of limited space
Vertical gardens are becoming popular in cities as a way of making the most of limited space. Suitable indoors or out, they can be a feature wall or a divider in a courtyard, and can be positioned in a sunny or a shady location, depending on plant requirements. They are efficient temperature regulators that can absorb excess heat and, when correctly sited, reuse water run-off from a roof.

### Plant choices
The plants that you can use are limited by size, drainage needs, foliage type and pedestrian access. Liriope, mondo grass, low-mounding *Helichrysum* and *Carex* species, dianellas and blue fescue (*Festuca glauca*) all work well. Succulents are good for low water use in full sun.

### Frameworks and modules
A vertical garden is supported by a framework, which is secured firmly to the wall. It usually contains individual lightweight stackable modules, which may be made from recyclable materials and hold the growing medium in which roots take hold. Inbuilt drip irrigation keeps the plants hydrated, and collection trays at ground level capture and recycle water. The growing medium of, for example, felt or biodegradable foam, distributes moisture evenly to the plant roots and retains moisture in extreme conditions.

## VIEWS AND PERSPECTIVE

### Getting it together
In larger gardens, natural perspective makes the distance between parallel lines appear to narrow and converge in the distance. In smaller gardens, you can use tricks that will deceive the eye into believing that the garden is longer and narrower or shorter and wider than it is.

### Altering perspective
The technique of false perspective is simple to master. To create the illusion of length, position large plants near the house and plant progressively smaller plants down the garden. Emphasise this effect by using colours: pale blues and mauves will recede into the distance, while bright oranges and reds will appear closer. Similarly, plants with smaller leaves will seem further away and those with larger leaves will seem closer.

### Create an illusion
Use the garden's sight-lines to create the illusion of length in the garden. Sight-lines usually run from windows, doors and seating places towards an interesting focal point some distance away. Slightly narrowing paths and flower borders or the spaces along the sight-lines will give the illusion of length.

### A turn for the better
A garden will seem bigger if it is not seen all at once but is instead discovered gradually. Plan lawns and paths so that they meander

## VIRUSES

Most plant viruses are spread by insects such as leafhoppers and aphids, but certain viruses can be spread by pollen and seed, while those affecting roots are spread by nematodes and soil protozoa.

### Plants affected
Many garden plants.

### Symptoms
Small, crinkled and irregularly shaped leaves. Streaks, puckering and mottling on leaf stalks and stems; mosaic on leaves; plants wilt. White, pale or yellow streaks on flower petals.

### Treatment
* Dig up and destroy or safely dispose of affected plants.

* Maintain good garden hygiene and discourage aphids and other pests that spread diseases.

* Practise crop rotation in the vegetable garden.

* Grow virus-resistant cultivars or buy certified virus-free plants.

* Disinfect tools after handling virus-infected plants; do not propagate from these plants.

VIEWS AND PERSPECTIVE | VIOLETS

around the corners or curves of borders or groups of plants, perhaps under arches, arbours or tunnels, to disappear into hidden areas of the garden. These will create an impression of further spaces beyond, with something of interest always to be discovered there – a seat, wall fountain, pool, pond or statue. In a small garden a doorway, real or false, would hint at mysteries lying beyond.

### All done with mirrors
Mirrors in shapes and sizes to suit most garden settings can be made to order, ready-cut and foil-backed, from glass and mirror specialists. Outdoor mirrors must have a lead foil backing, which protects the silvering from the effects of weather, and must be sealed with a waterproof sealant.

If well placed, a large mirror can add considerably to the apparent length of the garden. Site it to back a pergola at the end of the garden, or place it on a wall with its edges concealed by climbing plants. Position the mirror so it does not reflect the viewer or the sun or glare directly, as this can be annoying and will also destroy the illusion.

### Flaunting the view
If you have a garden with a view, make the most of your good fortune. The foreground should be kept as uncluttered as possible. Further enhance the view by framing it in some way, perhaps with a gate or with a handsome tree or clump of shrubs planted on each side.

### Screening an eyesore
Evergreens can be used to frame an attractive view inside or outside the garden. They can also be used to make ugly objects outside your garden invisible all year round. It is easier to hide an eyesore by planting a smaller evergreen nearer the viewing point than by planting it at the boundary, where you would need a much taller plant to do the same job.

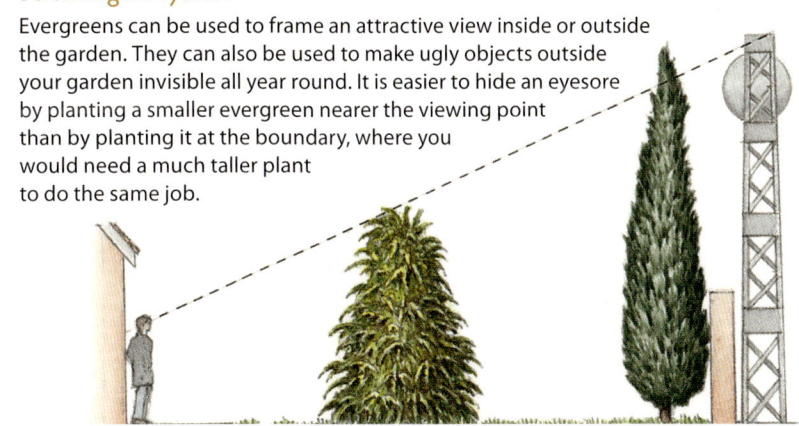

## VIOLETS

### Rich soil
Grow sweet violets (*Viola odorata*) in soil enriched with plenty of compost or manure. A mulch of manure mixed with well-rotted leaf mulch will encourage good strong growth and keep the soil cool in summer.

### Winter sun
Sweet violets need winter sun but benefit from a cool, sheltered spot in summer as they don't like scorching sun or wind. They will not flower well in full shade so select an area under a deciduous tree or that faces east. For a moist spot in constant shade, try the native violet (*V. hederacea*); it will grow and flower well there.

### Encourage flowers
Where violets are growing in an ideal location, they can form a dense and attractive groundcover. However, violets that are allowed to spread will produce fewer flowers than those that are kept compact. Trim plants regularly and divide large clumps every 3–4 years for plentiful flowers.

### Pruning for better growth
A quick way to prune violets in autumn to encourage new growth is to run over the violet patch with the lawnmower. If this sounds too extreme, simply prune away the old leaves with shears or secateurs. When violets are flowering, picking them will also promote more flowers – pick them with long stems.

**Native violet**

## WALL PLANTING

### Against the wall
When planting espaliered shrubs and climbers against a wall, put up the support first, then dig the planting hole at least 30 cm from the wall. (Check that the wall isn't damaged, because a climber will only make it worse.) Add plenty of moisture-retentive, bulky organic matter, such as well-rotted compost or manure. To encourage quick establishment, make sure the plant leans slightly towards the wall. Choose lime-loving plants for concreted areas.

To keep them growing close to the wall, the branches of espaliered shrubs must be tied in to their supports. Most climbers will need a trellis or support to cling to.

### Wall warmth
Brick walls absorb heat during the day and release it at night. So in cooler areas plants close to a wall will be protected from frost.

### Cosmetic cover
Hide an ugly wall by growing evergreen plants with dense foliage on or over it. If there is no soil at the base of the wall, plant climbers in large tubs or troughs for colour and interest; provide supports unless the climbers are self-clinging. Fix hanging baskets or wall pots filled with trailing lobelias, petunias or ivy-leaved geraniums to a wall for summer colour. Scrambling, spreading or trailing plants will cascade over ugly or utilitarian terracing walls.

### Planting under the eaves
The narrow strip of garden bed, often only 30–60 cm wide, that lies under house eaves receives little rainfall. Without careful planning and good plant selection, it can be difficult to establish a thriving garden bed there.

When improving soil, don't raise the soil level to block ventilation outlets or damp courses. Choose plants that thrive in very dry conditions with a limited nutrient supply. To reduce the likelihood of termite infestation in affected areas, don't use a wood-based mulch near the house. Pebbles or gravel are better choices.

*See also* Climbers, Espaliers

## WASPS

### Enjoy beneficial wasps
Many native wasps will frequent your garden to clean up aphids, caterpillars and other pests. Some wasps build mud nests, while others construct large papery nests attached to a tree, fence or under the eaves of a house. Take care not to get too close to a paper wasp nest, however; if the nest is disturbed, the inhabitants may attack and sting.

### Galling behaviour
The lumps and bumps, known as galls, found on leaves and stems are sometimes caused by wasps laying their eggs into young stems or foliage. The leaves and stems of acacias, eucalypts and coral trees are particularly favoured by gall-forming wasps. Citrus plants may also be attacked. As the larva develops, the surrounding plant tissue grows abnormally and forms a gall.

Galls can usually be ignored as they don't affect the long-term health of the plant. And as the insect is inside the plant tissue, chemical control is difficult unless a systemic insecticide is used. If only a small area is affected, you could snip off the gall before the insect hatches.

# WATER PLANTS

## Planting for ornamental effect
Choose a mixture of aquatic plants with contrasting foliage shapes and colours for your pond or pool. Plant waterlilies for their soft pads of leaves, irises and grasses for spiky foliage, and for a rounded shape, plants such as marsh marigolds. Variegated foliage will create interest when flowering has finished.

## Selecting the right plants
There are four main groups of pond plants: submerged, floating, deep-water and marginal plants. Submerged plants are vital for the wellbeing of the pool because they mop up excess nutrients, which algae would feed on otherwise, and produce life-giving oxygen for plants and fish. They also provide cover for spawning fish. Many floating plants offer colour and interest. Even though some floating plants spread rapidly to cover the water surface, they are easily scooped out and can be used to make good compost.

Deep-water aquatic plants include waterlilies and other decorative plants; choose varieties that suit the depth of your pond. Marginal plants grow in the shallows and provide an important transition zone around the edge of a pond.

## Clean up before planting
Don't place aquatic plants in your pool immediately after buying them because the leaves and roots may contain larvae, eggs or pests. Clean the plants first by washing them under the cold tap before setting them out.

## Acclimatising deep-water plants
Vigorous deep-water aquatic plants such as waterlilies need to be acclimatised gradually. Stand the plant on a stack of bricks so that its leaves are just below the surface, then remove the bricks one by one as the leaf stems grow and the leaves reach the surface. Divide the plants every 3–4 years.

## Beware vigorous plants
Floating aquatic plants such as the fairy mosses (*Azolla* spp.) and duckweeds (*Lemna* spp.) are prolific; if left unchecked, they can cover the entire surface of a pond. Avoid invasive plants such as water mint (*Mentha aquatica*) and pond sedge (*Carex riparia*), which will swamp their neighbours even when confined in planting baskets.

See also Bog gardens, Ponds and pools

---

### Water plants for a pond

**Deep-water plants** Waterblommetjie (*Aponogeton distachyos*) ✻ Waterlilies (*Nymphaea* spp. and cvs) ✻ Water fringe (*Nymphoides peltata*) ✻ Golden club (*Orontium aquaticum*) ✻ Swamp lily (*Ottelia ovalifolia*)

**Marginal plants** Sweet flag (*Acorus calamus*) ✻ Marsh marigold (*Caltha palustris*) ✻ Tassel sedge (*Carex fascicularis*) ✻ Rabbit-ear iris (*Iris laevigata*) ✻ Flag irises (*I. pseudacorus, I. versicolor*) ✻ Louisiana iris ✻ Water primrose (*Ludwigia peploides* subsp. *montevidensis*) ✻ Water forget-me-not (*Myosotis scorpioides*) ✻ Pickerel rush (*Pontederia cordata*) ✻ Dwarf bulrush (*Typha minima*) ✻ Calla lilies (*Zantedeschia* spp.)

**Floating plants** Water ferns (*Azolla filiculoides, A. pinnata*) ✻ Duckweeds (*Lemna, Spirodela* and *Wolffia* spp.) ✻ Pondweed (*Potamogeton octandrus*) ✻ Liverworts (*Riccia* spp.) ✻ Purple-fringed riccia (*Ricciocarpus natans*) ✻ Yellow bladderwort (*Utricularia australis*) ✻ Floating bladderwort (*U. gibba*)

**Submerged plants** Hornwort (*Ceratophyllum demersum*) ✻ *Eleocharis acicularis* ✻ Common water moss (*Fontinalis antipyretica*) ✻ Water violet (*Hottonia palustris*) ✻ Water milfoils (*Myriophyllum papillosum* 'Red Dragonfly', *M. simulans*) ✻ Curly pondweed (*Potamogeton crispus*) ✻ Water crowfoot (*Ranunculus aquatilis*)

*Waterlily*

# WATER TANKS

## Making a choice
Installing a rainwater tank is a big project, both financially and logistically. Take some time to research the different sizes and styles available, to ensure that you end up with the tank that has the capacity you need and the look you want at the price you prefer. Also make sure that your roof and gutters are in the right condition for rainwater collection.

**Slimline steel tank**

**Bladder tank**

## The right size
Tanks range in size from a capacity of about 300 litres up to 50,000 litres or more. When you're deciding what size tank you need, you must consider the size of your catchment area (that is, the area of your roof surface), the amount of rainfall in your area and the sort of applications for which the stored water is intended.

If you're only using the tank for outdoor applications, such as watering the garden and washing the car, it would use a little less than 100,000 litres of water a year. In most cases, this need can be met by a tank with a capacity of between 2000 and 4000 litres.

## Above-ground tanks
A tank elevated above ground has the following considerations:

* It is easy to notice a crack or a leak and deal with it.

* The elevated position produces better water pressure.

* It is easier to drain the tank when required, for example for the biannual maintenance.

* It is usually less expensive.

* It takes up land space.

* It is exposed to UV radiation, wind and damage from bushfires.

## Below-ground tanks
With a tank underground or under the house, consider the following:

* It doesn't intrude on land space.

* A pump is required to access the stored water.

* It is more difficult to detect leaks or water contamination and to address any problems.

* Maintenance can be more labour-intensive, and expensive.

## The right type
When reviewing the options, think about the logistics and cost of installation as well as what you intend to use the rainwater for.

## Polyethylene tanks
Lightweight polyethylene, or 'poly', tanks are UV-resistant and immune to rust. They come in corrugated cylindrical forms that mimic the shape of the classic metal tank, but also in a variety of shapes that suit different applications. Some polyethylene tanks can be installed under the ground. These tough tanks will easily withstand bumps and knocks, but heat from bushfires will damage them irreparably.

## Steel tanks
The classic Australian rainwater tank – a cylinder of corrugated steel – is still in production and certainly has enduring popularity. There are colour-coated and galvanised-finish tanks available that are lined internally with a high-grade plastic surface. This improves water quality and may increase the life of the tank. Metal tanks must be installed above

## Equipping the system
A tank must be fitted with devices that will keep the collected rainwater clean and ensure that you can access it as you need it. These devices include:

* Rain heads

* Gutter screens and guards

* First-flush water diverter

* Taps, also known as draw-off points

* An overflow outlet

* Mains top-up system (only required if the collected tank water will be used inside the house)

* Backflow prevention device

* Pipes for a wet or a dry system (A wet system has its pipes below the tank, so the pipes are permanently full of water – they do not dry out. A dry system's pipes are above the tank and remain dry until it rains, when they channel the rainwater to the tank then dry out again.)

* Pump for water pressure.

WATER TANKS

ground on a concrete platform or on a suitable metal stand.

### Concrete tanks

Concrete tanks generally sit directly on the ground or they are installed underground. Those that are well designed and constructed can last a lifetime and should be considered in rural or semi-rural areas because they will not melt or buckle in bushfires. In urban areas, underground concrete tanks built in new residences can be topped with load-bearing lids and installed under driveways, garages or other concrete slabs. However, there can be issues with access for general maintenance or for repairing cracks or leaks.

### Bladders

Several manufacturers produce rainwater bladders, pioneered in Australia. They store water in large sacks of flexible, puncture-resistant PVC tucked away in the sub-floor area of the house. The bladders sit inside protective steel frames and are installed below the floorboards or under the deck of the house. They are particularly suited to small properties. They come in a range of sizes and can be pieced together in a modular system to fit perfectly between the piers of a sub-floor area.

### Roof and gutter

The size of your roof affects the volume of water your tank will catch; the type of roof will affect water quality. Ask the tank supplier about the suitability of your roofing material and the tank's warranty beforehand.

Gutters form the first collection point from the roof and they must have the correct angle of fall to the catchment outlets. Keep the roof and gutters as clean as possible, and fit mesh screens to the gutters to divert leaf and other debris away from the roof. Also fix gutter outlets to the underside of gutters so that the flow of water is not obstructed.

## set up a Water harvesting system

Most gardeners configure their rainwater-harvesting system in one of three ways.

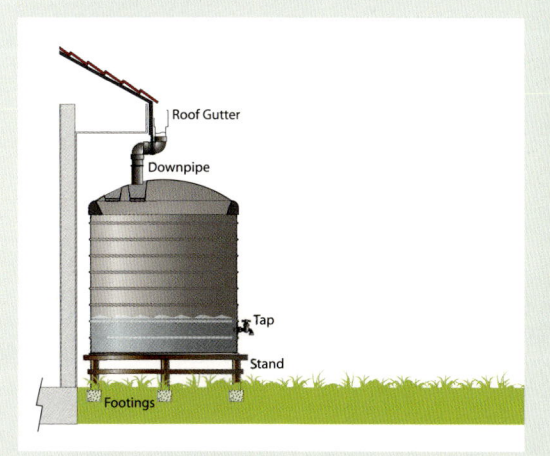

**Basic tank** This is the simplest type of installation, with the tank set on a stand, and a tap outlet. The stored water can be accessed for gardening as well as for filling buckets for washing cars and pets or for children's play.

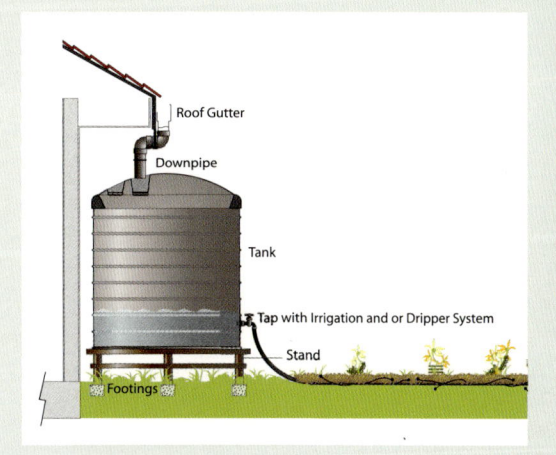

**Tap with basic irrigation** This relatively simple configuration for irrigation has a dedicated above-ground tank with a tap, connected to a soaker hose or drip system. It operates by gravity.

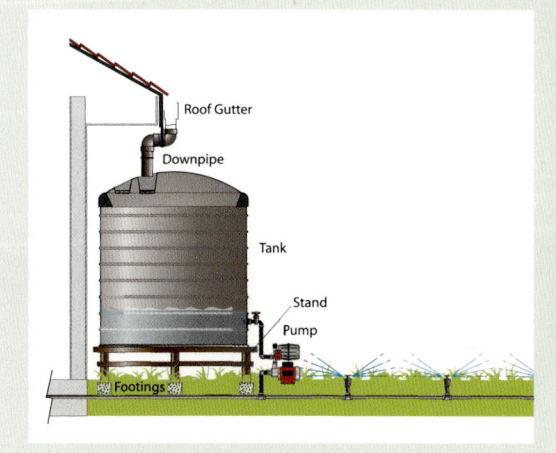

**Pump connected to irrigation system** A pump is necessary to provide the pressure required for a large, complex irrigation system or a system connected to spray or sprinkler heads. The rainwater tank can be above ground or below ground.

# WATERING

*Installing surface dripline irrigation*

## WATERING

### The right time
If your schedule permits, water in the morning during spring and autumn. This protects the foliage from the damaging effects of night frosts by allowing it to dry in the relative warmth of the day. During the summer, always water in the cooler parts of the day; if you water in the heat of the day during summer, much of it will be lost to evaporation and your plants may also be scorched.

No matter what season it is, always avoid watering during strong winds. In windy districts, apply water slowly with the nozzle set to a moderately heavy spray.

### Give a good soaking
The goal is to water slowly and deeply, so moisture has a chance to soak deep down into the soil without running off or pooling. It is better to soak the soil from time to time rather than water lightly every few days. Deep soaking encourages your plants to grow deeper, stronger root systems that can tap reserves of water during drought. Light watering does not penetrate deep into the soil, so roots look for water at the surface, resulting in a shallow-growing root system that is vulnerable to drought.

### How often?
Let the soil, light and climate be your guide as to how frequently you need to water. Heavy clay soil holds moisture longer than sandy soil, which lets water pass right through. Also, plants growing in light shade or in cool climates will stay moist longer than those in full sun, a northerly aspect or a warm climate. The time of year and the weather also play a part.

### Regulating the flow
Hand-held hoses can be fitted with a trigger-operated spray gun nozzle. These usually have lots of adjustable settings for fine jets, mists and spray patterns. The nozzle setting that delivers large droplets like the coarse rose on a watering can or natural rainfall is best for established plants, but use a fine mist or rose when watering seeds and seedlings. You could even use the fine spray setting on a spray bottle for seeds. It won't disturb the soil or seeds, or flatten the young plants.

### Make the most of it
Mulch well-watered soil with a thick layer of well-rotted compost, composted bark chips or straw. Provided the layer is at least 5 cm deep, it will limit evaporation and suppress weeds that will take the moisture your plants need.

## make a Watering basin

A watering basin will allow water to slowly seep into the soil that surrounds a plant's root system, ensuring that the plant is kept as well watered as possible.

**1** Build a raised ring of soil 30–50 cm away from the plant stem to concentrate water where it is needed most.

**2** Scoop out some soil from around the plant stem to create a natural basin. Firm the edge, gently sloping it towards the stem.

**3** Fill the basin with water, but be careful to avoid damaging the retaining ridge. Repeat until the soil is soaked.

### Spray foliage
When it is very dry and dusty, plants will benefit from a light spray of water to clean the leaves of dust and pollutants, especially in cities. In coastal areas, foliage plants should be sprayed quite frequently to remove traces of salt. However, don't water when strong winds are blowing. It is better to wait until the afternoon sea breeze has dropped.

### Needs of pot plants
The potting mix surrounding most pot plants should be kept moist but not saturated. Adjust the frequency of watering to suit the season and climate. Plants require less frequent watering during their dormant season.

# understand Watering equipment

| Type | Advantages | Disadvantages |
|---|---|---|
| Watering cans | They are good for watering pot plants, especially hanging baskets, indoor and balcony plants; applying tonics or liquid fertiliser; and watering in new plants. If high-level water restrictions are in place, they may be the only mains-connected watering method allowed. | When full of water, large watering cans are very heavy. Don't overdo it – use a smaller 5 litre can for higher pots and hanging baskets. |
| Hand-held hoses | They are ideal for watering containers and individual plants. They can also be adjusted to a hard squirt setting for washing off aphids or to a gentle shower for watering newly planted seedlings. | During water shortages, their use is restricted. Most water authorities require trigger spray guns. Watering a garden thoroughly with a hand-held hose takes time and patience. |
| Sprinklers | Cheap and easy to install, sprinklers mimic natural rainfall and they also distribute water evenly. | Most water authorities in Australia prohibit sprinklers connected to mains water. A lot of water is wasted from overwatering, applying water too quickly to be absorbed or droplets blowing away on windy days. |
| Weeper and soaker hoses | They are often made from recycled materials, such as old tyres, and are cheap to buy and easy to install. Place beneath mulch to direct water to the root zone, where it's needed. | You may need several hoses to deliver enough water to the plants in a large garden bed. The slow rate of delivery means water may need to run for a long time. |
| Micro-irrigation | It can be an efficient irrigation method if properly installed. The small spray heads give a good range of coverage and can be tailored to individual areas. Individual drippers work well for plants in pots and troughs. | It is high maintenance – spray heads can get blocked with dirt or insect nests – and easy to damage when digging in the garden. The fine spray is blown away in windy areas. Many water authorities prohibit its use with mains water. |
| Surface dripline under mulch | It is a highly efficient system as water is directed to the roots and there is little loss through evaporation. It is effective where water pressure is low, so a good choice for water tanks, and is essential for delivering diverted grey water (recycled from household washing). | It can be expensive and very labour-intensive to install because it requires pressure regulators and many metres of dripline. Sandy soils are difficult to wet evenly, and you may need to run it for up to an hour. It's also easy to damage the dripline when digging in the garden. |
| Subsurface dripline | This is an efficient system for lawns and gardens as water is delivered low in the soil profile, encouraging good root development. It can be used in a gravity-feed system and also for delivering diverted grey water. | It is only practical for new gardens or a lawn retrofit because of the digging needed for installation, which makes it very labour-intensive and expensive. The dripline can be damaged when digging in the garden. |

**WATERMELONS** *see page 294*

# WATERWISE GARDENING

Waterwise gardens can survive on little more than the rain that falls from the sky, which is important in areas where rainfall is scarce or unpredictable. The secret lies in good groundwork and well-researched plant selections.

### Do the groundwork

Get to know the particular characteristics of your garden soil. Plants tend to have a natural preference for one type of soil or another, and trying to force a plant to grow in a patch of ground that simply does not suit it will usually result in a waste of your time, money and energy as well as precious water.

The next step is to nourish your soil. Dig in plenty of organic materials, such as compost and well-rotted manure, and continue doing this regularly. This will enrich your soil and improve its water-holding capacity.

### Protect with mulch

The improvements made to your soil can be protected with mulch. Mulch comes in four forms: loose organic mulch (woodchips, straw, compost and grass clippings); inorganic loose mulch (pebbles and gravel); living mulches of groundcovers; and sheet mulch (blankets of newspaper or woven polypropylene mulch mat). Mulch reduces the amount of moisture that evaporates from the soil. It can also inhibit weeds, which will rob your plants of the water they need to survive.

### Select climate-compatible plants

Become familiar with your local climate as well as your soil type, and choose plants that suit those conditions, that are adapted to them and will be water-efficient when growing in them. Be aware that a plant that needs little water in its natural climate conditions may become a water guzzler in a different climate.

Plants that need only limited amounts of water to flourish tend to share certain properties. They may have plump and fleshy water-storing leaves; or fuzzy silver leaves with downy surfaces that protect from the evaporative powers of the sun; or the glossy, waxy or leathery leaves that also resist evaporation. Roots, trunks, stems, even flowers can also have adaptations to survive dry times.

### Buy big or small?

Buy smaller plants rather than large, well-established plants. Young plants in small containers are usually cheaper than large plants and they tend to establish more quickly and grow vigorously once they are planted.

### Get a good start

Ideally, time your planting so that it occurs during the evening, or on a mild, cloudy day, or at a time when rain is forecast. If that's not possible and you end up planting out in bright, sunny conditions, then think about setting up a temporary shade cover. Remove the protective shading after the first 2–3 days. All plants need some supplementary water from when they are first planted out until they're well established.

# WATERWISE GARDENING

## Make the most of irrigation
The best irrigation options for a waterwise garden are dripline systems. They usually involve a brown poly hose with pre-formed drip holes every 30–40 cm, which emit water directly into the root zone, where it is of most use.

The poly hose is laid over the soil and covered with mulch or it is buried (subsurface). Water isn't discharged into the air, making it very water-efficient. Subsurface dripline loses the least amount of water to evaporation, and it can also be connected to grey water diverters, which stop once-used household water from entering the storm-water system and redirect it to the garden instead.

Don't forget the humble watering can. It gives you a lot of control over where water is distributed, ensuring that very little water goes to waste.

## Casting cool shade
Trees and taller shrubs cast pools of shadow which provide relief from summer heat, help to reduce evaporation and shelter smaller plants. But remember that the large root systems of mature trees, especially shallow-rooted trees, will force plants to compete for scarce water and nutrients.

## Companion planting
You can save water by grouping plants according to their water needs. Put all the water-misers together, so there are large areas of the garden that don't need to be watered at all. Have another area for plants that need minimal watering, and consolidate all the thirsty plants together in a mulched bed or an area that you water more frequently than the rest of the garden. Some plants do better and need less water if they are grown in light shade, so team sun-filtering plants with lovers of light shade.

## Terracing to trap rain
Mound your garden beds into attractive contours, which have drainage channels in between. These dips will retain moisture when it rains, while the mulched mounds will provide well-drained beds that have underlying access to moisture – conditions that many plants enjoy. Other ways to conserve water include reducing the lawn area, creating sunken beds and planting windbreaks.

*See* Drought-tolerant plants, Dry conditions, Xeriscaping

## Good plants for a waterwise garden
Most drought-tolerant plants are not very demanding and look their best when they get only the minimum amount of water. But always check that their water needs are low in your particular climate zone before you plant them.

**Annuals**  Cosmos ✽ Baby's breath (*Gypsophila paniculata*) ✽ Alyssum (*Lobularia maritima*) ✽ Love-in-a-mist (*Nigella damascena*) ✽ Poppy ✽ Sun plant, rose moss (*Portulaca grandiflora*) ✽ Marigold (*Tagetes* spp.) ✽ Nasturtium ✽ Zinnia

**Bulbs, corms and tubers**  Ornamental allium (*Allium* spp. and cvs) ✽ Belladonna lily (*Amaryllis belladonna*) ✽ Bulbine ✽ Freesia ✽ Bearded iris ✽ Ixia ✽ Grape hyacinth (*Muscari* spp.) ✽ Spider lily (*Nerine* spp.) ✽ Star of Bethlehem (*Ornithogalum* spp.) ✽ Harlequin flower (*Sparaxis* spp.)

**Perennials**  Yarrow (*Achillea* spp.) ✽ Agapanthus ✽ Bromeliads ✽ Kangaroo paw (*Anigozanthos* spp.) ✽ African daisy (*Arctotis* x *hybrida*) ✽ Wormwood (*Artemisia* spp.) ✽ Clivia ✽ Dianella, flax lily (*Dianella* spp.) ✽ Grasses ✽ Sea holly (*Eryngium* spp.) ✽ Blanket flower (*Gaillardia* x *grandiflora*) ✽ *Helichrysum* spp. ✽ Catmint (*Nepeta* spp.) ✽ Geranium ✽ New Zealand flax (*Phormium tenax* and cvs) ✽ Rudbeckia ✽ Salvia ✽ Pincushion flower (*Scabiosa* spp.) ✽ Strawflower ✽ Strelitzia ✽ Thyme

**Groundcovers**  Cut leaf daisy (*Brachyscome* cvs) ✽ Pigface (*Carpobrotus glaucescens*) ✽ Snow-in-summer (*Cerastium tomentosum*) ✽ Pinks (*Dianthus* spp.) ✽ Gazania ✽ Goodenia ✽ Guinea flower (*Hibbertia* spp.) ✽ Fan flower (*Scaveola* spp.) ✽ Lamb's ear (*Stachys byzantina*)

**Succulents and cacti**  Aeonium ✽ Agave ✽ Aloe ✽ Cereus ✽ Cotyledon ✽ Crassula ✽ Echeveria ✽ Kalanchoe ✽ Sedum ✽ Senecio ✽ Sempervivum ✽ Yucca

**Shrubs**  Abelia ✽ Lillypilly (*Acmena*, *Syzygium* spp.) ✽ Barberry (*Berberis* spp.) ✽ Butterfly bush (*Buddleja* spp.) ✽ Flowering quince (*Chaenomeles* spp.) ✽ Ceanothus ✽ Rock rose (*Cistus* spp.) ✽ Correa ✽ Escallonia ✽ Euphorbia ✽ Euonymus ✽ Grevillea ✽ Hakea ✽ Hibiscus ✽ Lavender ✽ Tea tree (*Leptospermum* spp.) ✽ Leucadendron ✽ Mahonia ✽ Murraya ✽ Boobialla (*Myoporum* spp.) ✽ Nandina (*Nandina domestica* and cvs) ✽ Oleander ✽ Daisy bush (*Olearia* spp.) ✽ Photinia ✽ Plumbago ✽ *Potentilla* spp. ✽ Rosemary ✽ Roses ✽ Viburnum ✽ Native rosemary (*Westringia* spp.)

**Trees**  Dry-area wattles (*Acacia* spp.) ✽ Willow myrtle (*Agonis flexuosa*) ✽ Banksia ✽ Brachychiton ✽ Bottlebrush (*Callistemon* spp.) ✽ Eucalypt, gum (*Corymbia*, *Eucalyptus* spp.) ✽ Cypress (*Cupressus* spp.) ✽ Fig (*Ficus carica*) ✽ Juniper (*Juniperus* spp. and cvs) ✽ Crepe myrtle (*Lagerstroemia indica*) ✽ Paperbark (*Melaleuca* spp.) ✽ White cedar (*Melia azedarach*) ✽ Olive ✽ Pomegranate ✽ Dry-climate palms

Strawflower

# WATERMELONS | WATTLES

## WATERMELONS

Growing watermelons is easy, even if your summers are only very brief. The secret is to select the right varieties for your conditions.

### Planning the crop
A watermelon plant is a heat-loving, frost-tender annual, and it will need the sunniest position possible and good air circulation. It will tolerate a range of soils, including acid soils down to pH 5.5, but the soil must be enriched with compost and well drained. Planting in raised beds or hilled-up soil is recommended.

### Growing tips
Watermelon seedlings can be set back by transplanting, so sow four or five seeds in each position in the growing bed in spring and later thin to the two strongest seedlings. Sow running varieties 1.5–1.8 m apart, and bush varieties 1.2 m apart.

In cool districts, raise seedlings under protection and plant them out when the soil is warm, in late spring or early summer. Be sure to water your crop regularly.

### Ripe and ready indicators
Harvest watermelons when they are fully ripe, in late summer to early autumn. Look for these signs to be able to tell when a melon is ready: the part in contact with the ground turns white or yellowish, and the vine tendrils near the fruit turn brown. If you knock the side of the fruit with your knuckles, a ripe melon will make a dull, hollow noise.

## WATTLES

### Fast-growing and short-lived
Wattles (*Acacia* spp.) are well known for their short but rapid life, although there are some long-lived wattles, such as the blackwood (*A. melanoxylon*). They range from groundcovers and shrubs to stately trees. Their most popular use in the garden is as a fast-growing tree for shade, shelter and privacy.

### Quick and easy
Wattles are quick to establish and easy to grow. Water newly planted specimens well during their first summer, but after that most will survive on natural rainfall, except during extended dry periods. However, it is these very survival qualities that mean some wattles have become weeds outside their native range. Always check if the wattle species you want to plant has weed potential in your area, and if possible, select wattles that are native to where you live.

### For a quick screen
Wattles are perfect for a quick privacy screen or windbreak. Choose species with dense leafy growth, such as the Flinders Range wattle (*A. iteaphylla*) or sticky wattle (*A. howittii*). On the coast or in exposed locations, try the coast myall (*A. binervia*), a 3–4 m tree with silver foliage that is tolerant of salt breezes.

### Plant a nurse tree
Use fast-growing, short-lived wattles as 'nurse' plants around slower-growing, more vulnerable long-term plantings. The wattles will shelter these trees and shrubs from strong sun, hot or cold winds and even frost until they are well established. Remove the nurse wattles after a couple of years to allow the permanent plantings to grow to full size.

### Growing from seed
Wattles can be grown readily from seed but the seeds need some help to germinate. Place them in a cup of boiling water. Stand for 30 seconds, then pour off the hot water and cover the seeds with cold water. Soak for around 12 hours. Immediately plant the swollen seeds into a container of seed-raising mix. Discard any that aren't swollen.

### Allergy fallacy
Many allergy sufferers blame the pollen from wattles for their woes. But wattle pollen is very heavy and does not disperse far. Lighter pollens from flowering grasses, weeds and exotic trees travel long distances on winds and are more likely to cause allergy problems.

294

# WEED MANAGEMENT

### Weed before seed
Always remove annual weeds before they have the chance to flower. Then there is no risk of 'one year's seeds becoming seven years' weeds', as the old saying goes. Digging brings dormant weed seeds to the soil surface where they will germinate. A couple of weeks after digging, check the site and hoe off any seedlings that have developed.

### Paths and driveways
Using 100 per cent vinegar spray, organic herbicides, steam weed killers, hand-held weed flamers or even boiling water can help keep paths and driveways weed-free.

### Using herbicides
Organic herbicides (weedkillers) have been developed from pine oil or alpha-terpineol. There are also citrus oil-based sprays. Protect your garden plants, as organic herbicides can still do harm.

Used with great care, a systemic-type herbicide such as glyphosate is useful against both soft and woody perennial weeds. Spray or paint it onto the leaves and the plant will absorb it into its roots. Established weeds may need several applications to kill them. Woody weeds can be cut down and the stump painted immediately with herbicide to kill the roots.

Selective herbicides can be used on lawns to get rid of broad-leaved weeds. Most lawn grasses will resist the herbicide, although buffalo can be damaged.

### Beware of accidents
Herbicides will kill garden plants if any of the chemical gets on the leaves. You can wrap adjacent plants in old sheets or plastic bags to protect them. And if a plant is sprayed accidentally, wash the leaves immediately with clean water and also water the soil thoroughly until it is soaked to minimise any absorption. Water again 24 hours later.

### Prevention is possible
Blotting out sunlight kills even the toughest weeds. Cover a weed-infested area with a layer of weed mat, black plastic, old carpet or newspapers that excludes all light. Leave it in place for at least 6 months to a year, by which time the weeds should be dead and you can remove the covering. A thick layer of mulch will help to stop weeds germinating. To keep couch, buffalo and kikuyu grass runners from an adjacent lawn invading garden beds, install deep edging around the beds.

### Weed risk
Many plants have survival mechanisms that can turn them into invasive weeds, especially when grown in a more hospitable environment than the one where they originated. Never bring a plant into your garden without first assessing its potential for weediness. If a plant is a declared weed in your state or a potentially invasive weed in your area, do not plant it in your garden. Contact your local council for advice on plants classified as weeds, their identification and control.

---

### Chemical herbicides
For particularly tough perennial weeds that spread by invasive rhizomes, tubers, roots and bulbs, digging and hoeing can spread the problem. The only answer may be chemical herbicides (weedkillers).

**Contact herbicide** Kills leaf growth; for example, bromoxynil.

**Systemic herbicide** Absorbed by the leaves and works through to the roots, killing the whole plant; for example, glyphosate.

**Selective herbicide** Works only on broad-leaved or narrow-leaved plants. Use on lawns to get rid of broad-leaved weeds.

**Residual herbicide** Applied to the soil to attack the roots; for example, sodium chlorate. Use with care near other plants as it tends to creep outwards from the point of application.

Probably the most useful types for gardeners are contact and systemic herbicides, which are inactivated when they reach the soil.

# WEEDS

### Annual weeds
Annual weeds spread by seeding. In flower and vegetable beds, hoe or pull them out by hand as soon as they emerge and before they have a chance to flower and set seed.

### Chickweed *Stellaria media*
Thrives in moist soil and forms seeds even in winter. Spray with a contact or systemic herbicide.

### Shepherd's purse *Capsella bursa-pastoris*
Hand-weed or control with a contact or systemic herbicide before flowering.

### Hairy bitter cress *Cardamine hirsuta*
Likes dry ground and rock crevices. Spray with a contact or systemic herbicide, peferably when weed is still young.

### Groundsel *Senecio vulgaris*
Spray with a contact or systemic herbicide, which acts faster if it is applied in bright sunlight.

### Milk thistle *Sonchus oleraceus*
Can grow up to 75 cm high, depending on the soil. Hand-weed before flowering.

### Bindii *Soliva pterosperma*
Avoid dryness and close mowing, which encourage bindii in lawns. Cut out young plants with a knife or apply corn gluten meal – an organic pre-emergent that won't damage lawns – in early spring. Try herbicides that contain dicamba; these can kill nearby trees, so follow directions strictly.

### Sow thistle *Sonchus asper*
Has spiny leaves and grows taller than the very similar milk thistle. Hand-weed before flowering.

# WEEDS

## Perennial weeds
Perennial weeds multiply by invasive rhizomes, tubers, roots or bulbs, and can be much more challenging to eradicate.

### Curled dock
*Rumex crispus*
All docks can be controlled by improving drainage, adding lime and digging out mature plants; or use glyphosate repeatedly.

### Perennial thistle
*Cirsium arvense*
Reproduces by creeping rhizomes, also by seed. Repeatedly hand-weed just before flowering; or spot-treat with either glyphosate or glyphosate-trimesium.

### Stinging nettle
*Urtica dioica*
Pull out with a gloved hand in light soil; or treat repeatedly with glyphosate or glyphosate-trimesium.

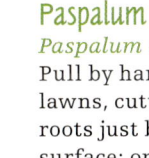

### Paspalum
*Paspalum dilatatum*
Pull by hand in lawns, cutting roots just below soil surface; or spot-treat with glyphosate.

### Couch grass
*Cynodon dactylon*
Easy to fork up but difficult when underground runners intertwine with roots of other plants. Usually, persistence is rewarded.

### Nut grass
*Cyperus rotundus*
Difficult to control. Cover with weed mat or black plastic for 12 months; or apply glyphosate repeatedly in hot weather.

### Sour sob
*Oxalis pes-caprae*
Regularly apply lime. Hand-weed with great care to avoid dispersing the small bulbs; glyphosate is more effective, but it may take several years to control.

### Pellitory, asthma weed
*Parietaria judaica*
Spray young plants with glyphosate. New seedlings will emerge for years from dropped seeds. Use a steam weed killer.

### Onion weed
*Nothoscordum inodorum*
Hand-weeding only breaks up the bulb clusters and propagates the plant. Never allow flowers to remain; cover with weed mat or black plastic for 12 months; or spray repeatedly with glyphosate. It will take years to control.

### Dandelion
*Taraxacum officinale*
Usually easy to dig up. Spot-treat with glyphosate or glyphosate-trimesium when growing among the roots of fruit bushes or trees.

### Wandering jew
*Tradescantia fluminensis*
Can reshoot from small pieces. Rake away, removing every piece; spray regrowth with glyphosate and re-treat when necessary. Cover area with newspaper and mulch.

297

# White Flowers

White can be used to enhance and bring out the best in any other colour. Combined with pale shades, it cools and calms; with bright colours it adds vitality and contrast. Many gardeners consider an all-white garden to be the epitome of style.

## All white
All white looks fresh even in the hottest weather, although large swathes can give off a lot of glare in full sun in hot climates. Soften the effect with green or silver foliage, and off-white and cream flowers. Even the palest pink, yellow or blue can create enough of a contrast to enhance bright whites.

## Luminous by night
White flowers reflect light, appearing luminous at night, especially at dusk. Many white flowers take advantage of this effect and open only at night to attract nocturnal-pollinating insects. Dragonfruit (*Hylocereus undatus*), flowering tobacco (*Nicotiana alata*) and evening primrose (*Oenothera* spp.) open their petals as evening draws on. Highlight paths and driveways by lining the edges with white flowers, and use white to brighten shady spots around an entertaining area. White is also found in foliage; look out for striped and spotted leaves, and variegated forms of your favourite species.

## A backdrop of white
There are many white-flowering climbers that can be used as a backdrop for other colours. In spring, clematis, climbing roses and the magnificent white wisteria (*Wisteria sinensis* 'Alba') are all in flower. Moving into summer, star jasmine (*Trachelospermum jasminoides*) starts to flower, while the many white rambling roses and *Pandorea* 'Lady Di' continue into autumn. Plant the climbers together so that they intermingle and provide months of colour.

### choose White flowers

**For temperate and cool climates**
* Japanese windflower (*Anemone × hybrida*)
* Sage-leaf rock rose (*Cistus salviifolius*)
* Silverbush (*Convolvulus cneorum*)
* Perennial candytuft (*Iberis sempervirens*)
* *Lamium maculatum* 'White Nancy'
* Snowflakes (*Leucojum* spp.)
* Alyssum (*Lobularia maritima*)
* Mock orange (*Philadelphus* spp.)
* Roses
* May (*Spiraea cantoniensis*)

**For warm and hot climates**
* Native clematis (*Clematis aristata*)
* Gardenia
* Hydrangea
* Magnolia
* Snow-in-summer (*Melaleuca linariifolia*)
* Murraya (*Murraya paniculata*)
* Osteospermum (*Osteospermum* cvs)
* *Pandorea* 'Lady Di'
* Madagascar jasmine (*Stephanotis floribunda*)
* Star jasmine (*Trachelospermum jasminoides*)

Magnolia

Alyssum

Clematis

Hydrangea

## WHITEFLIES

### Plants affected
Many, including brassicas, beans and tomatoes.

### Symptoms
Minute white, moth-like insects on the undersides of leaves, and black sooty mould.

### Treatment
* Encourage parasitic wasps.

* Grow French marigolds (*Tagetes patula*) around the crop.

* Only spray large infestations. Use insecticidal soap, petroleum oil sprays, white oil or pyrethrum.

* Release the parasitic wasp *Encarsia formosa* in the greenhouse; use a hand vacuum to suck up whiteflies, or hang yellow sticky traps nearby.

* Keep plants well watered to reduce the damage from attack.

* Bury or safely dispose of all affected plant remains to break the cycle.

## WILDFLOWER MEADOWS

### Poor soil is best
You don't need any particular type of soil to grow a wildflower meadow – in fact, the lower the fertility, the better. First, remove all weeds and grass. Then rake the exposed surface lightly to form a seedbed, removing any stones you find. Leave for a few weeks before sowing, so that any deep-rooted weeds that grow back can be dug out as soon as they appear.

### Sow a meadow
The best time to sow seeds for a wildflower meadow is autumn when the soil is still warm and seedlings are less likely to dry out in hot sunshine. Use a standard meadow mixture of grass and flower seeds – usually made up of 80 per cent grass and 20 per cent flowers – and sow it shallowly. Water regularly until the new plants are established.

### In the mix
Sow ephemeral and annual plants that are native to the southern hemisphere, such as the paper daisies. The wildflowers in seed mixes are usually a combination of European and American field flowers and include plants such as oxeye daisies and field poppies. All wildflowers grow best among clumping grass.

### Spring or summer flowers?
Wildflower meadows will either flower in spring (September to November) or summer (December to January). Unfortunately, you cannot combine the two because they require different mowing regimes. Special seed mixes are widely available and you should follow the instructions on the packet for recommendations on maintenance and mowing.

It is not easy to predict how your wildflower meadow will develop. Many seeds will only germinate in a dry summer; others need plenty of rain. Birds and insects or even the wind will introduce seeds from elsewhere.

### Mowing a meadow
Delay mowing until midsummer for spring-flowering meadows and autumn for summer-flowerers to give them time to produce seeds. Set the mower blades to a height of 5–7.5 cm. After mowing, leave the cuttings for a few days so that any seeds can ripen and drop to the ground to develop, then clear the cuttings (add to the compost) so that excess nutrients are not returned to the meadow. Cut the meadow at the same height two or three times during that year.

## WILDLIFE HAVENS

### Prize the untidy
If you provide food and shelter, animals, birds and insects will visit and may even make your garden their permanent home. 'Untidy' areas are prized. A tree hollow or a weathered wall makes an ideal shelter. Clumps of weeds provide food for birds in the form of seeds and the insects that the seeds will attract. A patch of unmown grass can be turned into a wildflower meadow.

### Welcoming refuge
The reflected warmth from a wall attracts butterflies, while birds may nest in natural holes in your trees or in nesting boxes. Closely planted trees and shrubs offer birds the safety of dense branches in which to build a nest as well as berries to eat. Butterflies and other insects, small animals and ground-dwelling birds will all visit a dense thicket or hedge of shrubs such as banksias, hakeas, grevilleas, Indian hawthorn (*Rhaphiolepis indica*) and wild hip-bearing roses. A few prickly shrubs will make access more difficult for a cat.

### Feeding time
A bird table will attract a great variety of birds, especially in winter. A birdbath placed nearby will give them a spot for bathing and drinking. However, if you have a cat, remember to put a bell on its collar!

### Meadow magic
Create a meadow of wildflowers and grasses in a sunny corner of the garden, where it doesn't matter if plants are left to grow straggly. Butterflies and bees will feed on the nectar of clover, cornflowers, dandelions and field poppies. Insects, ground-dwelling birds and small animals may take up residence among the grasses.

### A bed of nectar
Dedicate a sunny border to bees and butterflies collecting nectar. Nectar-producing flowers include butterfly bush, ceanothus, daisies, honesty, showy sedum, verbena and many native shrubs; asters and foxgloves will make a nectar attraction later in the summer.

### Rocky hideaway
In an out-of-the-way corner of the garden, a pile of rocks set in leaf litter will serve as a hideaway for lizards and frogs. Don't include this feature in areas where snakes or funnel-web spiders are present.

### Water world
A pond (with an underwater safety mesh) provides a home for frogs, fish and aquatic insects. Dragonflies, water beetles and pond skaters will make their own way to the pond, but you may have to introduce amphibians. Birds, possums and lizards may also come to quench their thirst.

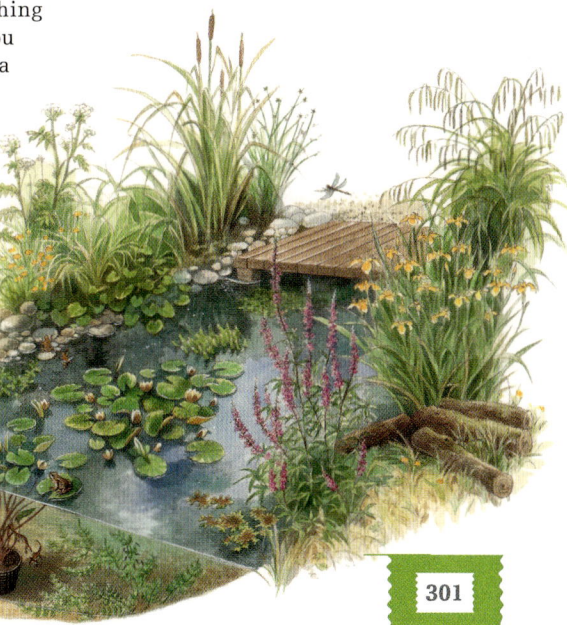

# WIND

## Windbreaks and shelterbelts
A windbreak excludes hot summer and freezing winter winds, salty ocean breezes and seasonal storm blasts. Windbreaks composed of several layers of plants are called shelterbelts. They can deflect and reduce the strength of wind, and other less resilient plants can thrive in their protection.

## Rows of protection
If you have the space, rows of wind-tolerant plants of different heights will reduce the strength of the wind more effectively than one thick hedge. Arrange short plants at the front to face the full brunt of the wind. Back these up with a row of intermediate-sized plants, then with tall evergreen trees closest to the garden or house. Winds are lifted up and over the shelterbelt; the house and garden rest in a protected pocket.

## Shelter the young
Wind not only damages plants. It also slows growth by increasing water loss through evaporation. It is essential to protect new plants – especially evergreens – because they are particularly susceptible. Provide them with temporary windbreak netting until they are well established. Position it on the windward side of the plants and leave the screen in place during their first two winters. Also keep all new plants well watered.

## An artificial alternative
Use firmly anchored, stout poles to support two sheets of lattice, one on either side of the poles and slightly offset from the other. This will reduce the force of the wind as it weaves through the lattice.

## Vulnerable vegetables
Windy sites are not ideal for vegetables. Try shorter varieties of brussels sprouts, such as 'Peer Gynt', and choose bush rather than upright tomatoes. Continual buffeting and moisture loss from the wind can greatly reduce yields of many vegetable crops. Also, pollinating insects avoid windy areas. So protect vegetable beds with windbreak netting, and grow fruit trees in a sheltered spot.

### Netting windbreak
If lack of space prevents you from growing a hedge windbreak in your garden, make a windbreak by attaching special fine-mesh or broad-banded plastic netting to sturdy posts. The netting is available in different densities.

# WINDOW BOXES

## A succession of colour
Use bedding annuals, or potted colour, to ensure that there is no break in floral continuity when it is time to remove exhausted plants and change the displays in your window boxes. Choose simple colour schemes such as red geraniums with ivy, or pastel petunias with silver-leaved helichrysum. For south-facing windows, which get lots of shade, choose ferns and impatiens. Try culinary herbs such as thyme, basil, mint and parsley in a box close to the kitchen.

## Wall-mounted window box
If the windowsill that you want to use is too narrow for a box, attach brackets, strong enough to hold the window box firmly in place, to the wall beneath the window. If the window opens outwards, take care to leave sufficient space above the box so that the fully grown plants will not obstruct it.

## Neighbourly precautions
Water window boxes regularly, as near to the plant roots as possible. If you live above other people, or if your box overhangs a pavement, put a drip tray under it so that passers-by don't get showered. Prevent tiny particles of potting mix from splashing up onto the window panes during watering by covering the surface of the mix with a layer of fine grit.

WINDOW BOXES | WINTER DISPLAY

# WINTER DISPLAY

## For a varied winter display
To brighten up the long dull days of winter, include plants with flowers or interesting evergreen foliage to offset the bare branches of deciduous trees. Golden flowers act like a pool of sunlight and are particularly welcome when light levels are low. Where it's too cold to spend much time outdoors, place plants with winter interest where you can appreciate them from indoors.

### June
**Flowers** Chinese lantern (*Abutilon* spp.) ✳ Aster ✳ Bergenia ✳ Sasanqua camellia ✳ Chrysanthemum ✳ Cyclamen ✳ Euryops ✳ Gordonia ✳ Winter iris (*Iris unguicularis*) ✳ Pansy ✳ Poinsettia ✳ Primula ✳ Mexican sage bush (*Salvia leucantha*) ✳ Strelitzia ✳ Witch hazel

**Foliage or bark** Aucuba ✳ Conifers ✳ Dwarf sacred bamboo (*Nandina domestica* 'Nana') ✳ Ornamental kale

**Fruit** Australian laurel (*Auranticarpa rhombifolia* syn. *Pittosporum rhombifolium*) ✳ Blueberry ash (*Elaeocarpus reticulatus*) ✳ Citrus ✳ Crab apples ✳ Hawthorn

### July
**Flowers** *Banksia* 'Giant Candles' ✳ Sasanqua camellia ✳ Flowering quince (*Chaenomeles* spp.) ✳ Coral tree (*Erythrina* spp.) ✳ Geraldton wax (*Chamelaucium uncinatum*) ✳ Grevillea ✳ Hardenbergia ✳ Kalanchoe ✳ Magnolia ✳ Poppies

**Foliage or bark** Conifers ✳ Crepe myrtle ✳ Dogwood ✳ 'Sango-kaku' maple

**Fruit** Beautyberry (*Callicarpa* spp.) ✳ Rock cotoneaster (*Cotoneaster horizontalis*) ✳ Cumquat ✳ Mahonia ✳ White cedar (*Melia azedarach*) ✳ Coralberry (*Ardisia crenata*)

### August
**Flowers** Azalea ✳ Japonica camellia ✳ Calendula ✳ Clivia ✳ Daisies ✳ Diosma (*Coleonema pulchrum*) ✳ Silk tassel bush (*Garrya elliptica*) ✳ Hellebore ✳ Hippeastrum ✳ Leucadendron ✳ Snowflake (*Leucojum vernum*) ✳ Polyanthus ✳ Protea ✳ Japanese apricot (*Prunus mume*) ✳ Flame vine (*Pyrostegia venusta*) ✳ Waratah ✳ Wattle

**Foliage or bark** Conifers ✳ Bromeliads ✳ Deadnettle (*Lamium* spp.) ✳ New Zealand flax ✳ Silver birch (*Betula pendula*)

**Fruit** Silverberry (*Elaeagnus* spp.) ✳ Japanese skimmia (*Skimmia japonica*) ✳ Snowberry (*Symphoricarpos* spp.)

**Waratah**

## make a Window box

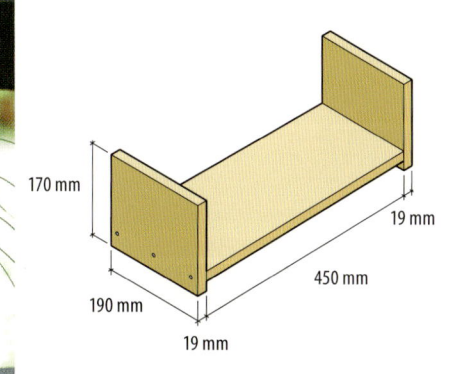

**1** Cut a 900 x 190 x 19 mm piece of radiata pine into 1 x 450 mm length for the base and 2 x 170 mm lengths for the ends. Then cut a 2100 x 42 x 19 mm piece of radiata pine into 4 x 488 mm lengths. Sand all the edges and corners.

**2** Drill 3 holes in each of the end pieces 30 mm up from the bottom, with one hole 10 mm in from each side and one hole in the centre. Nail the ends to the base, one end at a time.

**3** Position a 488 mm length on each side of the box, level with the tops of the ends. Drill 2 holes into each end of these lengths. Hammer in nails. Repeat on the other side. Position remaining 2 x 488 mm lengths 30 mm below the top rung on each side and repeat drilling and hammering.

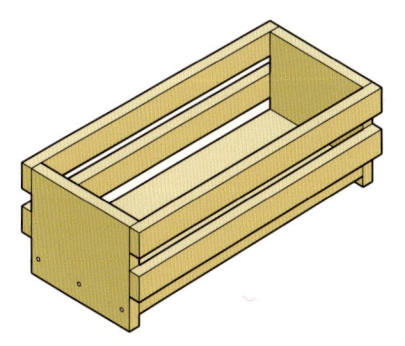

**4** Sand the timber all over. Punch nail heads and putty over them. Seal with one coat of undercoat, then sand again and apply two topcoats of your chosen colour. Allow each coat to dry before sanding. If you want the box to have a rustic, distressed look, sand the final coat.

## WISTERIA

### Graft is best
When selecting a new wisteria from a garden centre or nursery, choose a grafted plant. These are more reliable and flower earlier than plants that have been raised from seed. They will also remain true to type.

### Give space and support
Wisterias need plenty of space for their roots as well as their top growth to give their best. If your wisteria is planted near a path or paved area, check the surface regularly for any signs of lifting. Wisterias are also heavy and will need a strong support. Attach the support with strong wire or thick battens, so the plant doesn't pull it away from the wall.

### Small garden
If space in your garden is limited, grow a wisteria in a container. This will restrict its roots, and with careful pruning, it can be trained as a standard. Provide a steel pole for support as the standard becomes top-heavy.

### How to prune
To encourage a wisteria to bloom, establish a regular pruning routine. Cut back after the main spring flowering, when the new growth has begun. Then around 6 weeks after this initial prune, in summer, cut back unwanted branches to two or three leaves. However, don't cut back after autumn as you may be removing dormant flower buds. Pruning will become less arduous after the first few years of growth as the plant produces fewer new shoots.

### Extra warmth
Although wisterias are frost-tolerant climbers, the warmth of the sun is essential if their flower-producing wood is to ripen. For the best blooms, plant them against a north- or northwest-facing wall or a sun-drenched pergola or trellis.

## WORM FARMS

### A compact alternative
If you can't find enough materials for a compost heap or you don't have the space, you could set up a worm farm to deal with kitchen scraps. Worm farms produce excellent garden compost in the form of worm manure (usually referred to as worm castings), which can be added to soil or potting mix as a fertiliser or a mulch. The liquid that is drained off is an excellent liquid feed for potted and garden plants.

### Starting a worm farm
For the beginner, a worm farm kit is a good way to begin. Kits are readily available and contain everything you'll need to get started, including the worms. A worm farm is made up of a series of shallow trays stacked one on top of the other. As the worms feed, they migrate from one tray to the next. Specially designed plastic boxes are available from some nurseries and hardware stores to contain your worm farm. You simply add fresh food scraps to the box, and it is easy to look after and keep clean. Also, a tray in the base with a tap makes it easy to siphon off the liquid.

## WOOLLY APHIDS

### Plants affected
Apples, cotoneaster, hawthorns, mountain ash, pears, *Prunus* spp. and pyracanthas.

### Symptoms
Woody swellings; conspicuous white woolly wax develops on twigs, new branches and pruning scars; honeydew and sooty mould also appear.

### Treatment
* Prune off and destroy or safely discard damaged branches.
* Encourage parasitic wasps, which will often control the problem, and small birds that eat overwintering aphid eggs.
* Spraying for other pests may kill the wasps.
* Grow wisteria varieties that have resistant rootstocks, because the aphids also feed on the roots of plants.
* Spray with a petroleum oil spray, soap spray, pyrethrum or organic plant-based oil sprays, omethoate or dimethoate if this becomes necessary.

# WORM FARMS | WORMWOOD

## make your own Worm farm

1. Use a waterproof container such as an old (untreated) wooden or polystyrene box, no more than 30 cm deep, with a wide opening. A rectangular shape about 60 cm wide, 90 cm long and 30 cm deep is ideal.

2. Drill 10 to 20 drainage holes in the base of the container. Position it in a cool, shady spot, standing it on four bricks so it's elevated above the ground.

3. Line the bottom of the container with two sheets of newspaper, then half-fill it with a mixture of compost, grass clippings and moist shredded newspaper.

4. Add the compost worms – about 500 per box is a good number. Don't add too many as they breed and grow in direct proportion to the amount of food available and the size of the worm farm.

5. Water till moist, then cover the container with a plastic sheet. Place another plastic sheet or tray under the farm to collect the liquid.

6. Add a small quantity of kitchen scraps in the first week. Feed the worms once a week, gradually increasing the amount of food over the next 6 months.

7. Add water every few days to stop the worm farm from drying out. The mixture should be moist but not soggy.

8. If the worms outgrow the container, remove the lid and add another level on top. See steps 1–3. Place food in the new container to attract the worms up into it.

### Special worms
You must use special compost worms: tiger worms (*Eisenia foetida*) or red worms (*Lumbricus rubellus*) are good in cooler climates; blue worms (*Perionyx excavatus*) are ideal for the tropics. The worms do the work of breaking down waste materials. They are available from some nurseries or by mail order from commercial worm producers. Don't use garden earthworms.

### Creating the right conditions
The worms will eat the equivalent of about half their weight each day. Never give them oils, fats or meat, and only add citrus peel or onion skins in very small amounts and always well mixed with other materials. A few crushed egg shells or a little manure will add grit, which helps the worms grind their food.

Be sure to keep your worm farm moist, otherwise the worms may die. Also, very high temperatures in summer (over 40°C) will cause them to overheat and die. In hot weather move them to a cool spot and cover with moist hessian.

### Harvesting castings and liquid
To remove the worm castings from your worm farm without also removing too many worms, expose the surface to light. The worms will dig deeper into the container, leaving the top soil layer worm-free. Scoop out what you need with a small fork.

Drain off the liquid occasionally, too, so the worms don't drown.

# WORMWOOD

### Hardy and beautiful
Grown for their lovely silver-grey foliage, these plants of the *Artemisia* genus are extremely hardy and versatile in the garden. They thrive with little care as long as they have well-drained soil and plenty of sun and air to keep their felt-textured leaves dry. Most need a hard prune once a year to remain compact.

### Henhouse or hedge
Wormwoods are traditionally grown near the henhouse to deter parasites. They come in a range of sizes, from 15–90 cm tall, and can hug the ground or grow into shrub-sized specimens. The silver foliage contrasts well with other plants, although the flowers are insignificant. Some make good informal hedges: *A. arborescens* grows to 1.5 m high, while 'Powis Castle' forms a broad hedge 60 cm to 1 m high.

### Increasing the bounty
Most wormwoods root from stem cuttings taken in late summer, but it is simpler to divide clumps in early spring. Dig up a clump and pull its roots apart into two or three equal sections. Or dig up a section from the outer edge of the clump and replant immediately.

# XERISCAPING

## What is xeriscaping?
Xeriscaping is designing a garden to reduce or eliminate the need for supplementary watering. It lets you grow the plants you want to grow, as long as you are prepared to offset those that need plenty of extra water with those that require little if any. Ideally, you would harvest rainfall in tanks to water these thirsty plants.

## The best possible use
Prioritise how you allocate water to get the best value for what you do use. The key principles are:

* Create watering zones where you group together plants with similar water requirements.
* Use drought-tolerant plants.
* Reduce or rationalise unnecessary areas of lawn.
* Apply a generous layer of mulch.
* Only give your plants as much water as they really need, for as long as they need it, by using efficient irrigation techniques.

## Don't mix drought-tolerant with thirsty
Many garden beds contain plants that need lots of water right next to plants that need very little, such as hydrangeas growing with lavender and rosemary. The entire bed is watered when only a few plants need a drink. This wastes water, and overwatered drought-hardy plants are more susceptible to pests and diseases.

### Water allocation
You allocate a percentage of your property to the different zones. A good template to aim for is:

* No water zone = 50 per cent
* Low water zone = 25 per cent
* Moderate to high water zone = 25 per cent

## Creating watering zones
Divide your garden into three zones, in which you group plants that have similar water needs.

**Zone 1: No water zone** The plants in this area of the garden survive with no supplementary watering once established. You will never need to water this zone, except during long dry spells or drought.

**Zone 2: Low water zone** The plants in this area have low water requirements. If it hasn't rained, you will need to water this zone every 2–4 weeks; this is based on observing the plants and the soil.

**Zone 3: Moderate to high water zone** The plants in this area are those with moderate to high water requirements. If it hasn't rained, you will need to water this zone between once a week and several times a week, based on observing the plants and the soil.

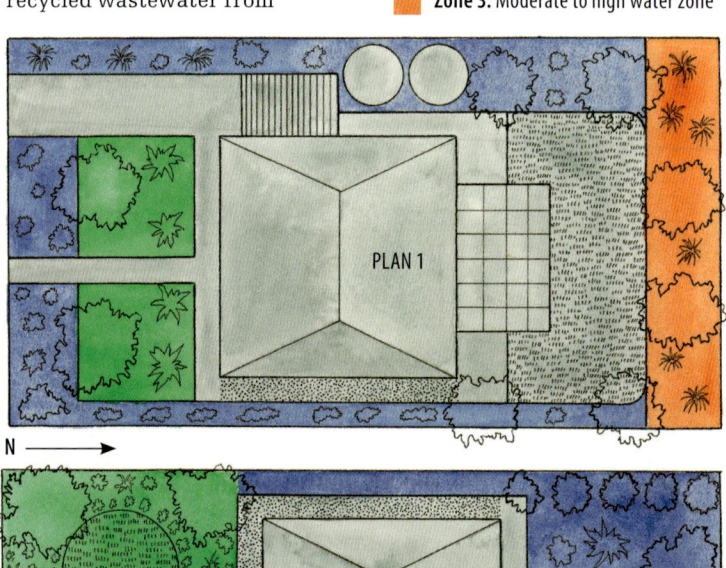

### Zone a Xeriscape garden
Both plans have the high water zone on the cool (southern) side of the house. The large trees in Plan 1 make the zone cooler and reduce its water needs – as long as the tree roots aren't too aggressive. The lawn is watered with grey water (the recycled wastewater from household washing) via a subsurface irrigation system, so the lawn is not included in the water zone equation.

- **Zone 1:** No water zone
- **Zone 2:** Low water zone
- **Zone 3:** Moderate to high water zone

# YELLOW FLOWERS | YUCCAS

Frangipani

Sunflower

## YELLOW FLOWERS

### Cheer up
Yellow brings light, brightness and cheeriness to the garden. Who can't help but smile when looking at a sunflower? This is the colour of the sun and it gives the feeling of warmth.

### In winter and summer
Luckily, there are many winter- and spring-flowering bulbs, including crocus, daffodils and jonquils, that arrive with a vivid splash of yellow just when it seems that the cold weather will never end. In summer, on the other hand, a mass of yellow can be overpowering, especially when the days are at their hottest. Plant yellow summer-flowerers, such as daylilies and heleniums, in small groups rather than en masse, and tone them down with white, cream and silver.

### A good mixer
Yellow looks good with almost every colour. Yellow and blue is a classic combination that always works. Try tall blue delphiniums with yellow pansies at their feet, or blue irises alongside yellow daisies or Flower Carpet ground-cover roses. Being complementary colours, yellow and purple are delightful together, especially if the paler shades of these colours are chosen.

### Be bold
For a bold and vibrant colour combination, mix yellow with red or orange. Many species flower in a range of these colours, making it easy to create this look. Poppies, wallflowers, daylilies, yarrows (*Achillea* spp.) and nasturtiums are all good plants for achieving this brilliant mix.

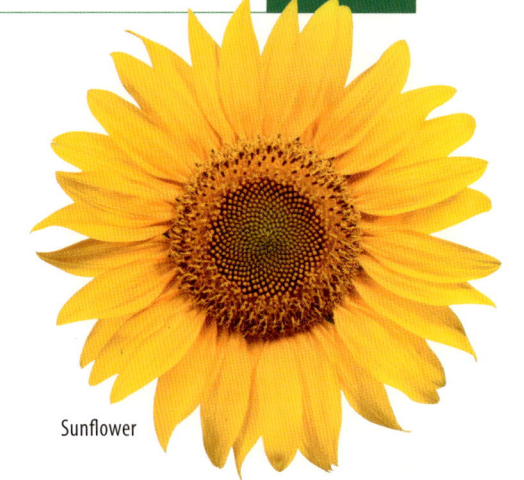

### Choosing yellow flowers

**For temperate and cool climates**
* Yarrow (*Achillea* spp.) * Wallflower (*Erysimum cheiri* syn. *Cheiranthus cheiri*)
* Forsythia (*Forsythia* x *intermedia*)
* Witch hazel (*Hamamelis virginiana*)
* Helenium, common sneezeweed (*Helenium autumnale*) * Sunflower (*Helianthus annuus*)
* Daylilies (*Hemerocallis* x *hybrida*)
* Jerusalem sage (*Phlomis fruticosa*)
* Roses * Banksia rose (*Rosa banksiae*)
* Coneflower (*Rudbeckia* spp.)

**For warm and hot climates**
* Chinese lantern (*Abutilon* x *hybridum*)
* Wattle (*Acacia* spp.) * Banksia
* Grey-leaved euryops (*Euryops pectinatus*)
* Carolina jasmine (*Gelsemium sempervirens*)
* Golden guinea vine, snake vine (*Hibbertia scandens*) * Hibiscus
* Frangipani (*Plumeria rubra*) * Yellow flax (*Reinwardtia indica*) * Strawflower, everlasting daisy (*Xerochrysum bracteatum* syn. *Bracteantha bracteata*)

## YUCCAS

### Sharp spines, scented flowers
These hardy plants from Central and North America form rosettes of strappy leaves, each ending in a sharp spine, and produce a spike of scented, white flowers. Because of their sharp spines, position yuccas a good distance from paths and high-traffic areas. They need well-drained soil.

There are many *Yucca* species and cultivars, ranging from shrubs and trees with woody stems, such as the 2 m spineless or giant yucca (*Y. elephantipes*), to the clumping perennial Adam's needle (*Yucca filamentosa*). Foliage colours range from green to grey-blue. There are variegated forms, too.

### Perfect for pots
Not only do yuccas look attractive in containers, but in cooler areas they can be moved to the sunniest spots of the garden in the summer and to sheltered corners when the weather becomes colder. Pile gravel over the roots in autumn or apply a mulch of bark.

### Sucker problem
Be careful which variety of yucca you choose because some, such as Adam's needle, sucker freely in warm climates. Getting rid of the rampant shoots can be a nuisance.

### Propagating yuccas
Detach young suckers from the base of the plant in spring and pot them up individually. The new plants may take 5 years to flower. Yuccas can also be propagated by seed, but these will take even longer to flower.

### Hot and dry combinations
Pair yuccas with other plants that flourish in heat, drought and sun. White-flowered zinnias and green-and-white variegated yuccas make a particularly striking match. Yuccas with leaves striped yellow combine well with chartreuse-flowered euphorbias.

# Z

ZINNIAS | ZUCCHINI

## ZINNIAS

### Every colour but blue
These bright summer- and autumn-blooming annuals are easy to grow, and seed mixes come in a variety of shades that includes every flower colour except blue – there is even pale green. They range in height from 30 cm dwarfs, such as the Lilliput and Thumbelina series, to 1.2 m 'Gold Medal', with large, almost dahlia-like flowers.

### Warmth for sowing
Zinnia seeds germinate quickly in warm soil, so it's best to wait until spring and summer to sow seeds or transplant seedlings. In cold climates, sow in pots indoors on a sunny windowsill in early spring, transplanting them when all danger of frost has passed.

### A longer run
To keep zinnias blooming as long as possible, trim off dead flowers when they fade, cutting their stems back to where new growth is starting. If the plants become leggy after midsummer, put in fresh ones for an autumn display rather than trying to rejuvenate them by cutting back hard.

All zinnias naturally develop numerous flowering stems, so no pinching out is required. Nor do they need staking.

## ZUCCHINI

### Summer squash
Zucchini are a type of summer squash, also known as courgettes. Essentially, they are small marrows, at their tastiest and best when picked young. Marrows are varieties that are bred for their tender flesh when fully grown. Patty pan squash, also known as scallop squash, are shaped like miniature pies and have scalloped edges. They can be used like zucchini when young and like marrows when older.

The summer squash provide a good yield from a modest area.

### Planning the crop
All these squash require a sunny position and a deep, rich soil. They can be sown or planted directly in the soil or on an old heap of thoroughly rotted manure or even on the compost heap if it won't be needed for a time. Both bush and trailing types are available.

### Water well
Once temperatures and soil have warmed up sow seeds 2.5 cm deep, with bush varieties 60 cm apart and trailing types 1–1.2 m apart. Water well after planting and also throughout the growing season during dry periods. Also apply a mulch to help retain soil moisture.

### Mark the spot
Trailing varieties have dense foliage and can spread over a wide area. When planting out the seedlings, drive a stake into each planting hole so that you know where to direct the water once the plants have grown, ensuring a good soaking for the roots.

### Pick them all
Ideally, you should start cutting and eating zucchini and patty pan squash when the fruit are about 10 cm and still young and tender. To harvest, use a knife to cut through the stalk. Marrows are best harvested and eaten in summer when the fruit are about 25–30 cm long. If it seems likely you'll have a glut of zucchini, you can pick the flowers (along with the stem). Use them raw in salads, stuffed or dipped in batter and deep-fried.

Be vigilant when you're picking zucchini. If you leave just one fruit to turn into a marrow, further zucchini production will be slowed down.

If you don't have enough ground space for trailing varieties, train them up a teepee of bamboo canes or cultivate the more compact bush varieties.

### Male and female flowers
All summer squashes produce male and female flowers. Females have an embryo fruit behind the flower, whereas males have no swelling there at all. The first few flowers are male, which will abort after opening.

308

ZINNIAS | ZYGOCACTUS

## A fiesta of cut flowers
Zinnias are one of the easiest and most plentiful cut flowers to grow for arrangements. Given fresh water every 2–3 days, zinnias will stay in prime condition for more than a week in a vase.

## Water carefully
Although they withstand drought, zinnias perform best when given supplementary water early in the growing season if rain doesn't fall. They are prone to fungal diseases such as powdery mildew in humid weather. To minimise this, keep leaves dry by watering at soil level. Also avoid watering in the evening, and space plants well for good air circulation.

Marrow 'Long Green Trailing'

Young zucchini

# ZYGOCACTUS

## Well-drained potting mix
Zygocactus, or leaf cactus (*Schlumbergera* spp.), do best in pots of very coarse, well-drained potting mix. They are ideal for hanging baskets on a well-lit veranda or under a tree. The most common zygocactus have a bright cerise pink flower, but there are many colours, including mauve, red, orange, white and bicolours.

## Light response
If leaves begin to yellow, it means that the light levels are too high – move your plants to a spot with less direct light. Zygocactus bloom in response to shortening daylight hours, so they flower naturally in late autumn and winter. Don't fertilise plants from late summer until the buds form, as this may result in a complete failure to flower. After buds are initiated, liquid-feed occasionally through autumn. Apply a slow-release fertiliser in spring.

## Grow from a leaf
New zygocactus plants are easy to grow from leaf segments taken in early spring. Allow the segments to dry out for several weeks before planting in well-drained potting mix. Water sparingly to avoid root rot. When moving the cuttings into larger pots, take care not to damage the roots as this can allow root rot to enter.

309

# INDEX

Page numbers in **bold** print refer to main entries

## A

abelias, **8**, 76, 90, 99, 213, 244, 293
acacias *see* wattles
acanthus, 77, 192
acephate, 14, 50
acid soils, **8**, 10, 20, 34, 62, 125, 134, 160, 246, 247, 280
acid-tolerant plants, 8, 10, 55
acidic mulches, 10, 134
Adam's needle, 307
adaptation, 292
aeoniums, 256, 257, 293
aerial layering, **152**, 160
*Aesculus*, 204
African daisies, 67, **79**, 99, 187, 192, 293
African marigolds, 164
African violets, **9**, 137
agapanthus, **9**, 32, 67, 74, 87, 90, 94, 187, 192, 232, 293
agaves, **10**, 38, 67, 256, 257, 293
air drying, 89, 128, 130
air pollution, 218, 244
Alexandra palm, 183
alfalfa sprouts, 250
algae control, 207
alkaline soils, 8, **10**, 55, 56, 57, 62, 117, 134, 160, 246, 247, 280
Allard's lavender, 147
allium, 293
almonds, **177**
aloes, **11**, 178, 256, 257, 293
alpine strawberries, 124, 245
alpine water ferns, 34
*Alstroemeria*, 204
aluminium fences, 100
aluminium foil recycling, 220
aluminium sulfate, 134
alyssum, 13, 99, 112, 193, 223, 242, 293, 298, 299
amaryllis, 41
Amazon lily, 238
ammonium sulfate, 34, 55, 174
amphibians, 301
  *see also* frogs
anemones, **11**
angelica, 131
angel's trumpets, 276
angel's wing begonias, 28
angel's wing jasmines, 140–1
animal manures *see* manures
animals, native *see* native animals; wildlife havens
anise hyssop, 93
annual weeds, **296**
annuals, **12–13**, 26, 67, 80, 99, 211, 213, 232, 269, 293, 301
*Anthemis* spp., 192, 199
anthracnose, **15**, 86, 162
ants, 138, 165, 196, 232
aphids, **14**, 29, 62, 114, 143, 146, 182, 196, 220, 228, 264, 284, 286, 291, **304**
apple mint, 166
apple moths, 220

apples, **14**, 92, 95, 108, 110, 128, 160, 211, 304
apricots, **15**, 98, 108, 110, 263
aquatic plants *see* water plants
Arabian jasmine, 141
arbours and arches, **15**
arctotis daisies *see* African daisies
armillaria, 86
artichokes, **17**, 233, 245
arugula *see* rocket
arum lilies, 238
Asian vegetables, **16**, 281
Asiatic lilies, 156, 157
asparagus, 233
asparagus chicory, 230
aspidistras, 67
assassin bugs, 50, 120, 138
asters, **17**, 75, 87, 99, 192, 215, 301, 303
asthma weed, pellitory, **297**
astilbe, 238
aubergines *see* eggplants
aucuba, 21, 126, 238, 303
Australian laurel, 303
autumn colours, **18–19**
avens, 180
avocados, 15, **20**, 108
awnings, 187
azalea petal blight, 20
azaleas, 8, **20**, 21, 55, 67, 97, 137, 152, 174, 180, 199, 211, 237, 238, 241, 245, 247, 270, 279, 303

## B

babianas, 40
baby beet, 28
baby bok choy, 16
baby donkey tail, 236
baby's breath, 293
baby's tears, 21
*Bacillus thuringiensis*, 30, 39, 45, 50, 159, 182, 195, 261, 264
bacterial diseases, 86, 162
balcony gardens, **21**, 61, 68, 134, 230, 291
bamboo fences, 100
bamboo palm, 183, 276
bamboo screens, 21
bamboos, **22**, 105, 219, 260
banana bunch top, 22
banana passionfruit, 185
bananas, **22**
bangalow palm, 183, 219, 260
banksia rose, 307
banksias, **23**, 27, 57, 60, 90, 91, 173, 197, 205, 214, 232, 293, 301, 303, 307
baobabs, 90
barberry, 293
bare-root plants, **200–1**, 251
Bartlett's rata, 173
basil, **23**, 27, 93, 124, 129, 130, 138, 198, 245, 249, 264, 302
Basil pesto sauce (recipe), 23

bauhinias, **24**, 104, 237
bay leaves, 130
bay trees, **24**, 94, 232, 245, 252, 268
beach fescue, 60
beach spinifex, 60
beach tamarind *see* tuckeroo
bean sprouts, 250
beans, 15, **25**, 38, 39, 54, 62, 114, 120, 160, 162, 235, 245, 281, 282, 283, 300
beautyberries, 82, 303
bedding begonias, 13, 28, 238
bedding plants, **26**, 238
bedrock, 247
beds and borders, **26–7**, 40, 295
bee stings, **27**
beer traps, 243
bees, **27**, 45, 138, 194, 250, 261, 263, 301
beetles, 54, 132, 181, 196, 243, 301
beetroot, **28**, 233, 281, 282
begonias, 13, **28**, 38, 67, 75, 90, 198, 199, 234, 238, 248
belladonna lilies, **29**, 75, 293
beneficial creatures, **29**, **30**, 119, **138**, 182, **286** *see also under name eg* bees
Benjamin's fig, 103
bent grass, 150
bergamot, 93
bergenia, 192, 303
berries and fruits, decorative, **82**, 104, 161
Betchel crab apple, 73
bicarbonate of soda spray, 86
biennials, 12
billbergias, 238
bindii, **296**
biological controls, 29, **30**, 119, 283
biological pesticides, 195
birch *see* silver birch
bird of paradise, 180, **258**
bird scarers, 171, 220
bird tables, 301
birdbaths, 30, 113, 301
birds
  beneficial, 29, **30**, 50, 60, 119, 121, 171, 172, 182, 194, 218, 261, 301, 304
  pest, **30**, 31, 34, 53, **109**, 160, 171, **190**
  plants that attract, 30, 60, 119, 121, 171, 172, 173, 184, 218, 301
bird's nest fern, 101, 219
black-eyed Susan vine, 236
black mulberry, 167
black sapote, 275
black spot, 86, 228
blackberry hybrids, **31**, 110, 152
blackcurrants, 110
blackwood, 294
bladders, rainwater, 289

bladderworts, 287
blanket flowers, 232, 293
*Blechnum articulatum*, 101
*Blechnum camfieldii*, 34
bleeding heart, 67, 70
blood and bone, **31**, 174, 197, 281
bloodleafs, 238, 276
blue chalk sticks, 256
blue fescue, 284
blue flag iris, 34
blue flowers, 27, **32–3**, 43, 61, 94, 105, 134, 180, 199, 215, 231, 284, 307
blue ginger, 32, 192
blue hibiscus, 215
blue lechenaultia, 32
blue marguerite, 32, 79
blue sage, 32
blue worms, 305
bluebeard, 32
bluebells, 67, 239, 279
blueberries, **34**, 109
blueberry ash, 82, 104, 171, 219, 303
bog gardens, **34**, 139, 173
bog sage, 231
bok choy, 16
bolting, 154
bonsai, **35**
boobialla. 293
borage, 27, **35**, 93, 264
Bordeaux mixture, 86, 228, 271
borders and beds, **26–7**, 40, 295
borecole *see* kale
borers, **35**, 143
borlotti beans, 282
boron, 176, 233, 270
boronias, 199, 238
borrowed landscape, 244
Boston fern, 137
Boston ivy, 18, 58
botanical pesticides, 195
botrytis, **121**
bottle recycling, 220, 243
bottle trees, 90
bottlebrushes, 27, **36**, 172, 173, 221, 261, 293
bougainvilleas, **36**, 38, 58, 81, 88, 122, 180, 194, 199, 245, 276
bow saws, 265, 266
bower of beauty, 173, 199
box, 21, **37**, 94, 113, 126, 152, 238, 241, 242, 252, 268
box elder, 163, 237
boxleaf honeysuckle, 268
boysenberries, 31
brachychitons, 293
brachyglottis, 173
brake ferns, 101
brassicas, 39, 43, 45, 88, 114, 170, 220, 270, 278, 280, 282, 300
Brazilian jasmines *see* mandevillas
Brazilian plume flower, 199
Brazilian snapdragon, 32

310

# INDEX

brick fences, 100
brick steps, 252
brick walls, 262, 286
brinjal *see* eggplants
broad beans, 25, **37**, 62, 119, 232, 282
broad-leaved lillypilly, 159
broad-leaved paperbark, 60, 173
broad mites, **38**
broccoli, **38**, 171, 232, 270, 280, 282
bromeliads, **38–9**, 137, 178, 219, 238, 250, 274, 276, 279, 293, 303
bromoxynil, 295
bronze fennel, 105
bronze orange bugs, 56, 196
*Brugmansia*, 204, 276
brush cherry, 159
brushwood structures, 100, 243
brussels sprouts, **39**, 233, 270, 281, 282, 302
budding grafts, 116
budworms, **39**, 196, 264
buffalo grass, 150, 295
bugles, 32, 42, 67, 99, 122, 215, 238, 244
building codes, 81, 100, 224, 262
bulb mites, **41**
bulb planters, 267
bulbines, 40, 293
bulbs, 26, **40–1**, 80, 87, 138, 149, 232, 238, 245, 293
Bull Bay magnolia, 160
bulrush, dwarf, 287
burrawang, 173
bush germander, 99
bush regeneration, **42**
bushfires, **42**
bushman's friend, 238
busy lizzies *see* impatiens
butterflies, 30, **43**, 45, 263, 301
butterfly bush, 43, 76, 193, 241, 293, 301
butterhead lettuces, 155
buying plants, **44**, **272**

## C

cabbage tree palms (*Livistona australis*), 219
cabbage trees (*Cordyline australis*), 68, 137, 173, 198
cabbage white butterflies, 16, 43, **45**, 170
cabbages, 43, **45**, 170, 224, 233, 238, 280, 282
cacti, **46**, 178, 256, 293, **309**
caladiums, 238, 279
*Calathea* spp., 276, 279
calcium, 176, 233
calendulas, 67, 75, 93, 138, 164, 180, 199, 303
California lilacs *see* ceanothus
California poppies, 90, 180, 199, 208, 234
calla lilies, 287
calliandras, **45**
camellias, 8, 10, 38, **47**, 55, 67, 95, 97, 126, 137, 152, 174, 199, 232, 237, 238, 241, 244, 245, 247, 303

campanulas, 12, 27, 32, 67, 70, 112, 192, 198, 215
Canary melons, 165
candles, garden, 158, 167
candytuft, 75, 223, 298
canker, 143, 271
cannas, **47**, 192, 221, 260
canopy trees, 218, 219
cantaloupes, 165
cape chestnus, 104
cape gooseberries, 82
cape primroses, 137
capsicums, 38, **48**, 108, 120, 128, 134, 198, 264, 282
carbaryl, 39, 50, 120, 132, 159
carbon, 176
cardamom, 248, 249
cardinal flower, 221
carexes, 173, 284
carnations, 39, **48**, 70, 80, 93, 174, 193, 198, 199
carnivorous plants, **49**
Carolina jasmine, 58, 140, 307
Carpentaria palm, 183
carpet grass, 8, 150
carrot flies, 85, 224, 262
carrots, **49**, 62, 85, 128, 224, 263, 281, 282
casaba melons, 165
cassava, 219
cassias, 38, 276
cast-iron plant, 137
casuarina spray, 86
catalpas, 104
caterpillars, 30, 39, 43, 45, **50**, 107, 159, 182, 196, 283, 286
catmint, 43, **50**, 67, 192, 232, 293
catnip, 50
cats, **50**, 54, 166, 171, 301
cattleya orchids, 181
cauliflowers, **51**, 270, 280, 282
ceanothus, 32, 33, 43, **51**, 55, 90, 293, 301
celeriac, 162, 282
celery, **52**, 128, 162, 280, 282
celerywood, 219
centipedes, 138
century plant, 10
cereus, 293
cestrums, 193
chamomile, 62, 122, 123, 165, 253
chard, 245, 249
chaste tree, 193
Chatham Island akeake, 232
Chatham Island forget-me-not, 173
chemicals, **52**, 86, 88, 93, 108, 119, 120, 121, 165, 171, 182, **229**, **250**, 283, **295**, 304
cherries, **53**, 92, 109
cherry guava, 82
cherry tomatoes, 264
chervil, 93, 130, 131
chestnuts, **177**
chewings fescue grass, 150
chickens, 194
*see also* poultry manure
chickweed, **296**
chicory, 230

children
  fountains &, 105
  gardening by, **54**
  mandarins &, 161
  play areas for, 54, 84, 167
  swimming pools &, 260
  *see also* poisonous plants
Chilean jasmine, 161
chillies, **48**, 198, 264
Chinese broccoli, 16
Chinese cabbage, 16
Chinese fan palm, 183
Chinese flat cabbage, 16
Chinese gooseberry *see* kiwi fruit
Chinese lanterns, **54**, 198, 303, 307
Chinese pink, 48
Chinese pistachio, 18, 237
Chinese plumbago, 32
Chinese silver grass, 105
Chinese tallow tree, 18, 273
Chinese windmill palm, 183
Chinese wisteria, 58
chives, **54**, 93, 124, 129, 130, 171, 232, 245, 264
chlorine, 176, 233, 270
chlorosis, 10, **55**, 169, 176, 270
chlorothalonil, 121
chocolate cosmos, 193
Christmas bells, 173
Christmas rose, 128
chrysanthemums, 38, **55**, 67, 75, 87, 93, 192, 198, 303
cinerarias, 13
citronella, 167, 261
citrons, 56
citrus, 8, 15, 21, **56**, 67, 92, 95, 108, 160, 232, 245, 270, 303
  *see also* grapefruit; lemon trees; lime trees; mandarins; oranges; pomelos; tangelos
citrus drop, 107
citrus gall wasps, 56, 286
citrus mealybug, 165
city gardens, small, **244–5**
clarkias, 12
clay soil, **57**, 85, 87, 89, 102, 246, 280
clematis, **57**, 58, 67, 75, 81, 152, 173, 194, 215, 236, 274, 298, 299
clematis wilt, 57
climate-compatible plants, **292**
climbers, **58**, 236, 252, **274**, 276, 286, 298
climbing flame pea, 173
climbing roses, 225, **226**, **228**, 274, 298
clivias, **59**, 67, 82, 87, 90, 180, 192, 204, 238, 293, 303
cloches, **59**, 220, 234, 235, 248, 255
clothes drying areas, 84
clove pinks, 93
clover, 119, 175, 280, 301
club root, 16, 45, 278
coast banksia, 23, 60, 173, 232
coast myall, 294
coastal beard heath, 60

coastal gardens, 23, 51, **60–1**, 68, 96, 98, 100, 135, 143, 166, 172, 173, 236, 243, 253, 261, 280
coastal rosemary, 60, 173
coastal saltbush, 60
coastal she oak, 173
coastal tea tree, 60, 261
coastal wattle, 173, 232
coconut coir, 191
codling moth, 30, 107
*Colchicum*, 204
coldframes, **59**, 235
coleus, 67, 76, 198, 219, 245
colour
  annuals &, 12, 13
  autumn, **18–19**
  bedding plants, 26
  beds and borders, 27
  butterflies &, 43
  combinations of, 180, 199, 215, 221, 307
  dried flower, 89
  false perspective &, 284
  foliage, 105
  front gardens &, 94
  grasses &, 118
  hydrangeas &, 134
  marigolds &, 164
  native plants &, 173
  overview of, **61**
  planting plans &, 202
  rock gardens &, **223**
  shady gardens &, 238
  shrubs &, **241**
  window boxes &, 302
  *see also under colour eg blue flowers
columbines, 12, 70, 94, 105, 192, 239, 279
comfrey, 27, 119, 210, 232
common chive, 54
  *see also* chives
common jasmine, 140
common lilac, 215
  *see also* lilacs
common maidenhair fern, 173
common sneezeweed *see* heleniums
common water moss, 287
companion planting, 23, **62**, 85, 114, 182, 224, 232, 264, **282**, 283, **293**
complete fertilisers, 102
compost, **62–3**, 84, 119, 168, 175, 194, 197, 231, 232
compost bins, 63, 280
compost worms, 305
compound fertilisers, 102
concrete, 244–5
concrete driveways, 188
concrete pots, 65, 66
concrete steps, 252, 253
concrete tanks, 289
coneflowers (*Rudbeckia* spp.), 307
coneflowers, purple (*Echinacea purpurea*), 43, 192
confetti bush *see* diosmas
conifers, **64**, 67, 92, 126, 212–13, 233, 239, 272, 303
contact herbicides, 295, 296, 297

# INDEX

container gardening, **66–7**, 92, 108–9, 170, 224, 244, **282**
containers, 21, **65**
controlled-release fertilisers, 102
*Convallaria*, 204
copper, 176, 270
copper-based sprays, 86, 88, 182
copper deficiencies, 180
copper oxychloride, 234
coprosmas, 67, **68**, 173
coral trees, 286, 303
coralberry, 21, 82, 303
cordylines, 50, 67, **68**, 105, 173, 245, 276
coriander, **69**, 130
corkwood, 219
corms, 80, 293
corn, 39, **69**, 128, 171, 232, 245, 281, 282
corn plant, 137
corn poppies *see* Flanders poppies
corn salad *see* lamb's lettuce
cornflowers, 32, 67, 234, 301
correa, 293
Corsican mint, 166
cos lettuces, 155
cosmos, 12, 13, 67, 99, 193, 293
cotoneasters, 82, 303, 304
cottage gardens, 32, **70–1**, 158
cottage pinks, 48
cotton lavender, 42, 99, 199
cottonwood, 132
cotyledon, 256, 293
couch grass, 150, 295, **297**
courgettes *see* zucchinis
courtyard gardens, **72**, 188
cow manure, 163
crab apples, **73**, 82, 95, 104, 303
cranesbill *see* geraniums and pelargoniums
crassulas, 256, 293
creeping bent grass, 150
Crenshaw melons, 165
crepe myrtle, 18, 67, **73**, 104, 211, 263, 273, 293, 303
cress, 230, 250
crickets, 196
crimson bottlebrush, 173
crimson clover, 175
crimson rata, 173
crocking, 211
crocuses, 40, 307
crop residues, 283
crop rotation, 15, 45, 88, 94, 111, 162, 171, 175, 182, 282, **283**, 284
crotons, 75, 105, 137, 219, 238, 276
crowea, 199
crown gall, 189
crown of thorns, 97
crown rot, **73**
crown vetch, 119
cucumbers, **74**, 134, 234
cucurbits, 15, 88, 234, 282
culinary herbs, 129, **130**, **131**, 164, 302
cumin, 248
cumquats, 56, 82, 245, 303

cunjevoi, 219
cup and saucer vine, 236
curl grubs, 196
curled dock, **297**
curly pondweed, 287
currants, 110
cushion spurge, 97
custard apple, 274
cut flowers, **74–5**, 78, 97
cut leaf daisies, 79, 173, 192, 232, 242, 293
cuttings
  African violet, 9
  cacti &, 46, 309
  geranium and pelargonium, 115
  hardwood, 76
  herbs grown from, 130, 261
  impatiens, 135
  lavender, 147
  overview of, **75–7**
  poisonous plants, 75
  rex begonia, 28
  root, 75, 77
  semi-hardwood, 76, 147
  softwood, 76
  understanding, 76
cutworms, 220
cycads, **77**
cyclamens, 38, 41, 137, 238, 303
cymbidium orchids, 181, 219
cypress pines, 35, 112, 293
*Cyrtomium* spp., 101

## D

daffodils, 40, 41, 67, 74, 75, **78**, 133, 149, 223, 239, 246, 279, 307
dahlias, 38, 41, 70, 74, **78**, 192, 198, 199, 221, 237
daikons, 217
daisies, 26, **79**, 112, 173, 301, 303, 307 *see also* paper daisies
daisy bush (*Brachyglottis greyi*), 173
daisy bush (*Olearia* spp.), 60, 79, 293
daisy grubbers, 267
damp courses, 188
dampieras, 32
damping off, 174, 182, **234**
dandelions, 8, 62, **297**, 301
daphnes, **80**, 90, 97, 193, 232
date palms, 183, 260, 276
daturas, 38, 277
Davidson's plum, 219
Dawson's creeping lawngrass, 150
daylilies, 67, 78, **80**, 84, 99, 180, 192, 221, 231, 307
deadheading, 26, 40, **80**, 93, 103, 136, 147, 158, 213, 228, 242, 275
deadnettles, 67, 99, 122, 303
de-caning, 213
deciduous trees and shrubs, 97, 119, 200, 237, 239, 244, 270, 272
decks, 81, 260
decorative fruits and berries, **82**, 104, 161

delphiniums, 32, 70, 71, 80, **82**, 87, 204, 307
dendrobium beetles, 181
dendrobiums, 181
desert cacti, 137
desert plants, 46
design
  bed and border, 26
  herb garden, 129
  lawn, 84
  native plants &, 172
  path, 186
  photographic guide, 83
  planting plan, **202**
  plants to fit, **83–4**
  plotting and planning, 83
  seasons &, 84
  small city garden, **245**
devil's ivy, 137
dianellas, 32, 87, 219, 232, 279, 284, 293
dibbers, 267
dichlorophen, 167
dieback, 86, 143
dietes, 192
digging, **85**, 266, 269
dill, 45, **85**, 93, 129, 130, 138
dimethoate, 107, 108, 304
diosmas, 76, **86**, 99, 303
disbudding, 55
diseases, 62, **86**, 182, 189, 264, 282 *see also* under name eg powdery mildew
division, 78, **87**, 101, 119, 130, 138, 258
dock *see* curled dock
dog rose, 173
dogs, 84, **88**, 166, 171
dog's tooth violet, 238
dogwood, 199, 241, 303
dolomite, 8, 160, 189, 280
donkey tail, 236
dot plants, 231
downy mildew, 86, **88**
dracaenas, 38, **88**, 105, 219
dragon tree, 88
dragonflies, 301
dragonfruit, 298
drainage, **89**, 187, 242
dried flowers, 70, **89**
drip-irrigation, 272, 284, **291**, **293**
driveways, 188
drought, 92, 237, 239, 260, 273
drought-tolerant plants, 88, **90–1**, 96, 98, 105, 117, 128, 150, 187, 218, 256, **293**, 306
dry conditions, **92**
drying herbs, 130
ducks, 243
duckweeds, 287
dumb canes, 75, 137, 204
duranta, 32, **94**
Durban grass, 149, 237
Dutch irises, 138
dwarf date palm, 183
dwarf plants, **92**, **94**

## E

earthworms, 29, 85, **93**, 194, 305
earwigs, 196
easter lily *see* November lily

eastern redbud, 18, 19
eau de cologne mint, 166
eaves, planting under, 286
echeverias, 157, 256, 257, 293
edging knives, 267
edible flowers, **93**
eelworms *see* nematodes; root knot nematodes
eggplants, **94**, 108, 134, 198, 264
elders, 82, 93
electric mats, 212
*Eleocharis acicularis*, 287
elephant's ears, 219, 276, 277, 279
elkhorn fern, 173, 219
endives, 230
English irises, 138
English lavender, 147
English spinach, 249
entertaining areas, 84, 187
entrances, **94**
epiphytes, 38, 218, 219
Epsom salts, 113, 160
ericas, 8
escallonias, 60, **96**, 126, 293
espaliers, **95**, 190, 263, 286
eucalypts and gums, 42, 90, **96**, 112, 172, 173, 198, 205, 221, 232, 237, 239, 273, 286, 293
eucarist lily, 94
euonymus, 18, 204, 238, 252, 293
euphorbias, 67, 75, **97**, 192, 204, 238, 256, 293
European box, 37
European nettle tree, 18
European pear, 190
euryops, 303, 307
evaporation, 90, 290, 292, 293
evening primrose, 298
evergreens, 61, 72, 82, **97**, 113, 137, **238**, 239, 241, 243, 244, 252, 268, 270, 272, 285, 302
everlasting daisies *see* paper daisies
extension leads, 229

## F

fairy fan flower, 215
fairy mosses, 287
fan flowers, 60, **98**, 99, 215, 243, 293
fan-training, **98**
fast-growing plants, **99**, 121
fastigiate yew, 268
feijoa, 82
fences, 60, 61, 72, 88, **100**, 171, 196, 205, 238, 245
fennel, 93, **99**, 105, 129, 130, 138, 192
fenthion, 108
fenugreek, 269
ferns, 34, 67, **101**, 105, 173, **219**, 232, 239, 243, 245, 250, 279, 302
fertilisers
  blood and bone, **31**, 174, 197, 281
  choice of, **102**
  container gardening &, 67
  fruit trees and bushes, 109, 154

312

# INDEX

hydroponics &, 134
indoor plants, 136, 137
lawns &, 102, **148**
nitrogen in, 174
N:P:K ratio &, 176
phosphate in, 197
roses &, **228**
storage of, 102
timing &, 102
trees and bushes &, 102, 121
vegetable gardens, 154–5, **280**, 281, 282
fescue, 60, 105, 150, 284
fibreglass pots, 65
field poppies *see* Flanders poppies
figs, 21, **103**, 293
finocchio *see* fennel
firs, 212–13
fish, ornamental, **206**, 269, 287
fishbone water fern, 101
five finger, 173
flag irises, 34, 138, 287
flagstones, 188
flame pea, climbing, 173, 180
flame trees, 90, 173
    *see also* Illawarra flame trees
flame vine, 180, 303
flaming glory bower vine, 58, 219, 221
flamingo flower, 137
Flanders poppies, 208, 221, 301
flapjacks, 144
flares, garden, 158
flax, 172
    *see also* New Zealand flax
flax lilies *see* dianellas
fleas, 138, 166
flies, 138
Flinders Range wattle, 294
florence fennel *see* fennel
floribunda roses, 225, **226**
flower meanings, **75**
flowerbeds and borders, **26–7**, 40, 295
flowering dogwood, 199
flowering gum, 273
flowering plants, **103**, 238
flowering plum, 18, 203
flowering quince, 180, 216, 241, 293, 303
flowering tobacco, 298
flowering trees, **104**
flowers, edible, **93**
flycatchers, 29
flying foxes, 171
foliage, **105**, 238, 241, 256, 284, 287, 292
foliar feeding, 250, 270
forest bell bushes, 238
forest lobelia, 219
forget-me-nots, 11, 12, 34, 75, 173, 238
forks, 266, 267
forsythias, 18, 307
fountain grasses, 105
fountains, **105**, 113, 119, 206, 244, 269, 285
foxgloves, 12, 26, 62, 70, **106**, 192, 204, 238, 301
foxtail agave, 10

foxtail palm, 183, 276
framework pruning, 213
frangipanis, 38, 104, **106**, 244, 276, 307
frangipanis, native, 106, 173
freesias, 40, 41, **106**, 149, 193, 223, 232, 293
French beans, 25, 258
French lavender, 147
French marigolds, 45, 164, 171, 232, 282, 300
French tarragon, 130, 261
fringe flower, 199
fringed lavender, 147
frogs, 29, 50, 119, 194, 243, 301
front door, 94
frost, **107**
fruit drop, **107**, 109
fruit flies, 94, 107, **108**, 189, 264
fruit fly traps, 30, 94
fruit salad bush, 82
fruit trees and bushes, 39, 92, 95, 107, **108–10**, 171, 198, 199, 200, 204, 210, 232, 245, 263, 271
fruits
    decorative, **82**, 104, 161
    heirloom varieties of, 128, 264
    tropical, **274–5**
fuchsias, 38, 67, 76, **110–11**, 173, 198, 245, 252
fumigants, 254–5
fungal diseases, **86**, 94, 103, 111, 117, 182, 195, 196, 228, 234, 271, 278
fungi kits, 169
fungicides, 15, 52, **86**, **111**, 162, 195, 211, 228, 229
furalaxyl, 88, 234
furniture, 21, **112**, 238, 269
fusarium wilt, 86

## G

gai choy *see* mustard greens
gai larn *see* Chinese broccoli
galangal, 248, 249
gall midges, **112**
gall wasps, citrus, 56, 286
galls, 286
garden candles, 158
garden feature lighting, 158
garden flares, 158
garden furniture *see* furniture
garden hygiene, 108, 111, **113**, 121, 229, 233, 254–5, 284
garden lines, 267
garden ornaments, **113**
garden propagators, 176
garden shears, 126, 213, 242, 266, 267, 268
garden thyme, 263
garden transformation, **269**
garden waste, 213
gardenias, 8, 21, 39, 55, 76, 94, 97, **113**, 137, 152, 160, 193, 241, 270, 298
gardenias, native, 219
garlic, 62, **114**, 162, 165, 255, 281
garlic chives, 54, 93
garlic sprays, 45, 50, 283
gauras, 27, 103, 192

gazanias, 42, 67, 99, **114**, 122, 180, 192, 223, 232, 253, 293
gazebos, 112, 187
geckos, 29
Geralton wax, 303
geraniums and pelargoniums, 8, 42, 60, 67, 78, 90, 91, 93, 94, 99, 113, **115**, 122, 193, 198, 221, 223, 238, 286, 293, 302
germination, **248**
gherkins, 74
giant chives, 54
giant rush, 173
giant snowdrop, 246
giant umbrella sedge, 173
giant white bird of paradise, 258
giant yuccas, 307
ginger, 248, 249
ginger mint, 166
gingers, 192, 219, 238, 245, 260, 276, 277, 279
gladioli, 41, 70, 74, 75, **115**
glazed pots, 65
globe artichokes, **17**, 233, 245
globe beetroot, 28
globe onions, 179
glory bower vines, 276
glory bushes *see* tibouchinas
gloxinias, 75
glyphosate herbicides, 22, 42, 295, 297
goat manure, 163
goat's beard (*Aruncus dioicus*), 238
goat's beard (*Clematis aristata*), 173
golden cane palm, 183, 219, 276
golden club, 287
golden feverfew, 62
golden garlic, 138
golden guinea vine, 219, 307
golden oregano, 164
golden penda, 219, 273
golden-rayed lily, 156
golden shower tree, 273
golden trumpet vine, 58
goodenias, 293
gordonias, 303
gourds, 215
grafting, **116**, 162, 204
grape hyacinths, 40, 41, 67, 279, 293
grape ivy, 137
grapefruit, **117**
grapevines, 18, 88, **117**, 211
graptoverias, 256, 257
grass seed, 148
grass trees, **118**, 172, 173
grasses, 67, 90, 237
    annual cut-down, 213
    coastal garden, 60
    drought-tolerant, 293
    invading, 250
    lawn, 148, 149, **150**, 295
    ornamental, 105, **118–19**, 244, 287
    vertical garden, 284
    wildflower meadow, 301
grasshoppers, 196
gravel, 84, 89, 112, 168, 244
gravel paths, **186**, 193, 238

graviola *see* soursop
grease bands, 50
grecian windflower, 41
Greek oregano, 164
green corridors, 171
green flowers, 174
green manures, **119**, 175, 232, 280, 283
green vegetable bug, **120**
greener gardening, **119**
greenhouses and shadehouses, 113, **120**, 121, 134, 235, 278
grenadilla *see* passionfruit
grevilleas, 27, 30, 57, 90, 99, **121**, 126, 172, 173, 180, 197, 204, 214, 223, 241, 261, 293, 301, 303
grey mould, 86, **121**
grey water, 92
groundcover roses, 225, **226**, 242
groundcovers, 42, 61, 99, **122–3**, 239, 243, 244, 276, 293
groundsel, **296**
group plantings, 125
guanábana *see* soursop
guavas, 108
guinea flowers, 293
gum vine, 219
gums *see* eucalypts and gums
gutters, 289
gymea lilies, 173, 172, 173
gymnosperms, 77
gypsum, 57

## H

hairpin banksia, 23
hairy bitter cress, **296**
hakeas, 30, 42, 173, 214, 293, 301
Halloween lanterns, 214
hanging baskets, **124**, 129, 264, 286, 291
happy plant, 137
harakeke *see* New Zealand flax
hardenbergia, 173, 215, 303
hardening off, 235, 270
hardwood cuttings, 76
hare's foot ferns, 101
harlequin flower, 293
haworthias, 256, 257
hawthorns, 21, 61, 82, 193, 301, 303, 304
hay, 93, 269, 281
hazelnuts, **177**
healing plants, 11, **165**, 184, 261
heartsease, 93, 183
heat, **125**
heat shields, 236–7
heath banksia, 23
heaths, **125**
hebes, 32, 60, 76, 112, 172, 173, 241
hedge trimmers, **126**, 127, 213, 242
hedges, 82, 96, 244
    bamboo, 22
    bottlebrush, 36
    box, 37, 126
    camellia, 47, 126
    coastal garden, 60, 68, 96
    conifer, 64, 126
    fast-growing, 99, 126

313

# INDEX

hibiscus, 126, 132
lillypilly, 126, 159
paperbark, 184
photinia, 197
planting, **127**
plumbago, 202
privacy &, 126
pruning and training, 64, 126, 127, 213
wormwood, 305
heirloom varieties, **128**, 264
heleniums, 307
helichrysums, 293, 302
*Heliconia* spp., 276, 277
heliotropes, 215
hellebores, 67, 122, **128**, 192, 204, 238, 239, 279, 303
hen and chicken fern (*Asplenium bulbiferum*), 101
hen and chicks (*Echiveria elegans*, *Sempervivum* cvs), 67, 114, 122, 123, 223
herald's trumpet, 58, 219
herb gardens, 84, 89, 93, 129
herb lawns, 112, 122
herbicides, 22, 42, 52, 195, 229, 250, **295**
herbs, 124, **129–31**, 245, 282
heritage roses, 93, 226
heucheras, 238
hibiscus, 38, 54, 67, 126, **132**, 180, 215, 221, 276, 293, 307
hibiscus flower beetles, 132
hildaberry, 31
Hill's weeping fig, 103
hippeastrums, 41, 303
hoes, 267
holidays, **132**
holly, 82
hollyhocks, 12, 70, 71, 93, 94
home offices, 84
honesty, 12, 238, 301
honey fungus, 271
honeydew, 153
honeydew melons, 165
honeyeaters, 29
honeysuckle, 21, 75, 252
Hong Kong orchid tree, 24
hormone rooting powder, 75, 76
hornwort, 287
horse manure, 163, 169
horseradish, 131
horsetails, 34
horticultural fleece, 248
horticultural oils, 195, 283
hoses, hand-held, 290, **291**
hoses, weeper and soaker, **291**
hostas, 34, 67, 78, **133**, 219, 238, 279
hoverflies, 14, 29, 50, 138
hoyas, 75, 137, 219
hyacinths, 40, 41, 67, 75, **133**, 193, 204, 279, 293
hybrid tea roses, 225, **226**
hydrangeas, 32, 33, 55, 67, 74, 94, **134**, 238, 244, 245, 298, 299, 306
hydrogen, 176
hydroponics, **134**
hypericums, 239
hyssop, 93, 131

## I

ice plants, 13, 223
iceberg lettuces, 155
Iceland poppies, 13, 180, 208
Illawarra flame trees, 173, 221
imidacloprid, 14, 56, 165
impatiens, 13, 43, 67, 76, 101, **135**, 198, 238, 245, 248, 302
Indian hawthorns, 21, 61, 301
indigenous plants, **135**, 172
indoor plants
　care of, **136–7**, 291
　carnivorous, **49**
　choice of, 9, 88, 101, 133, **137**, 203
　group benefits, **136–7**
　holidays &, 132
　light &, 137
　scale insects &, 232
ink spot disease, 145
inorganic fertilisers, 102
insect pests, **30**, **138**, 195, **196**
insect predators, **29**, **138**, 182, **286**
insecticidal soaps, 56, 138, 153, 165, 182, 195, 278, 300, 304
insecticides, 52, 111, 138, 195, 220, 286, 300, 304
iodine, 233
*Ipomoea* seeds, 204
irises, 32, 33, 34, 75, **138–9**, 287, 293, 303, 307
Irish strawberry tree, 273
iron, 176, 270
iron chelates, 55
iron deficiency, 10, **55**, 176, 232
iron sulfate, 10, 167
irrigation, 242, 272, 284, 289, **291**, **293**, 306
Italian arum, 238
ivory curl tree, 219
ivy, 21, 38, 113, 122, 137, **139**, 233, 238, 243, 302
ivy mite, 139
ivy tree, 137
ixias, 40, 149, 293
ixoras, **139**, 180

## J

jacarandas, 38, 90, 104, **140**, 215, 237, 244, 276
jacobean lily, 221
Japanese apricot, 303
Japanese barberry, 18
Japanese beautyberry, 82
Japanese blood grass, 118
Japanese box, 37, 67
Japanese cherry, 244
Japanese crab apple, 73
Japanese flag, 138
Japanese glory vine, 18
Japanese iris, 34
Japanese maples, 18, 19, 67, 163, 237, 241, 244
Japanese mock orange, 60, 97, 200
Japanese skimmia, 238, 303
Japanese windflowers, 26, 77, **142**, 192, 238, 279, 298
Japanese wineberry, 31

jasmines, 67, 93 **140–1**, 173, 194, 276, 298
jelly bean plants, 90, 91, 223, 236
Jerusalem artichokes, **142**, 237
Jerusalem sage, 307
Johnny-jump-ups, 183
jonquils, **78**, 133, 307
Judas tree, 104
junipers 122, **143**, 293
juno irises, 138
justicia, red, 221

## K

kaka beaks, 172, 173
kalanchoes, **144**, 257, 293, 303
kale, 67, **144**, 245, 282, 303
kalmias, 238
kangaroo paws, 67, **144–5**, 172, 173, 180, 192, 221, 293
kangaroo vines, 219
kanukas, 172
karo, 173
kelp seaweed, 233
kentia palm, 183
Kentucky bluegrass, 150
kikuyu grass, 150, 250, 295
king protea, 214
kiwi fruit, **145**
kneeling pads, 265
knotted club rush, 173
kohuhu, 173, 200
kowhais, 50, **145**, 172, 173, 232
kowhais moths, 50, 145
kumara *see* sweet potatoes
kunzeas, 173

## L

labelling, **146**, 176
laburnums, 95, 104, 204
lace bugs, 196
lacebarks, 172
lacewings, 14, 29, 138, 278
lady palms, 183
ladybirds, 14, 29, 38, 138, **146**, 182, 232, 278
lady's mantle, 112, 192
lamb's ears, 67, 90, 99, 122, 199, 223, 253, 293
lamb's lettuce, 230
*Lamium maculatum* 'White Nancy', 298
lantana, **146**
lanterns, 158
larkspurs, 13, 26, 70, 99
lasiandras, 263
lattice, 259, **274**
laurustinus, 238
lavenders, 32, 60, 62, 67, 70, 75, 76, 90, 91, 93, 97, 129, 130, 133, **147**, 152, 180, 182, 187, 193, 241, **242**, 244, 253, 282, 293, 306
lawn chamomile, 112, 122
lawn clippings, 150
lawn mowers, **151**
lawn mowing, **150–1**
lawns, 244, 269, 284, 306
　aerating, 148, 167
　bulb clusters in, 40, 41, 149
　design &, 84
　de-thatching, 148–9

dogs &, 88
dry conditions &, 92
fertilisers for, 102, **148**
garden seats &, 112
grass for, 148, 149, **150**, 295
groundcover, 122
laying of, 148, **149**
moss in, 167
tools for, **267**
top-dressing of, 148
trees &, 237
turf for, **148**, **149**
watering of, 148, 237
layering, 130, **152**, 160
leaf cactus *see* zygocactus
leaf colour, 44
leaf cuttings, 9, 46, 309
leaf polishing products, 136
leaf spot, 16, 86
leafhoppers, **153**, 196
leafminers, 56, 196
leafrollers, **159**, 220, 261
Lebanese oregano, 164
leeks, **153**, 162, 238, 245, 282
*Legionella* bacteria, 168
legless lizards, 29
legumes, 10
lemon balm, 130, 131, 198, 238, 245
lemon basil, 23
Lemon butter (recipe), 154
lemon grass, **153**
lemon mint, 166
lemon-scented jasmine, 141
lemon thyme, 263
lemon trees, 38, 92, 95, **154**
lenten rose, 128
leopard plants, 34, 238
lesser periwinkle, 122, 239
lettuces, 15, 39, 88, 134, **154–5**, 162, 174, 179, 230, 234, 236, 238, 245, 263, 281, 282
leucadendrons, 90, 214, 293, 303
leucospermums, 214
lichen, **155**
lighting, 84, 119, **158**, 171, 205, 212
*Ligustrum* berries, 204
lilacs, 74, 75, **158**, 215
lilies, 40, 41, 67, 70, 94, **156–7**
lillypillies, 82, 90, 104, 113, 126, **159**, 171, 173, 219, 241, 252, 268, 293
lily of the valley, 75, 279
lily-of-the-valley shrub, 238
lime sulfur spray, 86, 228, 232
lime trees, **154**
liming agents, 8
line trimmers, 150, 151
lipstick plant, 137
liquid feeds, 102
liriopes, 67, 94, 122, 215, 284
liverworts, 287
living mulch, 168, 269
lizards, 29, 50, 171, 243, 301
loam soil, **159**, 246
lobelias, 13, 32, 67, 219, 221, 234, 238, 248, 286
local authority regulations, 81, 100, 194, 212, 224, 262
loganberries, 31

# INDEX

lomandras, 105, 118
long-tailed mealybug, 165
loopers, **159**, 196
looseleaf lettuces, 154, 155
loppers, 213
Louisiana iris, 287
lovage, 130, 131
love-in-a-mist, 105, 293
lucerne, 93, 269, 280, 281
lungwort, 192, 238
lupins, 70, 71, 80, 119, 192, 204, 232, 235, 269, 280
lychees, 274

## M

macadamias, **177**
machaerina, 173
mâche see lamb's lettuce
macro-nutrients, 176
Madagascar jasmine, 298
madonna lilies, 156, 193
magnesium, 8, 176, 233
magnesium deficiency, **160**, 176, 270
magnesium sulfate see Epsom salts
magnolias, 8, 75, 104, 132, **160**, 298, 299, 303
mahonias, 97, **161**, 241, 293, 303
maidenhair fern (*Adiantum* spp.), 101, 137, 173
maidenhair tree (*Ginkgo biloba*), 18, 19
mail order, 44, 281, 305
maldison, 14, 50, 56, 120, 165, 232, 261, 278
mancozeb, 15, 88, 121, 228
mandarins, **161**
mandevillas, 58, 67, 81, **161**, 194, 274, 276
manganese, 176, 270
manganese deficiency, **162**, 176, 270
manganese sulfate, 162
mangoes, 15, **162**
mangosteen, 275
manual cultivators, 267
manuka, 173, 261
manures, 102, **119**, **162–3**, 169, 175, 197, 232, 239, 269, 280, 283
maples, 18, 19, 89, **163**, **198**, 303
marantas, 219, 260, 276
March lilies see belladonna lilies
Marguerite daisies, 79, 99
marigolds, 13, 32, 34, 45, 67, 70, 75, 80, 103, 138, **164**, 171, 232, 244, 282, 293, 300
marjoram, 93, 129, 130, **164**, 198
marrows, 198, 214, 220
marsh marigolds, 34, 287
mat rush, 219
may, 298
meadow rue, 238
mealy sage, 231
mealybugs, 46, **165**, 182, 196
measuring rods, 267
medicinal plants, 11, **165**, 184, 261
Mediterranean fruit fly, 108

Mediterranean gardens, 113
Mediterranean spurge, 97
melaleucas see paperbarks
melons, 15, **165**, 234
Menzies banksia, 22
metal fences, 100
metallic flea beetle, 54, 132
metrosideros, **166**, 172, 173
Mexican orange blossom, 97, 193
Mexican sage bush, 231, 303
mibuna, 16, 230
Michaelmas daisies, 43
micro-environments, 218
micro-irrigation, **291**
micro-nutrients, 176
mignonette, 12, 193
mildew, 17, 73, 74, 86, **88**, 111, 117, 162, **211**, 228
milk sprays, 86
milk thistle, **296**
millipedes, 138, 196
miltonias, 181
mineral pesticides, 195
miner's lettuce, 230
mini mondo grass, 118, 122
miniature roses, 225, **226**
mint, 93, 129, 130, **166**, 198, 238, 245, 302
mint bush, 97, 215, 241
mirror bush, 60, 61
mirrors, 244, **285**
mites, 29, **38**, 41, 143, 146, 195, 196, 264, **278**
miticides, 195
mizuna, 16, 230
mock orange (*Philadelphus* spp.), 193, 241, 244, 298 see also Japanese mock orange; murrayas
molluscicides, 195
molybdenum, 176, 270
mondo grass, 21, 67, 90, 118, 122, 244, 284
monkey flowers, 238
monkshood, 192, 204
monstera, native, 219
Moreton Bay fig, 103
Moroccan glory vine, 32, 99, 122
mosaic virus, 196
mosquitoes, 138, **167**, 261
mosses, **167**, 287
moth orchid, 181
mother-in-law's tongue, 137
moths and moth traps, 30, 50, 107, 145, 220, 261
mould, grey, 86, **121**
see also sooty mould
mountain ash, 104, 304
mountain cabbage tree, 68
mountain ebony, 24
mulberries, **167**
mulch, 93, **168**, 169, 174, 175, 286, **292**, 306
mulch mat, 168, 292
mulching, 20, 85, 92, 93, 96, 109, 114, 168, 218, 232, 238–9, 290
mullein, 70
muriate of potash, 210
murrayas, 90, 97, **168–9**, 193, 242, 244, 270, 293, 298

mushroom compost, 57, 109, **169**, 218, 239, 269
mushrooms, **169**
mustard clover, 232
mustard greens, 16, 119, 269
mustard seed sprouts, 250
myclobutanil, 211, 228
myrtles, 97, 268

## N

'naked ladies' see belladonna lilies
nandinas, 18, **170**, 213, 241, 293
napuka see purple hebe
narcissus, 40, 41, **78**, 193, 204
nashi pears, 190
nasturtiums, 26, 43, 54, 58, 67, 88, 93, 99, **170**, 180, 236, 249, 253, 264, 293, 307
Natal plum, 82
native animals, **171**, 172
native bees, 27
native clematis, 173, 298
native frangipani, 106, 173
native gardenia, 219
native ginger, 238, 279
native monstera, 219
native plants, 8, 27, 42, 60, 82, 90, 99, 103, 112, 135, 171, **172–3**, 181, 218, 219, 232, 301
native rosemaries, 99, 173, 293
see also coastal rosemary
native violets, 122, 219, 253, 279, 285
necklace fern, 173
nectarines, 92, 95, 98, 108, **189**, 263
nematicides, 195
nematodes, 16, 164, **171**, 195, 196, 232, 264
nerines, 40
nettles see stinging nettle
New Zealand cabbage tree moth, 50
New Zealand Christmas bush see pohutukawa
New Zealand flax, 26, 38, 67, 105, **172**, 173, 219, 293, 303
New Zealand jasmine, 173
New Zealand spinach, 249
New Zealand tea tree, 261
newspaper, **174**, 281, 295
ngaio, 173
nicotianas, 70, **174**, 193, 238
night flowers, **298**
night-scented stocks, 193, 253
nikau palm, 183
nitrate of potash, 210
nitrate of soda, 174
nitrogen, **174**, 176, 179, 210
nitrogen deficiency, 176
no-dig gardening, **175**, 281
noise reduction, 194, 218, **244**
Norfolk Island hibiscus, 60
Norway maple, 163
November lily, 156, 157
'nurse' plants, 99, 294
nursery areas, **176**
nut grass, **297**

nutrient deficiency, 10, 55, 160, 162, **176**, 232, 270
nutrients, **176**
nuts, **177**

## O

oak-leaf hydrangea, 134
oaks, 18
oats, 280
obelisk supports, 259
offsets, **178**
old-fashioned roses, **226**
oleanders, 60, 67, 75, 90, 126, **178–9**, 204, 293
olives, 90, **178–9**, 293
omethoate, 304
onion flies, 262
onion weeds, **297**
onions, 41, 62, 88, 160, 162, 171, **179**, 232, 263, 281, 282
orange flowers, 61, 164, **180**, 221, 284, 307
orange jessamine see murrayas
oranges, **180**
orchid cactus, 137
orchid tree, 24
orchids, 90, 137, **181**, 249, 250, 276
oregano, 124, **164**, 198
Oregon grape, 18, 161
organic fertilisers, 102, 194
organic gardening, **182**, 194, 269, **283**
organic sprays, 295, 304
oriental poppies, 80, 221
ornamental cherries, 53, 104
ornamental grapevines, 117
ornamental grasses, 105, **118–19**, 244, 287
ornamental kale, 303
ornamental pear, 18
ornamental plum, 273
ornamental rhubarb, 105
osmanthus, 193, 238
osteospermum, 298
outdoor mirrors, 244, **285**
oxeye daisies, 301
oxygen, 176

## P

paintbrush lily, 238
painted lady, 137
pak choy see bok choy
palms, 67, **183**, 218, **219**, 245, 260, 276, 293
Panama disease, 22
panda plants, 144
*Pandorea* 'Lady Di', 298
pansies, 11, 13, 67, 80, 103, 174, **183**, 303, 307
papaya fruit fly, 108
papayas see pawpaws
paper daisies, 13, 67, 79, 199, 232, 301, 307
paper wasps, 286
paperbarks, 90, 99, 173, **184**, 198, 261, 293
papyrus, 34
parasitic pests, 29, 30
parasitic wasps, 29, 50, 120, 153, 159, 182, 232, 300, 304
parent bedrock, 247

315

# INDEX

parsley, 124, 129, 130, **184**, 238, 245, 302
parsnips, **185**, 281, 282
paspalum, **297**
passionfruit, 58, 120, **185**, 245, 274
Paterson's curse, 200
paths, 94, **186**, 245, 284
patio plants, 92, 143, 187, 264
patios, **187**, 188, 262
patty pan squash, 308
pavers and paving, 187, **188**, 244, 245
pawpaws, **189**
pea straw, 281
peace lily, 137
peach leaf curl disease, 189
peaches, 92, 95, 98, 104, 108, 110, **189**, 263
pears, 95, 104, **190**, 304
peas, 39, 113, 119, 120, 162, **190**, 232, 235, 245, 282
peat and peat substitutes, **191**, 211
pecans, **177**
pelargoniums *see* geraniums and pelargoniums
pellitory asthma weed, **297**
pennyroyal, 138, 166
penstemons, 192, 198
peonies, 74, **191**, 199
pepepe *see* machaerina
peppermint, 166
perennial candytuft, 298
perennial rye grass, 15
perennial thistle, **297**
perennial weeds, 295, **297**
perennials, 67, 211, 232, 269
    beds and borders, 26
    butterflies &, 43
    cottage garden, 70
    deadheading, 80
    dividing, 87
    drought-tolerant, 293
    fast-growing, 99
    overview of, **192**
    pruning, 213
    shady garden, **238**
    tropical garden, 276
perfumed plants, 97, 112, 113, 115, 132, 158, 168, **193**, 241, 253, 259, 279
pergolas, 117, 187, **194–5**, 233, 236, 285
periwinkles, 122, 239, 279
perlite, 57, 134
permaculture, **194**
permethrin, 39, 50, 232
Persian violet, 137
persimmons, 82
perspective and views, **284–5**
pesticides, 14, 39, 50, 93, 107, 108, 119, 182, **195**, 229, 232, **250**, 283
pests
    bird, **30**, 31, 34, 53, **109**, 160, 171, **190**
    creature, **196**
    insect, **30**, **138**, 195, **196**
    *see also under name eg* caterpillars

petal blight, 196
petroleum oil sprays, 14, 56, 165, 195, 232, 300, 304
petunias, 12, 13, 67, 80, 94, 103, **196–7**, 198, 234, 242, 244, 253, 286, 302
pH tests *see* soil pH
pheromones, 30
philodendrons, 75, 94, 137, 152, 219
phlox, 74, 174, 193
phosphates, **197**
phosphorus, 176, 197
phosphorus deficiency, 176
photinias, 90, 126, **197**, 241, 244, 293
phytophthora root rot, 86, 184, **198**
*Phytoseiulus persimilis*, 278
pickerel rush, 287
pickling, 74
pickling onions, 179
pigeon manure, 163
pigface, 42, 60, 90, 243, 293
piggyback plant, 137
pinching out, 12, 23, 55, **198**, 213, 264, 273
pincushion flower, 215, 293
pine trees, 42, 62, 212–13
pineapple, 274
pineapple mint, 166
pink flowers, **199**
pink jasmine, 140
pink lasiandra, 263
pinks, **48**, 67, 122, 193, 198, 199, 223, 232, 253, 293
pirimiphos-methyl, 165
pittosporums, 99, **200**
plant names, **200**
planting, **200–1**, 292
planting and sowing tools, **267**
planting plans, **202**
plastic pots, 65, 66
play areas, 54, 84
plectranthus, 122, 192, 215, 219, 239, 279
plumbago, 32, 33, **202**, 242, 293
plums, 18, 92, 109, **203**, 263
poached egg plant, 138
pohutukawa, 60, 166, 173, 221, 232
poincianas, 104, 237
poinsettias, 90, 97, 137, 198, **203**, 221, 303
poisonous plants, 75, 77, 106, 128, 179, **204**, 222
polka dot plant, 137
pollination, **204**
pollution, 218, 244
polyanthus, 13, 67, **205**, 303
polyethylene water tanks, 288
pomegranates, **205**, 293
pomelos, 117
pompom tree, 104, 199
pond sedge, 287
pond skaters, 301
ponds and pools, 194, **206–7**, 242, 269, **287**, 301
pondweed, 287
poppies, 80, 99, **208–9**, 221, 293, 303, 307

Port Jackson fig, 103
port wine magnolia, 160
portulaca, 67, 230, 293
possums, 160, 171, **205**, 301
pot marigolds *see* calendulas
pot marjoram, 164
potash, 103, **210**
potassium, 176, 233
potassium deficiency, 176
potato blight, 182
potato vine, 81, 274
potatoes, 41, 62, 160, 194, **210**, 220, 264, 280, 282
*Potentilla* spp., 192, 299
pots
    balconies &, 21
    blueberries &, 34
    bonsai &, 35
    choosing plants for, **67**
    chrysanthemums &, 55
    cleaning of, 113
    coastal gardens &, 61
    cordylines &, 68
    courtyard gardens &, 72
    drainage &, 66, 67
    fruit trees/bushes &, 67, 92, **108–9**
    herb gardens &, **129**, 245
    hyacinths &, 133
    hydroponics &, 134
    olives &, 179
    orchids &, 181
    patios &, 92, 129, 187
    perennials &, 192, 245
    recycling &, 220
    rooftop gardens &, 224
    small city gardens &, 244, **245**
    sowing seeds in, 248
    standards &, 252
    strawberries &, **255**
    succulents &, 41, 46, 245
    tomatoes &, 264
    trace elements &, 270
    trees &, 67, **272–3**
    types of, **65**, 66
    vegetables grown in, **282**
    watering strategies for, **67**, 290, 291
    yuccas &, 307
    *see also* indoor plants; repotting
potting mix, **67**, 181, **211**, 256, 282, 309
potting on, 222
poultry manure, 163, 281
powdery mildew, 17, 73, 86, 162, **211**, 228
power tools, 85, **229**
pratia, 122
prayer plant, 219, 260, 276
predatory insects, **29**, **138**, 182, **286**
pressed flowers, 89
pricking out, 235
pride of De Kaap, 24
pride of Madeira, 60, 215
primroses, 75, 239
primulas, 137, 204, **205**, 238, 303
privets, 193
propagating mix, 76, 77, 248

propagation equipment, **212**, 248
proteas, 8, 57, 163, 197, **214**, 303
pruning
    annuals, 213
    grevilleas, 121
    hedges, 126, 127, 213
    hydrangeas, 134
    lilacs, 158
    perennials, 213
    roses, **225**, **228**, **252**
    shrubs, **241**
    tips on, **212–13**
    tomatoes, 264
    topiary &, **268**
    trees and bushes, **110**, 180, **212–13**, 271, 273
    violets, 285
    wisteria, 304
pruning cuts, 213
pruning tools, **213**, 233, 265, **266–7**, **268**
psyllids, 159, 196
puka, 173, 219
pumpkins, 120, 198, **214–15**, 245
purple flowers, **215**, 221, 307
purple fountain grass, 118
purple-fringed riccia, 287
purple hebe, 173
purple sage, 75
purple wreath, 276
purslane, 230
pyracanthas, 82, 88, 304
pyrethrum, 14, 39, 45, 50, 56, 132, 182, 195, 300, 304
pyrethrum daisies, 232

# Q–R

quassia, 182, 205
Queensland blue couch, 150
Queensland fruit fly, 108
Quince jam (recipe), 216
quinces, 108, 180, **216**, 303
rabbit-ear iris, 287
rabbits, 258, 273
radicchio, 230
radichetta, 230
radishes, 54, 62, **217**, 281
rainbow chard, 245, 249
rainforest gardens, **218–19**, 239, 250, 276, **279**
rainwater tanks, 84, 92, **288–9**, 291, 306
raised garden beds, 57, 89, 175, **217**, 242, 245, 269
rakes, 265, 266, 267
rambling roses, 225, 226, 236, 252, 274, 298
rambutan, 275
rangoon creeper, 276
raspberries, 109, 110, 114, 121, **220**
ratas, 166, 173
recipes, 23 154, 216
recycling, 213, **220**, 243, **253**, 254, 269, 284, 291
red currants, 110
red-flowering gum, 173
red flowers, 61, 96, **221**, 284, 302, 307
red heather, 125

316

# INDEX

red hot pokers, 61, 84, 87, 180, 192
red justicia, 221
red worms, 305
redbuds, 18, 19, 95, 237
reeds and rushes, 34, 173
renga lily, 173
repotting, **222**
residual current device, 229
residual herbicides, 295
retaining structures, 243, 262
rewarewas, 214
rex begonias, 28, 238
rhododendrons, 8, 55, 62, 152, 198, **222**, 237, 238, 270, 276
rhubarb, **222**
riberries, 82, 104, 159
riccia, 287
robinias, 67, 104
rock cotoneaster, 303
rock garden violet, 279
rock gardens, **223**, 243, 301
rock lily, 181, 219
rock mobility, **254**
rock orchid, 218, 219
rock phosphate, 197
rock rose, 60, 67, 293, 298
rocket, **224**, 230
rockmelons, 165
rockwool, 134
rooftop gardens, **224**
root cuttings, 75, 77
root flies, 224
root knot nematodes, 171, 232, 264
rosary vine, 137
rose apple, 219
rose hips, 82, 226
rose of Sharon, 132
rosemary, 42, 60, 93, 97, 122, 129, 130, 152, 182, 187, 193, 223, **224**, 241, 245, 253, 268, 282, 293, 306
rosemary, native, 99, 173, 293
roses, 70, 80, 88, 293
  care and maintenance of, **225**, **228**
  climbing, 57, 58, 193, 225, **226**, 228, 274
  coastal gardens &, 60
  companion plants for, 62, 114
  container gardening &, 67
  deadheading, 228
  drying, 89
  floribundas, 225, **226**, 227
  flower meanings &, 75
  groundcover, 122, 225, **226**
  hardwood cuttings of, 76
  heritage, 93, 226
  hybrid teas, 225, **226**, 227
  miniature, 225, **226**
  old-fashioned, **226**
  perfume of, 193
  pests and diseases of, 39, 121, 211, **228**, 232, 233
  pinching out, 198
  planting of, 200, **225**, 228
  pruning of, **225**, **228**
  rambling, 225, **226**, 228, 274
  shrub, 225
  standard, 225

training of, 228, 274
watering of, **225**
wild, **226**, 227
rosy maidenhair, 173
rotary hoes, 85, 269
rotenone, 50
rough tree fern, 173
royal agave, 10
royal fern, 34
royal palms, 219, 276
rubbish bins, 84
rudbeckias, 32, 192, 293
runner beans, 25, 26, 58, 62, 88, 113, 220, 235, 237, 281, 282
rushes and reeds, 34, 173
Russian sage, 192
Russian tarragon, 261
rusts, 86, 111, 143, 196
rye, 119
rye grass, 15

## S

sacred bamboo, 18, 94, 303
safety
  chemicals &, 52, 93, **229**, **250**, **295**
  clothing &, **229**
  digging &, 85
  edible flowers &, 93
  garden lighting &, 158
  garden tools &, 126, **229**, 265
  hot weather &, 125
  ivy &, 139
  lawn mowing &, 150, 151
  organic mulches &, 168
  poisonous plants &, 75, 77, 97, 103, 106, 179, **204**
  potting mix &, 211
  swimming pools &, **260**
  trees &, 272
saffron, 249
sage, 45, 93, 130, 193, 198, **229**, 282
sage bush, 303
sage-leaf rock rose, 298
salad burnet, 93
salad leaves, **230**, 281, 282
salad sprouts, 250
salt-tolerant plants, **60**, 61
saltbush see coastal saltbush
salvation Jane see Paterson's curse
salvias, 13, 26, 32, 67, 80, 99, 180, 192, 198, 199, 215, **231**, 293
sand dune stabilisation, 60
sandpits, 54
sandstone, 188
sandy soil, 60, 160, **232**, 246, 270, 280
'sango-kaku' maple, 303
satsumas, 56
savory, 93, 131
sawdust, **231**
sawfly larvae, 196
saws, 213, **265**, 266
scabs, 86
scale insects, 56, 143, 182, 195, 196, 228, **232**
scallions, 179

scallop squash see patty pan squash
scarlet oak, 18
scarlet sage, 231
scaveola see fan flowers
scoria, 134
Scotch heather, 125
screening and privacy, 173
screens and cover-ups, **233**, 261, 274, 282, 285, 294
screw pine, 173
sculpture, 113, 269
sea holly, 192, 232, 293
sealing wax palm, 183
seaside daisy, 122, 192, 253
seaside gardens see coastal gardens
seasons and design, 84
seating areas, 187
seaweed, **233**, 269
seaweed liquid fertilisers, 233, 270
secateurs, 213, **233**, 266
sedge, giant umbrella, 173
sedge, pond, 287
sedums, 26, 43, 67, 192, **236**, 244, 257, 293, 301
seed purchase, 235
seed-raising mix, 76, 234, 248
seed savers/saving, 128, 235
seed trays, 234, 235
seedlings
  hardening off, 235, 270
  preventing damping off in, **234**
  pricking/thinning out of **235**, **262–3**, 281
  transplanting of, **270**
  vegetable, **281**
seeds
  birds &, 235
  buying and saving, **235**
  firming in, **248**
  growing medium for, 234, **248**
  helping germination of, **234–5**, **248**
  sowing dates for, 247
  storage of, **235**
  testing viability of, **247**
  vegetable, 234, **235**, 248, **281**
  see also sowing seed
seeds, culinary, 130
selective herbicides, 295
semi-hardwood cuttings, 76
sempervivums, 257, 293
  see also hen and chicks
senecios, 257, 293
shade, **236–7**, 293
shade calculations, 236
shade lovers, 122, 279
shade trees, **237**, 272
shadecloth, 120, 125
shadehouses see greenhouses and shadehouses
shady gardens, 173, **238–9**, 243
shallots, 162, **179**, 238, **240**, 282
she-oaks, 60, 173, 232
shearing plants, 213, **242**
shears, 126, 213, 242, 266, 267, 268
sheds, 84, **254–5**

sheep manure, 163
sheep shears, 268
sheet mulches, 168
shell ginger, 199
shelling peas, 190
shelterbelts, 302
shepherd's purse, **296**
Shirley poppies, 208, 209
shopping for plants, **44**
shore juniper, 143
showy sedum, 236, 301
shrubs, **240–1**
Siberian flag, 138
sideshoots see offsets
sight-lines, 284
silica gel, 89
silk tassel bush, 82, 303
silky oaks, 90, 121, 219
silver birch, 303
silver cushion bush, 60
silver leaf, 189
silverbeet, 249, 281
silverberry, 303
silverbush, 298
skinks, 29
slate, 188
slaters, 196
slender bamboo, 260
sloping sites, 89, 100, 122, 223, **242–3**, 262
slugs, 133, 195, 196, 197, 220, **243**, 258, 283
small gardens, 104, 230, **244–5**, 272, 273, **284–5**, 304
smoke bush, 18
snails, 133, 195, 196, 197, 220, **243**, 283
snake vine see golden guinea vine
snapdragons, 12, 13, 67, 80, 174, 198, 221, 234
sneezeweeds, 87, 180
  see also heleniums
snow-in-summer (*Cerastium tomentosum*), 99, 122, 253, 293
snow-in-summer (*Melaleuca linariifolia*), 298
snow on the mountain, 97
snow peas, 190, 281
snowball bush, 82
snowberries, 82, 303
snowdrops, **246**
snowflakes, 41, 67, **246**, 298, 303
soaps see insecticidal soaps
sodium, 233
sodium chloride, 295
soft tree ferns, 101, 173
softwood cuttings, 76
soil
  acid, **8**, 10, 20, 34, 62, 125, 134, 160, 246, 247, 280
  alkaline, 8, **10**, 55, 56, 57, 62, 117, 134, 160, 246, 247, 280
  annuals &, 12, 103
  clay, **57**, 85, 87, 89, 102, 246, 280
  compacting of, 85, 269
  courtyard garden, 73
  digging, **85**
  drainage &, **89**

317

# INDEX

frost &, 107
fruit trees and bushes &, **108**
greener gardening &, 119
liming of, 8, 10, 280
loam, **159**, 246
magnesium deficiency in, **160**
manganese deficiency in, **162**
perennials &, 103
phosphates &, 197
preserving, 135, 247, 262
sandy, 60, 160, **232**, 246, 270, 280
texture of, **246**
vegetable gardens &, 280
waterwise gardening &, 292
wildflower meadows &, 300
see also crop rotation
soil analysis **246–7**
soil erosion, 243, 262
soil pH, 8, 10, 134, 182, 246, 247, 270, 280
soil profile, **246–7**
solar power, 119, 158
Solomon's seal, 238
sooty mould, 153, 196, 300
sour cherries, 53
sour sob, **297**
soursop, 274
sow thistle, **296**
sowing and planting tools, **267**
sowing seed
  directly, **234**, **235**, 248
  pots or trays &, **234**, **235**, 248
  preparation for, 234, **246–7**
  vegetables &, 234, **235**, 248, **281**
  wildflower meadows &, 300, 301
spades, 85, 266
spaniards, 173
Spanish irises, 138
sparaxis, 40
spearmint, 166
sphagnum moss, 191
spices, **248–9**
spider lily, 293
spiders, 29
spinach, 162, 236, **249**, 281, 282
spined citrus bugs, 56
split trunks, 271
sports areas, 84
spraying, **250**
spring beauty see miner's lettuce
spring onions, **179**, 281, 282
spring starflower, 41
sprinklers, **291**
sprouting seeds, 250
spurges, 97
squashes, 198, 214, 245, 308
staghorns, 218, 219
stains (timber), 81
stakes and staking, **251**, 264, 273
standards, **252**
star gardenia, 113
star jasmine, 58, 94, 122, 140, 233, 253, 274, 298
star magnolia, 160
star of Bethlehem, 293
statice, 70, 215
statues, 113, 269

steel tanks, 288–9
stepping stones, **254**
steps, **252–3**
sticky wattle, 294
stinging nettle, **297**
stocks, 67, 193, **253**
stone, 188, 223, 252, **254**, 262
stone mulch, 254
stonecrop, 43
storage, **254–5**
straw, 168, 269
strawberries, 62, 108, 109, 121, 124, 128, 134, 182, 198, 245, **255**
strawflowers see paper daisies
strelitzias, 90, 180, 192, **258**, 293, 303
string of hearts, 137
stringybark eucalyptus, 42
subsoil, 247, 262
succulents, 178, 187, 223, 232, 236, 245, **256–7** 284, 293
sugar snap peas, 190, 281
sugarbush, 214
sulfate of potash, 210
sulfur, 34, 38, 55, 88, 134, 162, 176, 182, 232, 233
summer savory, 131
summer squash, 198, 214, **308**
sun plant, 293
sunflowers, 54, 75, 237, 245, **258**, 307
superphosphate of lime, 197
supports
  bare-root tree, 251
  bean, **25**, 37, 245
  bed and border, 26
  bulb, 40, 251
  cleaning, 113
  clematis, 57
  climber, 58, 245
  coastal garden tree brace, 60
  creative, **259**
  dahlia, 78
  delphinium, 82
  geometric, **258–9**
  gladioli, 115
  kiwi fruit, 145
  lily, 156
  passionfruit, 185
  pea, 190, 245
  ready made, 258
  shrub, 240
  small city garden, 245
  sweet pea, 259
  tomato, 264
  tree, 273
  types of, **258**
  vertical garden, **284**
  wall plantings, 286
  wisteria, 304
  see also stakes and staking; trellises
swamp foxtail, 118
swamp lily (*Crinum pedunculatum*), 219
swamp lily (*Ottelia ovalifolia*), 287
swamp musk, 173
swamp she-oaks, 232
swedes, **278**, 282

sweet basil, 23
sweet box, 97, 193
sweet cherries, 53
sweet daphne, 193
sweet flag, 287
sweet marjoram, 164
sweet peas, 12, 13, 26, 58, 62, 67, 70, 75, 198, 199, 234, **259**
sweet peppers see capsicums
sweet potatoes, 194, **260**
sweet viburnum, 126
sweet violets, 279, 285
sweet William, 48, 67
swimming pools, 84, 88, 183, 188, **260**
Swiss chard see silverbeet
switch grass, 105
sycamore maple, 163
systemic insecticides/herbicides, 286, 295, 296

## T

*Tabebuia chrysantha*, 244
tall fescue grass, 150
tamarillo, 275
tangelos, **161**
tanks see rainwater tanks
tansy, 138
tarragon, 198, **261**
tassel flowers, 221
tassel sedge, 287
taufluvalinate, 50
*Taxus*, 204
tayberries, 31
tea tree oil, 184, 185, 261
tea tree web moth, 261
tea trees, 27, 42, 60, 90, 172, 173, **261**, 293
terraces, 242, **262**, 286, 293
terracotta pots, 65, 66, 109, 113
tetanus injections, 229
*Thevetia* berries, 204
thinning, **262–3**, 281
thistles, 296, 297
three kings climber, 173
thrift, 192, 199
thrips, 196, 220, 278
thymes, 27, 67, 93, 112, 122, 124, 129, 130, 165, 182, 193, 245, 253, **263**, 282, 293, 302
ti kouka see cordylines
tibouchinas, 215, **263**
tiger worms, 305
timber bench seats, 112
timber decks, **81**, 187
timber fences, 100
toads, 29
tobacco plants see nicotianas
tomatillos, 264
tomato caterpillars, 264
tomato hook worms, 264
tomatoes, 15, 23, 39, 108, 124, 128, 134, 160, 162, 182, **198**, **264**, 281, 282, 300, 302
tools, 76, 174
  care and maintenance of, 113, **265**, 284
  digging and cultivating, 85, **266–7**
  grafting, 116
  lawns and lawn care, **151**, 267

planting and sowing, **267**
pruning and trimming, **213**, **233**, 265, **266**, 268
safety &, 126, **229**, 265
shearing, **126**, 127, 242
weeding, **267**
topiary, 21, **268**
topsoil, 247, 262, **269**
*Toxicodendron*, 204
trace elements, 176, 232, 233, **270**
training
  balcony plants, 21
  blackberry branches, 31
  clematis, 57
  conifers, 64
  deck climbers, 81
  espaliers, **95**, 190, 263, 286
  fan, **98**
  fruit trees, 14, 98, 110, 198
  fruit vines, 117
  lollipop bay trees, 24
  passionfruit, 185
  pears, 190
  roses, 198, 228, 252, 274
  standards, **252**
  tibouchinas, 263
  trellises &, 274
  see also bonsai; topiary
transforming a garden, **269**
transplant shock, **270**, 281
transplanting, **271–2**, 281
traps, 30, 107, 153, **243**
traveller's palm, 276, 277
tree begonias, 28, 101, 238
tree collars, 196, 205
tree ferns, **101**, 105, 173, 219, 239
tree fuchsias, 173
tree guards, 273
tree houses, 167
tree ivy, 75
tree peonies, 191
tree repairs, **271**
tree ties, 251, 273
tree tomatoes, 82
trees
  advice on, **272**
  autumn planting, **272–3**
  choice of, **272**
  drought &, 237, 293
  fertilising, 102
  flowering, **104**
  gardens size &, **244**, **273**
  lawn under, 237
  planting, **272–3**
  pruning, **212–13**, 271, 273
  rainforest garden, 218, 219, 239
  repairing, **271**
  safety &, **272**
  shade, **237**, **238**, 272
  sleeve protectors for, 273
  transplanting, **270–1**
  tropical garden, 276
  watering, 237, 272, 273
  see also fruit trees and bushes; stakes and staking; topiary
trellises, 259, **274**, 286
triangle palm, 276

318

# INDEX

trident maple, 163
triforine, 228
tropical fruits, 274–5
tropical gardens, **276–7**
trowels, 267
true myrtle, 97
trumpet lilies, 156
trumpet trees, 104, 237, 276
trumpet vine, 58, 274
tsoi sum *see* bok choy
tubular fences, 100
tuckeroo, 60
tulip tree, 18
tulips, 40, 41, 67, **275**
tulipwoods, 237
tummelberries, 31
tupelo, 18
Turk's cap lily, 156
turmeric, 248, 249
turnips, 160, 224, **278**, 282
tussock grasses, 118
two-spotted mites, 143, 146, 182, 196, **278**

## U

umbrella plant, 137
umbrella sedge, giant, 173
umbrella trees, 219
underplanting, **279**
understorey plantings, 218, 219, **279**
uplighting, 158
urea, 174

## V

valerian, 192, 221
vanilla pods, 249
vegetable gardens, 62, 84, 88, **280–3**
vegetables, 211
  climatic considerations &, **282**
  companion crops, **282**, 283
  container growing of, **282**
  crop rotation &, **282**, **283**
  feeding, 154–5, **280**, 281, 282
  grouping, 282
  heirloom varieties of, 128
  marking rows in, **281**
  no-dig gardening &, **175**, **281**
  organic gardening &, **283**
  permaculture &, 194
  pests and diseases &, 282, **283**
  planting know-how, 281
  raised garden beds for, **217**
  record keeping &, 283
  seed or seedlings, 234, 235, 248, **281**
  shade &, 236, 237, 238
  small city gardens &, 245
  sowing, 234, **235**, **248**, **281**
  storing, 255
  thinning, 281
  windy sites &, 302
  *see also* Asian vegetables
veitchberries, 31
veldt daisies *see* African daisies
velvet elephant's ears, 144
verbenas, 67, 174, 242, 301
vermiculite, 57, 134, 218, 248
vertical gardens, **284**
verticillium wilt, 94

viburnums, 74, 97, 126, 293
views and perspective, **284–5**
violas, 11, 13, 75, **183**, 238
violets, 93, 238, **285**
violets, native, 122, 219, 253, 279, 285
violets, rock garden, 279
violets, sweet, 279, 285
Virginia creeper, 18, 19
Virginia stock, 253
viruses, 86, 182, 220, **284**

## W

walking stick palm, 219
wall-mounted window boxes, 302
wallflowers, 70, 193, 215, 307
walls
  brick, 262, 286
  courtyard garden, 72
  espaliers &, 95, 286
  hiding, 286
  ivy &, 139
  planting, **286**
  small city gardens &, 244
  terraces &, 262, 286
  vertical gardens &, 284
walnuts, **177**
wandering jew, **297**
waratahs, 57, 214, 221, 303
warrigal greens, 249
wasps, 14, 29, 45, 50, 56, 120, 153, 159, 182, 232, **286**, 300, 304
water beetles, 301
water chestnuts, 194
water crowfoot, 287
water features, 158, **206–7**, 243, 244, 285
  *see also* fountains; ponds and pools
water ferns, 287
water forget-me-not, 287
water fringe, 287
water harvesting systems, **289**
water irises, **138**, 139, 287
water milfoils, 287
water mint, 287
water moss *see* common water moss
water plants, 206, **287**
water primrose, 287
water recycling, 92, 284, 291, 293
water restrictions, 92, 260, 290, 291
water snails, 207
water-storing crystals, 61, 67, 124, 230
water tanks, 84, 92, **288–9**, 291, 306
water taps, 84
water violet, 287
waterblommetjie, 287
watercress, 230
waterfalls, 243
watering
  container gardens, 67, 282, 290, 291
  deep soaking, 290
  dry conditions &, 92, 237, 239, 290

  foliage &, 290
  hanging baskets, 124, 291
  holidays &, 132
  hot weather &, 125
  indoor plants, 136, 137, 291
  lawns, 148, 237
  methods of, **290**, **291**
  mulch &, 290
  rainforest gardens, 218
  roses, **225**
  spinach and silverbeet, 249
  times for, **290**
  waterwise gardening &, **293**
  wind &, 290
  *see also* xeriscaping
watering basins, **290**
watering cans, **291**, 292
watering equipment, 290, **291**
watering systems, 239
watering zones, **306**
waterlilies, 287
watermelons, **294**
waterwise gardening, **292–3**
wattles, 27, 30, 60, 90, 99, 112, 172, 173, 174, 197, 232, 235, 286, 293, **294**, 303, 307
wax flower, 137
waxflower, 97
weaver's bamboo, 22
wedge grafts, 116
weed mats, 254, 295
weeding tools, **267**
weedkillers, 52, 119, **295**
weeds, 82, 269
  annual, **296**
  bamboo as, 22
  blackberries as, 31
  bog garden, 34
  bush regeneration &, 42
  buying plants &, 44
  companion planting &, 62
  composting of, 63
  digging &, 85
  heather as, 125
  invasive, 295
  lantana as, **146**
  management of, **295**
  mulching &, 168, 292
  nasturtiums as, 170
  paths and driveways &, **295**
  patios &, 187
  perennial, 295, **297**
  perfumed, 193
  recycling &, 220
  seed of, 295
  stone &, 254
  types, of, **296–7**
  vegetable gardens &, 281, 283
weeping figs, 21, 103
weevils, 196
weigela, 241
Welsh onions, 179
whauwhaupaku *see* five finger
wheelbarrows, 265
wheki *see* rough tree fern
white cedar, 219, 293, 303
white correa 60, 243
white currants, 110
white flowers, 61, **298–9**
white kunzea, 60
white louse scale, 232

white mulberry, 167
white oil, 56, 232, 300
white wisteria, 298
whiteflies, 16, 30, 164, 170, 182, 196, 264, **300**
wild marjoram *see* oregano
wild rocket, 224
wild roses, **226**, 301
wildflower meadows, **300–1**
wildlife havens, 207, 218, **301**
wildlife ponds, 84
willow myrtle, 198, 293
wilts, 86, 264
wind, 290, **302**
windbreaks, 60, 61, 126, 218, 293, 294, **302**
window boxes, 94, 129, **302–3**
window pane palm, 183
winter daphne, 97
winter display, **303**
winter field beans, 175
winter iris, 303
winter jasmine, 140
winter melons, 165
winter oil, 165, 278
winter purslane *see* miner's lettuce
winter savory, 131
winter squash, 214, 215
wisterias, 58, 67, 81, 113, 194, 204, 252, 298, **304**
witch hazel, 241, 303, 307
witlof, 230
wong bok *see* Chinese cabbage
wonga wonga vine, 58, 173
wood ash, 103, 210
woodchips, 168
wooden containers, 65, 66
woodland tobacco, 174
woodlands, 239, **279**
woolly aphids, **304**
worm farms, **304–5**
wormwoods, 97, 105, 138, 232, 293, **305**
wreath plant, 58, 276
wrens, 29

## X–Z

xeriscaping, 92, **306**
yarrows, 67, 70, 74, 99, 192, 293, 307
yellow bladderwort, 287
yellow flax, 307
yellow flowers, 61, **307**
yellow jasmine, 141
yesterday, today and tomorrow, 97
yew, 113, 213, 252, 268
youngberries, 31
yuccas, 38, 67, 256, 293, **307**
Yulan magnolia, 160
zebra plant, 137
zephyranthes, 40
zinc, 176, 270
zineb, 15, 88, 228
zinnias, 13, 54, 67, 180, 199, 293, 307, **308–9**
zucchinis, 54, 198, 214, 282, **308–9**
zygocactus, 137, **309**

# A–Z OF GARDENING SECRETS

**Consultant** Debbie McDonald
**Project Editor** Bronwyn Sweeney
**Project Designer** Jacqueline Richards
**Proofreader** Kevin Diletti
**Indexer** Diane Harriman
**Senior Production Controller** Monique Tesoriero

**READER'S DIGEST GENERAL BOOKS**
**Editorial Director** Lynn Lewis
**Managing Editor** Rosemary McDonald
**Art Director** Carole Orbell

*A–Z of Gardening Secrets* is published by Reader's Digest (Australia) Pty Limited
80 Bay Street, Ultimo, NSW, 2007
www.readersdigest.com.au; www.readersdigest.co.nz;
www.readersdigest.co.za; www.rdasia.com;

First published 2013
Copyright © Reader's Digest (Australia) Pty Limited 2013
Copyright © Reader's Digest Association Far East Limited 2013
Philippines Copyright © Reader's Digest Association Far East Limited 2013

Some material in this book has originally appeared in some other Reader's Digest (Australia) gardening titles.

All rights reserved. No part of this book may be reproduced, stored in a retrieval system, or transmitted in any form or by any means, electronic, electrostatic, magnetic tape, mechanical, photocopying, recording or otherwise, without permission in writing from the publishers.

® Reader's Digest and The Digest are registered trademarks of The Reader's Digest Association, Inc.

National Library of Australia Cataloguing-in-publication data:

Title: A–Z of gardening secrets.
ISBN: 978-1-922083-61-6
Notes: Includes index.
Subjects: Gardening.
Other Authors/Contributors: Reader's Digest (Australia)
Dewey Number: 635

Prepress by Sinnott Bros, Sydney
Printed and bound by Leo Paper Products, China

We are interested in receiving your comments on the content of this book. Write to: The Editor, General Books Editorial, Reader's Digest (Australia) Pty Limited, GPO Box 4353, Sydney, NSW 2001, or email us at: bookeditors.au@readersdigest.com

**Note to readers:** This publication is designed to provide useful information to the reader concerning gardening issues and related gardening problems. It is not intended as a substitute for the advice of an expert in any of these areas. Many plants grown in Australia and New Zealand are also suitable for South Africa however some are regarded as invasive alien plants. Readers should obtain their own information on this issue. The writers, researchers, editors and publishers of this work cannot be held liable for any errors and omissions, or actions that may be taken as a consequence of information contained within this book.

To order additional copies of *A–Z of Gardening Secrets* please contact us at:
www.readersdigest.com.au or phone 1300 300 030 (Australia)
www.readersdigest.co.nz or phone 0800 400 060 (New Zealand)
www.readersdigest.co.za or phone 0800 980 572 (South Africa)
or email us at customerservice@readersdigest.com.au

**IMAGE CREDITS** Front and back cover all Shutterstock; 2 all Shutterstock, except tl Clive Nichols/Corbis; 6 Clockwise from top left Shutterstock, iStockphoto, Shutterstock, Photolibrary, RD, Shutterstock, RD, iStockphoto, Shutterstock, Shutterstock, Shutterstock, RD; 8 t iStockphoto; 9 c Shutterstock, bl iStockphoto; 10 Dreamstime; 11 Shutterstock; 12-13 Shutterstock; 13 t iStockphoto, b Shutterstock; 14 l Apple & Pear Australia, r Apple & Pear Australia;16 tl David Cavagnaro, Photolibrary, inset, all Andre Martin; 17 Shutterstock; 18 Shutterstock; 19 tl Getty Images, tr Shutterstock, bl Shutterstock, br Shutterstock; 21 Shutterstock; 22 Shutterstock; 23 l Shutterstock, r iStockphoto; 24 tl Shutterstock, cr Shutterstock; 28 b Shutterstock; 29 t Visions Pictures/Minden Pictures; 29 c Dreamstime, b iStockphoto; 31 t Mark Salter/Alamy, b Shutterstock; 32 Shutterstock; 33 all Shutterstock; 35 Shutterstock; 36 t Shutterstock, b Shutterstock; 37 Shutterstock; 38 bl Shutterstock; 39 all Shutterstock; 40 bl Shutterstock; 41 bl Shutterstock; 43 t Shutterstock, bl Shutterstock; 44 bl Shutterstock; 45 Shutterstock; 46 Shutterstock; 47 t Shutterstock, b Shutterstock; 48 t Shutterstock, b Shutterstock; 49 Shutterstock; 51 t Shutterstock, b Shutterstock; 53 Shutterstock; 54 t Shutterstock, b Shutterstock; 55 t Shutterstock, b Shutterstock; 56 l iStockphoto, r all Shutterstock; 57 b Shutterstock; 58 all Shutterstock; 59 tl Shutterstock; 60 Andrea Jones/Garden World Images; 62-63 Shutterstock; 63 Shutterstock; 64 tl Shutterstock; 65 Shutterstock; 68 Kathrin Ziegler/Getty Images; 69 tr Shutterstock, br iStockphoto; 70 t Shutterstock, b Shutterstock; 71 tl Shutterstock, bl Shutterstock, br Shutterstock; 72 t Andreas von Einsiedel/Alamy, b Shutterstock; 73 Shutterstock; 74 l Shutterstock, r Shutterstock; 75 tl Shutterstock, cl Shutterstock, bl Shutterstock; 77 tr Shutterstock, br Shutterstock; 78 t Shutterstock; 82 Shutterstock; 83 t Shutterstock, b Shutterstock; 85 t iStockphoto, b Shutterstock; 86 t Adrianne Yzerman/Alamy, bl Frank Blackburn/Alamy, bc Shutterstock, br Shutterstock; 87 Island Images/Alamy; 88 l Shutterstock, r Bramwell Flora/Alamy; 89 t Shutterstock, b Shutterstock; 90 Shutterstock; 91 all Shutterstock; 92 Paul Hobart/Alamy; 95 Shutterstock; 96 t John Glover/Alamy, b Dreamstime; 97 t Horticultural Picture Library, b Shutterstock; 98 t Shutterstock, b Shutterstock; 99 t Shutterstock, b Shutterstock; 101 Shutterstock, r Shutterstock; 103 Shutterstock; 104 tl FLPA/David Hosking, tr iStockphoto; 105 Shutterstock; 106 all Shutterstock; 107 Shutterstock; 108 t Shutterstock, b Shutterstock; 109 l Shutterstock, r Shutterstock; 110 t Shutterstock, b Shutterstock; 111 Shutterstock; 113 br Shutterstock; 114 t Shutterstock, b Shutterstock; 115 all Shutterstock; 116 c iStockphoto, bl Shutterstock; 117 all Shutterstock; 118 t Shutterstock, b Andrea Jones/Garden World Images; 119 Shutterstock; 121 tc Chris Hellier/Corbis; 121 tr Plantography/Alamy; 122 Fancy/Alamy; 123 Clive Nichols/Corbis; 125 t Shutterstock, b Shutterstock; 126 t Shutterstock, b Image Source/Alamy; 126-127 Shutterstock; 127 l Shutterstock, c Getty Images/Dorling Kindersley; 128 t Shutterstock, b iStockphoto; 129 b Shutterstock; 132 Shutterstock; 133 tl Shutterstock, tr Shutterstock, b Clive Nichols/Corbis; 134 t Shutterstock, b Dreamstime; 135 Shutterstock; 136 all Shutterstock; 137 all Shutterstock; 138-139 all Shutterstock; 140 Shutterstock; 141 tl iStockphoto, tr Dreamstime, b CuboImages srl/Alamy; 142 t Shutterstock, b Shutterstock; 144 t Shutterstock, b Shutterstock; 146 t Dreamstime, b Dreamstime; 147 bl Shutterstock; 148 t Shutterstock; 150 Shutterstock; 150-151 Shutterstock; 154 Shutterstock; 155 MAP/Nicole et Patrick Mioulane/Garden World Images; 156 Shutterstock; 157 all Shutterstock; 158 t Shutterstock, b Shutterstock; 159 Science Photo Library/Alamy; 160 t Shutterstock; 160 b Mike Walker/Alamy, bl Dave Zubraski/Alamy; 161 br Shutterstock, cr Shutterstock; 163 t iStockphoto, b Shutterstock; 164 t Shutterstock; 166 tr iStockphoto; 167 tc Shutterstock; 168 Shutterstock; 169 Science Photo Library/Alamy, inset clockwise from tl, RD, Shutterstock, RD, Shutterstock, RD; 170 t Shutterstock, b Shutterstock; 171 Shutterstock; 172 tr Dreamstime, br GWI/Garden World Images; 173 Shutterstock; 174 Dan Sams/Photo Library; 175 Shutterstock; 176 Shutterstock; 178 br Shutterstock; 179 Shutterstock; 180 tr Shutterstock, cr Shutterstock; 181 Shutterstock; 183 t Shutterstock, b Florapix/Alamy; 184 tr Shutterstock; 185 t imagebroker/Alamy, b Shutterstock; 186 l Shutterstock, r Shutterstock; 188 b Shutterstock; 190 bl Shutterstock, br Shutterstock; 191 Shutterstock; 192 Shutterstock; 193 all Shutterstock; 194 t Ambient Images Inc./Alamy, b Shutterstock; 195 l Tsuneo Yamashita/Getty Images, r Shutterstock; 196 t Shutterstock, b Shutterstock; 197 Science Photo Library/Alamy; 198 Shutterstock; 199 all Shutterstock; 200 Adrian James/Garden World Images; 201 b Shutterstock; 202 Shutterstock; 203 tr Shutterstock; 204 Shutterstock; 205 all Shutterstock; 206 r Shutterstock; 208 Shutterstock; 209 GAP Photos/Lynn Keddie; 211 Shutterstock; 214 t Shutterstock, br Shutterstock; 215 all Shutterstock; 216 Shutterstock; 218 t Shutterstock, b Shutterstock; 219 t Shutterstock, b Shutterstock; 220 Shutterstock; 221 all Shutterstock; 222 tr Meredith Hebden/Positive Images, cr Shutterstock; 223 t Shutterstock, b Shutterstock; 224 t Andre Martin, b Shutterstock; 225 Shutterstock; 226 Shutterstock; 227 tl David Dobbs/Alamy, tr John Glover/Alamy, bl Shutterstock, br View Photos/amanaimages/Corbis; 228 bc Mike Booth/Alamy, br Shutterstock; 229 t Shutterstock, b Shutterstock; 230 tl iStockphoto, tr Andre Martin; 230 c Andre Martin, bl Jacqui Hurst/Photolibrary, br Shutterstock; 231 Shutterstock; 232 Shutterstock; 234 GAP Photos/Friedrich Strauss; 235 b iStockphoto; 236 Shutterstock; 237 t Shutterstock; 238 Shutterstock; 240 Shutterstock; 242 b Shutterstock; 243 Shutterstock; 244 t iStockphoto; 245 Shutterstock; 247 Shutterstock; 249 b Shutterstock; 250 Shutterstock; 251 Apply Pictures/Alamy; 253 Shutterstock; 254 Shutterstock; 254-255 iStockphoto; 256 Shutterstock; 257 all Shutterstock; 258 Shutterstock; 259 Shutterstock; 261 Suzanne Long/Alamy; 263 t FLPA/Krystyna Szulecka; 264 Lynn Keddie/Photolibrary; 265 Shutterstock; 268 Shutterstock; 269 Jaime Plaza Van Roon/Auscape; 271 Shutterstock; 272 t Shutterstock; 273 Shutterstock; 274 all Shutterstock; 275 all Shutterstock; 276 Shutterstock; 277 tl Shutterstock, tr Shutterstock, bl Getty Images/Perspectives, br Shutterstock; 278 Shutterstock; 279 t Shutterstock, b Shutterstock; 282 Ron Sutherland/Photolibrary; 284 Shutterstock; 285 Shutterstock; 287 Shutterstock; 293 b Shutterstock; 294 Shutterstock; 298 Shutterstock; 299 all Shutterstock; 300 Shutterstock; 303 Shutterstock; 304 Shutterstock; 305 b Shutterstock; 307 all Shutterstock; 308 t Shutterstock; 309 Shutterstock

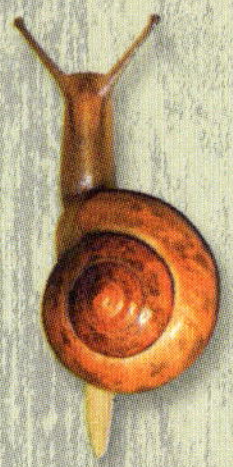

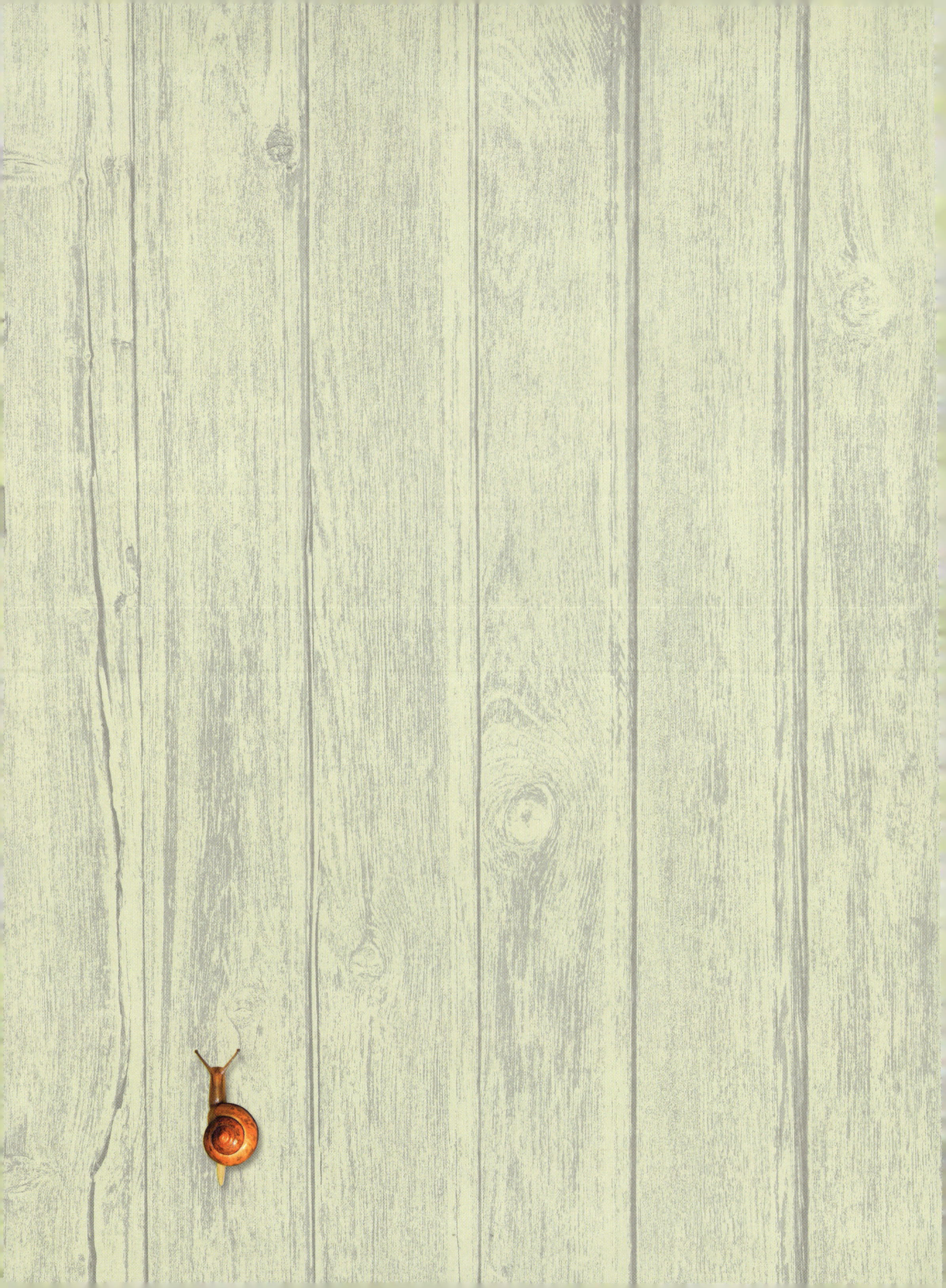